Library of
Davidson College

**Courts of Appeals
in the Federal Judicial System**

# Courts of Appeals
## in the Federal Judicial System

A Study of the Second, Fifth, and District of Columbia Circuits

J. Woodford Howard, Jr.

Princeton University Press
Princeton, New Jersey

Copyright © 1981 by Princeton University Press

Published by Princeton University Press, Princeton, New Jersey
In the United Kingdom: Princeton University Press, Guildford, Surrey

All Rights Reserved

Library of Congress Cataloging in Publication Data will be
found on the last printed page of this book

This book has been composed in VIP Melior

Clothbound editions of Princeton University Press books
are printed on acid-free paper, and binding materials are
chosen for strength and durability

Printed in the United States of America by Princeton
University Press, Princeton, New Jersey

To **Valerie Hope Barclay Howard**

# Contents

|  |  |
|---|---|
| List of Appendixes | ix |
| List of Tables | xi |
| List of Figures | xv |
| Preface | xvii |

### Part I · **The Flow of Federal Litigation**

|  |  |
|---|---|
| One · Courts of Appeals in the Governing Process | 3 |
| Two · The Flow of Litigation in Three Courts of Appeals | 23 |
| Three · The Flow of Litigation in the Supreme Court | 57 |

### Part II · **The Roles of Circuit Judges**

|  |  |
|---|---|
| Four · The Making of Circuit Judges | 87 |
| Five · The Purposes of Courts of Appeals | 125 |
| Six · Judicial Values and Judicial Votes | 159 |
| Seven · Consensus and Conflict in Circuit Courts, an Informal View | 189 |
| Eight · Leadership in the Allocation of Work | 222 |

### Part III · **Perspectives on Reform**

|  |  |
|---|---|
| Nine · Strategies of Reform | 261 |
| Appendixes | 297 |
| List of Abbreviations | 345 |
| Bibliographic Notes | 347 |
| Index | 399 |

# List of Appendixes

| | | |
|---|---|---|
| 1 | Methodological Notes | 297 |
| 2 | The Business of the Three Courts of Appeals and of the Supreme Court, FY 1965-1967 | 315 |
| 3 | Rates of Appeal from Contested Judgments in U.S. District Courts by Source of Civil Jurisdiction, FY 1967-1970 | 319 |
| | Rates of Appeal from Contested Civil Judgments and Convictions of Guilt in U.S. District Courts, FY 1967-1970 | 321 |
| 4 | Subjects of Circuit Court Decisions after Hearing or Submission, FY 1965-1967, 2d Circuit | 322 |
| | Subjects of Circuit Court Decisions after Hearing or Submission, FY 1965-1967, 5th Circuit | 325 |
| | Subjects of Circuit Court Decisions after Hearing or Submission, FY 1965-1967, D.C. Circuit | 328 |
| 5 | Sources of Supreme Court Decisions, FY 1965-1967, 2d Circuit | 331 |
| | Sources of Supreme Court Decisions, FY 1965-1967, 5th Circuit | 332 |
| | Sources of Supreme Court Decisions, FY 1965-1967, D.C. Circuit | 334 |
| 6 | Subjects of Supreme Court Decisions, FY 1965-1967, 2d Circuit | 335 |
| | Subjects of Supreme Court Decisions, FY 1965-1967, 5th Circuit | 338 |
| | Subjects of Supreme Court Decisions, FY 1965-1967, D.C. Circuit | 341 |

# List of Tables

| | | |
|---|---|---|
| 1.1 | Cases Commenced in Federal Courts, FY 1961-1979 | 12 |
| 2.1 | The Nature of Cases Disposed of by Three Circuit Courts (After Hearing or Submission, FY 1965-1967) | 26 |
| 2.2 | Terminations in Three Circuits and All Circuits (After Hearing or Submission, FY 1961-1979) | 27 |
| 2.3 | Governments as Parties to Litigation (Appellant or Appellee, FY 1965-1967) | 28 |
| 2.4 | The Business of Three Circuit Courts (After Hearing or Submission, FY 1965-1967) | 30 |
| 2.5 | Rates of Appeal from Contested Civil Judgments and Convictions after Trial in U.S. District Courts, FY 1967-1970 | 35 |
| 2.6 | Rates of Appeal from Contested Judgments in U.S. District Courts by Source of Civil Jurisdiction, FY 1967-1970 | 36 |
| 2.7 | Rates of Appeal from and Reversal of Contested Civil Judgments and Convictions after Trial in U.S. District Courts, FY 1967-1970 | 39 |
| 2.8 | Circuit Court Decisions (After Hearing or Submission, FY 1965-1967) | 40 |
| 2.9 | Circuit Court Finality (After Hearing or Submission, FY 1965-1967) | 43 |
| 2.10 | Sources of 2d Circuit Decisions (After Hearing or Submission, FY 1965-1967) | 44 |
| 2.11 | Sources of 5th Circuit Decisions (After Hearing or Submission, FY 1965-1967) | 45 |
| 2.12 | Sources of D.C. Circuit Decisions (After Hearing or Submission, FY 1965-1967) | 46 |
| 2.13 | 2d Circuit Rate of Disturbing Decisions of U.S. District Judges, FY 1965-1967 | 48 |
| 2.14 | 5th Circuit Rate of Disturbing Decisions of U.S. District Judges, FY 1965-1967 | 49 |
| 2.15 | D.C. Circuit Rate of Disturbing Decisions of U.S. District Judges, FY 1965-1967 | 51 |
| 3.1 | Supreme Court Review of Three Courts of Appeals (After Hearing or Submission, FY 1965-1967) | 58 |

| | | |
|---|---|---|
| 3.2 | Supreme Court Decisions in Appeals Heard from Three Circuits, FY 1965-1967 | 59 |
| 3.3 | Comparison of Appellate Court Business, FY 1965-1967 | 61 |
| 3.4 | Rates of Appeal to the Supreme Court and Rates of Certiorari Petitions Granted in Selected Subjects, FY 1965-1967 | 66 |
| 3.5 | Supreme Court Certiorari in Appeals from Three Circuit Courts, FY 1965-1967 | 68 |
| 3.6 | Intercourt Relations | 69 |
| 4.1 | Party Affiliation of Circuit Judges | 91 |
| 4.2 | Political Participation of Circuit Judges | 92 |
| 4.3 | Apprenticeship in Government of Circuit Judges | 92 |
| 4.4 | Pre-Judicial Experience and Career Preferences of Circuit Judges | 97 |
| 4.5 | Religious Affiliations of Circuit Judges | 103 |
| 4.6 | Social Class of Circuit Judges: Father's Occupation | 104 |
| 4.7 | Social Class of Circuit Judges: Self-Identified | 104 |
| 4.8 | Birthplace of Circuit Judges | 106 |
| 4.9 | Geographic Mobility of Circuit Judges: Place of Birth | 107 |
| 4.10 | Initial Interest of Circuit Judges in Politics | 109 |
| 4.11 | Initial Interest of Circuit Judges in Judicial Office | 111 |
| 4.12 | Paths to Courts of Appeals | 114 |
| 4.13 | Pre-Judicial Experience of Circuit Judges in Government: Elective-Appointive | 115 |
| 4.14 | Political Values of Circuit Judges before Becoming a Federal Judge | 116 |
| 4.15 | Circuit Judges' Evaluations of Preparatory Experiences for Service on Courts of Appeals | 119 |
| 5.1 | The Missions of Circuit Courts | 127 |
| 5.2 | Supreme Court Reversal of Decisions in Which 2d Circuit Judges Participated, FY 1965-1967 | 139 |
| 5.3 | Supreme Court Reversal of Decisions in Which 5th Circuit Judges Participated, FY 1965-1967 | 140 |
| 5.4 | Supreme Court Reversal of Decisions in Which D.C. Circuit Judges Participated, FY 1965-1967 | 141 |
| 5.5 | Judicial Perceptions of Whether Circuit Judges Resent Being Reversed by the Supreme Court | 141 |
| 5.6 | Citation of Other Circuits, FY 1965-1967 | 143 |
| 5.7 | Perceived Influence of Circuit Courts on Public Policy | 148 |

| | | |
|---|---|---|
| 5.8 | Perceived Influence of Related Actors on Circuit Decisions | 151 |
| 5.9 | Audiences of Written Opinions | 152 |
| 5.10 | Primary Reference Groups of Circuit Judges | 152 |
| 5.11 | Permissible Political Activity by Circuit Judges | 153 |
| 5.12 | Permissible Activity in Recruiting Federal Judges | 154 |
| 5.13 | Permissible Professional or Civic Activity by Circuit Judges | 155 |
| 6.1 | Attitudes toward Judicial Lawmaking | 161 |
| 6.2 | Precedent Orientations in Decision Making | 164 |
| 6.3 | Unclear Precedents in Decision Making | 165 |
| 6.4 | Social Backgrounds of Circuit Judges and Attitudes toward Judicial Lawmaking | 168 |
| 6.5 | Professional Backgrounds of Circuit Judges and Attitudes toward Judicial Lawmaking | 168 |
| 6.6 | Political Backgrounds of Circuit Judges and Attitudes toward Judicial Lawmaking | 170 |
| 6.7 | Political Orientations of Circuit Judges and Votes in Selected Subjects, FY 1965-1967 | 174 |
| 6.8 | Attitudes toward Judicial Lawmaking and Votes in Selected Subjects, FY 1965-1967 | 177 |
| 6.9 | The Effects of Political Orientations and Role Perceptions on Voting Outcomes in Selected Subjects, FY 1965-1967 | 180 |
| 6.10 | The Effects of Selected Background Characteristics of Circuit Judges on Voting Outcomes in Selected Subjects, FY 1965-1967 | 183 |
| 7.1 | Dissent Rates of Circuit Judges, 2d Circuit, FY 1965-1967 | 194 |
| 7.2 | Dissent Rates of Circuit Judges, 5th Circuit, FY 1965-1967 | 195 |
| 7.3 | Dissent Rates of Circuit Judges, D.C. Circuit, FY 1965-1967 | 196 |
| 7.4 | Perceived Influence of Legal Factors on Circuit Decisions | 199 |
| 7.5 | Judicial Perceptions of Whether Blocs Exist on Three Courts of Appeals | 206 |
| 7.6 | Judicial Perceptions of Whether There Is Give and Take on Three Courts of Appeals | 208 |
| 7.7 | Judicial Perceptions of Whether Sufficient Collegial Deliberation Exists on Three Courts of Appeals | 211 |
| 8.1 | Judicial Perceptions of Whether a Freshman Period Occurs on Courts of Appeals | 224 |

| | | |
|---|---|---|
| 8.2 | Judicial Perceptions of Whether the Office of Chief Judge Gives Incumbents Advantages in Influencing Adjudication | 227 |
| 8.3 | Judicial Perceptions of Personal Characteristics That Affect a Judge's Effectiveness on Circuit Courts | 230 |
| 8.4 | Panel and Opinion Assignments in the 2d Circuit, FY 1965-1967 | 236 |
| 8.5 | Panel and Opinion Assignments in the 5th Circuit, FY 1965-1967 | 237 |
| 8.6 | Panel and Opinion Assignments in the D.C. Circuit, FY 1965-1967 | 238 |
| 8.7 | Panel Assignments in Personal Status Cases, 5th Circuit, FY 1965-1967 | 242 |
| 8.8 | Participation in Civil Rights Cases and Support for Civil Rights Claims, 5th Circuit, FY 1965-1967 | 243 |
| 8.9 | Distribution of Panel Assignments in Civil Rights Cases in the 5th Circuit, by Groups, FY 1965-1967 | 245 |
| 8.10 | Comparative Opinion Assignments in Personal Status and Criminal Cases, 5th Circuit, FY 1965-1967 | 251 |
| 8.11 | Opinion Assignments in Criminal Cases, D.C. Circuit, FY 1965-1967 | 254 |
| 9.1 | Comparative Rates of Increase in Cases Terminated in Circuit Courts and Number of Circuit Judgeships, FY 1961-1978 | 263 |
| 9.2 | Circuit Judges' Perceptions of Whether They Felt Overloaded or Overworked, 1969-1971 | 264 |
| 9.3 | Profile of Productivity in Circuit Courts, FY 1979 | 266 |
| 9.4 | Participation by Active, Senior, and Visiting Judges, FY 1979 | 267 |
| 9.5 | Summary Calendar Percentage by Subject Matter, 5th Circuit, FY 1974-1976 | 280 |

# List of Figures

| | | |
|---|---|---|
| 3.1 | Federal Appeals Flowchart, 2d, 5th, and D.C. Circuits, FY 1965-1967 | 74 |
| 6.1 | A Professional Model of Judicial Decision Making | 172 |
| 6.2 | A Political Model of Judicial Decision Making | 172 |
| 6.3 | A Log Linear Model of the Effects of Political Orientations and Judicial Role Perceptions of Circuit Judges on Voting Outcomes, FY 1965-1967 | 178 |
| 6.4 | A Log Linear Model of the Effects of Class Origins, Political Party Affiliations, and Prior Judicial Experience of Circuit Judges on Voting Outcomes, FY 1965-1967 | 182 |

# Preface

There are twelve Courts of Appeals in the American national judiciary. They serve, according to statute, as intermediate appellate courts between ninety-five federal district courts and the Supreme Court of the United States. Even passing familiarity with federal circuit courts, as they are commonly called, suggests that they are important power centers in the American polity. As courts of last resort in the vast majority of federal cases, and as primary organs of judicial review of federal administrative agencies, they shoulder heavy responsibilities in enforcing national law, declaring federal rights, and holding bureaucrats to account. Controversies over the Pentagon papers, the Nixon tapes, and the Alaska pipeline illustrate how Courts of Appeals filter and shape great issues of public policy on their way to Congress and the Supreme Court.[1] Appointed for life by the President and confirmed by the Senate, the 132 federal circuit judges are major actors in American government.

Beyond general impressions, however, knowledge of the functions and operations of circuit courts is largely intuitive and fragmentary. Until the last two decades, few analysts followed the lead of Frankfurter and Landis by treating Courts of Appeals as integral parts of the federal legal system.[2] Only a handful of monographs, articles, and dissertations differentiated their operations from appellate decision making generally or focused on circuit judges as human instruments of federal power.[3] Not until court congestion reached a "near crisis" in the mid-1970s was a U.S. Commission on Revision of the Federal Court Appellate System formed to study their unique problems of adjudication and administration.[4] Collectively these studies provide a solid base on which this and future works will build. Still, Courts of Appeals remain among the least comprehended of major federal institutions. Revered though their leaders may be in the legal profession, to many citizens they are courts "nobody knows."[5]

The object of this study is to help improve understanding of intermediate federal courts by analyzing the business and functions of three major tribunals in the flow of federal litigation and the attitudes of the judges toward their job and its chief problems. The unifying threads of the inquiry are two classic questions in American federalism and jurisprudence, both bearing on problems of institutional cohesion. First, what provides the glue binding federal courts into a judicial system? Second, what controls the personal discretion of circuit judges to make law and policy in the course of adjudication? To explore these questions we shall view the three tribunals from twin perspectives. The focus of Part I, formal and telescopic, is on intercourt relations. After setting the stage in Chapter One for readers unfamiliar with the organization of federal courts and their political setting, we shall analyze the business of the three circuits and their decisions in the stream of federal litigation (Chapters Two and Three). Of particular concern are their functions in the federal judicial system and their relations with other courts. How uniform or unique is the work of the circuit courts? How strong are formal controls—appellate review and reversal—in supervising lower courts at both appellate levels?

Having explored the functions and relations of circuit courts as institutions, we then shift perspective in Part II to a more informal and microscopic analysis of the roles of circuit judges in the appellate process. Using judges, attitudes, and votes as units of analysis, we shall address a basic question of whether, in light of limited appellate supervision, shared political and professional values among the judges support the system of formal review. This inquiry dissolves into several subsidiary questions. Who are the judges, how were they chosen, and how did they learn what is expected of them as jurists? (Chapter Four) How did they perceive their judicial roles and evaluate various elements of decision? (Chapter Five) What relationships existed if any, among their political and professional orientations and their voting behavior on the bench? (Chapter Six) Is personal discretion restrained by judging in groups? How do circuit judges reach consensus and resolve conflicts? (Chapter Seven) Did administrative powers affect opportunities for leadership in adjudication? How was judicial work and therefore power distributed among the members? (Chapter Eight) Finally, the two perspectives come together in Chapter Nine, which considers the chief problems faced by the circuit courts in the current law explosion together with alternative solutions to these problems. Thus, without pretending to answer all the questions raised, or even most of them, we shall explore the integration of the federal judicial system, as seen from without and within three major Courts of Appeals.

**The Research Design**

Because the analysis draws upon social science concepts that may be unfamiliar to some readers, the basic conceptions and limitations of the research design should be understood from the start. (Further details regarding methodology appear in Appendix 1.)

Ideally, all twelve Courts of Appeals should be studied in a common framework. Because of time and financial constraints, this study was narrowed to three tribunals—the 2d, the 5th, and the District of Columbia circuits—during the period 1960-1979. The three intermediates were chosen on a priori grounds of significance, subsidiary grounds of convenience, and because they were different. The 2d circuit, a court of eleven judges covering the states of New York, Connecticut, and Vermont, has long been regarded as the nation's leading commercial court. The far-flung 5th circuit was the largest intermediate tribunal in number of judges and volume of business. Covering the six Gulf states of Florida, Georgia, Alabama, Mississippi, Louisiana, and Texas, plus the Canal Zone, this tribunal bore the brunt of implementing the Supreme Court's broad decrees in racial desegregation. Before being split into two circuits in 1981, it also became a paradigm of a circuit overloaded by burgeoning demand.[a] The D.C. circuit, a court of eleven judges with limited geographical scope, has special responsibilities over administrative appeals and, until 1973, had a unique local jurisdiction that made it the counterpart of a state supreme court in the nation's capital.

Together, the three tribunals traverse the range of activities circuit judges over the country are expected to perform. To determine the functions of these courts and the votes of their judges, all of their nonconsolidated decisions reported during fiscal years 1965-1967 —a total of 4,941 cases—were analyzed, coded on computers, and traced as they flowed through the circuits and the Supreme Court. The cases from the mid-1960s, which we shall call the base period, comprised roughly 40 percent of total decisions made by all circuit courts after hearing or submission on briefs during these years. The period is a useful basepoint because it was the last span of relative stability before an avalanche of appeals descended upon larger circuits, forcing expansion of judicial manpower by one-third after 1978. At the same time, most of the key legal issues of the 1970s were germinating in the litigation. To capture longer-term trends, we shall also draw from the reports of the Administrative Office of the United States Courts from fiscal 1960 to 1979.

The data concerning political values and role perceptions derive from not-for-attribution interviews conducted by the author with thirty-five active and senior judges from these circuits during 1969-1971. One retired Justice of the Supreme Court and three circuit

[a] The 11th circuit was carved from the 5th circuit while this book was in press. Thus, references to the 5th circuit are to the predivided circuit, except as noted.

court clerks were also interviewed. The interviews, combining mostly open-ended with a few structured questions, lasted from thirty minutes to six hours, for an average of about one hundred minutes. Turnover caused some differences between the judges in the cases and the interviews; but thirty judges, slightly less than a third of all federal circuit judges at that time, participated in both the interviews and the decisions. Spread geographically from Hartford to Houston, the judges interviewed, and listed below, included some of the country's most eminent jurists, such as Friendly and Lumbard in New York, Tuttle and Wisdom in the South, and Bazelon and Wright in Washington. Most of them still serve on Courts of Appeals. To protect their anonymity, only one remark quoted in the text will be attributed to its source. Also respected are judges' wishes to keep a few comments off the record. In addition to Mr. Justice Tom C. Clark, interviews were conducted with the following:

*Second circuit*
    Robert P. Anderson
    Wilfred Feinberg
    Henry J. Friendly
    Paul R. Hays
    Irving R. Kaufman
    J. Edward Lumbard
    Harold R. Medina
    Leonard P. Moore
    J. Joseph Smith
    Sterry R. Waterman
    A. Daniel Fusaro, clerk

*District of Columbia circuit*
    David L. Bazelon
    Charles Fahy
    Harold Leventhal
    Carl McGowan
    Roger Robb
    Spottswood W. Robinson III
    Edward A. Tamm
    J. Skelly Wright
    Nathan J. Paulson, clerk

*Fifth circuit*
    Robert A. Ainsworth, Jr.
    Griffin B. Bell
    John R. Brown
    G. Harrold Carswell
    Charles Clark
    James P. Coleman
    David W. Dyer
    Walter P. Gewin
    John C. Godbold
    Irving L. Goldberg
    Warren L. Jones
    Lewis R. Morgan
    Richard T. Rives
    Bryan Simpson
    Homer Thornberry
    Elbert P. Tuttle
    John Minor Wisdom
    Edward W. Wadsworth, clerk

Two influential concepts from the social sciences provide the organization and analytical framework for this book. First is the premise of *system*.⁶ Though avoiding the jargon of systems analysis, this study is set in a systems framework in order to make explicit my assumptions that the federal appellate process fits neither the classic model of mechanical jurisprudence, in which judges ratiocinate in splendid isolation from the environment, nor the legal realist model in which judges' predilections are all that matter when courts attempt to settle other people's disputes. Rather, I assume that Courts of Appeals function on a complex stage of loosely related parts, including judges and a large company, in continuing processes of conflict resolution and policy making. By virtue of their intermediate positions, Courts of Appeals fit naturally within a systems framework. They are the hub of an interlocking network of relations linking circuit judges to district courts, federal agencies, and the Supreme Court, and thence to other appellate courts, branches of government, and a wide array of individuals and interest groups who compose their chief constituencies. Simultaneously as litigants make demands on circuit courts, the judges convert the stimuli of cases, collegial relations, and their own values into decisions (output). The responses of their clienteles in the form of new litigation and other reactions then return "to haunt the system" (feedback).⁷ What happens in one part of the system, moreover, usually affects the rest.

The study is not a full-fledged systems analysis of the three circuit courts. The emphasis is on court relations and judicial roles as preliminary steps. Yet, the idea of system underlies Part I, because it offers several advantages. For one thing, the system premise prevents us from falling into the trap of projecting the Supreme Court onto the whole judicial process and assuming that what occurs in our least typical tribunal characterizes all of them. Focusing on Courts of Appeals as one among several power centers enables us to differentiate their unique functions and relationships with other tribunals without losing sight of their uniformities.

Another advantage is that the system premise places circuit courts in their working environment. Strong though judicial independence may be, the American judicial tradition has always linked federal courts to the political process.⁸ As described in Chapter One, politics determines the missions, organization, and jurisdiction of federal judges as well as who sits. Politics also restricts the options available for court reform.

The idea of a judicial system, though to some more a statement of aspiration than of reality, also locates common ground among those who study federal courts. A common core of systemic assumptions unifies several law-related disciplines. When lawyers Shepardize cases, forum shop, or take a "functional approach," they assume, as did Frankfurter and Landis, that the federal judiciary "articulates as a system."[9] When social scientists convert common observations into the special language of systems analysis, they do so to compare decision making across a broad and less obvious range of institutions and social contexts. Such comparisons are not only essential steps in constructing viable theories of judicial decision but also have practical implications for rational allocation of business among government institutions. As federal judges participate more and more in ruling the country, what problems are they equipped to handle and what should be left to other tribunals and institutions?[10]

The organizing concept for Part II of the book is *judicial role*. These chapters draw explicitly from a substantial social-science literature which applies so-called role theory to the study of decision makers' values. In particular, this analysis owes a heavy debt to Wahlke, Eulau, Buchanan, and Ferguson, *The Legislative System*, a pioneering study of American state legislators, since replicated for several legislatures and courts over the globe.[11] Because role theory rests on a theatrical metaphor—and judging is anything but play acting—it suffers from an unfortunate ambiguity in terms. The term "social role" is commonly used to describe both what persons or groups do in a social system and the norms guiding their action. In this study the terms "function" will be used for the former, and "role" will be restricted to the latter or normative sense.[12] The basic notion is that human behavior is guided by mutual expectations held by actors in a given position and those with whom they deal. A social role by definition is neither behavior nor idiosyncratic conduct; it is a reciprocal web of shared expectations about how a given task should be performed.[13] Just as actors in most plays are expected to act a part rather than themselves, so roles in different circumstances turn a person into a father, a daughter, a lover, a lawyer, a judge, or even a thief. Shared role expectations are what convert a collection of individuals into a legislature or a court. The norms of work also differentiate legislatures from courts.

Presumably, common understandings of how jobs should be performed affect how they are performed. Hence, determining the role perceptions and self-images of incumbent judges should provide information about the values of an important governmental elite and clues about why they decide as they do. These theories, too, have practical implications for the cohesion of federal courts. A central thesis is that shared values from the legal and political "cultures," carried into circuit courts by overlapping processes of socialization and recruitment, and reinforced by formal supervision and peer pressure, serve as sinews of judicial solidarity.

Studying judicial values in this way has several analytical advantages. One is that role perceptions of incumbents mediate between how an office looks to insiders and to outsiders. The concept of social role, integral to social systems, also helps to relate individual and collective behavior in judiciaries.[14] Judicial roles may be conceived as a set of job prescriptions shared by the participants of the legal system, which links "judges & co." while distinguishing courts from other institutions. So viewed, judicial roles become intervening variables between institutional and personality factors in the judicial process. For roles by definition are both interpersonal and, through processes of learning and internalization by individuals, part of the common property Roscoe Pound called "the trained intuition of the judge," passed from one generation to the next.

Judicial roles—the dos and don'ts of judging—have long figured prominently in justifications of judicial power. Especially in the United States, where federal judges exercise uncommon lawmaking authority, what prevents their personal predilections and policy values from determining the rules by which we live? Theoretically, the main defenses against judicial lawmaking are internalized professional norms regarding the control of precedent and the limits of judicial choice. Given the significance of "moralities of decision" in the theory of separation of powers, we shall consider in Part II how the judges of the three circuits learned and perceived of their duties as jurists and the implications of this informal value structure for problems of institutional integration. Analytical difficulties apart, this section requires few mental leaps for lawyers and judges. Role metaphors imbue their work. The tasks of the various components of our legal system—police, prosecutors, advocates, jurors, trial judges, appellate judges, and so on—are so elaborately prescribed and delineated by custom, statute, and professional codes that judges are among the most role conscious of American public officials.[15] These judges, at any rate, soon undermined my efforts to avoid the fuzzy word "role" in the interviews by introducing it themselves. One judge, quick to discern the research design, remarked: "We all have an idea of what the job of a circuit judge is supposed to be from reading formal statutes, and we can infer some things from the cases. But aren't you saying that the job is really the way judges see it? I like that approach. I think it's true."

Perhaps it goes too far to say that perceptions are reality. Certainly the proposition poses vexing problems of proof. We can never be sure that what judges think coincides with what they say or do. Even if thoughts and words are similar, observers cannot guarantee that they understood a judge in a hurried interview or structured questionnaire. More serious, what judges perceive as their duty does not necessarily constitute the judicial role. Because roles are relational, and perceptions may vary according to where one sits, we need to discover how the other participants in the judicial system see that job, too. Neither can we assume that judicial role perceptions actually affect judicial behavior. *This is the hypothesis to be proved.* That professional prescriptions affect judicial conduct is a plausible working hypothesis for the self-conscious judges of today; but too many variables, such as personality or the context of a case, intervene in judicial decision making to equate "ought" with "is."

We cannot even assume that judicial role conceptions are monolithic or static. Well-structured roles permit variations in individual behavior or style.[16] Just as Hamlet performed by Orson Welles or Laurence Olivier differs, though the words are the same, so our expectations of appropriate judicial conduct may vary by function, field, or forum. Certainly our impressions and conclusions are limited to these three tribunals in one place and time. Something must give, moreover, when the rules of judging are ambiguous or collide. These problems illustrate the difficulty of establishing the boundaries of role-influenced behavior. And they suggest why this study does not purport to solve all the riddles in the theory of judicial decision. In the final analysis, ample room is left for the play of individuals and the politics of one and the many.

This suggests a final limitation in the work, which, to my mind, exacts the dearest price. Concentration on the abstractions of litigation flow and judicial roles leeches the flesh and blood from litigants and judges in action. That is a serious loss for these Courts of Appeals. All three tribunals are populated by jurists rich in intelligence, character, and experience. All three tribunals during this period confronted a wide variety of social conflicts, ranging from shipwrecks to flag burnings, from desegregation to railroad mergers, from the legality of the Vietnam War to dirty movies and hairstyles in the public schools. Not least at issue were the courts' own functions in the governmental scheme. Circuit judges became the objects of political struggle while this study was in progress. The D.C. circuit, long the target of controversy because of its innovations in criminal justice, underwent a little-noted ideological reconstruction during the Nixon administration. At the same time, Congress and the judges were redefining the court's functions of administrative oversight as well as its relations to a metropolitan capital struggling to achieve home rule. Presidents and senators also locked horns over replacements in the 2d circuit that could effectively create a new court majority. Meanwhile, bombs were planted in the federal courthouse on Foley Square. Judicial politics was even more pronounced in the 5th circuit as both presidential parties vied for control of the federal judiciary. Two of its judges, Homer Thornberry and G. Harrold Carswell, were nominated to but failed to reach the Supreme Court. In the unfolding of President Nixon's "southern strategy," Attorney General John Mitchell publicly rejected a distinguished Republican prospect, John Minor Wisdom, for being "a damn left winger. He'd be as bad as Earl Warren."[17] Twice reporters interrupted my interviews to ask other circuit judges, such as future Attorney General Griffin B. Bell, about their chances of winning the prize. In the meantime, the court slipped into a crisis of exploding volume.

This is a book about the job of three United States Courts of Appeals and how their judges see it. Almost five thousand cases and thirty-five judges are abstracted into litigation flow and judicial roles for the same reason that busy judges spared me their time: to advance understanding of Courts of Appeals in the American government. I trust that readers will do their share by remembering that each statistic represents human beings bringing their conflicts, large and small, to other human beings cast in the role of judges for a just resolution through law.

## Acknowledgments

Any work of this scope bears heavy debts to others who receive scant reward. In particular I am indebted to several gifted students—Alan Betten, John P. Crumrine, Jerry Goldman, James Hirschorn, Joel Ish, Durwood Littlefield, James S. Nathanson, Michael Nelson, John E. Schofield, J. Randall Smith, and Mark Thomas—who helped to construct the code, analyze the cases, and compile the data. Without their aid I never could have contemplated this study, much less completed it. The same holds for The Johns Hopkins University and the Ford Foundation. Johns Hopkins contributed research leave, computer facilities, and all those intangible supports that make it a scholar's haven. The study was launched under a faculty research fellowship granted by the Ford Foundation. However, the conclusions, opinions, and other statements are those of the author and not necessarily those of the Ford Foundation. I should also like to thank my daughter, Elaine Hope Howard, for proofreading; Mrs. Evelyn Scheulen, Mrs. Evelyn Stoller, and Mrs. Catherine Grover for skillful typing of the manuscript; William Ascher, Alan Betten, Matthew

Crenson, Jerry Goldman, Richard Katz, Thomas Marvell, Austin Sarat, Stephen V. Stephens, and John T. Wold for helpful criticism; Joseph F. Spaniol and James A. McCafferty of the Administrative Office of the United States Courts for aid in locating unreported cases and data for three-judge district courts; the Federal Judicial Center for sponsoring research reports at a critical time; and the *George Washington Law Review*, the *Law and Society Review*, and the *Journal of Politics* for permission to reprint portions of Chapters Two, Three, and Six. I am grateful to the *New Yorker* for permission to reprint two cartoons. Jerry Goldman graciously consented to reprinting in Chapter Two and Appendixes 2 and 3 parts of an article we wrote together for the *George Washington Law Review*. Special gratitude goes to the circuit judges, who generously gave their time and thoughts about federal appeals. For me the interviews were a rewarding personal experience from which I learned much about life as well as law. Most of all my thanks go to my wife who, in her many roles, more than merits the dedication of this book.

# Part I
# The Flow of Federal Litigation

The federal judiciary "articulates as a system."
Felix Frankfurter and James M. Landis, *The Business of the Supreme Court* (1927), 3.

# One · Courts of Appeals in the Governing Process

United States Courts of Appeals were created in the 1890s to help the Supreme Court enforce the supremacy and uniformity of federal law. From the start they have been enmeshed in a paradox between the missions and organization of federal courts. On the one hand, the basic object of the national judiciary is to uphold federally created rights as the supreme law of the land. On the other hand, that centralizing task has been dispersed among the most decentralized institutions of the government. In theory, of course, federal judges form a pyramid that supports the will of the Justices. In reality, federal judicial power is widely diffused among lower court judges who are insulated by deep traditions of independence, not only from other branches of the government but also from each other. So strong are the sources of fragmentation, in fact, that the most challenging questions are: what keeps the federal judiciary from flying apart? Why is consensus actually more characteristic of circuit courts than conflict?

To comprehend how Courts of Appeals mirror this paradox of purpose and practice requires preliminary mapping of their origins and organization in the governmental process as well as their links to the external political environment.

### Origins and Organization

The United States is one of the few federal countries to establish lower national courts to enforce the law of the central government.[1] Other federations, such as Australia, entrust national interests to state or provincial judiciaries, subject to final review by a national supreme court. The American arrangement of dual courts is usually justified on two main grounds: (1) state judges, regardless of their constitutional oaths, cannot be trusted to execute national laws or to prevent prejudice against nonresidents; and (2) one supreme court cannot secure federally created rights throughout so vast a country.[2] Argument never dies as to whether distrust of state judiciaries is warranted, or whether federal courts should retain jurisdiction over state questions involving citizens of different states, now that localism is less rampant and federal judges no longer profess to define state common law.³ Still, the basic premise underlying so-called inferior federal courts was, and remains, state infidelity to national law. Federal district courts and Courts of Appeals were designed to extend national power over individuals within the states—and clearly do so today. The leading part played by the Supreme Court in American life since the Civil War is scarcely imaginable without the supporting cast in lower federal courts.⁴

Despite the goal of national supremacy, however, the actual structure and authority of Courts of Appeals evolved incrementally during continuing struggles over the organization of federal judicial power. These contests, played against a backdrop of competing conceptions of American federalism and public policy, usually produced compromises in institutional structure as a result of resistance to a strong national judiciary, which was overcome only after the Civil War and the industrial revolution. The framers of the Constitution, having set the stage by straddling the issue, authorized inferior federal courts but left their creation to Congress. When Congress acted in 1789, opponents of national power compelled the new tribunals to be organized on a state basis with limited jurisdiction. Not until the close of Reconstruction in 1875 were federal district courts empowered to decide controversies concerning the federal Constitution, treaties, and statutes, even though federal enforcement of federal law was a prime object of a separate national judiciary.⁵ Before 1875, in consequence, most federal questions had to filter through state tribunals before reaching the Justices.

Intermediate national courts designed to combat localism in federal trial courts met a similar fate. Apart from an early attempt by lame-duck Federalists, which the Jeffersonians promptly aborted, circuit courts were judicial stepchildren through much of the nineteenth century.⁶ Possessing limited appellate jurisdiction, they served mainly as trial courts in diversity of citizenship cases, offering refuge to nonresidents in issues involving state law, while federal district courts concentrated on admiralty. Lacking independent personnel until 1869, the circuit courts consisted of long-complaining members of the Supreme Court, who rode circuit from the forests of Maine to the mud flats of Arkansas, and federal district judges who reviewed their own judgments. As American territory expanded, circuit riding atrophied. Federal district judges developed strong traditions of localism and independence, and the Justices in Washington struggled to develop uniform legal standards over a continental empire that guaranteed to every federal litigant a right to review in the country's highest court.⁷

This system operated three tiers of courts with only two sets of judges. What saved it from collapse in the early years was light judicial business. The growth of the nation and of government regulation after the Civil War, coupled with judicial activism on behalf of property rights, produced a virtual breakdown in federal appeals by the 1880s. As the Supreme Court's docket fell over two years in arrears, the high tribunal could not maintain a coherent body of national law over both state and federal courts without somehow restricting the right to appeal. The Justices, who aggravated the problem by retaining control over commercial common law while stimulating massive appeals from public economic regulation, sought relief through reorganization.[8] Congress responded by reviving Oliver Ellsworth's original concept of intermediate appellate tribunals to relieve Supreme Court congestion and to provide "uniformity to the proceedings" of diverse federal trial courts.[9] Nine regional Circuit Courts of Appeals were created under Article III of the federal Constitution in 1891. The District of Columbia circuit was gradually absorbed into the system after 1893, the 10th circuit was carved from the 8th in 1929, and the 11th from the 5th in 1981. Their official names are now Courts of Appeals.[10]

The capstones of the modern structure came in a series of statutes after World War I, which reallocated appellate responsibilities in vital ways. In response to lobbying by Chief Justice Taft and others in the mid-1920s, Congress empowered federal appellate courts to decide all civil and criminal appeals rising from federal district courts, while restricting access to the Supreme Court.[11] The Justices were granted discretionary control over their own docket, except for direct appeals from state supreme courts and three-judge federal district courts which, in cases of paramount national interest defined by statute, bypassed Courts of Appeals. In 1976, such cases were narrowed to the Civil Rights Act of 1964, the Voting Rights Act of 1976, legislative reapportionment, or as Congress specifies.[12]

These organizational changes were designed to conserve the energies of the Supreme Court for its historic missions of umpiring intergovernmental disputes and determining legal issues of national significance. To Courts of Appeals went the primary responsibility of deciding federal appeals. As tribunals of general federal jurisdiction, they are authorized to hear appeals as a matter of right from the final judgments and certain interlocutory orders of federal district courts within each region. These include appeals from essentially administrative functions of district courts (e.g., bankruptcy, naturalization, and parole) as well as issues of state law rising in diversity jurisdiction. Hence, alongside the specialized and limited subjects of federal law, circuit judges apply overlapping and sometimes conflicting state rules over a far broader range of subjects. In 1979, diversity cases composed 12 percent of their business rising from district courts.[13]

In addition, Congress gave Courts of Appeals special responsibility to review the actions of federal regulatory agencies and to reconcile their conduct with the rule of law. Circuit courts may hear directly petitions to review or enforce the orders of major federal agencies, such as the Federal Communications Commission, the National Labor Relations Board, and the Securities and Exchange Commission, many of which exercise both rule-making and adjudicatory powers. Although administrative appeals constituted only 10 percent of cases heard by circuit judges in 1979, they can involve complex issues and substantial social interests. Can the Federal Communications Commission impose prospective bans on common ownership of newspapers and broadcasting media in the same communities?[14] Under what conditions can the Environmental Protection Agency curb economic growth or energy development to prevent significant deterioration of air already cleaner than national standards?[15] Can government contracts be denied to companies that violate a president's wage-price guidelines against inflation?[16] Reviewing agency behavior puts Courts of Appeals in the forefront of policy formation and implementation in the modern regulatory state. As a commissioner of the Federal Energy Regulatory Commission put the point recently, "We live with the Courts of Appeals!"

Besides acquiring a fully matured jurisdiction, circuit courts became focal points of federal judicial administration. To bolster judicial independence from the executive branch during the New Deal, Congress in 1938 transferred the management of the federal judiciary from the Department of Justice to federal judges themselves.[17] Managerial control was not lodged in the Supreme Court, largely at Chief Justice Hughes's insistence, but distributed among several institutions, committees, and circuits. The chief policy-making arm of the federal judiciary is the Judicial Conference of the United States, a body required to meet annually, which is composed of the Chief Justice of the United States, the circuit chief judges, and elected representatives from district courts. Administrative command, at least in theory, is decentralized among the Courts of Appeals, which in their managerial capacity are called circuit judicial councils. The premise was that circuit judges, being closer to the problems and personnel of district courts, could supervise their activities better by informal techniques compatible with traditions of judicial independence and self-government. Regional administration would also husband the energies of the Justices and keep them out of the politics of federal judicial administration. The Supreme Court, as a result, was excluded from managing lower courts except indirectly via litigation, defining rules of federal procedure, and whatever Chief Justices make of their positions as heads of the Judicial Conference.

In theory, circuit judges oversee the management of lower federal courts, but increasingly they have delegated administrative burdens to an allied bureaucracy. A centralized Administrative Office of the United States Courts, located in Washington, maintains tight reins on fiscal management, housekeeping, and data collection. The Federal Judicial Center, created in 1969, is active in research, development, and training of personnel. Since 1971, professional circuit executives also assist circuit councils and chief judges in judicial administration; and larger circuits employ central staff attorneys to help separate the wheat from the chaff in litigation. As in hospital administration, the new bureaucrats are supposedly on tap rather than on top of the dominant professionals. It is a good question whether over the long run judges will be any more successful than doctors in maintaining their supremacy.[18]

These shifts in responsibility profoundly altered the character of federal appellate courts. The Supreme Court changed from a forum, heavily engaged in private law, to a public-law tribunal increasingly concerned with constitutional issues, and all that means for the high court's roles in the polity and the politics of its support. Courts of Appeals moved from the periphery to the hub of federal adjudication and court management. In effect, Congress built a double division of labor into the appellate process. One division lies between the function of "error correction," in which appellate courts hold trial courts and agencies accountable under law, and the function of "institutional review," in which appellate courts umpire conflicts among different branches of government and declare general principles of legal policy.[19] This distinction is at one with that between individual and national interests in federal appeals. The high court serves essentially national purposes. The person in the street may exclaim—"I'll take my case to the Supreme Court, by God!"—but that is unlikely by act of Congress, even if he can afford it. Unless a litigant can convince four Justices that the claim has general import, transcending personal stakes, the right to appeal essentially stops at state supreme courts and federal Courts of Appeals.

The price of concentrating the power of the Supreme Court on institutional review was to divert error correction in particular cases into eleven regional intermediates. As these tribunals may decline review in only three situations, virtually all of their business is mandatory.[20] Because their decisions are final except when the Justices grant review, circuit courts are courts of last resort for the great mass of federal litigants.

Congress also attempted to separate the functions of judicial policy making and administration at every level. Chief judges and court administrators are expected to manage federal courts effectively without affecting the merits of adjudication. Though the realism of this distinction is open to question, the administrative obligations of circuit judges, such as tending dockets or supervising application of the Bail Reform Act of 1968, are increasingly demanding.

For both adjudication and administration, then, it is fair to conclude with Frankfurter and Landis that the rise of the Supreme Court has been marked chiefly by progressive contraction of its jurisdiction and progressive expansion of the responsibilities of Courts of Appeals.[21] In the process these tribunals have acquired triple missions in the national government: adjudicating federal appeals, supervising federal agencies, and administering lower federal courts. Expected to pull together the loosely related parts of the federal judiciary, courts in between serve as more than stepchildren or way stations in litigation. Collectively, they are "the vital center of the federal judicial system."[22]

The vital center, however, is composed of eleven centers, not one. Several sources of destabilization inhere in their modern form. Regional organization, for all the relief to the high court, impedes unity of command in both legal doctrine and procedure. By virtue of jurisdiction and administrative independence, no two Courts of Appeals are alike. Their business tends to reflect the characteristics of each region. Notwithstanding uniform rules of appellate procedure adopted in 1968, their power to define subsidiary rules lends surprisingly little standardization to internal decision making or administrative practice. These peculiarities inevitably constrict comparisons among the three circuits.

Regionalism is also a source of conflict among the eleven circuits over issues of national law. These conflicts the Supreme Court is supposed to resolve. Variety, to be sure, adds creative spice to federal jurisprudence and court management. Decentralization nonetheless converts lower courts into potential nodes of competition and conflict, which litigants may exploit. Woven into the fabric of federal judicial organization is a potential flaw circuit courts were created to control: Balkanization of national law.

What's more, the composition of Courts of Appeals encourages diversification *within* circuits as well as *among* them. To maximize appellate resources, Congress authorized circuit courts to decide appeals by divisions of not more than three judges.[23] All intermediate courts distribute cases among rotating panels of three members. These panels *are* Courts of Appeals. It takes little imagination to recognize the potential of rotation for intracircuit conflicts. A tribunal of nine members can yield eighty-four different combinations of judges.[24] A majority of active members may convene the full court (en banc) to reconcile differences; but circuit judges tend to avoid en bancs as cumbersome devices of conflict resolution. Even when major issues are at stake, the path of least resistance is to tolerate disagreement and pass the buck on up. Cracks in circuit cohesion thus go concealed and unmended.[25]

Panel rotation is to the circuits what regionalism is to the Supreme Court, a potential source of disharmony in federal law. Inconsistent decisions are not the only hazard. Courts of Appeals are expected to rotate panel memberships randomly to ensure impartial decisions. Rightly or wrongly, few circuits have escaped suspicion of panel packing to steer results.[26] Subtler threats to circuit coherence are the physical dispersion of judges, at least one per state, and obstacles to collegial deliberation among autonomous individuals increasingly swamped with work. The busier the court the stronger the temptations to delegate labor, bureaucratize internal operations, and mass-produce decisions. Such practices jeopardize the collegiality and quality of decisions on which judicial accountability and community acceptance depend.

These sources of instability, inherent in the organization of federal courts, have been magnified in recent years by a law explosion. Since the 1960s, Courts of Appeals have been in the vortex of great changes in American conceptions of law and the judicial function. These changes, particularly in federal public law, are both qualitative and quantitative in character. Qualitatively, judges confront a rapid rise in the range and complexity of disputes they are asked to resolve. "Over the last two decades," as Abram Chayes observed in 1976, "courts have assumed responsibility for desegregating school systems, reapportioning legislatures, regulating employment practices of major companies, supervising land use planning in municipalities, directing credit practices of banks and credit card companies, monitoring environmental quality and even managing mental institutions and prison systems. What has happened is much more than a doctrinal shift. It adds up to a radical transformation of the role and function of the judiciary in American life."[27]

The transformation involves both what judges do and how they work. Drastic departures are being taken from the classic model of adjudication, shaped largely by private-law actions, in which neutral umpires apply established legal rules to disputes initiated by private adversaries. Traditional notions of appropriate subjects and methods of adjudication are in flux. Standards governing access to courts and standing to sue have been relaxed. Cases encompass broad policy principles and social interests. Rights and remedies have not only expanded enormously but become more flexible. So has judicial power. When federal judges take command of state school systems in Mississippi or mental hospitals in Alabama to protect individual rights; when federal judges close jails in New York City or order southern municipalities to spend or to change their form of government in pursuit of social equality, it is apparent that inherited boundaries of judicial authority under the doctrine of separation of powers have substantially eroded. As governing becomes more complex, and courts take on more of the burdens of solving social problems, institutional differences recede in the administrative state.[28]

The slippage involves more than a recurring cycle of government by judiciary, in which jurists impose checks on legislative majorities. Federal judges, as Felix Frankfurter feared, have become surrogate lawmakers in the vacuums of public choice. Courts, seizing the initiative, have become catalysts of social change—motors as well as brakes of the body politic. Lower federal courts, their discretion stretched to implement broad decrees, resemble administrative agencies. They oversee great public enterprises in education, housing, and economic development. They also serve as ombudsmen for relief of official abuse.[29] And in the process of enlarging their sphere of influence federal judges have enlarged their political risks. Small wonder that the proper role of judges has become the subject of intense dispute both on and off the bench. For a comparable period of judicial creativity one must recall England before equity followed law.

These changes have improved the quality of American justice enormously. Yet, they have also contributed to a quantum leap in caseloads, which strain courts as organizations and adjudication as a process of decision. Federal courts are awash with litigation. As shown in Table 1.1, the number of cases commenced between 1961 and 1979 doubled in the trial and supreme courts and quadrupled in Courts of Appeals. Growth of cases outstripped growth of judgeships at every level. The gap between demand and supply, though widely publicized for the Supreme Court, is most acute for courts in between. The rate of growth in circuit filings during this period exceeded that of judicial manpower by 336 percent, as compared to 44 percent for district courts and 144 percent for the supreme bench. Cases disposed of after hearing or submission on briefs, a better measure of judicial work, outpaced the growth of circuit judges 162 percent (for details see Table 2.2). In 1978, after a ten-year hiatus, Congress enlarged the number of circuit judgeships by over a third; but a companion increase of 30 percent in district judges makes it doubtful if the imbalance between levels was corrected.[30] It is even doubtful whether the stock cure of more judges and courts will long satisfy spiraling demands for appellate services. What has happened is much more than workloads swelling in step with national growth. It adds up to a massive inflation in both gravity and volume of federal appeals.

What accounts for this extraordinary surge in federal appeals? As with most great inflations, the causes are complex and not fully understood.[31] Population increases, economic growth, and crime waves no doubt are partly responsible. So are sweeping expansions of federal rights launched in response to demands for centralized government solutions for problems formerly handled elsewhere. Though the law explosion encompasses state judiciaries as well, a fundamental trend is the steady maturation of the dual-court structure. Both the Supreme Court and Congress, clinging to the federal purse and premises of state infidelity, have pursued national alternatives down the course of their logic. The drift is most pronounced in criminal justice. A judicially inspired revolution in criminal procedure in the era of the Warren Court, including nationalization of most of the federal Bill of Rights and expansion of rights of prisoners to attack convictions and prison conditions in federal courts, stimulated a massive tide of criminal appeals and prisoner petitions.[32] Between 1961 and 1979, state prisoner petitions alone rose roughly 1,700 percent in both district courts and Courts of Appeals. Congress, too, has spurred federal criminal litigation by sponsoring bail reform, speedy trial, and above all subsidized rights to counsel. Hesitating to ascribe the steep climb of federal criminal caseloads to decisions of the Warren Court, Casper and Posner attribute it mainly to a combination of more affluent defendants and the provisions of the Criminal Justice Act of 1964, providing compensation to the attorneys of indigent defendants. Indigents now have little to lose by appealing; after *Anders v. California* their attorneys risk liability if they do not.[33] The result is that criminal justice has become a major responsibility of Courts of Appeals in less than one generation. Still greater caseloads loom on the horizon if Congress recodifies federal criminal law and provides for appellate review of sentencing.[34]

Though criminal justice involves the most dramatic increases, ap-

TABLE 1.1
Cases Commenced in Federal Courts
FY 1961-1979

|  | 1961 N | 1979 N | % Increase 1961-1979 |
|---|---|---|---|
| **U.S. District Courts** | | | |
| Criminal | 30,268 | 32,688 | 8.0 |
| U.S. civil | 18,254 | 51,341 | 181.3 |
| Private civil | 37,430 | 80,324 | 114.6 |
| Prisoner petitions | 2,609 | 23,001 | 781.6 |
| Federal | (1,589) | (4,499) | (183.1) |
| State | (1,020) | (18,502) | (1,713.9) |
| Sums | 88,561 | 187,354 | 111.6 |
| Number of authorized judgeships | 308 | 516 | 67.5 |
| **U.S. Courts of Appeals** | | | |
| Criminal | 616 | 4,102 | 565.9 |
| U.S. civil | 609* | 3,208 | 426.8 |
| Private civil | 1,423* | 6,259 | 339.8 |
| Prisoner petitions | 290* | 2,753 | 849.3 |
| Federal | (179)* | (775) | (333.0) |
| State | (111)* | (1,978) | (1,682.0) |
| Bankruptcy | 115 | 423 | 267.8 |
| Administrative appeals | 846 | 2,922 | 245.4 |
| D.C. Court of Appeals | 18 | — | (−)100.0 |
| Original proceedings | 89 | 552 | 520.2 |
| Sums | 4,006 | 20,219 | 404.7 |
| Number of authorized judgeships | 78 | 132 | 69.2 |
| **U.S. Supreme Court** | | | |
| Appellate docket | 842 | 2,379** | 182.5 |
| Miscellaneous docket | 1,098 | 2,335** | 112.7 |
| Original docket | 0 | 17** | 1,700.0 |
| Sums | 1,940 | 4,731** | 143.9 |
| Number of authorized judgeships | 9 | 9 | 0.0 |

SOURCE: AO Annual Reports (1960, 1961, and preliminary 1979).
* 1960 data
** 1978 term

pellate workloads, as Table 1.1 shows, have ballooned along all fronts. The example set by the Supreme Court in *Brown* v. *Board of Education* and the willingness of federal judges to respond to the "punting syndrome" of inactive state officials have undoubtedly contributed to the conditions critics scorn as the "imperial judiciary."[35] It would be hard to prove, however, that an oligarchy of judicial activists is more responsible for expanding judicial roles and swollen dockets than other branches of government. Congresses and presidents, without displacing old business or sharing the burden with state judiciaries, have added vast enforcement responsibilities to federal courts in civil rights, welfare, consumer protection, energy, and the environment. Swollen appellate dockets merely reflect a general trend during this period toward nationalization of law.[36]

In the end, perhaps the root cause is the oft-noted litigiousness of the American people. It seems that the less they participate in voting, the more they litigate in the belief, however mistaken, that law is a fit instrument of social change and that federal courts offer cheaper, faster, and more effective solutions to their problems.[37] More and more litigants are turning to the formal machinery of adjudication to resolve disputes. For example, civil cases filed in federal district courts more than doubled between 1961 and 1979. The ratio of federal criminal cases reaching trial also rose from 10 percent in 1950 to 24 percent in 1975, thereby expanding the pool out of which appeals may rise.[38] Yet, it is unwise to assume that "the volume and nature of appellate work depends largely upon the intake of *nisi prius* courts."[39] Litigation pressures vary widely among different levels of the judiciary and sections of the country.[40] Federal appeals have risen over three times faster than federal trials. Expectations must be rising about the potential of federal justice on appeal.

No one knows the extent to which the quest for appellate justice represents falling faith in a sluggish political process or simply searches for responsive forums. Nor do we know exactly how much changing concepts of law and the judicial function have fed the caseload inflation. What's certain is that the transformations of recent times have far-reaching implications for Courts of Appeals. They are undergoing significant expansion in public responsibilities and corresponding shifts in their clienteles. To traditional functions of norm enforcement, circuit judges have added policy making and management. As losers and weaklings at the polls resort to adjudication to achieve their goals, federal courts are being converted into representative bodies and lawsuits into political weapons.[41] Circuit judges are also reaching beyond their traditional constituencies of economic elites—corporations, unions, government agencies—and extending their services to the mass. Intensified in the process are perennial debates over the *legitimacy* of judicial power.[42] Increasingly, too, critics ponder neglected questions of judicial *capacity* to make and administer social policy. Given the limitations of adjudication as a process of decision, does policy making by lawsuit actually work?[43]

Mushrooming demands also aggravate worrisome pathologies in the operations of federal courts. Overload breeds delay. Overload shrinks appellate oversight at the very time that discretion in trial courts and agencies expands. Preoccupation with policy problems and processing cases, in larger circuits as well as the Supreme Court, intensifies the tension between the goal of uniformity and localized operations. Fears mount that national appellate capacity is inadequate.[44] Unlike decisions in like cases are lamented no less in the circuits. Even more serious is the impact of quantity on the quality of adjudication. The influx of so-called junk litigation, such as prisoner petitions and social security claims, has forced virtually all Courts of Appeals to shift part of their business from handcrafted to mass-production techniques of decision. These include limited oral argument, per curiam opinions, and summary decisions from the bench. Pressures for greater efficiency have led to increased delegation and bureaucratization of authority inside Courts of Appeals. The three circuits, as discussed in Chapter Nine, are in the vanguard of these experiments. Their experience, however essential in keeping them abreast of their work, points to basic tensions between rising tides of litigation and changing expectations of federal appellate justice. If the "triumph of equity" is converting federal courts into something more than the traditional judiciary, so assembly-line adjudication is converting them into something less.[45]

In many ways Courts of Appeals now confront the same symptoms of overreach that gave them birth. Their roles and resources have stimulated considerable government concern. The Burger Court has attempted to reduce the intake by restricting access to federal courts.[46] The Carter administration has created a new office in the Department of Justice devoted to improving the administration of federal justice, and many reform proposals are before Congress.[47] These reactions raise vexing issues not unlike those plaguing other public services, such as education and welfare, that we attempt to dispense en masse. Is expansion of federal appeals ultimately self-defeating? Can review be rendered in large volume without cheapening the quality and uniformity of the product on which the legitimacy of judicial power rests? Can access to federal appeals be limited without offending fundamental norms of due process and equal justice under law? In short, are rising flows of litigation compatible with changing judicial roles?

These questions may merely reflect larger problems of government overload in the United States, but it is essential to understand that the answers are only partly within the control of judges. Just as critical sources of appellate demand are embedded in the external environment, so the remedies for the ills of circuit courts are rooted in—and restricted by—the politics of federal courts.

## The Political Setting

The question is often asked whether American courts are legal or political institutions. For the Supreme Court, Archibald Cox's short answer is both.[48] Courts of Appeals, too, are bifocal. Politics, meaning authoritative allocation of values as opposed to partisan brawls, pervades their goals, composition, and working milieu.[49] To understand them as instruments of government, even as courts of law, is to link them to the political universe in which they orbit.

This theme naturally invites dispute. Americans still cling to an official ideology of "a government of laws and not of men," a vision of the rule of law in which politics and law are separate worlds and judging is objective judgment. These distinctions have traditionally loomed large in reconciling judicial power with popular democracy. Defining law as right reason, Alexander Hamilton and John Marshall solved the conundrum of judicial legislation by denying its existence. According to their classic model, judges do not make the law but merely declare it; judges exercise neither political power nor personal will but merely judgment, a process bridled by law and the discipline of a professional craft.[50]

Legal realists in the twentieth century have had a field day debunking these official ideologies of law and the judicial function. The conduct of judges in every generation has demonstrated that independence from Congress or president does not divorce federal judges from political life. Nor does the principle of judicial neutrality toward litigants imply that legal rules are neutral. Because law itself is purposive, judging in appellate courts is necessarily value laden rather than value free. Especially is this so in the United States where courts participate in lawmaking, legitimation, and even public education.[51] However much discretion may be veiled behind legal categories that appear to routinize decisions, judges cannot escape the "leeways of choice."[52]

It is easier to debunk worn myths of judicial objectivity, however, than to replace them with realistic conceptions of the policy functions of courts that do not overstate the case. Recognizing that judges legislate is the beginning rather than the end of sophistication. "The problem," as Justice Frankfurter once wrote Justice Black, "is not whether the judges make the law, but when and how and how much."[53] The same is true of their newer roles in public administration. To grapple with these subtler issues of degree, social scientists have developed models depicting federal judges as political actors with distinct constituencies and constraints, as functionaries in legal bureaucracies, and as members of separate, small groups. A substantial consensus exists about the major links between federal courts and the political process.[54]

The most basic connections, often taken for granted, are between judicial organization and jurisdiction. The missions and structure of federal courts, their budgets and boundaries with other institutions, are not made in heaven but mostly in Congress with earthly ends in view. A fundamental lesson of American experience is that politics limits organizational change of federal courts. Illustrations riddle our history. Just as the Founding Fathers delegated to Congress the power to organize the federal judiciary, so Congress fashioned district courts along state lines to temper national power, as we have seen. Within each circuit, positions on Courts of Appeals are also allocated by state, a custom that gives senators considerable leverage over their membership. These compromises, like representation in the Senate, mean that state interests help to compose the very organs of national judicial power interposed between states and the people to secure federal rights.

State and national judicial authority is further divided by jurisdiction—what cases courts are empowered to decide. Though technical in appearance, questions of jurisdiction are questions of public policy, because jurisdiction rations judicial power and access to it. Not everybody uses circuit courts or has equal opportunity to do so. Ability to tap judicial resources depends formally on satisfying jurisdiction over the subject matter or the parties, as well as technical standards of standing to sue and "justiciability," which serve as gatekeepers controlling the controversies federal courts can remedy. Circuit judges, their work "largely predetermined by the jurisdictional ambit" of lower courts and agencies, have little control over these matters.[55] The scope of federal jurisdiction is a policy question to be decided primarily by national politicians. If history is any guide, they usually find it easier to expand the supply of judicial resources than to contract demand. Layers of jurisdiction, once added, are rarely discarded to make room for new responsibility. The

House of Representatives' refusal to allow the Hruska Commission even to consider jurisdiction is but a recent case in point.[56] What could be more "political" than the people's access to federal courts?

The power to initiate legal action, moreover, is highly decentralized. Litigants, not judges, set court agendas. Though circuit judges are not entirely powerless, as we shall see, their passivity conditions many things. Ability to litigate, for one, depends on ample purses and effective mobilization of legal services, which vary greatly among different classes, groups, and sections of the country.[57] Consumers of circuit services, for another, may differ over field and time. Commercial interests in diversity jurisdiction dominated circuit dockets in the beginning. The Great Depression and World War II brought continuing relations with powerful social aggregates concerned with labor relations, taxation, and public regulation of basic industries. Today, Courts of Appeals are under mounting pressure to stretch their services to an expanding universe of individuals, groups, and less material interests.[58] Such pressures do not pulsate with equal volume or intensity. Behind a formal facade of federal uniformity flourishes great variety in litigious activity and outcomes from one locality to another. These, in turn, spur intercircuit conflicts, some accidental and some on purpose. Federal agencies, such as the NLRB and the Internal Revenue Service, regularly relitigate issues in different circuits in order to have important principles of law decided adversely to them resolved nationally by the Supreme Court.[59] Shopping for a favorable forum, in law as in politics, is an old tactic among adversaries in a government of separate institutions sharing powers.

Selection of federal judges is another critical nexus between politics and national courts. Complex political processes filter who, of the many qualified lawyers available, will decide federal appeals. Federal judgeships are among the richest prizes politicians may bestow. Choosing judges rarely occurs in a vacuum. As examined more closely in Chapter Four, a multitude of participants including presidents, senators, bar associations, and other interests, at both state and national levels, may be active in recruiting circuit judges. Though each appointment may be discrete, the recipe usually boils down to three related ingredients—professional competence, political participation, and personal ambition—plus a pinch of luck.[60] As one recent appointee summarized his experience:

> It's a unique process. Nobody gets to be a circuit judge unless a high-powered politician has an interest in that man. There are as many highly qualified men who don't make it as those who

do. There's got to be an element of friendship and admiration on the part of a politician to select you out of the herd. Of course, you've got to have some basic qualifications. You can't pick just anybody in the face of the American Bar Association ratings. But at the same time I can't say the honor always goes to the most qualified.

Though President Carter's merit nominating commissions were designed to reduce reliance on "high-powered politicians" in recommending candidates, these facts of life condition Courts of Appeals fundamentally. The politics of recruitment affects the kinds of persons who become circuit judges and the decisions they make. Skillful replacement of judicial turnover, whether labeled "court packing" or "balancing," is a customary method of influencing the ideological hue of federal courts. New judgeships have traditionally lubricated passage of structural or jurisdictional reforms through Congress. Even without conscious attempts at external control, the selection process tends to hoist certain kinds of individuals onto the bench while excluding others. Only lawyers customarily serve. Besides ensuring a professional monopoly, the many filters through which candidates must pass tend to eliminate political extremists, mavericks, and outsiders. This means more than that circuit judges tend to be members of a legal "establishment" or political elite. It means that professional values are strong on Courts of Appeals. It means further that political values of moderation blend with professionalism and formal review in controlling judicial discretion.

As discussed more fully in Part II, courts in the middle tend to attract men in the middle, politically and professionally. Because their vocational choices and training tend to interact with the politics of their recruitment, a certain symbiosis or "fit" has developed between the office and its members. Common values learned en route to office contribute to a broad consensus in the judges' conceptions of judicial roles and public policy. Contrary to official theory, moreover, professional norms do not shield judicial decisions from political predilections. In the 2d, 5th, and D.C. circuits, the two sets of values tended to meld. Overlapping judicial values became a primary source of cohesion, offsetting decentralization of institutions, because they narrowed the range of conflict and the window of essential Supreme Court review.

Judicial politics as well as judicial philosophies helps to integrate the federal judiciary. For all the rhetoric decrying the penetration of politics into the judicial process, it is far from certain that political considerations should be eliminated from the selection of judges, even if they could be. So long as circuit judges participate in governing the country much is to be said for courts being responsive, as distinct from responsible, to the governed.[61] Political appointment serves to harmonize federal judicial power with popular tolerances and concomitant lawmaking coalitions in other branches of government. So do permeating professional and social contacts among federal judges and their communities. Federal judges may not feel beholden to their patrons or represent certain constituents, but those who occupy these posts are usually individuals of affairs who rose to power by developing an impressive array of professional and political contacts. Such people naturally become conscious of constituencies in the bar and their communities and are sensitive to what their publics will bear.[62] Reacting to a headstrong Supreme Court, Theodore Roosevelt once blustered: "I may not know much about law but I do know one can put the fear of God into judges."[63] Interlocking processes of socialization, recruitment, and professionalization make such methods seldom necessary for Courts of Appeals.

Beyond these ties to the policy process, judicial behavior is affected by the attitudes of individual jurists and constrained by internal decision-making processes of collegial courts. Just as attitudes are a blend of personal and professional values acquired en route to the bench, so external expectations affect methods by which judges make decisions and achieve consensus within each group. Also relevant to judicial functions are the politics of compliance with court rulings and the impact of judicial decisions on public policy. After *Brown* v. *Board of Education*, it is hardly necessary to argue that judges set policy goals in this country.[64] Considering the difficulties of implementing that decision, it is also unnecessary to belabor Brooks Adams's warning that the universe will not obey the judicial decree.[65] Because appellate courts are highly dependent on others to set their agendas and enforce their rulings, effective policy making by judges depends on support from other actors, including other jurists, with whom they share power. These broad relationships have been thinly substantiated for Courts of Appeals, and those concerning compliance and impact are beyond the scope of this study; but they suggest a final modality worth noting in the political setting of circuit courts.

Reform of the federal judiciary is at heart a political process with distinct patterns and rhythms. Since most of the pressures and remedies are beyond judicial control, the capacities of circuit judges to correct the pathologies of overload are severely limited. Even so, judges and allies at the bar have historically been the catalysts of change, activated after chronic distress became acute. Certainly the massive reallocations of judicial responsibility of this century owe much to prolonged pressure on Congress from Justices, who were goaded by docket congestion and administrative neglect. Yet, judges are reluctant lobbyists. Inhibited by law and custom from political activity, and supported by few interest groups, they can seldom mobilize winning coalitions in favor of institutional changes, much less of jurisdiction. Innovations, as a result, tend to be internal and incremental adjustments rather than overhauls. Often they come too little, too late. The natural bias of federal courts, institutionally as well as doctrinally, is toward the status quo.[66]

These patterns prevail today. Courts of Appeals were designed to relieve clogged appellate dockets but possess few means to protect themselves from the same affliction. In view of political realities, the remedies are likely to be slow and piecemeal until breakdown threatens, thus increasing tension between their functions of timely error correction and lawmaking in test cases, not to mention uniformity. Precisely because both Congress and the Supreme Court depend on intermediate appellate courts to implement their programs and to oversee bureaucracies, those who control judicial structures are likely to increase physical resources or to tinker with judicial machinery before curtailing access to circuit services. External demands from the political environment, far more than principles of judicial administration, tend to shape the structure and functions of courts in between.

As agents of the national government, circuit judges feel the tug of these environmental connections in several directions at once. In the federal system they serve as more remote authorities sufficiently insulated from community or partisan pressures to make unpopular decisions that local officials or even federal district judges find hard to make. Middle positions, however, cut both ways. The twelve circuits are in some degree competing power centers, potential checks on as well as extensions of Supreme Court authority.[67] At the same time that they enforce national policies they also mediate between national law and various political and professional constituencies in regional communities. Middlemen, too, face difficulties in securing consistency in and conformity with their rulings. Beyond their traditional duties of adjudicating controversies they are expected to administer federal courts effectively and to cope with changing demands from litigators—private and public, elite and mass—to enforce federal law and shape public policy. Their everyday working world, consequently, is hardly a closed system of legal reasoning, concerned exclusively with cases or even personal predilections. As intermediates in many dimensions of responsibility, they look down to district courts and agencies, up to the Supreme Court and the central government, in to themselves, their colleagues and staffs, across to rival appellate courts, and all around to various groups and individuals who compose their attentive publics.[68] In ways both subtle and crude Courts of Appeals are inevitably part of the shifting lawmaking coalitions that compose the pluralistic world of American politics.

As the vision of circuit judges is necessarily expanded by these broader relationships, so should the complexities of the judicial environment be taken into account in assessing Courts of Appeals in the governmental process. Given their purposes, powers, and political settings, what are the contemporary functions of the three circuits and their relations with other courts in the judicial system? Are they way stations, mirror images of the Justices, or nerve centers of the federal judiciary? How diverse is their business and how final their decisions?

Courts of Appeals were created to assist the Supreme Court when the Justices confronted about 1,500 appeals annually. What holds the federal judiciary together over eight decades later when the Justices, facing 4,000 cases a year with capacity to hear less than 200, can provide only limited supervision to fifty state supreme courts, twelve federal circuits, and a cluster of specialized tribunals? Has the growth of federal appeals outstripped the ability of the Supreme Court and the Courts of Appeals to supervise trial courts and agencies or are more tribunals required? What contains the discretion of judges to make law according to personal preferences? How do circuit judges resolve their conflicts and allocate their work? What remedies are available to resolve tensions between rising demands for appellate relief and judicial resources?

Without pretending to provide all the answers, we shall address these questions by examining two basic dimensions of control on judicial discretion in three major Courts of Appeals. In the next two chapters, from the perspective of courts, we shall consider the reach of formal review at both appellate levels in the flow of federal litigation. Then, in Part II, from the perspective of circuit judges, we shall examine the informal norms and values that circuit judges shared as members of the interpretative community. The analysis of litigation flow shows that in the mid-1960s federal courts were, indeed, decentralized. Appeals were widely and unevenly spread. Formal supervision was limited. Reliance on internalized constraints to maintain judicial solidarity, both among and within circuit courts, was heavier than reliance on external review. Contrary to declaratory or legal realist theories, however, the values apparent in the circuit judges' votes were neither exclusively professional norms nor political predilections, but complex congeries of both depending on the subject and context. The political orientations and role conceptions of these judges, overlapping and mutually supporting, contributed informally to circuit consensus. A similar mix of informal expectations with formal decision rules also guided conflict resolution within the circuits and the distribution of judicial work.

Either to diagnose the problems of Courts of Appeals or to fashion remedies for them without considering the interplay of formal practice and informal custom may well be counterproductive. So it is of the uniformity and uniqueness of Courts of Appeals.

# Two · The Flow of Litigation in Three Courts of Appeals

"Inflexible execution of the national laws," in Alexander Hamilton's phrase, is a primary object of federal courts.[1] Unity of legal doctrine is difficult to achieve in any case-law system, but the task is the more formidable when the organs of judicial power are decentralized across a "teeming continent."[2] It is a common error to assume that all federal courts are alike.[3] Notwithstanding strong forces of cohesion in the federal judiciary, substantial discretion and diversity flourish among the very tribunals Congress created to harmonize national law. Just as the doctrine of *stare decisis* gives federal judges leeway to reconcile the values of continuity and change, so regional organization enables them to accommodate local and national interests in federal law enforcement. How much so—the independence of lower courts and agencies from formal review—is central to the functions of Courts of Appeals and the integration of the federal judiciary.

In this chapter and the next, we shall examine the mix of uniformity and uniqueness in court relations as litigation flowed through three widely different circuits. The theme is that variety in their work diversified supervision of district courts and agencies and thus their functions in federal law enforcement. Despite a long-term trend toward greater uniformity in circuit dockets, regionalism flourished alongside nationalization of judicial values.[4] For evidence we shall compare (1) the business of the three tribunals, (2) the mobilization of appeals to them from different sources and subjects, and (3) the character and policy outcomes of their decisions. Then in Chapter Three we shall compare the work of the Supreme Court in the same cases in order to estimate the finality of circuit decisions and the reach of formal appellate controls.

The basic goal is to determine, at least formally, what litigation the three intermediate courts controlled in the federal judicial system. For this purpose it is necessary to track the same cases and their outcomes through both the circuit courts and the Supreme Court.[a] Al-

---

[a] The main reason for independent tracking is that published government data are designed to monitor workflows horizontally at each level of the federal judiciary, not vertically between levels. Data about the subjects and sources of appeals decided after hearing or submission on briefs are reported only in very broad categories at both

though a case may pass through successive appeals before completion, we shall make the simplifying assumption that each case is an independent unit in one cycle of litigation from district courts or agencies to the Supreme Court in order to estimate the extent to which the three tribunals became courts of last resort. A short-hand expression for that is "finality," which is the stage when a judicial decision becomes officially binding on the parties because it either is not appealed or is upheld. Because of limited resources, no attempt was made to discover who had the final word after one cycle of appeal, though Judge John R. Brown is surely right that, "unlike their military counterparts, many cases neither die nor fade away. They simply go on."[5]

The cases consist of all nonconsolidated decisions made after hearing or submission on briefs by the three circuit courts during three fiscal years, 1965-1967. These decisions include 4,135 cases published in the *Federal Reporter*, plus 806 unpublished cases obtained from the Administrative Office of the United States Courts—a total of 4,941 cases. Decisions after hearing are examined, rather than cases commenced, because they are better measures of judicial work.[b] Together, these decisions constitute roughly 40 percent of all appeals disposed of by circuit courts after hearing or submission on briefs during this period, a time of relative stability before the sharp acceleration of federal appeals after 1968.

A few disclaimers are in order at the start. There is a view that counting decisions is an unilluminating way to study federal courts. Because appellate adjudications are shaped by many participants, so the argument goes, the formal decisions of Courts of Appeals do not necessarily express their influence. For many students the critical product of litigation is not who wins or formally decides law suits, but doctrine. Incremental case law is at once the policy product of courts and the main medium of communication among multiple actors in the legal process.[6] Building blocks of judge-made law, opinions not outcomes are what count.

It is a perennial issue, as we shall see in Chapter Five, whether the fruits of appeal are reasons or results. Though professors, judges,

---

levels, making it difficult to gauge intercourt supervision and impossible to link the particular district courts, agencies, or judges involved. One must also assume that appeals commenced were terminated in the same fiscal year, though this convention proved to be less distorting than originally feared. See Appendix 1 for discussion of the methods used to analyze litigation flow.

[b] Henceforth the Administrative Office will be abbreviated as AO, and references to fiscal years will be dropped in the text for easier reading. Decimal points will also be rounded off in the text, though retained in the tables with one exception: sums in the tables and appendixes will be rounded off to 100.0%.

and litigants may assign them different weights, the truth is that both error correction and lawmaking are integral and interrelated functions of federal appeals. The aggregate decisions of appellate courts are critical in transmitting federal policies to the people and in enforcing individual rights.[7] Law, by like token, is often on trial with litigants because of the pressure of facts on legal principles. New doctrine also tends to stimulate new litigation, sometimes to the point of institutional strain. In evaluating systems of justice, no less than in grading students of law, it is well to recall Justice Holmes's "warning against thinking dramatically rather than quantitatively."[8]

Making inferences from aggregate decisions is undoubtedly hazardous for circuit courts, sandwiched as they are between two other tiers and composed of rotating members. The procedures used here offer no escape from subjectivity in classification or from the vagaries of analyzing influence. No commonly accepted definition of finality exists; nor does the concept differentiate among the indeterminate causes that may explain it.[9] Rates of appeal and reversal, moreover, are inevitably static and partial estimates of finality in continuous adjudications, not to mention less formal chains of causation or compliance. Danger also lurks in interpreting results. To assume that the legal order is a democracy of numbers in which all cases are equal is to exaggerate the discretion and workloads of lower courts.

These difficulties are by no means unique to the study of judicial decision making, however. Though what follows is not the only way to study federal appeals, analyzing the flow of litigation is a useful ally of doctrinal analysis in assessing circuit courts as institutions. Clarifying what happens in the same cases at different judicial levels highlights the regularities as well as the variations in judicial work. It pinpoints the division of labor among different tribunals and permits comparison of judicial behavior within them. This information enables us to explore intercourt relations in ways that judicial opinions alone may obscure. Just as scientists study the moon both microscopically and telescopically, so Courts of Appeals, intermediate planets in the judicial solar system, bear scrutiny at ranges both near and far.

## The Business of the Circuit Courts

The first tasks are to describe the business of the three Courts of Appeals during the base period and the major trends since 1960 to provide historical perspective. The nature of the cases decided by each circuit after hearing or submission during 1965-1967 is reported in Table 2.1. These data indicate that the basic directions of the three courts in the next decade were well set.[10]

TABLE 2.1
*The Nature of Cases Disposed of by Three Circuit Courts*
(After Hearing or Submission, FY 1965-1967)
% of circuit caseload

| | From U.S. District Courts | | | | | | | | |
|---|---|---|---|---|---|---|---|---|---|
| | | Civil | | | Adminis- | Original | | | |
| | | Prisoner | | | trative | Proceed- | | | |
| | Criminal | Petitions* | Other | Bankruptcy | Appeals | ings | Other** | Total | |
| Circuit | % | % | % | % | % | % | % | N | % |
| 2d | 21.7 | 10.0 | 43.9 | 6.2 | 14.4 | 3.8 | 0.0 | 1,357 | 100.0 |
| 5th | 16.1 | 15.2 | 53.2 | 3.5 | 9.7 | 2.1 | 0.2 | 2,248 | 100.0 |
| D.C. | 39.0 | 8.5 | 30.5 | 0.0 | 16.2 | 2.6 | 3.1 | 1,336 | 100.0 |
| Sums | 23.8 | 12.0 | 44.5 | 3.3 | 12.8 | 2.7 | 1.0 | 4,941 | 100.0 |

* Prisoner petitions, including habeas corpus, mandamus, parole review, and motions to vacate sentences, are considered civil actions in conformity with AO practice.
** Includes D.C. Board of Tax Appeals and other D.C. boards and commissions.

For example, direct criminal appeals and prisoner petitions constituted at least 30 percent of the cases in each circuit. The volume crisis was also beginning to engulf southern judges. The 5th circuit, then a court of nine to thirteen members, had nearly as many cases as the other two circuits combined. By 1970, in fact, the fifteen judges of the 5th circuit decided almost one-quarter of the national total.

Four things become noteworthy when these data are put in the context of trends since 1960. First, appeals from district courts dominated the caseloads of the three tribunals, both in the mid-sixties (84%) and in 1978 (83%). Appeals from federal administrative agencies, including U.S. Tax Courts, constituted only 13 percent of the cases in the base period. Even in the D.C. circuit, where half the cases by 1977 involved agency appeals, the politically significant function of administrative review rested on a small sampling of presumably select cases.[11]

Second, civil litigation, constituting two-thirds of the caseload, also dominated the dockets of the three circuits and of Courts of Appeals generally. But, third, as shown in Table 2.2, there have been major shifts in business over time. Criminal appeals for all circuits rose from 16 percent of total volume in 1961 to 29 percent by 1979.[12] Criminal cases in the three circuits jumped 503 percent—at least twice as fast as bankruptcy, civil, or administrative appeals.

Fourth, although the rising criminal trend is evident everywhere, the three circuits differed markedly in energies devoted to criminal law. In our cases the D.C. circuit's percentage of criminal appeals (39) was almost double the all-circuit average (22%). In fact, the D.C. circuit's criminal work leaped dramatically in two decades—from only 7 percent of total volume in 1950 to 56 percent in 1970—while its "private civil" ratio fell threefold. It goes too far to suggest a displacement of roles for any circuit court. Criminal business fell drastically after 1973 as appeals and habeas corpus petitions under the D.C. code were transferred to local courts. Comparisons among circuits and over time nonetheless suggest that federal appellate courts are better reflexes of society than is sometimes supposed.[13] Even before Congress mandated that criminal cases be given priority, criminal justice shifted from a peripheral to a central responsibility of Courts of Appeals in one generation.[c]

TABLE 2.2
*Terminations in Three Circuits and All Circuits*
(After Hearing or Submission, FY 1961-1979)

|  | Three Circuits | | | | All Circuits | | |
| --- | --- | --- | --- | --- | --- | --- | --- |
|  | 1961 N | 1970 N | 1979 N | % Increase 1961-1979 | 1961 N | 1979 N | % Increase 1961-1979 |
| Criminal | 195 | 780 | 1,176 | 503.1 | 448 | 2,720 | 507.1 |
| U.S. civil | 236 | 380 | 632 | 167.8 | 621 | 1,882 | 203.1 |
| Private civil | 439 | 1,045 | 1,236 | 181.6 | 1,101 | 3,650 | 231.5 |
| Bankruptcy | 18 | 39 | 53 | 194.4 | 93 | 140 | 50.5 |
| Administrative appeals | 211 | 304 | 350 | 65.9 | 457 | 887 | 94.1 |
| D.C. Court of Appeals and other | 5 | 7 | — | (−)100.0 | 18 | — | (−)100.0 |
| Original proceedings | 32 | 12 | 0 | (−)100.0 | 68 | 6 | (−) 91.2 |
| Total civil and criminal | 1,136 | 2,567 | 3,447 | 203.4 | 2,806 | 9,285 | 230.9 |
| Number of authorized judgeships | 27 | 33 | 48 | 77.8 | 78 | 132 | 69.2 |

SOURCE: AO *Annual Reports* (1961, 1970, and preliminary 1979), Table B1.

Prisoner petitions inflated criminal concerns even more, but moderated the differences among the circuits. If prisoner petitions are added to the criminal litigation in Table 2.1, 48% of the cases in the D.C. circuit concerned criminal matters, as compared to 32% in the 2d circuit and 31% in the 5th circuit.

A related comparison concerns who uses Courts of Appeals. Table 2.3 distinguishes the 1965-1967 cases according to federal, state, and nongovernmental litigants before the three circuit courts. These data underscore the theme that the three tribunals, though forums for private litigation, serve primarily to enforce federal law. The federal government, both as appellant and appellee, was their prime consumer. The law enforced, moreover, was largely statutory in character. Classified by subject matter, only 9 percent of this litigation involved constitutional questions while 63 percent involved statutory or federal-rules questions. Despite the growth of criminal appeals, the federal government as a litigator was engaged mainly in civil (63%) rather than criminal (37%) disputes.

TABLE 2.3
*Governments as Parties to Litigation*
(Appellant or Appellee, FY 1965-1967)

| Circuit | U.S. % | State % | Private % | Total N | Total % |
|---|---|---|---|---|---|
| 2d | 51.7 | 8.0 | 40.3 | 1,357 | 100.0 |
| 5th | 48.5 | 14.4 | 37.1 | 2,248 | 100.0 |
| D.C. | 70.5 | 1.0 | 28.4 | 1,336 | 100.0 |
| Sums | 55.3 | 9.0 | 35.7 | 4,941 | 100.0 |

These elementary characteristics have basic implications for federal judicial functions. For one thing, recognition of the resistance potential of lower courts and agencies should not obscure the underlying premise that *both* Congress and the Supreme Court depend on these tribunals to enforce federal policy. Innovation from the top is difficult to imagine without their support.[14] For another, the growth of criminal business without corresponding loss of "private civil" litigation in most Courts of Appeals implies that intermediate federal courts have acquired new roles in national law enforcement without discarding old, private-law responsibilities, including diversity jurisdiction, that mingle federal judges in state judicial policy. For chronically overloaded circuits, one or the other may have to give.[15]

Table 2.3 also reflects unique characteristics of the three circuits. The court in Washington is primarily a U.S. government tribunal having little to do with state law or corporate disputes, though in the base period it served uniquely as the equivalent of a state supreme court for the District of Columbia in roughly one-fourth of its business. Its personality as a result was split between regulatory affairs of national import and the minutiae of life in Washington. The 2d and 5th circuits had similar mixes of private and federal litigation, but the 5th had more cases involving states or state agents as parties and a disproportionate share of civil liberties claims. State business was almost totally civil in character in all three circuits.

Central to the diversification of judicial power is the tendency of the three courts to concentrate on different subjects as a result of distinctive locations and jurisdiction. Table 2.4 classifies the cases by twelve broad fields of litigation that summarize sixty-two subjects contained in Appendix 2. At first glance, the spread of business among the three circuits appears quite even, but closer analysis supports conventional wisdom about their differences. The 5th circuit, by virtue of prisoner petitions and civil rights disputes, had the largest share of personal status cases. The D.C. circuit had little tax litigation and the heaviest concentration of crimes against persons and property. Though the 2d circuit decided the highest percentage of commercial cases (16), it heard relatively more morals offenses than the others and fewer tax, tort, and contract cases than anticipated from its location in the nation's leading commercial center. In contrast to the D.C. circuit, the 2d and 5th circuits concentrated more on economic issues (62% and 60% respectively) than on personal status issues and crimes.

These broad categories, of course, gloss over the legal issues at stake and the underlying structural and social conditions giving rise to them. Those conditions emerge more clearly when the cases are divided among the sixty-two subjects reported in Appendix 2. Coastal locations surely explain the dominance of the 2d and 5th circuits in admiralty, just as the D.C. circuit's monopoly of rape and FCC licensing cases can be attributed to its unique jurisdiction. Because most "morals offenses" involved narcotics convictions, which received short shrift in all three circuits, it is not surprising that the proportions of circuit decisions concerning narcotics descend (from 9% to 6% to 1%) as one moves south. Auto-theft cases, by contrast, rose in the opposite direction. More surprising is that civil rights consumed a smaller share of the 5th circuit's caseload (4%) than labor-relations statutes (7%), federal taxes (12%), and prisoner petitions (15%). Even at the crest of the civil rights revolution the grist of federal appeals in the Gulf States was predominantly economic in character.[d]

---

[d] The expectation of some judges that the 5th circuit would have the largest per-

TABLE 2.4
The Business of Three Circuit Courts
(After Hearing or Submission, FY 1965-1967)

| Subjects | 2d<br>N = 1,357 | 5th<br>N = 2,248 | D.C.<br>N = 1,336 |
|---|---|---|---|
| Contracts | 9.3 | 12.9 | 10.3 |
| Torts | 13.8 | 14.8 | 7.1 |
| Commerce | 16.3 | 9.1 | 13.8 |
| Labor | 11.5 | 10.8 | 7.3 |
| Taxation* | 10.8 | 12.4 | 2.5 |
| Personal status** | 12.9 | 23.0 | 9.1 |
| Crimes against persons | 0.3 | 0.2 | 8.8 |
| Crimes against property | 5.5 | 6.8 | 18.7 |
| Morals offenses | 9.4 | 1.8 | 6.9 |
| Miscellaneous offenses | 2.7 | 1.1 | 1.4 |
| Local | 0.0 | 0.0 | 4.0 |
| Other | 7.6 | 6.9 | 10.2 |
| Sums | 100.0 | 100.0 | 100.0 |

NOTE: Because both civil and criminal sanctions exist in several categories, criminal appeals spread beyond the ostensibly criminal categories as follows. Commerce: 1 criminal case in the D.C. circuit, 2 in the 2d, and 4 in the 5th. Labor: 4 in the 2d circuit. Taxation: 3 in the D.C. circuit, 24 in the 2d, and 84 in the 5th. Personal status: 3 each in the D.C. and 2d circuits and 10 in the 5th. Other: 33 in the D.C. circuit, 19 in the 2d, and 43 in the 5th.

* Includes tax fraud and wagering taxes.
** Includes civil rights, immigration, and suffrage cases, plus prisoner petitions.

Caseloads, to be sure, crudely measure judicial workloads. Criminal appeals and prisoner petitions normally are less time consuming than regular civil cases, especially in administrative law. Dissecting circuit business by substantive fields also fails to capture precise issues before the courts. It is the nature of appeals that a dispute concerning, say, tort or criminal liability is often narrowed on appeal to a specific legal question or problem of procedure. Did the police transgress evolving rules of searches and seizures in obtaining evidence of tax fraud? Did the FPC consider environmental impact in approving construction of a pipeline? Do environmental groups

---

centage of labor-management cases because of the South's economic growing pains failed to materialize, though the relatively high incidence of appeals concerning wage-hour and social security standards in the 5th circuit may support the view of some judges that the court confronted labor issues settled in the North a generation before.

have standing to raise such questions in court? No statistical system yet devised captures this shift of emphasis on appeal.[16] Clouded in consequence is the heavy concentration of Courts of Appeals on problems of process—how the game of government is played.

Comparisons of substantive business are instructive, even so, because they show that Courts of Appeals participate intermittently rather than uniformly in federal law enforcement. It is fallacious to assume that appeals move evenly into various circuit courts at any given time.[17] Analysis of Appendix 2 yields at least three distinct classes of circuit activity on which the courts' policy functions depend.

First are fields of *staple litigation* common to all three circuits. Actually, these are quite limited in number. If 2 percent of a circuit's caseload is chosen as a basepoint of sustained activity—an average of one panel annually per judge—all three circuits met that standard in only six of sixty-two subjects: labor relations, habeas corpus, and the residual categories of "other contracts," "other personal injury," "other torts," and "other commerce," a group containing many administrative appeals. Taken together, even the more typical 2d and 5th circuits would add only seamen's injuries, bankruptcies, income taxes, and "other taxation" to the list.

Rising from these diverse substantive fields, it is true, were several common issues, such as the wagering tax under the Fifth Amendment, the insanity defense, or the "unseaworthiness" doctrine in admiralty. Yet, the fact remains that all three circuits provided sustained supervision of tribunals below in only a few areas of public policy, notably labor relations, taxation, and criminal procedure. From a quantitative perspective, the three courts concentrated in common on a limited range of policy issues and clienteles.

The impression of intermittent review is accentuated by a second class of litigation—fields of *marginal activity* common to the three circuits. Several subjects were sparsely adjudicated anywhere. There were no kidnapping appeals, for instance, and only a handful concerning embezzlement, extortion, racketeering, food and drugs, migratory birds, and "other sex offenses." Presumably these subjects generated little original litigation. Hence, circuit courts figured in these fields mainly as potential threats, with severely restricted opportunities to supervise trial judges or to fashion new law.

These sectors of shared high and low activity should be contrasted with a third class of litigation—fields of *circuit concentration*. Each circuit adjudicated most of the appeals in some subjects while the other circuits decided only one, two, or sometimes no appeals at all for three years. For example, the D.C. circuit had sparse litigation concerning admiralty, civil rights, and social security, which were heavily litigated in the 5th circuit. The distribution of business by source in Tables 2.10–2.12 shows parallel variety in administrative review. Though the three circuits had similar percentages of administrative appeals (2d, 14; 5th, 10; D.C., 16), the composition of their work contrasted sharply when appeals from the NLRB and the Tax Courts were put aside. Then it became clear that the D.C. circuit decided most of the cases from the federal regulatory agencies, such as the CAB (24 of 25), FCC (60 of 61), FPC (8 of 15), and FTC (8 of 11), while the 2d circuit heard four-fifths of the appeals from the Immigration and Naturalization Service. The 5th circuit heard no appeals from the CAB, FCC, SEC, or even the Secretary of Agriculture.

The frequencies are too small to prove that the D.C. circuit, because of its location in the nation's capital, served as the special watchdog over the federal bureaucracy. The days when this tribunal was virtual overlord of the CAB and FCC also appear to be over, judging by its overall support of these agencies and the FCC's ultimate victory over the judges in standards governing radio programming.[18] Still, the data highlight a tendency toward specialization in administrative review. Circuit judges in Washington dominated judicial oversight of federal regulatory agencies dealing with transportation and communication industries; other circuits carried the main burden in labor relations, taxation, and immigration. Meanwhile, Congress extended the administrative specialization of the D.C. circuit by giving it exclusive or alternate appellate jurisdiction in such matters as the Clean Air Act of 1970.

Widespread does not mean evenly spread.[19] Because their business varies by subject and locality, circuit judges do not have equal opportunities to make judicial policy. From a personal standpoint as well, they seldom concentrate on one subject at a time. Weekly panels might find routine tax and criminal appeals interspersed with complex corporate battles, a new round in the endless "post-*Catco* fallout" from regulation of natural gas prices, plots to blow up the Statue of Liberty, or pornographic films allegedly so disgusting as not to appeal to prurient interests of average Americans.[20] Such breadth of business inevitably stretches the judges' span of attention and limits the ability of rotating members to specialize or to plan. It also constrains their collective capacity to sustain policy leadership in many fields at once. While the most pressing legal issues of the era—mass demonstrations, environmental protection, prison administration, the rights of welfare mothers, the efficacy of plea bargaining—were already germinating in these circuits, their policy-making potential was highly diffused according to which circuits heard them and which judges sat.

Why, for instance, did the D.C. circuit have no bankruptcy or selective service appeals? Why did the 5th circuit have such a large caseload in the fields of insurance, social security, and workmen's compensation? Why did the 2d circuit have the smallest share in patents? The cases and interviews suggest that in addition to jurisdiction and location, ideology is a factor, as in the hospitality of Texas courts to workmen's compensation awards and the relative inhospitality of the 2d circuit to patents.[21] Both conditions would invite forum shopping. At this point we cannot confirm such answers, but rampant forum shopping in patents surely sustains one warning: beware of generalization about the policy role of Courts of Appeals. Regionalization of appellate structures, for some subjects at least, may well spawn regional specialization and regionalized national law.

## The Mobilization of Appeals

Enhancing the diversity of circuit business are varied pulses of appeal in different fields and places across the country. For all their common jurisdiction, circuit judges have little control over their intake of cases. Their command of federal adjudication depends at the threshold on what is appealed to them and how these cases are decided. Because Courts of Appeals vary materially in what they are asked to review, a useful measure of their work is the rate at which litigants challenged decisions in cases subject to appeal. Rates of appeal help us gauge consumer demand for appellate judicial services as well as the adequacy of institutional resources to meet that demand. When coupled with circuit decisions, they also illuminate intercourt relations and the scope of appellate supervision of lower courts.

Given the significance of rates of appeal for diagnostic purposes, one might assume that standard measures of appellate demand would have been developed long ago. Unfortunately, such measures are not readily available, in part for want of a common definition of what judgments are appealable. Rates of appeal in administrative cases are virtually impossible to calculate precisely because of scattered reporting and varying standards of appealability among federal agencies. Consequently, we shall sidestep administrative appeals momentarily and accept Martin Shapiro's best guess that of thousands of formal adjudications and appealable orders made annually in federal agencies, only 1 to 2 percent are appealed to the courts, which perforce reverse very few.[22] The primary reasons for the paucity of administrative appeals are the heavy reliance on informal bargaining in the regulatory process and tight screening of the government's appeals by agency counsel, appellate sections of the Justice Department, and the Office of the Solicitor General.[23]

To estimate demand from U.S. district courts, on which we shall concentrate, we shall use as a baseline Jerry Goldman's unpublished data for "contested judgments" in civil cases and convictions of guilt after trial.[24] These measures, though they do not track cases, are preferable to those in common use because they better reflect statutory guidelines governing appealability.[e] Regrettably, this information is lacking for the base period, and the AO ceased compiling it after 1970; but the rates of appeal from district courts to the three circuits are presented in Appendix 3 and summarized in Tables 2.5-2.7 for the last four fiscal years, 1967-1970, in which data regarding contested judgments are available. Circuit decisions during the same period are also shown in Table 2.7.

Overall, litigants in this period appealed 32 percent of appealable district court decisions. Adjusting for appeals that were terminated before hearing or submission on briefs, as in Table 2.7, we estimate that these circuit judges reviewed about 20 percent of contested judgments and convictions after trial in the federal district courts. The all-circuit figure was about 17 percent.

Whether review of one case in five sufficed for effective supervision of district courts requires differentiation. Striking variations occurred in appellate oversight of different districts and subjects. For example, Table 2.5 shows that litigants of the 2d and D.C. circuits were much more prone to challenge decisions of district judges (42% and 68%) than the national average (30%). In criminal litigation both circuits were bellwethers of things to come. Long before the mid-1970s, when the national ratio of appeals to criminal convictions after trial reached 75 percent, direct appeal in their criminal cases was virtually automatic.[25] By 1970, this ratio was 96 percent in the 2d circuit and 105 percent in the District of Columbia.[f] In the 5th circuit, by contrast, appeals from district courts were below national averages in both civil and criminal cases. The subsequent swamping

---

[e] The most common measures, "cases commenced" or "trials completed" in district courts produce substantial distortions. So do "appeals commenced" as distinct from "appeals decided after hearing or submission on briefs," used above. For details, see Appendix 1.

[f] In theory rates of appeal cannot exceed unity. How much the excess in this instance is attributable to multiple appeals or measurement errors is unknown.

of this tribunal may well only have entailed southerners catching up with the rest of the country.

Consumer demand also differed by source of civil jurisdiction, as reported in Table 2.6. In the D.C. circuit three-fifths of the district court's decisions involving federal questions were appealed, compared to one-third in the 2d circuit and one-fourth in the 5th. The high rate of appeal in diversity cases, moreover, refuted notions that docket pressure in this artery of appellate litigation is insubstantial.[26] Even though federal judges in diversity cases ostensibly serve merely as convenient forums to enforce state-created rights, litigants challenged one-fourth of their decisions in the 5th circuit, half in the 2d circuit, and almost a third country-wide. Of the four main sources of civil litigation in federal courts—U.S. plaintiff, U.S. defendant, federal questions, and diversity jurisdiction—appellate demand was as great or greatest in diversity, where federal interests are weakest.

By virtue of variable demand, circuit supervision of individual trial courts diverged sharply, particularly among some urban and rural districts. As shown in Appendix 3, litigants in the Southern District of New York challenged at least half the decisions in all but one category of litigation, including 61 percent of the diversity cases and 85 percent of the criminal convictions after trial. In Vermont, on the other hand, only one-fifth of the civil and one-third of the criminal decisions were appealed. Except for the districts of Northern

TABLE 2.5
*Rates of Appeal from Contested Civil Judgments and Convictions after Trial in U.S. District Courts, FY 1967-1970*

| Circuit | Civil Rate of Appeal % | Civil Contested Judgments n | Criminal Rate of Appeal % | Criminal Convictions after Trial n | Total Rate of Appeal % | Total Appealable Judgments N |
|---|---|---|---|---|---|---|
| 2d | 35.7 | 6,911 | 72.4 | 1,400 | 42.0 | 8,311 |
| 5th | 20.6 | 21,194 | 50.2 | 2,704 | 24.0 | 23,898 |
| D.C.* | 32.5 | 2,630 | 93.2 | 1,699 | 67.7 | 4,329 |
| Sums, three circuits | 25.0 | 30,735 | 68.1 | 5,803 | 31.9 | 36,538 |
| All U.S. circuits | 25.5 | 90,222 | 54.9 | 16,263 | 30.0 | 106,485 |

SOURCE: Data courtesy of Jerry Goldman and the Federal Judicial Center; AO *Annual Reports*, Table B1, and *Federal Offenders in United States Courts*, Table D7, 7a.
* Local jurisdiction excluded.

TABLE 2.6
Rates of Appeal from Contested Judgments in
U.S. District Courts by Source of Civil Jurisdiction, FY 1967-1970

| Circuit | U.S. Plaintiff | | U.S. Defendant | | Federal Question | | Diversity of Citizenship | | Total | |
|---|---|---|---|---|---|---|---|---|---|---|
| | Rate of Appeal % | Contested Judgments n | Rate of Appeal % | Contested Judgments n | Rate of Appeal % | Contested Judgments n | Rate of Appeal % | Contested Judgments n | Rate of Appeal % | Contested Judgments N |
| 2d | 23.0 | 534 | 36.4 | 1,161 | 33.4 | 4,173 | 50.2 | 1,043 | 35.7 | 6,911 |
| 5th | 9.6 | 3,354 | 22.2 | 4,547 | 22.1 | 8,955 | 24.5 | 4,338 | 20.6 | 21,194 |
| D.C.* | 24.9 | 177 | 31.2 | 2,304 | 59.7 | 149 | — | 0 | 32.5 | 2,630 |
| Sums, three circuits | 12.0 | 4,065 | 26.9 | 8,012 | 26.1 | 13,277 | 29.5 | 5,381 | 25.0 | 30,735 |
| All U.S. circuits | 12.8 | 9,769 | 27.2 | 21,897 | 26.2 | 42,235 | 29.1 | 16,321 | 25.5 | 90,222 |

SOURCE: Data courtesy of Jerry Goldman and Federal Judicial Center; AO Annual Reports, Table B7.
* Local jurisdiction excluded.

Alabama, Southern Mississippi, and Middle and Southern Florida, where criminal defendants and U.S. attorneys were active, rural areas of the South also generated relatively little demand for appeals, especially in civil suits. Even the districts encompassing Houston, New Orleans, and Miami spawned relatively fewer appeals than those containing Washington or New York.

A significant anomaly is that some of the lowest rates of appeal occurred in districts where judges were most resistant to circuit courts in civil rights. In the district of Southern Georgia, for example, appeals were taken in less than 13 percent of the civil and 20 percent of the criminal litigation, even though in 1965-1967 the circuit court had reversed nearly half of the decisions appealed from this trial court. Whether self-screening or, more likely, lack of legal services was responsible, appeals were skimpy in the very areas where federal appellate review was one of the few effective avenues open to defend individual rights.

Reflection dispels most mysteries as to why such disparities in demand on appellate courts exist. Circuit judges in Washington and New York attributed them to an aggressive, litigious bar conveniently located near federal courthouses. Southern judges stressed the Sunbelt's economic boom. "My gosh!" one judge commented with obvious respect. "Some of the most unusual cases come out of Miami. Anywhere you get Jewish businessmen you get some of the most complicated legal problems." Conflicts concentrate in cities. In rural regions there is apparently more reluctance to litigate, and fewer legal services are available. Only three black attorneys practiced in Mississippi in 1965; only forty-nine served a black population of 800,000 in 1973.[27] In Vermont also, where low rates of appeal accompanied high rates of reversal, appellate demand was more inelastic, that is, unresponsive to the chances of relief, and probably more selective as well.

The stakes involved probably account for the opposite experience in diversity and criminal cases. Congress gave indigents "a free ride to the Court of Appeals" in the Criminal Justice Act, and the Supreme Court in *Anders v. California* strengthened the incentives of attorneys to appeal.[28] Increasingly, also, litigants are turning to the formal machinery of adjudication to resolve disputes. The portion of federal criminal cases reaching trial swelled from less than one-tenth in 1960 to one-fourth in 1975, thus expanding the pool from which appeals may rise.[29] The proportion of all civil cases ending in contested judgments doubled from 18 to 37 percent in the decade 1960-1970. This suggests that parties are compromising less and adjudicating more. Added business is generated for Courts of Appeals even when rates of appeal remain constant. Except for criminal cases, where rates of appeal doubled between 1960 and 1970, expansion in the base of appealable district court judgments is actually more responsible for swollen appellate dockets in this period than growth in *rates* of appeal.[30]

Mistaken calculations, what judges condemn as "the conspicuous consumption of clients" or the "ego trips of counsel," further account for docket growth. The fee system of payment by the hour reinforces the lawyers' professional instinct to leave no stone unturned for the client. That over half the appeals commenced in the D.C. and 2d circuits in 1978 "washed out" before hearing or submission highlights the use of appeal as leverage to induce settlement or to delay judgments. Because settlement is the object of so much corporate litigation, judges in the 2d circuit encourage prehearing conferences to foster settlements and thereby reduce their workloads, although the effectiveness of such conferences has yet to be substantiated.[31]

Whatever its causes, the uneven flow of appeals into the circuits plainly diversifies the capacity of Courts of Appeals to police lower courts. Outcomes, too, teem with variety. Even though some demands for review may be inelastic, superior-subordinate relationships in the federal judiciary tend to be unique. General evidence for this conclusion is provided in Table 2.7, which compares rates of appeal from and reversal of district courts during 1967-1970. Circuits with higher rates of appeal tended to have lower rates of reversal. The odds of achieving relief for dissatisfied litigants were one in four in the 5th circuit, but only one in eight in the 2d circuit.[g] Thus, the mobilization of appeals bears no necessary connection to the odds of judicial relief. Uniqueness, for all the efforts to unify the federal judiciary, is a hallmark of relations between judges at the front line and courts in between.

The above estimates perforce exclude original proceedings as well as appeals from administrative agencies. For completeness, Table 2.8 reports how the three circuit courts decided *all* appeals, including those previously excluded, for cases tracked in the base period of 1965-1967. The overall reversal rate was 21 percent. The addition of "mixed" decisions increases the rate of "disturbed" decisions to 26 percent. These are similar to AO estimates for the period and our estimates for the subsequent four years. In aggregate, at least, there appears to be little relation between rates of appeal and reversal. As in

[g] By 1975, however, as so-called junk litigation fell in the D.C. circuit but rose in the other two, reversal rates shifted to 1 in 6 cases in the 2d and 5th circuits and 1 in 5 in Washington. Since 1971, the all-circuit rate of reversal has hovered around 17%.[32]

TABLE 2.7
Rates of Appeal from and Reversal of Contested Civil Judgments
and Convictions after Trial in U.S. District Courts, FY 1967-1970

| Circuit | Rates of Appeal | | | Rates of Reversal | |
|---|---|---|---|---|---|
| | (1) Contested Judgments and Convictions after Trial N | (2) Appeals Commenced % of N | (3) Appeals Disposed of after Hearing or Submission % of N | (4) Total Judgments Reversed % of N | (5) Judgments Reversed after Hearing or Submission [(4)÷(3)]x100 |
| 2d | 8,311 | 42.0 | 21.8 | 3.6 | 13.7 |
| 5th | 23,898 | 24.0 | 16.3 | 4.4 | 26.7 |
| D.C.* | 4,329 | 67.7 | 32.7 | 6.1 | 18.6 |
| Sums, three circuits | 36,538 | 31.9 | 19.5 | 4.2 | 21.8 |
| All U.S. circuits | 106,485 | 30.0 | 16.7 | 3.6 | 21.5 |

SOURCE: Data courtesy of Jerry Goldman and the Federal Judicial Center; AO *Annual Reports*, Table 31.
* Excludes local jurisdiction.

1967-1970, the 5th circuit had the lowest rate of appeal and the highest rate of reversal. Adding administrative appeals results in southern judges disturbing roughly one in three decisions after hearing compared to one in four for the other two circuits.

Slippery though they may be, these estimates of review and reversal by three circuit courts contain some basic implications for the problems of federal appeals. Above all is the necessity of taking an integrated view of the judicial system. On the input side, the data demonstrate the significance of consumer choices in determining the business of federal courts.[33] Because judges "lack a self-starter," litigants and their counsel are in pivotal positions to set court agendas and the boundaries of judicial policy making.[34] Contrary to conventional wisdom that federal appeals merely reflect external social forces or the intake of trial courts, at each level these choices have a life of their own. Litigant motivations, though beyond the scope of this book, are sorely in need of investigation. Rational allocation of judicial resources requires knowledge of why people litigate and appeal in such numbers and variety.[35]

Second, trial courts are vital in the administration of federal justice. The great majority of district court decisions are neither reviewed nor reversed. Speaking generally from the 1967-1970 experi-

TABLE 2.8
Circuit Court Decisions
(After Hearing or Submission, FY 1965-1967)

| Circuit | Affirm % | Mixed* % | Reverse % | Avoid** % | Other*** % | Total N | % |
|---|---|---|---|---|---|---|---|
| 2d | 73.6 | 5.8 | 17.2 | 1.7 | 1.6 | 1,357 | 100.0 |
| 5th | 63.9 | 6.0 | 24.4 | 1.5 | 4.3 | 2,248 | 100.0 |
| D.C. | 68.9 | 2.9 | 19.6 | 3.6 | 4.9 | 1,336 | 100.0 |
| Sums | 67.9 | 5.1 | 21.1 | 2.1 | 3.7 | 4,941 | 100.0 |

\* This category contains decisions affirmed in part and reversed in part.

\*\* In this category the issue of appeal was avoided, usually by procedural techniques.

\*\*\* A residual category for appeals that were dismissed or had missing information.

ence, litigants appealed about one case in three to the circuit courts. These tribunals reviewed a fifth of appealable district court decisions after hearing or submission and reversed one in five of those heard. In effect, courts of first instance became courts of last resort in over two-thirds of the cases and made decisions that prevailed in 96 percent. Trial courts determine the vast majority of federal adjudications. The rod of reversal is used sparingly. "That's a hard lesson for a lawyer to learn," observed one circuit judge. "There is seldom any relief at the Court of Appeals."

Third, circuit supervision of trial judges, while substantial in most jurisdictions, varies abundantly by field and clime. Uneven case flows make it risky to project from one court to another in assessing the adequacy of appellate control of particular courts. Not every circuit court is overloaded. Not every overloaded court faces identical pressures. Trial judges in some subjects and jurisdictions were relatively free from supervision. Rapid growth of direct criminal appeals, by contrast, is transforming some urban circuits from monitors of criminal justice to automatic courts of error, irrespective of prospects of relief. If present trends continue, reduction of plea bargaining or appellate review of sentencing, coupled with the dictates of the Speedy Trial Act, could play havoc with circuit as well as district courts, increasing their conversion from civil to criminal courts.[36] Appeals from some rural districts, on the other hand, were sparse and perhaps insufficient to supervise trial courts and enforce federal rights where such appellate activities were needed most.

Because the overall rate of appeal seldom fell below one in five in any jurisdiction, it would be wrong to conclude that many trial judges were beyond effective oversight. From the standpoint of enforcing national law, nonetheless, an excess of appeals in some sectors coexisted with pockets of deficient demand, particularly in certain southern areas where federal litigation provided the only channel for redressing civil rights violations. In short, the rate of appeal can be both too high and too low. All-purpose tonics may be inappropriate for both conditions.

Finally, the adequacy of appellate supervision depends on a complexus of incentives and strategies among litigants and trial judges, only partially subject to formal appellate controls. To enforce and harmonize national law, circuit judges perforce rely heavily on informal constraints such as precedent, professionalism, and ideological affinity as distinct from formal reversal. That circuit judges reviewed so many decisions but upset so few suggests that these mechanisms produced considerable legal cohesion within the circuits. Whether that condition remains under the workloads of the 1980s is an open question. Uneven review and reversal among the circuits point to substantial differences in values among district courts, agencies, and Courts of Appeals, especially in the 5th and D.C. circuits, which circuit judges are expected to overcome.

## The Decisions of Circuit Courts

So far we have shown that the mixture and mobilization of appeals diversify appellate capacity in different subjects and places. That alone would not destabilize national law were circuit decisions alike in like circumstances. Comparing Courts of Appeals on a third dimension—the nature of their decisions and their outcomes—reveals a similar blend of common and varied experience in their reviewing functions. Courts of Appeals, as a result, participated in both national and regional policy networks.

That judicial decisions and policy leanings differ from circuit to circuit has been documented by case studies in various fields, such as patents and taxation.[37] The challenge is to chart the differences across the board.

Though gross rates of appeal and reversal tell us something about the range of appellate oversight, the cohesion within circuits, and the frequency of formal decisional controls, they are crude indicators of judicial functions and relationships with other courts. In the first place they reveal little about the *form* of decision. Courts of Appeals, despite obligatory intake, are not devoid of tools to ration judicial work. "Filings" measure clerk-work, not judge-work. Over one-fourth of the cases commenced in this period were terminated without hearing or submission. Circuit judges consolidated another tenth and reduced the remaining cases requiring full opinion by half. One-third were disposed of per curiam and the remainder without published explanation. Only 1 percent were *in forma pauperis* or had amicus briefs. Less than 1 percent (N = 42) were en bancs. Streamlined decision making to keep current was proceeding full steam.

Without dispelling judges' complaints of overwork, these shortcuts mean that circuit courts are hardly at the mercy of litigants. Their ability to screen and consolidate cases, to define issues and differentiate the treatment accorded to various litigants, enables circuit judges to shape their doctrinal output—and their opinion-writing workload. Hence, both qualitatively and quantitatively, intermediate courts exercise important functions as gatekeepers, directing traffic in the stream of federal appeals.

A simple reversal rate also obscures internal disagreements. The overall rate of nonunanimous decisions in the three courts was 8 percent, with the D.C. circuit leading the pack (16%), the 2d in the center (9%), and the 5th trailing behind (4%).[h] Dissents were more likely when Courts of Appeals disturbed (14%) rather than affirmed (6%) decisions below.[38] Dissent rates also varied considerably by subject. Fields provoking the greatest dissension in one circuit court might generate the least in another. Morals offenses, for instance, drew the highest dissent rate in the D.C. circuit (24%) and no dissent at all in the 5th.

Further, in contrast to the conclusion of Richardson and Vines that transformation of issues is a primary function of Courts of Appeals, only 7 percent of these opinions offered any evidence that circuit judges reformulated controlling issues.[39] Revolt in the ranks was even rarer, though sometimes intense. Resistance to prior appellate rulings was evident in 2 percent of the cases (19 cases in the D.C. circuit, 12 in the 2d, and 61 in the 5th). Resistance concerned mostly criminal procedure in Washington and New York, civil rights in the South.[40] The tactics ranged from subtle evasions, such as distinguishing away precedents like *Escobedo* in New York, to some spectacular acts of defiance by southern district judges that provoked angry threats from the bench and external cries for impeachment.[i][41]

[h] For dissent rates of individual circuit judges, see Tables 7.1-7.3.

[i] As visiting judges on the Court of Appeals, however, certain well-known resisters like William H. Cox, who once charged that his erstwhile superiors did not "know what they are talking about," quietly enforced on fellow district judges rules they had personally opposed.[42]

Further complicating intercourt relations are varying *degrees of finality* of appellate commands. Flat reversals differ from remands, which may leave some degree of lower court discretion intact. Given the special opportunities for resistance by lower courts after remand, this form of decision is distinguished from straight affirmances, reversals, and other disposition of the caseload during the base period in Table 2.9.

TABLE 2.9
*Circuit Court Finality*
(After Hearing or Submission, FY 1965-1967)

| Circuit | Affirm % | Reverse % | Remand % | Other % | Total N | % |
|---|---|---|---|---|---|---|
| 2d | 73.1 | 7.4 | 13.6 | 5.9 | 1,357 | 100.0 |
| 5th | 63.1 | 7.1 | 24.5 | 5.3 | 2,248 | 100.0 |
| D.C. | 68.7 | 8.8 | 18.6 | 3.8 | 1,336 | 100.0 |
| Sums | 67.4 | 7.7 | 19.9 | 5.1 | 4,941 | 100.0 |

Because most remands are reversals, and vice versa, the primary effect of distinguishing remands is a sharp drop in the reversal rate from 21 to 8 percent. Admittedly, this estimate of finality rests on an assumption, not always valid, that remand preserves some discretion in lower courts. Remand sometimes may be no more than a face-saving formality. Even so, the use of remands was higher in civil (22%) than in criminal cases (14%), higher also in cases from district courts (21%) than from federal agencies (16%), and higher in the 5th circuit (25%) than in the D.C. (19%) or 2d circuits (14%), all of which may signify appellate tactics at work. By reminding us of the discretion that often passes to lower courts after appeal, these estimates are a useful counter to "upper court myths" implicit in hierarchical models of judicial power.[43] When we recall that the great majority of cases are never tried or appealed in the first place, the finding that 87 percent of almost 5,000 appeals were either affirmed or returned for further consideration reinforces a "bottom-up" view of decision making in the federal judiciary.[44] It also highlights the use of remands as an appellate technique. Tribunals below are seldom flatly overruled.

More fundamentally, to assess the policy functions and controls of intermediate courts we need to know who reverses whom for what. Government statisticians seldom report what happened to appeals from different sources and in different subjects.[45] For this purpose, in Tables 2.10-2.12 the distributions of disturbed decisions in each circuit during 1965-1967 are linked to their origins among district courts and a sampling of administrative agencies. "Disturbed decisions" constitute those reversed in whole or in part by Courts of Appeals. Although little significance attaches to percentage differences among small numbers of cases, basic regularities among the circuits are accompanied by intriguing dissimilarities in outcomes.

In general, district courts fared better on appeal than administra-

TABLE 2.10
Sources of 2d Circuit Decisions
(After Hearing or Submisson, FY 1965-1967)

| Sources | Decisions Reviewed | | Decisions Disturbed | |
|---|---|---|---|---|
| | N | % of Total | n | % (n/N) |
| U.S. District Courts | 1,110 | 81.8 | 244 | 22.0 |
| Connecticut | 84 | 6.2 | 17 | 20.2 |
| New York | | | | |
| Northern | 57 | 4.2 | 11 | 19.3 |
| Eastern | 141 | 10.4 | 32 | 22.7 |
| Southern | 756 | 55.7 | 163 | 21.6 |
| Western | 47 | 3.5 | 13 | 27.7 |
| Vermont | 25 | 1.8 | 8 | 32.0 |
| *Boards and Commissions* | 196 | 14.4 | 61 | 31.1 |
| U.S. Tax Court | 66 | 4.9 | 20 | 30.3 |
| National Labor Relations Board | 88 | 6.5 | 27 | 30.7 |
| Civil Aeronautics Board | 1 | 0.1 | 0 | 0.0 |
| Federal Communications Commission | 1 | 0.1 | 1 | 100.0 |
| Federal Power Commission | 2 | 0.1 | 0 | 0.0 |
| Federal Trade Commission | 1 | 0.1 | 0 | 0.0 |
| Secretary of Agriculture | 0 | 0.0 | 0 | 0.0 |
| Securities and Exchange Commission | 2 | 0.1 | 0 | 0.0 |
| Immigration and Naturalization Service | 8 | 0.6 | 2 | 25.0 |
| Other boards and commissions | 27 | 2.0 | 11 | 40.7 |
| *Original Proceedings* | 51 | 3.8 | 8 | 15.7 |
| *Other* | 0 | 0.0 | 0 | 0.0 |
| Sums | 1,357 | 100.0 | 313 | 23.1 |

TABLE 2.11
Sources of 5th Circuit Decisions
(After Hearing or Submisson, FY 1965-1967)

| Sources | Decisions Reviewed N | % of Total | Decisions Disturbed n | % (n/N) |
|---|---|---|---|---|
| U.S. District Courts | 1,978 | 88.0 | 584 | 29.5 |
| Alabama | | | | |
| Northern | 74 | 3.3 | 25 | 33.8 |
| Middle | 60 | 2.7 | 19 | 31.7 |
| Southern | 55 | 2.4 | 23 | 41.8 |
| Florida | | | | |
| Northern | 38 | 1.7 | 13 | 34.2 |
| Middle | 187 | 8.3 | 57 | 30.4 |
| Southern | 258 | 11.5 | 64 | 24.8 |
| Georgia | | | | |
| Northern | 138 | 6.1 | 40 | 29.0 |
| Middle | 79 | 3.5 | 26 | 32.9 |
| Southern | 72 | 3.2 | 33 | 45.8 |
| Louisiana | | | | |
| Eastern | 217 | 9.7 | 50 | 23.0 |
| Western | 91 | 4.0 | 22 | 24.2 |
| Mississippi | | | | |
| Northern | 51 | 2.3 | 14 | 27.5 |
| Southern | 112 | 5.0 | 47 | 42.0 |
| Texas | | | | |
| Northern | 177 | 7.9 | 56 | 31.6 |
| Eastern | 66 | 2.9 | 22 | 33.3 |
| Southern | 203 | 9.0 | 45 | 22.2 |
| Western | 94 | 4.2 | 28 | 29.8 |
| Canal Zone | 6 | 0.3 | 0 | 0.0 |
| Boards and Commissions | 218 | 9.7 | 86 | 39.4 |
| U.S. Tax Court | 63 | 2.8 | 17 | 27.0 |
| National Labor Relations Board | 115 | 5.1 | 54 | 47.0 |
| Civil Aeronautics Board | 0 | 0.0 | 0 | 0.0 |
| Federal Communications Commission | 0 | 0.0 | 0 | 0.0 |
| Federal Power Commission | 5 | 0.2 | 3 | 60.0 |
| Federal Trade Commission | 2 | 0.1 | 1 | 50.0 |
| Secretary of Agriculture | 0 | 0.0 | 0 | 0.0 |
| Securities and Exchange Commission | 0 | 0.0 | 0 | 0.0 |
| Immigration and Naturalization Service | 1 | 0.0 | 0 | 0.0 |
| Other boards and commissions | 32 | 1.4 | 10 | 31.3 |
| Original Proceedings | 47 | 2.1 | 12 | 25.5 |
| Other | 5 | 0.2 | 2 | 40.0 |
| Sums | 2,248 | 100.0 | 684 | 30.4 |

TABLE 2.12
Sources of D.C. Circuit Decisions
(After Hearing or Submission, FY 1965-1967)

| Sources | Decisions Reviewed N | % of Total | Decisions Disturbed n | % (n/N) |
|---|---|---|---|---|
| U.S. District Courts | 1,042 | 78.0 | 210 | 20.2 |
| U.S. jurisdiction | 739 | 55.3 | 105 | 14.2 |
| D.C. jurisdiction | 303 | 22.7 | 105 | 34.7 |
| Boards and Commissions | 217 | 16.3 | 65 | 30.0 |
| U.S. Tax Court | 5 | 0.4 | 1 | 20.0 |
| National Labor Relations Board | 62 | 4.6 | 19 | 30.6 |
| Civil Aeronautics Board | 24 | 1.8 | 4 | 16.7 |
| Federal Communications Commission | 60 | 4.5 | 9 | 15.0 |
| Federal Power Commission | 8 | 0.6 | 3 | 37.5 |
| Federal Trade Commission | 8 | 0.6 | 1 | 12.5 |
| Secretary of Agriculture | 1 | 0.1 | 0 | 0.0 |
| Securities and Exchange Commission | 3 | 0.2 | 0 | 0.0 |
| Immigration and Naturalization Service | 1 | 0.1 | 0 | 0.0 |
| Other boards and commissions | 45 | 3.4 | 28 | 62.2 |
| D.C. Board of Tax Appeals | 18 | 1.3 | 6 | 33.3 |
| Other D.C. Agencies | 14 | 1.0 | 2 | 14.3 |
| Original Proceedings | 35 | 2.6 | 12 | 34.3 |
| Other | 10 | 0.7 | 4 | 40.0 |
| Sums | 1,336 | 100.0 | 299 | 22.4 |

tive agencies. The three circuits together upset one out of three agency decisions as compared to one out of four decisions of district courts. The NLRB and the Tax Courts, which accounted for over half of the administrative appeals and reversals in this group, received especially rough treatment in the 2d and 5th circuits, whose judges commonly complained that too many labor appeals involved merely factual issues.

For kindred reasons, perhaps, the D.C. circuit was twice as inclined to reverse district courts in local as in national jurisdiction. The circuit was also more favorably disposed toward the FCC and

CAB than the FPC, which also met rough water in the 5th. Such divergencies, needless to say, buttress our conclusions about discrete relationships between circuit courts and their subordinates. So do comparisons of support for individual district courts and judges. Though variations in overall support were not extreme, the D.C. circuit, for instance, disturbed district court decisions in comparable U.S. jurisdiction at substantially lower rates (14%) than the other two circuits (22% and 30%). Metropolitan districts in the 5th circuit, such as Eastern Louisiana (New Orleans, 23%) and Southern Texas (Houston, 22%), were in closest harmony with the Court of Appeals. Badly out of step were three less urbanized districts: Southern Georgia (46%), Southern Mississippi (42%), and Southern Alabama (42%). Like Vermont, the district court with the highest rate of disturbed decisions—Southern Georgia—had the lowest rate of appeal, again suggesting inelasticity of demand.

As most U.S. district courts have more than one member, these tables mask individual differences and a tendency, well known to court observers, of appellate courts to single out individual judges for reversal. Though incomplete information, especially in Washington, prevents a full analysis of agreement between Courts of Appeals and trial judges, their experience is portrayed in Tables 2.13, 2.14, and 2.15 by ranking district judges (who had ten or more decisions challenged) according to the percentage of appealed decisions disturbed, in whole or in part, in each circuit.[j] The small number of appeals involved for each person makes percentage rankings treacherous, but basic relationships of high and low support emerge with considerable clarity. In general, both the D.C. and 5th circuits followed Judge Augustus Hand's rule of thumb that "a decent trial judge ought to be affirmed about two-thirds of the time."[46] Hand's own circuit was even more supportive (77%). Individual experience, however, ranged widely. Each circuit disturbed the decisions of some district judges at roughly four times the rate of others.

In the D.C. circuit, Richmond B. Keech and Luther W. Youngdahl had the highest degree of support. John J. Sirica of Watergate fame was somewhat above average in decisions upset. The lowest support went to Henry A. Schweinhaut, first director of the Civil Liberties Unit in the Department of Justice, and Edward A. Tamm, a former FBI executive, whose promotion to the circuit may well have resulted from these disagreements. Alexander Holtzoff was surpris-

[j] Because of different reporting practices the identities of district judges were found in only 53% of cases from district courts in the D.C. circuit compared to 85% for the 2d circuit and 96% for the 5th circuit. The rates for the D.C. circuit are artificially high as a result of nonreported cases.

TABLE 2.13
2d Circuit
Rate of Disturbing Decisions of U.S. District Judges, FY 1965-1967
(In 10 or More Cases)

| Judge | District | % Decisions Disturbed (Reversed or Mixed) | Total Decisions Reviewed N |
|---|---|---|---|
| Weinfeld | S.D.N.Y. | 10.8 | 37 |
| Cooper | S.D.N.Y. | 10.8 | 46 |
| MacMahon | S.D.N.Y. | 11.5 | 26 |
| Brennan | W.D.N.Y. | 11.8 | 17 |
| Herlands | S.D.N.Y. | 12.5 | 16 |
| Clarie | Conn. | 12.5 | 16 |
| Metzner | S.D.N.Y. | 14.3 | 21 |
| Tenney | S.D.N.Y. | 16.0 | 25 |
| Rayfiel | E.D.N.Y. | 16.7 | 18 |
| Palmieri | S.D.N.Y. | 17.1 | 35 |
| Bruchhausen | E.D.N.Y. | 18.1 | 22 |
| Cannella | S.D.N.Y. | 20.9 | 43 |
| Blumenfeld | Conn. | 21.1 | 19 |
| Bryan | S.D.N.Y. | 23.1 | 26 |
| Bartels | E.D.N.Y. | 23.1 | 13 |
| Murphy | S.D.N.Y. | 23.3 | 43 |
| Foley | N.D.N.Y. | 23.5 | 17 |
| Levet | S.D.N.Y. | 24.1 | 54 |
| Bonsal | S.D.N.Y. | 24.4 | 41 |
| Henderson | W.D.N.Y. | 25.0 | 28 |
| Croake | S.D.N.Y. | 25.1 | 32 |
| Tyler | S.D.N.Y. | 26.2 | 42 |
| Zampano | Conn. | 26.7 | 15 |
| Dawson | S.D.N.Y. | 26.7 | 15 |
| McLean | S.D.N.Y. | 27.0 | 37 |
| Burke | W.D.N.Y. | 27.2 | 22 |
| Wyatt | S.D.N.Y. | 27.6 | 29 |
| Sugarman | S.D.N.Y. | 27.8 | 18 |
| Timbers | Conn. | 28.6 | 28 |
| Dooling | E.D.N.Y. | 30.7 | 26 |
| McGohey | S.D.N.Y. | 33.3 | 15 |
| Mishler | E.D.N.Y. | 33.3 | 18 |
| Cashin | S.D.N.Y. | 33.3 | 18 |
| Gibson | Vt. | 35.0 | 20 |
| Rosling | E.D.N.Y. | 35.3 | 17 |
| Ryan | S.D.N.Y. | 40.0 | 30 |
| Port | N.D.N.Y. | 40.0 | 10 |
| All judges (N = 37) | | 23.4 | 955 |

## TABLE 2.14
## 5th Circuit
### Rate of Disturbing Decisions of U.S. District Judges, FY 1965-1967
(In 10 or More Cases)

| Judge | District | % Decisions Disturbed (Reversed or Mixed) | Total Decisions Reviewed N |
|---|---|---|---|
| Hunter | W.D.La. | 8.6 | 23 |
| Smith | N.D.Ga. | 9.1 | 11 |
| Estes, J. | N.D.Tex. | 13.0 | 23 |
| Ainsworth | E.D.La. | 15.0 | 40 |
| Thornberry | W.D.Tex. | 15.0 | 20 |
| Garza | S.D.Tex. | 15.1 | 33 |
| Christenberry | E.D.La. | 15.2 | 46 |
| Dyer | S.D.Fla. | 15.4 | 52 |
| Connally | S.D.Tex. | 16.7 | 42 |
| Ingraham | S.D.Tex. | 20.6 | 63 |
| Young | M.D.Fla. | 22.9 | 35 |
| Fulton | S.D.Fla | 23.3 | 56 |
| Simpson | M.D.Fla. | 23.4 | 47 |
| Sheehy | E.D.Tex. | 24.3 | 37 |
| Clayton | N.D.Miss. | 25.0 | 48 |
| Dooley | N.D.Tex. | 25.0 | 28 |
| Hannay | S.D.Tex. | 25.0 | 28 |
| Hughes | N.D.Tex. | 26.2 | 42 |
| Lieb | M.D.Fla. | 26.2 | 42 |
| West | E.D.La. | 26.3 | 80 |
| Whitehurst | M.D.Fla. | 26.4 | 19 |
| Dawkins | W.D.La. | 29.7 | 40 |
| Spears | W.D.Tex. | 27.5 | 29 |
| Mehrtens | S.D.Fla. | 28.6 | 14 |
| Putnam | W.D.La. | 28.6 | 21 |
| Hooper | N.D.Ga. | 29.2 | 48 |
| Morgan | N.D.Ga. | 29.4 | 51 |
| Johnson | M.D.Ala. | 29.9 | 57 |
| Bootle | M.D.Ga. | 30.0 | 40 |
| Grooms | N.D.Ala. | 30.7 | 26 |
| Choate | S.D.Fla. | 32.3 | 96 |
| Allgood | N.D.Ala. | 33.3 | 30 |
| Lynne | N.D.Ala. | 33.3 | 21 |
| Sloan | N.D. Ga. | 33.3 | 27 |
| Suttle | W.D. Tex. | 33.3 | 15 |
| Carswell | N.D.Fla. | 33.4 | 30 |
| Noel | S.D. Tex. | 35.5 | 31 |
| McRae | N.D. Fla. | 36.8 | 57 |

TABLE 2.14 (cont.)

| Judge | District | % Decisions Disturbed (Reversed or Mixed) | Total Decisions Reviewed N |
|---|---|---|---|
| Cox, W. | S.D. Miss. | 37.7 | 69 |
| Brewster | N.D.Tex. | 37.8 | 37 |
| Ellis | E.D. La. | 40.0 | 35 |
| Fisher | E.D. Tex. | 40.0 | 35 |
| Elliott | M.D.Ga. | 40.5 | 42 |
| Thomas | S.D.Ala. | 42.0 | 50 |
| Davidson | N.D.Tex. | 46.5 | 43 |
| Scarlett | S.D. Ga. | 48.6 | 72 |
| Thomason | W.D.Tex. | 50.0 | 12 |
| Mize | S.D.Miss. | 51.7 | 31 |
| All judges (N = 48) | | 29.5 | 1,874 |

ingly absent from their company. Holtzoff, a leader in federal procedure, became a testy trial judge whose resistance and antics on the bench provoked harsh appellate rebukes, including occasional removal from cases.[47] His temperament and high jinks in print, rather than overall record of support, perhaps were responsible for Holtzoff's having the largest number of decisions challenged in the D.C. circuit.

Except for Brennan and Ryan at the extreme ends, the strongest support in the 2d circuit tended to go to judges in the Southern District of New York, Weinfeld and Cooper, for example, while the least went to judges outside. Considering the ABA Standing Committee on the Federal Judiciary's vigorous opposition to Irving Ben Cooper's confirmation on grounds of narrow legal experience, his record of having the lowest rate of decisions disturbed must stand as some vindication.[48] That reversal rates have little bearing on judicial selection is illustrated by William H. Timbers of Connecticut, who was promoted to the circuit bench in 1971 despite an above-average disturbance rate of 29 percent.

Of the nine district judges subsequently promoted to the 5th circuit—Ainsworth, Thornberry, Dyer, Ingraham, Simpson, Clayton, Morgan, Carswell, and Johnson—only Carswell fell below par in circuit support. Though twice as prone to reversal as Homer Thornberry, another unconfirmed nominee to the Supreme Court, Carswell was not the circuit's low man. Those honors went to Frank M. Scarlett of Southern Georgia, Sydney Mize and William H. Cox of South-

TABLE 2.15
D.C. Circuit
Rate of Disturbing Decisions of U.S. District Judges, FY 1965-1967
(In 10 or More Cases)

| Judge | % Decisions Disturbed (Reversed or Mixed) | Total Decisions Reviewed N |
|---|---|---|
| Keech | 11.4 | 35 |
| Youngdahl | 20.0 | 25 |
| McGarraghy | 23.9 | 46 |
| Jackson | 25.0 | 20 |
| Robinson, S. | 25.0 | 20 |
| Walsh | 27.5 | 40 |
| Curran | 30.3 | 33 |
| Pine | 30.8 | 13 |
| Gasch | 31.3 | 16 |
| Corcoran | 33.3 | 27 |
| Hart | 33.4 | 51 |
| Sirica | 35.7 | 28 |
| Holtzoff | 38.0 | 92 |
| Matthews | 38.1 | 21 |
| Jones | 43.4 | 23 |
| Schweinhaut | 47.4 | 19 |
| Tamm | 48.2 | 29 |
| All judges (N = 17) | 32.0 | 538 |

ern Mississippi, D. Holcombe Thomas of Southern Alabama, and T. Whitfield Davidson of Northern Texas, most of whom openly resisted the civil rights revolution.[49] Illustrating the fate of judges on both ends of the ideological spectrum, Frank M. Johnson, Jr., champion of racial equality in Alabama and expansive judicial supervision of state prisons and mental institutions, fell just below the median of circuit support.[50]

Reversal rates, it should be stressed, measure agreement, not judicial quality. When linked to the sources and subjects of appeal, however, they shed considerable light on the policy functions of intermediate courts. These turn out to be somewhat issue specific. The distribution of circuit decisions by subject is provided in Appendix 4. On the whole, labor decisions in this period were disturbed most (36%); morals offenses (13%) and crimes against property (16%) were disturbed least. Contrary to popular impressions, criminal appeals were overturned at a lower rate (17%) than were civil appeals (29%). This was true even in the District of Columbia where so much controversy developed over criminal standards.[k]

Telling evidence of conflicting values occurred among individual circuits. The D.C. and 5th circuits were twice as prone to grant relief in prisoner petitions as the 2d circuit (15%). The 5th circuit, known for its tendency to disturb decisions concerning civil rights (45%) and suffrage (58%), was just as inclined to upset decisions concerning labor relations acts (44%) and fair labor standards (56%). The tribunal's high reversal rate was not simply a function of enforcing civil rights against hostile communities, but also of policy disagreements with federal officials in other fields, especially labor.

This independent motif in labor law, prevalent in the 5th circuit since passage of the Wagner Act, parallels long-standing skepticism of patent claims among judges of the 2d circuit.[52] Southern judges, by contrast, were far more favorable to patent validity claims than their counterparts in New York or Washington.[l] In the 1970s, the 5th circuit also became more sympathetic to producer interests in oil and gas regulation than its consumer-minded counterpart in Washington.

Powerful, indeed, is the "law of the circuit" in giving a regional stamp to federal appeals. A simple reckoning of case outcomes in terms of who won or lost shows that the potential for regional policy making was realized in these Courts of Appeals.[m] Some of the most pronounced patterns of reversal or support occurred in the very fields in which circuit business and doctrinal leadership were concentrated. In its few income tax cases, for example, the D.C. circuit tended to favor individuals (9-6), whereas the 2d and 5th circuits favored the government by more than two-to-one margins. The court

[k] The rates of disturbing decisions were: D.C., 25% civil and 19% criminal; 2d, 26% civil and 12% criminal; 5th, 33% civil and 18% criminal.

During the late 1960s, the D.C. circuit's reversal rate in criminal cases appeared to be declining while its civil reversal rate increased, a condition that one circuit judge attributed to neglect of civil dockets by district judges struggling to absorb rapid changes in criminal law. "Unless we're at fault," the judge observed, "that means in the one area of litigation in which U.S. district courts ought to offer the best forum—United States litigation—they're doing the worst job."[51]

[l] In cases whose outcomes could be scored the 5th circuit favored patent claimants (10 pro, 14 anti) more than the D.C. circuit (2 pro, 13 anti) or the 2d circuit (3 pro, 9 anti). The frequency of patent appeals in the D.C. circuit probably had less to do with policy differences than with the presence of the Board of Patent Appeals in Washington. Eleven of 13 anticlaimant decisions by the circuit court were affirmances.

[m] Only a third of the D.C. circuit's decisions could be scored accordingly, compared to two-thirds for the 2d circuit and four-fifths for the 5th circuit. These decisions approximate those in which analysis of opinions was possible.

in Washington also split evenly in habeas corpus outcomes, whereas the 5th circuit favored the government by over two-to-one and the 2d circuit by almost five-to-one margins.ⁿ The 5th circuit, heavily laden with labor and civil rights cases which it reversed, favored workers two to one in workmen's compensation (22-11) and fair labor standards cases (20-9). Deciding 100 of the 113 civil rights and suffrage cases in this group, the court also favored individuals rather than the government by two-to-one margins. In immigration, by contrast, the 2d circuit not only had the most cases, but favored the government over individuals in all scorable instances (0-12).ᵒ

Because cases differ, these results do not mean that one circuit was necessarily more liberal or conservative than another. Though they suggest that Courts of Appeals served to "federalize" local judicial values, proof of this proposition would require linking all decisions at every level of the federal judiciary.[54] Still, these patterns of decision illuminate important dynamics of the federal appellate process during the era of the Warren Court. In general, decisions favoring the government tended to be affirmances; those favoring individuals tended to be reversals. Strong patterns of either type clustered in the circuits' magnetic fields. Policy values manifest in leading opinions were reflected in frequencies of litigation, too.

More revealing than whether these tendencies produced liberal or conservative results is what they tell us about the clienteles and policy functions of the circuit courts. Appeal by definition is an attempt to undo a government decision. Litigants do not have equal motivation or equal resources to mount the challenge. Successful parties have little incentive to do so. Recurrent litigants, such as government agencies, corporations, and unions, are often in a position to choose favorable forums. Federal prosecutors in the 1960s hesitated to appeal unfavorable decisions for fear of nationalizing their defeats, a condition that changed under the Burger Court.[55] It stands to reason that appeals in the 1960s were weighted with individual claims against the government and that appellate support of those claims would take the form of reversal and vice versa. At the first level of appeal the government was primarily on the defensive. Nationalization of policy values, as it were, inhered in the dynamics

---

ⁿ The D.C. cases were split 9-9. The 5th favored the petitioners in 59 cases and the government in 141. The 2d circuit granted petitions in 15 cases and denied 71.

ᵒ Chief Judge Irving R. Kaufman, comparing the "baffling skein" of statutory provisions that the Immigration Service and the courts must interpret to "King Minos' labyrinth in ancient Crete," once cited tax laws and immigration statutes as examples "of Congress' ingenuity in passing statutes certain to accelerate the aging process of judges."[53]

of appeal, not simply the attitudes of regionally insulated circuit judges, however mutually supportive they may have been.

In consequence of diversity in the composition and pulse of appeals, circuit courts are likely to serve particular clienteles and policy values at any given time. Their dockets have split personalities in which masses of error-correcting claims, often subsidized and significant only to the litigants, are mixed with a select sample raising policy problems that tax traditional bounds of judicial power. Financially, this implies a squeeze on the poor and the middle between jailhouse lawyers and the well-to-do.[56] Functionally, it implies that Courts of Appeals filter cases not simply by gatekeeping before hearing but also by inviting and discouraging, sifting and refining, federal appeals. It is no accident that in the era of the Warren Court these circuits often appeared to champion national over parochial points of view. The three tribunals faced a loaded sample, weighted with claims against the government, margin for reversal, and policy-making potential.

The other side of the coin is that decentralization of the judicial process did not stop with judges but stretched far among members of the litigating community. Decisions to settle or to forgo appeal are part of the process no less than decisions to litigate. The stronger the pressure to appeal, the more important the question of whether litigants, judges, or staff screen wheat from chaff. Monolithic and formal in appearance, the federal appellate process breeds decentralization and informality in practice.

## Conclusions

Federal courts are united by purpose, general jurisdiction, and a hierarchy of doctrine. Beneath the formalities of the legal process, nevertheless, teems substantial variety in business and behavior. Pluralism, though perhaps exaggerated by focusing on three disparate Courts of Appeals, pervaded the composition of their cases, the demand for their services, and the subjects and sources of their decisions in the flow of appeals. Outcomes differed, too. Differentiation of their policing and policy functions, as a result, becomes a central theme. The three intermediate courts exercised not one but several types of supervision of tribunals below—staple, marginal, concentrated. They provided sustained oversight in a few major sectors of public policy, such as labor relations and criminal justice, which brought the three courts into continuing relations with corporations, unions, government agencies, and various elements of the criminal process, along with substantial opportunity to decide similar questions of law. The notion of Courts of Appeals as the vital center of the national appellate system, in these circumstances, was close to the mark.

So sparse was litigation in other fields, at the same time, that the intermediate courts were hardly even way stations. More important were regional policy networks. Each circuit became a magnet for certain subjects of federal law by virtue of location, special jurisdiction, and predilections, which produced division of labor and tonal variations in federal adjudication. The D.C. circuit was chiefly responsible for supervising regulation of the transportation and communication industries, while the 2d and 5th circuits dominated appeals in diversity jurisdiction, taxation, and admiralty. Distinctive outcomes intensified these differences because they tended to cluster in areas of circuit concentration. Judges in Washington tended to favor consumers and criminal defendants. The 5th circuit strongly supported workers and blacks. The 2d circuit supported public rights in patents and the government in immigration. Diverse treatment of district courts and agencies, publicized in the Carswell nomination fight, also occurred within each circuit. The potentials for forum shopping, specialization, and Balkanization of federal law hardly require elaboration. Slack pervades the system. What could be better proof of regionalization than unseemly races to friendly courthouses or the Hruska Commission's ground rule of minimal interference with settled circuit law?[57]

The variety of circuit experience calls for caution in "dealing with diversity by means of uniform rules."[58] Heterogeneity also bears on the adequacy of appellate supervision in the law explosion. Generally speaking, litigants in the late 1960s appealed approximately one-third of contested judgments and convictions of guilt after trial in federal district courts to the three circuit courts, which actually reviewed about one-fifth and reversed 4 percent of the original number. The finality of administrative decisions was probably higher. However pressed circuit judges may feel by bloated dockets, the appellate boom has hardly altered the "bottom-up" character of the federal judicial system. Because reversal rates tend to fall as caseloads rise, the system, if anything, is becoming more bottom heavy over time.

Fears of appellate overextension are justified, but there is little cause for panic. Raw filings exaggerate the pressure on judges, and overall averages are not very useful in assessing the supervision of particular courts or policies.[59] Whether appellate capacity is adequate depends on the subject and locality. The scope of administrative review in these circuits ranged from a surfeit of factual disputes in labor relations to a few blockbusters in energy and environmental regulation. The explosion of criminal appeals, in turn, is transforming federal Courts of Appeals from monitors of criminal trials to automatic courts of error in big-city districts. The pressure of appeal also was high in diversity cases, and apparently on judge-time as well.[60] If New York and Washington generate too many appeals, some rural districts may well spawn too few. As demands on circuits differ, so does the adequacy of their checking functions.

Numbers, furthermore, are only part of the story. The deterring effects of review and reversal on the discretion of agencies and district judges, to whom reversal is disruptive and distasteful, should not be minimized. It is not necessary to review or reverse every case to oversee circuits effectively.[p] So long as the threat of reversal remains credible, review may reinforce the "rule of anticipated reactions," at least over the basic "premises of decision" of subordinates who apply law in particular cases.[62] The relatively high rates of review and low rates of reversal in most subjects in the mid-1960s suggest that lower courts were not out of control. Except for urban criminal justice, however, the risks of reversal were too low for circuit judges to rely exclusively or even primarily on formal review to coordinate the activities of the federal judiciary. In a system of adjudication so decentralized and diverse, review presupposes conformity to informal norms of conduct. Two complex processes, only partially subject to formal judicial control, thus emerge as critical in charting the relationships among original and appellate courts: (1) *filtering*—the selection of appeals by litigants and judges, and (2) *judicial role*—the internalized constraints on decision making that underlie formal review and reversal.

Equally important is the extent to which the three intermediate tribunals themselves became courts of last resort. Just as circuit judges share with litigants and tribunals below the task of shaping their product, so the power of the middlemen depends on how much they, too, escaped direct supervision. What causes did the Courts of Appeals determine? How often did they have the final say? To these questions we now turn in order to gauge how much the three circuits effectively became regional Supreme Courts.

---

[p] For example, after the Supreme Court reversed Muhammad Ali's conviction for draft evasion, district judge William H. Cox dismissed similar charges against two conscientious objectors as "a waste of time and money," reportedly remarking to the defendants: "Go back to preaching."[61]

# Three · The Flow of Litigation in the Supreme Court

To casual observers federal courts look alike. They form a unitary, centrally controlled pyramid held together by Supreme Court review and adherence to precedent. In reality, the national judiciary, as Graham Allison describes all governments, "consists of a conglomerate of semi-feudal, loosely allied organizations, each with a substantial life of its own."[1] That is true of Courts of Appeals both horizontally and vertically.

The pluralism of their functions and relations becomes pointed when we assess the finality of circuit decisions and compare their work with the Supreme Court's in the same cases, using the methods of Chapter Two. In spite of common jurisdiction, the business of the Supreme Court was not a reflex of circuit activity or of external pressures. Requests for review pulsed unevenly in different pathways of litigation. By dint of docket control, the high court's fare was selective, scattered, and issue specific. Supervision of lower courts was sporadic. Courts of Appeals in the process were quasi-autonomous organs of judicial authority in some networks of national policy and mini-Supreme Courts in others.

## The Finality of Circuit Decisions

A basic condition of the American judicial system is that the Supreme Court exerts very little direct supervision over lower courts. Certainly this was true of the three Courts of Appeals during the late 1960s. In Table 3.1 their decisions in the base period that were not appealed to the high court are distinguished from those that were appealed and declined or accepted by the Justices. Litigants took 1,004 or 20 percent of these circuit decisions to the Supreme Court, which granted certiorari in 9 percent of those appealed. Discounting 11 dismissals, the Court heard 92 cases or 1.9 percent of the entire group of 4,945 circuit cases and rendered full opinions in 62 cases or 1.3 percent of the original number.[a] If we consider cases that were

[a] The total number of circuit decisions becomes 4,945 to account for 2 circuit cases that were unconsolidated by the Justices and 2 that were consolidated but treated separately with appeals from other circuits.

TABLE 3.1
Supreme Court Review of Three Courts of Appeals
(After Hearing or Submission, FY 1965-1967)

| Circuit | No Appeal % | Declined or Dismissed % | Certiorari Granted % | (n) | Circuit Decisions N | % |
|---|---|---|---|---|---|---|
| 2d | 70.3 | 26.7 | 2.9 | (40) | 1,359 | 100.0 |
| 5th | 80.3 | 18.2 | 1.6 | (35) | 2,249 | 100.0 |
| D.C. | 88.3 | 10.5 | 1.3 | (17) | 1,337 | 100.0 |
| Sums | 79.7 | 18.4 | 1.9 | (92) | 4,945 | 100.0 |

consolidated, pending, and reported in the Supreme Court but not below, the ratio of decisions reviewed remains the same; but the rate of appeal from the three circuits climbs to 30 percent and certiorari granted falls to about 7 percent.[b]

Supreme Court oversight plainly was projected through a narrow prism of federal appeals. The proportion heard, moreover, though smaller than estimates from AO reports (2.4%), has declined since then. By 1975, the ratio of certiorari petitions granted was less than 1 percent of all circuit decisions and between 5 and 6 percent of decisions appealed.[c]

It is also characteristic that the Justices intervened primarily to alter decisions. Table 3.2, which classifies their decisions in the base period according to the same categories of reversal as in Table 2.8 for the circuits, shows that the Justices disturbed two-thirds of the decisions they heard. Their reversing rate, triple that of the circuits, was below the theoretically optimum use of scarce resources by appellate courts with discretionary docket control. Although any affirmance is a "mistake" from the standpoint of error correction, the Justices affirmed over one-fourth of the circuit decisions they heard.

Formally, therefore, the three Courts of Appeals became courts of last resort in 98.1 percent of this cycle of federal appeals and made decisions that prevailed in 98.6 percent. Courts of Appeals are mini-Supreme Courts in the vast majority of their cases. The jobs of circuit judges and Justices thus differ, as circuit judges suggest, less

[b] For details, see Appendix 1.
[c] Years in the text are fiscal years. Estimates from AO reports are the ratios of cases disposed of by the three circuits after hearing or submission (Table B1) and petitions for certiorari granted to them in the same period (Table B2), assuming that both actions occur in the same years. See Appendix 1.

TABLE 3.2
Supreme Court Decisions in Appeals Heard from Three Circuits
FY 1965-1967

| Circuit | Affirm N | Mix N | Reverse N | Avoid N | Other* N | Total N |
|---|---|---|---|---|---|---|
| 2d | 11 | 0 | 28 | 1 | 8 | 48 |
| 5th | 11 | 4 | 20 | 0 | 2 | 37 |
| D.C. | 3 | 1 | 13 | 0 | 1 | 18 |
| Sums | 25 | 5 | 61 | 1 | 11 | 103 |

* Assorted dismissals.

in terms of the finality of decisions than of the geographic reach and selectivity of their business.

It bears emphasis, however, that the three circuits were not forty-nine times more influential over these federal appeals than the Supreme Court. Just as intermediate appellate courts are highly dependent on litigators and adjudicators below in shaping their dockets, so they are theoretically bound by other Supreme Court decisions in like circumstances as well as by state decisions in diversity jurisdiction. Rulings of other circuits influence them, too. Like a giant's paw, one decision by the Justices may sweep aside dozens of contrary holdings in the circuits.[2] In a case-law system no one should assume that a lower court must be reversed before it will follow a higher one. Certainly not every controversy before the circuits was equal in social significance to those—for example, *Butts, Wade, Gojack, Afroyim,* and *Red Lion*—that the Justices heard.[3] For that matter neither were all of the high court's decisions of equal consequence. Gross frequencies help to establish the range of opportunity to adjudicate federal appeals; but as with circuit decisions before, aggregate rates of appeal and reversal are only the beginning of inquiry into relationships among federal courts on which the cohesion of the national judiciary depends.

## The Business of the Supreme Court

The Supreme Court *disturbed* over two-thirds of the circuit decisions it heard from the base period; Courts of Appeals *affirmed* two-thirds of theirs. This contrast alone should dispel casual assumptions that federal appellate courts are alike. Even the face of decisions showed greater variety between appellate levels than among the three circuits. Although the proportion of decision by full opinion (60%) in the high court was not much higher than in the circuits (50%), for example, there was greater relaxation of representational standards. The *in forma pauperis* rate was 13 percent compared to 1 percent for the circuits.[d] Amicus briefs appeared in 27 percent of the cases compared to 1 percent for the circuits.[e] Disagreement also was far more prevalent among the Justices. Dissents occurred eight times as frequently (64%) as among the circuits. Whatever else may be said for the federal appellate process, it successfully screened into the high court a heavy sampling of issues that divide federal judges.

The Supreme Court and the Courts of Appeals also differed in the composition of their business and how they disposed of it. The Justices decided a larger mix of constitutional questions (32%) than the three circuits (9%). They heard relatively more criminal cases (30% versus 24%), and a larger share of administrative appeals (22% versus 13%). Of the thirty-three constitutional cases, twenty-five concerned the rights of criminal defendants and only four involved the First Amendment. None involved elections or civil rights.[4] The Warren Court, in cases rising through the three federal circuits during this period, clearly concentrated on commercial regulation and criminal law. And unlike circuit practices, the Court affirmed only one criminal case.[5]

A comparison of the business of the Supreme Court and the three circuits combined in Table 3.3, which includes cases in the "other" columns for consistent comparison, also runs counter to the popular notion that the Warren Court in this period was essentially a civil liberties tribunal. Over half of the Court's cases, like the circuits', was economic in character, though the Justices decided a lower rate of contract and tort cases than the circuits and a higher proportion of commerce and tax cases. As these differences were not simply a function of what was appealed, the upshot is uneven supervision of circuit courts by the Justices, suggesting extensive selectivity and specialization among federal appellate tribunals.

The variety of appellate concerns is best illustrated by the taxonomy of substantive fields from Appendix 2. By comparing subjects in which these appellate courts met the 2 percent standard chosen in the last chapter as a baseline of sustained activity, we find that the Supreme Court had broader coverage than the circuits, deciding 2 percent of its cases in twenty-three fields as opposed to seventeen for

[d] All but 2 were decided by per curiam opinions.
[e] All but 5 were decided by full opinions.

TABLE 3.3
*Comparison of Appellate Court Business, FY 1965-1967*
(Including Dismissals)

| Subject | Three Circuits N | Three Circuits % | Supreme Court % | Supreme Court N |
|---|---|---|---|---|
| Contracts | 554 | 11.2 | 3.9 | 4 |
| Torts | 615 | 12.4 | 8.7 | 9 |
| Commerce | 613 | 12.4 | 27.2 | 28 |
| Labor | 497 | 10.0 | 6.8 | 7 |
| Taxation | 459 | 9.3 | 14.6 | 15 |
| Personal status | 814 | 16.5 | 15.5 | 16 |
| Crimes against persons | 125 | 2.5 | 0.0 | 0 |
| Crimes against property | 477 | 9.7 | 8.7 | 9 |
| Morals offenses | 261 | 5.3 | 2.9 | 3 |
| Miscellaneous offenses | 81 | 1.6 | 5.8 | 6 |
| Local | 54 | 1.1 | 0.0 | 0 |
| Other | 395 | 8.0 | 5.8 | 6 |
| Sums | 4,945 | 100.0 | 100.0 | 103 |

the 5th circuit, fifteen for the D.C. circuit, and thirteen for the 2d circuit. Such breadth of attention raises the question of whether the Justices cast their nets over so many pools of policy as to limit their catch within each.[6] The question is less loaded than first appears, because the continuity of the Court's review and the narrowing of appeals tend to unify seemingly disparate issues into coherent legal objectives. Eliminating pressures on the Fifth Amendment privilege against self-incrimination, for instance, which the Court found in wagering taxes, firearms registration, and immunity statutes, accounted for ten decisions recorded in taxation, weapons, and narcotics. Still, the problem of overextension persists in view of the varied relationships inherent in the distribution of substantive workloads among the three circuits and the Supreme Court.

First were fields of *staple activity* among all the federal appellate courts. The Supreme Court provided sustained supervision in the same six staple fields the circuits had in common: labor-management relations, habeas corpus, and the residual categories of "other contracts," "other personal injuries," "other torts," and "other commerce," all but one of which concerned administrative problems. To them may be added seamen's injuries, bankruptcies, income tax, and "other tax," in which the Supreme Court shared regular caseloads with the 2d and 5th circuits. Also shared with the D.C.

and 2d circuits were procedural problems rising from narcotics and robbery cases. Reasonable persons may differ whether two to five cases were adequate for effective oversight of three leading circuits in fields so complex and heavily litigated as labor relations and taxation over a three-year span. Certainly no one contends that the Justices should take a representative sample of cases that vex tribunals below. Considering the transformation of issues on appeal and the high court's review of other circuits, however, the business of the Justices bore a sufficient likeness to that of the three circuits to justify the notion that both appellate levels were regular participants in national policy networks concerning labor relations, economic regulation, and criminal procedure.

The same holds for the reverse situation of *shared inactivity* at both appellate levels. Certain fields (such as kidnapping, migratory birds, extortion, embezzlement, obscenity through the mails, and "other sex offenses") generated few appeals, presumably because they spawned few trials. Here again the coverages of the circuits and of the Supreme Court were reasonably similar, and district courts were on their own. In their high and low areas of concentration, then, the two levels had parallel concerns and clienteles.

There the resemblance stopped. For a third group of subjects involved *relatively low circuit but high Supreme Court activity*. Though circuit judges may have helped to structure issues on their way to the top, the Justices intervened in a disproportionate number of cases in select subjects. This category, including antitrust, tax fraud, immigration, and civil rights, is a litmus of Supreme Court discretion in action. Two small fields—food and drug and firearms regulation—illustrate the point. Together they generated one-tenth as many appeals at the circuit level as labor relations but consumed an equal volume of Supreme Court decisions.[f] However the Supreme Court's preoccupations may shift over time, its selectivity is marked.

In contrast were fields of *high circuit activity but Supreme Court indifference*. For three years during which they handled roughly 40 percent of total circuit business after hearing or submission, the three Courts of Appeals were largely their own masters in broad expanses of public policy. The Supreme Court heard only one appeal each in the fields of forgery, negotiable instruments, patents, and copyrights. The Court exercised no supervision at all over these circuits concerning insurance and marine contracts, real property,

---

[f] Of 11 food and drug cases in the three circuits, 4 were appealed to the Supreme Court, which took 2 from the 2d circuit and affirmed both. The 5th circuit decided 9 of the 20 appeals concerning federal firearms statutes, 2 of which were appealed to the high court. The Justices took both and reversed.

workmen's compensation, fair labor standards, bribery, parole, social security, suffrage and elections and school desegregation. Granted, some of these fields involved state law in diversity jurisdiction; other issues such as reapportionment and school desegregation arose directly from three-judge district courts. In major arteries of federal litigation, nevertheless, the three Courts of Appeals were not way stations. They were the end of the line.

In some fields, moreover, two circuits operated without Supreme Court intervention. Only the D.C. circuit provoked a grant of certiorari in patents. Only the 2d circuit was reviewed in antitrust, food and drugs, copyrights, and immigration. The 5th circuit was singled out in negotiable instruments, motor vehicle injuries, "other torts," and weapons. As a result, the circuit courts escaping review became final arbiters in precisely their magnetic fields, such as patents, social security, insurance, workmen's compensation, civil rights (though not immigration), where autonomous policy flavorings were strong. Stimulated thereby were divisions of labor in federal appeals and regionalism in federal law enforcement. Courts of Appeals, though "merely a reflector, serving as a judicial moon," refracted light of their own.[7]

## The Mobilization of Appeals

Expanding the policy-making responsibility of the federal judiciary inevitably contracts the Supreme Court's surveillance over individual subordinates and enlarges their freedom of action. Because the staple business at both appellate levels is limited, policy variations flourish among regional federal courts. Courts of Appeals are not simply "the courts of last resort in the run of ordinary cases," as the Justices recognized in 1941, but also quasi-independent units competing for "voice" in the formulation of public policies at different levels of the judicial system.[8]

From either a functional or a policy standpoint, key relationships among the Supreme Court and courts below thus turn on the screening processes by which litigants and the Justices select what the Supreme Court reviews. To explore this dimension of intercourt relations, we shall consider three questions. First, what were the rates and sources of appeal to the high court? Second, was there a connection between appellate demand and what the Justices heard? Third, as a barometer of the high court's priorities, whom did the Justices support in the cases they took?

At the threshold is the mobilization of appeals. The rate of appeal to the high court—20 percent for reported cases, 30 percent for all cases—was virtually the same as our estimate from district courts to the circuits. These figures again demonstrate inelasticity of appellate demand. Litigants persisted in appealing to the high court at the same rate as below in the teeth of nine to one odds against acceptance.

At the same time, sharp contrasts prevailed in the origins and outcomes of appeal. The 2d circuit, as shown in Tables 3.1 and 3.2, had a disproportionate share of its decisions appealed and reversed. Litigants challenged almost one-third of that prestigious tribunal's decisions. The D.C. circuit, on the other hand, fared worse after certiorari was granted. This court had four decisions upset for every affirmance as compared to roughly two to one for the other two circuits.

The majority of certiorari petitions—and those granted by the Justices—were challenges to decisions of the federal government. The United States sought or supported review in only 3 percent of the 1,004 petitions to the Court, but was respondent in 59 percent. Appeals from state action consumed only 9 percent of the petitions; disputes between private parties constituted another 28 percent. These figures reflect the tight screening of government litigation by the Solicitor General, whose faucetlike control of appeals of adverse decisions by the federal government gives that official powerful leverage over the high court's intake.[9] Solicitors General during this period authorized certiorari petitions in only 10 percent of the cases requested from all federal sources, including only 6 of 312 criminal cases, in order to focus the Court's attention onto problems of taxation, labor relations, and economic regulation.[10] In our cases, the federal government sought or supported review in half of the administrative appeals heard by the Court (12 of 22)—and won all but 3 of them.[11] The United States supported review in only 2 criminal cases—*U.S. v. Wade* and *Greenwood v. Peacock*—in both instances to temper the libertarian thrust of decisions by the 5th circuit concerning police lineups and civil rights removals.[12] Even the Solicitors General of the Johnson presidency, Thurgood Marshall and Archibald Cox, sought review far less on behalf of defendant's rights or civil liberties than to defend the government's position in economic regulation and the administrative process.

The federal government, as usual, was far more successful in obtaining review for its few petitions (67%) than in the more frequent instances when it was respondent or states and private litigants were parties. Indicative of the credibility that Solicitors General have developed with the Justices by virtue of careful screening of government requests for review, not to mention *in forma pauperis* petitions, these data document the shared objectives of the Justices and the Solicitor General, as an officer of the Court, in seeking resolution of major issues of national scope.[g] The Supreme Court is less a national umpire than a ballplayer on the federal team.

Screening was not confined to Justices or government attorneys. Despite chilling odds, litigant strategies worked wide variations in demands on the high court. Table 3.4, which samples the subjects of appeal in Appendix 2, shows that litigants challenged over half of the circuit decisions involving tax fraud compared to one-fourth of those concerning civil rights, income tax, or habeas corpus. Only one-tenth of the bankruptcy appeals went beyond the circuits.[13] Between these extremes, was there any connection between the rate of appeal and what the Supreme Court took?

Apart from some overlap in the 2d circuit, the answer is negative. For large aggregates, moderate differences among rates of appeal were met by large differences in the Court's response. For example, though litigants appealed criminal cases at a slightly higher rate (26%) than civil cases (19%), the Justices decided an even larger proportion of criminal cases (34%). For particular subjects in Table 3.4, the broad variations in rates of certiorari sought and granted indicate that what the Supreme Court heard was not a function of appellant demand.

Linking the subjects of appeal to their sources, as in Appendixes 5 and 6, we find that, though circuit decisions from district courts and agencies were appealed at the same rates (21%), the Justices were much more inclined to hear cases rising from federal agencies (30%) than from district courts (8%). In particular, the Justices accepted only one appeal from the D.C. circuit concerning its three most prolific sources of administrative review—the NLRB, the FCC, and the CAB—yet they took six of the ten appeals from that circuit concerning the FPC, the FTC, and "other boards and commissions," reversing all of them. This was the only instance in which the Supreme Court's reversing rate was 100 percent.

The Supreme Court was more responsive to demand from the 2d circuit. Where the rate of appeal was relatively low, for example,

[g] Summarized below are rates of certiorari petitions granted by the nature of the parties for cited circuit decisions during FY 1965-1967:

| Type of Party | % | N |
| --- | --- | --- |
| U.S. petitioner | 66.7 | 30 |
| U.S. respondent | 8.3 | 591 |
| States or state agents | 8.9 | 101 |
| Private parties | 4.6 | 282 |
| Sums | 9.2 | 1,004 |

TABLE 3.4
Rates of Appeal to the Supreme Court and Rates of Certiorari
Petitions Granted in Selected Subjects, FY 1965-1967

(From Appendix 2)

| Subject | Circuit Decisions Appealed to Supreme Court | | Certiorari Petitions Granted | |
|---|---|---|---|---|
| | Total Decisions N | Rate Appealed % | Total Certiorari Petitions N | Rate Granted % |
| Tax fraud | 34 | 50.0 | 17 | 11.8 |
| Fraud | 62 | 48.4 | 30 | 6.7 |
| Antitrust | 38 | 42.1 | 16 | 12.5 |
| Narcotics | 235 | 29.8 | 70 | 4.3 |
| Immigration and deportation | 34 | 29.4 | 10 | 40.0 |
| Copyright | 44 | 27.3 | 12 | 8.3 |
| Habeas corpus | 346 | 24.9 | 86 | 5.8 |
| Income tax | 244 | 23.4 | 57 | 7.0 |
| Civil rights | 113 | 23.0 | 26 | 15.4 |
| Labor relations | 325 | 19.7 | 64 | 6.3 |
| Bankruptcy | 163 | 10.4 | 17 | 23.5 |
| Suffrage | 45 | 6.7 | 3 | 0.0 |

from the NLRB (1 in 7) or Vermont (1 in 5), so was certiorari. Where the rate of appeal was high, as in antitrust, tax fraud, and the Southern District of New York, all of which generated petitions for review approximately half the time, the Justices responded generously. The 5th circuit produced only one prominent pattern—a repetition of lower rates of appeal from rural areas, including the four most rebellious district courts, than from urban districts, such as Eastern Louisiana or the Southern Districts of Florida and Texas. Accented were the critical parts played by litigants in defining court business and by the 5th circuit in serving as the main channel to enforce civil rights. The Supreme Court is not well positioned to correct deficient supervision of district courts by the circuits. Without appeal its hand is stayed.

What emerges from this stream of appeals is the selectivity of both appellants and the Justices in setting the Supreme Court's agenda. Except in the 2d circuit, as already noted, there was little correspondence between rates of certiorari sought and granted. The Justices relied more on circuit supervision of district courts than of federal agencies. They also exerted little control over pockets of circuit specialization, such as the D.C. circuit in communications law or the 5th circuit in civil rights, thanks in part to the reluctance or inability of litigants to climb the last mountain.

All this perhaps overproves the point that demands from appellants, though shaping the initial pool of cases that Justices see, have less to do with what the Court hears than the policy goals of the Justices. It is well understood that among the Court's most important decisions are what it decides to decide.[14] Discretionary jurisdiction is governed officially by Supreme Court Rule 19, which articulates that the primary reasons for granting review are to determine important federal questions, settle conflicts among federal circuits, and secure compliance with settled legal rules. Because the Justices rarely explain denial of certiorari—or over 90 percent of their decisions—social scientists have attempted to infer the priorities governing the Court's screening process.

In a leading study of the Supreme Court's certiorari jurisdiction, Joseph Tanenhaus and his students developed the theory that certain cues in certiorari petitions guide the Justices in separating frivolous appeals from those deserving serious attention.[15] The cues found were dissension within lower courts, civil liberties issues, and the federal government's requests for review. No attempt will be made here to replicate Tanenhaus's study, but we shall explore certain characteristics of these appeals bearing on their first cue, the Supreme Court's responsibility to control dissension among lower courts. Our hypotheses, based on the work of Richardson and Vines, are that the Justices were inclined to hear (1) reversed decisions more than affirmed decisions, (2) nonunanimous decisions more than unanimous decisions, and (3) en banc decisions more than panel decisions.[16]

Clearly, all three manifestations of conflict are related to Supreme Court review. The comparative rates of certiorari petitions granted in these situations, reported in Table 3.5 for the ninety-two cases heard, support each hypothesis. The hypothesis for reversed decisions received weaker support than the hypotheses for split and en banc decisions. One reason may be that reversals were weaker cues to appellants than split and en banc decisions. Reversals were appealed at a lower rate than affirmances, a phenomenon that supports the contention of Richardson and Vines that litigants tend to keep on appealing until they win a reversal or exhaust their remedies.

Disagreements between levels in a circuit may project weaker signals of relevance to the Supreme Court than disagreements within Courts of Appeals. As the data in Table 3.5 mix the motives of appellants and Justices, it is impossible to unravel them conclusively. The

TABLE 3.5
Supreme Court Certiorari in Appeals from Three Circuit Courts
FY 1965-1967

| Type of Circuit Decision | Circuit Decisions Appealed | | Certiorari Petitions Granted | |
|---|---|---|---|---|
| | Total Decisions N | Rate Appealed % | Total Certiorari Petitions N | Rate Granted % |
| Affirmance | 3,357 | 23.0 | 772 | 7.9 |
| Reversal & mixed | 1,300 | 16.2 | 211 | 13.7 |
| Other & avoid | 288 | 7.3 | 21 | 23.8 |
| All cases | 4,945 | 20.3 | 1,004 | 9.2 |
| Unanimous | 4,535 | 18.7 | 848 | 7.5 |
| Split | 410 | 38.0 | 156 | 17.9 |
| All cases | 4,945 | 20.3 | 1,004 | 9.2 |
| Panel | 4,903 | 20.1 | 987 | 8.9 |
| En banc | 42 | 40.5 | 17 | 23.5 |
| All cases | 4,945 | 20.3 | 1,004 | 9.2 |

results after certiorari was granted, however, reinforce the significance of initial screening, because there was little difference in the treatment of circuit decisions accepted for review. The Court upset reversals and mixed decisions at about the same rate as affirmances (72%). No difference existed between its rate of disturbing unanimous and split decisions (71%). Thus, despite impressions that *intra*circuit conflict no longer interests the Justices, a relationship between internal disagreement and Supreme Court judgments actually emerged from what the Justices decided to hear.[17] These data also illustrate the inelasticity of some appeals. Litigants challenged affirmed decisions at a higher rate than disturbed decisions even though their cases were less likely to be accepted. Are judges right about the waste of resources on unmeritorious appeals?

Additional light on the Supreme Court's priorities is provided in Table 3.6, which juxtaposes decisions at both appellate levels in order to discover who supported whom. The nebulous data in the "avoid-other" column are excluded from much of the following analysis. Both disturbed decisions and conflicts between levels consist of reversals in whole or in part.

Our conclusions are, first, that the Supreme Court had little overt interest in resolving conflict *within* circuits. The Court disturbed

TABLE 3.6
Intercourt Relations

|  | Circuit Decisions (N = 4,842) | | Supreme Court Decisions (N = 103) | | | |
|---|---|---|---|---|---|---|
|  | No Appeal | Review Declined | SC Affirm | SC Disturb | SC Avoid-Other | Total |
| CA affirm | 2,585 | 708 | 16 | 41 | 7 | 3,357 |
| CA disturb | 1,089 | 177 | 8 | 21 | 5 | 1,300 |
| CA avoid-other | 267 | 16 | 1 | 4 | 0 | 288 |
| Sums | 3,941 | 901 | 25 | 66 | 12 | 4,945 |

NOTE: SC = Supreme Court; CA = Courts of Appeals.

more circuit affirmances (N = 41) than it reaffirmed (N = 16). Hence, the Justices themselves injected more court conflict into the cases they took than they averted or resolved (N = 34). The Supreme Court also upset more circuit reversals and mixed decisions (N = 21) than it affirmed (N = 8). Hence, when conflict already existed between two tiers below, the Justices disturbed more circuit resolutions of the conflict than they sustained and sided more often with original than with appellate tribunals. Thanks to the high degree of consensus below, however, the Supreme Court also upset more district court and agency decisions (N = 41) than it sustained (N = 37).[h] We cannot leap to the conclusion that the Supreme Court was basically supportive of original tribunals. Reaffirming consensus and settling conflict below in about the same proportions (1 in 4), the Court actually extended roughly the same degree of support to district courts and Courts of Appeals in all three circuits.

Rather, reversals tended to involve substitution of the Justices' judgment for a consensus reached in lower courts. That occurred in almost two-thirds of the circuit decisions that were disturbed. Hence, the effect of Supreme Court reversal in appeals rising from district courts was more to upset regional harmony than to compose conflicts.[i]

[h] The Justices upset 41 original decisions by disturbing 41 circuit affirmances. They sustained 37 original decisions by affirming 16 circuit affirmances and disturbing 21 circuit reversals and mixed decisions.

[i] A striking example is *General Electric Co. v. Gilbert*, 429 U.S. 125, 147 (1976), in which the Supreme Court rejected the conclusion of all six circuits that addressed the question of whether, under Title VII of the Civil Rights Act of 1964, failure of employers' disability plans to cover pregnancy-related disabilities discriminated against women.

In administrative appeals, by contrast, the Justices supported agencies more than Courts of Appeals (13-9). The main thrust of review was to reinstate decisions of the FPC and the FMC upset by the D.C. and 5th circuits and to change decisions of the Tax Court and Immigration and Naturalization Service approved by the 2d circuit.[j]

These patterns resolve into a deceptively simple conclusion that the Justices supported whoever agreed with them in whatever interested them in appeals before them. A 100 percent reversal rate, the theoretical optimum use of Supreme Court resources for error correction, is unlikely because the Justices obviously grant certiorari to settle intercircuit conflicts and to affirm decisions below that they approve.[k] Our conclusions, therefore, amend some implications of cue theory; the Supreme Court was less interested in resolving intracircuit disagreements as such than in resolving the policy disputes with which those disagreements were correlated. Supreme Court review of the three Courts of Appeals in this period was less the resolution of lower court conflicts than "applied politics"— securing the supremacy of highly selective policy values regardless of levels.[l] [18]

Resolving conflicts *among* circuits, a major objective of Supreme Court review, also appeared secondary to policy formation. The Court's own explanation for granting certiorari in these cases indicates that uniformity played second fiddle to policy making. Of the fifty-eight cases in which reasons for certiorari were offered, the Justices stated a substantial federal question in thirty-seven, intercircuit conflict in only twelve, both in seven, and circuit compliance in two. Only one decision in five involved intercircuit conflict or problems

---

[j] The Justices disturbed the agency position in 1 out of 6 cases from the FPC, 1 out of 3 from the FMC, 2 out of 4 from the NLRB, and 2 out of 3 from the INS and the Tax Courts.

[k] Resolving intercircuit conflicts and monitoring compliance were responsible for less than half (11 of 25) of the affirmances by the Supreme Court, including 2 cases in which conflict was present but unacknowledged as a reason for review. Because the 14 remaining affirmances involved 3 major labor disputes and frontier issues concerning immigration, searches and seizures, and civil rights removals, these decisions on their face can hardly be attributed to "mistakes." The Court evidently granted certiorari in order to nationalize important decisions below. The Justices have a method to eliminate their screening mistakes—dismissal—which they employed freely. (Litigants were responsible for 8 dismissals under Rule 60; the Court dismissed 2 as improvidently granted and 1 for mootness.) The three circuits, incidentally, "lost" half (N = 10) of their decisions involving intercircuit conflicts.

[l] To answer objections that resolving *intra*circuit conflict is irrelevant, as this object is unrecognized in Rule 19, one should note that circuit judges increasingly justify avoidance of en bancs for this purpose on grounds that the Supreme Court will decide the important issues anyway. See p. 218.

of conformity.[19] Though complete proof requires comparative analysis of briefs, the signs from these appeals point in the same direction: the Supreme Court gave higher priority to its lawmaking or supremacy functions than to its conflict-resolution or uniformity functions. Absent significant issues of national policy, or decisions offensive to four Justices, Courts of Appeals were left largely alone.

## The Sources and Subjects of Supreme Court Decisions

What then were the Justices' policy objectives and their implications for relations with Courts of Appeals? Did the high court's policy-making priority leave these circuits insufficiently supervised?

Some light may be shed on these questions by linking the sources and subjects of Supreme Court review with case outcomes. Except for taxation, in which five decisions favored the government and nine favored individuals, the Warren Court overwhelmingly supported libertarian goals. The Justices sided against claimants in all contract cases ($N = 3$), supported workers and claimants in all tort cases ($N = 8$), and favored workers and unions in all labor relations cases ($N = 6$) decided in the base period. In marked contrast to the Vinson Court, where civil liberties claimants lost more often than they won, the Warren Court favored individuals against the government in twelve of sixteen personal status cases and in all but one of nineteen remaining criminal cases—a search in Washington warily sustained.[20] Given the decisional tendencies of the circuits, and the inelasticity of appellate demand, these results support the thesis of Richardson and Vines that the federal appellate process in this era served as a screen through which nonlibertarian decisions were successively challenged until judicial remedies or purses were exhausted.[21]

The range of Supreme Court responsibility is so broad, though, that its review at any given time is apt to be spasmodic and its relationship with each circuit discrete. We have seen that, apart from the six staple fields that the Justices policed in common with the three circuits, these Courts of Appeals were final arbiters in major areas of litigation, such as reapportionment, desegregation, social security, and patents, some of them precisely those in which the circuits asserted substantial regional independence. The impression that the high court exerted little control over circuit specialties is reinforced by further analysis of Appendixes 5 and 6. For example, notwithstanding the uproar over criminal law in the nation's capital, and a high rate of appeal in local cases, the Supreme Court traditionally defers to local judges concerning affairs in the District of Columbia.ᵐ Except for voiding a local juvenile delinquency act, the Warren Court was no different.²² Its supervision of the D.C. circuit centered on select issues of administrative law.

The administrative decisions of the 2d circuit, by contrast, fared well on review. This circuit was reversed in only one labor-management case, an impressive record in view of the volume. Except for taxation and torts, the court in New York received solid support in commercial cases. This circuit collided with the Justices mainly in immigration and criminal procedure.

The 5th circuit, almost all of whose decisions in contracts and torts were upheld, was strongly supported in civil rights by what the Justices refused to review. Though this circuit decided 100 of the 113 civil rights cases in the base period, litigants appealed 20 decisions to the Court, which heard only 2, with mixed results. What's more, the Justices took only one case from the four rebellious district courts in the 5th circuit and none from the heavily reversed district court of Vermont. To the circuits fell the job of keeping wayward district judges in line, in part because their decisions were sparsely challenged.

It pushes the point to suggest that the Supreme Court defers to expertise, but it is apparent that the same selectivity that characterized the subjects of the Supreme Court's review extended to the objects of its support. When called to account, each circuit court was found to be in step in some fields and out of line in others. Reversals of the D.C. circuit were concentrated in administrative law, especially concerning the Federal Maritime Commission and the Federal Power Commission. The 2d circuit was reversed mostly in immigration, seamen's injuries, and criminal procedure, particularly concerning confessions and the Fifth Amendment in which circuit judges like Henry J. Friendly and J. Edward Lumbard were openly critical of the Warren Court. While the 5th circuit was also in error regarding self-incrimination, it was reversed mainly in bankruptcy, gas regulation, and labor relations. For the most part, however, the three Courts of Appeals were not reversed at all. No more telling example could be found than school desegregation. During three years of sound and fury in which the 5th circuit led the country toward an affirmative constitutional obligation to integrate public schools by whatever means "that work and work now"—including

---

ᵐ The D.C. circuit's review of district courts in local jurisdiction was challenged at double the rate (1 in 5) of district courts in national jurisdiction (1 in 10), though the Justices took only 2 of the former cases and 8 of the latter.

threatened criminal contempt against Mississippi's governor, Ross Barnett—not one of its decisions was upset.[23]

The short of it is that 1.9 percent supervision did not stretch very far over an expanding range of Supreme Court responsibility. As head of a vast, but diffused legal apparatus involving many tribunals, the Court must practice parsimony in overseeing any single court or subject. Even when they intervene, the Justices often delegate to lower courts substantial discretion in implementing their commands. Not only was their remand rate in these cases (35%) almost twice that of the three circuits, their mandates were often so general as to leave the doctrine of *stare decisis*, in Julius Stone's choice phrase, more like a muumuu than a straitjacket.[24]

The result is broad autonomy for Courts of Appeals. Officially, to be sure, denial of certiorari signifies nothing about the merits, only that a petition failed to muster the requisite four votes for review. Practically speaking, denial of certiorari means plenty. Unless the Court subsequently decides a similar case to which intermediate tribunals are obliged to conform, circuit decisions become regional law, and, as Chief Judge William Denman recognized in 1937, the large circuits become "the Supreme Courts for 98% of the circuits' Federal litigation."[25] The notion that the Supreme Court review, buttressed by the doctrine of *stare decisis*, compels uniformity in every circuit is a mirage and has been for some time.

These conclusions are graphically illustrated by the flowchart in Figure 3.1, which summarizes the formal finality of circuit decisions in this cycle of federal appeals. We have found that the three Courts of Appeals affirmed two out of three and disturbed about one in five of 4,941 decisions in three fiscal years. Over one-fifth of these decisions—or 30 percent adjusting for consolidated and uncited cases—were appealed to the Supreme Court, which accepted one in eleven for review and disturbed over two out of three of those heard. Of 4,945 circuit decisions, the Supreme Court exercised direct control over 1.9 percent, affirming 0.5 percent and disturbing 1.3 percent. In effect, the three tribunals became courts of last resort in 98 percent of the cases and made decisions that formally prevailed in 98.6 percent. From a starting point of about 120,000 cases filed in federal district courts and almost 5,000 appeals disposed of after hearing or submission in the three circuits, the Supreme Court heard 92 cases and rendered only 62 full opinions.

Notwithstanding the high court's propensity to reverse, the Justices intervened so rarely and selectively in these federal appeals that controls on the discretion of circuit judges would appear to

FIGURE 3.1
*Federal Appeals Flowchart*
*2d, 5th, and D.C. Circuits, FY 1965-1967*

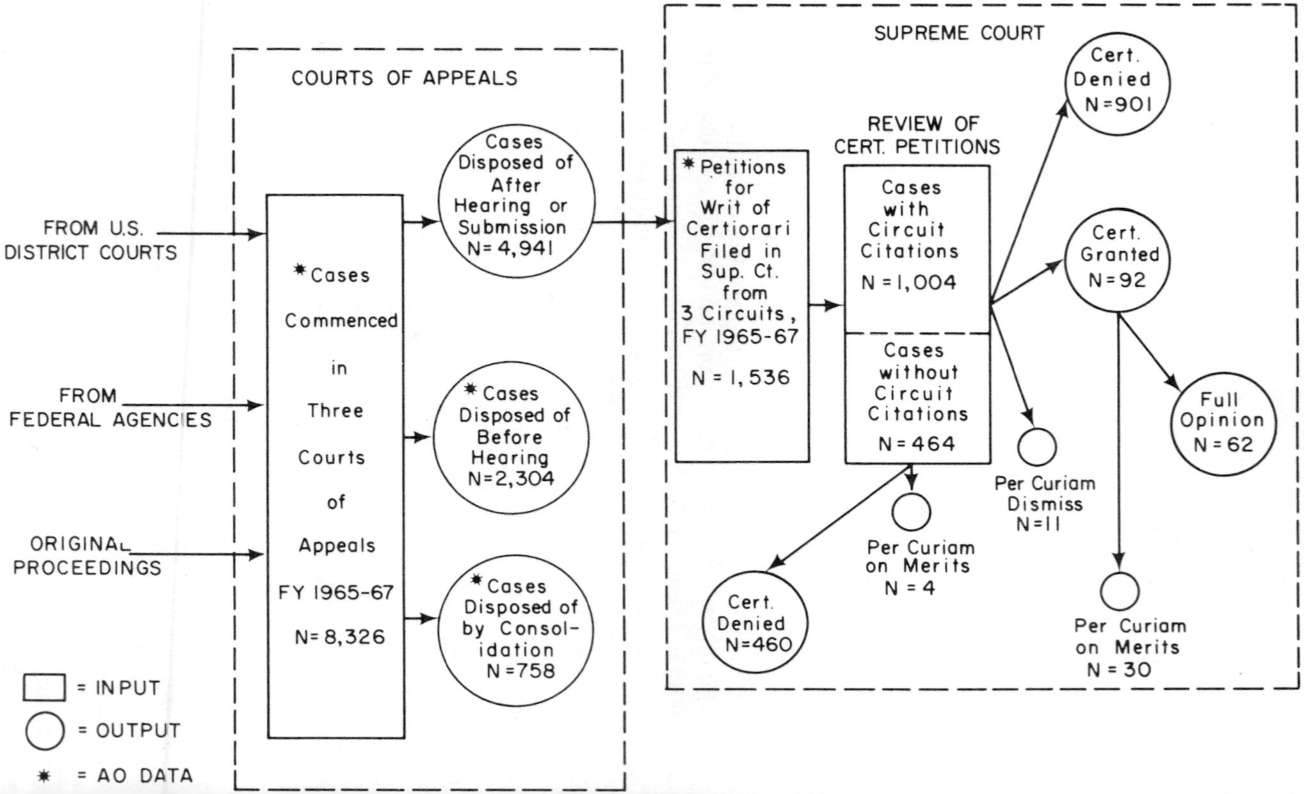

depend less on fear of formal reversal than on informal constraints derived from a community of professional and political values. Interviews with thirty-five judges from the three circuits support that inference. As we shall see in Chapter Five, Supreme Court review looms as too uncertain and unpredictable for rotating circuit judges to worry greatly about reversal or to anticipate the reactions of Justices, who appear less interested in correcting error or arbitrating court conflicts than in advancing select policy goals.[26] To harmonize the work of lesser federal courts, the high tribunal perforce must rely heavily on voluntary compliance with its commands. Strong internalized norms requiring lower court conformity with Supreme Court directives are critical elements of cohesion in the federal judiciary, the more so under the appellate crunch of the mid-1970s, when the proportion of decisions reviewed inevitably fell at the very time lower court responsibilities increased. What then unifies the regional supreme courts and constrains judicial discretion in the law explosion?

## Conclusions: Roles and Relations of Federal Appellate Courts

To anyone reasonably familiar with the American judiciary, it is hardly news that Supreme Court Justices, in the course of deciding cases, make public policies selectively. That is what they are supposed to do. Nor is it news that harmonizing judicial decisions is subordinate in practice to resolving major federal questions. Experts have suspected as much for some time.[27] Wise readers will also be wary of projecting these samplings beyond their own time and place. Since 1967, the D.C. circuit has lost its local jurisdiction, the 5th circuit has suffered stinging reversals in school desegregation cases, all three circuits but especially the 2d have undergone substantial personnel changes—and the Warren Court is no more.[28] President Nixon's pledge to "balance" the federal courts, aided by a record number of appointments, worked deep changes in the federal judiciary at every level. Massive additions of judicial manpower in lower courts augured more changes after 1978.

All the same, this analysis of the flow of litigation supports several conclusions about the roles and relations of federal appellate courts in the crisis of volume. First of all, the distribution of labor among the Supreme Court and the Courts of Appeals, implicit in the Judiciary Act of 1925, has matured into fully differentiated functions for federal appellate courts. Substantively, the Supreme Court has become more and more a constitutional tribunal. Courts of Appeals concentrate on statutory interpretation, administrative review, and error correction in masses of routine adjudications. Functionally, the Supreme Court, for all its commanding doctrinal influence, is better understood as a general staff or a selective formulator of policies than as a court of error or overseer.[29] Even though the Justices address most of their full opinions to circuit courts, at best they can only sample legal error and intercourt conflicts. Policy making, resolving important national issues as distinct from arbitrating court conflicts or stabilizing uncertain law, takes top priority.

Furthermore, the Supreme Court is quite selective about its policy objectives. The Court does not attempt to police the entire range of federal court business, much less all fields of federal policy.[30] The Justices reviewed the work of these circuits with regularity in only two broad classes of litigation: (1) six areas of staple federal adjudication, for example, income tax, labor relations, and criminal law, which the circuits had most in common, and (2) select fields, for example, antitrust, immigration, and natural gas regulation, in which the Justices appear to have exercised a kind of "policy-shot" function—picking from appeals before them targets that furthered their view of what was good for the country. Because the Justices were limited to a few and sometimes ambiguous directives even within those favored concerns, the Courts of Appeals normally went about their business without close surveillance by their superiors or effective challenge by their constituents.

The Supreme Court is a policy court; Courts of Appeals are courts of appeals. In consequence, the relations between the high court and each circuit were usually discrete, centering on specific issues such as administrative law in the D.C. circuit or admiralty in the 2d. The dynamics of appellate review and the physical limitations on the Court may alter the issues according to the changing enthusiasms of incumbents, but the basic allocation of appellate resources is likely to remain unaltered. The Supreme Court, too, is one among many power centers—and a highly selective one at that.

The selectivity and limited surveillance of the Supreme Court perforce mean that Courts of Appeals exercise several overlapping functions in the federal legal system. Most basic is *error correction*— supervising the application and interpretation of national and state law in district courts and agencies and holding them to account. The Justices exerted so little direct control over this process that those concerned with the administration of individual justice or of national policy through law should look not only up to Mt. Olympus but also down and around. Tribunals of first instance carry the principal burden of determining the quality of federal justice. Courts of

Appeals are the primary monitors of their performance. This responsibility is explicit in the Judiciary Act of 1925, which gave Justices discretionary docket control and circuit judges the main job of adjudicating federal appeals. That the Supreme Court intervened in less than 2 percent of this litigation is indicative of its dependence on the circuits to perform the central appellate task of ensuring correct legal determinations and fact finding in lower courts and agencies.

The same is true for *settling disputes* and *enforcing national law*. As Courts of Appeals provide finality in the vast majority of federal appeals, these functional objectives of the 1925 statute have clearly succeeded. Circuit courts are the end of the road in all but a tiny fraction of federal appeals. Not that litigants failed to challenge the decisions of trial judges. Nearly a third of their judgments were appealed in 1967-1970; appeal in criminal cases is becoming automatic. Nor were circuit courts themselves unchallenged. Almost a third of their decisions, too, were taken to the Supreme Court. But the Justices intervened so intermittently that the three circuits became courts of last resort in the vast majority of cases.

With finality goes *filtering*, sorting and shaping review-worthy claims on their way to the Supreme Court. Filtering is harder to gauge than finality, because so many actors—litigants, judges, clerks—take part in it and because one of its forms, transformation of issues, is so subjective. Yet, intermediate courts have important tasks in shaping federal appeals. Circuit judges come to grips with legal issues sooner than the Justices and are less insulated from the environment that produces them. Circuit judges also have at their disposal powerful tools of gatekeeping and docket management. Since 1969, every circuit has developed techniques of mass production, such as screening, to expedite decision making. These devices give Courts of Appeals formidable means of docket control and considerable impact on the ultimate work of the high court.

Beyond that, circuit courts filter doctrine by regional experimentation and by structuring issues on their way to Congress and the Supreme Court. Circuit judges interviewed were less than sanguine about their ability to predict or to provoke certiorari. Still, some of them fight doggedly for en bancs and "all but write certiorari petitions" to encourage review. However a Learned Hand might complain about the futility of passing on constitutional questions— "Who in hell cares what anybody says about them but the Final Five of the august Nine?"—the Justices continually avow the value of dress rehearsals below, much as circuit judges themselves value the work of *some* district courts.[31]

Error correction, conflict resolution, law enforcement, filtering, all add up to a more controversial function for Courts of Appeals, not explicit in the 1925 Act—*lawmaking*. There is an old adage that those who administer a policy help to make it. This adage has particular force in a case-law system because, as Martin Shapiro observes, judges develop policy less by giant leaps than by "the day-to-day power over small decisions."[32] Unless we assume that 92 cases screened into the Supreme Court exhausted all important policy issues in almost 5,000 appeals, this sampling indicates that circuit courts perforce make public policy when they decide appeals. The real problem is "when and how and how much."[33]

Close analysis of the flow of litigation shows that complex, subtle concentrations of business exist among federal appellate courts. Consequently, rather than serving as mirror images of the Supreme Court, intermediate tribunals have multiple policy roles affecting lower courts. As we saw in Chapter Two, the three circuits provided sustained supervision, in common with the Justices, over some sectors of public policy, for example, labor, taxation, and criminal justice. They participated marginally in other fields and concentrated in still others with substantial regional independence. Their dockets were hybrids containing masses of routine claims and factual disputes interspersed with trail-blazing cases pressing the edges of legal change. Surfeits of appeals in some jurisdictions and subjects coexisted with pockets of questionable sufficiency. Tracking these appeals at both appellate levels also showed that for three years these circuits were final arbiters in major areas of federal policy. Some of them, such as school desegregation, were precisely those in which the circuits dominated litigation and doctrinal independence flourished. Though many factors may inhibit circuit judges from fashioning changes out of whole cloth, numerous examples come to mind of cases in which these courts made ground-breaking decisions that became final.[34] To that extent the circuit courts became potentially competitive power centers. It can be argued that these courts did just that in the late 1960s for race relations in the 5th circuit, criminal law in Washington, and vigorous enforcement of environmental protection statutes in all three circuits until the Burger Court trimmed their sails after 1972.[35]

Thus, circuit courts not only screen, filter, and apply federal law so that the Justices may innovate. As courts of last resort in the overwhelming majority of cases, they *make* national law residually and regionally. The magnitude of their finality and specialization, in contexts of regional recruitment and organization, yields considerable potential for independent policy making and adaptation of federal policy to regional environments. Unless an extremely small portion of cases is coterminous with the policy potential of federal appeals, regionalization is an inescapable adjunct of adjudicating appeals in one of the oldest regional operations of federal power in existence.

These conditions magnify the paradox of seeking unity through decentralized courts. For one thing, they may engender conflict over judicial roles and priorities, as discussed in Chapter Five. The broad autonomy of circuit courts in adjudication and administration also makes them more independent of the Supreme Court—and of each other—than organizational charts convey. The federal judiciary may articulate a system, as Frankfurter and Landis maintained, but the system is composed of loosely related parts whose connections are not only hierarchical but heterogeneous.[36] Conceptually, this condition increases the temptation to replace the traditional view of circuit courts as intermediates in a pyramid with a bureaucratic or even a pluralist political model in which circuit judges, coupled with allied constituencies and clienteles, are semiautonomous competitors for a voice in policy formation along with the Justices and everybody else.[37] So viewed, Courts of Appeals participate in both national and local policy networks, their decisions becoming regional law unless intolerable to the Justices.

In practical terms, the diversification of federal judicial authority also raises serious issues regarding the adequacy and quality of appellate review. On the one hand, it suggests limits on what is amenable to uniform rule.[38] On the other, to enforce national policies the Supreme Court increasingly must rely on the very courts in a position to Balkanize federal law. To cope with swelling dockets and expanding judicial functions, Courts of Appeals are transforming the process of decision. Does the dispersal of judicial power threaten the uniformity of national law *among* Courts of Appeals? Are the cohesion and quality of appellate decisions being eroded *within* them?

Though projecting past experience from only three circuits has obvious limits, this analysis suggests that the answers depend on the interplay of diversity and informality of court relations at each level. At first glance, the variety of business and behavior that flourishes in inferior federal courts reinforces fears that the federal judiciary has overextended its central nervous system. Despite common diets in staple fields, these circuits specialized, decided similar issues differently, and shaped regional policies. Whether these centrifugal forces justify institutional centralization, nevertheless, requires careful differentiation of appellate functions and intercourt relations at each rung of the national judiciary.

The adequacy of appellate resources depends in large measure on the presumed functions of federal appeals and the strength of informal controls on judicial discretion. The new National Court of Appeals, proposed by the Hruska Commission to relieve the Supreme Court, is a good example.[39] If error correction is the primary aim of Supreme Court review, then its coverage is "patently inadequate," as former judge Shirley M. Hufstedler once charged; because the Justices hear less than 1 percent of the cases decided by federal circuit courts, which "can neither be right nor harmonious 99 percent of the time."[40]

If the main purpose of the Supreme Court is setting policy directions rather than error correction or conflict resolution, however, the evidence of inadequate supervision is much less compelling. To begin with, 1 percent supervision, an estimate based on filings, is misleading. As noted earlier, the Justices and their clerks screened almost one-fifth of these circuit decisions after hearing in the mid-1960s and heard almost 10 percent of those appealed.[n] Even though the latter ratio declined to between 5 and 6 percent in the mid-1970s, as so-called junk cases increased, Justice Brennan estimated that 30 percent of docketed cases still reached the Supreme Court conference room.[41]

Rising appellate demand may consume time in screening better spent in other decision-making activities, but it makes a big difference whether appeal turns on uncertain rules of law or mere sufficiency of the evidence. A large and growing share of federal appeals are "programmed decisions," prisoner petitions, for example, involving routinized factual review. These the Supreme Court can largely ignore and circuit courts can mass-produce. According to these circuit judges, only about one in ten of their cases presented inescapable lawmaking opportunities—an estimate that has changed little over the years. Though the doctrine of *stare decisis* affords appellate courts more "leeways of choice" than formal theory permits, the Supreme Court regularly policed the major sectors of appellate business the three tribunals had in common while pursuing selective policy goals.[42] Assuming that the judges' estimates of overt judicial legislation are reasonably accurate, and that most of the fertile tenth are appealed, the quantitative evidence is hardly overwhelming that Supreme Court review is insufficient to control circuit lawmaking.

The strongest case for inadequate review involves uniformity. The

---

[n] Adjusting for uncited cases in FY 1965-1967, the ratios are 30% appealed and 7.3% certiorari petitions granted. See Appendix 1.

appeals explosion and the high court's policy priority have fanned concern that the Supreme Court's workload exceeds its ability to give binding resolution to legal issues of national scope. Experienced practitioners, such as former Solicitor General Erwin N. Griswold, argue forcefully that the Justices must pass over "certworthy" appeals they would have decided in the past. Uncertainty stemming from unsettled circuit conflicts is perhaps a greater evil.[43] Whether these problems justify some of the cures proposed, however, is highly debatable. Uniformity, after all, is not an absolute but an organizational objective to be weighed against competing goals. Perfect harmony, indeed, is an undesirable obstacle to legal growth.[44] Just as the doctrine of *stare decisis* affords appellate judges sufficient leeway to bridge the values of the past and present, so the quest for uniformity contains room for regional experimentation and adaptation of national law to continental diversity.

Apart from patents and taxation, the proof of Balkanization is thin. That the Warren Court devoted only one-fifth of its certiorari grants to this problem makes it highly doubtful that these circuits were then out of control. The problem may have been worse for all circuits a decade later; but given the actual potential for intercircuit conflicts, close students of the subject were impressed how few of them lacked resolution in reasonable time.[45] Paul D. Carrington, among the first to warn of threats to national law, concluded that "direct and unresolved conflict is a rare phenomenon."[46]

As for uncertainty, the government itself shares the blame. Federal attorneys regularly relitigate adverse decisions in other circuits in hopes of converting regional defeat into national victory. The Solicitor General's policy is that adverse circuit rulings are not authoritative until three circuits concur.[47] A new National Court of Appeals undoubtedly would increase the delay and cost of federal appeals, at some risk of diminishing the stature of Courts of Appeals, without necessarily reducing the workload of either circuit judges or the Justices. The institution may become unavoidable if the number of circuits proliferates. But surely the government's litigation policy, among other less drastic alternatives, should be reconsidered before launching a new appellate structure on such slender evidence of need.[48]

Especially is this so when informal norms governing lower courts are taken into account. Formal sanctions presuppose that adherence to higher court rulings is customary professional conduct. The stronger the internalized constraints on judicial discretion the fewer cases the Justices must review to secure compliance with their commands. Though the effects of review on the calculations and conduct of subordinates are hard to measure, appellate judges no more need to review every decision below than a teacher must admonish every child to maintain order on a playground.⁴⁹ Just as the threat of trial keeps the whole process of induced consent moving in trial courts and agencies, so the Supreme Court has only to maintain a credible threat of review and reversal to guide the behavior of "judges & co." in inferior courts.⁰ ⁵⁰ Anticipating the reactions of superiors may be less prevalent in intermediate than in district courts, which are reviewed more regularly. It is also less necessary. The object of *stare decisis* and Supreme Court review, to borrow from Herbert Simon's theories of organizational leadership, is not to control specific outcomes but the "premises of decision" of subordinates who exercise discretion in particular cases.⁵² For the premises of decision, at least, Griffin B. Bell's general conclusion appears sound that the Supreme Court provides sufficiently close scrutiny to hold circuit courts in bounds.⁵³

Thus, the adequacy of national appellate resources turns on the presumed functions of federal appeals and intercourt relations in different fields. Though appellate functions obviously overlap, Supreme Court review of circuit courts is "patently inadequate" for error correction, probably adequate for broad policy making, and inadequate for uniformity in a few technical subjects. The bonds are looser than in yesteryear, but the symptoms of Balkanization so far suggest only a "very low grade infection" rather than a crisis requiring drastic institutional surgery.⁵⁴

Similar conclusions hold for courts in between, even though their caseloads have grown three times as fast since 1960 as that of the Supreme Court. As seen in Chapter Two, circuit judges in the late 1960s reviewed about 20 percent of contested judgments and convictions after trial in federal district courts and reversed about 4 percent of the original number. Despite the relative infrequency of reversal, it is hard to conclude as a general proposition that review was insufficient for the multiple functions of circuit courts, except perhaps for a few rural pockets of inadequate demand. For error correction, a major objective of circuit review, supervision if anything was excessive in criminal cases, where appeal is becoming automatic. The same is true in diversity jurisdiction and in litigious environments such as Washington and New York. Assuming rational mobilization of legal interests, the rate of appeal was not on its face

⁰ Judge Learned Hand once made the point pungently: "A burnt child dreads the fire and Felix [Frankfurter] singed my fanny."⁵¹

insufficient for circuit courts to control the premises of decision or to maintain credible threats of reversal in district courts and agencies.

The main problem of the circuits is actually the reverse of the Supreme Court's, not overextension, but overload and its effects on Courts of Appeals as institutions. Circuit control of maverick or rebellious trial judges is no longer a major challenge as in the 1960s. Panel conflicts, though more serious, are easily exaggerated. While the 9th circuit may be too cavalier about inconsistent panel rulings, self-studies by the 5th circuit show that the primary reason for holding en bancs was not to settle inconsistent rulings but to assure majority rule in path-breaking decisions.[55] Circuit judges also appear to give higher priority to lawmaking than to conflict resolution. Intracircuit conflict, as Shirley M. Hufstedler observed, involves head-on collisions less than sideswipes, for which en banc procedures are inadequate.[56] In the face of a 250 percent increase in federal appeals between 1968 and 1978 without any increase in judicial resources to do the work, the central dilemma of circuit judges is whether they can adjudicate federal appeals without sacrificing the quality of decision, on which their prestige depends, by resort to assembly-line techniques that are the bane of American trial courts. Can federal adjudication be transformed from an elite to a mass service without cheapening the coin of federal appeal?

Filings exaggerate the burdens, to be sure. Pressures vary by locality and field. Intermediate courts are not bereft of docket controls. Still, two basic conditions should be understood in fashioning remedies for the undoubted problems of Courts of Appeals. One is that the Supreme Court did not and cannot rely primarily on formal sanctions to maintain coherent law within these circuits. Neither can courts in between. The threat of reversal was so slim—roughly 1 percent of circuit decisions and 4 percent of district court decisions—that informal rather than formal checks must have been largely responsible for the consensus in the system. In the final analysis the adequacy of appellate resources boils down to whether review is sufficiently regular and rigorous to nourish informal constraints on judicial discretion. For this purpose our rough estimates of review in the late 1970s—5 percent at the top and 17 percent at the middle—may well suffice.

Finally, from every angle we hit a bedrock condition that the central characteristics of American government—decentralization and informality in decision making—apply fully to the most hierarchical and formalized institutions in the polity. The uniformity of federal law and the accountability of federal judges are matters of degree, depending on a variety of business and behavior over which courts have only partial command. Harmony, like certainty, is a chimera.[57] Uniformities coexist with uniqueness. That is why so much controversy has flared in modern times over the judicial function. To acknowledge diversities, to offset their centrifugal potential by informal controls, is to open a formal system of law to personal responsibility and to politics. The coherence of the legal system depends on who the judges are and how they perceive their roles. Effective enforcement of federal law and control of judicial discretion hinge on conceptions of judicial duty that are undergoing transformation in both federal courts and society at large.

Yet, that is the theme to follow. Appellate review, however instrumental in enabling the Supreme Court to serve as the gyroscope of the legal order and Courts of Appeals as the monitors of federal adjudication, is not enough to provide system to the judicial department. Appellate review is a necessary catalyst to keep a vast network of expectations and informal decisions working. At a time when proposals abound to overhaul appellate structures, it is well to remember that norms of judicial office and shared social values, learned in advance by professional training and enforced on the job, are primary bonds of judicial union. Proliferation of appellate courts will not alter the basic tendency of trial judges to have the final word.[58] Nor will proliferation alter the fact that the unity and accountability of federal judges depend vitally on a conjunction of professional and political values over which reasonable persons may contend.

Part II
## The Roles of Circuit Judges

"Work, I submit, is in all human societies
an object of moral rule . . ."
Everett Cherrington Hughes, *Men and Their Work*
(1958), 101.

# Four · **The Making of Circuit Judges**

In the world of legal realists judicial decisions are determined less by formal logic or precedent than by individual discretion in settling disputes. A less-noted corollary is that legal systems persist because the chaos of choice is contained within a community of judicial values in a common political and legal culture.[1] To comprehend why courts cohere, therefore, is to plumb informal processes that make judges and their decisions more alike than different.

Little empirical proof has established the links between cultural values and judicial consensus, but it is logical that the weaker the external controls on judges' decisions the more their integration depends on informal constraints and internalized norms. The relative insulation of Courts of Appeals from external checks or Supreme Court supervision increases the significance of personalities and professionalism on the bench. How are circuit judges chosen and how do they learn what is expected of them in office? What standards shape their work and guide their personal choices?

In this chapter we shall explore how members of three federal circuits attained their positions and brought the professional and political values they developed in the process onto the Courts of Appeals. The central theme is that, however idiosyncratic and fortuitous their occupational histories, three interrelated processes in the making of circuit judges—recruitment, socialization, and professionalization—tended to filter into these tribunals judges of similar mold. Their recruitment, a process beginning much earlier than actual appointment, was closely related to their vocational development and training as "political lawyers." Professionalism penetrated the circuits, as a result, but so did shared political outlooks. Because the judges' political and professional experiences on their way to the bench overlapped, their perceptions of appropriate public policy and judicial duty were not necessarily incompatible. Instead, their orientations tended to merge consistently with the duality of their governmental functions. Courts in between generally attracted judges in between in professional and political values. The making of circuit judges, consequently, may provide major sources of cohesion for Courts of Appeals—a proposition to be tested empirically in Chapters Five and Six.

Without pretending to offer a systematic theory of leadership selection, let alone of judicial learning, we shall examine a collective profile of thirty-five judges on the three Courts of Appeals, using data drawn from published biographical sources and their own recollections, to explore these themes. Interested in how political and professional orientations are formulated and reinforced, we especially want to know what the judges themselves consider to be critical turns in their own paths to a judicial career and what they bring to the office by way of value-shaping experience. The reader should be warned, however, against projecting the results onto other courts or assuming that the patterns described here are necessarily standard sequences.

That judges learn their roles en route to office is a hallmark of the American judiciary. The Constitution and laws of the United States impose few qualifications for the office of federal circuit judge. Except for procedures of appointment and provisions to secure judicial independence, federal law leaves the staffing of Courts of Appeals largely to politics and custom. There are no age, citizenship, or residency requirements. Officially, circuit judges do not even have to be lawyers.

The lack of formal job specifications differs markedly from European countries, such as France, where prospective judges are civil servants in ministries of justice. The openness of American judicial selection, enabling lawyers to alternate between private practice and public service in a profusion of levels and branches of government, has long nurtured the dominance of the legal profession in American political leadership.[2] The absence of fixed vocational criteria and ladders of advancement does not mean, however, that choosing circuit judges is without pattern, nor that professional controls are absent from federal courts. Rather, the regularities in recruitment and training that do exist are all bound up with the occupational experience of incumbents and the politics of judicial selection. Choosing judicial leaders, for all the byways and blind alleys, involves a series of hurdles—personal, professional, and political—which progressively screen out aspirants like rounds of a spelling bee.

The reciprocal nature of judicial recruitment links the value structure of court personnel to their working environments. Regardless of rhetoric about being "called" to the bench, federal judgeships usually go to those who seek the office and subject themselves to its discipline. Well-traveled paths to Courts of Appeals exist. The normal course is to make one's mark politically and professionally beyond local levels. These experiences, we shall argue, tend to homogenize the social composition of circuit courts; they also tend to weed out ideological extremes. Because circuit judges are expected to learn their jobs in advance of appointment, their prior occupational choices condition their eligibility for and normative conceptions of federal appellate work. Socialization is both anticipatory and reciprocal in matching recruits and jobs. The very training and experience that made them eligible for national office predisposed them to accept its obligations *before* appointment.

More tentatively, the related processes of recruitment and vocational development fostered professionalization—the seeds of a profession within a profession—in federal courts. Besides the capstone of life tenure with good salaries on a prestigious tribunal, these circuit judges shared most of the elements that students of the subject consider requisite for the professionalization of an occupation: a basic body of theory or specialized techniques, authority recognized by clientele groups and sanctioned by the community, a code of ethics regulating relations of professionals with clients and colleagues, self-consciousness and a "professional culture" sustained by at least the rudiments of formal associations to guard over standards of training, performance, and mutual protection.[3] Unique though the personalities and life histories of individual members may be, on the whole there were sufficient uniformities in their induction, training, and occupations to speak of Courts of Appeals in terms of an appellate career. Therein lie clues to the coexistence of judicial cohesion and independence.

## Elements of Recruitment

Who are the judges and how are they chosen? These are perennial questions, because most court watchers take for granted that the personalities of judges, their social philosophies, and even their conceptions of judicial duty, are basically formed before they don their robes. Nomination battles otherwise are meaningless. The essential problem is whether the method of judicial recruitment, viewed broadly as a continuous and reciprocal process, makes a difference in the way judges view their jobs and behave in office.[4] Do federal judges appointed for life come from different social strata or have different values from those who must stand election? Are different kinds of people attracted to judicial as distinct from other political posts? Or, within the pool of eligibles, is selection fortuitous?

Becoming a judge, as Joel S. Ish observed, "is a process far more complicated than the final selection of a handful of lawyers to sit on the bench."[5] Though reformers traditionally concentrate their efforts on formal selection procedures, close students of judicial recruitment increasingly view the mode of induction as merely the last leg of a long journey, less critical in determining judicial qualifications than the "progressive winnowing" processes that filter the few who judge from the many who are judged.[6] Gradual, cumulative, and reciprocal, these processes are offshoots of larger species by which individuals choose occupations and the society picks political leaders. To understand how judges reach Courts of Appeals is to dissect long-term interaction between professional development and political recruitment.[7]

Conversations with circuit judges reinforce this broad view of judicial selection. When asked to isolate "the most important factors" in their own appointments, their recipes boiled down to four related ingredients—political participation, professional competence, personal ambition, plus an oft-mentioned pinch of luck.

*Political Participation*

If politics enlarges the career opportunities of American lawyers, so it restricts eligibility for high judicial office. Judgeships normally are rewards for political service. As a distinguished federal judge observed: "You can't get on the federal bench in this country without a political claim. I had a political claim, and so did every one of my colleagues."[8] Because staffing federal courts is too important to be left to lawyers, selecting circuit judges has always been more deeply rooted in politics than the visible jockeying among presidents, senators, and the bar over final choices would suggest.[9] Adjusting only for professional standards, Kenneth Prewitt's model of political recruitment is a useful guide to the successive stages by which prospects for judgeships establish their political claims. "Every political community," he wrote, "has a comparatively large number of citizens who meet the minimal legal requirements for holding political office. From these citizens come some persons who are attuned to political matters—the politically attentive public. From this public comes another and yet smaller group which is politically active. And from this group comes an even fewer number of citizens who are actually recruited into channels which can lead to public office. From these are chosen the candidates and from the candidates are chosen the few who will hold public office."[10]

The most elementary sieve is party affiliation. While membership in political parties may signify little about a person's predilections, who is chosen usually depends on which party is in power. In recent years nine out of ten appointees to the federal bench belonged to the same party as the nominating president.[11] The two-to-one preponderance of Democrats in these circuits, as shown in Table 4.1, mirrors that history. Though one southerner was an independent in na-

TABLE 4.1
*Party Affiliation of Circuit Judges*

| Circuit | Democrat N | Republican N | Other N | Total N |
|---|---|---|---|---|
| 2d | 4 | 5 | 1 | 10 |
| 5th | 11 | 5 | 1 | 17 |
| D.C. | 7 | 1 | 0 | 8 |
| Sums | 22 | 11 | 2 | 35 |

tional politics and Paul Hays led the Liberal Party in New York, these circuit judges for the most part were seasoned partisans in the two-party system.

To the politically active as well as to the party faithful go the prizes. These circuit judges participated in politics far more actively than most Americans. Table 4.2, which arrays their political participation across a continuum ranging from mere voting to candidacy, shows that over 70 percent of them were either candidates for office or party activists at some point in their careers. Even though few were successful candidates for very long, over a third of them had ventured into electoral waters for government or party posts before reaching the bench. The most common targets were state legislatures, judgeships, and law enforcement positions, often part-time and early in their careers. Only five judges, two of them governed by the Hatch Act, restricted their participation to voting. Another five were contributors or campaign workers. Though political participation was strongest in the 5th circuit, two-thirds of these judges figured among the relatively small band of politically active Americans whose manning of the machinery of politics made them eligible for public office.[a]

Circuit judges, as a result, bring a rich governmental experience to the appellate process. If like government paymasters, we count clerking for federal judges and serving on government commissions as public employment, all but five of these judges had some experience in public office before appointment to a Court of Appeals—every judge in the D.C. circuit, nine-tenths in the 2d, and two-thirds in the 5th. Only two were bystanders in party or bar-association affairs. The variety of public posts held, as summarized in Table 4.3,

[a] Two judges, both former advocates in major civil liberties decisions by the Supreme Court, considered themselves to have been politically inactive. Otherwise, subjective recollections substantiated external inferences about political activity.

TABLE 4.2
Political Participation of Circuit Judges

| Circuit | Voter Only N | Party Worker, Contributor N | Party Official, Campaign Manager, Adviser N | Candidate* N | Total N |
|---|---|---|---|---|---|
| 2d | 1 | 3 | 2 | 4 | 10 |
| 5th | 1 | 1 | 5 | 10 | 17 |
| D.C. | 3 | 1 | 3 | 1 | 8 |
| Sums | 5 | 5 | 10 | 15 | 35 |

* Includes 3 for party posts only.

ranged widely among local, state, and national offices. Local positions included a city councilman and mayor of Austin, Texas (Thornberry) and numerous public defenders, prosecutors, judges, and legislators. State posts included an attorney general, supreme court justice, and governor of Mississippi (Coleman), as well as multiple memberships on state commissions. National offices included two members of Congress (Thornberry and Smith), and clerks to Justices Brandeis (Friendly), Stone (Leventhal), and Reed (Leventhal). The group also contains former U.S. attorneys (Lumbard, Moore,

TABLE 4.3
Apprenticeship in Government of Circuit Judges
(Number of mentions)

| Type of Experience | Federal | State |
|---|---|---|
| District attorney | 4 | 4 |
| Assistant district attorney | 5 | 5 |
| Public defender | — | 1 |
| Legislator | 2 | 5 |
| Legislative assistant | 2 | 0 |
| Trial judge | 14 | 4 |
| Law clerk | 3 | 0 |
| Governor | — | 1 |
| Government attorney | 8 | 5 |
| Boards and commissions | 5 | 3 |
| U.N. delegate | 1 | — |
| Mayor | — | 1 |
| City council | — | 1 |
| None | 5 | 5 |

Wright, and Carswell) and several prominent bureaucratic lawyers, such as an assistant attorney general (Bazelon), a chief counsel of the Treasury Department (Tuttle), and a Solicitor General, legal adviser to the State Department, and U.N. delegate (Fahy). Almost half—38 percent in the D.C. circuit, 41 percent in the 5th, and 60 percent in the 2d—had previous judicial experience. If fewer of them served on state appellate courts than in prior years, their range of federal exposure was broader.[12] Considered as preparation for Courts of Appeals, theirs was a composite apprenticeship in keeping with future responsibilities.

*Professional Competence*

"For me, becoming a federal judge wasn't very difficult," former Attorney General Griffin B. Bell once remarked. "I managed John F. Kennedy's presidential campaign in Georgia. Two of my oldest and closest friends were the two senators from Georgia. And I was campaign manager and special, unpaid counsel for the governor." Bell then quipped, "It doesn't hurt to be a good lawyer either."[13]

Jokes aside, professional competence—or at least the reputation for it—is a prerequisite for a circuit judgeship. Of all the filters through which potential judges must pass, the one with the most far-reaching implications is the dictate of custom and the bar that circuit judges must be qualified lawyers. This occupational requirement alone reduces eligibles to 0.5 percent of the nation's civilian labor force.[14] Beyond creating a lawyers' monopoly, demands for professional skills transform the organized bar into an active pressure group in judicial recruitment. The American Bar Association's Standing Committee on the Federal Judiciary, in close cooperation with leading local attorneys, rates prospective candidates and brings considerable influence to bear on politicians in the final stages of nomination and confirmation.[15] Eligibility in the process is usually narrowed to leading members of the legal community.

The requisite professional standards profoundly shape the composition of Courts of Appeals. Circuit judges are members of an educated elite. This in turn tends to stratify federal courts in terms of social class and professional standing. Though many of these jurists came of age in the Great Depression, all but one of them attended college and almost two-thirds had college degrees. Only two lacked law degrees. Over 40 percent were educated at the prestigious Harvard, Yale, or Columbia law schools; another 15 percent at such "national" law schools as Cornell, George Washington, Georgetown, Michigan, and Northwestern.[16] In fact, nine of the ten judges interviewed in the 2d circuit attended Harvard, Columbia, or Yale law schools. Three-fourths of those in the D.C. circuit were trained in so-called national law schools, though only a third in the 5th circuit attended such institutions.

The educational achievements of these jurists went beyond advantageous schooling. Academically, despite several having to work their way through school, two-thirds of them ranked in the upper half of their class. One-fifth were either among the top three students of their class or made the law review. These circuit judges were not merely members of a professional elite; educationally, many of them were the elite of the profession.

Their work histories, too, bear the marks of successful careers. Only two of them, Edward A. Tamm and J. Skelly Wright, both primarily professionals in federal service, spent less than five years in private practice. The median experience as practicing attorneys, the prime qualification for judges in the eyes of the bar, was twenty years. Because all but three received top ratings (a.v.) in the Martindale-Hubbell Law Directory, a publication in which lawyers rate their peers professionally, these men were hardly "lawyers on their own," solo practitioners struggling to survive in a scramble for clients and prestige.[17] They were lawyers of high professional standing. Heavy joiners in bar associations, legal fraternities, and the American Law Institute, this group of judges includes one former president of a state bar association (Gewin), one former head of the American Judicature Society (Waterman), and a former dean of Howard University law school (Robinson), as well as professors of law at Northwestern (McGowan) and Columbia (Hays). Among several inducted from leading law firms were chief counsels of the Chicago and Northwestern Railroad (McGowan) and Pan American Airways (Friendly).

By and large they represented national enterprises, such as companies, unions, and public agencies, in metropolitan legal centers. At the same time, most of them came from a broader professional spectrum than "corporation lawyers," the leading figures in professional stature and political satire.[18] Less than one-third of them described their practices as corporate. Two-fifths described theirs as general, including both criminal and civil work, and another fifth described theirs as general-civil. Almost half classified their former firms as small. Three-fourths of them, as already noted, had some governmental experience—half at some point in criminal prosecution, almost half in judgeships. Contrary to occasional innuendo, these circuit courts were not preserves for corporate specialists or retread politicians. The typical recruits were successful lawyers, neither from the pinnacle nor the bottom of a stratified profession, whose careers more often than not straddled law and politics in mutually supportive ways.[b] Prepared by experience for roles as generalists, most of them can be called, for want of a better term, political lawyers with extensive litigious experience.[19]

*Vocational Choice*

Neglected in the study of judicial recruitment are individual career objectives. Though a circuit judgeship is often assumed to be the goal of "any lawyer of an age to be eligible," the office in fact is not always sought or accepted. Compressing the large field of eligibles to a handful of active candidates are the efforts of individuals to find congenial and rewarding work. Social psychologists theorize that "the choice of a vocation is an expression of personality."[20] However facile the notion of "judicial temperament," we know that judgeships exert a greater pull for some members of the profession than for others. William Howard Taft, for instance, long yearned to be Chief Justice of the United States, an ambition that politics and his wife frustrated for many years. John W. Davis, on the other hand, declined a Supreme Court seat saying, "I have taken the vows of chastity and obedience but not of poverty."[21] Francis Biddle accepted a circuit judgeship only as a stepping-stone to the position of Solicitor General. Why, apart from chance, do some lawyers aspire to judicial office while others of equal attainment prefer politics or private life?[c] [22] Do career choices involve efforts to align personal needs and occupations?

To explore the personal motivations of these careers, without searching for personality traits as such, we asked these circuit judges whether, on looking back, they had been "more inclined toward a political or judicial career." The norm that the office seeks the judge is so strong that even this mild sally into ambition drew some curt rebukes: "What's the relevance to your study? You take the court as you find it." "I didn't seek it" was a common response among a minority of eight judges who denied having aspired to any public

[b] Perhaps this explains why the ABA committee ratings were concentrated in the middle—i.e., "well qualified"—category. Of the 16 judges for whom ABA committee ratings are available, only 1 was in the lowest category of "qualified" and only 4 in the highest category of "exceptionally well qualified."

[c] Expressing fondness for academia, Felix Frankfurter once wrote Eugene V. Rostow that he "could never understand why a dean of an important law school should, from the point of view of intrinsic significance, give up a deanship for a circuit judgeship. (Tom Swan's was a different case because he had been an active practitioner at least as long as he had been an academician.) I say a circuit judgeship, and I don't mean to be snooty about it." Frankfurter added: "I never felt that I was translated to the kingdom of Heaven when I passed from my chair at Harvard to a seat on the Supreme Court."[23]

office until a judgeship "fell my way." Others, with the ring of truth, recalled having declined the position when first offered and recounted arm twisting by Justice Department officials in both Democratic and Republican administrations. Describing how Attorney General Robert F. Kennedy had dispatched his deputy, Burke Marshall, to persuade him to accept a district judgeship at a time when private practice and local politics beckoned, one southerner commented:

> The judiciary was something that seemed to come along. My goal was to be a successful lawyer. I didn't want to hold office. I was roped into state senator. I wanted to be a successful lawyer. Practice came first, that third—even when I was in the deepest political work. Life is a game of opportunities. To my great amazement, it was being thrust on me by the Attorney General of the United States. He was asking: "Why don't you want this job?" That's what made me do it. But I had my doubts afterward. Oh, Lord, the first two or three years I was not happy at all.

Still, most of these jurists assumed that "every lawyer wants to be a judge—80 percent anyway."[d] The overwhelming majority, as Table 4.4 shows, confessed gravitating toward judicial careers. Only three, all southerners, acknowledged a preference for politics at the time they entered the Courts of Appeals. Vocational preferences, moreover, were clearly associated with pre-judicial backgrounds. No judge without electoral experience favored political office. Of the twenty-three having judicial aspirations, only three had faced electorates. And offsetting those who denied seeking judgeships were seven for whom appointment satisfied a "long-term ambition." "I always felt this life would suit me," one of them remarked. The work of a federal judge, as Harold R. Medina wrote a schoolmate on the bench, "is just what my whole career has fitted me to do."[24]

This response encapsulates Harold D. Lasswell's hypothesis about the selective effect of personality on political participation.[25] Going beyond the old prescription that courts should be staffed with persons possessing judicial temperament, the theory is that individuals gravitate consciously or unconsciously to jobs that suit their abilities and personalities. Because recruitment is in part reciprocal and self-selective, some occupational experts argue that "people in a vocational group have similar personalities." Lawyers generally have

---

[d] One judge said: "That's a foolish question. Do you suppose that there are many successful lawyers of an age to be eligible who would not welcome appointment to a Court of Appeals? When I say there was a vacancy—that's it!"

TABLE 4.4
Pre-Judicial Experience and Career Preferences of Circuit Judges

| Career Preference | Appointive Experience N | Elective Experience N | Both N | None N | Total N |
|---|---|---|---|---|---|
| Political | 0 | 2 | 1 | 0 | 3 |
| Judicial | 14 | 2 | 4 | 3 | 23 |
| Neither | 5 | 1 | 0 | 2 | 8 |
| Unknown | 1 | 0 | 0 | 0 | 1 |
| Sums | 20 | 5 | 5 | 5 | 35 |

been classified as "enterprisers," persons skilled in the arts of persuasion and leadership, of manipulating events and getting along with others.[26] If this notion could be refined further to differentiate judging from other occupations, it would have profound theoretical and practical significance by providing a psychological dimension to the theory of separation of powers. Do personality differences help to explain why persons of similar professional and political backgrounds seek judicial rather than legislative office—or no public office at all?

These judicial careers lend interest to personality theories of vocational choice. Several judges themselves used occupational stereotypes to explain their ambitions for the bench. Expressing the standard antipathy of lawyers for judicial elections, one southerner said:

> My desire to be a judge was a professional one. I wouldn't go onto the state bench for anything. I would be totally ineffectual. The only time I ever stood for election was for the board of [my] country club. I was defeated. It hurts when your friends don't want you!

A fifth of these judges even invoked personality to differentiate suitability for trial and appellate work. Of a former politician who smarted from public isolation, a colleague observed: "Judge—
——misses public life. Lots of district judges prefer their job for that reason. I wouldn't care to be a trial judge and don't now. It's a good thing, too. I don't have the temperament."[e]

The recollected incentives of these judges, however, involved more than affinity between office and personalities. Judges who discussed their career goals exposed a mixture of motives as well as

[e] For further evidence on this point, see p. 137.

qualifications of time and circumstance, that softens even the evidence of self-selection. For example, six judges developed a preference for the judiciary only after their political comets fizzled in one-party states or fell at the polls. Jocularly, two of them thanked victorious opponents for stifling their state political ambitions. Then, too, attraction to the bench occasionally involved a quest for a change of pace from politics or private practice—withdrawing, as it were, from a life of advocacy. One judge put it this way:

> You'd have to admit, after a man has fooled around as a *pro bono publico* man as long as I have, his idea of enjoying the benefits of government gets broadened. He realizes he has a responsibility. I got tired in a practice like mine—all over this region. . . . I said: "What the hell? When the opportunity comes along, I'll take it." I was tired of practice and fighting. I had a duty other than to represent litigious people. A judge has only one client who pays regularly. I don't want to gush, but. . . .

The desire to change pace suggests that the "anatomy of dissatisfaction," which Jerome Carlin found among solo practitioners at the bottom of the professional heap in Chicago, can also afflict those near the top.[27] Because professional skills can be transferred from private practice to public office, it is easier for lawyers than for other professionals to switch occupations and styles of life. For those interested in judgeships, moreover, economic incentives appear secondary to professional prestige, autonomy, and the sense of performing valuable public service.[28] Sixty percent of those jurists suffered sizable losses of income—some "a real boot in the tail" of over $50,000 annually—to join the federal government. Independent wealth was not really mandatory even before salaries were increased in 1977 to $57,000.[f] Short-term sacrifices were moderated by in-service promotion, cost-of-living increases, and above all by retirement at full pay. Financial considerations nonetheless may affect the timing of a recruit's availability, making judgeships more attractive for older prospects whose children are grown and educated.

Whatever the economic balance sheet, judicial recruitment is in

---

[f] "You hear people moan about the sacrifice they are making," an elderly judge observed. "Most of it is not true. The overhead in my office was $6,000 per month." The same judge even challenged as "another figment" the grumbling about overwork. Declaring that the life of a circuit judge was "much less strenuous" than private practice, he recalled that after a few weeks on the 5th circuit "Chief Judge Hutcheson asked me, 'Isn't this harder?' I replied: 'Judge Hutcheson, it's been too long since you practiced law, met all those dates and deadlines, sat up all night coaching witnesses, and spoke to strange juries over kingdom come.' . . . Being a judge involves severe responsibilities, but it is not the same nervous strain."

large measure reciprocal and self-selective. These circuit judges for the most part sought personal fulfillment in judicial careers and made the necessary material sacrifices to gratify their ambitions.

## Chance

Even if a person possesses the requisite political claims, professional qualifications, and vocational aspirations, "the odds are high against anyone making it" to a Court of Appeals. The passage from the sea of eligibles to the narrow channels of candidacy, these judges generally agreed, requires luck. This usually meant a chance convergence of basic credentials with the politics of final selection—"knowing the right people at the right time."

The wheel of fortune at this stage turns on the mix of ingredients. By themselves neither political claims nor professional merit were considered sufficient for appointment. The many judges who emphasized their political assets insisted that a "good reputation as a lawyer" was essential. The few who attributed their selection to professional standing in turn conceded that a surrogate for partisan activity, such as strong bar endorsement or knowing a powerful politician or public official, had been necessary to acquire a sponsor and to neutralize opposition. Besides reflecting the party and political philosophy of appointing presidents, nominees needed a patron to single them out and push their cause. Being a crony of a high legislative or administrative official, as Earl Warren complained in 1969, was a minimum requirement for a federal judgeship.[29]

One reason recruitment at this stage appears so haphazard is that the politics of selection varies by office and circuit.[30] In the distribution of power, circuit judgeships lie somewhere between Supreme Court appointments, which presidents tend to dominate, and district judgeships, which senators regard as their prerogative. The custom of earmarking circuit judgeships among the states of each circuit gives senators from the state in line extra leverage. When the senator's party is not in power, the administration and the bar have greater influence. President Eisenhower's nominees in the 5th circuit, for example, owed little to Democratic senators. Most of them were recruited by Justice Department officials from leading southern supporters of General Eisenhower in the 1952 Republican convention. Often reared outside the Deep South, and carefully screened to be in sympathy with desegregation, most of them rejected the dominant culture of white supremacy. Democratic choices, by contrast, owed more to bargaining among senators, including James O. Eastland of Mississippi, then chairman of the Senate Judiciary Committee. President Nixon overtly selected southern conservatives. Ironically, Eisenhower's appointees were sometimes more reconstructed in race relations than those named by presidents Kennedy, Johnson, and Nixon—or Eisenhower himself. And the country confronted in the 1960s an uncustomary sight: elderly judges of a southern court serving as pacesetters for the Union in civil rights.

Senator Jacob K. Javits' stalling of Nixon nominees in New York shows how senatorial courtesy may temper presidential control of judicial selection.[31] Bar politics in New York City also appears to play a stronger part in recruiting circuit judges than in the other circuits or even other states of the same region. No circuit judge sitting in this period was recruited from upstate New York, though the fact that the overwhelming majority of the circuit's litigation comes from the Southern and Eastern districts may make this more palatable.

As senatorial power is weakest in the D.C. circuit, the politics of selection turns mainly on presidential patronage and policy. This mixture has several consequences. The court may be used to reward faithful supporters or to promote district judges whose advancement is blocked by a home-state senator. The promotion of J. Skelly Wright, vigorous supporter of desegregation in New Orleans, is a case in point. For similar reasons, the D.C. circuit is frequently staffed by former bureaucrats and activists in national party organizations. Generally having fewer local ties prior to appointment than in the other two circuits, judges in Washington were the only ones to cite professional merit exclusively as the reason for their selection. If their backgrounds jibe with their national jurisdiction, however, their composition, like that of the Supreme Court, is especially sensitive to partisan political change. Small wonder that outsiders complain that decision making in this tribunal is a lottery. Recruiting members with sharp political differences tends to inhibit development of a cohesive role structure on any collegial court.

Politicking by the candidates is usually a final element in the broth. Because rival candidacies with supporting coalitions usually spring up for each vacancy, a prospect can seldom wait passively for the call. Though a few eminent attorneys had only "to let it be known that I was available," most nominees participated actively, though usually discreetly, in campaigns to mobilize sponsors and support. These may include incumbents on the federal bench.[g] One southern judge put the matter bluntly:

---

[g] For example, Chief Judge John R. Brown wrote a letter to the Senate Judiciary Committee in support of Homer Thornberry's nomination to the Supreme Court, and several of G. Harrold Carswell's colleagues on the 5th circuit did likewise.[32] For judicial perceptions of the propriety of participating in selection of federal judges, see Table 5.12.

I didn't do any pointing for a judicial appointment. There was a death. The appointment was to come to [my state]. . . . I don't mean that I waited for people to pound on my door. People don't get judgeships without seeking them. Anybody who thinks judicial office seeks the man is mistaken. There's not a man on the court who didn't do what he thought needed to be done.

For all the play of luck, staffing Courts of Appeals is rarely left to chance. Circuit judges, like Supreme Court Justices, are usually former political activists, nominated by politicians and confirmed by politicians, in furtherance of political objectives.[33] Yet, because professional interests tend to be more effectively mobilized in recruiting circuit judges than on other levels of the national judiciary, professionalism may be more significant at the middle tier of federal courts than above or below. Even the final stages of recruitment were far from being a simple reflex of presidential and senatorial patronage, but involved an intricate web of vocational and political contacts developed long before the denouement. The virtue of this system of selection is that progressive winnowing ensures that the job will be performed by persons experienced in both law and public affairs. Those endowed with life tenure also will have passed muster among their principal constituencies and veto groups, including their peers. The defect of the system is that circuit judgeships do not necessarily go to the most qualified persons.

In 1977 President Carter established by executive order U.S. Circuit Judge Nominating Commissions to improve the quality of judges as well as the representation of women and ethnic minorities on Courts of Appeals.[34] Despite potential tension between the two goals, initial evaluators praised the new procedure of recommending candidates to the president for its openness, emphasis on professional qualifications, and reduction of senatorial patronage.[35] Candidates have been recommended who lacked the political muscle to be considered under the traditional method, and affirmative action is taking root in filling vacancies and new postitions. But doubters regard the commissions as more window dressing than a fundamental reform eliminating politics from judicial selection. Merit selection no less than patronage systems presupposes that appointing the "best qualified" is good politics. The same goes for affirmative action.[36] As long as presidents nominate, and positions are earmarked by state, only modest differences in the type of judges chosen may be expected. Circuit judges are still likely to be moderate to liberal, political lawyers of the president's party, formed in that sector of the profession where legal and political careers intersect.[37]

## Political and Professional Socialization

The interweaving of political and professional criteria in the selection of circuit judges, besides conditioning eligibility for service, affects their preparation for and outlooks on the bench. Caution should be observed, of course, in attributing to individuals values commonly associated with general experiences or groups. Some scholars are skeptical about whether experiences prior to appointment are sufficiently uniform to speak of common socialization or learning.[38] For the judges in this study, however, similarities in development enhanced their cohesion in several vital respects. The process of recruitment, viewed broadly, tended to homogenize the social composition, training, and value structure of members of circuit courts.

### Social Screening

Virtually every study of the social origins of American political leaders indicates that those who govern are not a cross-section of the governed. High offices tend to be occupied by members of middle-to-upper-class elites who have acquired the education and professional skills, as well as the time and interest, to engage actively in public affairs.[39] Though social mobility is too high for the country to be governed by a ruling class, Donald R. Matthews's conclusion is that American voters prefer candidates who are not like themselves but what they would like to be.[40]

What characterizes the national legislature holds also for these Courts of Appeals. The process of selecting judges effectively biased the social composition of these tribunals on nearly every available barometer. Women had no representation on the three courts until 1979. Neither did the young. The median age of entry into the office for these judges was fifty-five, the upper end for occupational elites in this country, and a shade higher than that (53) of contemporary Supreme Court justices or of circuit judges a generation ago.[41] Only one circuit judge, David L. Bazelon, was appointed before he was forty.

Anomalies also appear in their religious affiliations and ethnic mix. The distribution of religious affiliations in Table 4.5 shows that minority religions were overrepresented in the D.C. circuit and underrepresented in the others. The presence of Catholics and Jews in the 5th circuit was both recent and token. Despite heavy black and Spanish-speaking populations, no Negro or Chicano sat there until 1979. Between 1965 and 1978, only one black judge, Spottswood W. Robinson III of the D.C. circuit, served on any of these tribunals,

TABLE 4.5
Religious Affiliations of Circuit Judges

| Circuit | Protestant N | Catholic N | Jewish N | None/Unknown N | Total N |
|---|---|---|---|---|---|
| 2d   | 6  | 1 | 3 | 0 | 10 |
| 5th  | 15 | 1 | 1 | 0 | 17 |
| D.C. | 2  | 3 | 1 | 2 | 8  |
| Sums | 23 | 5 | 5 | 2 | 35 |

though Thurgood Marshall was a member of the 2d circuit when elevated to the supreme bench.

One may concede that representativeness is less relevant to courts than to legislatures, if only to avoid Senator Roman L. Hruska's trap that mediocrity, too, merits a place on the highest court.[42] The social makeup of the judiciary, nevertheless, has symbolic significance bearing on the efficacy of federal courts in the public mind as well as equal opportunity and mobilization of talent for the bench. Within limits, circuit judges themselves shared the view that social diversity strengthens collegial decision making.[h]

All the same, circuit judges tend to be drawn from the middle to upper reaches of social class. Examination of their parents' occupations, a common measure of class distinction in America and a major influence on career choices, shows that two-thirds of their fathers were professionals or businessmen (see Table 4.6). The judges' own rankings of their families in community class structure, shown in Table 4.7, were similar. Two-thirds regarded their families as middle to upper class. Despite a slight upward weighting in the 2d circuit, no judge came from "high society," and only two judges, both in Washington, considered their families as lower class.

These careers, on the other hand, offer little support for the notion that appellate judges are co-opted from a self-perpetuating "power elite." Because prospective lawyers, in common with other professionals, tend disproportionately to be members of higher social

[h] For example, one 5th circuit judge commented: "The strength of this court can be largely discerned from its diversity—men of every kind of background. We have a Catholic, a Jew for the first time, all kinds of Protestants; a former congressman, a former governor, several former state legislators, a former national committeeman—Harvard graduates and graduates of schools of lesser repute; intellectuals, practical men, and in every instance hardworking men. It's a unique group in that everybody likes everybody else. Oh, there's a little backbiting sometimes. But no hatred. There's a lot of loyalty between us. These men are in a blend to the benefit of 35 million people."

TABLE 4.6
Social Class of Circuit Judges:
Father's Occupation

| Occupation | N |
|---|---|
| Judge | 2 |
| Lawyer | 4 |
| Doctor | 3 |
| Merchant | 10 |
| Businessman | 6 |
| Teacher | 2 |
| Farmer | 2 |
| Minor local official | 3 |
| Unknown | 3 |
| Sum | 35 |

TABLE 4.7
Social Class of Circuit Judges:
Self-Identified

| Class | 2d N | 5th N | D.C. N | Total N |
|---|---|---|---|---|
| Upper | 3 | 4 | 1 | 8 |
| Upper middle | 1 | 0 | 0 | 1 |
| Middle | 5 | 6 | 3 | 14 |
| Lower middle | 0 | 3 | 0 | 3 |
| Lower | 0 | 0 | 2 | 2 |
| Other | 0 | 1 | 2 | 3 |
| Unknown | 1 | 3 | 0 | 4 |
| Sums | 10 | 17 | 8 | 35 |

classes, the complexion of these circuits may merely reflect parental influence on early career choices and the profession at large. Like senators, moreover, almost half of the judges' parents were merchants and businessmen, too busy on the whole to engage in politics.[43] Only Roger Robb of the D.C. circuit followed his father's footsteps onto a federal circuit court, though J. Joseph Smith's father was a jurist in Connecticut and Bryan Simpson had uncles on the 5th circuit and in the U.S. Senate.

Otherwise, the social histories of these judges resemble serial sagas of middle America. Besides professionals and merchants, their parentage includes paternalistic mill-owners, and self-made men, along with plumbers, ne'er-do-wells, and "genteel poor." Amid success stories were hints of broken hopes, divorce, and hardships. An uncommon number of these judges (one-fifth) had fathers who died in their youth, aggravating the economic struggles of the depression years. There were regional variations, too, ranging from the "jaded aristocracy" in the South, where brothers scrimped on legal educations so that sisters might continue music lessons, to rugged individualists from the Midwest and New England who, for all their social advantages, denied that they thought in class terms—"and still don't." Far from a ruling class, these men were part and parcel of a broad middle stratum of families, neither very rich nor poor, who managed to give their sons a head start in the scramble to success.

Were this all, curiosity about these jurists could be satisfied by concluding that the typical circuit judge, like the typical U.S. senator, is "a late-middle-aged or elderly, white, Protestant, native-born man" of upper-middle-class origins, a college-educated lawyer, and a "joiner," who at some point came close to centers of power.[44] It might be added that in personality they gave every appearance of being "enterprisers," persons skilled in the arts of leadership and persuasion and of getting on with others. None seemed excessively fat or skinny, jovial or dour, and none wore beards.

Yet, beneath the generality that circuit judges tend to be members of a successful "establishment," like appellate judges in most countries, lie some significant modalities that distinguish these jurists from federal legislators and other elites.[45] Beyond superior educational attainments are more cosmopolitan origins, urban upbringing, and occupational mobility. These characteristics are of interest in view of the attitudes commonly associated with rural versus urban rearing and the need to insulate federal judges from local pressures. The distribution of judges by place of birth in Table 4.8 indicates that, in contrast to national legislators, Main Street did not "win out."[46] While judges born in rural areas and small towns dominated the 5th circuit by two to one, nearly all the members of the D.C. and 2d circuits were born in cities that were over 25,000 in 1920. Most were reared in urban communities as well.

Their urban roots were strengthened by occupational mobility. These judges overwhelmingly pursued their vocations in large metropolitan centers such as New York, Washington, Houston, or Miami. Only four of them—one in the 2d circuit and three in the 5th—remained in rural or small-town areas to practice law. Country lawyers, even in the South, still appear more likely to reach state judicial posts than federal Courts of Appeals.[47]

Occupational mobility went beyond a drift to the cities. Table 4.9

TABLE 4.8
Birthplace of Circuit Judges

| Circuit | Rural N | Small Town N | Urban N | Total N |
|---|---|---|---|---|
| 2d | 1 | 0 | 9 | 10 |
| 5th | 6 | 6 | 5 | 17 |
| D.C. | 1 | 2 | 5 | 8 |
| Sums | 8 | 8 | 19 | 35 |

NOTE: Rural = under 2,500; small town = 2,500-25,000; urban = over 25,000 (1920 census).

shows that over 40 percent of these jurists were born outside their circuits. Their regional movement, albeit inflated by the D.C. circuit and lower than that of political executives in the last two decades, was twice that of congressional leaders (19%) or the general population (14%). Even in the 2d and 5th circuits movement *across regions* (30% and 24%) roughly paralleled the mobility of U.S. district judges *across districts within states*.[48] While no judge was recruited from outside the circuit except in the District of Columbia, the geographic origins and working environments of these circuit judges were typically more urban, cosmopolitan, and geographically mobile than those of their counterparts in Congress or lower federal courts. Such choices early in life can make a difference not only in who reaches the bench but also in judicial perspectives. In examining indicators of support for civil rights among 5th circuit judges—birthplace, age, party affiliation, and the like—Mary H. Curzan found only one positive correlation: geographic mobility in work experience.[49]

*Stages and Agents of Socialization*

However circuit judges may differ from legislators in terms of education, upbringing, and occupational mobility, these differences alone do not distinguish them from other lawyers who shunned public service or other political lawyers who failed to become judges. Social screening leaves unexplored two critical transitions in the selection process: (1) how politically attentive citizens become political activists, eligible for appointment, and (2) how political activists become judges. Because various attempts at relating social backgrounds with voting behavior have met with little success for either legislators or jurists, perhaps Lon L. Fuller is right that researchers have looked at the wrong spectrum.[50] Instead of trying to explain

TABLE 4.9
Geographic Mobility of Circuit Judges:
Place of Birth

| Circuit | In Circuit N | Out of Circuit N | Total N |
|---|---|---|---|
| 2d | 7 | 3 | 10 |
| 5th | 13 | 4 | 17 |
| D.C. | 0 | 8 | 8 |
| Sums | 20 | 15 | 35 |

judicial conflict by reference to static background characteristics, which most political elites share anyway, maybe we should study social backgrounds in the dynamics of building consensus, namely, how the political and vocational development of judges narrowed their selection as jurists and homogenized their attitudes on the bench.

The term "socialization" refers to the processes of education by which persons acquire the skills, interests, and values that equip them for various social roles and guide their performance of them.[51] As these are obviously individual experiences, they can be studied fruitfully from the standpoint of learning theory or of personality development.[52] The concept of social role offers another fruitful approach, especially for learning by adults. Socialization in large part concerns how group standards are imparted to individuals; it can be defined as the learning of one's social roles.[53] Training youth for citizenship has been a central concern of politics since Plato. Preparing individuals for the highly specialized tasks of modern life, including the professions or politics, has long since passed from family hearth to formal academies and the experiences of the adult world. Learning the skills and codes of conduct in occupations is among the most important aspects of adult learning.[54]

This is particularly true of judges. The lack of formal training for judgeships, in a society that sharply distinguishes judicial from other government roles, means that judges must learn what is expected of them as jurists by advance preparation (anticipatory socialization), by adjusting to demands of the new group (freshman socialization), or by doing (occupational socialization).[55] Though most judges presumably learn their trade by an amalgam of all three processes, the code of the legal profession is strongly anticipatory. In theory, the best training for appellate courts is practical experience in advocacy and on a trial bench.[i] Judicial roles, consequently, are to be assimilated primarily through the same experiences that qualify judges, politically and professionally, for appointment. It would be strange if their resulting political and professional orientations were not connected on the way to the bench.

The process of socialization, for everyone but mental fossils, is continuous and cumulative. Though the basic political orientations and party allegiances of most Americans tend to be set by adolescence, political awakening may occur at different stages of life. The catalytic agents also may range from family, friends, or schoolmates to specific experiences including office itself. Yet, somewhere during a person's life one either acquires or rejects political interests and chooses a part to play. Of special concern are experiences that point toward a judicial career.

Because knowledge is so skimpy about the socialization of appellate jurists, these judges were asked a series of questions, focusing more on process than on content, concerning the stages and primary agents of their interest in politics and judging.[57] Their answers, subject to the usual reservations about adult recall, reflect accumulating experiences and drift rather than conscious steering toward the bench. Their recollections, even so, tended to cluster into basic patterns. The political awakening of most circuit judges, like most professional politicians, occurred *before* law school as a result of association with family and friends. Political participation and ambitions for judgeships, in contrast, tended to develop *after* law school as a result of cross-cutting experiences as advocates. Circuit judges differed somewhat from professional politicians in their initial occupational choices; by the time they ascended to the bench their professional ambitions and career lines were sharply focused toward judicial careers. Their belief systems, in the process, had much in common. The socialization of circuit judges, in short, *was* in large measure anticipatory.

In political awakening, these circuit judges differed little from other political elites.[58] Over half of them, as shown in Table 4.10, located their initial political interest in their youth, some in early childhood. Politics was in "my family blood," noted one judge whose family tree was studded with politicians. Another, "brought

---

[i] These qualifications figure prominently in ABA ratings of prospective appointees as well as in perennial professional prescriptions for the ills of wayward courts. The development of orientation and training programs for new judges reflects a challenge to the traditional view that experience as a lawyer is sufficient preparation for judges, particularly for trial procedure and court administration. The format and coverage of these programs, however, have yet to penetrate Courts of Appeals significantly.[56]

TABLE 4.10
Initial Interest of Circuit Judges in Politics

| Stage of Initial Political Interest | Judges N | Primary Agents of Political Interest | Mentions N |
|---|---|---|---|
| Childhood | 7 | Family | 15 |
| Youth | 12 | Friends | 7 |
| University | 4 | University | 6 |
| As lawyer | 8 | As lawyer | 6 |
| Other | 0 | Other | 4 |
| No interest | 1 | No interest | 1 |
| Unknown | 3 | Unknown | 4 |
| Sum | 35 | Sum | 43 |

NOTE: The question was: "Can you tell me how you first became interested in politics?"

up in Washington," caught Potomac fever. "You can't escape it. Politics was table talk in my house since I first understood anything."

Though the majority became politically attentive by adolescence, others formed their political identity in later stages of maturity. Unlike Woodrow Wilson, who studied law to prepare for politics, over a fifth of these judges recalled being drawn to politics as lawyers. Just as Louis D. Brandeis launched his social crusades from the law, so several circuit judges vaulted over "the doorbell-ringing side of politics by an aspect of legal work."[59] As one judge observed: "My entire life has been law—in practice, as a teacher, as a judge. I was always interested in legal problems. When those were reflected in legislation, I got active. They always had to do with the law. I didn't get interested enough in those other things." Only one judge denied any interest in politics; despite having a high elected official for a law partner, his activity stopped at voting.

Since most judges placed their political awakening in their youth, it follows that the primary agents were family and friends. Though there was little evidence of deliberate ideological indoctrination, some fathers explicitly instilled in their sons a sense of civic obligation.[60] "My father constantly preached that we should vote and take an interest," an elderly southerner declared. "If we failed to vote, he would have undertaken to punish me and my two brothers at any age!" Grandparents also engaged their charges in political learning, which stirred one hopeful adolescent to read the *Congressional Record* regularly and to memorize the names of every congressman and senator in the United States. As a small boy another judge invented and played games in American history, placing famous characters in simulated situations, asking, for example: how would old Ben Franklin have voted on the League of Nations? "I was fascinated with politics," he said. "At seventeen I made my way to the Democratic National Convention of 1920 by begging, borrowing, and stealing."

Youthful stirrings apart, less than half the judges cited their families as the chief agents of their political awakening. This accords with other studies of government leaders in many countries, which qualify earlier assumptions that families are the dominant stimuli in political learning. Rather, from the acquisition of basic political awareness and party identity to the development of personal ideology, the political education of citizens tends to be cumulative and gradual.[61]

It is also a big step to pass from the mass of politically attentive citizens to the relatively small group of political activists who become eligible for public office. This distinction between interest and action was well understood by the judges, less than 20 percent of whom recalled their parents having been active beyond voting.[62] Though the questioning was not systematic about this critical passage in their own lives, they tended to recollect their interest in terms of action, so that two major impressions formed about their entry into active political life. (1) Getting started in politics usually came later, and the catalytic agents were more diffused, than becoming politically alert. Most of them were initially activated as adults, though a few judges "always" had their eye on public office, and several southerners identified their state universities as breeding grounds of political leaders. The judges also identified a host of influences on their political entry—the magnetism of Woodrow Wilson and the example of public-spirited lawyers like Emory Buckner, who attracted bright young lawyers into public service; the shock of the Great Depression and "the desire to do something about it which affected so many of my generation."[63] (2) More important, most of them entered politics *as lawyers*. The intersection of political and professional life generally involved a coupling of selfish and altruistic motives—for example, gathering professional experience as a law clerk or an assistant prosecutor, the attraction of higher pay in public office, the desire to help elect a president, such as Eisenhower or Truman, even boredom in private practice. Far more than political interest, developing personal ideologies and entering politics stemmed largely from diverse influences in adult stages of their legal careers.

The significance of this convergence of political activity with vocational development emerges when the judges' careers are compared with those of professional politicians. In general, these circuit judges first entered public life at older ages and at higher levels of responsibility than did legislators. They also started in appointive more than in elective jobs.[64] Whereas almost half the senators of Matthews's study had achieved public office before they were thirty, only a third of these judges had done so at the same age. Whereas the initial office of senators was distributed rather evenly between positions in law enforcement (28%) and state legislatures (21%), circuit judges started primarily by appointment as government attorneys (49%), rather than by election to state legislatures (14%). The seeds of role differentiation, first evident in their educations, sprouted at the outset of their public careers.

Furthermore, professional incentives were paramount in their ambitions and training for the bench. Their recollections about their initial interest in judgeships, summarized in Table 4.11, indicate that judicial ambitions, like political activity, developed primarily after law school in conjunction with being active lawyers. Six judges, to be sure, recalled "always" wanting to be a judge. One fixed his sights on the judiciary so firmly that his life insurance stopped at age fifty on the assumption that he would obtain a judgeship by then, a goal he met with five years to spare. The delicacy of confessing such ambitions and the odds against satisfying them are such that over a quarter of these judges denied any serious aspirations for a judgeship until opportunity knocked. The timing of their interest, however, was overwhelmingly associated with advancing legal careers.

TABLE 4.11
*Initial Interest of Circuit Judges in Judicial Office*

| Stage of Life | N |
|---|---|
| Youth | 6 |
| Law school | 1 |
| As lawyer | 17 |
| At vacancy or offer | 8 |
| None/no answer | 3 |
| Sum | 35 |

NOTE: The question was: "Can you tell me how you first became interested in serving as a judge?"

It is surprising that only one judge mentioned law school in the stirring of judicial ambitions. Kornberg and Thomas found that American national legislators often aspired for public office at this stage.[65] These recollections also jar with the favorable evaluations these jurists, particularly the graduates of "prestige" law schools, gave to the influence of formal professional training on their subsequent careers and legal thought. "Terrific," "tremendous," "the greatest thing that ever happened to me," rang a refrain interrupted by only a few sour notes—"a complete bust . . . I am ashamed to admit."

The attributed influence of law schools was not confined to prestigious institutions, nor to the classroom. One judge asserted that some of his former Yale professors "shanghaied me" onto the federal bench. Most of them maintain relations with law schools by lecturing, serving on moot courts and visiting committees, and employing revolving law clerks. Still, judging from these recollections, professional schools appear to have been more influential in forming general approaches to legal method and professional reference groups than in generating political ideologies or ambitions for the bench.[j]

So Dan Lortie and others have found for the training of lawyers.[66] Laymen become lawmen less in laws schools than on the job. Accordingly, we would expect that the lessons learned while these men made their way as advocates, entering politics and developing judicial ambitions in concert, would have particular potency and hold on their learning of judicial roles. Further, their perceptions of how judges ought to behave should reflect the expectations of general practitioners and government attorneys more than those of academics, corporate specialists, or professional politicians. Because their political and professional careers dovetailed en route to judicial office, so should their political and professional orientations interact. That is the design. The making of appellate judges is essentially anticipatory, a cumulative and largely adult enterprise heavily dependent on the interplay of vocational development and political opportunity.

## Paths to Courts of Appeals

Besides sharing similar social backgrounds and passing through similar stages of socialization, most of these judges followed similar and relatively stable channels to Courts of Appeals. Their collective

[j] For example, one Harvard graduate, noting that he had thought little about the question, observed that the school was "in the tradition of developing law out of precedent, that it wasn't the business of judges to be activist—to make law for themselves. That is the business of legislatures."

journeys, diverse though individual motives and career lines may be, are worth retracing because they suggest that a structure existed in an ostensibly haphazard selection process and because they bolstered elements of moderation and professionalism in appellate values.

Already observed are how most of these recruits enjoyed superior educations, succeeded as political attorneys in regional centers, and "inclined" to the bench. To follow the dynamics of their vocational development, their first and last governmental posts are juxtaposed in Table 4.12 with their primary occupation before appointment to circuit courts. Though the gradualness of career decisions should be remembered, several conclusions are noteworthy. First, these careers conformed poorly to conventional teachings about the surest road to Courts of Appeals. Becoming assistant U.S. attorneys and ascending the ladder through U.S. attorneyships and federal district courts—the classic advice to young lawyers—was the path followed least. True, over half of these men had prosecutorial experience; but only J. Skelly Wright held all of these federal posts, and even his chain was not continuous. Equally inapposite are common complaints that politics thwarts in-service promotion. Over 40 percent of these circuit judges were promoted directly from U.S. district courts. Their conceptions of appropriate circuit conduct were shaped by the most concrete of experiences—being on the receiving end of appellate power and serving occasionally on Courts of Appeals by designation.

Second, these recruits followed three basic paths to the circuit courts, paths apparently related to the politics of recruitment in each circuit. (1) *Private practice* buttressed by national party service or an important local sponsor. This pattern, apparent in all three tribunals, was especially prominent in the 5th circuit. (2) *In-service promotion* either within the federal judiciary or as government attorneys. The former was notable in the 2d circuit, the latter in the D.C. circuit. (3) *Lateral entry* at an older age, sometimes from service as a U.S. attorney after co-option from private practice. This also occurred in every circuit, but especially in the 2d, where some judges gave high marks to senators, such as Robert F. Kennedy, for sharing high professional standards of recruitment.

Finally, though the judges tried their wings in various elective and appointive positions, especially in the South, these careers contained considerable evidence of reciprocity. Just as service on city councils and state legislatures are customary springboards to Congress, so appointive positions as government attorneys are breeding grounds for federal circuit judges.[67] The bulk of these recruits, as

TABLE 4.12
Paths to Courts of Appeals

| Previous Occupations | Initial Public Office | | | Last Public Office before Court of Appeals | | | Primary Occupation before Court of Appeals | | Private Practice or Academic |
|---|---|---|---|---|---|---|---|---|---|
| | Federal N | State N | None N | Federal N | State N | None N | Federal N | State N | N |
| District attorney | 2 | 2 | — | 2 | 1 | — | 2 | 0 | 1 |
| Assistant district attorney | 5 | 5 | — | 0 | 1 | — | 0 | 0 | 1 |
| Public defender | — | 1 | — | 0 | 0 | — | 0 | 0 | 0 |
| Legislator | 0 | 2 | — | 0 | 1 | — | 0 | 0 | 1 |
| Legislative assistant | 1 | 0 | — | 0 | 0 | — | 0 | 0 | 0 |
| Trial judge | 2 | 0 | — | 14 | 0 | — | 14 | 0 | 0 |
| Law clerk | 3 | 0 | — | 1 | 0 | — | 0 | 0 | 1 |
| Government attorney | 3 | 1 | — | 4 | 2 | — | 2 | 0 | 5 |
| Boards and commissions | 2 | 1 | — | 2 | 1 | — | 0 | 0 | 2 |
| U.N. delegate | 0 | — | — | 1 | — | — | 0 | 0 | 1 |
| Private practice | — | — | 5 | — | — | 5 | — | — | 5 |
| Sums | 18 | 12 | 5 | 24 | 6 | 5 | 18 | 0 | 17 |

shown in Table 4.13, gravitated toward appointive rather than elective offices throughout their public careers.[k] Electoral insecurity and rebuff at the polls accelerated this trend so that, by the final selection stage, their electoral careers had ended and their primary occupations had narrowed to two basic channels: (1) a major position as a federal lawyer or judge, and (2) private practice or teaching. None

TABLE 4.13
Pre-Judicial Experience of Circuit Judges in Government:
Elective-Appointive

| Circuit | Appointive N | Elective N | Both N | None N | Total N |
|---|---|---|---|---|---|
| 2d | 7 | 1 | 2 | 0 | 10 |
| 5th | 6 | 4 | 2 | 5 | 17 |
| D.C. | 7 | 0 | 1 | 0 | 8 |
| Sums | 20 | 5 | 5 | 5 | 35 |

was inducted from a principal occupation in state government. Their political credentials were little shaped by exposure to state electorates. The cleavage between pathways to two judicial services, state and federal, noted by Rodney L. Mott since 1900, continues unabated.[68] It was as lawyers in regional practice or federal service, not as local politicians, that most of them prepared for federal appellate roles.

*Offices and Values*

This channeling of careers, even if peculiar to three circuits, not only consolidated paths to the bench, it also produced considerable matching between institutional roles and the values of recruits. The multiple filters through which they passed, besides affecting eligibility, served as screens that moderated ideological cleavages and strengthened judicial insulation from local pressure. Flocking toward the middle is a major source of cohesion in circuit courts, both politically and professionally.

In political ideology, the majority of these jurists regarded them-

[k] Although every judge in the D.C. circuit had seen public service, only one, Charles Fahy, ever held elective office, as city attorney of Santa Fe. (John A. Danaher, a senior circuit judge and former U.S. senator from Connecticut, was not interviewed.) In the 2d circuit only J. Joseph Smith was ever elected for office higher than state's attorney, and those in the 5th circuit were evenly split.

selves as having been moderates before ascending the federal bench. In accordance with the pragmatic nature of American politics, no judge recalled his political awakening or activity in ideological terms. Judicial ambitions were seldom fired in programmatic coals. As shown in Table 4.14, when asked to classify their political beliefs *before* becoming a federal judge, half of those who answered positioned themselves among moderates on a liberal-conservative continuum. A third were liberal or shades between. One judge labeled his past political orientations as "liberal-radical." Another considered himself conservative toward economic rights and liberal concerning human rights, a distinction substantiated by his voting record on the bench.

TABLE 4.14
Political Values of Circuit Judges before Becoming a Federal Judge

| Circuit | Liberal N | Moderate-Liberal N | Moderate N | Conservative N | Other/No Response N | Total N |
|---|---|---|---|---|---|---|
| 2d | 2 | 0 | 4 | 1 | 3 | 10 |
| 5th | 4 | 2 | 9 | 1 | 1 | 17 |
| D.C. | 2 | 0 | 3 | 2 | 1 | 8 |
| Sums | 8 | 2 | 16 | 4 | 5 | 35 |

NOTE: The question was: "*Before* you became a federal judge, how did you classify yourself according to political beliefs or values—conservative, moderate, liberal, other?"

Crude though these indicators may be, they show how political recruitment links the ideological universe of judges to their external worlds. In a study by John T. Wold the same question yielded a totally conservative response among members of the Virginia Supreme Court and contrastingly liberal leanings in the New York Court of Appeals. Different political ideologies prevailed on state appellate courts despite varied schemes of selection to insulate judges from them. More than that, the judges' political orientations correlated strongly with their disagreements about the judicial function.[69]

A general landscape of moderate liberalism is precisely what we would expect in the three federal circuits, especially when regional variations are kept in mind in the successive funneling of recruits. A moderate in Washington like Carl McGowan, as one southerner observed, would be considered "a flaming liberal down here." Judges professed differing political views, but a basic effect of professional and political screening was to weed out mavericks and ideological extremes. Reduced thereby was the strain of ideological conflict between judges and their constituencies. Though the D.C. circuit may be an exception, a concert of political values tended to reduce tension over proper judicial roles.

The roads to the bench likewise tended to broaden the vision of recruits and thicken their insulation from parochial pressures. The dynamics of career development, for these judges at least, suggest that their superior detachment from popular winds was not simply a product of regional organization or life tenure, which district judges share, but was anchored in an underlay of attitudes evident in their backgrounds and aspirations before they assumed office.

Although resisters in district courts like William H. Cox went to Harvard and enjoyed top professional ratings, too, it is commonly suggested that circuit judges tend to be more cosmopolitan in outlook than many constituents and local politicians by virtue of their social origins and occupational experience.[70] In contrast to state judges and attorneys general whose affiliations and ambitions were often state bound, these circuit judges, as we have seen, worked in a wide universe of expectations and affiliations. As lawyers they practiced in the nation's legal centers. As political activists they gravitated away from state politics to federal service, which necessarily broadened the interests to which they would be accountable for approbation and promotion.

Future aspirations, moreover, were as important as their backgrounds.[71] After *Brown v. Board of Education* in 1954, it was no secret that prospective federal judges might face severe conflict between local ties and national responsibilities.[72] Most of these judges crossed that divide in the process of obtaining office. They aspired for positions whose claims were unmistakably national.

It is no accident that local and federal officials in the South, all equally bound by supreme federal law, could respond so differently to their colliding roles as public officials and local citizens.[73] Circuit judges were not only further removed from the heat; their accumulated experiences, associations, and aspirations made them less sensitive to it to begin with. Political recruitment, professional development, and organizational structure were all mutually supporting in attracting members willing to accept the obligations of federal office in the teeth of popular opposition. In a striking example of anticipatory socialization and reciprocal recruitment, most of these judges assimilated the roles of their office in the process of achieving it.

## Professionalization

Just as the matching of men and office tended to moderate and nationalize the political horizons of circuit judges, so were professional values imported and reinforced in Courts of Appeals. Perhaps the most obvious point is that recruits to circuit courts are generally of high quality. Selection was not "all politics." Staffing circuit courts tends to be more professionalized and less politicized than on other levels of the national judiciary. These winners, certainly, accented professional incentives and standards of performance. That their tribunals satisfy most of the formal conditions for professionalization of an occupation was already discussed at the beginning of this chapter. That circuit judges were imbued with professional orientations is also demonstrable from their occupational histories and ambitions. Nascent professionalism appeared in their educations, standing as lawyers, appointive apprenticeships, and in-service promotions. Dual tracks to circuit judgeships further suggest that, when inducted, these judges probably had a stronger commitment to law practice than average recruits to legislatures.[74] Despite the desire of a few to escape the treadmills of private practice, only prime federal legal positions were attractive enough to lure them away.

Another mark of professionalization is that the financial rewards of a job play second fiddle to psychic satisfactions. Most of these jurists made economic sacrifices in accepting the office and remained after 1969 in the face of diminishing real income and increasing work. Morale may have suffered, as the resignation of Griffin B. Bell or the lawsuit of federal judges for pay increases attests; but the great majority of them regarded their jobs as terminal positions, filled with professional gratification, a perception that reinforces their independence.[75]

One index of job satisfaction is the extent to which incumbents view their position as a rewarding climax or capstone to a career.[76] Though a few southerners demurred when asked whether they viewed their occupation this way, the judges generally expressed a deep sense of professional fulfillment and pride of association that vindicated traditional views of judgeships as the highest calling in the legal profession.[1] "Yes, there's a great deal to that," judges com-

---

[1] One southerner commented: "I attach no great significance to the office. I regard it as the terminal point of a lawyer's career because it is not feasible to take this position and resign for something else. I was so happily occupied in the practice of law, however, that I would not look at this job as a capstone. I have great respect for judges. I don't think a lawyer can fail to respect the office and function of a judge. But I don't

mented with feeling. "I'm signed up for life. There's nothing I'd rather do." "It was taking the veil, the end for me." "I wouldn't think of doing anything else. I don't regard it as a stepping-stone to anything else. When I feel I am disintegrating, I'll quit." Expressing contempt for "those fellows who make a reputation on the bench, then leave in order to clean up in practice," one who had cleaned up beforehand stated the prevailing norm: "When a man goes on the bench, he takes that job for good." As for Supreme Court prospects, one judge stated the general feeling: "I'm not dreaming that dream."

The belief that a circuit judgeship is a terminal occupation, containing seeds of a profession within a profession, reflected a bias toward the advocate's viewpoint.[m] So did the judges' evaluations of various forms of preparation for Courts of Appeals. The results of this structured question, tabulated in Table 4.15, indicate that these judges shared the general consensus of the organized bar that extensive legal practice, preferably trial experience, strongly outweighs formal education and even prior judicial service as training for a cir-

TABLE 4.15
*Circuit Judges' Evaluations of Preparatory Experiences for Service on Courts of Appeals*

| Type of Experience | Very Important N | Moderately Important N | Not Important N | No Response N | Total N |
|---|---|---|---|---|---|
| Extensive legal practice | 21 | 12 | 0 | 2 | 35 |
| Experience as trial lawyer | 19 | 13 | 2 | 1 | 35 |
| Prior judicial experience | 11 | 17 | 5 | 2 | 35 |
| Training in leading law school | 10 | 16 | 7 | 2 | 35 |
| Experience in civic affairs | 1 | 28 | 5 | 1 | 35 |
| Bar-association leadership | 1 | 10 | 22 | 2 | 35 |
| Political experience | 0 | 15 | 19 | 1 | 35 |

regard them individually as holy, and I don't think I'm a damn bit better in any respect than I was as a lawyer."

[m] One judge expressed concern over conflict between the two ideas in an organization without mandatory retirement. "I believe in young judges," he said. "The old judges who get on the court as a capstone of their careers don't turn out well. They look upon it as retirement. That's what's wrong with the system. In my view it's a profession. It takes three-four years to get into it and more than that to develop judges who are scholars. So when a judge looks at it that way—as a capstone of a legal career—he takes the icing on the cake. It will finally undo us. We just got one on our court aged 67, though he had been a district judge a long time. You can't complain about giving a man a reward. But if all were like that, how long would we last?"

cuit bench.[77] The low impact of law schools in these recollections is less surprising than the fact that not all judges who actually served on lower courts ranked that experience as "very important." This goes against the expected upgrading of personal experience, not to mention the drumbeating by members of the bar that prior judicial service is essential equipment for appellate judges. Political, civic, and bar-association leadership, however vital to their recruitment, were downgraded even more.

All professions and institutions tend to develop occupational ideologies. The disjunction of political experience and professional evaluations by these jurists reflects both a professional monopoly in judicial selection and their successful socialization as lawyers, who traditionally regard law and politics as separate and the politics of judicial selection as a necessary evil. Notwithstanding the penetration of politics in their own development, the evidence is impressive of the cumulative effect of professionalism on their selection and training for the bench. Politics, for most, was ancillary to professional incentives and standards of performance.

The legal profession is far too heterogeneous, and idiosyncracies of personality and recruitment too prevalent, to offer professionalism as either a functional equivalent of formal training of jurists abroad or a surrogate for Supreme Court supervision. Still, the continuities in these careers show that vocational goals were strong propellants toward judicial careers and catalysts in learning judicial roles. It would be extraordinary if professional norms, internalized en route and reinforced at work, did not constrain individualism in the appellate process. The real question, to be faced in Chapter Six, is whether they outweigh political values acquired simultaneously on the way to the bench.

## Conclusions

The work histories of thirty-five circuit judges, though limited in number and design, yield more by way of conclusion than that Courts of Appeals, like other high offices or professions, are staffed by members of social and political elites. In an ostensibly open system of selecting and training judges the related processes of political recruitment, anticipatory socialization, and professional development produced basic patterns in the kinds of judges inducted and in their values. In the matching of men and offices lie elements of cohesion that provide continuity to institutions and shape to norms of appellate conduct.

## Recruitment

It is important to recognize that formal instruments of judicial recruitment, though much debated, are mostly intramural sortings among candidates whose eligibility has been much narrowed by longer and more intricate processes of social screening and leadership selection. Becoming a circuit judge, for all its regional variations, involves a complex winnowing process involving four main ingredients: political participation, professional standing, personal ambition, and luck. Broadly speaking, this combination tends to reward supporters of the presidential party; weed out incompetents, mavericks, and ideological extremists; and ensure substantial professional and political experience among those who wield federal appellate power. Forged thereby are continuous links between judges and their political and professional surroundings. Restricted thereby are the types of persons inducted into Courts of Appeals. The multiple filters through which recruits must pass put a premium on moderate, middle-class, and political lawyers, successful people advantaged in life.

## Socialization

Because training for federal judgeships is largely anticipatory, the requirement that recruits satisfy multiple criteria is of central importance in structuring judicial roles in these circuits. It oversimplifies reality to pose political attitudes and perceptions of judicial duty as polar opposites. Far more likely, considering the shaping experiences of these recruits, is a convergence in practice of political and professional ideologies. The trend toward moderate liberalism, in two circuits at least, relieves the strain of competing role expectations and supports a system of *stare decisis* for the simple reason that circuit judges tend to be alike.

It is also an oversimplification to treat circuit judges as berobed politicians. However close they may have been to other public officials in the ages and agents of their political awakening, the accent of their political activity and professional development differed from professional politicians. If the sorting did not begin in law school, their activation in politics, their movement to regional centers for employment, their apprenticeships in government and escalating ambitions for judgeships, even the training they valued most—all were seen through predominantly professional prisms.

The significance of these patterns for the study of American political leadership is that the socialization of these judges was not merely anticipatory, but also self-selective and often professional in basis.

For all the overlap between political and professional experience, professional perspectives became dominant. Most of them entered Courts of Appeals more as professional lawyers than as professional politicians. Their concepts of judicial office were heavily shaped by adult experiences as attorneys. More urban than rural, more appointed than elected, more generalist than specialist, more regional than local, these men were absorbing the skills and roles of federal appellate judges in the very process of recruitment.

*Professionalization*

As a result, more professionalism permeates these circuits than appears on the surface. Though the pathways to American appellate courts are more politicized than in Japan, France, or Great Britain, certainly these judges shared with lawyers a vocational ideology whose strength must be considered in assessing the cohesion of the federal judiciary. As a rule, the stronger the professionalization of an occupation, the more will conformity to occupational expectations be achieved through internalized values and peer-group pressure and the less through formal, external controls. Whether or not the general public expects lawyers to hold appointed judges accountable, the present system of appellate review presupposes that judicial discretion is checked by professional discipline.[78]

This is not to say that professionalism necessarily supplants personal predilections in Courts of Appeals, nor that the three tribunals met professional criteria in the same degree. The 2d circuit appears to be the most professionalized and the least divided in terms of social backgrounds, party affiliations, and political predispositions. This court presumably should be more united regarding judicial roles than the D.C. circuit, which is not only the most diverse in social composition but also the most sensitive to national constituencies and partisan political change. Because the 5th circuit was the most politicized in conventional terms of senatorial patronage and the least cosmopolitan in social backgrounds, one would expect that court to have the strongest ties to local constituencies. Compared to state or federal district courts, however, the regional Court of Appeals would still be expected to attract persons whose vision had been widened and hide thickened, so to speak, on the way to the bench. The vocational development and aspirations of recruits during this period not only reinforced the cleavage between state and federal judiciaries, but tended to replace local reliance with broader allegiances that anticipated judicial insulation.[79] Professional values acquired while achieving national office helped to shield circuit judges from the pull of constituency and local hostility during the turmoil of desegregation.

Finally, because judicial selection relates individuals to working environments, perfect harmony in role conceptions or policy preferences is hardly to be expected among thirty-five jurists with disparate backgrounds and personalities. Progressive winnowing produces modalities, not identities. The patterns in these work histories, nevertheless, suggest a series of expectations or hypotheses about the value structure and informal cohesion of circuit courts to be considered in following chapters. Ideological conflict, in the first place, should be relatively moderate. The social backgrounds of circuit judges are probably better explanations of consensus than of conflict. As these judges were more alike than different, so should be their decisions.

Except perhaps for the D.C. circuit, moreover, role strain and policy disputes among circuit judges should occur within a basic professional consensus about organizational missions and appropriate judicial conduct. Because professional status and prestige were their primary incentives in becoming judges, their role conceptions would probably slant toward the advocate's rather than the politician's viewpoint. Professional constituencies should serve as their primary reference groups. Similarly, informal exchanges among fellow professionals should be favored modes of management and conflict resolution inside Courts of Appeals.

Presumably such highly educated and experienced judges would hold conceptions of judicial duty and articulate them without difficulty or dissimulation.[80] Presumably, too, these men of affairs should not be insensitive to their surrounding political world nor to the reach of appellate power. In view of their development as political lawyers neither should their professional and political orientations be presumed to be antithetical, though professional values should have greater weight. As candidates who lack appropriate skills or values are weeded out, so circuit courts should be expected to attract persons who are technically equipped, loyal to organizational goals, and capable of identifying themselves as agents of the national government rather than as state ambassadors.[81] Judges so inclined toward federal service and imbued with a belief in its efficacy would be expected further to subject themselves willingly to its discipline—to arrive, as one said, "knowing what was expected of me" and to perform the job with a minimum of freshman dislocation, thereby increasing each court's effectiveness as an institution. For the open system of judicial training presupposes that circuit judges, if not born, are made in processes of becoming. That is why in the traditional scheme "men count more than machinery."[82] "I've got the best job in the United States," concluded one newcomer, as experienced in private practice and southern politics as in judging on a federal trial court. Thus by fitting judges and jobs do circuit courts endure as institutions, and recruits learn their roles en route to Courts of Appeals.

# Five · **The Purposes of Courts of Appeals**

"In this quarter century how much the character of the job has changed! And how much what is thought to be the proper function of the judge!"[1] So Judge Learned Hand, apostle of judicial self-restraint, greeted new judicial activism in 1946. Imagination soars as to how the salty Hand might have viewed changing conceptions of judicial duty since. Although the federal judiciary's basic mission of enforcing the supremacy and uniformity of national law remains unchanged, rising litigiousness, as we saw in Chapter One, is revolutionizing traditional ideas about the roles of law and courts in American society.[2] The expanding scope and volume of federal appeals simultaneously challenge the quality of judicial decisions and generate concern whether judicial self-discipline—the traditional "steadying factors in our appellate courts"—suffices to keep the federal judiciary from becoming all sail and no anchor.[3]

Changes of function and volume compound the problem of harmonizing national courts. Their coherence depends more than ever on conformity by individual judges to informal codes of conduct and professional standards which are themselves in flux. The appropriate roles and functions of intermediate appellate judges have never been fixed or universally accepted. Remedies for the ills of circuit courts presuppose an understanding of how the incumbents comprehend their job and its problems. To what extent are circuit judges united by a common sense of purpose? What activities take priority? To what communities, state and national, do circuit judges relate? What are the bounds on their civic and political participation? Are they "properly mindful of the nine big brothers on the telescreen?"[4]

The concept of judicial role refers to normative expectations shared by judges and related actors about how a given judicial office should be performed. In this chapter we shall consider the content of judicial roles as perceived by members of the three tribunals concerning two fundamental dimensions of their work on Courts of Appeals. First are *purposive role* orientations—that is, their conceptions of the main missions of their courts as government institutions, including how they differentiate their jobs from those of district judges and Supreme Court Justices. Included in this section also are assessments of their psychic distance from their superiors and other circuits. Second are their *community role* orientations—that is, their concepts of obligation toward various constituents and publics in the surrounding environment. These include their orientations to regional and national constituencies ("areal roles") as well as their appraisals of court influence on public policy, of relevant reference groups, and of the permissible range of extracurial participation by judges in community affairs. Both dimensions are analytically distinct from *decisional role* orientations, to be discussed in Chapters Six and Seven, inward-looking expectations toward the decision-making process, including judicial lawmaking and methods of resolving internal disputes.

By itself, of course, what judges expect of themselves encompasses neither judicial roles nor judicial behavior. Role orientations are merely the judges' understandings of anticipated conduct in performing their duties.[5] Because these assessments were gleaned from in-depth interviews, moreover, the inherent limitations of this method of ascertaining judges' role perceptions should be kept in mind.[6] What follows, even for the limited number of judges interviewed, are exploratory rather than definitive approximations of how circuit judges view their jobs.[a]

**Purposive Roles**

*The Missions of Circuit Courts*

What are the primary purposes and priorities of Courts of Appeals? To discern their perceptions of institutional objectives by questions comparable with those used in studies of other courts and organizations, members of the three tribunals were asked a broad, open-ended question which permitted them to define their goals any way they liked.[7] The question was: "How would you describe the job of being a judge on the U.S. Court of Appeals—what are the most important things you should do here?"

Because organizational goals are so inclusive, the judges were expected to offer multiple answers to this query and occasionally to stumble over its breadth. "God, what a question!" exclaimed the first judge to be interviewed. "And on one foot, too?" A colleague underscored the difficulty of establishing priorities, "because everything happens at once." Still, the inquiry was seldom misunderstood; and the net result was a basic consensus, heavily influenced by official

[a] For discussion of these limits see pp. xxii-xxiv. For methods and the interview schedule, see Appendix 1.

theories of judging and their attendant contradictions, within which flourished evident tension over priorities. As summarized in Table 5.1, these responses yield two basic and three ancillary orientations toward the primary objectives of circuit courts, which will be cast here in terms of ideal types.

TABLE 5.1
*The Missions of Circuit Courts*

| Purposive Orientations | Total Purposes Mentioned N | Primary Purpose Inferred N |
|---|---|---|
| Adjudicator | 29 | 20 |
| Ritualist | 12 | 10 |
| Administrator | 11 | 3 |
| Lawmaker | 18 | 1 |
| Educator | 10 | 1 |
| Sums | 80 | 35 |

ADJUDICATOR   The strongest orientation, both in frequency and emphasis, concerned the most visible task of adjudicating appeals. Over four-fifths of these judges articulated this function; over half gave it top billing. An example of this ordering of priorities was the judge who, "thinking out loud," said he would "cut from several angles":

> First, to make adjudications. . . . It is the starting point; no matter how the question is phrased it will come back to this. . . . So number one, I go about adjudicating tasks with all the labor I can summon. Number two . . . to make the right decision, i.e., to correctly apply the law. Number three, I've got to write an opinion explaining carefully why the decision was made. . . . After countless hours spent in reaching a decision, we must be careful before it comes down to make the opinion clear to those without the same degree of contact with the case. This is not the primary responsibility, but it is a good illustration of an adjudicative function.
>
> Thus adjudication is one angle. Everything else is secondary to that. At the same time there is a second angle—an administrative angle. I'm not at all surprised at your interest in litigation flow. It is an ancient problem.

No judge was assigned to the adjudicator category unless he mentioned some larger governmental purpose than merely deciding appeals. The concept of adjudication is so inclusive, however, that several nodes of stress emerged. Most prominent was the finality of circuit decisions. Half of the judges referred to their finality during the interviews; one-third volunteered this theme at the start. As one judge in the 5th circuit began:

> I perceive of the job in a broad sense. There are 35-40 million people in my circuit who look to me as one of fifteen men who decide some of the most important things they have in daily life—in their commercial lives. Thus, I'm in a position unique in authority and power and therefore must use it well. In my mind's eye I see a map of the South. My 40 million people are like pins all over. They say, "You're affecting me directly as virtually a court of last resort."

Beyond mentioning finality, over a third of these judges (N = 13) echoed classic formulas of legal literature, such as "making the right decisions," "correctly applying the law," and "administering justice between the parties," even while recognizing potential conflict among these aims. Older judges especially emphasized that activities such as writing opinions, aiding the Supreme Court, or protecting litigants from unfair procedures and "the so-called expertise of the agencies," all were subordinate to the fundamental task of finding "the justice under law of the case."

> That's the essence of his responsibility, [declared a senior judge]. Of course, there's a larger way of looking at it—the effect in the governmental system—but it is not the most important. People who man the courts do have a part to play in our plan of government, but I would emphasize the duty with respect to cases that come to us to decide. . . . There is no substitute for deciding the immediate case with justice for the parties.

The result orientation of these judges was surprising in that so few of them explicitly linked it to their supervisory responsibilities of assuring fair and legally correct determinations in trial courts and agencies. Rather than focus on their relations with other tribunals, these judges emphasized the law and justice of discrete cases—and sparred about which took precedence. More than one circuit judge assailed the erosion of precedent resulting from emphasizing justice in the case. "*Stare decisis* is becoming a forgotten doctrine in appellate jurisprudence in the 5th circuit as elsewhere," one southerner complained.

Judges decide each case as it comes down now. Starting with the war cry of the ABA—Justice under the Law—they stress justice forgetting the law. Nobody agrees what justice is. It is a purely personal concept, I think. The law is what the legislature has enacted or courts have declared. But judges no longer regard it as their duty to apply or enforce the law. They sense their obligation is to administer justice in particular cases. District judges don't do that as much as appellate courts. Of course, we weasel on those cases with the pretense of making no changes. But it's difficult to get the tongues out of our cheeks when we send opinions to the printer.

At the other extreme, counterparts in Washington underscored their service in problem solving, a creative "process of reexamining society and evolving rules responsive to the needs of orderly change which take account of the aspirations of the people." "Though some judges don't do it," observed one of them, "this requires a reexamination of the past in light of the present."

Tensions between law and justice, between cases and their principles, are no less intrinsic in the common-law tradition than reconciliation of continuity and change.[8] Classic conflicts over priorities in deciding appeals were present in these circuit courts. Even though their expressed aims were steeped in professional lore, it is striking how these jurists injected basic issues of appellate adjudication at their first opportunity. The traditional contrast between styles of judging in code-law and common-law countries, pitting freedom to particularize against the chains of precedent, was thus blurred in these courts. So were their supervisory responsibilities over tribunals below. Traditional functions of error correction and dispute settlement were either taken for granted or subordinated to case results and the larger roles of the Courts of Appeals as instruments of government. What unifies these adjudicators, accordingly, was not political values or even philosophies of judicial activism and restraint, but their common perspective toward adjudication as something more than deciding appeals, a process involving larger social ends. Because those ends were broad and potentially conflicting, the ideal type of adjudicator included judges of every background and philosophic bent.

RITUALIST   The second major orientation—in emphasis though not in frequency—involved concentration on the task of judging itself. The term "ritualist," used here for consistency with other studies, does not imply that judges so disposed were unsophisticated about the larger roles of appellate courts in American life.⁹ Whatever ritualists may be like on state tribunals, included here were some of the most learned and respected leaders in the federal judiciary. The central distinction between them and adjudicators is that ritualists were so preoccupied with judging that deciding cases was considered "the most important thing we do." The external goals of circuit courts were either unarticulated or assumed. One judge of the 2d circuit, for instance, smiling at what he doubtless regarded as a naive question, replied:

> I can give you the trite answer. You decide appeals. That's the most important. My first year on the bench I once talked to Learned Hand about a difficult case. It was close. I was swinging like a pendulum. He said, "God damn it, Joe, decide the case. That's what you are paid for."[b] The first job therefore is to decide—that's not always easy. Beyond that, all kinds of questions open up. After the result, is it a case in which we should say as little as possible? Is it the case in which we should try to elaborate the more important reasons? Let your mind roam, is it useful to say more than necessary because of the problems before lower courts? . . . Sometimes there is no choice. The case is obviously important. With us there is always the question of what does it matter, because we don't have the final say—but on lots of types of cases we really do—admiralty, for example. I am working now on a case involving an owner's lien problem. [Laughter] There is no great Supreme Court interest in that one!

Ritualists also emphasized the burdens of administering their courts and, above all, of producing satisfactory opinions. "Writing opinions," said one judge in New York, "—that's the job as I see it."

The weight given to opinions by seven judges points to a key difference between adjudicators and ritualists. For the former, opinion writing was usually an important but subsidiary task. "Administration of justice is the function," as a leading southern jurist declared. "The thing is to get the right decision out, then satisfy the law professor if you can."[10] For ritualists, opinions were paramount. "Three-fourths of my time is spent writing opinions," countered a contemporary in Foley Square. "That's the only function that counts."[c]

[b] Name changed from original.

[c] Because his court was "generally speaking, a court of last resort," another judge in the 5th circuit put judgments and opinions on an equal plane: "My view of it is, while it is very important to have a sound basis for the judgment, it is equally important to portray it in intelligent, understandable form so the case can serve as precedent. That

Whether reasons or results should take primacy is an old bone of contention in jurisprudence. The tension, cutting deeper than fears of stating wrong reasons for right results, or even a natural tendency among judges to make too much of their cases, reflects different job expectations and demands. The mandatory jurisdiction of circuit courts implies that their main mission should be "to decide appeals fairly and promptly."[11] In practice, justifying decisions appears to attract greater attention. The 3rd circuit's time study showed that preparing and clearing opinions consumed more judge-time than all other elements of the job combined.[12] A residual function of developing precedent appears to be displacing the traditional objective of correcting erroneous applications of law.

Colliding priorities of processing cases and policy making reflect different volume pressures as well as role perceptions.[13] Sound decisions were most commonly stressed in the overloaded 5th circuit, which has severely restricted opinion production to stay current with docket growth. Opinion writing was ascendant in New York. Suggestive also is that many of those who emphasized explanation were former academicians or U.S. district judges, several of them new to circuit courts. Whereas adjudicators came from more diverse backgrounds and projected a variety of external objects onto Courts of Appeals, ritualists concentrated on making decisions and explaining them, goals in keeping with the professional expectations of a relatively narrower audience of judges, advocates, and academics. Consequently, it is unsafe to assume that they simply took the larger governmental purposes of Courts of Appeals for granted. For ritualists, too, said little about supervising lower courts as their primary end.

ADMINISTRATOR   An ancillary set of objectives, mentioned by a third of the judges and emphasized by three, concerned effective administration of federal courts. These functions included not simply court management and supervision of district courts and agencies, but also filtering—that is, winnowing less important cases and issues from the appellate stream. Filtering involved dress rehearsals as well as gatekeeping. Some judges mentioned different strategies of writing opinions in "certworthy" cases, even though that form of influencing the Justices provoked demurrers: "I doubt that. They don't read! [Laughter]"

Southern judges, some of whom viewed circuit courts as labora-

---

means writing opinions is a very important function. Perhaps I'm a little too conscientious about it." Still another judge minimized the conflict—"having to write helps achieve the right result."

tories of regional experiment, were especially sensitive about their administrative responsibilities. In addition to the difficulties of managing their own circuit and innovating under the gun of swollen dockets, they offered desegregation cases as a special reason for transforming courts from adjudicative into administrative bodies. Bargaining and negotiating with school boards and HEW officials were "not anything like what courts are supposed to be," observed one judge active in this field. "I don't know what to call it—it's just part of life in the South."

LAWMAKER  A related function, second in frequency though not in priority, concerned lawmaking. Half of these circuit judges explicitly recognized their impact as legislators. Two comments, the first from the 2d and the second from the 5th circuits, give the flavor of their observations:

> Here in this jurisdiction we constantly get cases which in some regard plow new ground. So we do have some effect on molding the law, working on its growing points. I can't say we have had an overwhelming influence on the Supreme Court, but we have to think that a very high percentage of our cases are the end of the trail for litigants. We don't have that half-comforting feeling I had as a district judge that if I make an egregious error, the Court of Appeals will correct it. You can never tell if the Supreme Court will review or not.

> To some extent Courts of Appeals are required to develop the law and in broad terms are somewhat legislative in effect. Every judge, practically speaking, has to fill in the interstices in broad general statutes. Thus a federal Court of Appeals has to that extent an important role to play in the development of a judicial philosophy—or broadly speaking a political philosophy, a social philosophy. Isn't it interesting that on the whole question of race, a lay body as to morals took the lead over the press, the religions, the teachers—the sociological bodies? The areas of greatest progress—where fortunately courts took the first step—have been those in which the courts were supported by a good paper, a mayor, or a governor. We haven't had many good governors around here.

Judicial legislation, nevertheless, was endorsed cautiously. Only one judge accented lawmaking as his principal purpose. Only two ritualists even mentioned it. Some raised the issue to register intense opposition to "the social architect approach to judicial matters." The rest hedged, as for instance the 2d circuit judge who said:

Purposes of Courts of Appeals · 133

> The majority of the informed would say that our function is to mold the law so it will serve its purpose in society and not to pay so much attention to this case so long as the law is being developed logically and rationally and is serving the community. I feel that way, too, but not nearly so strongly as the other fellows. To me, you're administering justice whether you're on the Court of Appeals or you're a justice of the peace. The first consideration is doing justice to the parties, finding a just and proper result. That doesn't mean to flout authority or the Supreme Court. But I am more interested in doing justice between the parties than I am in molding the law.

The fact that half of these judges injected this issue themselves in response to a broad opening question, coupled with the emotional intensity of their remarks, introduces the strain among them concerning the proper boundaries of judicial legislation. To this conflict we shall return in the next chapter.

EDUCATOR  A final orientation was the goal of educating various publics—the bar, administrative agencies and their constituents, the Supreme Court, and the people at large. Only one judge gave primacy to "launching new ideas," but several judges stated that they should and did educate from the bench. That this goal was related to tensions between writing opinions and processing cases was illustrated by the southerner who observed:

> Well, we have the scholar's job, the teaching job. One of the most important roles of the circuit judge is to teach. I don't worship at the shrine of succinctness. My colleagues say I am prolix. I'd rather be clear and prolix than unclear and succinct. I think we have an obligation beyond the mere deciding process, an obligation to show what we thought about a problem. And that's why I'm slower than some of the others.

Some judges believed that they had influenced the Supreme Court's solution of public problems, including race relations. Others consciously altered their styles of writing when addressing the general public. Tactics apparently vary according to lesson and audience. No judge in the 2d circuit mentioned this function, however, even though several members actively engaged in teaching, lecturing, and writing on legal topics. Notwithstanding Justice Brandeis's sermon that government is "the omnipresent teacher," 2d circuit judges appear to heed Learned Hand's contrary admonition against converting jurists into platonic guardians or communal mentors.[14]

In sum, divided though circuit judges may be over such ancillary functions as lawmaking or education, they were quite cohesive about the central missions of Courts of Appeals. The large majority were either adjudicators, focusing on the justice or social effects of deciding appeals, or ritualists, who were immersed in decision making. Other studies have found similar orientations among appellate jurists, though ritualism appears stronger on state supreme courts.[15] At its simplest, the emphasis of these intermediate judges on administering justice and writing opinions as their main tasks highlights the hold of traditional ideologies of the legal profession on their self-images as judges and a basic consensus among them concerning organizational goals. For all their recognition of courts as legislators, only one judge saw lawmaking as a primary duty, and none lumped circuit courts with legislatures as policy makers without differentiation. The mental world of these circuit judges was a far cry from that of tribunes, brokers, or politicos in state and national legislatures.[16] Theirs was primarily a professional world, perceived largely through the lens of former advocates, in which judicial legislation is essentially a by-product of adjudicating cases and therefore a unique form of policy formation. In that world also their focus fixed more on discrete controversies than on intercourt relations or larger functions in the governmental scheme. Within this basic consensus, disagreements centered over priorities assigned to just results versus explanation and above all to molding versus applying the law.

## The Tasks of District Judges, Circuit Judges, and Supreme Court Justices

To explore their conceptions of courts in between, the judges were also asked to compare their jobs with those of federal district judges and Supreme Court Justices. This query, though concerned more with "is" than "ought," revealed that role differentiation was a congenial mode of thought and, perhaps because almost half (46%) of these judges had served previously on trial courts, cracked orthodox molds. Expected responses were either that trial courts concentrate on facts and appellate courts on law or that district judges have greater responsibility to ensure justice in individual cases while circuit judges grapple more with legal doctrine. In fact, no judge gave the former response and only three the latter. Instead, these jurists stressed three operational differences—pacing, insulation, and responsibility—and disagreed about the consequences.

The main functional distinction drawn between trial and circuit courts was pacing—that is, instant versus reflective judgments. One southerner compared the two positions this way: "Our work is far more deliberate and supported by reason. The district judge must decide on the spur of the moment most of the time. . . . The chief difference is that they shoot from the hip; we do it deliberately. Our mistakes are not hurriedly made—and we make mistakes."

Closely connected to different pacing was the circuit judge's relative isolation from attorneys, witnesses, jurors, and "the world outside." "You wouldn't believe how isolated we are here," declared a former district judge, one of several who missed "the hurly-burly of an active trial court" as compared to "this cloistered existence."

A third difference between district and circuit courts turned on solo versus collective responsibility. Even though trial courts may be more subject to review, circuit judges saw the federal district judge as "more of his own boss." "Oh, you'll get mandamused occasionally," ex-trial judges said, "but your calendar is your own . . . and yourself is the only person you have to convince." "A Court of Appeals decides by committee."[d]

Circuit judges often disagreed, however, about the practical implications of these differences for the pressures and personal satisfactions of office. Different pacing, for instance, produced considerable speculation as to which position was more demanding. One southerner, echoing the customary refrain that district judges are the workhorses of the federal judiciary, found "circuit work in some ways less personally confining." But the prevailing view was that trial judges face less pressure. Having observed several trials to decide if he preferred an appointment to a federal district court, a circuit judge recalled:

> It was so boring! All that time spent on the calendar, getting the case to trial. The pace was so slow. . . . How they have the patience to listen! Some enjoy it, however, God bless 'em.
> Of course, they have to make spur-of-the-moment rulings, but most are not reversed whichever way they make them. We have time to study things out. But presiding over a ten-week trial—is that harder than hearing forty to fifty appeals, which we would do in the same period?

---

[d] Commented a former trial judge: "The transition between a district judge and circuit judge is not an easy one, primarily because of, shall I say, the autocratic position occupied by the district court judge. He is the sole decider. He decides as he sees fit, when he sees fit, and files the decision in a form as he sees fit. A Court of Appeals decides by committee. One of the first traumas I had was when opinions were sent back by the other judges asking me to add this sentence, change that, etc., to get concurrence. I admit at the beginning I resisted that. It was pride. I learned it was a joint project, but it was a very difficult thing. I see the same in others."

One reason circuit work was considered more demanding was that "everything comes all at once, whereas a district judge has one decision at a time." "When all are combined," judges said, "it becomes a great pressure." Trial judges can get "rid of them and get them off their mind." Then, too, the weight of responsibility was thought heavier, even though shared. As the reach of circuit rulings is broader, so are the errors. "Doctrine has a way of spreading like oil on water," remarked a judge in Washington. "That's the way our mistakes spread, too." Circuit judges have less confidence that their mistakes will be corrected. Final responsibility "weighs on you."[e]

The relative isolation of district and circuit courts likewise aroused mixed feelings. The same remoteness that insulated them from popular pressure also removed them from the popular pulse. A few judges feared becoming mental prisoners, as it were, of bench and bar. The trial judge's closeness to the people, in turn, saddles district courts with more routine cases and fewer intellectual challenges. Routinization of work frustrated several former trial judges, as one of them explained:

> I felt my talents were not being used. That sounds immodest, but it's true. Here's why. The docket was heavy with auto acci-

[e] One 2d circuit judge, who found both jobs so attractive that he "would do either for nothing if I could afford it," explained why he thought the Court of Appeals imposed greater pressure. "When I was a district judge we all thought circuit judges didn't work very hard; that was based on lack of knowledge, measuring work by hours spent in court. We had the feeling that we were working in the courtroom while they were loafing in their offices. I was surprised how busy you are as a circuit judge if you do the job right, giving close attention to every case. It's a very full job. The district court, oddly enough, while it has very urgent emergencies at times, doesn't produce the same feeling of urgent pressure. Only rarely does a Court of Appeals get an urgent emergency, like motions which call for overnight rulings, and when they do the record has been winnowed—the district judge has ruled. The district courts are really by themselves. In motions you sink or swim . . . but the sustained pressure is greater in the Courts of Appeals, much to my surprise. A trial has its own pace. It may be difficult, but the judge can concentrate on that trial's problems with no distractions.

"Contrast the Court of Appeals. Every month you hear cases, you read the briefs, and if you don't get your opinions out, you fall further and further behind. There's month-in, month-out pressure. . . . The best way to understand it is to look at the calendar of a Court of Appeals. There has been an increase to about 20 cases when you sit. You are supposed to read the briefs ahead of argument. I do, most people do. It takes a good part of the preceding week. I do it nights and on weekends. Then the entire week is spent hearing cases. You can't do anything else that week. The voting memorandum system takes an enormous extra expenditure of time. You won't finish that week unless you're fast. Then you go into the next week—two weeks have gone by already—for the conferences. There are 20 cases. Opinions must be written in only two to three weeks. And one of those weeks is occupied with reading briefs again. If I didn't like it, the pressure would be terrible."

dent negligence cases. The district court I was on was a personal injuries court. I got sick of broken legs and cracked skulls. . . . My performance was okay. . . . My docket was as up as it could be. I was on the job nine to five. Still, I never quite felt my full potential was being used. The difference is that here there is no limitation on the variety, diversity, or importance of cases. It's a better platform. I could write the same opinion as a district judge, but no one would pay any attention.[f]

Irrespective of disagreements over the relative burdens of each office, these circuit judges easily differentiated the functions and operations of trial and intermediate appellate courts. The contrasts they drew were not between fact finding and lawmaking, but in pacing, insulation, and relative responsibility. At bottom these differences boil down to the familiar distinction between line and staff. Differentiating sharply between these functions, seven judges even distinguished the talents required according to personal "temperament."[g]

At appellate levels, on the other hand, these judges saw few intrinsic distinctions between deciding appeals in the circuits or the Supreme Court, beyond the obvious differences of the Justices' selectivity and final authority. ("In all humility I think I could wade in, pick up, and not miss a stride.") Likening the responsibilities to those of general practitioners and specialists in medicine, circuit judges stressed most often that docket control freed the Justices from their daily lot of routine cases, which produced the divisions of appellate labor examined in Chapter Three. Quoting Chief Justice Warren to capture the difference—"You're a court of appeals. We're a court of review. We don't have to take the case. Right or wrong, you do"—one chief judge concluded: "Our work is different. We have to rectify error. We can't say, as they do, the system can tolerate this."

[f] Contrast the retort of one chief judge: "Everybody has his role and function. The apex ought to be the district court—and the Supreme Court at the bottom—where it is so important to get a fair hearing from a careful judge, because it is win or lose there."

[g] Consider, for example, these observations: "I was never interested in becoming a district judge. I would be bored to death listening to witnesses. I am interested in broad questions, in principles. After a while most district judges harden. They have to. It would hurt me too much seeing other people's troubles. I identify too much with suffering." Or: "I couldn't be a district judge. I don't have confidence in myself to make quick decisions daily or to have to listen all day to inept lawyers." Role differentiation according to distinctive rather than monolithic "judicial temperaments" also surfaced among several 5th circuit judges who opposed using visiting district judges to help meet their caseload on grounds that trial judges often found it difficult "to think like appellate judges." Mentioned as exceptions were future circuit judges Frank M. Johnson, Jr. and G. Harrold Carswell. For discussion of the fit between personality and office, see pp. 96-97.

Because selectivity narrows the docket of the Supreme Court to the Justices' special concerns, while Courts of Appeals hear "everything under the sun," some circuit judges thought the Supreme Court was "not a law court but a political court."[h] A few southerners, criticizing the Justices for being "overly conscious of the political implications of their decisions," complained that lower appellate courts, both state and federal, were being reduced to "a valley between two mountains."

Yet, no judge disputed that having the "last word" imposed more "awesome" responsibility on the Justices and institutional constraints on themselves. It was universally conceded that "we are bound by what the Supreme Court says." Circuit judges also concurred that the higher the court, the greater the freedom to innovate. Hence, their ability to mold the law is restricted to subjects the Justices have not preempted.[i] The doctrine of *stare decisis*, to the extent that judges conform to norm, *does* enable the Supreme Court to control their policy premises.[17]

## The Independence of Appellate Courts

The duty of obedience, on the other hand, hardly implies that circuit judges are legal eunuchs. Middle positions oblige them, if not to anticipate the reactions of Justices, at least to aid in legal development. Though some of them opposed holding en bancs for this purpose, circuit judges were conscious of the advantages of dress rehearsals in appellate litigation. "When we have a bear by the tail," as one judge said, "I do my best to set it up so that, if it does go upstairs, it goes up intelligently."

What's more, by virtue of their organization and finality, circuit judges enjoy considerable psychic independence in the hierarchy of work. The fate of their decisions in other courts had little effect on individual reputations for leadership or, as discussed in Chapter Eight, the distribution of labor. Judicial prestige, as distinct from judicial power, was perceived at all levels largely in terms of personal and professional capacities rather than of institutional authority.

[h] One 5th circuit judge commented: "When *Brown* v. *Board of Education* was before the Supreme Court, the Justices made a political decision. It was extremely important and extremely necessary. If the case was before the Court of Appeals when I was on the panel, I would have felt our court had no right to overturn the precedent of 100 years, that we had to follow the law as found in the books. The Court since *Marbury* v. *Madison* has amended the Constitution whenever it felt political necessity required it."

[i] For example: "We have to follow the lead of the Supreme Court. We can move into areas where they haven't entered. Where they have acted they can bar us, and we can't act. Further, they can reverse themselves, and we can't reverse them."

These conclusions are based on both vertical and horizontal evidence. To capture vertical relationships between the circuits and their superiors, the rates of Supreme Court reversal of decisions in which each circuit judge participated in 1965-1967 are presented in Tables 5.2-5.4. Though extreme caution is required in interpreting such small numbers, the data indicate little association between circuit leadership and agreement with the Justices. Some circuit leaders, such as Lumbard, Brown, and Bazelon, had the highest reversal rates.[18] Tuttle, by contrast, was among the lowest. Less prominent figures at the time, such as Kaufman or Waterman, fared better on review. Circuit reputations appear to be independent of Supreme Court support.

Also reinforcing the impression of psychic independence on different judicial planes were reactions to queries as to whether circuit judges resented being reversed by the Supreme Court. Table 5.5 summarizes how these judges, overwhelmingly and often laughingly, toed official lines: reversal seldom causes resentment. Though "I can't say I enjoy it," judges said, "not at all. That's their job." "How can you resent disagreement? It's merely a matter of institutional supremacy." "There has to be a rule of finality. . . . The last guess may be a different view."

TABLE 5.2
Supreme Court Reversal of Decisions in Which
2d Circuit Judges Participated, FY 1965-1967
(Adjusted for Dissent)

| Judge | Rate of Reversal % | Decisions in Which Certiorari Was Granted N |
|---|---|---|
| Swan | 100.0 | 4 |
| Lumbard | 77.8 | 18 |
| Smith | 69.6 | 23 |
| Friendly | 60.0 | 15 |
| Moore | 58.8 | 17 |
| Hays | 57.1 | 7 |
| Waterman | 55.5 | 18 |
| Anderson | 55.5 | 9 |
| Kaufman | 50.0 | 14 |
| Medina | 50.0 | 2 |
| Feinberg | 33.3 | 6 |
| Marshall | 33.3 | 3 |
| Sums | 61.0 | 136 |

TABLE 5.3
Supreme Court Reversal of Decisions in Which
5th Circuit Judges Participated, FY 1965-1967
(Adjusted for Dissent)

| Judge | Rate of Reversal % | Decisions in Which Certiorari Was Granted N |
|---|---|---|
| Coleman | 100.0 | 3 |
| Dyer | 100.0 | 3 |
| Thornberry | 100.0 | 1 |
| Goldberg | 100.0 | 1 |
| Jones | 75.0 | 4 |
| Brown | 70.0 | 10 |
| Ainsworth | 66.7 | 3 |
| Hutcheson | 66.7 | 3 |
| Rives | 63.6 | 11 |
| Gewin | 62.5 | 8 |
| Wisdom | 60.0 | 5 |
| Bell | 57.1 | 7 |
| Tuttle | 33.3 | 6 |
| Godbold | 0.0 | — |
| Simpson | 0.0 | — |
| Sums | 66.2 | 65 |

Sometimes circuit judges are persuaded they were wrong. More often, they react to reversal like the parson to his God: "Though vanquished I can argue still."[j] Talking back normally occurs in private more than in public.[19] A few conservatives, "proud of their disagreement" with the Warren Court, wore reversals as badges of honor. "Our function is to expose ideas," said one lawmaker; "winning or losing isn't important." Just as professional norms restrain personal conflict among judges, so disagreements with the Supreme Court were submerged in vocational expectations of obedience. What circuit judges resented most were breaches of standards of craftsmanship by superiors, such as reversal "without listening" or "even a respectable funeral oration."

[j] The one judge who admitted resentment said: "Oh, well, everybody minds it. Don't believe that business about 'I don't mind a bit'—at least from any judge who is any good. You carry on the argument in your head where they didn't seem to understand the case the way you did. I don't resent it in the sense of bleeding about it. But I never acquiesce without reargument in my own head."

TABLE 5.4
*Supreme Court Reversal of Decisions in Which D.C. Circuit Judges Participated, FY 1965-1967*
(Adjusted for Dissent)

| Judge | Rate of Reversal % | Decisions in Which Certiorari Was Granted N |
|---|---|---|
| Prettyman | 100.0 | 1 |
| Bazelon | 80.0 | 5 |
| Fahy | 80.0 | 5 |
| Edgerton | 75.0 | 4 |
| Tamm | 71.4 | 7 |
| Burger | 66.7 | 6 |
| Danaher | 66.7 | 3 |
| Miller | 62.5 | 8 |
| McGowan | 60.0 | 5 |
| Wright | 50.0 | 6 |
| Washington | 50.0 | 4 |
| Leventhal | 50.0 | 2 |
| Bastian | 0.0 | 1 |
| Robinson | 0.0 | — |
| Sums | 64.9 | 57 |

Thus, circuit judges, expecting policy disagreement, judged the Justices largely through professional and ideological lenses. Though a few took reversal personally, keeping careful track of their record, rarely did they gauge the influence of their peers in terms of Supreme Court support. The gentle gibes at unsuccessful efforts by col-

TABLE 5.5
*Judicial Perceptions of Whether Circuit Judges Resent Being Reversed by the Supreme Court*

| Circuit | Yes N | Sometimes N | No N | No Response/ Don't Know N | Total N |
|---|---|---|---|---|---|
| 2d | 0 | 1 | 8 | 1 | 10 |
| 5th | 0 | 4 | 11 | 2 | 17 |
| D.C. | 1 | 0 | 6 | 1 | 8 |
| Sums | 1 | 5 | 25 | 4 | 35 |

NOTE: The question was: "Do you resent being reversed by the Supreme Court?"

leagues to educate the Justices, and the not-so-gentle agitation over en bancs for this purpose in the 2d circuit, were symptoms of regionalization with only limited external interference. Neither judicial prestige nor opinion leadership among peers depended on relations with the high court. For individual judges, as for circuit courts as institutions, an older judge summed up the central credo of judicial independence: "My show is mine, and theirs is theirs."

Independence was even stronger among equals. To gauge whether cross-circuit ties might serve as a further bond among federal courts, the judges were asked whether the 2d circuit still enjoyed the reputation it won in the 1950s as the ablest court in the country.[20] Then the frequency of citing other circuit decisions was analyzed for the base period as a measure of intercircuit influence.

Though some southerners mounted a testy challenge to the 2d circuit's primacy, the court in New York was still regarded as the front-runner for reasons of its business, its bench, and its bar.[k] Conscious that "this is the court of the Hands," which "makes us strive for perfection a little more than the others," judges in Foley Square assumed that other circuits "look to us for leadership."

> This court [one member commented] has enormous prestige which gives it a position of more influence on the direction of federal law in general than any other Court of Appeals, except possibly the D.C. circuit. The present membership, while it wouldn't have won the enormous prestige of the Hands and Swan, is able enough to sustain the prestige won for it by our predecessors. The 2d is cited more frequently than other Courts of Appeals when they go outside their circuit for authority. Of course, any circuit court cites itself most. Other Courts of Appeals pay deference to us in terms of quality. It is striking the way they discuss a 2d circuit case—with deference. Another qualitative factor is that I get the impression we reverse less than the other circuits. This reflects the high quality of district court judges in this circuit. At the same time there are considerable

---

[k] For example, a judge in the 5th circuit said: "I think we're better than all of them, myself. I hate to be that immodest, but you asked me. I think we could make a valid claim to greatness, relative greatness. With an increasing number of demands we found the resources in the form of visiting judges to keep our head above water and handling all that time the most intense, sensitive, and controversial items—decisions which were invariably disturbing to the people. And we did it!"

Discounting the importance of administrative innovation, a colleague disagreed: "If nothing else, they [the 2d circuit] flatly confront the most intricate problems, problems I would quail before. I read the *Federal Reporter* through and through. They are far and away the ablest—by necessity."

differences in the quality of business before the court. Once commenced, cases are more likely to be appealed. I sat on the 5th circuit as a visitor. There is no comparison, though recently I have to admit that the 2d has more of the less important business.

Previous analysis of the flow of litigation supports the accuracy of this judge's impressions, except for circuit citations. Judging from the conduct of the three tribunals in 1965-1967, the 2d circuit was a clearer leader in *citing* the decisions of other circuits than in being *cited* by them. Table 5.6 shows that, while judges in the 5th circuit cited the 2d circuit most often, judges in Washington cited the 2d less frequently than they did the 9th circuit, a consistent leader in all three. In neither cases nor comment did the 5th circuit impress colleagues in New York or Washington as much as it impressed its own members. Though southerners often attributed their lower reputation to a lack of scholars on the bench, judges in the other two circuits regarded the 5th as simply too sprawling, overloaded, and politicized for a position of leadership.

Citations, of course, only go so far as a measure of cross-court in-

TABLE 5.6
Citation of Other Circuits, FY 1965-1967

| Other Circuits | D.C. Cites N | 2d Cites N | 5th Cites N | Total Citations N |
|---|---|---|---|---|
| First | 7 | 15 | 4 | 26 |
| Second | 13 | — | 47 | 60 |
| Third | 7 | 44 | 23 | 74 |
| Fourth | 12 | 27 | 24 | 63 |
| Fifth | 10 | 38 | — | 48 |
| Sixth | 7 | 26 | 26 | 59 |
| Seventh | 12 | 28 | 35 | 75 |
| Eighth | 9 | 27 | 29 | 65 |
| Ninth | 17 | 45 | 40 | 102 |
| Tenth | 6 | 19 | 31 | 56 |
| D.C. | — | 16 | 6 | 22 |
| Sums | 100 | 285 | 265 | 650 |
| % of total cases with citations to other circuits | 3.7 (n = 1,336) | 10.3 (n = 1,357) | 6.6 (n = 2,248) | 6.8 (N = 4,941) |

NOTE: Cases with citations = 337; total number of cases = 4,941.

fluence. Kindred business may help to account for the 2d circuit's heavy citation of decisions by the 3rd circuit, which has headquarters in another financial center (Philadelphia), or the common thread of admiralty among the coastal circuits. Judges also cite cases to indicate homework done as well as for support. Frequency of citation, at bottom, is a matter of personal style. Some judges, such as Henry J. Friendly, habitually comb relevant case law from over the country and abroad; others follow John Marshall's example of emphasizing principles unencumbered by precedent. Most striking in these decisions is the scant reference (7%) to other circuits at all.[1] Much as opinions in a case-law system serve as media of professional communication or as materials of legal growth, the three tribunals relied far more on their own case law (and the Supreme Court) for guidance than on sister tribunals. Judicial prestige, apparently dispersed among circuit judges over the country, turned less on institutional than on individual reputations for sound judgment and craftsmanship.[m21]

The emphasis on individuals rather than institutions reflects a national legal culture. But accentuated the more is the independence of Courts of Appeals in the chain of command. Cross-circuit influence, a volitional element of cohesion in the federal judiciary, is no substitute for Supreme Court review and intracircuit pressures to enforce the rule of law. Because review from above is uncertain, circuit roles

[1] Express adoptions or rejections of holdings of other circuits in this court were as follows:

|  | Adopting Holdings of Other Circuits N | Rejecting Holdings of Other Circuits N |
|---|---|---|
| 2d | 4 | 1 |
| 5th | 14 | 5 |
| D.C. | 1 | 0 |
| Sums | 19 | 6 |

[m] Among judges singled out for approbation were Wisdom in the 5th circuit ("a scholar!"), Fahy from the D.C. circuit ("There's a human being!"), and, above all, Henry J. Friendly ("the ablest of all circuit judges." "In oral argument," remarked a southern judge, "if a lawyer cites the 2d circuit, I ask: 'Who wrote it?' If he replies, 'Friendly,' I read it very carefully").

Cross-pollination also occurs when judges sit by designation in other circuits. For example, Sterry R. Waterman, having lost a battle in the 2d circuit for rights to counsel in police lineups, supplied the margin of victory for this principle as a visiting judge in the 5th circuit in *U.S. v. Wade*.[22] Also see *North Carolina Utilities Commission v. F.C.C.*, 552 F. 2d 1036 (1977), in which Richard T. Rives and Elbert P. Tuttle, sitting by designation in the 4th circuit, upheld the FCC's program to give customers "freedom of choice" in telephone equipment sales over the dissent of 4th circuit judge, H. Emory Widener, Jr. Widener was the only active judge of this court who had not disqualified himself, thus precluding en banc review.

of filtering and finality probably encourage circuit judges to emulate Justices more than does anticipating commands.[23] Whatever the fit between personalities and offices, moreover, judicial roles differ by institutional layer. The jobs of trial and appellate judges, irrespective of the impetus for promotion, evoked different talents and expectations.[24] And amid a common conception of appellate work, circuit courts displayed considerable independence, both from their superiors and from each other. The more they served as "semiclosed systems" of law and policy, the more significant became relations with colleagues and the external community.[25]

## Community Roles

### National versus Regional Obligations

So far we have seen that circuit judges have common orientations toward their basic mission of deciding appeals in the institutional division of labor. Uniting them further is a general duty to obey the Supreme Court. Additional bonds of cohesion are shared perspectives toward their "areal roles" and their relations with their publics. Given their potential autonomy in the enforcement of federal law, how circuit judges conceive of their place in the polity—as agents of national policy or as regional power centers—is no minor matter in the federal judicial system. Nor is the answer free from complexity. Just as their duty to follow the Supreme Court is conditional in practice, so general understandings regarding their community roles tend to be qualified by countervailing norms of judicial independence and modes of enforcement.

The basic premise of decision is nationalism. Despite local influences in their selection and organization, these judges were acutely aware of their obligation, as arms of the federal government, to maintain national supremacy. A few southerners even put service as a national court at the head of their list of duties. As one of them stated at the outset:

> I think you first have to realize that you're not a sectional judge, not an Alabama or a southern judge, but a United States judge. Your decisions affect Alaska, Hawaii, Washington, you, me, and every other man. That's the first thing you've got to decide. In every case you must remember—was it Achilles?—"I'm part of all I meet." It's true from my own experience.[n]

[n] The function of a Court of Appeals as a national court "influences me greatly," another southern judge commented at the outset. "I am very interested in whether the

As expected from their socialization and recruitment, judges in all three circuits responded to specific questions about their areal roles with overwhelmingly national rather than regional leanings. Two-thirds of thirty-one respondents expressed national loyalties without hesitation or qualification. Five of them said that regional obligations had never occurred to them. Though a nameless southerner was accused of speaking for "his state instead of for the court—a kind of senator from state X"—only one jurist, a lone deviant on more than this question, voiced states' rights sentiments.°

The geographic issue was most salient among southern judges, not merely because of desegregation scars or fears that circuit realignment would parochialize the court. A third of the judges, all but one from the 5th circuit, also saw regional organization as a paradoxical source of strength in American federalism. Proper performance of federal duties included accommodation of national and local values. "It's fundamentally a national court to enforce national policy," one of them remarked, "though I try to be conscious of local interests. Resolving conflicts between national and local units is the job."

Far from viewing the regional distribution of appellate resources as a contradiction between institutional purpose and design, these judges viewed it as a healthy compromise that satisfied the people's desire to have judges from their own areas pass on their problems and the need to adapt federal law to local conditions. "Regionalism works both ways," they argued. Even if decentralization "makes it tougher for the Supreme Court to go adverse to section," the history of desegregation demonstrated that the Justices cannot implement policies without the support of circuit judges who take "a more national view than can be expected of a single judge in a single state." "Courts of Appeals took the heat off and expended it."

Offsetting inroads on uniformity, in other words, was better fed-

---

question will be decided on a parochial or national basis. On a Court of Appeals we have to pull a lot of chestnuts out of the fire for district judges who must face lots of parochial pressures. Also, the Court of Appeals has a function to save the Supreme Court from having to decide cases unnecessarily that ought to be decided at our level. You can't decide on the assumption that the Supreme Court can correct our errors. I feel this way especially regarding conflicts between states' rights and federally created rights. A Court of Appeals is a national court."

° He said: "The regional idea has completely dissipated, and that's bad. My frank opinion is that this circuit would be twice as effective and twice as influential if it were divided and could go back to a 9-man court. This would permit more intensive consideration of problems. The opposition say it would make a parochial court. I don't accept that at all. Provincialism is a thing of the past. Oh, there are a few fragments left, but darn few—some I'd like to preserve."

eral law. One southerner, a champion of the circuits as national courts, commented at length:

> I would accept the regional concept if it meant something beyond my state. I don't sit as ambassador from some state. Judge Cameron sat as ambassador from Mississippi. The same is true for the South as a region. It's a paradox. We're better at interpreting the South than any other court. I'm more optimistic we'll reach a better conclusion in civil rights than the North.
>
> I feel strongly our courts should be readily open to persons who want national rights protected. One of the problems with the whole situation in the country is that there would not have been all these problems if the courts had been open. Compare the 2d circuit. They don't understand this. Take removals, for example. They see the problem in terms of workload. They say: "That question can be tried in state courts." I've heard that argument all my life: "The state court is as well qualified to decide constitutional questions as federal." That's for the birds in the crunch. Maybe they can, but they don't. This conflict goes all the way back through our history.<sup>p</sup>

National allegiances do not preclude sharp divergences over particular public policies. Impressive, all the same, is how strongly diverse circuit judges embraced institutional obligations as agents of the national government. Even in the 5th circuit, which felt the anticipated tug of sectionalism, anticipatory socialization spawned strongly national loyalties. "I have no difficulty answering that," concluded one Nixon appointee, chosen ostensibly to balance the Gulf Coast circuit in response to local pressures. "I think purely in a national sense. I doubt if any of the judges thinks otherwise. I never ran into it consciously or even suspected it. They all think that way, nationally."[26]

*Perceived Influence on Public Policy*

Dominant though nationalism and institutional obedience may be as premises of decision, working in regional centers tempered the judges' conceptions of themselves as instruments of national power.

<sup>p</sup> One judge in the 2d circuit agreed with this diagnosis. Though "the country is a different country than in 1881," he argued, after World War II the "Hand-Swan philosophy" of abstention, "which was the philosophy of the early twentieth century, still pervaded our basic approach to the issues before us, despite the fact that we had Frank and Clark who were really . . . 'neutralists,' men who recognized that we are becoming a unitary nation whether we like it or not. Federalism is on the way out, and modified legal conceptions are the result."

This tempering, already observed in institutional separation and sectional pull, was also evident in the judges' perceptions of their influence on public policy and primary reference groups. Norms of office may be national and professional in content; but, except for Supreme Court review, enforcement mechanisms are informal and diffused. As intermediates, Courts of Appeals may synthesize "cultures"—local and national, legal and political—in deciding federal appeals.[27]

One barometer of the judges' functional understandings, in an operational as well as normative sense, is the estimated influence of their courts on public policy. This question troubled a fourth of the judges.[28] Some, distinguishing sharply between law and politics, equated public policy with legislation. Somehow, judge-made rules of tort or contract were not policies.[29] Others, finding influence impossible to measure from the inside, merely repeated general reputations without explanation.[q] Yet Table 5.7 shows that, on the whole, at least 60 percent of them ranked their own tribunals as "influential" or "very influential," because of both the volume and the importance of litigation in particular fields.

Each court's policy impact naturally was greatest in its own region. Influence outside each circuit was perceived largely in terms of leadership in their magnetic fields. In weighing policy leadership,

TABLE 5.7
Perceived Influence of Circuit Courts on Public Policy

| Circuit | Very Influential N | Influential N | Not Influential N | No Response/ Don't Know N | Total N |
|---|---|---|---|---|---|
| 2d | 3 | 3 | 2 | 2 | 10 |
| 5th | 8 | 6 | 0 | 3 | 17 |
| D.C. | 1 | 4 | 2 | 1 | 8 |
| Sums | 12 | 13 | 4 | 6 | 35 |

[q] For example, southerners commented: "I just can't answer the question. When I travel, I feel we are looked on as one of the leading circuits. The 2d, the 5th, the D.C. circuits—law school people say they are the leaders. I don't know why. The 6th and 10th have some excellent men. I think we are living on the reputation of old personnel to an extent—Sibley, Hutcheson, Tuttle. I do the same with the 4th; I think of Parker." "At meetings the other judges tell me, every time, what a load the 5th carries, how they appreciate what we've done, how it took guts to do what we've had to do. Some say, 'I don't see how you stand it.' I've been to meetings of the Civil Rights Commission. They all show great obeisance to us. But I suspect that some don't think we do a good job."

moreover, these jurists usually discussed leading personalities and doctrines rather than institutions or aggregates. Judges in Washington praised their court for having "opened up the law to seminal ideas" concerning criminal responsibility and rules of representation before administrative bodies. Judges in New York considered their court influential primarily "because it is at the heart of so much that affects policy—commerce, finance, industry, the media," though there were complaints of poor press coverage.[r] Some southerners, going beyond a natural tendency to inflate their own tribunal's significance, held an expansive view of their influence, attributable perhaps to their circuit's size, distance from Washington, and battles in racial desegregation. Even when recognizing that theirs was "reflected glory," they took pride in their leadership in civil rights.

> This court probably made as great a contribution to liberalism and humanity and broad-mindedness as any institution operating in the South, [one newcomer declared]. It was way ahead of the legislatures, the chambers of commerce, the churches, and other institutions dealing with public opinion. I also think the mores of a community often flow from leadership rather than toward leadership. Education of itself would never have liberalized. It took law to do it. People are changing. We're in the mores stage now.

Gallup polls showing increasing willingness by southern white parents to accept school desegregation support this view of law as a catalyst of social change.[30] A few doubting Thomases in each tribunal, to be sure, were skeptical of their influence. "The Supreme Court doesn't pay the slightest attention to what lower courts say on policy," a New Yorker maintained. "They have no alternative but their own policy views and shouldn't." Some judges in Washington believed that their prestige had fallen because of permissiveness on law-and-order issues. "This court is on the defensive before the bar of public opinion," one member commented. "Every time I go out to

---

[r] A 2d circuit judge argued: "No other court surpasses us. In certain definite areas we are almost the court of last resort, the court to which all other courts defer. [Probe: what areas?] Wall Street control, securities, mergers, banking, and the rest of it. I am almost afraid to say criminal conspiracy also, because of the big white collar cases. But where the money is, is where people steal. . . . Then, of course, figures speak for themselves. We have more admiralty—seamen's injuries—than anybody else. Worse than all that, New York is New York. Major corporations have their headquarters here, their executive offices. Anybody dissatisfied with American affluent society can sue here and go after the big boys, and they do. In public law, the D.C. circuit probably outranks us in administrative battles and all that. Outside of that field, we've got it."

dinner, people ask me why we let all those criminals back on the streets." In the 5th circuit, too, judges feared that their influence had been diluted by overload and preoccupation with civil rights.[s] Generally speaking, however, the judges saw their tribunals as influential instruments of public policy, both regionally and nationally.

*Reference Groups and Community Participation*

Recognizing their policy discretion at both levels necessarily entwines the normative dilemmas of judge-made law with circuit relations in the larger community. Even if demands on circuit judges are changing and their formal links to other courts are weak, circuit judges are not necessarily their own masters. Traditional professional values permeated their perspectives toward their constituencies and relations with the public. In theory, reference groups are the "related others" who help to define, impart, and enforce the prescriptions of any social role.[31] That circuit judges tended to define their jobs more professionally than politically, as a profession within a profession, finds strong support in their evaluations of the influence of various actors in the appellate process. So does the norm of judicial independence. Hence, despite their ties to a national legal culture, in each region their primary reference groups were colleagues and constituents. The effect was to qualify their national identities, though not to the point of conceding that Courts of Appeals were regional centers of power.

These conclusions are based on responses to a structured questionnaire reported in Tables 5.8-5.10. Of the participants in the appellate process evaluated in Table 5.8, only the opinions of other panel members were rated as "very important" influences on their own decisions. The views of nonpanel judges, law clerks, and law review commentators figured modestly—and surprisingly closely—in their rankings. Community values, public opinion, and interest groups were even less relevant and, for a few judges, fighting words. However cognizant of their policy-making roles or of the expanding universe of litigants before them, most circuit judges rejected an interest-group theory of the judicial process. The related others that counted most for them, following tradition, were fellow judges and, secondarily, members of the legal fraternity. Colleagues, in intermediate as in supreme courts, remain a judge's "severest critics."[32]

[s] Accurately reflecting reactions of colleagues outside, a judge in the 5th circuit observed: "I am afraid that . . . we almost have too much to do to be influential. Maybe I'm wrong. It's hard to know from the inside. But the school cases and civil rights—I am weary of people who think that's all we do. I fear we are spending so much time worrying about them, problems so social and psychological in character, that we're not paying enough attention to the main problems of our business."

TABLE 5.8
Perceived Influence of Related Actors on Circuit Decisions

| Opinions of Related Actors | Very Important N | Moderately Important N | Not Important N | No Response N | Total N |
|---|---|---|---|---|---|
| Judges on panel | 22 | 12 | 0 | 1 | 35 |
| Nonpanel judges | 7 | 18 | 7 | 3 | 35 |
| Law clerks | 6 | 22 | 6 | 1 | 35 |
| Relevant law review article | 5 | 21 | 6 | 3 | 35 |
| Community values | 3 | 14 | 12 | 6 | 35 |
| Respected members of bar | 1 | 13 | 16 | 5 | 35 |
| Public opinion | 2 | 8 | 22 | 3 | 35 |
| Interested groups | 0 | 7 | 25 | 3 | 35 |

NOTE: The question was: "In reaching your decisions, how influential do you consider the following factors?"

Horizons expanded somewhat, it is true, when attention shifted from making decisions to explaining them. Of the various audiences of judicial opinions considered in Table 5.9, party litigants were the ones circuit judges seemed most eager to reach. Members of the bar, judges below, and to a lesser extent law schools and the Supreme Court also were moderately important targets of judicial opinions. Striking, even so, is how the immediate participants in adjudication—colleagues, counsel, clerks, litigants—were viewed as more influential touchstones and targets of judging than the external interests emphasized in political or realist theories of judicial decision. Though some judges acknowledged shifts in writing style when addressing major public issues, they were more sensitive to professional criticism and consumers of federal appeals than to public opinion or even the Supreme Court. And they stuck to their guns when asked to select the group whose approval gave them greatest personal satisfaction. Table 5.10 shows that, except for the addition of "fellow judges" by four jurists and "none" by one, party litigants and members of the bar remained their primary reference groups.

Demonstrated again is the hold of professional values, particularly those of former advocates, on these judges' conceptions of their jobs. In the last chapter, we saw how professional experience far outweighed political factors in their evaluations of preparation for their work, regardless of political debts acquired in their selection. So now, consistent with their backgrounds and orientations as ad-

## Table 5.9
### Audiences of Written Opinions

| Audience | Very Important N | Moderately Important N | Not Important N | No Response N | Total N |
|---|---|---|---|---|---|
| Party litigants | 27 | 2 | 3 | 3 | 35 |
| Members of bar | 16 | 16 | 1 | 2 | 35 |
| Judges below | 14 | 13 | 5 | 3 | 35 |
| Law schools | 8 | 16 | 7 | 4 | 35 |
| Supreme Court Justices | 6 | 12 | 13 | 4 | 35 |
| General public | 2 | 15 | 14 | 4 | 35 |
| Other government officials | 2 | 11 | 18 | 4 | 35 |
| Interest groups | 1 | 6 | 23 | 5 | 35 |

NOTE: The question was: "In writing opinions, which audience are you most eager to reach?"

## Table 5.10
### Primary Reference Groups of Circuit Judges

| Reference Group | N |
|---|---|
| Party litigant | 8 |
| Bar | 8 |
| Law schools | 5 |
| Fellow judges | 4 |
| Supreme Court Justices | 3 |
| Judges below | 2 |
| General public | 1 |
| Interest groups | 0 |
| None | 1 |
| No response | 3 |
| Sum | 35 |

NOTE: The question was: "The approval of which group above gives you greatest personal satisfaction?" "Fellow judges" and "none" were not included in the questionnaire.

judicators and ritualists, they held fast to traditional models of adjudication. This was true despite recognition of their legislative function and their contact with an ever-widening conglomeration of interests in judicial policy making. Because the sway of traditional professional ideologies of the judicial function seems unaffected by contrary experience, these disjunctions may represent "role lag"—that is, resistance in theory to changing appellate functions in practice.[33]

Professionalism, even if regionally enforced, likewise constrained judicial participation in community affairs. Judging from responses to structured questions about the permissible range of extrajudicial activity, there was a stronger consensus about participating in political and professional activities than in civic organizations. Of the political activities evaluated in Table 5.11, voting was unanimously seen as permissible, endorsing political candidates or policies almost unanimously seen as not. Only a few shades of disagreement appeared between these extremes, such as whether it was proper to make private recommendations of political candidates to friends or to postpone retirement so that one's party could appoint the successor. Oddly, two judges thought campaign contributions were acceptable, even though outlawed by the Hatch Act.

TABLE 5.11
Permissible Political Activity by Circuit Judges

| Political Activity | Permissible N | Not Permissible N | Qualified N | No Response N | Total N |
|---|---|---|---|---|---|
| Vote | 34 | 0 | 0 | 1 | 35 |
| Postpone retirement so party can appoint successor | 8 | 26 | 0 | 1 | 35 |
| Recommend candidate to a friend | 6 | 25 | 2 | 2 | 35 |
| Make campaign contribution | 2 | 30 | 2 | 1 | 35 |
| Advise politicians behind the scenes | 0 | 32 | 1 | 2 | 35 |
| Attend party meeting | 0 | 32 | 1 | 2 | 35 |
| Speak publicly in support of policies only | 0 | 32 | 1 | 2 | 35 |
| Endorse candidates publicly | 0 | 33 | 0 | 2 | 35 |

Strictures against political participation weakened closer to home, namely, in staffing federal courts. Table 5.12 reflects wide agreement that circuit judges properly may advise appointing authorities on request, but should not take the initiative or politick openly for candidates. Advising senators or other politicians about judicial selection was thought less legitimate than advising Justice Department lawyers, again reflecting professional biases.[34] Like maidens in Victorian courtship, their reticence concerned appearances more than substance.

Rules governing the political and financial activities of federal judges are prescribed by statute and codes of professional responsibility developed by the American Bar Association, which the Judicial Conference adopted in 1973.[35] Standards of participation in professional and civic organizations, though partially covered by professional canon, are largely proprieties evolved by custom, which permit individuals greater freedom of choice.[36] As shown in Table 5.13, most of these judges regarded membership in bar associations as permissible, though one resigned from the ABA after his appointment. Most also approved the reciprocal honoring of service as trustees of eleemosynary institutions, but a vocal minority disapproved of judges teaching or assuming active leadership in bar asso-

TABLE 5.12
Permissible Activity in Recruiting Federal Judges

| Recruitment Activity | Permissible N | Not Permissible N | Qualified N | No Response N | Total N |
|---|---|---|---|---|---|
| Advise Justice Department on request | 32 | 1 | 0 | 2 | 35 |
| Advise senators and other politicians on request | 24 | 8 | 1 | 2 | 35 |
| Recommend names to Justice Department | 4 | 27 | 2 | 2 | 35 |
| Recommend names to senators and other politicians | 2 | 31 | 0 | 2 | 35 |
| Politick openly for qualified candidates | 1 | 30 | 2 | 2 | 35 |
| Politick behind the scenes for qualified candidates | 0 | 31 | 2 | 2 | 35 |

TABLE 5.13
Permissible Professional or Civic Activity by Circuit Judges

| Professional or Civic Activity | Permissible N | Not Permissible N | Qualified N | No Response N | Total N |
|---|---|---|---|---|---|
| Member of bar or civic organization | 33 | 1 | 0 | 1 | 35 |
| Contribute financially to bar or civic organization | 30 | 4 | 0 | 1 | 35 |
| Trustee of hospital, art museum, university, etc. | 28 | 6 | 0 | 1 | 35 |
| Teach in accredited law school | 24 | 8 | 2 | 1 | 35 |
| President or committee head of bar association | 12 | 16 | 6 | 1 | 35 |
| President or committee head of civic organization | 9 | 23 | 2 | 1 | 35 |
| Head of public investigating committee | 2 | 28 | 4 | 1 | 35 |

ciations and civic groups. At a time of agitation over professional ethics, when circuit judges were sensitive to conflicts of interest raised in the Haynsworth nomination and resentful of Chief Justice Warren's attempt to impose standards of financial disclosure on lower federal courts (but not the Supreme Court) with little consultation, a certain ambiguity reigned over appropriate relations with the external community.[37] Their de facto power led some judges to feel the more popular contact the better.[38] ("If a judge wants to eat veal cutlets and sing at Rotary meetings, let's let him.") Others, cloistered for the same reason, were attracted to Charles de Gaulle's axiom: the general dines alone.

Though more latitude surfaced among these judges about civic than political or professional relations, their responses further illustrate the expected strength of professional and organizational values in the normative structure of intermediate courts. Partisan political activity, once heavily engaged in and often essential to selection, is forbidden. Participation in professional organizations is permissible. Politicking for lawyers' causes, such as staffing or improving federal courts—like their own recruitment—lies somewhere between. Leadership in bar activities is also more acceptable than leadership in civic organizations. Marginal disagreements and occasional breaches apart, the expectation that circuit judges would bring to office common understandings of their roles in the community, understandings heavily laden with professional ethics, is borne out by their perceptions of relevant others and appropriate relations with fellow citizens. For all the transformation of judicial functions in the modern state, the symbiosis of professionalism and judging was too strong to make much dent in the way circuit judges saw their world.

## Conclusions

"Complete freedom—unfettered and undirected—," Benjamin N. Cardozo once reminded judges, "there never is. . . . The inscrutable force of professional opinion presses upon us like the atmosphere, though we are heedless of its weight."[39] Having seen in the last chapter how deeply professional experiences affected the selection and training of circuit judges, we now find that members of the three intermediate courts learned their lessons well. Professional and official ideologies permeated their perceptions of judicial duty. Regardless of differences over priorities, these judges were united by a common understanding that the central mission of circuit courts is to adjudicate appeals as agents of the national government. They differentiated their jobs from other federal courts in common ways. Nationalism and *stare decisis* were fundamental premises of decision.

Each premise of decision, to be sure, was qualified by competing considerations. The judges not only felt obliged to obey the Supreme Court but also to assist in legal growth, and their psychic independence was probably too strong for frequent rule by anticipated reactions. They identified themselves with a national community, though these allegiances were tempered by institutional separation and regional reference groups, especially in the South. Informal norms are national in scope but regionally enforced. In the crosswinds of office and constituencies, Courts of Appeals may mediate cultural values—national and local, professional and political—in federal appeals.

Otherwise, professionalism tended to offset recognition of courts in between as regional power centers. The judges differed little in evaluating the major components and clienteles of their craft or the proper extent of their contact with the surrounding community. Broadly speaking, they were more sensitive to constituent parts of the appellate process—litigants, judges, counsel—than to the external objects of judicial power. Colleagues and lawyers in each circuit remained their primary reference groups in the teeth of changing public functions and widening audiences. These elements of the legal profession, accordingly, would be expected to have substantial sway over judges' innovations in rules of law and in court reform.

Harmony hardly prevailed, of course, amid great changes in the work of federal courts. Tensions flourished between the priorities of making decisions and accounting for them as well as between processing cases and making policy. A major question is how these differences affected adjudication. As we turn to conflict and its resolution on Courts of Appeals, nevertheless, it is well to remember the central baseline. The work of Courts of Appeals is subject to moral rule. By virtue of related processes of recruitment, socialization, and professionalization, circuit judges were sensitive to both professional norms and political realities in keeping with the duality of their governmental functions. For all the flux in their functions, conflict among them occurred within a basic accord, heavily influenced by official and professional norms, absorbed en route to office, concerning the purposes and clienteles of appellate adjudication.

Drawing by Handelsman; © 1971. The New Yorker Magazine, Inc.

# Six · Judicial Values and Judicial Votes

The sharpest conflicts among members of the three tribunals concerned judicial lawmaking. Time and again they raised this classic problem of appellate jurisprudence, and their answers to specific questions demonstrated that the controversy over judicial activism in the modern Supreme Court has enveloped Courts of Appeals. The appropriate limits on judicial creativity—to one judge "the stinking question"—was a major point of contention in their decision-making roles.

It is easy to understand why. Judicial legislation, however responsive to sluggish political institutions, collides with two leading principles of American government: separation of powers and popular representation in lawmaking. Innovation in lower courts also aggravates problems of harmonizing national law, not to mention the effectiveness of courts as instruments of social policy.[1] How to reconcile the interests of legal growth and stability without stifling justice or transforming adjudication in the process is an enduring challenge to the legal order.[2]

Long debated is whether judges' philosophies of the judicial function actually guide their decisions or merely rationalize personal policy preferences.[3] In this chapter we shall focus on the issue of judicial innovation against a backdrop of the political values of circuit judges. Specifically, we shall consider: (1) how members of the three courts viewed the permissible range of lawmaking discretion, (2) the relations of their role conceptions to their professed political orientations before becoming federal judges, and (3) the extent to which both sets of attitudes, taken as indicators of political and professional ideologies, affected voting outcomes in selected fields of public policy. To supplement the evidence, we shall correlate certain background characteristics of the judges—social class origins, political party affiliations, and prior judicial experience—with their role concepts and voting behavior. The analysis of values and votes, though riddled with methodological land mines and bound by time and place, addresses a central issue in the theory of judicial decision—are judges' prescriptions causes or covers of their performance?—in the context of dual legal and political functions in American government.

## The Limits of Judicial Innovation

Role conflicts among American legislators appear to center on the purposes of representation.[4] Appellate judges tend to be strained more by their functions as legislators.[5] Members of the three Courts of Appeals, especially in the 5th and D.C. circuits, were no exception. Yet, it is critical to understand that these federal circuit judges differed over issues of degree rather than kind.[6] Unlike some members of state supreme courts, virtually all of them agreed that lawmaking was inherent in their jobs. While bold renovations of law like *Brown v. Board of Education* should be left to the Supreme Court or Congress, *stare decisis* was "not an unbreakable rule."[a][7] Within these extremes, their responses to questions about the propriety of judicial innovation fell into three broad groupings along a continuum which for convenience will be summarized in Table 6.1 as ideal types.[b]

### Innovator

Five judges left the impression that they felt obliged to make law "whenever the opportunity occurs." Creative opportunities were usually described as legal vacuums created by unclear precedents, unanticipated situations, and political stalemates. In aiding the Supreme Court, innovators also emphasized their filtering or gatekeeping functions less than their experimentation. As one senior circuit judge declared:

> The Supreme Court cannot be expected to be supermen. The Courts of Appeals should take a definite lead in innovating in the law—even at the risk of being overruled. Of course, we've got to be cautious, but we shouldn't leave it to the Supreme

---

[a] A typical example was this reaction by a southern judge: "If you mean by innovation radical departures from existing law, my feeling is to sit tight. But I mean that in a limited way. Practically every sitting judge has a case in which to some extent we're plowing new ground. That's why the term 'activist' is so difficult; it covers such a wide spectrum of degrees. Any court doing its job has to be an activist court. We have to face up to change and the necessities of life. We have to cut and trim the law to meet them, and we do it every time we sit. If you're thinking of revolutionary changes like *Brown v. Board of Education*, that's different. I'd leave that to the Supreme Court. On our court, some judges feel we should advise the Justices . . . but they have had little success. [Laughter]"

[b] Role perceptions were inferred from the judges' responses to open-ended and structured questions, including the following query about innovation: "Some people think circuit judges should be legal innovators, thus illuminating issues for the Supreme Court; others argue that circuit judges should merely apply the law, leaving legal innovations to legislatures and the Supreme Court. What do you think?"

TABLE 6.1
*Attitude toward Judicial Lawmaking*

| Circuit | Innovator N | Realist N | Interpreter N | Other N | Total N |
|---|---|---|---|---|---|
| 2d | 0 | 8 | 1 | 1 | 10 |
| 5th | 2 | 9 | 6 | 0 | 17 |
| D.C. | 3 | 3 | 2 | 0 | 8 |
| Sums | 5 | 20 | 9 | 1 | 35 |

Court.... Courts of Appeals are a laboratory to try out ideas on a regional basis.

The most unqualified expression of this view came from a jurist who considered the best part of the job to be "launching new ideas." "The formal checks and balances system most people talk about is a naive notion," he argued. "That isn't the way the checks work. If one branch pulls too hard, the others pull less and vice versa." Did this mean that circuit courts participate in policy formation? "Certainly," he said. "And the greatest abuse of power is failure to exercise it."

Innovators lauded such judicial initiatives as the *Durham* rule in Washington and the Jefferson County school case in the South.[8] ("People say it was legislative. It was.") Even though the 2d circuit sponsored policy initiatives during the same period, none of its judges espoused such ambitious notions of circuit authority. As predicted from the politics of recruitment, the 2d circuit was the most cohesive, and the D.C. circuit the least, on issues of judicial originality.

*Interpreter*

At the opposite pole were nine judges, mostly southerners, who emphasized that judicial lawmaking should be held to a minimum. Two judges, harboring a "phobia" against "the modern trend of judicial legislation," bitterly denounced jurists who "can't wait for the people's representatives; they must seize power for themselves." "Activism," a term the interviewer avoided, was a favorite pejorative, which one judge defined as follows:

> It means 15 percent concentration on personal justice, about 20 percent on sociological values, 20 percent on psychiatry, 15 percent on economics, and on through the social sciences. An activist is a kind of Leonardo, a master of many crafts. Non-

activists believe courts are confined to the law of cases. I am a nonactivist, which means of course that I am a reactionary. I believe courts should confine themselves to legal problems. You know where that places me on the animal farm, among progressive sheep and reactionary goats.

Only one judge unqualifiedly endorsed the view that judges should merely interpret the law, a traditional conception of judicial duty still prominent on several state supreme courts and trial courts.[9] Recognizing that lacunae inevitably occur in statutes and case law, these judges objected most to courts legislating "beyond the case." Almost a paradigm of modern "strict constructionism" was this soliloquy from a Nixon appointee:

> I certainly do have views on that. There is a lawmaking power in every judge, whether he likes it or not. It is inescapable. You can't just leave the law blank because Congress did. To that extent the judges fill in the gaps to determine the rights of parties and get on to decisions. You can't be a pink funk and do nothing!
>
> However [with emphasis], the judge should avoid this process whenever possible. He should leave innovation within the confines of the particular case and leave wholesale innovation to the legislature, where Madison said it should be left. . . . Some judges just go way out of line beyond the case. . . . This is a great hazard in circuit work, deciding in the ambit of one case unrelated things without realizing it. It's a grand forum, you know. The opinions get printed. Lawyers have to read them. Some judges just can't resist temptation. I call it diarrhea of the pen.

*Realist*

Almost two-thirds of these circuit judges, including the majority of the 5th circuit and all but one member of the 2d circuit, took hybrid positions, recognizing more demands for judicial creativity than interpreters and more restraints than innovators. Like innovators, realists saw no conflict with *stare decisis* when precedent is absent or ambiguous. Pragmatic problem solvers, willing to fill power vacuums, they sometimes viewed the issue of inadequate appellate capacity as a reflex of legislative atrophy. ("Judges legislate when Congress abdicates." "Suppose Congress doesn't legislate. I wish Congress would legislate!")[c] On the other hand, like interpreters,

---

[c] Typical were these comments from the 5th and 2d circuits: "We have no right to get way out and experiment with our social theories; but by the same token, in the climate of today, we must interpret so as to give life to the law. Then I am an

realists cautioned against anticipating the Justices and emphasized "the professional way" of initiating legal change. What distinguished realists most from the other judges was their common tendency, when acknowledging legislative responsibilities, to differentiate carefully various types of judicial lawmaking and appropriate occasions for innovation. For example, some judges saw more room for creativity in civil rights or torts than in commercial law, in which the advantages of planning and stable rules outweighed those of change. The conservatism of the 2d circuit was attributed in part to its heavy commercial docket. A few judges, following Karl N. Llewellyn, stressed the innovative potential of "shaping the rules to the facts." Others, shading close to interpreters, believed that judicial policy making should be restricted to the Judicial Conference and the Supreme Court's power to define procedural rules. Conceding that "there are degrees and gradations in lawmaking by judges, that every time judges interpret a statute I suppose they leave an imprint on the law, one way or another," one senior judge criticized the Supreme Court for going "too far, too fast" in reforming criminal justice. "They ought to do it by the rule-making power—the established procedures for judicial influence," he said. "*Miranda* was in process by the rule-making power. The Supreme Court jumped the gun."

This summary scarcely captures the subtlety with which these jurists pondered the dilemmas of lawmaking by intermediate courts in a federal republic. But it helps to delimit the problems of relating roles and behavior in circuit courts. On the one hand, these men plainly shared what Chief Justice Burger has called a "basic divergence between two schools of thought among professors, lawyers and judges as to the proper role of judges," a divergence ranging from emphasis on precedent and the status quo to innovation and policy making.[10] On the other hand, sophisticated about the

---

innovator—when precedent is no longer usable. I am not an 'activist.' I don't like the word. But I'm trying to be practical. The Constitution was written when men were powdered and wore knee britches. If they wore that today, they would be arrested. Yet the broad principles of the Constitution are still applicable. We should innovate, but we have no right to rewrite the Constitution or clear statutes to suit our personal views of how law ought to be. We have arguments about that in conference, especially when words are clear."

"You ask me two questions. (1) Anticipating overrulings. That's not a very profitable enterprise unless the occasion for it is patent. That is rare. (2) Innovation. There are different kinds of innovation. Often it is a brand new problem. That is no violation of *stare decisis*. No one has faced the question before. You have to innovate in those cases. In other cases, waiting for the legislature is not productive. The legislature doesn't legislate. Courts have had to do a good deal of stuff that would be better for the legislature to have done. But it's better for courts to do them than no one."

melding of modern judicial functions, they differed over issues of degree within a relatively narrow range of creative opportunities. Despite a robust commitment to rendering justice in individual cases, observed in the last chapter, nearly all of them felt strongly constrained by the norms of *stare decisis*. This is evident in their evaluations of various elements of decision, summarized in Tables 6.2 and 6.3. Adherence to precedent commanded the allegiance of the overwhelming majority. Common sense, an elusive "situation sense" not free from subjectivity, was also valued highly.[11]

TABLE 6.2
Precedent Orientations in Decision Making

|  | Very Important N | Moderately Important N | Not Important N | Other/ Unknown N | Total N |
|---|---|---|---|---|---|
| Precedent, when clear and relevant | 32 | 2 | 0 | 1 | 35 |
| Common sense | 27 | 6 | 0 | 2 | 35 |
| Personal views of justice in the case | 17 | 14 | 2 | 2 | 35 |
| Respect for judge below | 6 | 23 | 5 | 1 | 35 |
| Public needs and demands | 6 | 14 | 11 | 4 | 35 |
| Anticipated response of Supreme Court | 4 | 15 | 13 | 3 | 35 |
| Precedent, when unclear and uncertain | 2 | 21 | 11 | 1 | 35 |

NOTE: The question was: "In reaching decisions how influential are these factors?"

Even when precedents are clear, however, tension exists between law in place and justice in the case, as Table 6.2 reflects. This conflict sharpens considerably when legal rules are uncertain. In those situations, though most judges still ranked as "very important" the closest circuit rulings, Table 6.3 shows that precedent and the dictates of justice were at a standoff. In neither situation was the anticipated Supreme Court response rated as important as the needs of public policy. Nor did many judges concede the relevance of public opinion. Searching for justice in adjudication, no matter how legislative in effect, was not considered a representative function. Considering the relative rarity of reversal by the Supreme Court or

TABLE 6.3
Unclear Precedents in Decision Making

|  | Very Important N | Moderately Important N | Not Important N | Other/ Unknown N | Total N |
|---|---|---|---|---|---|
| Dictates of justice | 26 | 6 | 0 | 3 | 35 |
| Closest precedent in circuit | 24 | 9 | 0 | 2 | 35 |
| Needs of public policy | 18 | 11 | 3 | 3 | 35 |
| Closest precedent in any circuit | 6 | 25 | 2 | 2 | 35 |
| Views of court's most expert member | 6 | 18 | 8 | 3 | 35 |
| Decision of most prestigious court | 5 | 19 | 7 | 4 | 35 |
| Anticipated response of Supreme Court | 4 | 16 | 11 | 4 | 35 |
| Public opinion | 1 | 8 | 22 | 4 | 35 |

NOTE: The question was: "When precedents are absent or ambiguous, what do you do? Please rank the following factors according to which you are most likely to follow in this situation."

Congress, circuit judges, as noted before, approached lawmaking via adjudication with substantial intellectual independence.

Whether precedent appears clear or cloudy, needless to say, is a matter of individual vision, and abstract recollections are not the same as action. Yet most of these jurists agreed that, lacking docket control, their opportunity to fashion new legal rules seldom exceeds a tenth of their cases. This estimate has changed little over time.[d] Claims calling for creativity are apparently offset by burgeoning routine. Though individuals may differ as to what cases properly constitute the fertile tenth, these judges felt obliged to lead as well as

[d] These estimates, based on total caseloads, are smaller than those in the literature of jurisprudence which presume that appeals are limited to cases involving uncertain rules of law. Judge Charles E. Clark once estimated that 70% of circuit cases could be decided only one way, 10% called for Cardozo's method of social values, and 20% were of certain outcome, but "counsel might be forgiven for thinking they had a bare chance of success."[12]

Surprisingly, innovators in this study did *not* give higher estimates of creative opportunity than the others, though one innovator did complain that "one of the troubles with this job is that it is only 10%." [Why?] "For several reasons. (1) Interest declines through the years. (2) I'm older. You lose your reformist fires. It's inevitable. I can't take sitting up until 4:00 A.M. stewing over a problem like I used to."

to follow. By virtue of their training and functions, they were more imbued with the teachings of legal realism, more in the middle concerning their duty to legislate, than contemporaries in state appellate courts or trial courts.[13] Hence, their conflicts over judicial lawmaking are inadequately caught by such popular dichotomies as activism versus restraint, or the so-called objective role of adherence to precedent versus subjective preference.[14] For them as for Chief Justice Burger, "the question is perhaps more one of pace and timing, not essentially one of function."[15] Just as no single tradition of representation links congressmen with constituencies, so judicial duty was perceived in these Courts of Appeals as a mixture of elements and leanings.[16] The real issue is how they combine in an estimated tenth of the cases in which circuit judges confront gaps in the law.

Because circuit judges are called upon to reconcile values of continuity and change in adjudication, usually in advance of the Justices and with little assurance that their mistakes will be corrected, tension is inherent in their positions. Strain among expectations *within* a role perhaps characterizes their situation better than does the concept of conflict *between* roles.[17] In any event, ambiguity of appropriate limits on lawmaking by intermediate courts softens the control of received interpretations and elevates the significance of situational factors in decision making. *Stare decisis* is thus an "open norm," to use Richard Lempert's term, which cannot specify precise forms of action in all cases.[18] When norms are open to further specification, individuals or groups can establish socially approved rules of conduct of greater particularity.[e] That is why these jurists often illustrated their disputes over lawmaking with specific policy issues, such as criminal responsibility in the D.C. circuit or civil rights in the 5th circuit, in which policy conflicts were sharp and the law in flux. That is also why the socialization of circuit judges and the politics of their selection are vital in understanding their expectations as sponsors of legal change. When judges are free to choose, personalities, predilections, and group relations perforce fill the

---

[e] Justice Holmes, for instance, made dissent respectable. The cohesive role structure of the 2d circuit illustrates the capacity of a group to "resocialize" members of diverse backgrounds and political values. Consider these remarks of a self-styled former "liberal-radical": "All of us have personal views on that. *It is a personal matter.* I'm a law judge rather than an innovating judge myself. Let me stress that, of course, it's a matter of emphasis. I have initiated a number of en bancs to change past decisions. But the court as a whole is not an innovating court. It is oriented toward applying the law as it stands. It's a matter of emphasis; we consciously leave it to the Supreme Court. We'd rather that they overrule us than we overrule them. The matter comes up frequently. It's a general attitude on our court."

void. Open or ambiguous roles inevitably enlarge the personal discretion of judges.

## Political and Professional Values

What then guides a circuit judge's conception of judicial duty when rules and roles are unclear? Of the welter of factors that may bear on this issue—psychological, social, institutional—we shall focus on political and professional values. Both are central to popular theories of adjudication. According to political interpretations, judicial decisions are heavily influenced by the political philosophies that judges bring to the bench. *Stare decisis* is more personal than institutional, and legal formulas mask value judgments latent in judicial choices.[19] In traditional legal theory, contrarily, professional norms shield judges' decisions from policy and other personal preferences so that results conform to law. Professional discipline thus serves as a surrogate medium of accountability, accommodating judicial power with popular rule.[20]

The trouble with these formulations is that the political and professional values of judges are not mutually exclusive. In keeping with the duality of their backgrounds and missions, both sets of attitudes among these circuit judges tended to be complementary. In plumbing the sources of role conceptions, we find intriguing associations between the judges' political orientations before ascending the bench and their attitudes toward judicial lawmaking. Though other background factors and judicial attitudes overlapped as well, the strongest links were political in character.

These impressions arise initially from juxtaposing three clusters of background characteristics—social, professional, and political—with the judges' attitudes toward judicial lawmaking. Though each characteristic is reported independently in Tables 6.4-6.6, they are assumed to be related and their effects cumulative. Their interaction will be considered later; for now it suffices to call attention to a few high points on the surface of the terrain.

Social backgrounds, of the three sets of indicators, were weakest in relation to judges' role concepts. Table 6.4 shows no notable association between urban upbringing or class origins and attitudes toward judicial legislation. The numbers are too small to prove that Catholic and Jewish judges drifted toward innovative positions, as one might expect from other studies of political elites.[21]

Somewhat stronger were connections between role perceptions and professional backgrounds in Table 6.5. Most innovators attended "prestige" law schools, where legal realism flourishes. Most interpreters did not. Most innovators and interpreters were recruited

### TABLE 6.4
### Social Backgrounds of Circuit Judges and Attitudes toward Judicial Lawmaking

| Social Background | Attitudes toward Judicial Lawmaking | | | |
|---|---|---|---|---|
| | Innovator (5) N | Realist (20) N | Interpreter (9) N | Total (35)* N |
| *Upbringing* | | | | |
| Urban | 3 | 12 | 4 | 20* |
| Nonurban | 2 | 8 | 5 | 15 |
| *Social class* | | | | |
| Upper/upper-middle | 1 | 6 | 2 | 9 |
| Middle | 1 | 9 | 3 | 14* |
| Lower/lower-middle | 1 | 3 | 1 | 5 |
| Other/unknown | 2 | 2 | 3 | 7 |
| *Religion* | | | | |
| Protestant | 2 | 14 | 7 | 23 |
| Catholic | 1 | 2 | 1 | 5* |
| Jewish | 1 | 4 | 0 | 5 |
| None/unknown | 1 | 0 | 1 | 2 |

* Includes one unscorable response.

### TABLE 6.5
### Professional Backgrounds of Circuit Judges and Attitudes toward Judicial Lawmaking

| Professional Background | Attitudes toward Judicial Lawmaking | | | |
|---|---|---|---|---|
| | Innovator (5) N | Realist (20) N | Interpreter (9) N | Total (35)* N |
| *Legal education* | | | | |
| Prestige law school | 4 | 10 | 3 | 18* |
| Other | 1 | 10 | 6 | 17 |
| *Last occupation* | | | | |
| U.S district judge | 0 | 10 | 3 | 14* |
| U.S. attorney | 1 | 2 | 1 | 4 |
| Private practice/academic | 4 | 8 | 5 | 17 |
| *Tenure as circuit judge* | | | | |
| 1-5 years | 0 | 7 | 4 | 11 |
| 5-10 years | 1 | 7 | 3 | 11 |
| 10-15 years | 0 | 2 | 1 | 4* |
| Over 15 years | 4 | 4 | 1 | 9 |

* Includes one unscorable response.

from private or academic careers, most realists from other federal posts. It is significant that no former U.S. district judge espoused a highly innovative view of his job. Prior training and judicial service, as bar associations maintain, may instill in appellate judges the creed of judicial restraint.

However, the political indicators in Table 6.6, including political party affiliation, participation, and orientations prior to appointment, do not permit a conclusion that professionalism preempted politics in federal courthouses. Instead, as suggested by the judges' backgrounds as political lawyers, their attitudes and experiences overlapped. For example, four of the five innovators were Democrats with lengthy tenure, three of them appointed by Presidents Roosevelt and Truman. All but one interpreter was a Republican or a southern Democrat. Few circuit judges at the extreme ends in role perceptions had significant electoral exposure. The most active former politicians, contrary to lawyers' myths, did *not* become judicial activists. Except for our constant maverick, an interpreter, former professional politicians gravitated toward moderate and realist positions, just like former district judges. Behavior comported with attitudes, moreover. The most activist circuit judges, measured either in terms of propensity to disturb decisions or of antigovernment results, were former bureaucrats and private practitioners. Facing either electorates or litigants across the bench apparently tempered attitudes toward appellate power in these Courts of Appeals.

The most intriguing association was between the judges' political orientations before appointment and their attitudes toward judicial lawmaking. Though the relationships are weaker than those found by John T. Wold in the supreme courts of New York and Virginia, the dotted squares in Table 6.6 indicate that political and professional outlooks were congruent.[22] Four of the five innovators identified themselves as having been political liberals before becoming federal judges; only one of nine interpreters did so. The most ardent innovator called himself a former political conservative, perhaps as a joke. Otherwise, the large majority were men in the middle, self-styled moderates before becoming jurists, who likewise straddled the conflict over lawmaking.

The fuzziness of both political and role categories, let alone the small number of judges involved, warns against pushing attitudinal associations very far. Compatible attitudes do not prove that philosophies of the judicial function are berobed political ideologies. Nevertheless, these jurists tended to favor conceptions of judicial duty in accord with their prior political convictions. Hardly surprising given the realities of their recruitment, this connection is an important bridge between personal values and the judicial proc-

## Table 6.6
### Political Backgrounds of Circuit Judges and Attitudes toward Judicial Lawmaking

| Political Background | Attitudes toward Judicial Lawmaking | | | |
|---|---|---|---|---|
| | Innovator (5) N | Realist (20) N | Interpreter (9) N | Total (35)* N |
| *Political party affiliation* | | | | |
| Democrat | 4 | 13 | 4 | 22* |
| Republican | 1 | 6 | 4 | 11 |
| Other | 0 | 1 | 1 | 2 |
| *Political participation* | | | | |
| Voter only | 0 | 3 | 2 | 5 |
| Party worker | 0 | 2 | 3 | 5 |
| Party official | 3 | 6 | 1 | 10 |
| Candidate** | 2 | 9 | 3 | 15* |
| *Political values before appointment* | | | | |
| Conservative | 1 | 0 | 3 | 4 |
| Moderate | 0 | 11 | 4 | 16* |
| Moderate-liberal | 1 | 0 | 1 | 2 |
| Liberal | 3 | 5 | 0 | 8 |
| Other | 0 | 4 | 1 | 5 |

\* Includes one unscorable response.
\*\* Includes 1 innovator and 2 realists who were candidates for party posts only.

ess. Because the socialization of American judges is largely informal and anticipatory, as we saw in Chapter Four, their perceptions of judicial roles are likely to interact with their prior political beliefs, developed from the same antecedent experiences. The distinction between politics and law, so prominent in professional ideologies, tends to blur among those who staff Courts of Appeals. Their philosophies of politics and the judicial function, notwithstanding official efforts to separate the two, are entwined in resolving and rationalizing the normative ambiguities of their work. And in that entwining may lie glue of unsuspected strength in a national system of law.

### Values and Votes

The proof of the pudding is whether political values and role conceptions affect adjudication. Historically, the conduct of appellate judges supplied sufficient evidence for most observers to take the general relationships for granted. Yet, social scientists contend over relative weights, that is, whether political predispositions and job prescriptions should be conceived of as independent, intervening, or dependent variables in the theory of judicial decision.[23] In the jargon of the trade, is judging "political behavior" or "judicial role behavior"?

The reader should keep in mind the many pitfalls confronting efforts to answer this question. Theoretically, a person's political self-images and role perceptions are but single aspects of a vast cognitive network, which may be rooted in the irrational.[24] Even discounting disparities between what people say and think, a direct relationship is seldom to be expected among an individual's social roles, role concepts, and conduct.[25]

Methodological snares inhibit the discovery of links. The most formidable are subjectivity in classifications; a multiplicity of competing variables (e.g., collegial decision making or personality) mediating between general attitudes and specific choices; and the lack of transitivity among aggregated votes.[26] Panel techniques were used to reduce the bias in inferred role perceptions, but disagreement among the author and two assistants regarding six of thirty-five judges on both margins of the realist category indicates that standardization of terms remains a serious problem in judicial role analysis. Similarly, self-estimates of political orientations eliminated neither regional differences nor the vagaries of recall. Problematic as well is the assumption that votes accurately mirror individual attitudes on collegial courts, where give and take is also expected.[27] More troublesome is violating the principle of transitivity (i.e., that all judges participated in the same cases) for purposes of aggregation in rotating courts.[28] Even though we are dealing with over 5,000 votes, relaxation of transitivity standards became necessary because panel rotation and low dissent rates in these tribunals yielded frequencies too small for conventional analysis of variance among different subjects and individuals. Finally, the difficulty of objectively isolating the cases that comprised the creative opportunities of circuit judges precluded testing of judicial attitudes toward innovation in exclusively lawmaking situations.

Political orientations and role perceptions, like most analytical constructs, are riddled with oversimplification. Still, for exploratory purposes, it is useful to establish whether different political and professional predispositions affected aggregate performance on the bench. Ideally the test should be whether judicial role conceptions shielded judicial votes from political values in lawmaking situations, as in Figure 6.1. Since we cannot objectively isolate lawmaking situations, we shall invert the hypothesis and test whether judges' prior political outlooks and attitudes toward judicial innovation were related to their voting behavior *defined politically*, as in Figure 6.2. Presumably, different role conceptions that were consis-

FIGURE 6.1
A Professional Model of Judicial Decision Making

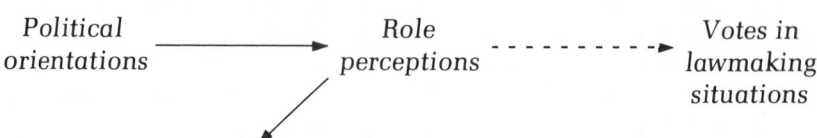

tent with divergent policy results did not block political values from these decisions, as traditional legal theory suggests, but interacted with them. Evidence of interaction would buttress the theme of overlapping socialization and value systems, developed in Chapter Four and Table 6.6, in keeping with the duality of court functions in modern American society.[29] Interaction also would support the notion that judicial role perceptions serve as intervening variables or cues regulating when policy values appropriately may enter decision.[30]

FIGURE 6.2
A Political Model of Judicial Decision Making

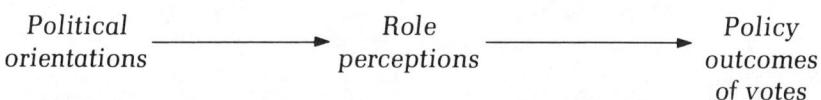

For these purposes we shall examine relations among the judges' values and votes in three ways: simple correlations, multivariate analysis in which each variable is controlled and their interaction assessed, and a supplementary, multivariate analysis of the effects of judicial background characteristics on voting outcomes.

First, the judges' political orientations and attitudes toward judicial lawmaking will be correlated with the policy outcomes of their votes in selected subjects. Of course, few concepts in the American political lexicon are more elusive than "liberal" and "conservative." While these jurists readily classified their prior political values on a liberal-conservative continuum, they often affirmed common observations that neither label describes a unitary ideology but rather a cluster of attitudes toward different subjects.³¹ To capture some of this complexity, broad policy fields are differentiated in Tables 6.7 and 6.8, which compare the political orientations and role perceptions of these jurists with the outcome of their votes during 1965-1967. The political hypotheses, following Nagel, Vines, and Glick, are that self-styled former liberals, more than other political animals who became circuit judges, would tend to favor workers in employee-injury cases and claimants in other personal injury cases while opposing claimants in patent and copyright suits.³² Similarly, self-styled former liberals would tend to defer to the NLRB and the government in income tax litigation while supporting individuals in civil rights controversies, prisoner petitions, and criminal cases. Conversely, self-styled conservatives would resolve doubts in opposite directions.

The distribution of votes in Table 6.7 lends little support to these hypotheses. The proportions of liberal voting were virtually the same across the political spectrum. Nor were different political orientations statistically significant when correlated with mean percentages of liberal voting per judge, a procedure that preserves differences among individuals.ᶠ Within separate policy fields, no strong differences emerged in criminal justice. Political orientations were statistically significant in "other personal injury" and civil rights, but the associations were not strong.ᵍ While the direction of voting conformed to expectations in three fields—employee injuries, income tax, and civil rights—only the civil rights correlations ($\gamma$ = .194) were noteworthy. In civil rights self-styled former liberals favored individuals against governments more than did self-styled conservatives by almost a three-to-one margin.

ᶠ "Other" judges, plus one moderate with only 9 votes, were omitted from the following distribution of liberal votes:

|  | Mean % | Standard Deviation % | Total Votes N |
|---|---|---|---|
| Conservative (N = 3) | 41.0 | 14.1 | 531 |
| Moderate (N = 12) | 39.6 | 8.3 | 2,471 |
| Moderate-liberal and liberal (N = 10) | 42.1 | 4.1 | 2,101 |

Using the two-sample difference of means test, the null hypothesis of sameness could not be rejected for the following political categories: conservative/moderate (df 13, t = 0.207, p > .10); moderate/moderate-liberal and liberal (df 20, t = 0.803, p > .10); and conservative/moderate and moderate-liberal (df 11, t = 0.201, p > .10).³³

ᵍ Though a one-sample $\chi^2$ test may not be strictly appropriate when a hypothesis takes order into account, the values are given in Tables 6.7 and 6.8. Both liberal and nonliberal votes are included in computations of $\chi^2$ and gamma. The "other" column is omitted.³⁴

TABLE 6.7
Political Orientations of Circuit Judges and Votes in Selected Subjects
FY 1965-1967

| | Political Orientations before Becoming Federal Judges | | | | | | | | | | | |
|---|---|---|---|---|---|---|---|---|---|---|---|---|
| | Liberal (8) Votes | | Moderate-Liberal (2) Votes | | Moderate (13) Votes | | Conservative (3) Votes | | Other (5) Votes | | Total (31) Votes | |
| Subject | % | (N) | % | (N) | % | (N) | % | (N) | % | (N) | % | (N) |
| Employee injury, pro-employee | 66.3 | (95) | 61.7 | (60) | 53.8 | (143) | 48.6 | (35) | 59.7 | (62) | 58.5 | (395) | $\chi^2 = 5.33, p > .10$; $\gamma = .135$
| Other personal injury, pro-claimant | 39.4 | (109) | 64.7 | (51) | 45.5 | (198) | 48.9 | (43) | 42.4 | (59) | 46.1 | (460) | $\chi^2 = 9.21, p < .05$; $\gamma = (-).098$
| Patent and copyright, anti-claimant | 59.6 | (57) | 39.1 | (23) | 66.7 | (96) | 73.3 | (15) | 64.0 | (25) | 62.0 | (216) | $\chi^2 = 6.95, p > .05$; $\gamma = (-).066$
| Labor-management, defer to agency | 60.3 | (146) | 55.9 | (68) | 63.6 | (228) | 58.8 | (51) | 61.8 | (55) | 61.1 | (548) | $\chi^2 = 1.53, p > .50$; $\gamma = (-).002$
| Income tax, pro-government | 76.6 | (141) | 75.0 | (76) | 70.2 | (218) | 69.0 | (42) | 63.0 | (54) | 71.8 | (531) | $\chi^2 = 2.44, p > .30$; $\gamma = .078$
| Civil rights, pro-individual | 62.7 | (118) | 60.0 | (60) | 53.5 | (172) | 23.3 | (30) | 54.2 | (48) | 54.9 | (428) | $\chi^2 = 15.75, p < .003$; $\gamma = .194$
| Prisoner petitions, pro-individual | 25.2 | (333) | 25.4 | (130) | 28.2 | (522) | 28.3 | (92) | 24.5 | (106) | 26.7 | (1,183) | $\chi^2 = 1.17, p > .70$; $\gamma = (-).037$
| Criminal pro-individual | 24.2 | (458) | 19.3 | (176) | 23.7 | (894) | 29.6 | (223) | 18.4 | (201) | 23.6 | (1,952) | $\chi^2 = 6.39, p > .05$; $\gamma = (-).036$
| Sums | 41.5 | (1,457) | 43.0 | (644) | 39.7 | (2,471) | 39.0 | (531) | 38.5 | (610) | 40.3 | (5,713) | |

NOTE: $\gamma$ = Goodman-Kruskal gamma, df 3.

The data may be too weak to prove the absence of a relationship between political ideologies and voting behavior, but they are strong enough to cast doubt on a common view that circuit decisions are dominated by the past political predispositions of the judges. For all the concern over their predilections during the selection process, broad political differences were not reflected significantly in the judges' votes, except feebly in civil rights.[35]

The relation of judicial role perceptions to voting behavior, albeit stronger, yields similar conclusions. Assuming that attitudes toward judicial innovation and political values were related in circuit decisions, as popularly thought during the era of the Warren Court and implied by the overlapping attitudes shown in Table 6.6, the hypotheses are as follows. Innovators should have been more likely than interpreters to favor workers and claimants in injuries cases, public rights in patent and copyright cases, and the government in NLRB and tax cases.[36] Innovators more than other judges also would be expected to support individuals in civil rights, prisoner petitions, and criminal cases. Interpreters, in turn, would tend to vote in opposite directions, and realists would cluster in the center.

The distribution of votes in Table 6.8 offers moderate support for the proposition that innovators generally were more libertarian in voting behavior than were realists and interpreters. The evidence bolsters confidence especially in the distinction between innovators and interpreters on the outer edges of the continuum. Voting by innovators listed toward "libertarian activism"; interpreters resisted it. Unlike prior political orientations, moreover, differences between innovators and the other judges were statistically significant when role perceptions were compared with mean percentages of liberal voting per judge.[h] Though prisoner petitions and criminal appeals were the only fields to satisfy normal standards of probability, the direction of voting between the two groups of judges followed the liberal-conservative continuum in every field save the ideologically

[h] Cf. notes f and g, this chapter. Two realists with only 22 votes and one unscorable respondent were omitted from the following distribution of liberal voting:

|  | Mean % | Standard Deviation % | Total Votes N |
|---|---|---|---|
| Innovator (N = 5) | 47.3 | 8.0 | 1,042 |
| Realist (N = 17) | 39.7 | 7.4 | 3,259 |
| Interpreter (N = 6) | 36.4 | 5.0 | 1,171 |

Using the two-sample difference of means test, the null hypothesis of sameness could be rejected for the innovator-interpreter comparison (df 9, t = 2.49, p < .025) and for the innovator-realist comparison (df 20, t = 1.89, p < .05), but not for the realist-interpreter distinction (df 21, t = 0.97, p > .10).

amorphous subject of income tax. Moreover, the strongest association between role conceptions and voting behavior occurred precisely in subjects, such as civil rights ($\gamma = .200$) and criminal justice ($\gamma = .282$), in which the judges illustrated their disputes over lawmaking. In criminal appeals innovators favored defendants more than did interpreters by a two-to-one margin. The odds that this occurred by chance were less than one in a thousand.

Granted, judges and cases are not fungible. Given the size of the voting universe and the low levels of dissent in these courts, even these modest relationships are nonetheless among the most positive yet uncovered between judicial role perceptions and aggregate voting behavior.[37]

The biggest surprise is that the judges' role orientations were more consistent with liberal-conservative voting than were their past political attitudes. If a relationship existed between only one set of values and votes, the expected tie would surely be with political rather than with role orientations. After all, voting behavior is defined politically in terms of who wins or loses.[38] Further, if the two sets of values were related, as suggested in Table 6.6, we would expect votes to be, too. Yet, civil rights is the only significant field in which the direction of votes was mutually reinforcing, and even there chance cannot be ruled out as the link with roles. Turning professional theories on their head, are role conceptions rationalizations of political choices? What accounts for the weak association of values and votes in these decisions? Do the anomalies in aggregate behavior contradict earlier impressions that political and professional values interact?

One obvious explanation is that the data reflect well-known vagaries in general categories of political ideology. This problem is accentuated by the tendency of these judges to flock toward the middle. In addition, the two orientations refer to distinguishable values, one to past and more remote political convictions, the other to the permissible scope of judicial lawmaking without reference to specific policies. The voting patterns also aggregate outcomes on a crude liberalism scale, not on the degree or the policy direction of innovation.[39] Lawmaking, as the Burger Court demonstrates, can travel diverse ideological paths.

Closely related is the generality of both evaluative dimensions. Because political orientations and role conceptions are seldom so specific as to command particular decisions, a judge may be an "activist" or a "liberal" in one subject and not another. Some judges confessed to being conservative about property rights and liberal about human rights—and voted accordingly. The scattered associa-

TABLE 6.8
Attitudes toward Judicial Lawmaking and Votes in Selected Subjects, FY 1965-1967

| Subject | Attitudes toward Judicial Lawmaking | | | | | | | | |
|---|---|---|---|---|---|---|---|---|---|
| | Innovator (5) Votes | | Realist (19) Votes | | Interpreter (6) Votes | | Total (30) Votes | | |
| | % | (N) | % | (N) | % | (N) | % | (N) | |
| Employee injury, pro-employee | 63.5 | (52) | 57.8 | (211) | 58.5 | (118) | 58.8 | (381) | $\chi^2 = 0.56, p > .70$ <br> $\gamma = .038$ |
| Other personal injury, pro-claimant | 54.2 | (72) | 44.2 | (265) | 45.2 | (104) | 46.0 | (441) | $\chi^2 = 2.32, p > .30$ <br> $\gamma = .085$ |
| Patent and copyright, anti-claimant | 61.5 | (39) | 65.9 | (129) | 54.3 | (35) | 63.1 | (203) | $\chi^2 = 1.64, p > .30$ <br> $\gamma = .078$ |
| Labor-management, defer to agency | 64.5 | (110) | 61.7 | (311) | 55.5 | (108) | 61.1 | (529) | $\chi^2 = 2.0, p > .30$ <br> $\gamma = .108$ |
| Income tax, pro-government | 69.1 | (94) | 73.9 | (307) | 69.8 | (106) | 72.2 | (507) | $\chi^2 = 1.2, p > .50$ <br> $\gamma = (-).004$ |
| Civil rights, pro-individual | 65.4 | (81) | 57.1 | (238) | 48.4 | (95) | 56.8 | (414) | $\chi^2 = 5.19, p > .05$ <br> $\gamma = .200$ |
| Prisoner petitions, pro-individual | 34.1 | (226) | 25.3 | (688) | 23.3 | (231) | 26.6 | (1,145) | $\chi^2 = 8.29, p < .02$ <br> $\gamma = .153$ |
| Criminal, pro-individual | 35.6 | (368) | 22.0 | (1,132) | 17.1 | (374) | 23.7 | (1,874) | $\chi^2 = 39.6, p < .001$ <br> $\gamma = .282$ |
| Sums | 47.3 | (1,042) | 39.7 | (3,281) | 37.0 | (1,171) | 40.6 | (5,494) | |

NOTE: $\gamma$ = Goodman-Kruskal gamma, df 2.

tions in particular fields buttresses an impression, akin to the conclusions of Miller, Stokes, and other analysts of legislative roll calls, that the effects of ideology may be issue specific.[40]

Simple correlations cannot distinguish cause from coincidence, nor separate the effects of each variable on voting outcomes, controlling for their overlap. To sort out both their independent effects and their interaction, the data were set in two log linear models, one using the same attitudinal variables and the other selected background characteristics. These additive or saturation models, similar to regression analysis, isolate the independent effects of each variable on voting outcomes by controlling for the others; they also measure the interaction among variables.[41]

FIGURE 6.3

A Log Linear Model of the Effects of Political Orientations and Judicial Role Perceptions of Circuit Judges on Voting Outcomes, FY 1965-1967

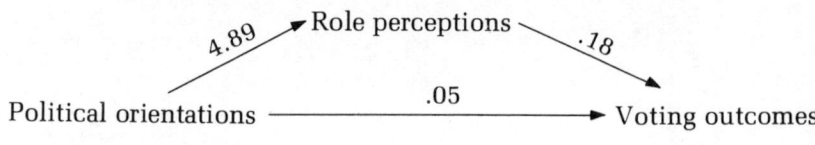

$\chi^2 = 31.5$, df 3, p < .01

The role model, illustrated in Figure 6.3, estimates the effects of political orientations and attitudes toward judicial lawmaking on voting outcomes, as previously defined. For all fields combined, though the lambda coefficients provide no standard scale of judgment, the data bolster the conclusions already reached and add potent evidence of interaction among political and professional values in decision making. As predicted, there was a strong link between the political orientations and role perceptions of these judges ($\lambda = 4.89$). Alone, however, neither variable was a major determinant of liberal-conservative voting behavior. Though each independently affected voting outcomes, their effects were weak and, ironically, stronger for role conceptions ($\lambda = .18$) than for political orientations ($\lambda = .05$). The links between political and professional predispositions of the circuit judges extended to their decisions. The significant chi square here (p < .01) implies that the effects of values on votes were independent of marginal distributions. One of two explanations would account for this result: either interaction among variables within the model or factors external to it. Intuitively, the strong relationship between political and role orientations suggests that political values did affect voting outcomes indirectly by filtering through role perceptions as intervening variables.

At the same time, the effect of these values on votes, taken singly or together, was issue specific. This point is demonstrated in Table 6.9, which deploys the same data by subject matter. The seeming independence of the variables (as in Table 6.8) stems largely from prisoner petitions and criminal justice, since the model "fits" or accounts for voting outcomes in the remaining six fields. In addition, though chance cannot be eliminated entirely, the effects of each variable when others are controlled varied considerably by subject. Political orientations, for instance, outweighed role conceptions in employee injuries and civil rights; role expectations had greater impact in prisoner petitions and criminal justice. To compound the mix, the interactive effects in the two criminal fields were not only stronger than in civil rights but ran in counterlibertarian directions. This indicates that the fusion of political and professional attitudes in voting behavior was not confined to a new breed of liberal innovators but flourished among their conservative-interpreter opponents as well.

Now, a number of alternative explanations could account for these results. Among the leading contenders are circuit influences, personality differences, and such methodological snags as the unfocused attitudes employed and the uneven participation of judges in the cases. Civil rights best illustrate the pull of the group. The 5th circuit dominated the cases, only two of its seventeen judges voting against civil rights more often than not. If we use Robert G. McCloskey's definition of activism as favoring individuals against governments, almost the whole court was activist.[42] By contrast, only one judge outside the 5th circuit voted in favor of civil rights claims more than half the time; and another judge, described by a colleague as "inclined to be activist," actually voted against civil rights claims in all recorded instances. Otherwise, the circuit variable had very weak effects on voting outcomes in the aggregate or in particular fields.[i]

The power of personality is illustrated by the ardent innovator, quoted earlier, who called himself a former political conservative. This judge had the second most libertarian voting record (61%). The

---

[i] Only in civil rights was the circuit variable stronger than attitudinal ones when included in the log linear model, and even that effect was negligible ($\lambda = .10$). In patents, the field of strongest expected effects, the actual impact was nil. Accordingly, the circuit variable was dropped from the model to highlight the interplay among values.

TABLE 6.9
The Effects of Political Orientations and Role Perceptions on Voting Outcomes in Selected Subjects, FY 1965-1967

| Subject | A<br>Political Orientations and Role Perceptions<br>$\lambda$ | B<br>Political Orientations and Voting Outcomes<br>$\lambda$ | C<br>Role Perceptions and Voting Outcomes<br>$\lambda$ | D<br>Probability<br>($\chi^2$, df 3) | E*<br>Interaction of Political Orientations and Role Perceptions on Voting Outcomes<br>$\lambda$ |
|---|---|---|---|---|---|
| Employee injury | 2.58** | .19 | (-).01 | .19 | (-).07 |
| Other personal injury | 2.90** | (-).02 | .22 | .23 | (-).48 |
| Patent and copyright | 2.18** | .03 | .08 | .19 | (-).08 |
| Labor-management | 3.00** | .02 | .07 | .16 | .43 |
| Income tax | 3.15** | .14 | (-).14 | .23 | .29 |
| Civil rights | 2.98** | .33 | .05 | .10 | .06 |
| Prisoner petitions | 3.71** | (-).01 | .31 | <.01 | (-).54 |
| Criminal | 3.94** | .12 | .47 | <.01 | (-).43 |
| Combined subjects | 4.89** | .05 | .18 | <.01 | (-).22 |

* Interaction scores are derived from a separate saturated model in which $\chi^2$ is always zero with a probability of 1.
** Standardized effect is greater than twice the standard deviation.

fact that the political moderate category contained both the highest and second-lowest extremes of so-called liberal voting (64% and 31%) also underscores regional variations in political labels.[j] Consequently, these connections between values and votes no more eliminate regional differences than they refute the Cardozo-Ehrlich caveat that "in the long run 'there is no guaranty of justice . . . except the personality of the judge.' "[43]

This raises the possibility that methodological shortcuts, notably the generality of ideological categories and intransitivity of votes, distorted the results. The variables chosen hardly exhaust the political and professional values that might have affected voting behavior in these courts.[k] The unequal distribution of votes opens the possibility that different combinations of judges dominated voting in separate fields. (The broader the range of coefficients in column A of Table 6.9, the more plausible this becomes.) In that event, discreteness of cases and panels may be the missing trump.

Ultimately, however, both professional and political ideologies should offset the uniqueness of cases and individuals if they have the causal power attributed to them in standard theories of judging. If not, we are left with two leading explanations of voting outcomes which may reduce to the same thing: scattered and overlapping effects of political and professional values in separate fields of public policy or discrete cases and personal preferences. Either interpretation deflates the force of general ideologies and elevates the significance of case situations and panel rotation in the appellate process.

To supplement the evidence for these conclusions, similar techniques were used to estimate the effects of key background characteristics, all prominent in the literature as indicators of judicial values, on voting behavior. These variables, also less subject to criticism for subjectivity and intransitivity, are the judges' social-class origins (self-defined), political party affiliations, and prior judicial experience. The hypotheses are that circuit judges with lower-class origins, Democratic party affiliations, and no prior judicial experience would have a greater tendency to cast liberal votes, as previously defined, than judges of middle- and upper-class origins, Republican party affiliations, and no prior judicial service.[l] [44]

[j] The lowest liberal voting score (28.5%) was registered by a conservative interpreter.

[k] That most role categories are meaningful, however, is supported in note h, this chapter.

[l] See Tables 6.4-6.6. The hypothesis that judges with previous judicial experience would tend to cast nonliberal votes derives from traditional arguments that judging is a conservatizing experience as well as from the findings that no former federal district judge espoused a highly innovative philosophy of the judicial function.

182 · Chapter Six

FIGURE 6.4

A Log Linear Model of the Effects of Class Origins,
Political Party Affiliations, and Prior Judicial
Experience of Circuit Judges on Voting Outcomes, FY 1965-1967

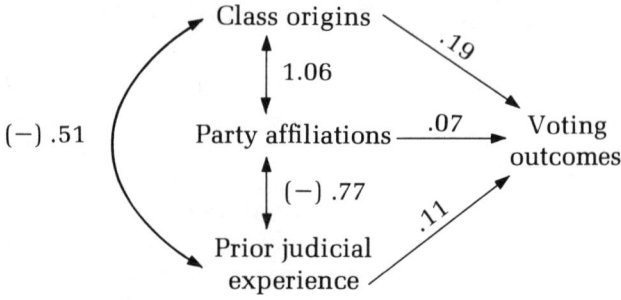

$\chi^2 = 17.29$, df 13, p = 0.20

The results, shown in Figure 6.4 and Table 6.10, counting both liberal and nonliberal votes, reveal a close fit of this model to voting outcomes in most fields. The combined distributions are not statistically significant; in income tax and labor relations the model fits or "explains" variances in voting almost perfectly.[m] Nevertheless, this evidence bolsters the conclusion that the impact of judicial background characteristics on voting outcomes was interactive and issue specific. Only two fields—civil rights and prisoner petitions—were independent of the marginals. No single background characteristic was a strong determinant of voting outcomes across the board. Class origin was the strongest of the three indicators, affecting votes significantly in taxation, prisoner petitions, and criminal justice. Party identification, contrary to other studies, was weakest.[45] Judicial experience, prime filter in the professional canon, significantly affected voting outcomes only in civil rights, where political orientations were at work, too (cf. Tables 6.7 and 6.9).

Interaction among background variables also affected voting in some fields, such as employee injuries, patents, labor relations, and prisoner petitions, but not all of them. Unless attributed to methodological gremlins, the signs from cross-tabulations, multivariate models, and participant interviews, all lead to the same destination: the effects of judicial values on voting outcomes in these tribunals were spasmodic, interactive, and issue specific. Far from

[m] The range of voting participation also was smaller than in the previous model. Compare column A in Table 6.9 with columns A and B in Table 6.10.

TABLE 6.10
The Effects of Selected Background Characteristics of Circuit Judges on Voting Outcomes in Selected Subjects, FY 1965–1967

| Subject | A<br>Class Origins and Party Affiliations<br>λ | B<br>Class Origins and Voting Outcomes<br>λ | C<br>Party Affiliations and Voting Outcomes<br>λ | D<br>Prior Judicial Experience and Voting Outcomes<br>λ | E<br>Probability ($\chi^2$, df 13) | F*<br>Class Origins, Party Affiliations, and Prior Judicial Experience<br>λ | G*<br>Interaction of Class Origins, Party Affiliations, and Prior Judicial Experience on Voting Outcomes<br>λ |
|---|---|---|---|---|---|---|---|
| Employee injury | .66** | .17 | .14 | .15 | .66 | .75** | (−).34** |
| Other personal injury | .81** | .18 | (−).05 | .16 | .76 | .67** | .14 |
| Patent and copyright | .75** | (−).18 | .25 | (−).05 | .91 | .97** | (−).53** |
| Labor-management | .77** | (−).09 | .09 | (−).14 | .98 | .91** | (−).36** |
| Income tax | .79** | (−).42** | .12 | .10 | .99 | 1.43** | (−).02 |
| Civil rights | .72** | .13 | .15 | .35** | <.02 | .50** | (−).03 |
| Prisoner petitions | .87** | .38** | .06 | .15 | <.01 | .95** | .41** |
| Criminal | .81** | .53** | .19 | .15 | .34 | 1.66** | .08 |
| Combined subjects | 1.06** | .19 | .07 | .11 | .20 | 1.66** | .05 |

* Interaction scores are derived from a separate saturated model in which $\chi^2$ is always zero with a probability of 1.
** Standardized effect is greater than twice the standard deviation.

direct causal paths, flowing through psychological or social experiences to political attitudes and role conceptions that shape behavior, the judicial process resembled a kaleidoscope in which these values, like lenses of an oculist's wheel, permit judges to see through all at once or separately as the case may be. In some fields, such as civil rights or prisoner petitions, several lenses may come together, altering and reinforcing the total vision. In other fields, such as taxation, a single lens or even chance factors like panel composition may dominate.[46] However at odds with the predictive impulse of social science or the normative impulse of legal theory, this kaleidoscopic view of relationships among values and votes in Courts of Appeals avoids the single-factor fallacy, accords with the fractured nature of political ideology among American political elites, and squares with every sophisticated account on record of deciding appeals in collegial courts.[47] As Justice Holmes concluded, though "the chief end of man is to frame them . . . no general proposition is worth a damn."[48] On the margins choice is personal, and judges know it. Just as concepts of law are ideological constructs vying for allegiance, so circuit judges are obliged to choose among competing conceptions of judicial duty in cases at the edges of legal change.[49]

**Conclusions**

A classic question in the theory of judicial decision is whether judging is political behavior or judicial role behavior. The short answer from these courts is a bit of both. The basic findings are that these circuit judges, by virtue of their recruitment and socialization, shared fairly common political orientations and conceptions of judicial duty, though substantial strain persisted over their lawmaking roles. Within a general consensus as to their mission as agents of national power and the obligations of precedent, changing philosophies of judicial action, responsive to lethargy among other policy makers, have extended the Supreme Court's perpetual tension over the appropriate scope of judicial lawmaking to the three Courts of Appeals. The effects of clashing philosophies, however, were not confined to so-called libertarian activists, but extended as well to opponents holding more passive views of judicial functions. Nor were these tensions powerful enough to break ligaments of cohesion underlying limited formal review. Though the appellate process accorded individual judges considerable latitude to choose among competing policy alternatives, the three tribunals were not riven by ideological cleavages. Consensus, on the whole, was more characteristic of their values and votes than conflict.[50] Circuit judges were more alike than different; so were their decisions.

A dimension of disagreement over policy outcomes was present, to be sure, a dimension not coextensive with dissent.[51] In accounting for these divergences, the analysis uncovered some of the strongest connections encountered thus far between aggregate judicial attitudes and behavior. But it is important to recognize how limited, complex, and counter to conventional theory these relationships actually were. Neither the judges' past political orientations nor their attitudes toward judicial lawmaking were totally consistent with voting behavior. Neither set of normative beliefs, alone or in concert with the other, dominated policy results. Relationships that did exist between divergent values and votes were modest, spasmodic, and issue specific. Different political orientations before appointment had virtually no bearing on adjudication, except feebly in civil rights. Different role perceptions, though untested in exclusively lawmaking situations, moderately affected liberal-conservative voting behavior primarily in criminal justice. Role conceptions, ironically, instead of shielding decisions from political preferences, were clearer cues to policy choices than were past political outlooks, in part because political values filtered through role perceptions in some subjects—and vice versa.

It is a major conclusion that the political and professional values of these jurists, depicted as antagonistic in much of our legal theory, were complementary and overlapping. The entwined orientations that lubricated the judges' paths to the bench interacted in their voting behavior in specific policy fields, though not all of them.[52] Similarly scattered relationships held for selected background indicators, such as social class, party affiliations, and judicial experience, which suffer fewer problems of definition and measurement.

Consequently, the combination of uniformity and pluralism that characterized the distribution of business among circuit courts extended to judges' values and votes within them. The paradoxical results were to intensify ideological conflicts in a few policy fields, notably civil rights and criminal justice, but to diffuse conflict in most. Converging political and professional values made agreement the norm in the great mass of cases; ideological differences tipped the balance at policy outcroppings, where open roles and close cases made personal preferences permissible guides to decision.[53] The net effect was to narrow the range of circuit conflict and of necessary Supreme Court intervention to control the policy premises of subordinates. In the compatibility of professional and political values, more than their antagonism, lay the reconciliation of their roles and the cohesion of national courts.

These conclusions, however at odds with conventional theories of judging, have several implications for the theory and practice of federal appeals. Theoretically most compelling is that the appellate process is too complex to be caught by a single explanatory net. The causal chains implicit in political, professional, or bureaucratic models of appellate adjudication, however useful as conceptual prisms to order complex experience, all tend to overestimate the impact of general ideological differences in the decision making of these circuits. For individuals the evidence may be sufficient to sustain the old notion that judges' predilections affect their decisions, but for circuit judges generally that proposition is less certain for broad social values used to answer "the stinking question." Prior political orientations of these jurists hardly triumphed over professional norms. The predictive power of political indicators was negligible and indirect. Judicial role perceptions, in turn, were neither so weak as to be subsumed under personal preferences nor so strong as to be considered "the most significant single factor in the whole decisional process."[54] The roles of judges were bonds rather than chains. Federal circuit judges enjoyed more discretion to make policy than presumed in deterministic theories of judicial decision, whatever the postulated control.

To recognize complexity of choice is not to cast a plague on simplifying theories, but rather to point up the need to develop finer measures of judicial values and to differentiate conditions under which they may be expected to affect judicial behavior in different courts. Capturing such differences will aggravate problems of measurement. But the evidence lends little support to ideological theories of judging, either political or professional, that are not further refined according to subject, situs, and situation. Just as relationships between judicial attitudes and behavior may be overlapping or issue specific, so may they vary by institution.[55] Contrasting role perceptions among the judges of these circuits and state supreme courts, for example, shake the notion that a uniform role structure controls American judges, regardless of jurisdiction or political environment. In this period interpreters apparently dominated the high courts of Virginia and Louisiana; innovators were prominent in New Jersey and New York.[56] These circuit judges clustered mostly in the center, both in values and votes, as befit their roots and roles. Such variations accentuate the trend, noted by Mott in the 1930s, toward separation of national and state recruitment systems and legal cultures—a trend that separate admission standards to practice in federal district courts would accelerate.[57] It is doubtful whether philosophies of judicial policy making reigning in one court will necessarily appeal to other courts. Trial judges regard the lawmaking issue as much less salient than clashing priorities of processing decisions promptly and fairly. These problems, as we have seen, are beginning to envelop circuit courts, too.[58]

Similar account needs to be taken of decisional situations. The slippage between general values and specific votes in these circuits supports not only those who emphasize the duty of rendering justice in each case but also the importance of context. Panel rotation is especially significant in Courts of Appeals, because it diffuses court membership. Role expectations, moreover, as Glen H. Stassen observed in a study of U.S. senators, tend to be determinative for routine questions whose rules of decision are settled.[59] So these circuit judges regarded roughly nine-tenths of their cases. Not for them was the basic assumption of legal realism that every case bristles with creative choice. Appeal by right and relentless demand induce assembly lines and delegation of routine. Role playing is also likely when issues are perceived in terms of an organization's victory over or defeat by rivals. The self-consciousness of the 5th circuit in civil rights and the 2d circuit in opinion writing offers examples. Discretion and role strain, in turn, coalesce with policy disputes on legal frontiers, where ambiguity breeds subjectivity.

Last, the cohesion among these circuit judges concerning the constraints of precedent and national office, which limit creative opportunities, warns against exaggerating judicial leeway into license. Shared normative beliefs help to institutionalize the federal judiciary. Role conflict, according to participants, is absent from the overwhelming majority of circuit cases. Adherence to precedent remains the everyday, working rule of American law, enabling appellate judges to control the premises of decision of subordinates who apply general rules to particular cases.[60] Even when superiors sound an uncertain trumpet, circuit judges maintain, the closest call rivals justice in the case as a guide to decision (see Table 6.3).[61] Affirmations of shared purpose and judicial roles in these tribunals strengthen the view that the absence of precedent does not necessarily cast judges adrift into seas of purely personal preferences.[62] Constraining judicial discretion are standards and expectations of a professional craft and, as we shall see, of the workplace itself.

Professionalism, furthermore, is only part of the story of why a decentralized judiciary fails to fall apart. The politics of federal courts, neglected as a cohesive in legal theory, is a major element in the integration of the national judiciary. Common policy values among judges cabin judicial choice. Past political outlooks were among the weakest explanations of divergent policy results. Far from polar opposites, the professional and political orientations of these jurists were entwined like marble cake. While the blending may occasionally aggravate disagreements on the growing edges of public policy, on the whole overlapping values tended to homogenize outlooks and outcomes on Courts of Appeals, just as rotation tended to diffuse personal disputes.

As a practical matter, of course, the general compatibility of professional and political norms may provide small comfort to counsel caught between factions of a tribunal fighting over a particular issue of unsettled law. And it is precisely in the "vacant spaces . . . when there is no decisive precedent," as Cardozo observed, "that the serious business of the judge begins."[63] From the standpoint of the judicial system, nonetheless, shared political values, in concert rather than collision with professional norms, were more important in sustaining a decentralized judiciary—and a system of *stare decisis*— than limited formal review. The short of it is that federal intermediate courts tended to attract political lawyers who by vocation and training fused elements of political and legal culture in appellate adjudication. An underlay of shared and mutually supporting values among members of the interpretative community narrowed the range of judicial conflict in the Courts of Appeals and the aperture of essential review by the Supreme Court. Diversity of circuit business was offset by homogeneity of judicial values in the "vital center." Underlying processes of judicial recruitment and socialization, for this reason, appear to be critical bonding agents in the national judiciary. Courts in between were melded more by modalities in membership than by manipulating machinery.[64]

All the more reason for caution, therefore, before revamping institutions to increase the appellate capacity of national courts. The practical problem is not whether nine Justices can effectively monitor all federal appeals in a law explosion, but whether they can do so at the creative margin in which judicial roles and policy directions are relatively open. This study suggests that professional discipline *is* an imperfect surrogate for institutional controls in cases of greatest policy-making potential. The irony is that pragmatic and middle-of-the-road policy values, dominant among federal circuit judges by virtue of their training, selection, and rotation, make it unlikely that circuit courts as institutions will stray far from the reservation.

# Seven · Consensus and Conflict in Circuit Courts, an Informal View

Problems of achieving unity amid diversity prevail within as well as among circuit courts. By law a Court of Appeals is a panel of three judges. The organizational principles of collegiality and random rotation, in environments of administrative independence and escalating caseloads, profoundly shape decision making in intermediate federal courts. No circuit judge, however motivated, is entirely a free agent. Judging is a collective enterprise governed by established rules and routines to which any individual member is expected to conform.

Group decision making thus ranks with Supreme Court review and professional discipline as a major potential limit on the personal discretion of circuit judges. How group dynamics and internal operating procedures affect the decisions of individuals has long been a subject of inquiry.[1] Lawyers and social scientists alike are interested, for example, in how appellate judges prepare for decisions, distribute their labor, and enforce standards of performance. How do members of collegial courts achieve agreement and contain internal disputes? Do the processes of accommodation and leadership formation in circuit courts resemble those of the Supreme Court? Of particular significance are methods of maintaining doctrinal consistency among rotating panel members with swelling dockets.

This chapter focuses on ways in which circuit judges reach consensus and resolve conflicts in the three Courts of Appeals. The problem of unification, ever present in organizations, is particularly acute in circuit courts. On the one hand, judges are expected to make joint decisions with a maximum of cohesion and a minimum of discord. Professional canons exhort them to restrain pride in personal opinion. Statutes and court rules provide formal mechanisms, such as conferences and en bancs, by which differences may be composed. On the other hand, the rules of decision within these tribunals are highly permissive and individualistic. Courts of Appeals are among the most decentralized of government institutions, fragmented, tolerant of individuality, and weak in imposing sanctions against nonconformity.[2] Decision makers are officially equal, undisciplined by party or personal loyalties, and insulated by deep traditions of judicial independence. To a considerable extent, moreover, the judges are physically dispersed. Face-to-face contact is limited even in Washington and New York. Turnover of members is relatively frequent.[a] Senior and visiting judges further diversify the membership. Not even the Supreme Court is more diffused in leadership and administration.

Panel rotation, above all, stamps Courts of Appeals with unique problems of integration. Panel division, to be sure, serves major institutional goals. Panels enable each circuit to adjudicate large numbers of appeals simultaneously without sacrificing the principle, established in the Judiciary Act of 1891, of collective appellate review on a regional basis. Rotation also decreases the ability of litigants to anticipate the court's exact composition and, by diversifying personnel, inhibits the formation of polarizing blocs or cliques.[3]

These fruits of organizational pluralism undoubtedly enhance the legitimacy of circuit decisions. They are purchased, however, in centrifugal coin. Rotation increases the chances of conflicting decisions and minority rule. A court of nine members can yield eighty-four different three-member combinations.[4] Senior and visiting judges increase the odds of disunity even more. Though judges sitting by designation tend to dissent less, they are reversed more by en bancs than are regular members.[5] Their unfamiliarity with the law of the circuit intensifies the difficulty of one panel of judges knowing what the others are doing, inherent in all circuits with rotating membership.

Uniquely in the federal judiciary, Courts of Appeals face a built-in tension between dual organizational principles to determine court policy: rotation and uniformity. Just as regional organization tends to Balkanize national law *among* circuits, so panel rotation breeds diverse outcomes *within* them. Uniformity is theoretically achieved by convening the whole court en banc, the official procedure to resolve inconsistent decisions; but judges tend to avoid en bancs as cumbersome devices that may exacerbate conflict. Scarcely any circuit judge regards them as satisfactory instruments to unify circuit courts.

These conditions on their face would appear to make Courts of Appeals sitting ducks for disintegration. In fact, they are not. Another paradox of the circuits is that such loosely organized tribunals appear to be so cohesive in practice. Dissent rates throughout the 1960s, far lower than on the Supreme Court, were well within

[a] During FY 1965-1975, a new judge was appointed on the average every 14.7 months in the 2d circuit, every 9.4 months in the 5th circuit, and every 22 months in the D.C. circuit.

the bounds of customary conduct in lower appellate courts.[6] If the acid test of the integration of a governmental body is its ability to make collective decisions without flying apart in the process, all three circuits must be considered reasonably coherent tribunals.[7] What's more, they continued to function without bursting their seams under increasing pressure in the 1970s.

What keeps these tribunals from disintegrating? Why are overt conflicts so contained? The thesis of this chapter is that at least partial answers may be found in the informal norms and procedures that guide decision making within circuit courts. Group politics, an internal counterpart of informal bonds among federal courts, should be added to formal review and the informal ties of the interpretative community as elements of cohesion in the federal judiciary. Just as these judges were substantially united in organizational goals (purposive roles), national missions (areal roles), and attitudes toward precedent, so they shared a working consensus regarding appropriate methods of making decisions and resolving internal disputes. These attitudes, brought by judges into courts from their previous professional workplaces and reinforced by their peers, are also part of the glue that binds circuit courts into a working system. A shared sense of participation and responsibility for organizational objectives enabled members to coordinate their activities largely through informal processes of mutual influence.[8]

To function, any group of decision makers must develop a minimum accord about procedures of operation to regulate how common undertakings should be performed.[9] Certainly this is so of lawyers, whose consciousness of the effects of procedure on substance elevates process values to virtually a professional ideology. Recognizing that the way courts organize decisional activity affects the way they think, most circuit judges simply presumed that the process of judging must be bounded by rules for the sake of efficiency and quality in rendering justice.

The rules of decision in Courts of Appeals are both formal and informal, their sources external as well as internal. Basic formal rules, such as circuit size, jurisdiction, or provision for en bancs, are fixed by Congress. So are the locations of panel sittings within each circuit. Deeply rooted principles of the adversary process and the appellate function, such as party presentation of disputes, are set by custom. Judicial rule-making power is an additional source of procedural controls. Uniform rules of federal appellate procedure nationalized many circuit practices after 1968. Each circuit also has independent power to establish local rules, usually in published form, covering such details as the docketing and screening of cases, the amount of time for oral argument, the records required, and the like. Beyond that, each court usually develops internal operating procedures, often unpublished but not secret, governing methods of panel and opinion assignment, conducting conferences, and forming en bancs.

Interlaced with formal procedures are informal conventions and understandings, commonly generated by the group itself, to facilitate the conduct of mutual business. Such conventions may be called "consensual roles," that is, norms guiding personal relations in the performance of collective tasks.[10] Students of legislatures and other decisional groups composed of equals often stress the significance of unofficial folkways and rules of the game in blending roles and personalities into an effective unit.[11] Rules of the game, according to Homans, "represent not an absolute imposed by a superior power . . . but a convention . . . accepted by a body of equals as the first condition of their cooperation."[12] Rules of the game may also be defined as "consensual norms," particular to each group, which members consider legitimately binding in order to hold the respect and cooperation of their colleagues.[13] Like other norms, they may be learned either in advance of appointment or through "freshman socialization." However learned, they embody normative guidelines that help to integrate individuals into a working group. In the nomenclature of social science, such rules of expected behavior intervene between individual values and collegial decisions, now tempering, now intensifying personal preferences as the group converts various elements of decision into a concrete, collective choice.

In this chapter we shall consider how selected formal procedures and informal conventions affect decision making and conflict resolution in the three courts. Because formal practices and local rules are described elsewhere, but are seldom evaluated, we shall concentrate on how circuit judges themselves appraised key processes and norms bearing on intracourt relations and the problem of cohesion.[14] These include the judges' perceptions of the severity of conflict and modes of managing it in their tribunals, including informal rules of the game and formal en bancs. In the next chapter we shall consider their perceptions of leadership as a medium of integration as well as the distribution of work. Since the data are largely impressionistic, no conclusions will be attempted in terms of small-group theory. Yet the discussion should contribute useful information about the inner workings of three circuit courts and thereby help to answer the central query: how do judicial decisions differ because they are made by groups rather than by individuals acting alone?[15]

## Conflict Resolution in Courts of Appeals

An initial question is: how much conflict actually exists on circuit courts? By any external standard the answer is not much. Consensus was far more prominent in the three tribunals than conflict. During both the base period and the subsequent decade, the number of en bancs seldom exceeded 1 percent of total decisions. Circuit judges also dissented sparingly. The overall dissent rate for individuals during 1965-1967, provided in Tables 7.1-7.3, averaged only 4 percent. In the 2d circuit the greatest disagreement came from so-called liberals—Marshall, Hays, and Smith—but the significant thing in both the 2d and 5th circuits was the paucity of public protest. The mean dissent rate in the 5th circuit was just over 1 percent. Indeed, Judge Tuttle dissented only 3 times in 611 cases and Judge Wisdom only twice in 527 cases. Three freshman judges, Dyer, Goldberg, and Simpson, registered no dissents at all. Even in the D.C. circuit, the tribunal most riven by dissension, the mean dissent rate was only 10 percent. The rate of nonunanimous decisions in Washington (16%) was lower than in the highest courts of ten states.[16]

Why were circuit dissent rates so much lower than in the Supreme Court? Many theories have been advanced to explain this common phenomenon in inferior appellate courts: theories of cognitive dissonance, in which judges seek to reduce the psychic discomforts of standing alone;[17] theories of exchange, in which judges accommodate competing preferences by bargaining over results and language;[18] power theories, in which judges either forge minimum winning coalitions to maximize internal influence or mass majorities to maximize external force;[19] institutional theories, in which the nonunanimity characteristic of the Justices is incompatible with lack of docket control and masses of routine business.[20] Though all are plausible, the magnitude of routine litigation in the circuits was undoubtedly a major factor in depressing dissent. If the Justices' denials of certiorari were included, their dissent rates would be minuscule, too. Increasing workloads and summary disposition, which leave little time for individual expression, were also powerful suppressants of dissent.

Still another factor is that the consensus of the circuits is in some ways synthetic. Public clashes in dissents and en bancs understate internal disharmony. They represent the end rather than the beginning of the conflict-resolution process, the differences judges failed to compose. Dissents measure neither the intensity of disagreement among circuit judges nor its reflection in voting blocs, bargaining

TABLE 7.1
Dissent Rates of Circuit Judges
2d Circuit, FY 1965-1967

| Judge | Dissent Rate % | Dissents n | Sittings N |
|---|---|---|---|
| Marshall | 4.5 | 7 | 155 |
| Hays | 4.4 | 16 | 364 |
| Smith | 4.1 | 16 | 393 |
| Friendly | 3.8 | 16 | 419 |
| Lumbard | 3.7 | 16 | 432 |
| Medina | 3.5 | 3 | 85 |
| Moore | 3.2 | 16 | 493 |
| Waterman | 2.4 | 10 | 411 |
| Kaufman | 2.3 | 8 | 351 |
| Feinberg | 2.2 | 4 | 180 |
| Anderson | 1.8 | 6 | 327 |
| Swan | 0.0 | 0 | 29 |
| Sums | 3.2 | 118 | 3,639 |

NOTE: Range = 4.5%.

over the language of opinions, and divergent outcomes among rotating panels. This gap between appearance and reality results in part from unique decision rules of circuit courts. The mechanics of panel division do not just produce lower statistical odds of dissent in three-judge panels than in larger courts. Rotation also permits "dissensus"—that is, discordant outcomes without dissent—to flourish among unanimous panels, which nonrotating tribunals would have to resolve. Distinguishing dissensus without dissent from overt conflicts in the same cases, Atkins and Green found that the dispersal of disagreement among rotating panels created an illusion of consensus in all federal circuits.[21] This condition, which presumes consistency in the policy content of cases allocated among various panels, we also encountered in Chapter Six. Rotation enables circuit judges to avoid personal conflict at the expense of institutional solidarity. The more their disagreement is dispersed among panels, the more diffuse becomes circuit policy.

The possibility that conflict may be submerged beneath a surface of consensus highlights the significance of informal techniques of conflict resolution in Courts of Appeals. Are circuit judges, like legislators, guided by consensual roles and rules of the game? If so,

TABLE 7.2
Dissent Rates of Circuit Judges
5th Circuit,* FY 1965-1967

| Judge | Dissent Rate % | Dissents n | Sittings N |
|---|---|---|---|
| Hutcheson | 3.4 | 5 | 147 |
| Rives | 2.7 | 13 | 479 |
| Gewin | 2.1 | 11 | 516 |
| Godbold | 2.0 | 2 | 100 |
| Jones | 2.0 | 9 | 460 |
| Brown | 1.9 | 11 | 575 |
| Bell | 1.3 | 7 | 531 |
| Coleman | 1.0 | 3 | 315 |
| Ainsworth | 0.7 | 1 | 151 |
| Thornberry | 0.6 | 2 | 323 |
| Tuttle | 0.5 | 3 | 611 |
| Wisdom | 0.4 | 2 | 527 |
| Dyer | 0.0 | 0 | 121 |
| Goldberg | 0.0 | 0 | 142 |
| Simpson | 0.0 | 0 | 26 |
| Sums | 1.4 | 69 | 5,024 |

NOTE: Range = 3.4%.

* Excluding Cameron, 1 dissent in 6 sittings.

what are these norms and how are they enforced? To explore the hypothesis that individual discretion is constrained by group relations, we asked the judges of the three tribunals several questions about the nature of conflict on their courts and whether rules of the game, analogous to those in legislatures, helped to control it. Further, they were asked whether blocs or factions existed, whether give and take and sufficient collegial deliberation existed in their courts, and whether judges disagreed over criteria for holding en bancs.

It speaks volumes about the autonomy of circuit judges that, in comparison with the elaborate rituals governing legislatures, informal rules of decision in Courts of Appeals were largely implicit, nonspecific, and poorly enforced. The concept of "rules of the game" itself was less meaningful to these circuit judges than to either legislators or other jurists. Several judges were puzzled by such questions. ("Really, I don't know what you are talking about.") Heavy probing usually elicited agreement that informal practices existed "to facilitate things," but they were often described as per-

TABLE 7.3
Dissent Rates of Circuit Judges
D.C. Circuit, FY 1965-1967

| Judge | Dissent Rate % | Dissents n | Sittings N |
|---|---|---|---|
| Miller | 23.4 | 30 | 128 |
| Bazelon | 14.2 | 40 | 281 |
| Danaher | 13.4 | 31 | 232 |
| Fahy | 12.9 | 34 | 263 |
| Wright | 11.5 | 30 | 261 |
| Tamm | 9.8 | 13 | 132 |
| Burger | 9.4 | 25 | 267 |
| Bastian | 9.2 | 12 | 130 |
| Prettyman | 8.6 | 6 | 70 |
| Washington | 6.3 | 9 | 143 |
| Edgerton | 4.7 | 6 | 128 |
| McGowan | 2.1 | 6 | 282 |
| Leventhal | 2.0 | 3 | 150 |
| Robinson | 0.0 | 0 | 24 |
| Sums | 9.8 | 245 | 2,491 |

NOTE: Range = 23.4%.

sonal strictures rather than joint rules, and many judges had difficulty volunteering more than one example. The general impression was that circuit courts, like the Supreme Court, were "citadels of jealously preserved individualism," bound by weaker normative expectations than legislatures or even state courts of last resort.[22] Members described Courts of Appeals as "institutions where all are individualists." "This is a body of individuals, not a club."

On the other hand, even though the judges felt no "body of strictures that are burdensome or give conscious worry," probing made clear that their intrinsic individualism was held in check by traditions and internal conventions within each tribunal. Just as most judges had common perceptions and evaluations of the main purposes, elements, and clienteles of their work, as we saw in earlier chapters, so also they felt obliged to follow certain courtesies and unwritten conventions in dealing with colleagues. Only a few of these informal expectations were rules of the game in the strict sense that deviations would result in sanctions or loss of respect. Most were looser norms and unwritten understandings, often transposed customs of the bar, geared to the functions of the courts. Though interrelated, these informal rules and expectations will be discussed, for convenience, according to their functions of (1) facilitating the execution of court business, (2) managing conflict, and (3) promoting circuit unity.[b]

*Rules to Facilitate the Execution of Court Business*

Inherent in the collegial condition are various mutual understandings and practices that "oil the wheels" of decision making. The foremost rule of the game is panel rotation. This convention, and methods of ensuring random selection, are not imposed by Congress but lie within the administrative prerogative of each court. Though the 5th circuit experimented briefly with standing panels in 1971 to prevent "an absolute state of chaos," and rationed time for oral argument by screening panels, which changed composition annually, random rotation is a basic rule of decision in most federal circuits.[23] Rotation presupposes a potential danger of bias in standing, small groups. However imperfectly past panels conformed to the norm (something we shall explore in the next chapter), these judges regarded disinterested panel composition as a fundamental ground rule guarding the impartiality of decisions, the equality of members, and the freedom of the court from factionalism.

Another set of conventions, under heavy pressure from workloads, concerned personal preparation for and participation in judging. Public complaints to the contrary, a strong norm prevailed that circuit judges should read the litigants' briefs prior to decision. As one judge in Washington described this standard, "There is nothing in writing, but it is understood that when you walk out on the bench you've done your homework. We announce that the judges have examined the case; counsel need not spend time explaining the facts. We know the issues. This is not peculiar to this court."

Virtually every circuit judge asserted that he *always* read the briefs before deciding cases and that colleagues did so "most of the time." A powerful deterrent against lapses from the norm is awareness that colleagues and "good lawyers" are hard to fool. Volume

---

[b] Curiously, rules to preserve the integrity of decision, frequently paramount in studies of other institutions, were seldom articulated. The closest was a remark by a southerner: "Perhaps the most sensitive rule would be not to try to get a man to change his opinion by what I'll call 'legislative means.' It's judicially appropriate to argue that 'you're wrong,' but that's the only reason on earth. Not because the chief would like it or Bill is your friend. That's sort of protocol—unwritten law—but there's not so much of it."

The judges were highly sensitive to conflicts of interest, because of contemporary controversies over the Haynsworth and Carswell nominations as well as the ABA's proposed code of professional conduct, but these involved external rather than internal relationships.

pressures, even so, are eroding such traditional standards of preparation. Many circuits, including the 2d, delegate to central staff attorneys the tasks of screening and proposing opinions in *pro se* petitions from indigents.[24] Some 5th circuit judges, finding it impossible to read every brief prior to screening cases, relied heavily on the memoranda and recommendations of law clerks in cases disposed of without oral argument. Though several members read "every brief and as much of the record" as they found necessary, proposed per curiams in roughly half the cases tended to be written by clerks before judges saw the case.[25]

Under modern conditions, moreover, intensive analysis of the record by judges prior to oral argument or decision is the exception rather than the rule. Some judges prefer not to read the record in order to avoid premature judgment; most refrain for lack of time. As one senior judge asserted:

> Judges say they read the whole record, but the plain truth is they don't have time. . . . Some judges sit two weeks per month. You can't do that and read all the briefs and records. It can't be done. So it is one of those honest misrepresentations. Before bar associations they'll swear blue that every judge reads every brief and every record. It's not so. Some do, some don't.

Prior to argument most circuit judges seldom do more than scan pertinent portions of the record called to their attention by clerks or counsel, a technique increasingly systematized in several circuits to streamline appeals. To prepare for oral argument, all but a handful of circuit judges rely upon bench memoranda prepared by their law clerks, plus their own notes from reading briefs. Oral arguments and judicial conferences also permit pooling of factual perceptions. Otherwise, intensive review of the record is normally restricted, *after* argument and decision on the merits, to the judge or the clerk who writes the opinion. That is why the innovation of pinpointing relevant passages in the record on appeal has become so important. For their perceptions of the issues prior to decision, circuit judges are increasingly dependent on the homework of others.

These standards of preparation are reflected in the judges' evaluations of various factors of decision, summarized in Table 7.4. Briefs of counsel and independent research drew considerably more "very important" rankings than oral arguments or the interests represented.

Though the need for intensive preparation before argument is debatable—"After all, I'm preparing to listen to oral argument, not to make a decision at this point"—some former trial lawyers, steeped

TABLE 7.4
Perceived Influence of Legal Factors on Circuit Decisions

| Legal Factor | Very Important N | Moderately Important N | Not Important N | No Answer N | Total N |
|---|---|---|---|---|---|
| Briefs of counsel | 30 | 4 | 0 | 1 | 35 |
| Independent research | 24 | 9 | 1 | 1 | 35 |
| Judicial conferences | 20 | 11 | 3 | 1 | 35 |
| Oral arguments | 17 | 16 | 0 | 2 | 35 |
| Amicus curiae briefs | 5 | 21 | 7 | 2 | 35 |
| Standing of counsel | 0 | 9 | 24 | 2 | 35 |
| Nature of parties | 0 | 5 | 26 | 4 | 35 |

NOTE: The question was: "How would you rank the following factors in terms of their influence on your perception of issues and your decision in a case?"

in habits of close factual analysis, were discomfitted by increasing remoteness from the record prior to decision. A judge in Washington declared:

> One of the great casualties in the litigation explosion is that judges don't have time to read the record the way they should. I can read the briefs, then thumb through the record for an hour or so, and have a different view of what happened. If you can't do that, the whole point of appellate review is lost. The point is we have to have time to reflect. Compare the district judge—the nature of his job is to shoot from the hip. Our function is to serve as a check on him from a reflective vantage point. What's the point if we shoot from the hip, too? I question whether it is very useful.

Distance from the record prior to the opinion stage worried these judges especially in three situations: cases that turn on the weight of the evidence; oral decisions from the bench or by summary order, which are frequent in the 2d and 5th circuits; and most appeals in the 5th circuit, where limited oral argument and face-to-face exchanges put a premium on advance preparation. "Study must precede argument," one southerner explained, "because the decision in the case in the majority of cases occurs right after argument. Then it's a question of reducing that to an opinion."

> Conferences . . . are said to be tentative. In over 80 percent they are actually final. . . . The assignee sometimes changes his mind and swings the other judges over, but in the majority of cases

tentative votes are final. I feel that once committed, it is hard to get a judge to change his views. . . . We have to prepare thoroughly before argument because we are a circuit-riding court.

Whether the standard of thorough preparation is sufficiently met by reading briefs, bench memos, and stipulated portions of the record remains a major unresolved issue in the law explosion.

Also under pressure are expectations that judges should write their own opinions. As part of a larger norm of personal responsibility for decisions, circuit judges expect one another to supervise closely the opinions produced in their offices; but there was little consensus on the degree of acceptable delegation of writing chores. Some judges claimed they "never" permitted law clerks to serve as ghostwriters. Others do so regularly. The matter is essentially left to each judge's discretion, as informed by his role conception, work habits, and caseload.[c]

In general, Learned Hand's view of the judge-clerk relationship—"I write, you criticize"—seems to be fading in favor of increasing reliance on law clerks and staff for research and writing. A common practice, once an opinion is assigned, is for the judge to set one or more clerks to writing a separate first draft, from which the judge may incorporate into the final opinion such portions as he sees fit. "That actually makes it harder," some judges felt. "You write over them, argue over shadings of language. The clerks are proud of their authorship." "And I tell you, these boys put up a fight."[26]

Small wonder that Learned Hand called law clerks "puisne [pronounced puny] judges."[27] With annual caseloads hovering around one hundred or more per judge by 1970, law clerks and staff attorneys have become integral parts of the judicial process. Circuit judges' offices resemble little law firms, in which the distribution of labor depends less on collective rule than on the individual styles and workloads of incumbents. Circuit judges insist that they control their decisional product, and much supports this view.[28] Traditional expectations that judges do their own work, to which Justice Brandeis attributed the Supreme Court's prestige, have nonetheless yielded to unremitting pressures on judges' time.[29]

---

[c] Several judges conceded heavy dependence on law clerks in drafting opinions. "I take what I like," said a judge with a large caseload. "I have little chance to do otherwise. We discuss the case. I tell them what I want—give them the slant. If the style differs too much, I have been known to write myself. [Laughter]"

"I don't hesitate to say that clerks write my bankruptcy opinions," another judge asserted. When a colleague challenged him to improve an opinion he had criticized, he recalled, "I got a clerk who was a bankruptcy specialist to write it. [My colleague] said of that opinion, 'I've been overwhelmed!' "

Bloated calendars, on the other side of the coin, reinforce a group principle of equal say, equal work. As circuit judges expect to have equal opportunity to influence decisions, so that right is earned by sharing the labor. In the face of common complaints that "we work like hell," peer-group pressure does surface against laggards. Irritation arose in the 5th circuit, for instance, against "one or two judges" who take "an interminable time to return an opinion."

> They are very much criticized for it in private. There is one judge who shirks his work. He'll say, for example: "I just don't agree; one of you fellows should write." That violates a general understanding that cases—both hard ones and easy ones—are to be evenly divided taking the week as a unit. If there is any doubt, the senior judge should take the harder cases.

Another general norm, far different from legislative practice, is that circuit judges should be generalists rather than specialists. Opinion assignments, accordingly, are expected to be diversified rather than concentrated in order to free the courts from the tunnel vision of experts.

Besides such general understandings are informal rules of decision peculiar to each circuit. Of necessity the 5th circuit was more formally structured than the other two. Size and distance dictated more explicit procedures, adopted "more or less by common consent," to facilitate joint action. Two examples are the order of speaking and voting. In panels, after the presiding judge outlined the case, the junior member normally spoke and voted first. This procedure, once followed in Supreme Court voting, was designed to protect newcomers from being overpowered by experienced members.[d] Speaking and voting orders were reversed in en bancs which, as in the Burger Court, followed the principle of descending seniority.[30]

Another southern custom is "the rule that disposing of other judges' opinions has priority over your own." The most frequent illustration of a rule of the game in this circuit, in fact, was that "the first priority is to respond to another judge's opinion." As one senior judge described the obligation,

> When a judge receives an opinion from one of the brothers, he should lay aside his own work and act upon it first—out of courtesy and to keep the court running. It doesn't work that way now. I never had one I kept more than a month. But I had one

---

[d] This practice was also defended as "a good educational process." "When I first came on the court," said one judge, "I sat right on top of everything in every case. I had to talk first. I didn't want to be embarrassed. It's a great institutional aid. It puts the judge on his mettle instantly."

recently which the judge held back nearly two years for dissent. That's dead wrong! I raised all the cain I decently could, but I'm not always successful. The court has slipped back.

To counter delays, the judges formalized this understanding into a rule that they have thirty days to indicate their concurrence or dissent and another thirty days to write. On the sixtieth day, "you have to file it or forget it." Whether the written rule has had the desired effect is questionable, because the reward system is weak.

The voting memorandum system of the 2d circuit, by contrast, is a strong rule of the game. Uniquely among Courts of Appeals, every judge on a panel is expected to prepare and circulate a memorandum explaining his views and his vote after hearing a case but before conference, which usually occurs about a week after the hearing. It is understood that judges may change their minds any time before filing the decision. Though avoided in simple cases, which may be decided orally from the bench or by summary order, this procedure is the regular method of deciding appeals in the circuit. The practice, "hallowed by tradition," was instituted over a generation ago in the teeth of the heaviest caseload among circuits to improve the quality of deliberation and to guard against one-judge decisions.[31] The question naturally arises whether this extra drain on judicial resources is worthwhile. Also, because of speculation that the practice institutionalizes conflict, by hardening positions and making dissenting opinions easier to prepare, the judges were asked to evaluate whether the procedure encourages dissent.[32]

There was a solid consensus that, for all the extra labor, the memorandum system improved the judges' performance. Having each member come to grips with the issues in writing was thought to be a "salutary discipline," productive of more careful consideration by everyone. Because judges tend to write to convince their colleagues and their "bright young clerks," the method was further defended as "the best way to squeeze out every drop of learning of individual judges in the case." Besides helping to clarify issues and to prevent important points raised by counsel from being overlooked, the practice was considered the most effective defense against one-judge judgments.

Though the system "has its angles," as members may jockey to avoid or win opinion assignments by what they write in memos, the judges discounted the disadvantage that voting memoranda encourage dissent.[e,33] For every member who conceded that preparing

[e] This hypothesis stems from Judge Charles E. Clark's argument that "the most questionable feature of the practice, even if we do not admit it," is the resistance of

memos might stiffen positions, others thought that exchanging views could stifle doubts. In one case the voting memos exchanged by two judges persuaded *both* men to switch sides! Yet, the judges perceived certain disadvantages in the memorandum system. Preparing voting memoranda entails extra work. Though the court has kept up with its docket better than other large circuits, one member argued that the cost of more composite decisions was less collegiality in writing opinions. The writing burden, others thought, had helped to sell the court on increasing summary dispositions and other gatekeeping innovations. Still another judge complained about colleagues withholding ideas to reap personal glory. For the system to work, he said, "everybody must play the game." Allegedly, one or two members did not, with consequent loss of respect.

Voting memoranda apparently are not what they used to be. Routinely they tend to be short position papers with cursory citation of authority. The judges remain wedded to the procedure, all the same. Perhaps the acid test of their commitment is that they chose alternative methods to improve productivity rather than discard a practice in keeping with their priority of producing high-quality opinions.[35] For judges of the 2d circuit, the real cause for concern was not whether preconference memoranda intensified disagreement, but whether a proven method of quality control would become "a casualty of the great increase in the court's workload."

## Rules to Manage Conflict

In addition to conventions to expedite mutual business were rules of reciprocity designed to control conflict. Though methods of reducing discord were characterized as "infinite," the most pervasive norm was a rule of civility in which judges are expected to prevent intellectual disagreements from becoming personal. As one judge stated the norm,

---

strongminded judges, having put their thoughts on paper, to changing their minds. Marvin Schick challenged Clark's view on the basis of memos from the 1941-1951 period, which revealed numerous instances when judges switched tentative votes.[34] A former colleague supported Schick's impression that Clark himself was the member least likely to do so: "Only one time do I know of Clark changing his mind after he got out his original memo. Clark used to say the memo system was baloney because every fellow would stick to his way Clark did. I believe the memo system is wonderful. There *is* give and take. . . . Lots of fellows give in. I don't know a single judge who won't except Clark. I don't mean to say the judge will do so when he feels strongly that he is right. But you don't mean that, do you? You mean, is he open to persuasion. The answer is, yes, except Clark. Clark just wouldn't yield. I've never seen anything like it."

You must keep things at an impersonal level, realizing that you're not in personal combat with those who disagree. You may think he's dead wrong, say so, and write so. You don't say he's a damn fool. Some district judges are also extremely sensitive on reversal. We have to be careful.

The precept that judges should disagree without being disagreeable was virtually a rule of the game, adapted from professional traditions of advocacy to minimize disruption of the court. Judges in all three circuits insisted that, despite their differences, personal animosity was rare. "It is difficult for people who are not judges to understand that we can disagree with a colleague and yet be on perfectly good terms," one judge commented. "It's important that they be so in order that lines of communication remain open so each case will be decided on its own merits."

Even in the D.C. circuit, reputed to be a jungle, personal relations were described as "all very civilized." "It's amazing how we can batter each other around in opinions and yet maintain cordial relations," judges in Washington declared. Of reports that some colleagues were not on speaking terms, a member fresh from hosting a dinner party for the brethren scoffed: "That's nuts. It couldn't be more friendly."[f]

The convention of personal civility does not require friendship. Fraternal feelings naturally tend to bloom among the like-minded. "That's true on all courts." Nor does it prevent occasional personal ruptures. Judges recalled bitter "correspondence wars" between liberals Charles E. Clark and Jerome Frank in New York during the 1940s, Ben F. Cameron's charge that four colleagues stacked panels in civil rights cases in the South, and acerbic battles between Warren E. Burger and David L. Bazelon in Washington over criminal justice.[36] Still, these episodes were regarded as exceptions to general conditions of mutual respect. A jurist in Washington spoke for many when asked whether there was much internal conflict on his court:

Intellectual yes, personal no. Being lawyers we all have the same end in view—discharging professional responsibilities. Initial disagreement means we talk it out. Talking it out is the

---

[f] Another colleague commented: "I make an effort to avoid personal ruptures. That wouldn't be good for the court or our own relationships. We maintain a civilized veneer at least. Even during the early 1960s, the outside world thought a dogfight was going on here. Not so. From the beginning the temper of conferences, the relationships among judges, were equable. The language used in opinions was not as strong as the Supreme Court's. When every lawyer assumed the place was tense, I was pleasantly surprised."

process. If you don't convert a colleague, there comes a time [to vote]. Nobody takes his marbles and goes home because he didn't prevail. A judge may write a dissent.

By providing legitimate outlets for protest, short of resignation, dissents actually serve contradictory purposes on Courts of Appeals.[37] They are both symptoms of unresolved conflict and approved modes of loyal opposition. Despite relaxation of professional strictures against dissent, some animus against ventilating disagreement did exist on these courts. ("Some guys take pride in not writing dissents.") But the animus hardly constituted a rule of the game, and there was no evidence of group suppression, such as the muzzling of Judge Musmanno by colleagues of the Pennsylvania Supreme Court, under principles of collective responsibility.[38] Workloads, not behavioral norms enforced by peer groups, the judges regarded as the chief depressant of dissent.[39] Another factor was mutual respect engendered by skilled professionals judging and being judged together. As one judge said, "You dissent on your own time. It's a good thing—the greatest deterrent. Also, after a while you develop a healthy respect for the capacities of your colleagues. If you feel strongly, you dissent." Most judges would not hesitate to dissent if they thought their protest would influence the Supreme Court or another circuit. Long justified as seeds of legal change, dissents on appellate courts also serve as safety valves that can foster group harmony by allowing freedom of individual expression.

More tainted than dissent to bench and bar is division of a circuit into voting blocs or factions. These judges were uncertain how well their courts adhered to the standard against factionalism.[g] Everywhere they conceded that "there are blocs in the sense of persons whose views can be guessed in advance." "Depending on who sits, the same case can have opposite results."

As indicated in Table 7.5, most members of the 2d and 5th circuits believed their tribunals to be substantially free from factions, because voting alignments shifted too much by subject for minority cliques to persist.[41] Judges in New York concurred that theirs was "a remarkably cohesive court," except during en bancs when "some

---

[g] Part of the uncertainty stems from disagreement about what constitutes a faction or bloc. Judges, like scholars, differ as to whether the term "bloc" covers coincidental voting alignments or should be reserved for collusive conduct.[40] "Anybody can take a computer and count votes, but that doesn't establish a bloc," said a former chief judge. Certain bloc studies were also condemned as "distortions" or "of limited insight." A southerner, on learning that he was labeled in one study as the most liberal member of the 5th circuit in terms of support for black litigants, was quoted by a colleague as having responded: "Say it's not so!"

judges seem to pair off." "We've been through hell in admiralty!" Similarly, the 5th circuit had evolved from intense polarization over civil rights to a condition in which judges perceived "a few identifiable personal predilections but no identifiable blocs." Even the one member who thought otherwise (our maverick friend) regarded blocs as no longer of "real importance." Two unanimous en bancs in the Mississippi and Houston school desegregation cases were regarded as watersheds of the judges' ability to function cohesively.[42] Three factions compromised their differences, as one member explained, because "we felt we owed an institutional duty to the public" to speak with one voice. "I don't know where you'd find fifteen judges who'd agree on such an emotional subject."[h][43]

In Washington, by contrast, though polarization has subsided, judges regarded voting blocs as important elements of decision.[i]

TABLE 7.5
*Judicial Perceptions of Whether Blocs Exist on Three Courts of Appeals*

| Circuit | Blocs Exist N | Blocs Exist Somewhat N | Blocs Do Not Exist N | No Answer N | Total N |
|---|---|---|---|---|---|
| 2d | 1 | 5 | 4 | 0 | 10 |
| 5th | 1 | 3 | 13 | 0 | 17 |
| D.C. | 4 | 3 | 0 | 1 | 8 |
| Sums | 6 | 11 | 17 | 1 | 35 |

NOTE: The questions were: "In recent years there has been a lot of talk about factions or blocs on the Supreme Court. Do they exist on the circuit court? Why?"

[h] While en bancs remain the primary arena for bloc formation, judges felt that alignments "shifted even in the old days from theme to theme." A member commented: "There were no factions even then, except Cameron. He was a faction by himself. This is no secret. He would brag about it. He wanted to fire on Fort Sumter tomorrow morning." "You can imagine what our conferences were like."

Muzzling differences in en bancs also may reflect tactical calculations. Explaining why he stifled dissent in the Houston en banc, a judge said: "In Cameron's day, we'd have wanted our positions known. To some extent the Supreme Court would pay attention to how we voted. Therefore, there may be a bloc [today], but it is not as pronounced or abrasive as formerly."

[i] Regarding earlier polarization, one member observed: "It is no secret that Burger and Bazelon were at swords' point. It erupted into public print. Burger is very outspoken; he expresses himself in a vivid way. The attention led to his appointment as Chief Justice. Bazelon's personality, and the fact that he is socially minded, led some more passive judges to get very angry. However, the same anger was not directed to others, such as Wright, who makes changes, but . . . there is no great bitterness now."

Blocs were conceived in terms of both coincidental voting along ideological lines—"If you count them, you get a group"—and collusive factions. "The bar says, with some justification, that the disposition of the majority of cases depends on who sits," judges said. "When the court sits en banc, the blocs close ranks, whereas in panels the bloc influence is dissipated." Even a member who contended that past tensions were exaggerated conceded that "we have five-to-four polarization in the criminal field, as at first, with two or three judges in the middle. In en bancs these two or three [Leventhal, McGowan, and Robinson] get a weighted influence on the result."[44]

These descriptions illustrate ambivalent attitudes toward conflict and its management in circuit courts. Disagreement is considered normal, even healthy. Dissensus is inevitable. As "every judge has a little bent," outcomes depend on membership. When judges of similar bent come together, they are likely to vote together. Because rotation disperses disagreement, personal conflicts are diluted and coalitions are relatively fluid in panels. Conflict and blocs surface most in en bancs. Even then most judges saw nothing wrong with coincidental voting or compromise. What they condemned were knee-jerk voting, collusive tactics, and personalizing disagreement. These standards, they conceded, are not always met, particularly in periods of experimentation and rapid change. Serious internal battles accompanied legal pioneering in both the 5th and D.C. circuits during the 1960s. Factionalism, personal hostility, and charges of breached rules of the game all erupted into public print.[45] Remedies for such conduct were weak, however, because the official procedure to compose differences, review en banc, is unwieldy and because sanctions collide with stronger norms of judicial independence and cooperation.

If individual conflicts are composed at the expense of institutional cohesion, collegiality also imposes informal expectations of open-mindedness or give and take in reaching joint decisons. Circuit judges are expected to be team players. Stubbornness can lead to loss of respect. These judges, as shown in Table 7.6, believed overwhelmingly that there was substantial give and take on their tribunals, with a few notable exceptions. Some colleagues in New York considered Charles E. Clark unyielding, and a conservative in Washington regarded discussion with four colleagues as "useless."[j] Judges, like most of us, tend to be more pliant with those who normally agree with them. (When they differ, "those who frequently

---

[j] See note e, this chapter. Even the maverick judge agreed: "Yes, there is also a great deal of give and take. Of course, others will say we have some men on this court who are stubborn and have strong views. If they tell you that, they include me! [Laughter]"

agree with them will back off and reconsider.") Tolerance was also said to be more prevalent in panels and in close cases where doubts abound than in en bancs.

Yet, the prevailing sentiment was that circuit "judges generally try to arrive at a decision acceptable to all." Finding common ground among experienced advocates with strong views can be

TABLE 7.6
Judicial Perceptions of Whether There Is Give and Take on Three Courts of Appeals

| Circuit | Yes N | Some N | No N | No Answer N | Total N |
|---|---|---|---|---|---|
| 2d | 5 | 0 | 0 | 5 | 10 |
| 5th | 14 | 1 | 0 | 2 | 17 |
| D.C. | 6 | 2 | 0 | 0 | 8 |
| Sums | 25 | 3 | 0 | 7 | 35 |

NOTE: The question was: "Is there much give and take among members of the court?"

bumpy. What is sometimes idealized as collegial deliberation can involve what in other forums is called bargaining and exchange. Consensus building in circuit courts resembles conflict resolution in the Supreme Court, where the methods range from persuasion to bargaining, from monitoring opinions to threats of dissent, rehearings, or "going public."[46]

Persuasion by colleagues was freely acknowledged and included episodes when judges assigned to write opinions changed their minds and convinced colleagues to follow suit.[k] Judges also related how they moderated the language of opinions at the behest of colleagues and held their noses en route. One judge translated the norm of open-mindedness into a personal guideline called the "no-goddam-difference rule," which he told his clerks "has two applications":

[k] For example, Judge Moore's dissent in *Empire Rayon Yarn Co. v. American Viscose Corp.*, 354 F. 2d 182, 188 (2d Cir. 1965) ultimately became the position of a unanimous en banc, 364 F. 2d 491 (2d Cir. 1966). In another instance, *Wolf v. Barkes*, (348 F. 2d 994, 998 [2d Cir. 1965]), Judge Waterman declared himself "reluctantly persuaded by the convincing language of my brother Friendly."

One, when a colleague wants a change and it makes no goddam difference, go ahead, and, two, when I want to suggest a change and it makes no goddam difference, don't suggest it. One or two judges [he said] have clerks who think it their duty to pick holes in everything that circulates, and the judges have the habit of slipping in whatever the clerks criticize. I don't like that. Hence my rule. Most of the judges do that without formalizing it into a rule. A couple don't.

Conferences are the main medium for bargaining over results, memos and telephones for opinions. Changes may result from threats to dissent or to call en bancs. A southern judge described the jostling this way: "To one judge I might say, 'If you don't modify that, I'll request an en banc.' If he is sure of his ground the other judge might reply: 'Just ask for an en banc!' Otherwise, he'll probably modify." When a conservative minority sought to amend a middle-of-the-road compromise by which the 5th circuit achieved unanimity in the Mississippi school case, for example, a former legislator reportedly threatened to bolt to the left.[47] "They came back into the fold in a hurry," a colleague remarked. "So you see, the judicial process is like legislation. All decisions are compromises."

The ultimate weapon, usually reserved for breaches of basic rules, is public exposure. Judge Cameron's famous charge of attempted minority control was not unique.[48] In 1967, Judges Burger and Danaher accused Bazelon, Fahy, and Wright of knowingly attempting to foist a minority view of criminal procedure on the D.C. circuit.[49] Another judge related how, as a freshman on the bench, he had threatened exposure to force a senior colleague to recall an opinion filed without his approval, a possibility he had been warned against by another member. "It was my first sitting as a circuit judge," he recalled. "It was not a major case. But there was strong give and take!"

In the final analysis the strongest stimuli of compromise on Courts of Appeals, as in most appellate tribunals, are conditions of collective responsibility and the shifting composition of majorities from case to case. Personal restraint of necessity is required to maintain working relations when antagonists in one appeal may be allies in the next. ("You have to keep on living with each other. In the next case the situation may be reversed.") A fine line also exists between massing a court and preserving judicial independence. No judge is expected to compromise principle. Then, too, searching for unanimity takes time, a scarce resource, which weakens pressure against nonconformity. The resulting tensions between solo and orchestrated opinions, between norms of collegiality and timely decision, were well captured by Judge Learned Hand, then on senior status, in response to Judge Clark's complaints about delay. Hand, despite "feeling that, when an Old Goat has cashed in, he ought to mind his own business and confine himself to what he is asked to do," agreed "to drop a light hint" because he, too, felt "troubled" and "stymied."

> I have tried to spread the gospel [he wrote] that in a court made up of a number of judges, one must accept what the writer of the opinion says unless one thinks it will come back to bother the court as a precedent. Good God! I used to have to swallow more unpalatable tripe from Manton and Rogers than I like now to think of, but I always had the practise of letting it pass provided the result was right and provided that it did not contain passages which . . . might serve as bad precedents. I don't know what else one can do. When I talk I try to encourage both dissents and concurrences.
>
> The English have apparently always felt free to have as many opinions as the individuals want except in the Privy Council; and I hate an enforced conformity. Indeed it seems to me that freedom of general expression is the sign of a living court. I know judges differ about this, but I am of that view, and when the evident conformity results in the delays that it apparently is resulting in here, it seems to be a major abuse.[50]

Meshing individual parts into a consensus of the whole inevitably constrains members of collegial courts.

*Rules to Promote Court Unity*

Closely related to conventions designed to prevent and control conflict are informal norms and procedures, mostly taken for granted, to unify the circuits. As each judge expects to make his influence count in decisions, so the decisions of each panel are expected to be collegial.[51] Uniformity of judgment among panels is likewise expected to prevent Balkanization of circuit law. It is considered improper for one panel to overrule the decisions of another, though judges admitted that "we fudge on it sometimes" by distinguishing cases, narrowing down rulings, and other tactics. The approved methods of integrating Courts of Appeals are internal negotiations and en banc review. A majority of circuit judges in regular active service may order hearings or rehearings en banc, at the request of either a party litigant or an active member. Court organization and workloads condition the members' capacity to confer, however, and the use of en bancs as a means of unification has troubled large circuits.[52] Their judges, as a result, settle differences largely by informal techniques, including avoidance and transformation of en bancs.

Given their twin goals of collective reasoning and institutional cohesion, the judges were asked whether collegial deliberation was sufficient on their tribunals and whether their colleagues disagreed over the criteria of calling en bancs. The prevailing view, as summarized in Table 7.7, was that either sufficient collegiality existed on the courts or as much existed as could be expected under current circumstances. The latter reaction was especially common among judges of the beleaguered 5th circuit.

TABLE 7.7
*Judicial Perceptions of Whether Sufficient Collegial Deliberation Exists on Three Courts of Appeals*

| Circuit | Sufficient N | Sufficient under the Circumstances N | Insufficient N | No Answer N | Total N |
|---|---|---|---|---|---|
| 2d | 3 | 4 | 1 | 2 | 10 |
| 5th | 2 | 12 | 2 | 1 | 17 |
| D.C. | 4 | 4 | 0 | 0 | 8 |
| Sums | 9 | 20 | 3 | 3 | 35 |

Different answers again reflected competing role conceptions and external demands. Judges who assigned opinion writing their top priority tended to have more misgivings than those who emphasized timely adjudication. Distinguishing decisions from opinions, no one thought that insufficient deliberation led to faulty decisions. Though several members complained that there was "never enough" time for collegial deliberation, that conferences were shorter and less penetrating than formerly, they fretted most about the quality of opinions. Without eschewing the value of collegiality, on the other hand, a minority challenged conventional wisdom that more cooks would necessarily improve the written broth.[53] A leading southern jurist, while conceding that panels "lack something in that regard," defended solo opinion writing. After conferences, he said,

> You go home to write. I don't feel litigants suffer. I wouldn't want more [collegial deliberation] because it might waste a lot of judicial time. Most judges are fairly lonely in writing opin-

ions. They don't like too much [interchange] while writing. They leave it to others to pick holes after opinions are written.

These differences cut to the heart of the appellate process. How much collective reasoning is necessary to ensure a quality product? How much should individuals work alone? In a pinch should the priority be deciding cases or developing legal principles?

Generally speaking, most judges expressed a desire for greater collegial deliberation to improve the quality of opinions, which they regarded as the main problem; but few saw much room for improvement under current conditions. Collaboration is easiest in Washington where all members have offices on one floor of the federal courthouse and no circuit-riding responsibilities. Because its business is so complex, this circuit remains one of the few that circulates every draft opinion to the whole membership, with ten days to respond, as a means of integrating the court.[54] When circuit judges meet monthly as a council to consider the calendar and other housekeeping responsibilities, moreover, they often turn to substantive matters. "We wouldn't be very bright," one judge remarked, "if we didn't take advantage" of such opportunities.[1]

Physical dispersion and heavier volume aggravate problems of communication in the two circuit-riding courts. The voting memorandum system of the 2d circuit, however effective in combating one-man rulings, may require so much writing before decision as to inhibit collegial drafting of opinions. According to one member, "We don't have any deliberation at all!"

> To that extent the memo system isn't good. The memo system doesn't lend itself to getting together. Only once do we get together—the conference on the case. Even that is to compare memos and take a vote. Then we withdraw to our ivory towers to do our writing. Such deliberation as there is comes via drafts. I would like more but there's no time. Every case could be a Ph.D. thesis.

Though judges in New York are housed in opulent chambers on the top floors of the federal courthouse in Foley Square, personal

---

[1] Judges in Washington complained, even so, that their discussion and analysis of cases were crimped by scarce time. Consider these two remarks: "When I first arrived some of our discussion was as good as the law school faculty club. Not now. Discussions are not as probing." [Is there sufficient collegial deliberation?] "Yes, except I wish we did have more time. Some lawyers cite cases in their briefs. I like to read their cases. I can't, except the important ones. But you can't take forever. It's better to decide our cases and get them out."

contact during opinion writing is limited.[m] Judges from Vermont and Connecticut have their main offices outside New York; "physically we don't see each other very much." Even those in New York often communicate through clerks and memos. Published reports, in effect, are the slip opinions for nonpanel members.

These barriers to collegial deliberation pale beside those imposed by the size and docket of the 5th circuit. The court's fifteen active members and five senior judges (in 1975) were not only geographically scattered and riding circuit, the volume of cases filed in their tribunal exceeded the intake of *all* federal circuits only a generation earlier.[55] To cope with explosive demand, up to half their cases were decided in the mid-1970s without oral argument after screening by panels of judges who neither rotated regularly nor conferred in person.[56] Physical contact in the remainder was limited to hearings and postargument conferences, plus occasional en bancs, council meetings, and annual conferences. It was entirely possible for members not to sit together for over a year in the normal rotation. That the circuit lacked its own central facility in New Orleans until 1972 was more than an administrative inconvenience; it symbolized the difficulties of institutionalizing courts in the vortex of the law explosion.

The circuit's main responses were to expand its membership and to accelerate decision making. Three times in the last generation Congress enlarged the size of the tribunal and considered dividing it into two circuits to increase judicial manpower. The judges, in turn, streamlined decision-making procedures and substituted informal methods of conflict resolution to avoid onerous formal procedures prescribed by statute. Each in its own way cut into collegial deliberation.

The maximum feasible size of an appellate court is often said to be nine judges. This principle, though embraced by a committee of the Judicial Conference of the United States in 1964 and advocated by the Commission on Revision of the Federal Court Appellate System in 1975, yielded twice to expanding business in the 1960s, when the

[m] A senior judge in New York observed that "the idea of conferring together to just knock the ball around has almost disappeared. When I first came on the court, things were different. In admiralty, Hand and Swan would position model ships on the table to determine the facts. Oh, they talk to each other [now] to iron things out. But the general sessions are gone." Yet, a newer judge wondered "if we have too much [collegial deliberation]. We haven't reached it, but I am struck by the number of times we get together—five or six decision points: (1) after argument, (2) voting memos, (3) conferences, (4) drafting and circulating opinions, (5) occasionally changing minds and resuming conferences, (6) petitions for rehearings. Each is a decision point at which we really have to look together."

5th circuit was enlarged to thirteen and then fifteen active members. Given their experience with enlargement, members of the court were asked to evaluate how expansion had worked.[57] The shifting responses in the brief period between the interviews in 1969-1971 and the Hruska Commission's hearings in 1973-1975 are barometers of the effects of external pressure on judicial outlooks toward court organization.[58] As the decade opened, the judges were sharply divided over the wisdom of enlarging their court. They split almost evenly among three basic viewpoints: (1) those who believed that the experiment had worked "admirably" or "at least better than expected"; (2) those with mixed reactions who preferred an enlarged tribunal, despite difficulties of administration and communications, to preserve its character as a "national court"; and (3) advocates of division who regarded size as "our biggest problem."

Policy preferences affected these positions, too. Proponents of desegregation successfully blocked division of the circuit in 1964 with arguments that two circuits of nine judges each would be too parochial to live up to national responsibilities in race relations and energy issues.[59] New appointees and a volume crisis softened such opposition a decade later. Overwhelmed by numbers, the court unanimously agreed in 1972 that further enlargement would "diminish the quality of justice"; and a majority of active judges, asserting publicly that even fifteen was too large for effectiveness, supported compromise proposals of the Hruska Commission to split the circuit into two independent divisions of nine judges on each side of the Mississippi River.[60] Congress, stalemated by political crossfire, expanded the tribunal to twenty-six members in 1978, but again refused to divide the circuit. Instead, any Court of Appeals having more than fifteen members was authorized to constitute itself into separate administrative units and to perform en banc functions by such number of members as prescribed by circuit rules. The 5th circuit acted on this authority until Congress finally accepted the unanimous petition of the circuit council to create a new 11th circuit, composed of twelve judges from Alabama, Florida, and Georgia and based in Atlanta, the division to take effect on October 1, 1981.[61]

Meantime, the judges coped by mass production, confident that as much collegial deliberation existed as could be expected under the circumstances. Some members, sensitive to criticism by colleagues outside, mounted an old southern defense that Yankees failed to practice what they preached. ("The telephone is a big factor in our collegiality," commented judges, who conferred by phone "all day, every day." "We may talk more than they do.") Making the best of limited contact, others saw two sides to the question. Ideally, the court would be "immensely more effective" if the judges lived and worked at the same place. ("I've often felt that I could probably resolve that problem if I could just walk down the hall and thrash it out face to face.") On the other hand, riding circuit brings judges closer to the community; colleagues can be too close for comfort. ("It would be tough with fifteen men as diverse as Coleman and Wisdom all in the same building.") Still, several of them voiced concern about the effectiveness of joint deliberations, particularly in screening panels, opinion writing, and en bancs.

The "outward appearance" of screening, judges admitted, "looks like short shrift." Despite assurances that cases not argued orally were seldom decided without written exchanges or telephone conferences, screening panels lacked "eyeball-to-eyeball discussion ... which is sometimes helpful." Limited personal contact after conference also bred one-judge opinions. Judges in the 5th circuit, of course, communicate about opinions. Often mentioned was "a tendency to change your mind half-way into a draft." When that happens, one judge said, "we burn the phones up." Yet, visiting judges from other circuits concluded that communication by telephone and letter were imperfect surrogates for personal encounters. As in other large, circuit-riding courts the judges live in personal isolation from their colleagues. The psychological differences are profound. Communications, hardly less than caseloads, made solo writing the circuit norm.[62]

The worst problem was en bancs. Even opponents of circuit realignment conceded that the problem of circuit cohesion, common to all except "the sleepy 1st," was acute in the 5th. Judges had difficulty keeping current with their colleagues' decisions when the stack of slip opinions to be absorbed annually was over four feet thick."[63] Ensuring majority control of circuit law and interpanel accord was no easier. The larger the court the greater the need for en bancs, but the harder they were to come by and administer. The logistics of getting everybody together, even consideration of whether to meet, was a serious drag on judicial energies and a source

---

[n] A proponent of circuit division declared in 1970: "I am more and more convinced that a court of 9 judges, possibly of 11, is the maximum. There's a geometric progression—more than half—in the workload. There's so much paper work when 15 judges are on the court. Opinions have to be read for all 15. Do you know how much reading that takes? And that's just one detail. Then there's correspondence concerning other duties. It all takes time. You can reach a point of collapse from your own weight. By adding judges you could reach the point that theoretically all they could do is read their own opinions. You can't have an institution if judges don't read all of them."

of delay.[64] An en banc in a major decision like the Mississippi school case, for example, consumed the equivalent of eighty regular cases in judge-time and, in the opinion of some members, exhausted the judges besides.[65] Time and again they complained that "with fifteen men it's impossible to get an en banc, and if you get one, it's impossible to function as an en banc." "It's more like a convention than a court."

The judges responded both formally and informally to this dilemma. Formally, they increased en banc determinations without oral argument, taking a cue from the 2d circuit, though in 1978 the 5th circuit alone conducted almost half (N=30) of the national total of en bancs, all with oral hearings. To offset assignment of school desegregation negotiations to presiding judges for the sake of efficiency, the tribunal circulated slip opinions concerning this special subject to the whole membership.[66] Digests of recent decisions were also distributed to every judge. Informally, the court found a way around statutory requirements of holding hearings in Fort Worth and Jacksonville in order to increase the sittings at a central location in New Orleans.[67] In addition, nonpanel members monitored slip opinions to forestall en bancs. Certain judges took it upon themselves to criticize slip opinions in order to iron out errors and inconsistencies before filing. The practice was formalized to the extent that when a nonpanel member circulated a letter of criticism to the full court, the panel advised the clerk to hold up publication pending an exchange of views among interested members. Changes in the opinion were then circulated with a deadline. "The panel is in charge," a proponent explained, but "nonmembers have an absolute right—a duty—to criticize. It is simply a system of advice . . . [that] obviates the need of en bancs."

Monitoring opinions is, in effect, an informal en banc. Other circuits have also bypassed en bancs and stepped up internal criticism to avert the "delay, costs, and continued uncertainty that can ill be afforded at a time of burgeoning calendars," especially when Supreme Court review seems certain.[68] This development illustrates an oft-observed phenomenon in organizations: the creation of informal surrogates to avoid onerous formal methods of decision making.

Subtle changes also transpired in the purposes of en bancs, a shift in which resolving panel conflicts was subordinate to ensuring majority rule in important issues of public policy when certiorari was uncertain.[69] Of sixty-five en bancs held by the 5th circuit in 1968-1972, for instance, only five were called to settle panel conflicts, mostly in criminal law, while the remainder were held to decide "troublesome" questions.[70] To meet rising demands for innovation, the Court of Appeals, no less than the Supreme Court, gave primacy to its policy-making rather than its uniformity functions.

These transformations were not painless, however. The monitoring of opinions by nonpanel members, secondary reference groups as we saw in Chapter Five, can ruffle judicial feathers. One reason the D.C. circuit appears so conflictual is that circulating opinions to everyone concentrates rather than disperses disagreement. Informal methods work better on smaller courts. Some judges denounced telephone conferences to avoid en bancs, an increasingly popular practice, as an "absurdity."

> We're becoming so overloaded [one southerner said] I'm fearful of the effect on the quality of our work. Fifteen judges are too many. We had a conference call the other day simply to avoid an en banc. Fifteen men spoke for an hour and forty-five minutes. Just to hold the phone that long my arm ached all day.

In the same vein, Judges Godbold and Bell openly decried the silencing and legislative effects when members compromised principles for the sake of harmony.[71]

Though the 5th circuit may be an extreme case, the truth is that most circuit judges regard en bancs as a "damned nuisance." The main dilemma, Judge Friendly has written, is that "as the federal courts are taking over more and more of the management of the country, many courts of appeals judges are experiencing considerable discomfiture in being committed to far-reaching policies in whose formulation they had no voice. On the other hand, the consequent desire for more en bancs is being held in check by the tremendous pressure of work due to the explosion of the business of the courts of appeals."[72]

Judges also resist en bancs because they "prefer peace." The procedure can intensify conflict and polarize courts. En bancs called to correct a "wrong decision" necessarily pit the judgment of one group of judges against others. When members deny oral argument by counsel, they tend to argue mainly "among ourselves." To call this tendency the "institutionalization of conflict" is perhaps an exaggeration.[73] Whether en bancs exacerbate or ease disputes depends on subsequent compliance with majority rulings, not the intensity of showdowns. Nevertheless, judicial resistance to en bancs and the bruises exposed in opinions call into question the success of this instrument of unification.[74]

Despite attempted guidance from the Supreme Court, these jurists, particularly in New York, were at odds over the purposes of en bancs. Basically, four standards justify convening a whole court: (1)

to overrule prior decisions, (2) to settle panel conflicts, (3) to correct error, and (4) to ensure majority control in policy issues of "exceptional importance," both as an aid to the Supreme Court and as a symbol of solidarity to circuit constituencies. In Washington, en bancs were described as "a confined open problem," less sore than during earlier disputes over criminal justice.[75] In the 5th circuit, en bancs were "no longer the big problem, though they are a big problem." In complex cases the tribunal splintered into "6⅞ and 7⅛ votes"; and sitting en banc was "often a euphemism for the full court deciding the case by mail."[76]

Judges of the 2d circuit agreed only that the full court should participate in overrulings—and that they disagreed about other criteria of holding en bancs. On one extreme were members who favored en bancs not only to correct errors, "sloppy writing," or minority decisions, but also to assist the Supreme Court by holding dress rehearsals and resolving intercircuit conflicts.[77] On the other side were judges, reportedly led by Chief Judge Kaufman, who believed that en bancs should be restricted to overrulings and rare cases of great public moment. According to this view, "en bancs should not be held simply for disagreement. We're not a miniature Supreme Court doing their job at a lower echelon." "The Supreme Court will decide the important ones anyhow. Why bother?"[78] Most judges described themselves as in between, as one said, "shifting along, like Dante's ghost, here and there." As a result, the circuit held only five en bancs with oral argument during the decade 1965-1975.[o]

This dispute, the one crack in the cohesion of the 2d circuit, illustrates anew how external pressures can erode internal decision rules in Courts of Appeals. Convening the full court is the official method to integrate federal circuits, but because en bancs "slow things down terribly," judges tend to avoid them, patching over differences by informal monitoring and "verbal contrivances" that "conceal judicial disharmony."[79] To reach consensus under great volume pressures,

---

[o] Commented two judges in New York: "I find it difficult to determine my own criteria! [Laughter]" "If you could tell me the criteria for en bancs, I would be delighted. Without question this is the one problem I don't have any answer to. It is clear that overrulings can only be by the entire court. But I have a theory, a Parkinson's law, that the importance of an en banc is a function of how close one is to writing the opinion."

A southerner also observed: "The big thing about en bancs when one finally gets down to it is they just don't deliver great law, but decide only the facts—unless the result is outrageous. . . . You can never articulate the criteria for en bancs. . . . You can't get absolute symmetry with 15 or 9 judges. The trouble with purists on en bancs is when you finally get together you vote on hunch. If there was time enough, you'd all see this is a———factual case."

in short, all three tribunals favored informal methods of conflict resolution. En bancs tend to be reserved for policy making and head-on collisions rather than the more frequent sideswipes.[80] Transformed in the process is the capacity of regional courts to unify circuit law.

## Conclusions

The larger and more diverse the court, the harder it is for judges to "promote solidarity of conclusion and the consequent influence of judicial decision."[81] These traditional norms of appellate judging are doubly challenging for intermediate tribunals with rotating memberships. Judicial perceptions of intramural conflict and its management in the three circuits suggest that canons of self-restraint are less useful in explaining the puzzle of unity in diversity than are external pressures, common judicial values, and informal dynamics in these small groups.

The consensus of the circuits, for one thing, is a partial illusion. Heavy workloads and routine litigation inhibit dissents and en bancs. Diffusion of disagreement among rotating panels also permits judges to sidestep disputes behind a facade of agreement. Paradoxically, individual conflicts may be reduced at the expense of the unity of the whole. Tensions exist among judges over how vital it is to resolve such differences in face of burgeoning caseloads. These tensions extend to the very modes of determining court policy, panels or en bancs. Consequently, unlike results in like cases are not strangers to circuit law. Outcomes depend on who sits.

Circuit court judges, like decision makers in other small groups, also rely heavily on informal means to coordinate their activities. In earlier chapters we saw how a broad normative consensus underlies the functioning of intermediate courts as organizations in the judicial system. These circuit judges were unified not just by Supreme Court review, but by substantial agreement regarding organizational goals, national missions, and overlapping policy values. Disagreements, though real, clustered at the margins of lawmaking. We also saw how judges shared common outlooks toward appropriate tools and clienteles of their craft. Now we see that they felt further constrained by unwritten rules guiding work in groups. Various traditions and unofficial conventions, some carried over from previous professional life, served to facilitate the execution of mutual business, control conflict, and foster cohesion in each tribunal. Several practices, such as speaking order or processes of bargaining, resembled those of the Supreme Court. Others, such as the memorandum system of the 2d circuit, reflected role expectations. Still others, such as screening or shifting priorities for en bancs, were unique responses to mounting external demands. Monitoring opinions manifested both the judges' dissatisfaction with formal procedures of conflict resolution and their capacity to develop informal surrogates to institutionalize their courts. Just as informal decisions and patterns of behavior offset potential diversity *among* federal courts, so informal understandings and professional standards guide conduct *within* them. The inner workings of circuit courts, too, are subject to moral rule.

The effect of these internal norms on particular decisions, however, should not be exaggerated. It may be doubted whether group controls explain away the gap between the surface cohesion and latent conflict among these judges.[82] Rules of the game in Courts of Appeals, weaker and less specific than those in American and Canadian legislatures, were so implicit that the judges had trouble articulating them. Except perhaps for panel rotation, nothing compares to the elaborate rules of legislative etiquette, which members violate at considerable risk. The mutual expectations circuit judges felt obliged to follow were professional courtesies and unwritten conventions to facilitate common work, not codes or taboos. They may vary from circuit to circuit to fit unique conditions; everywhere they tend to be poorly enforced, because sanctions rub against jealously guarded traditions of personal independence.

So again we reach the conclusion that judicial discretion is bridled by another dimension of informal constraints inherent in collective action, but not so much as to preclude individuality. Justices Jackson and Powell have described the Supreme Court as an institution whose members collaborate when they choose.[83] Circuit courts, too, are "pretty individual, not collegial." Fragmented, informal, and permissive, these small groups of equals are organized according to rival principles of independence and collegiality. Panel rotation tends to pluralize them, en bancs to polarize them. Rotation is to the parts what regionalism is to the whole—a decentralizing and destabilizing force. The wonder is that Courts of Appeals cohere as well as they do given the difficulties of collective action in the law explosion. Routinization of ordinary work and displacement of goals in en bancs signify that the function of uniformity, in the circuits as in the high court, is yielding to the priority of policy making. Intracircuit harmony is taxed no less than the national appellate capacity of the Supreme Court. Freedom of expression, expertise, and fluid coalitions flourish in this environment. So do discretion and informal means of conflict resolution and avoidance, including tolerance of circuit dissensus for the sake of peace. Because outcomes depend on panel composition, two questions become paramount in managing circuit courts. To what extent is leadershp a source of circuit cohesion? How is judicial work, and therefore judicial power, distributed in Courts of Appeals?

# Eight · Leadership in the Allocation of Work

It is a truism that loosely knit work groups require leaders to unite members in the performance of common tasks. Students of formal organizations often suggest an inverse relationship between leadership and conflict.[1] In Congress, for instance, representatives tend to take their cues in routine decisions from trusted colleagues who, by virtue of character and expertise, successfully mediate between the personal predispositions of members and party positions.[2] Even in voluntary organizations like political parties, whose workers may be torn between pragmatic and institutional loyalties, leaders, by whatever chemistry, manage to lower the intensity of disagreement and to mobilize individuals behind collective goals.[3]

However imperfect the analogies to larger organizations, these observations have a familiar ring in Courts of Appeals. Though specialization probably figures less in judicial than in legislative leadership, the tribunal least united in role orientations, the D.C. circuit, was the most divided over legal policy. The cohesion of the 2d circuit, in turn, some judges attributed to the leadership of their chief, J. Edward Lumbard. Yet, little is known about leadership formation in circuit courts. Are the leaders few or many? What is the basis of their influence? Do newcomers undergo apprenticeships in which their influence is wan while they learn their jobs? Do chief judges enjoy advantages in adjudication? Do policy objectives, seniority, or expertise affect panel and opinion assignments? These questions will be addressed in this chapter, using both perceptual and behavioral data, as we consider leadership in the distribution of work—and hence of judicial power—in three intermediate federal courts.

**Freshman Socialization**

Circuit judges, as noted earlier, generally learn their duties as jurists—their institutional missions and community obligations—en route to Courts of Appeals. Advance training is less apposite, though, to internal decision-making rules and the folkways of group life. New members of most government bodies commonly undergo a period of adjustment and familiarization as they learn the ropes and internalize group norms. The length and intensity of on-the-job training, of course, vary with different organizations and individuals. Legislatures, because of greater size, diversity, and committee specialization, tend to rely more than courts on rules of the game and freshman socialization to integrate their members.[4] The seniority system institutionalizes this process in most American legislatures. Courts, being smaller and less specialized, rely more on anticipatory socialization for the learning of judicial roles.

Freshman socialization, nonetheless, occurs at all levels of the federal judiciary. New district judges, particularly former specialists, attest to the fact that the demands of their jobs required considerable adaptation.[5] Supreme Court Justices as diverse as Cardozo, Stone, and Murphy—or Warren, Brennan, and Goldberg—all experienced a breaking-in period, commonly about three years in duration, before they felt fully effective on the high bench.[6] Their behavior during this transition was marked by deference to senior members, uncertainty and moderation in voting, relatively sparse opinion writing or dissent, and even discomfort over cloistered styles of life. Chief Justice Taft was not the only federal judge to complain about living in a monastery.

The freshman socialization of circuit judges, in keeping with their positions and functions, appears neither so critical to institutional integration as in legislatures nor so lengthy as in the Supreme Court. In response to direct questions about a freshman period, as summarized in Table 8.1, these circuit judges believed three to one that newcomers did undergo adjustments of about one year, though not as a result of institutional rules. "Generally, it's in the mind of the freshman," observed a circuit judge. "He feels the others don't pay as much attention to his opinions. He labors under an inferiority complex. I'm sure it doesn't take over a year. I felt it myself."[a]

Assimilation takes longer on the Supreme Court, the judges thought, because of its intricate jurisdiction and finality in close, controversial issues. For themselves the greatest discomfort arose from the central duty: adjudicating federal controversies "soundly." The flavor of these feelings is captured by the reactions of two newcomers, one a former district judge, who observed:

> I wouldn't say it's a freshman period. But I've got to gain the respect of members of the court in my ability to write opinions and not err and to be correct. So you have to prove yourself as a

[a] Another jurist in Washington said: "Yes, that's very true, for instance, Judge [the court's newest member]. It takes a couple of years before one becomes effective—and sound. I know Warren Burger has felt it [on the Supreme Court]. He told me so."

TABLE 8.1
*Judicial Perceptions of Whether a Freshman Period Occurs on Courts of Appeals*

| Circuit | Yes N | Some N | No N | No Response N | Total N |
|---|---|---|---|---|---|
| 2d | 4 | 2 | 2 | 2 | 10 |
| 5th | 8 | 2 | 4 | 3 | 17 |
| D.C. | 4 | 3 | 1 | 0 | 8 |
| Sums | 16 | 7 | 7 | 5 | 35 |

NOTE: The questions were: "Supreme Court Justices often mention a certain 'freshman' period before they became a fully effective member of the court. Is this true on the Court of Appeals? How long does the period last?"

man whose ability to write opinions they respect. I don't think that I'm very effective right now. I hope to be more effective.

It must be so, because I still feel very much a freshman. I hope I haven't acted sophomoric!

Because the depth and duration of freshman learning depend on each individual's background and personality, the process is largely ad hoc and unstructured. Former district judges were considered less troubled as newcomers than specialists and academics, because of broader exposure to federal law and experience in making judgments. Particularly was this so in the 5th circuit where several members had already served on the Court of Appeals by designation. Neophytes also felt less diffident in their specialties. ("I was no blushing violet in fields I knew something about. How effective I was is another question. [Laughter]") Because few felt familiar with the wide range of litigation or the function of reflection, however, even former trial judges expressed surprise that "it takes a while to learn the job—and I'm not addressing myself to personal relationships. . . . That's a very different job." One judge, universally acknowledged as a leader from the start, "remarked only yesterday that I don't know how I got through my first year."

Because the "agony" of decision is not confined to novices, some judges discounted the differences between regulars and newcomers who were otherwise qualified for the post.[7] ("We letter from the first day.")[b] Still, enough circuit judges regarded their first year or so on

[b] Commented a chief judge: "I haven't seen anything an experienced lawyer can't

Courts of Appeals as a period of on-the-job training to suggest several hypotheses about uniformities in their behavior. Freshman judges generally tend to speak less for the court or in dissent than experienced members. Some may wallow in indecision for a time, take longer to write opinions, and defer to chief judges. Regulars, broadened and toughened by experience, feel more confidence in themselves—and in their peers. Calmer about the responsibility of decision, they assume a greater share of the load. Therein, perhaps, lies the most persuasive argument for prior judicial service as a criterion for selection to the Supreme Court: "Things don't appear so earthshaking after some experience."

## Perceptions of Administrative and Adjudicative Leadership

Learning how to judge usually comes by doing. Pulling a court together usually requires leadership. Who are the leaders, and what is the basis of their influence, in rotating courts of equals? For Courts of Appeals, as for many other appellate tribunals, the starting points of analysis are the official distinction between administrative and policy leadership and the interplay of seniority and expertise in adjudication.

The administrative leader of each circuit, by statute, is the chief judge, chosen from regular active judges according to seniority with tenure up to age seventy. Administrative leadership, as in congressional committees, thus depends on accidents of recruitment rather than administrative talent or design. That Lumbard rather than Waterman became chief judge of the 2d circuit in 1959, for example, turned on a difference in seniority of only one day.[8] Policy leadership, that is, influence in deciding cases and developing legal doctrine, is officially divorced from administration. In adjudication, as E. Barrett Prettyman stated the theory, "the Chief is one of nine judges, no more and no less. His influence over his brethren is his power of persuasion, and he has exactly the same amount as he would have were he not the Chief Judge."[9] Most multimember courts in the United States are organized accordingly. In theory,

---

handle. Nothing is hard for me. It's no harder than the practice of law. Our only difficulty is having to decide. I disavow that I get down on my knees. I'm religious, I hope, and I want to do right, but judges are not on an altar. Too much wisdom is ascribed to judges. When did I get it? When I took an oath that lasted a few seconds? I'm the same person. I'm no smarter after. I have more power, but not more wisdom. It's amazing how much so-called capacity is ascribed to judges. I disavow it!

"I always say our biggest problem is: 'What's it going to do tomorrow?' I have no difficulty deciding a case. What it's going to do tomorrow is the problem."

court management is a ministerial function separated from judging to foster judicial independence and the natural flowering of legal ideas.

The trouble is that the attempted divorce of administration from policy making seldom succeeds in most organizations. Merely to recite the managerial tasks of chief judges is to cast doubt on the distinction in Courts of Appeals as well. The formal heads of circuit courts are key actors in federal judicial administration. Chief judges, aided by small staffs, administer the dockets and supervise panel assignments. Chief judges automatically preside at any panel or en banc hearing they attend and assign opinions when in the majority. Having psychological advantages as presiding officers, they are expected to lead discussions, clarify issues, and speak for the court in the most controversial cases.[10] Further, chief judges assign members of three-judge district courts, which decide major issues in civil rights and reapportionment, appealable directly to the Supreme Court. Chief judges share with the Chief Justice authority to designate visiting judges to, from, and within the circuit. They organize and preside over meetings of circuit councils, which are committees of the whole responsible for administration of all federal courts in each circuit. They arrange the programs of annual circuit judicial conferences and serve as ex officio members of the Judicial Conference of the United States, the main policy-making arm of the federal judiciary. Finally, "implicit in the designation," as Judge Prettyman observed, "is a definite responsibility, greater than that of any other member, for the intangible qualities which come to characterize the organization as a unit." To chief judges inevitably falls primary responsibility of safeguarding the "intangible attributes of a court as a court," of enforcing the rules of the game.[11]

"Chief judges are always trying to pull a court together," as one southerner put it. Though far from overlords, and clearly less influential than Chief Justices of the United States, the managers of circuit courts are of all members most expected to conform to group standards and to represent their tribunals to the outer world.[12] To explore whether their administrative authority affects adjudication, leadership was left undefined, and the judges were asked, first, if the position of chief judge gave incumbents advantages in deciding cases and, second, to rank those personal characteristics that determine effectiveness on the bench. The judges' perceptions of panel and opinion assignments were then compared with the distribution of work in the base period, 1965-1967.

Though chief judges are expected to assert task leadership, it is striking how little their formal powers figured in the judges' evaluations of interpersonal influence on the three courts. A two-to-one majority, embracing official theory, rejected the notion that administrative authority gave chief judges extra influence in adjudication. The dominant view, as shown in Table 8.2, was that doctrinal leadership derived from judicial rather than managerial capacity. As one 5th circuit judge remarked of his chief:

> We think John Brown has one vote and we have one. We stand up to John Brown and push him around a bit, I'm afraid. He takes it well. He has advantages in assigning judges and opinions. We respect him as a brilliant judge, but he's not infallible. He takes it upon himself to monitor everyone else's opinions. Sometimes he's off base, firing from the hip at us. However, it puts you on your toes. I'm glad he does that, though sometimes it's exasperating. He writes you to rewrite. He is vigorous in pushing his opinions. I don't mind. It contributes to the well-being of the court.

TABLE 8.2
*Judicial Perceptions of Whether the Office of Chief Judge Gives Incumbents Advantages In Influencing Adjudication*

| Circuit | Yes N | Qualified N | No N | No Response N | Total |
|---|---|---|---|---|---|
| 2d | 1 | 2 | 5 | 2 | 10 |
| 5th | 2 | 3 | 10 | 2 | 17 |
| D.C. | 1 | 2 | 5 | 0 | 8 |
| Sums | 4 | 7 | 20 | 4 | 35 |

NOTE: The question was: "Does the office of chief judge give the incumbent advantages in influencing other members?"

The office of chief judge, viewed mostly as a bundle of service functions, actually evoked "little more than sympathy" for incumbents—and praise for individuals, such as Lumbard of the 2d circuit and Brown of the 5th, who were regarded as exceptionally able administrators.[c] A chief judgeship, in this respect, is comparable to the chairmanship of an academic department or a Senate

---

[c] Though one colleague declared that "Eddie gives me fits!" Lumbard was described as "a perfectly wonderful administrator. He keeps them all busy. He puts fire

committee.[13] Responsible more than any other person for efficient operation of the organization, but lacking commensurate power to act alone, a chief judge must operate largely through informal consultations with his peers. The daily chores of housekeeping, docketing, reporting, financial accounting, and keeping laggards to the wheel, not to mention external representation and devising better methods of management, all require constant negotiation with individual judges and staff. These activities, which are bound to increase as the courts seek organizational remedies for the stress caused by increased demand, have been estimated to consume from one-third to one-half of a chief judge's time.[14] Simultaneously, chief judges are expected to carry an equal share of the caseload. Small wonder that incumbents harbored few illusions that the office makes the judge. Of a thankless job, one former chief said: "The only advantage is that the title sounds more imposing if you are speaking in public or writing an article. Otherwise it's a pain in the ass."

Whether members agree on "strategic premises" has much to do with the influence of chief judges on legal policy.[15] For example, Simon E. Sobeloff, the able chief judge of the 4th circuit, lacked majority support for vigorous desegregation which Elbert P. Tuttle enjoyed in the 5th. Parlaying the position into opinion leadership also depends on successful exploitation of powers to assign. Evaluating these prerogatives differently, a minority of judges in all three circuits insisted that administrative authority inevitably affected adjudication. A chief judge, observed one jurist in New York, has "tremendous influence."

> It depends on how your bloc reacts. In the normal course, the chief judge is just the same as the rest. I think unquestionably, for about two years, a new judge is influenced by the chief. By that time he's on his own feet. Administratively, good Lord, tremendous influence. Clark had the language: procedure is how your case is decided. That's why Clark was such a student of it. The chief judge has tremendous influence by careful and deliberate manipulation of administrative power.... The philosophic approach and orientation of certain individuals—their relation to current problems—are well known. If the chief judge

---

under their tails. The reason why we're up to date with our calendar is J. Edward Lumbard!"

Of John R. Brown, judges said: "We've got a great chief judge." "He's a dynamo—it's a good thing he is." "It depends on the individual. Hutcheson had no teamwork or imagination.... Brown is good—innovative and imaginative in administration. He's had to be." "Tuttle never cared for the administrative part. He is a great man, but he'd be the first to say that. Brown loves it. Frankly, he's more able at it, too."

is of a certain stripe, he will succeed in getting that certain stripe in panels. Clark succeeded in getting judges of a certain kind. Lumbard succeeds in getting the opposite kinds. None of us complains. We take it as it is. That's it.

Though other colleagues detected no favoritism in Lumbard's assignments, the same themes were echoed elsewhere.[d] "So many times judicial problems slop over into administrative problems and vice versa," Chief Judge Brown once confessed, that the real questions are where and when.[17] As with strong presidents, these judges argued, the spillover "depends on the personality of the chief" and the countervailing force of experienced colleagues. The impact of chief judges was most noticeable on freshmen and the composition of three-judge district courts. ("If all the judges are new, he'll pack a wallop out of proportion to one vote.")[e] Southern judges made no bones about packing three-judge district courts in race relations cases. ("Tuttle was not about to set up a three-judge court with Cameron or Cox on it; this occurs no more.") Of all administrative powers, plainly the most potent instruments of policy leadership involve the assignment of work.

Even so, most circuit judges maintained that formal administrative power determined policy leadership far less than did professional skill. For all the boy-scout quality of the alternatives, Table 8.3 shows substantial agreement in the judges' ranking of traits thought necessary for effectiveness on a circuit bench. Task rather than policy oriented, they tended to rate intelligence, integrity, and expertise higher than personality, conviction, or length of service. Furthermore, when asked if any colleagues were particularly effective in influencing other members, most answered affirmatively and, as anticipated in Chapter Four, explained why in professional terms. Effectiveness in all three circuits was perceived as a combination of factors, as one judge explained, "not necessarily in order—sound legal capacity, scholarship and personality, and qualities of leadership which would make a man a leader in any group."

A few judges thought interpersonal influence was "a function of agreement." ("I tend to listen to one judge more than to another. You

[d] Judge Friendly dismissed the danger of panel stacking by "evil-minded" chiefs as not "very serious." "But none of the chief judges I have known would think of doing that; if one were to attempt it, the secret would not last very long, and the response would be vigorous."[16]

[e] To illustrate, consider this comment from a freshman regarding his chief: "I don't know how he does it. Seriously, there is no real advantage on legal doctrine, in trying to persuade. It means a lot if he asks you to do something; if you can you should. That's an unwritten rule."

TABLE 8.3
Judicial Perceptions of Personal Characteristics
That Affect a Judge's Effectiveness on Circuit Courts

| Personal Characteristic | Very Important N | Moderately Important N | Not Important N | No Response N | Total N |
|---|---|---|---|---|---|
| Intelligence | 32 | 1 | 0 | 2 | 35 |
| Integrity | 32 | 0 | 1 | 2 | 35 |
| Learning/ expertness | 24 | 8 | 1 | 2 | 35 |
| Craftsmanship | 22 | 11 | 0 | 2 | 35 |
| Personality | 8 | 22 | 2 | 3 | 35 |
| Willingness to compromise | 4 | 23 | 6 | 2 | 35 |
| Intensity of conviction | 4 | 18 | 11 | 2 | 35 |
| Length of service | 2 | 25 | 6 | 2 | 35 |
| Party affiliation | 0 | 0 | 33 | 2 | 35 |

NOTE: The question was: "How would you rank the following personal characteristics as they affect a judge's effectiveness on a circuit bench?"

can't get away from it.") Personality factors, such as "character," "insistence and just plumb aggressiveness," were also considered significant, though it goes too far to say that leadership qualities were primarily attributes of personality rather than of attainment. In contrast to state judges, these jurists ranked neither ideological nor personality traits as highly as professional capacity and expertise.[f][18] Typical were these comments:

> Personality doesn't amount to so much as opinion-writing ability. Some judges are simply better than others. Some know more, think better. It would be strange if among nine men all had the same ability. Some simply have more respect than others.

> That's bound to be so in any group. The first thing is, is the judge particularly broad and experienced in the field? A couple of judges are acknowledged masters in admiralty. What they think carries more weight. I don't have much trouble being heard on criminal law or state government. I've been there. Ex-

[f] Regarding personality, one judge in Washington observed that "sometimes an en banc opinion assignment will be influenced by that. Maybe if Joe is the writer, Judge X will go along. If Judge Y writes there is slight chance."

district judges on Courts of Appeals certainly carry more weight in discussion of trial procedures, instructions to juries, etc. Every judge is recognized for a particular proficiency obtained before or after his appointment. It saves enormous spadework and drudgery [to assign opinions accordingly]. No one could develop an expertise in all these fields.

Of them all, Henry J. Friendly came closest to universal recognition as the most respected federal circuit judge.[g] Because of diverse specialization and panel rotation, however, no one was thought to dominate any circuit. Attempts to lead not only vary among individuals but may backfire.[h] One judge typically asserted:

Like any other group, some are more impressive than others. Some are more determined. Some are tenacious. They have strong convictions. But, on the other hand, that can cause the others to react—to hell with you. Unfortunately, judges are human beings. That doesn't happen often. Within a court you'll find that some judges don't want a role of leadership.

Consequently, a few judges cautioned against overestimating the impact of leaders on circuit decision making. ("You have to live with yourself. You don't try to persuade if they feel strongly.") Among a "group of men who are pretty able to make up their own minds," they regarded opinion leadership as spasmodic and situational, restricted to "a given time, a given case."[19] Day in, day out, they placed most members on an equal plane. If one generalization held, it was that circuit judges perceived the core elements of leadership to be intellectual integrity and professional skill. Impatient of probing about personality, one prominent activist summarized the prevailing view: "Yes, there is leadership, if you will, but leadership influenced by legal knowledge, legal insight, practical judgment, and ability to articulate them persuasively!"

---

[g] "Friendly is very effective," colleagues remarked. "I wouldn't hesitate to say I feel a great deal safer—that we haven't overlooked something, that nothing foolish is going out—if he's on a panel. He has a great deal of influence. Lumbard, too, and it is quite deserved in both cases." For Friendly's influence outside his circuit, see Chapter Five, note m.

[h] For example, judges in the 5th circuit observed: "Tuttle I give an 'A plus.' Hutcheson carried it to excess. He would lobby against an opinion he didn't like. He would call up immediately. We used to resent his overdoing it."

"We have dissenters who ask for en bancs all the time. I wouldn't name them. If Dyer asks for an en banc, I'll look. He doesn't dissent much. I don't think that Carswell, who hasn't sat for very long, would be ignored on a procedural question regarding district courts. We would listen to him before Judge X's opinion. Otherwise, it's the old story of hollering wolf."

The emphasis on expertise in perceptions of judicial leadership is a significant symptom of the informal decisional structure of the three tribunals. Lacking a captain, and unorganized by party, ideological factions, or personal loyalties, circuit judges naturally turn to their most informed members to satisfy role expectations of reasoned decisions under heavy volume pressures. Similar responses have been observed in Congress and small legislative councils.[20] Highly fragmented and permissive organizations with relatively low levels of internal conflict are conducive to reliance on expertise.[21] Especially is this so among peer groups, such as circuit judges, who are imbued with professional values, limited in personal contact, and bound by a broad consensus regarding group objectives and the irrelevance of personal and partisan loyalties. Knowledge is power and the road to group effectiveness.

Unlike legislatures, however, where specialization of labor is necessary for productivity and acquisition of respect, assigning work in Courts of Appeals according to policy preferences or expertise collides with internal norms of random rotation and equality among generalists.[22] A major empirical question is how circuit judges resolved this tension in expectations, especially in light of their capacity for tolerating dissensus and the potential policy leverage in the hands of administrative leaders who allocate judicial work.

## Perceptions of Panel and Opinion Assignments

From every perspective, the key to circuit decision is who decides. What litigant wins or loses, what doctrine or policy prevails, what judge leads or follows, all depend on the composition of the court. This is hardly a state secret. Even the Hruska Commission conceded that when the philosophies of judges and circuit law are known, as they usually are, the power to assign is the power to decide.[23] That is why the principle of random rotation is such a critical rule of the game.

Suspicions of panel stacking arise from time to time in every circuit.[24] A rigged panel, like a rigged jury or a bad umpire, is an easy scapegoat for losers. Specialization in opinion assignments also has been advanced as a rational way to alleviate workloads.[25] Though methods of selecting panels vary in each circuit, most of these judges insisted that panel composition, while not perfectly random, was disinterested. Panels fell short of perfection, they maintained, to accommodate competing interests, such as personal convenience, seniority, and geographic balance. In the 2d circuit, for instance, where the chief judge and his assistant select panel members, Judge Lumbard attempted to satisfy individual preferences as to when, as distinct from with whom, they wished to sit. Attempting to equalize caseloads in terms of presumed difficulty, Lumbard also arranged schedules so that judges would serve with one another at least once annually. He further juggled panel memberships according to seniority so that everyone but the freshman member (then Feinberg) would preside over at least one set of panels a year. Such careful knitting can be easily unraveled, however, because "the brethren display almost fiendish glee in trading assignments with each other" for reasons of personal convenience.[26]

Judges of the 5th circuit, charged with panel rigging by one of their own members in 1963, were especially sensitive to the issue of neutral selection. "Cameron's opinion on that," a colleague recalled, "put Tuttle into near hysterics."[i] [27] To allay suspicions, the succeeding chief judge, John R. Brown, developed a theoretically fail-safe method of ensuring randomness. The chief and his administrative assistant distributed the weekly sittings among judges without knowing the cases; the clerk and a calendaring judge assigned cases to panels without knowing the membership until the two parts were published simultaneously.[j] Foolproof in theory, even this system fell shy of mathematical perfection for several reasons. The chief judge, as in the 2d circuit, attempted to diversify panels according to seniority and geography. The calendaring judge distributed cases with an eye to location (to minimize litigant expenses) and weight ("How tough are they?"), a task later shared by three-judge screening panels and central staff. Screening, above all, qualified the rule of randomness. Roughly half the decisions in the mid-1970s were made unanimously without oral argument by screening panels whose members rotated but once a year.[28]

In the District of Columbia, where panel members were chosen in a monthly lottery held by the clerk, similar accommodations qualified strict adherence to chance.[29] A "very senior" staff person screens cases according to weight. Judges swap assignments, sometimes even to avoid sitting with antagonists or in fields they disliked. Though the gossip in Washington regarding systematic panel

[i] Though no judge admitted that Cameron's charges were true, denials were not always convincing. Said one victim of Cameron's attack: "The statistics speak for themselves on that question. Now it is not so . . . it is done strictly by rotation."

[j] Chief Judge Brown, who regarded mixing membership as part of the court's strength, declared: "Unlike every other circuit, this chief judge has nothing to do with calendaring cases. I can't. I have instructed the clerk not to listen to me if I try. That's an order. Other chief judges think I'm nuts." Quoted with permission.

stacking seems unwarranted, members conceded that "to say there is absolute chance is inaccurate."[30]

Hence, in principle, these judges were strongly attached to panel rotation. Critical of proposed specialized panels to increase productivity, most of them expressed confidence that their courts measured up in practice to public expectations of unbiased composition.[31] The shortfall from perfect randomness they attributed to justifiable reasons of convenience, seniority, geographic diversification, and the press of business. Division of labor at the panel stage, either to influence policy or to increase efficiency, was considered minimal.

Opinion assignments, by contrast, the judges saw as more purposive and specialized. Unlike the 6th circuit, whose chief judge selects court spokesmen, in these three tribunals opinions were assigned by the presiding judge, that is, the senior active judge in the majority of each panel. Guiding their selections were informal norms of equal work and diversification. "We try to be generous," judges said, "though the result is inevitably less than random." Specialization was perceived primarily in two forms: assignment to experts or to judges from states whose law governs in diversity cases. A "slight local tinge" thus colored diversity opinions as part of a general tendency of members to defer to colleagues most knowledgeable about the subject.

> There is no formal declared policy in this circuit [a southerner explained], but, sure, in diversity cases opinions usually go to a judge of the state involved or to a specialist in a highly specialized subject, such as admiralty to Brown, if he's on the panel. That's actual practice. It is not formally recognized and never to the extent of panel assignment. There, theoretically, every judge is qualified to pass on anything. On opinions, the presiding judge assigns to the best able man in that subject.

The best judge available, because of seniority and special interests, may be self-selected. Choosing spokesmen was described as highly informal and often voluntary.

> If someone doesn't like to write the opinion in a case, he can say so [a 2d circuit judge asserted]. Someone else may volunteer. There is assignment cooperation. Once in a while there will be a case in admiralty; they know I like it. They let me have it. But only once in a while. Take taxation, for example. I can't think of anyone on this court with a specialty or interest in it. The same with patents. Some courts have hotshots. We don't.[k]

[k] Southern judges commented in similar vein: "There was specialization of opinion assignment in Hutcheson's day, not today. The only time now is when a panel has a

Informality, together with panel rotation and recognition that no one was a universal expert, left these judges untroubled by opinion specialization. Some defended it as bringing their best minds forward, an intelligent allocation of resources in the appeals explosion. Others regarded it as too fluid to compromise seriously the norm of appellate review by generalists. All the same, these jurists were highly sensitive to expertise, able to identify specialists in various fields, and self-conscious about their own.[32] Professional skill more than formal authority was the foundation of mutual respect and influence. According to most judges, rotation virtually eliminated policy control from panel assignments, but an informal winnowing occurred in selecting opinion writers. Because power to assign turns on seniority, it follows that in Courts of Appeals, as in legislative committees, two principles of leadership—specialization and seniority—may merge as judges distribute their labor and choose their spokesmen.[33] The question is how much.

## Panel Assignments in Practice

The interplay of seniority and specialization can be observed at both stages of assignment in the three courts. Tables 8.4, 8.5, and 8.6 summarize the distributions of panel and opinion assignments among the judges who sat in one hundred or more cases during 1965-1967. The columns on the left show the frequencies of actual panel assignments per judge and the ratio of observed to expected panel assignments if perfectly random.[1] These distributions, which are significant at $p < .001$ levels either for all judges or full-time judges only in each circuit, tend to confirm the judges' contentions that panel selection during this period was neither perfectly random nor sufficiently nonrandom to justify lawyers' fears of gerrymandering—with the possible exception of the 5th circuit. Disparities in panel assignments were not grossly offensive to the norm of equal

---

difficult question of local law. If someone from that state is on the panel, he'll say: 'I'll take it.' Goldberg, for example, is an authority on the intricacies of oil and gas leases and tax problems in that area. He has tremendous experience as a lawyer, and he writes well. He is studious and turns out much better work than I would in that area. He's usually kind enough to volunteer. Brown is experienced in admiralty, and he likes to do it. This is the way it falls into line."

Countering suggestions that Judge Hutcheson during this period concentrated on cases from Texas because he shunned travel after suffering a stroke, one judge said: "Hutcheson just saw tough Texas questions others didn't see." Judges in Washington offered parallel explanations for Judge Bazelon's frequent utterances on criminal justice.

[1] For methods of randomization, see Appendix 1.

TABLE 8.4

Panel and Opinion Assignments in the 2d Circuit, FY 1965-1967

| Judge (Year Appointed) | Panel Assignments | | Total Majority Participations (Excludes per curiam) n | Opinion Assignments | | |
|---|---|---|---|---|---|---|
| | Actual Panel Assignments (Includes per curiam) N | Ratio of Actual to Randomly Expected Panel Assignments* % | | Actual Majority Opinions n | Randomly Expected Majority Opinions** (n) | Ratio of Actual to Randomly Expected Opinion Assignments % |
| Medina (1951) | — | — | 63 | 36 | (21.5) | 167.4 |
| Moore (1957) | 493 | 122.6 | 331 | 128 | (112.7) | 113.6 |
| Friendly (1959) | 419 | 104.2 | 299 | 114 | (101.8) | 112.0 |
| Hays (1961) | 364 | 90.5 | 248 | 85 | (84.5) | 100.6 |
| Lumbard (1955) | 432 | 107.5 | 309 | 102 | (105.2) | 97.0 |
| Anderson (1964) | 327 | 84.9 | 219 | 71 | (74.6) | 95.2 |
| Smith (1960) | 393 | 97.8 | 282 | 90 | (96.0) | 93.8 |
| Waterman (1955) | 411 | 102.2 | 289 | 91 | (98.4) | 92.5 |
| Marshall (1962) | 155 | 106.9 | 112 | 33 | (38.1) | 86.6 |
| Kaufman (1961) | 351 | 87.3 | 213 | 62 | (72.5) | 85.5 |
| Feinberg (1966) | 180 | 100.0 | 117 | 33 | (39.9) | 82.7 |
| Sums | 3,525 | 100.0 | 2,482 | 845 | (845.0) | 100.0 |

* Excludes judges with less than 100 assignments (Medina, N = 85 and Swan, N = 29). Expected frequencies are weighted by number of months served.
N judges = 11
df = 10
$\chi^2$ = 44.45
p < .001
Range = 37.7%

** Weighted by mean dissent rate per judge of 4.5% in cases with signed opinions.
N judges = 11
df = 10
$\chi^2$ = 17.9
p > .05
Range = 84.7%

N full-time judges = 10
N cases = 809
df = 9
$\chi^2$ = 8.0
p > .50
Range = 31.4%

TABLE 8.5
Panel and Opinion Assignments in the 5th Circuit, FY 1965-1967

| Judge (Year Appointed) | Panel Assignments | | Opinion Assignments | | |
|---|---|---|---|---|---|
| | Actual Panel Assignments (Includes per curiam) N | Ratio of Actual to Randomly Expected Panel Assignments* % | Total Majority Participations (Excludes per curiam) n | Actual Majority Opinions n | Randomly Expected Majority Opinions** (n) | Ratio of Actual to Randomly Expected Opinion Assignments % |

| Judge | Actual Panel N | Ratio Panel % | Total Maj Participations n | Actual Maj Opinions n | Randomly Expected Maj Opinions (n) | Ratio Opinion % |
|---|---|---|---|---|---|---|
| Hutcheson (1931) | 147 | 30.9 | 99 | 63 | (34.5) | 182.6 |
| Tuttle (1954) | 611 | 128.4 | 293 | 112 | (102.0) | 109.8 |
| Rives (1951) | 479 | 100.6 | 257 | 94 | (89.6) | 104.9 |
| Jones (1955) | 460 | 99.6 | 219 | 78 | (76.2) | 102.4 |
| Wisdom (1957) | 527 | 110.7 | 279 | 95 | (97.2) | 97.7 |
| Dyer (1966) | 121 | 91.7 | 67 | 23 | (23.8) | 96.6 |
| Brown (1955) | 575 | 120.8 | 328 | 110 | (114.2) | 96.3 |
| Ainsworth (1966) | 151 | 104.1 | 85 | 28 | (29.7) | 94.3 |
| Bell (1961) | 531 | 111.6 | 265 | 87 | (92.4) | 94.2 |
| Gewin (1961) | 516 | 108.4 | 271 | 88 | (94.4) | 93.2 |
| Coleman (1965) | 315 | 103.6 | 183 | 57 | (63.7) | 89.5 |
| Thornberry (1965) | 323 | 101.9 | 164 | 48 | (57.1) | 84.1 |
| Goldberg (1966) | 142 | 97.9 | 76 | 22 | (26.4) | 83.3 |
| Godbold (1966) | 100 | 69.0 | 54 | 15 | (18.8) | 79.8 |
| Sums | 4,998 | 100.0 | 2,640 | 920 | (920.0) | 100.0 |

\* Excludes judges with less than 100 assignments (Cameron, N = 6 and Simpson, N = 26). Expected frequencies are weighted by number of months served.

N judges = 14
N full-time judges = 13
N cases = 4,851
df = 12
$\chi^2$ = 62.49
p < .001
Range = 55.6%

N judges = 14
df = 13
$\chi^2$ = 319.7
p < .001
Range = 97.5%

\*\* Weighted by mean dissent rate per judge of 2.54% in cases with signed opinions.

N judges = 14
df = 13
$\chi^2$ = 29.45
p < .01
Range = 102.8%

N full-time judges = 13
N cases = 2,541
N opinions = 851
df = 12
$\chi^2$ = 5.3
p > .90
Range = 31.0%

TABLE 8.6
Panel and Opinion Assignments in the D.C. Circuit, FY 1965-1967

| Judge (Year Appointed) | Panel Assignments | | Opinion Assignments | | | |
|---|---|---|---|---|---|---|
| | Actual Panel Assignments (Includes per curiam) N | Ratio of Actual to Randomly Expected Panel Assignments* % | Total Majority Participations (Excludes per curiam) n | Actual Majority Opinions n | Randomly Expected Majority Opinions** (n) | Ratio of Actual to Randomly Expected Opinion Assignments % |
| Leventhal (1965) | 150 | 96.8 | 103 | 52 | (34.7) | 149.9 |
| Fahy (1949) | 263 | 126.4 | 138 | 58 | (46.5) | 124.7 |
| McGowan (1963) | 282 | 135.6 | 173 | 67 | (58.2) | 115.1 |
| Burger (1956) | 267 | 128.4 | 139 | 49 | (46.8) | 104.7 |
| Bazelon (1949) | 281 | 135.1 | 171 | 59 | (57.6) | 102.4 |
| Danaher (1953) | 232 | 111.5 | 134 | 44 | (45.2) | 97.3 |
| Tamm (1965) | 132 | 81.5 | 78 | 23 | (26.3) | 87.5 |
| Wright (1962) | 261 | 125.5 | 135 | 37 | (45.5) | 81.3 |
| Bastian (1954) | 130 | 62.5 | 67 | 18 | (22.6) | 79.6 |
| Miller (1945) | 128 | 61.5 | 60 | 14 | (20.2) | 69.3 |
| Edgerton (1938) | 128 | 61.5 | 79 | 18 | (26.6) | 67.7 |
| Washington (1949) | 143 | 68.8 | 77 | 17 | (26.0) | 65.4 |
| Sums | 2,397 | 100.0 | 1,354 | 456 | (456.0) | 100.0 |

* Excludes judges with less than 100 assignments (Prettyman, N = 70 and Robinson, N = 24). Expected frequencies are weighted by number of months served.
N judges = 12          N full-time judges = 8
df = 11                N cases = 1,868
$\chi^2$ = 216.31
p < .001
Range = 74.1%          Range = 45.3%

** Weighted by mean dissent rate per judge of 14.9% in cases with signed opinions.
N judges = 12          N full-time judges = 8
df = 11                N cases = 1,071
$\chi^2$ = 23.3        N opinions = 389
p < .02                df = 7
                       $\chi^2$ = 11.77
                       p > .10
Range = 84.5%          Range = 63.4%

work, so long as qualitative differences in cases and experience are taken into account. Yet, there was more evidence of nonrandom panel assignment than the judges admitted or perhaps perceived. Panel selection was exploited as an instrument of leadership, especially in the South.

One way to lead is to sit. Certain judges in all three circuits shouldered disproportionately large caseloads. Particularly striking were the chiefs. Despite heavy administrative duties, Judge Bazelon exceeded random expectations by 35 percent (13% considering only full-time judges), Tuttle by 28 percent, and Lumbard by 8 percent. As a result Lumbard participated in almost a third of the decisions of his circuit; Tuttle did so in 27 percent and Bazelon in 21 percent of theirs. In addition, one or two colleagues carried extra loads. These workhorses included (with the excess over randomly expected assignments in parentheses): Moore (23%) in the 2d circuit; Brown (21%), Bell (12%), and Wisdom (11%) in the 5th circuit; and McGowan (36%) and Burger (28%) in the D.C. circuit. Generally, these judges were either high in seniority or ideologically in the center. Most of them were leaders on doctrinal fronts as well.

Seniority also tempered the randomness principle for senior and freshman judges. Senior circuit judges, whose workload is discretionary, were at both extremes of panel assignment. Most judges on senior status, tailoring work to personal circumstances of age, health, and interest, limited themselves to part-time service. (See, for example, the bottom four judges in the D.C. circuit in Table 8.6.) But a few of them, such as Jones and Rives, who retired early to increase judicial manpower in the 5th, participated fully. Fahy in Washington, in fact, exceeded the expected workload by 26 percent. On the other hand, newcomers such as Dyer, Godbold, and Tamm sat less frequently than expected, thus confirming one hypothesis about freshman socialization in the 5th and D.C. circuits. The main exception was in the 2d circuit, where Feinberg sat more regularly than his more senior colleagues, Anderson and Kaufman.

It is unlikely that convenience accounts for these discrepancies as much as seniority.[m] Length of service cut both ways into the principle of random panel composition. Experienced full-timers, especially chief judges, shouldered disproportionately heavy caseloads; newcomers the lightest. Opportunities to lead in Courts of Appeals, as in Congress, were skewed more toward age than youth.

[m] The same patterns, also significant at $p < .001$ levels, occurred if part-time judges are eliminated. See Tables 8.4-8.6 and Appendix 1. Spearman rank correlation coefficients between seniority and ratios of observed to expected panel assignments of full-time judges were: 2d circuit, 10 judges, $r_s = .5758$, $p < .05$; 5th circuit, 13 judges, $r_s = .5598$, $p < .05$. Cf. D.C. circuit, 8 judges, $r_s = .4821$, $p > .05$.

Frequency of sitting, to be sure, does not fully measure any judge's influence on decisions, least of all their quality. Some cases are more difficult and time consuming than others. Jurists work at variable speeds. Some individuals, like Irving R. Kaufman, were more active than most in external judicial affairs. Well-crafted opinions, not frequency of decision, are the stuff judicial reputations are made of in the legal profession. A first condition of judicial influence, nevertheless, is the opportunity to decide. Because chief judges oversee the allocation of work, panel selection in these circuits, as the minority maintained, must be considered a potential leadership resource.[34] The administrative heads of these tribunals, like athletic coaches or committee chairmen in Congress, put a premium on experience in making panel assignments. Their bias, however understandable in terms of getting the job done, inevitably mingled administrative and judicial powers. Seniority not only determined the courts' administrative leaders but touched the heart of the judicial process: who decides?

To what extent did these administrative choices also yield specialization by subject? To explore this issue the actual and randomly expected panel assignments of each judge were compared in eight general fields of law.[n]

Though the subjects are too broad to capture steering in particular cases, there was little evidence of specialization by general field in the panel composition of the 2d and D.C. circuits. A few disparities occurred between expected and observed frequencies, but the composition of panels in both circuits was not statistically significant for any person or subject.[o] Though assignments to three-judge district courts were another story, neither tribunal appears to have engaged in systematic panel specialization to promote policy or productivity goals.[p]

[n] The fields were contracts, torts, commerce, labor, taxation, personal status, crimes, and "other," plus local in the D.C. circuit. These are the same fields analyzed in Chapters Two and Three, except that four criminal categories are consolidated here.

[o] In the 2d circuit, for example, Marshall had more labor assignments than randomly expected (23 versus 16); Waterman had fewer labor assignments than randomly expected (36 versus 44). The labor assignments of Hays, an expert in this field, exceeded perfectly random expectations by only 6%. In the D.C. circuit, Bazelon had more personal status assignments than expected (34 versus 24); Fahy had less (16 versus 23 expected).

[p] The requisite circuit members on three-judge district courts tended to be chosen with an eye to outcomes as well as to workloads.[35] Judge Lumbard, for example, assigned the largest share of 43 such sittings to Moore (7), Friendly (6), and Kaufman (5). Judge Moore received over half (9 of 17) of total assignments to three-judge district courts in civil rights cases in FY 1965-1967. Sheldon Goldman identified Lumbard, Moore, and Friendly as members of a conservative voting bloc.[36]

While assignments to three-judge courts were more evenly distributed in the Dis-

The 5th circuit's record is murkier. Whereas the judges' total panel assignments were the only distributions for the 2d and D.C. circuits that could not be attributed to chance (see Tables 8.4 and 8.6), in the 5th circuit assignments by subject were significant at p < .03 levels or lower for six individuals—Gewin, Goldberg, Jones, Rives, Thornberry, and Tuttle. Nonrandom assignment under acceptable odds also occurred in personal status and taxation cases, two fields of special concern to Chief Judge Tuttle and loci of the court's bloc divisions.[q][38]

What's more, the first impression of panel assignments in personal status cases looks suspiciously like residues of Judge Cameron's charges of rigging.[39] Table 8.7 shows the distribution among judges of all personal status cases on the left. On the right are the general category's two major components, civil rights cases and prisoner petitions. (Immigration and suffrage cases are omitted.) A new quartet composed of Thornberry, Rives, Wisdom, and Bell received most of the civil rights and prisoner petition assignments; a minority of Gewin, Jones, and Godbold disproportionately less. Thornberry's ratio of observed to expected panel assignments was almost twice that of Gewin's, generally regarded as a conservative in civil rights.

There are several reasons, however, why first impressions of attempted policy control are deceptive. One is the incongruity between Tuttle's own panel assignments and specialties. Brown and Bell had disproportionately higher caseloads in Tuttle's specialty of taxation; Tuttle's own sittings in personal status, civil rights, and tax cases fit random expectations almost perfectly.[r] Another reason is that chance cannot be eliminated if civil rights and civil rights removals cases are considered separately. Prisoner petitions are what lent statistical significance to the overall personal status category. Furthermore, the apparently random character of panel assignments in civil rights cases accords with the conclusions of a careful study by Atkins and Zavoina that panel steering in race relations occurred only during the critical period 1960-1963, when "The Four" liberals appeared to shuffle panels to keep the circuit in line with national policy.[40] Because the danger of retreat did not confront them either

---

trict of Columbia, Judge Bazelon assigned Tamm and Burger 7 of 10 Interstate Commerce Commission cases; Leventhal and Edgerton 6 of 8 civil rights cases. Goldman placed Tamm and Burger in a conservative bloc, and Leventhal in a moderate-liberal bloc.[37] Edgerton was a leading civil libertarian.

For assignments to three-judge district courts in the 5th circuit, see note u, this chapter.

[q] For details, see Appendix 1.

[r] That Tuttle's panel assignments withstood the null hypothesis of randomness is attributable mainly to his avoidance of marine personal injury cases and a disproportionately heavy share of criminal appeals.

TABLE 8.7
Panel Assignments in Personal Status Cases, 5th Circuit, FY 1965-1967

| Judge | Personal Status | | | Prisoner Petitions | | | Civil Rights | | |
|---|---|---|---|---|---|---|---|---|---|
| | Actual Panel Assignments N | Randomly Expected Panel Assignments (N) | Ratio of Actual to Randomly Expected Panel Assignments* % | Actual Panel Assignments N | Randomly Expected Panel Assignments | Ratio of Actual to Randomly Expected Panel Assignments % | Actual Panel Assignments N | Randomly Expected Panel Assignments | Ratio of Actual to Randomly Expected Panel Assignments % |
| Thornberry | 99 | (75.6) | 131.0 | 67 | | 129.6 | 26 | | 136.1 |
| Rives | 137 | (112.1) | 122.2 | 95 | | 124.0 | 33 | | 116.6 |
| Wisdom | 144 | (123.3) | 116.8 | 97 | | 115.1 | 39 | | 125.4 |
| Bell | 144 | (124.3) | 115.8 | 101 | | 118.8 | 40 | | 127.8 |
| Dyer | 29 | (28.3) | 102.5 | 20 | | 103.0 | 6 | | 84.5 |
| Goldberg | 33 | (33.2) | 99.4 | 25 | | 110.1 | 4 | | 47.6 |
| Ainsworth | 35 | (35.3) | 99.2 | 29 | | 119.8 | 4 | | 44.9 |
| Tuttle | 141 | (143.0) | 98.6 | 98 | | 100.2 | 35 | | 97.2 |
| Hutcheson | 33 | (34.4) | 95.9 | 19 | | 80.9 | 10 | | 114.9 |
| Coleman | 68 | (73.7) | 92.3 | 54 | | 107.1 | 12 | | 64.5 |
| Brown | 120 | (134.6) | 89.2 | 79 | | 85.9 | 29 | | 85.5 |
| Jones | 87 | (107.6) | 80.9 | 52 | | 70.6 | 27 | | 99.6 |
| Gewin | 87 | (120.7) | 72.1 | 54 | | 65.4 | 27 | | 88.8 |
| Godbold | 13 | (23.4) | 55.6 | 10 | | 62.5 | 3 | | 50.8 |
| Sums | 1,170 | (1,170.0) | 100.0 | 800 | | 100.0 | 295 | | 100.0 |

$\chi^2 = 39.8$, df 13, p < .001
* (Excludes Cameron, N = 2 and Simpson, N = 3.)

$\chi^2 = 36.7$, df 13, p < .001
(N judges = 13, N cases = 781;
$\chi^2 = 40.3$, df 12, p < .001)

$\chi^2 = 18.3$, df 13, p > .10
(Corrected for continuity)
(Freshman judges collapsed:
$\chi^2 = 16.7$, df 10, p > .05)

before Hutcheson retired as chief judge in 1959 or after the *Armstrong* showdown in 1963, when a majority declined to rehear Judge Gewin's challenge to vigorous circuit leadership in school desegregation, there was little need to pack panels subsequently. Notwithstanding tension over doctrines of affirmative action, by the mid-1960s new recruits and new issues had transformed this circuit.[41] The overwhelming majority of circuit judges, as shown in Table 8.8, responded favorably to civil rights claims. Links between support for civil rights and panel participation were weak.[s][42] However valid in 1963, stacking the deck in civil rights cases in the 5th circuit cannot be substantiated for 1965-1967.

How then can the nonrandom assignments of this period be explained? To reject Cameron's charge of minority control as outdated

TABLE 8.8
*Participation in Civil Rights Cases and Support for Civil Rights Claims, 5th Circuit, FY 1965-1967*

| Judge | Participation in Civil Rights Cases N* | Votes for Civil Rights Claimants % |
|---|---|---|
| Goldberg | 4 | 100.0 |
| Rives | 32 | 78.1 |
| Jones | 23 | 73.9 |
| Tuttle | 33 | 72.7 |
| Wisdom | 38 | 71.0 |
| Brown | 27 | 70.3 |
| Bell | 37 | 67.5 |
| Ainsworth | 3 | 66.7 |
| Gewin | 23 | 65.2 |
| Coleman | 10 | 60.0 |
| Thornberry | 25 | 60.0 |
| Dyer | 5 | 40.0 |
| Godbold | 3 | 33.3 |
| Sum | 263 | 69.2 |

$\chi^2 = 2.8$, df 12, $p > .99$.
* Excluding 10 votes by Hutcheson, 3 votes by Simpson, and 22 unscorable votes.

[s] The Spearman rank correlation coefficient between support for civil rights claims and the ratio of observed to randomly expected panel assignments in civil rights and civil rights removal cases for 13 judges (excluding Hutcheson) was $r_s = .1854$, $p > .05$; with freshman judges collapsed (N = 10), $r_s = .3227$, $p > .05$.

is not to rule out subtler strategies of panel management. Besides a chance strike, several hypotheses suggest themselves: the effect of geographic balancing, the bunching of cases in particular years, the reliance on proven competence and speedy workers to handle a sudden influx of litigation. The most plausible explanation, one that accords with internal role expectations and external political conditions, is consolidation of the court under pressure. After all, this was the time of James Meredith, Ross Barnett, Selma, and *Jefferson County*—the crisis time of civil rights enforcement.[43] No sooner had the court settled its own policies toward desegregation than enforcing those policies in a hostile community erupted into an acute national disturbance. No sooner had the new majority propounded advanced constitutional doctrines of affirmative action than storm warnings arose of a volume crisis ahead.[44] To speak plainly, the leadership apparently maintained a degree of panel management not so much to control doctrine as to compose internal conflict and to consolidate the court's external strength in a struggle over civil rights enforcement and an incipient law explosion. Panel assignments in civil rights, accordingly, were concentrated among distinguished and reliable senior colleagues—Rives and Wisdom, plus two moderate Kennedy-Johnson appointees, Thornberry and Bell—while the chief judge and his successor Brown assumed low profiles to dampen "near hysterics" aroused by Cameron's recent public charges of abused administrative power.

However conjectural, considerable evidence supports this inference of a more refined assignment strategy. First is that seniority bore a stronger relation to panel assignments in race relations cases than did support for civil rights claims—stronger even than the general tilt toward seniority in all cases.[t] Second, close comparison of assignments in civil rights and prisoner petitions in Table 8.7 shows that conservatives such as Coleman and Gewin received relatively meager rations in civil rights, irrespective of seniority. Freshman judges, such as Ainsworth, Dyer, Godbold, and Goldberg, were also slighted, despite their support for civil rights claims. Freshman judges received heavier diets of prisoner petitions, which few judges savor. The reverse held for Jones and Hutcheson, senior judges who followed Supreme Court mandates in desegregation. Moreover, the odds that civil rights panels were randomly chosen become less than

---

[t] Spearman rank correlation coefficients between seniority and panel assignment ratios in civil rights and civil rights removal cases were: 14 judges (including Hutcheson), $r_s = .6082$, $p < .05$; 13 judges (excluding Hutcheson), $r_s = .6229$, $p < .05$. Spearman rank correlation coefficients between the judges' overall and civil rights assignment ratios were: 14 judges, $r_s = .2176$, $p > .05$; 13 judges, $r_s = .3462$, $p > .05$. Cf. correlations between civil rights participation and support, note s, this chapter.

one in one thousand if three groups are differentiated, as in Table 8.9, according to this theme. A new quartet of reliables and moderates decided a fourth more than their randomly expected share of cases, the four freshmen barely half. If Tuttle was not about to assign civil rights cases to Cameron or Cox, neither did he assign them to newcomers.[u]

Chance cannot be eliminated from civil rights assignments, though they are a universe, not a sample. "And of course every molehill looks like a mountain when viewed through a microscope."[46] But the composite evidence is consistent with an interpretation that the 5th circuit, unlike the 2d or D.C. circuits, managed panel assignments in response to special conditions in the external environment. During a transitional period when a new majority was struggling to consolidate and extend doctrinal gains amid the initial

TABLE 8.9
*Distribution of Panel Assignments in Civil Rights Cases in the 5th Circuit, by Groups, FY 1965-1967*

| Group | Actual Panel Assignments N | Expected Panel Assignments (N) | Ratio of Actual to Expected Panel Assignments % | Mean N | Standard Deviation N |
|---|---|---|---|---|---|
| Reliables (4) (Thornberry, Bell, Rives, Wisdom) | 138 | (109.7) | 125.8 | 126.6 | 6.9 |
| Regulars (6) (Brown, Coleman, Gewin, Hutcheson, Jones, Tuttle) | 140 | (154.8) | 90.4 | 91.8 | 15.4 |
| Freshmen (4) (Ainsworth, Dyer, Godbold, Goldberg) | 17 | (30.3) | 56.1 | 57.0 | 16.0 |
| Sums | 295 | (295.0) | 100.0 | | |

NOTE: $\chi^2 = 14.7$, df 2, $p < .001$. Using a difference-of-means test, each category was significant as follows: reliables versus regulars, df 8, $t = 3.59$, $p < .005$; regulars versus freshmen, df 8, $t = 3.08$, $p < .01$; reliables versus freshmen, df 6, $t = 6.9$, $p < .0005$.

[u] Judge Tuttle's assignments to three-judge district courts in civil rights cases were similarly concentrated. Bell (12), Rives (11), Coleman (10), and Tuttle himself (8) participated in two-thirds of 62 civil rights cases. In turn, Jones (9), Brown (6), and Gewin (5) sat in 59% of 34 ICC cases. The latter trio had only 11 civil rights assignments altogether.[45]

shock waves of appellate overload, the chief judge appears to have leaned on certain reliables, slighted assumed conservatives and freshmen, and reduced the visibility of the senior administrative leaders, himself and Brown, in the center of controversy.

In prior years, the court had appeared to resolve conflicting role expectations by sacrificing an *internal* rule of the game—random rotation—to meet *external* obligations of compliance with national law. So, now, in a period of doctrinal consolidation and political struggle over civil rights enforcement, internal norms guiding panel composition yielded to collective obligations to unite as effective instruments of national policy in the regional community. As the crisis in civil rights enforcement faded into a new crisis of volume, the norms of equal work resumed their traditional strength.

From an institutional perspective, these compromises resembled familiar Supreme Court strategies: massing internal forces to maximize external power.[47] Tuttle, a courageous and creative jurist, earned much public praise for leading his court through the civil rights crisis by an adroit union of judicial and administrative powers.[48] The price was an appearance that panel membership reflected the values of the court's administrative leadership. Some specialization, in the sense of gravitating toward different policy issues, took place in the composition of 5th circuit panels. Of the six judges whose assignments were statistically significant, liberals decided a disproportionately large share of cases involving civil rights, prisoner petitions, and crimes and disproportionately fewer cases dealing with economic issues. Conservatives, such as Gewin and Jones, had the opposite experience.[v] At the least, sufficient patches of non-

Comparative Ratios of Actual to
Randomly Expected Panel Assignments among
Selected Judges in the 5th Circuit, FY 1965-1967
(Randomly Expected = 100%)

| Subject | Judge | Actual Panel Assignments N | Ratio % | Judge | Actual Panel Assignments N | Ratio % |
|---|---|---|---|---|---|---|
| Torts | Jones | 87 | 128 | Tuttle | 74 | 82 |
|  | Gewin | 94 | 123 |  |  |  |
| Commerce | Jones | 49 | 116 | Goldberg | 8 | 61 |
|  |  |  |  | Thornberry | 19 | 64 |
| Personal status | Thornberry | 99 | 131 | Gewin | 87 | 72 |
|  | Rives | 137 | 122 | Jones | 87 | 80 |
| Crimes | Goldberg | 26 | 182 | Rives | 30 | 62 |
|  | Tuttle | 75 | 121 | Jones | 38 | 82 |
|  |  |  |  | Gewin | 47 | 90 |

random panel selection remained in tax litigation and prisoner petitions after 1964 to warrant overhauling the circuit's assignment system when the administrative leadership changed in 1967. Regardless of motives, the circuit was not above suspicion that a few judges had disproportionate influence over major policy issues. As one member said bluntly in 1969: "One or two guys used to run this court. Others went along for the ride. Now that is no longer so."

**Opinion Assignment in Practice**

Since the shape of legal doctrine and court prestige depend on opinions, selection of court spokesmen also can be a potent instrument of judicial leadership. Chief judges who control writing assignments, as in the Supreme Court or the 6th circuit, wield considerable influence over the legal reputations of their colleagues, who sometimes chafe at lean diets and hunger for richer fare.[49] On the three Courts of Appeals, however, several competing factors weaken opinion assignment as a leadership resource. For one thing, increasingly large pools of decisions in all three circuits do not receive signed opinions. For another, panel rotation and seniority diffuse the power to assign. According to statute, judges most senior in commission preside and therefore assign opinions when in the majority, unless they waive the privilege.[w50] Though the animus against specialization is weaker in opinion than in panel assignment, the temptation to select spokesmen according to policy predilections or superior knowledge rubs against a general expectation that circuit courts should avoid concentrating opinions among experts.[52] Accommodating these competing objectives, Judge Harold R. Medina once declared, made assigning opinions "the hardest . . . the most interesting and the most delicate part of the job."[53]

How then did the three tribunals select their spokesmen? Were leaders in terms of panel participation also leaders in terms of writing opinions? Did seniority stimulate specialization? Even less than for panel assignment, of course, do ratios of opinion writing fully

---

[w] In the 5th circuit, so-called initiating judges in screening panels, to whom cases were assigned randomly, wrote the opinions in appeals decided without oral argument. In both the 2d and 5th circuits the presiding officer in cases with oral argument was the most senior *active* judge. This custom is another illustration of circuit courts developing informal surrogates for problematic formal procedures. Complaints arose in other circuits about the tendency of senior judges, refusing to waive the privilege of presiding, to assign opinions to themselves, with consequent delay. In response, the Senate passed legislation in 1979 restricting presiding judges to the most senior members in regular active service.[51]

measure leadership. Despite a drift toward one-judge opinions in ordinary cases, quantities convey nothing about the contribution made by colleagues and clerks in the give and take of drafting opinions nor about the quality of performance. Still, one must bat in order to score. Frequencies of assignment at least tell us something about opportunities to lead as well as the effects of administrative power on adjudication.

Some clues to the riddle of leadership may be found in the columns on the right side of Tables 8.4-8.6, which compare the distribution of actual opinion assignments with the randomly expected number, adjusted for dissent.[x] Since the expected frequencies are *proportions* of each judge's majority participations, part-timers are included, though the usual caveat holds for percentages based on small numbers.

The opinion-assignment data reflect three characteristics common to the circuits. First, considering the decentralized method of selection, the general distribution of opinions was remarkably even among *full-time judges*, active or senior. If the activities of part-timers on senior status are set aside, chance cannot be ruled out for any circuit. Parity among full-timers was especially impressive in the 2d and 5th circuits, where the range of assignments among full-time judges (31%) was half that of the D.C. circuit. Quantitatively, at least, the norm of equal work was carefully observed.

Second, seniority nonetheless qualified the principle of equal participation in patterns parallel to those of panel selection. Chief judges Tuttle and Bazelon (though not Lumbard) wrote a disproportionately large number of opinions. So did such workhorses as Moore, Fahy, and McGowan, to whom Friendly should be added in New York. Some who led in panel participation, such as Bell, Brown, or Wright, fell slightly below numerical par in writing majority opinions.[y] Judge Kaufman's scores were below expectations on both dimensions of productivity.

The effects of seniority, as in panel selection, were sharp for both senior and freshman judges. Senior circuit judges, such as Medina in New York, Hutcheson in Houston, and Fahy in Washington, wrote far more opinions than would be expected by random assignment, let alone relative age. Hutcheson was nearing ninety and Medina eighty even then. Junior judges, such as Feinberg, Tamm, Godbold, and Goldberg, had shorter rations, though the slippage was less pronounced for former district judges in the South, such as Dyer and

---

[x] For methods of randomization, see Appendix 1.

[y] As chief judge, Brown later wrote the highest number of opinions of any judge in the 5th circuit.[54]

Ainsworth. The major exception to the freshman effect was Leventhal, then new to the D.C. circuit, who led his entire court with half again as many opinion assignments as randomly expected.

The prominence of Leventhal and McGowan in opinion writing would seem to confirm the earlier suggestion that efforts to reduce conflict increased the influence of members in the ideological center. Intramural disputes in this circuit perhaps made equalization of work harder to achieve. In fact, however, the two centrists received less than randomly expected assignments in the areas of greatest controversy—criminal law and personal status issues—and more than expected in economic affairs.[55] Expertise is a more plausible explanation for their frequent writing than internal conflict resolution.

Otherwise, seniority structured ostensibly equal opportunities to explain decisions.[z] Writing opinions is a chance to lead. In practice, judges with longer service tended to assign opinions among themselves.[56] Just as chief judges were biased toward seniority in panel selection, so presiding judges emphasized experience in choosing court spokesmen. This may not be surprising in view of other collective goals, such as efficiency and quality, until one recalls the judges' commitment to the norm of equal say, equal labor—and their common cry against overwork. Far from shunting off the drudgery onto junior members, typical of old pros in other organizations, experienced circuit judges tended to assume extra responsibility in both sitting and speaking for their courts.

This tendency alone casts doubt on a popular theory, echoed in the judges' chambers, that law clerks are responsible for the proliferation of opinions. For what could be better proof of personal goals "to make a contribution," or, if one pleases, of the will to power, than carrying a disproportionate share of the work? Again, administrative power affected the central nerve of judging. Despite official equality, experienced members usually enjoyed disproportionate

---

[z] Largely because McGowan and Leventhal were relative newcomers, the association between seniority and opinion assignment ratios was negative in the D.C. circuit. Spokesman rates were closely related to seniority in the other two tribunals, particularly at the top and bottom ends.

The Spearman rank correlation coefficient between seniority and ratios of actual to randomly expected opinion assignments among all 12 judges in the D.C. circuit was $r_s = (-).4152$, $p > .05$; for 8 full-time judges (excluding Bastian, Miller, Edgerton, and Washington), $r_s = (-).0536$, $p > .05$. In the 5th circuit the Spearman rank correlation coefficients between seniority and opinion assignment ratios were: 14 judges (including Hutcheson), $r_s = .7907$, $p < .01$; 13 judges (excluding Hutcheson), $r_s = .6999$, $p < .01$. The comparable coefficients in the 2d circuit were: 11 judges (including Medina), $r_s = .6182$, $p < .05$; 10 judges (excluding Medina), $r_s = .4909$, $p > .05$.

opportunity, and freshman members less, to form and to express the opinion of the group.

Finally, a few spots of subject-matter specialization appeared beneath the surface of even participation. These concentrations were actually milder than in panel selection, though the norms themselves were weaker, if only because smaller numbers make division of labor harder to prove. Of the three circuits, the 2d adhered most to the standard of nonspecialization. The possibility of chance variation could not be rejected for any judge or field. Chief Judge Lumbard's assignments and the court's most unwanted business—crimes—fit random expectations almost perfectly.[aa] Assigning judges, nonetheless, occasionally tapped special skills. Judge Friendly, for instance, spoke for over 60 percent of the majorities in which he participated in "other commerce," a category laden with issues in his specialty of administrative law.[bb] Hays did likewise in labor cases. Moore strengthened his hold as the court's workhorse by writing 60 percent of the majority opinions when eligible in taxation, a field none claimed as his own.[cc] [57]

Specialization was more serious in 5th circuit opinions on subjects of greatest doctrinal dispute—personal status issues.[dd] If the assignments of freshman judges in these subjects are consolidated to reduce small cells, as in Table 8.10, opinion writing repeated the basic leadership configuration of panel selection.[58] The top five judges in proportionate panel participation—Thornberry, Rives, Wisdom, Bell, Tuttle—also led in proportionate opinion production.[ee] Freshman members and conservatives, such as Gewin and Coleman, again were shortchanged.

Though the distribution of criminal opinions in Table 8.10 could be attributed to chance, the contrast with personal status cases supports Atkins's conclusions from a study of opinion assignment in all

[aa] Lumbard, $\chi^2 = 2.1$, df 7, $p > .95$. Crimes, $\chi^2 = 1.9$, df 10, $p > .99$. The closest to statistical significance were Hays ($\chi^2 = 9.6$, df 7, $p > .20$) and labor ($\chi^2 = 11.5$, df 10, $p > .25$).

[bb] As majority spokesman in 13 of 21 "other commerce" cases in which he participated, Friendly thus wrote one-fourth of the court's total opinions in this area (N = 52), almost twice the 7.1 randomly expected.

[cc] Hays spoke for majorities in 18 of 30 labor cases, as compared to 10 randomly expected. Moore wrote 27 of 45 opinions when eligible in taxation, as compared to 17.2 expected, making him the spokesman in one-fourth of the circuit's total tax cases (N = 114).

[dd] In no other subject could the null hypothesis of chance variation be rejected in the 5th circuit. In taxation, the other field that was statistically significant in panel selection, the one-sample $\chi^2$ test yielded: $\chi^2 = 8.0$, df 10, $p > .50$.

[ee] The Spearman rank correlation coefficient between panel and opinion assignment ratios in personal status cases (with freshmen collapsed) was $r_s = .5455$, $p < .05$.

TABLE 8.10

Comparative Opinion Assignments in Personal Status and Criminal Cases, 5th Circuit FY 1965-1967

| | Personal Status Cases | | | Criminal Cases | | |
|---|---|---|---|---|---|---|
| Judge | Actual Opinion Assignments N | Randomly Expected Opinion Assignments (N) | Ratio of Actual to Randomly Expected Opinion Assignments % | Actual Opinion Assignments N | Randomly Expected Opinion Assignments (N) | Ratio of Actual to Randomly Expected Opinion Assignments % |
| Bell | 25 | (15.3) | 163.4 | 7 | (8.5) | 77.8 |
| Tuttle | 30 | (19.7) | 152.3 | 9 | (11.5) | 78.3 |
| Wisdom | 22 | (16.7) | 131.7 | 5 | (9.8) | 51.0 |
| Rives | 18 | (16.5) | 109.1 | 5 | (9.2) | 51.5 |
| Thornberry | 9 | (8.9) | 107.1 | 8 | (5.4) | 163.3 |
| Jones | 10 | (13.7) | 73.0 | 12 | (8.5) | 150.0 |
| Brown | 14 | (19.4) | 72.2 | 5 | (11.3) | 44.2 |
| Gewin | 11 | (15.5) | 71.0 | 11 | (9.6) | 120.9 |
| Freshmen* | 10 | (15.5) | 64.5 | 12 | (9.6) | 131.9 |
| Hutcheson | 7 | (11.1) | 63.1 | 8 | (7.0) | 123.1 |
| Coleman | 6 | (10.0) | 60.0 | 13 | (6.4) | 220.3 |
| Sums | 162 | (162.0) | 100.0 | 95 | (95.0) | 100.0 |

$\chi^2 = 21.93$, df 10, $p < .02$
(Corrected for continuity)
* Ainsworth, Dyer, Godbold, Goldberg

$\chi^2 = 22.2$, df 10, $p < .02$
(If corrected for continuity, $\chi^2 = 17.3$, df 10, $p < .10$)

circuits that general equity in workloads can camouflage specialization among particular subjects. Also, leaders in one field are usually followers in others.[59] Here, members slighted in personal status cases, such as Jones, Gewin, or Coleman, tended to write disproportionately more criminal opinions—and vice versa.[ff] The contrast was vivid for Coleman, considered a conservative in race relations but an experienced moderate in criminal justice.

Sharper still is the contrast in civil rights. The trio of Tuttle, Bell, and Wisdom wrote 62 percent of the total opinions when eligible—almost twice the randomly expected number. Eleven remaining colleagues wrote less than half. The probability that this distribution occurred by chance was less than one in one thousand.[gg] Thus, three judges, two of them leaders in panel participation as well, were the dominant voices in the court's magnetic field of civil rights. Because Tuttle was chief judge, Wisdom the intellectual leader of affirmative action doctrine, and Bell a moderate skilled in mediation, opinion assignments appear to have reflected the same strategies of consolidation that guided panel selection in civil rights.[hh][60]

The personal interests of senior members also produced a few patches of opinion specialization. The assignments of Sterry Water-

---

[ff] The Spearman rank correlation coefficient between the *highest* ratios of opinion assignment in personal status cases and the *lowest* ratios in criminal cases ($r_s = .5273$) barely exceeded normal standards of statistical significance at $p = .05$ ($r_s = .535$).

[gg] Opinion assignments in civil rights cases were as follows:

|  | Frequency Observed N | Frequency Expected (N) | Ratio % |
|---|---|---|---|
| Top three (3) | 32 | (16.6) | 192.8 |
| Regulars (6) | 17 | (26.9) | 63.4 |
| Freshmen + Hutcheson (5) | 3 | ( 8.5) | 27.7 |
| Sums | 52 | (52.0) | 100.0 |

$\chi^2 = 21.44$, df 2, $p < .001$.

A rival hypothesis that the distribution reflected seniority was weakly supported. The Spearman rank correlation coefficient between seniority and civil rights opinion ratios was $r_s = .2258$, $p > .05$; with freshman judges collapsed, $r_s = (-).1886$, $p > .05$.

[hh] Indeed, the evidence mounts that Griffin B. Bell, Judge Tuttle's junior colleague in Atlanta and future Attorney General, enjoyed a special relationship with his chief, as perhaps Moore did with Lumbard in New York. Tuttle and Bell were the only individuals in this study whose opinion assignments by subject overcame chance odds. (Bell, N opinions = 87, df 6, $\chi^2 = 14.18$, $p < .05$. Tuttle, N opinions = 111, df 6, $\chi^2 = 13.4$, $p < .05$.) Bell wrote 59% (10 of 17) of the opinions when eligible in civil rights. Tuttle spoke for 46% (17 of 37) of his majority panels in taxation. Their opinion writing, moreover, displayed an affinity for the same subjects, except for commerce. Both wrote more majority opinions than randomly expected in labor, taxation, and personal status cases; less in contracts, torts, and crimes. This correlation was significant according to a direction sign test: $N = 8$, $x = 1$, $p = .035$.[61]

man and John R. Brown, who assigned their own opinions when chief judges were not sitting, are instructive. Waterman wrote disproportionately few opinions in labor cases during 1965-1967 and none in 1966-1968.[ii][62] Brown, avoiding both personal status and criminal opinions, gravitated toward economic issues. Brown and Wisdom wrote almost half of the 5th circuit's thirty "other commerce" opinions during this period. Exploiting his expertise in admiralty, Brown alone wrote 75 percent of the opinions when eligible in marine personal injuries.[jj]

Such concentrations were usually compensated for by slack activity in other subjects. The trade-off was clearest between Bazelon and McGowan in Washington. Chief Judge Bazelon assigned himself 44 percent more personal status and criminal opinions than randomly expected, and 40 percent less in economic subjects such as contracts, torts, and taxation. McGowan's menu was virtually the opposite. In consequence, these two joined Brown as the only judges whose opinion assignments were statistically significant if dichotomized into economic versus personal status and criminal issues.[kk] Beneath opinion assignments evenly allocated on the whole, clear links existed among the established interests and writing assignments of a few judges in a position to pick panel spokesmen.

These patches of specialization confirm the judges' perceptions of a mild division of labor in opinion writing on an informal and volunteer basis. It probably oversimplifies complex choices to explain such disparities as mainly measures to improve efficiency in low-conflict courts.[63] The experience of the D.C. circuit reinforces the impression from the 5th that, aside from reflecting personal interests, selectivity is most likely in zones of doctrinal dissension.[64] In Washington the only subject to withstand the null hypothesis of randomness was crime. Table 8.11 shows that opinions in criminal cases, randomly distributed in the 2d circuit, were dominated by clashing wings of the court. Wright and Bazelon wrote a disproportionately large number of opinions in this field; so did their opponents Burger and Danaher. Since neither chance, seniority, nor overall workload accounts for this distribution, a fair inference is that opinion assignments reflected policy conflicts.[ll] Judges battling over

---

[ii] Waterman, who also sat less often than expected in this field, wrote opinions in only 25% (6 of 24) of his labor cases. Cf. Hays, note o, this chapter.

[jj] Writing 9 opinions for 12 majorities in which he participated, Brown wrote a fourth of the court's 36 opinions in this subject.

[kk] For details, see Appendix 1.

[ll] Spearman rank correlation coefficients for seniority and ratios of observed to randomly expected opinion assignments in D.C. criminal cases were: for 12 judges, $r_s =$

criminal justice not only attracted notice by the intensity of their rhetoric; they also exploited their opportunities to speak out.

It should be emphasized, in summary, that opinion specialization in these circuits was sporadic and selective, more a matter of informal gravitation than of central design.[65] No individual or faction monopolized the opinions of any tribunal. Concentrations in one subject usually offset shortages in others. Despite some overlap among those who led in both stages of decision, opinion leadership was not simply a reflection of who sat.[mm] Diffusion of assigning

TABLE 8.11
Opinion Assignments in Criminal Cases, D.C. Circuit, FY 1965-1967

| Judge | Actual Opinion Assignments N | Randomly Expected Opinion Assignments (N) | Ratio of Actual to Randomly Expected Opinion Assignments % |
|---|---|---|---|
| Wright | 19 | (11.7) | 162.4 |
| Burger | 22 | (15.5) | 141.9 |
| Edgerton | 8 | (5.7) | 140.4 |
| Danaher | 18 | (13.9) | 129.5 |
| Bazelon | 23 | (18.6) | 123.7 |
| Bastian | 5 | (5.7) | 87.7 |
| Leventhal | 14 | (16.4) | 85.4 |
| Fahy | 14 | (18.3) | 76.5 |
| Washington | 4 | (5.3) | 75.5 |
| McGowan | 12 | (21.2) | 73.2 |
| Miller | 2 | (4.4) | 45.5 |
| Tamm | 3 | (7.3) | 41.1 |
| Sums | 144 | (144.0) | 100.0 |

$\chi^2 = 20.1$, df 11, $p < .05$. (Corrected for continuity. If Miller is dropped, $\chi^2 = 18.34$, df 10, $p < .05$.)

---

.1827, $p > .05$; for 8 full-time judges, $r_s = .3155$, $p > .05$. The comparable coefficients for ratios of overall and criminal opinion assignments were: for 12 judges, $r_s = .0000$, $p > .05$; for 8 full-time judges, $r_s = (-).3333$, $p > .05$.

[mm] For courts as wholes, the association between ratios of panel and opinion assignment was weak in the 2d circuit and dependent on the mix of part-timers in the other two. The coefficient of correlation between ratios of actual to randomly expected panel and opinion assignments for 10 judges of the 2d circuit was: $r = .4831$, $F = 2.44$, df 1 and 8, $p > .05$. The comparable coefficients for the 5th circuit were: 14 judges, df 1 and 12, $r = (-).6511$, $F = 8.83$, $p < .05$; 13 judges, df 1 and 11, $r = .6066$, $F = 6.4$, $p < .05$. The coefficient of correlation for 12 judges in the District of Columbia was: $r = .5808$, $F = 5.09$, df 1 and 10, $p < .05$. For 8 full-time judges, $r = (-).0545$, $F = 0.018$, $p > .05$.

power, as the judges maintained, diversified circuit spokesmen. Many opinion leaders emerged on the three courts in terms of opportunity to write.

Beneath an umbrella of equalized work, nevertheless, significant sprinklings of specialization occurred, especially in the 5th circuit, by virtue of seniority, judicial strategies, and affinities between particular individuals and subjects. That leadership was compatible with equality becomes more evident when the opinion assignment practices of circuit judges are joined to their qualitative reputations. Invariably, the doctrinal leaders of these circuits—say, Friendly, Hays, Tuttle, Wisdom, Bazelon, Burger, McGowan, or Wright—led in either panel participation or opinion production and sometimes both. That this much subject-matter specialization existed in the teeth of panel rotation is a testament to the strength of seniority and the capacity of individuals to exploit leadership opportunities in pursuit of collective and personal goals.

Rotation, in short, diffused but did not eliminate panel and opinion assignment as instruments of leadership. In Courts of Appeals, as in other organizations of equals, certain individuals performed uncommon labor and reaped uncommon influence on the basis of their expertise and length of service.

## Conclusions

Courts of Appeals are highly fragmented organizations in which individuals and groups attempt to act as units. Atomistic though they may appear at first glance, some scaffolding does structure and coordinate the activities of diverse members. Circuit judges, as seen in the last chapter, felt constrained by informal norms and conventions engendered by each court. Among formal equals we now find patterns of leadership in their opportunities to work.

The distribution of labor inevitably affects the distribution of power within Courts of Appeals. Most circuit judges, it is true, perceived of judicial influence primarily in terms of craftsmanship. Most also embraced the official separation of administration from adjudication and the informal convention of equal work. Yet, in some respects these principles collide. Freshman socialization dilutes the influence of newcomers as they absorb the particular expectations of the job and the folkways of group life. The distinction between managerial and opinion leadership, the former resting on seniority and the latter on professional skill, creates even sharper tensions in the allocation of responsibility among circuit judges. Intended to insulate adjudication from organizational control, the distinction obviously affects judicial styles. Some chief judges have more ability and interest in judicial administration than in judicial philosophy. Some are also better at one activity than the other.

In practice, however, these circuits were no more successful in divorcing the two forms of leadership than other governmental bodies organized on similar distinctions between administration and policy making. Though there was little evidence of systematic panel rigging to control outcomes, as commonly charged, administrative discretion affected adjudication in several ways: (1) a bias toward seniority and experience in all three circuits in selecting panel members and spokesmen, (2) a tendency to compose three-judge district courts in tune with the policy preferences of chief judges, (3) an appearance of panel management in the 5th circuit to resolve clashing internal norms of random rotation and national obligations to enforce civil rights, and (4) spots of opinion specialization in keeping with the policy views and personal interests of assigning members. Because the numbers are small and the analysis emphasizes extremes, the data regarding opinion assignments especially demand cautious interpretation. Frequencies of assignment merely measure participation, not teamwork behind the scenes nor the quality of play on which judges themselves evaluated performance. Administrative leadership and adjudicative leadership, all the same, were entwined. The combination of formal rules of assigning work by seniority with informal role expectations and rotation of circuit judges contributed to the emergence of both experience and expertise as interlocking bases of leadership. This coupling of specialization and seniority, though more diffused and less critical to effective operations than in Congress, surfaced in each tribunal, sometimes at the expense of major rules of the game.

Seniority was the primary link between the two forms of leadership as well as the main inroad on the principle of equal participation. Despite panel rotation, all three circuits tended to concentrate decision making and opinion writing among the experienced. Several layers of leadership may be distinguished accordingly: *chief judges*, who took leading parts in sitting and speaking in spite of extra administrative burdens; *workhorses* and *experts*, on whom chiefs and presiding judges relied to meet both priorities of sound adjudication and quality opinions; and *senior circuit judges*, whose added manpower went so far beyond pinch-hitting that the most meaningful distinction was not between active or senior status, but between full and part-time service. Quantitatively, some judges with advanced seniority gravitated toward favorite subjects, avoiding others they disliked. Qualitatively, they also grasped choice assignments. Freshman judges generally received shorter rations except in fields of prior experience. Assignments in these circuits were neither equal nor weighted toward youth.

As a leadership resource, the spillover between administration and adjudication may involve strategies other than the will to power of judges most senior. Assignments based on convenience and geographical considerations are little controverted. Assigning judicial tasks according to experience and expertise may ease freshman transitions and help to reconcile norms of equality, efficiency, and quality.[66] Discretion to assign also can be used to compose internal conflicts, strengthen circuit courts against external opposition, and advance personal policy goals.[67]

Even so, because panels rotate and specialties are spread among autonomous individuals, tolerant of dissensus, it is important not to exaggerate the unity of command in circuit courts. Neither seniority nor specialization was as strong in these tribunals as in congressional committees or even the Supreme Court. No person dominated any tribunal or field. Generalists in background, circuit judges themselves usually prefer a mix. Specialization was spasmodic, informal, and often voluntary even in the assignment of opinions, a high-priority task by which many judges felt themselves held to account. The point is simply that allocation of work was not left entirely to chance. The coupling of formal powers to assign and informal role expectations provided pattern and purpose in supposedly random sharing of work. Power relations among the judges, as a result, were neither hierarchical nor equal. Balkanization, a diffusion of authority among ruling groups, characterized relations within Courts of Appeals no less than among them.[68] A tendency for circuit courts to concentrate on certain subjects trickled down to individuals in the same fields.

This condition, which naturally fluctuates across place and time, has some practical consequences worth noting. Seniority is a popular principle in many organizations, because it depoliticizes the choice of formal leaders and ensures experience in decision making. In circuit courts as in Congress, however, this seemingly neutral arrangement has potent effects in allocating authority. Who administers, presides, decides, and speaks, all hinge on who was recruited first. The Hruska Commission, in a preliminary report in 1975, severely criticized this method of selecting chief judges for failing to match managerial talent with administrative need, then quickly retreated when Warren E. Burger opposed the proposed remedy of appointment by the Supreme Court as creating more political problems than it would solve.[69] In recognition that seniority also sweeps beyond court management into central nerves of judging—who decides and explains—the Senate passed legislation imposing a maximum term of seven years for chief judges and curbs on the capacity of judges on senior status to preside (and hence assign opinions to themselves).[70] In the Omnibus Judges Act of 1978 Congress eliminated senior judges from sitting en banc, even as circuits across the country increasingly rely on them to shoulder the load.[71] Additional proposals to limit en bancs to the nine active judges most senior in service, for greater efficiency in large circuits, would further weaken the influence of new members and the sensitivity of circuits to appointing authorities.[72] In 1978, Congress authorized Courts of Appeals having more than fifteen members to organize en bancs according to the number of members prescribed by circuit rules.[73] If enlarged circuits like the 9th, authorized to expand to twenty-three members, rely on seniority to trim en bancs to manageable size, the effect would strengthen the bias, already present, in favor of experienced active judges.

Whatever one's view of these issues, such recommendations presuppose our basic conclusion: managerial and legal leadership, like political and professional values, tend to overlap in courts in between. However distinguishable administration and policy making may be in theory, the leaders of these tribunals in real life tended to be the same individuals who tapped multiple sources of power. Judicial leadership, in fine, was not simply a natural radiation of legal talent, as officially presumed, but also reflected the internal norms, decision rules, and politics of each group. That is why the office of chief judge, for all the official theory of *primus inter pares*, offers a formidable basis for leadership to strong personalities so inclined. It is also why this potential is the greater the more Courts of Appeals seek organizational solutions for the ills of the law explosion. Process affects product in the distribution of work—and therefore of judicial power.

Part III
**Perspectives on Reform**

". . . judicial reform is no sport for the short-winded . . ."
Arthur T. Vanderbilt, *Minimum Standards of Judicial Administration* (1949), xix.

Drawing by Dana Fradon; © 1979 The New Yorker Magazine, Inc.

# Nine · **Strategies of Reform**

The idea of a legal system, as Julius Stone observed, conveys an "overall vision of unity, despite the unending changefulness and conflict in what goes on beneath."[1] The concept also implies a dialectic between formal rules of decision and informal operations in the conduct of courts. It would be foolhardy to underestimate the force of formal rules and relations—such things as common jurisdiction, legal standards, and external review—as bonding agents among national courts. Yet, there is a growing awareness that the formalities of the judicial process breed a propensity "to see things whole and harmonious, when in fact they are fragmented and heterogeneous."[2] Obscured no less are informal values and channels through which courts, like other branches of government, actually operate.[3]

In preceding chapters we have analyzed three Courts of Appeals from the dual perspectives of formal, intercourt relations in the flow of federal litigation and of judges' attitudes, votes, and informal relations in collective work. These chapters underscored two principal themes: the diversity and informality of the federal appellate process. When these tribunals were viewed telescopically, as intermediates webbed in superior-subordinate relationships, it became evident how myopic was the assumption that "the federal judicial system is one."[4] For all the nationalization of law over time, circuit business was so varied and direct supervision so limited that the intriguing questions became: what provides the glue? Why was consensus more characteristic of these circuits than conflict? When the three tribunals were viewed microscopically, as collections of individuals attempting to function as groups, we saw how informal relations and internalized norms provided part of the answer. Circuit judges were more alike than different. Homogeneity in judicial values counterbalanced heterogeneity in court business. Informal and internalized restraints underpinned formal and external controls. Judicial roles and political orientations, instead of shielding federal judges from personal values or the external environment, were interwoven ligaments pulling national courts into a loosely coordinated whole.

Both perspectives now merge as our focus shifts from the theory of judicial decision to some practical implications of diversity and informality for the problems of the three circuits in the law explosion and for alternative strategies of reform. Against the specter of federal courts in crisis, brought on by expanding judicial responsibilities and attendant volume pressures, the informal bonds of judicial union should provide some comfort. The question is whether they are strong enough to withstand the strains of mushrooming appeals in one nation with many courts.

## Problems and Prospects

When Congress approved the Judges' Bill in 1925, Justice Louis D. Brandeis wrote Felix Frankfurter that its enactment contained an important moral: the Supreme Court was "venerated throughout the land" because "the official coat has been cut according to the human cloth." "Congress, executive departments, commissions and lower federal courts," by contrast, were "all subject to criticism and or execration," Brandeis thought, because too much work had been piled on them "regardless of human limitations. The high incumbents—in many instances—perform in name only. They are administrators—without time to know what they are doing or to think how to do it. They run human machines."[5]

The conditions Brandeis described a half-century ago are only "more so" today.[6] The paramount problem of federal Courts of Appeals in the 1970s was the pressure of quantity on the quality of appellate justice. Though the malaise varied considerably in different parts of the federal judiciary, symptoms of overload were national in scope. Qualitatively, as we saw in Chapter One, the functions of federal appellate judges have been expanding without corresponding adjustments in tools to do the job. The goal of uniformity, at both appellate levels, has been taking a back seat to accentuated responsibilities in lawmaking and error correction, especially in criminal justice. Quantitatively, whatever the causes of caseload inflation, there were too many appeals for too few judges.[7] Congress responded in 1978 by increasing circuit judgeships one-third, but this was a catch-up rather than a lasting solution.[8] Circuit courts attempted to keep pace by streamlining the process of adjudication. Increases in productivity were impressive, both for the three circuits and nationally. As Table 9.1 indicates, the number of cases terminated per judgeship in all circuits jumped over 250 percent between 1961 and 1978 and in the 5th circuit over 350 percent.

Gains in productivity nonetheless failed to keep pace with growth. The odds of review by the Supreme Court fell during the same pe-

TABLE 9.1
Comparative Rates of Increase in Cases Terminated in Circuit
Courts and Number of Circuit Judgeships, FY 1961-1978

| Circuit | Increase in Cases Terminated % | Increase in Cases Terminated per Judgeship % | Increase in Judgeships % (N) |
|---|---|---|---|
| 2d | 185 | 185 | 0 |
| 5th | 560 | 384 | 36 (4) |
| D.C. | 109 | 109 | 0 |
| All circuits | 338 | 252 | 24 (19) |

SOURCE: AO *Annual Report* (1978), Table 3, 162.

riod when policy-making discretion in lower courts increased.[a] And the methods of increasing output, shifting from handcrafted to assembly-line techniques of decision, shook confidence in the quality of adjudication at the very time when more and more litigants sought justice in Courts of Appeals. The combination of heavy volume pressures and increased policy making thus aggravated the tension between the roles of circuit judges and their capacity to satisfy rising expectations of justice on appeal.

By the mid-1970s, despite some easing in the rate of growth, the situation in some circuits became acute.[b] Burgeoning caseloads prodded lawyers, scholars, judges, and a national commission into sounding public alarms. Relentless waves of appeals were said to be swamping the courts, Balkanizing federal jurisprudence, debasing appellate standards, and lowering judicial morale.[11] Though experts disagreed about details, a rash of proposals, some dusted off from earlier battles over court reform, arose in professional circles and Congress. Overload, if not yet the "near crisis" that the Chief Justice and congressional committees proclaimed, once again pressed the roles and organization of intermediate federal courts onto the political agenda.[12] Collectively, policy makers face a basic dilemma of how judicial functions and institutions can be "cut to human cloth."

[a] The ratio of certiorari petitions granted by the Supreme Court to petitions filed from circuit decisions declined from approximately 1 in 14 in 1965-1967 to about 1 in 20 in 1978.[9] Years are fiscal years. See Appendix 1, p. 300.

[b] In 1978 the number of newly docketed cases fell 1%—the first decline in twenty years—but rose 6.9% in 1979. Cases pending increased 7.8% in 1978 and 1979.[10]

The three Courts of Appeals, along with the 9th circuit on the West Coast, are in the vortex of the law explosion. Even when under less pressure as the 1970s opened, a two-to-one majority of their judges already felt overloaded and overworked. Table 9.2 gives their number; their comments are more graphic, particularly in the 5th and D.C. circuits. "Harried," "straining," "under pressure all the time," doing more than judges could "comfortably handle" or "ought to do," they expressed anxiety about "shoddy work" and feared the future. Volume of litigation, of all the changing demands on their courts, was the strongest force. Except for one jurist who most feared court packing by President Nixon's men, the press of quantity on quality was universally perceived as their foremost problem.[c]

TABLE 9.2
*Circuit Judges' Perceptions of Whether They Felt Overloaded or Overworked, 1969-1971*

| Circuit | Yes N | No N | Don't Know/ No Response N | Total N |
|---|---|---|---|---|
| 2d | 4 | 5 | 1 | 10 |
| 5th | 10 | 2 | 5 | 17 |
| D.C. | 5 | 2 | 1 | 8 |
| Sums | 19 | 9 | 7 | 35 |

NOTE: The question was: "We hear much these days about overloaded dockets. Do you feel overloaded and overworked?"

By virtue of their diverse experience in managing large circuits at various stages of docket congestion, the three tribunals provide a useful prism to consider the main issues and alternatives in reform. Each court, adapting to its own circumstances and priorities, represents different organizational responses by large circuits to changing external demands.

[c] Even in 1969, when the 5th circuit disposed of only half as many cases per active judgeship (N = 77) as five years later (N = 144), two southern judges exclaimed: "I feel absolutely overpowered by the enormity of the task."[13] "We're becoming so overloaded that I am fearful of the effect on the quality of our work." Said a colleague in Washington: "There is insufficient time to do the important things well. We are straining. The little things constantly get in the way. I feel harried. I like some pressure, but not being harried. I am concerned for the quality of our product. Judges skimp a lot, greater than is good for the product. Delay is not so important as insufficient reflection."

Strategies of Reform • 265

The geographically compact 2d circuit is the last holdout against assembly-line justice, though that, too, is a matter of degree. Without screening cases to limit oral argument or scrapping its memorandum system of quality control, the court built an enviable record of productivity, procedural innovation, and dispatch. It was the only circuit to stay current with its docket every year between 1973 and 1979.[14] Fostering efficiency was relatively slow docket growth—caseloads actually fell 13 percent in 1978—but the court also effectively exploited practices that typify compact circuits during the initial stages of court congestion. The tribunal expedited criminal appeals in response to congressional urgings, filtered out over half its filings before hearing, and eliminated signed opinions in two-thirds of the cases heard (see Table 9.3).[d,15] Another important time-saver was temporary expansion in judicial manpower. Visiting judges and judges on senior status, as shown in Table 9.4, participated in almost 40 percent of the tribunal's cases in 1979.[e]

These practices, however, may not be portable or durable. Both high wash-out rates and affirmance-from-the-bench procedure are best suited to geographically concentrated circuits. The court, reluctantly forced to expand in 1978, projected a need for eighteen judgeships or their equivalent by 1980.[18] Having exhausted initial remedies compatible with its own self-image of opinion leadership and craftsmanship, the 2d circuit thus skirts the edges of basic change: expanding in size or altering the decisional process—and maybe both.

The D.C. circuit illustrates the temporary character of relief by diversion of business to other forums. Transfer of local jurisdiction to District of Columbia courts under the Court Reorganization Act, a program completed in 1973, radically reduced its private civil and criminal business. Contrary to fears of underutilization, the slack was soon filled by a richer mix of U.S. civil and agency actions. This litigation, clearly more demanding than the local cases displaced, constitutes over two-thirds of the court's docket.[19] Almost half of its filings involve agency appeals, the largest administrative load in the country.[20]

---

[d] The wash-out rate in 1978 was 51% in the 2d circuit, 66% in the D.C. circuit, and 36% in the 5th circuit. The all-circuit rate was 50%. The rates for 1979 were: 2d circuit, 57%; D.C. circuit, 70%; 5th circuit, 36%; all circuits, 51%.[16]

[e] The 2d circuit also experimented with a Civil Appeals Management Plan, involving preargument conferences between the parties and a court coordinator under Federal Rule of Appellate Procedure 33 to clarify issues, narrow the scope of litigation, and induce settlement. Evaluations of CAMP do not confirm success in reducing the volume of appeals, or inducing settlements.[17]

TABLE 9.3
Profile of Productivity in Circuit Courts, FY 1979

| Circuit | Authorized Judgeships N | Filings per Judgeship N | Terminations per Judgeship* N | Terminations without Oral Argument % | Terminations without Signed or Reasoned Opinions* % | Signed Opinions per Judgeship N | Median Interval between Filing of Completed Records and Final Disposition Months |
|---|---|---|---|---|---|---|---|
| 2d | 11 | 187 | 80.4 | 37.3 | 5.0 | 23 | 4.1 |
| 5th | 26 | 148 | 83.4 | 27.0 | 19.6 | 36 | 7.9 |
| D.C. | 11 | 129 | 35.8 | 35.2 | 35.5 | 13 | 13.4 |
| All circuits | 132 | 153 | 70.3 | 33.4 | 21.7 | 27 | 8.2 |
| SOURCE: AO Annual Report (preliminary 1979), | Table 3, 45 | Table 3, 45 | Table 11, 51 | Table 11, 51 | Table 11, 51 | Table 11, 51 | Table B4, A8 |

* Terminated after oral argument or submission on briefs. These figures deflate the actual productivity of circuit courts in 1979, because none of the 35 new circuit judgeships created by statute in 1978 was filled by June 30, 1979, the end of the AO's statistical year.

TABLE 9.4
Participation by Active, Senior, and Visiting Judges, FY 1979

| Circuit | Active Judges % | Resident Senior Judges % | Visiting Judges % | Total Nonactive Judges % |
|---|---|---|---|---|
| 2d | 61.5 | 22.2 | 16.3 | 38.5 |
| 5th | 88.0 | 10.1 | 1.9 | 12.0 |
| D.C. | 79.3 | 0.2 | 20.5 | 20.7 |
| All circuits | 77.8 | 9.3 | 12.9 | 22.2 |

SOURCE: AO *Annual Report* (preliminary 1979), Table 10, 51.

The court's business naturally breeds a policy priority, just as novelty spurs low rates of opinion production, dissension, and delay (see Table 9.3). For similar reasons, the judges insist on circulating slip opinions among the full membership to institutionalize the court, a luxury even the 2d circuit cannot afford.[21] They also take shortcuts. Two-thirds of the cases wash out before hearing. At the suggestion of a national crime commission in 1966, the court pioneered the rapidly growing practice of writing unpublished memo opinions for litigants only in preference to order judgments.[22] These accounted for over a third of its decisions in 1978. Screening eliminated oral argument in a tenth of the cases; in 1979 manpower was stretched another two-tenths by an "aggressive visiting judge program" (see Table 9.4).[23]

Still, the court fell further behind. The median time between filing and disposition, the worst in the country in 1979, was over a year (see Table 9.3). The court faced "a staggering backlog," a record number of filings, and worse projections for 1980.[24] The lesson seems plain that diverting local traffic merely kept this court open for more substantial federal claims. Even with two extra members after 1979, little lightening of judicial loads is in sight.

The 5th circuit is a paradigm of court "modernization" to meet a volume crisis. Besides holding doctrinal leadership in civil rights, this tribunal over the last two decades led all others in increasing productivity under pressure. The court not only kept abreast of exploding volume until 1975, but actually cut disposition time in half between 1966 and 1977.[f]

The keys to the court's productivity were enlargement, mass pro-

[f] The median interval between filing and disposition in the 5th circuit fell from 12 months in 1966 to 4.9 in 1973, but rose to 6.0 months in 1977 and 7.9 months in 1979.[25]

duction, and delegation of authority, usually begun as emergency measures that became standard after less onerous alternatives proved wanting. In the process the 5th circuit pioneered most of the remedies with which other circuits later experimented, including expansion and an experiment with designated district judges, later used in the 9th circuit, which was quickly scrapped in 1969 as a threat to court cohesion.[g] Then came a series of innovative techniques in docket management and decision making adapted from the states. Foremost were staff screening and order-type opinions under local Rule 21, affirming or reversing decisions without explanation.[27] Together with expedited criminal appeals, these procedures kept the 5th circuit current until the mid-1970s, even while deciding a volume of cases that all eleven circuits handled only fifteen years earlier.

The Hruska Commission praised these "innovative and imaginative" measures for averting "what might have been a failure in judicial administration of disastrous proportions."[28] But the price was high "both in the burdens imposed on the judges and in terms of the judicial process itself."[29] Too high, in fact, for the court's members and clienteles. As mass production shifted from the exception to the norm, circuit judges denounced the workload as "unreasonable, oppressive, and not in the public interest."[30] Griffin B. Bell, calling "frivolous litigation" and low pay a "debilitating experience," resigned.[31] Official bodies expressed fear that the lack of "mature consideration" of each case threatened "public acceptance of adjudications."[32] Even Chief Judge Brown, champion of modernization, conceded that "we are at the end of our rope. We can't do more."[33]

Modernization, too, failed to stem the tide. Despite a lull in growth in the late 1970s, a backlog developed when the court, responding to criticism, increased oral arguments and written opinions. Preemp-

---

[g] Most of these jurists approved of occasional exchanges by trial and appellate judges for purposes of familiarization, but members of the 5th circuit overwhelmingly condemned the district judge experiment, later used in the 9th circuit, as a disaster. Said one judge who "yelled the loudest" against it: "They've got their own work to do. You can't assign majority opinions to them. It's terrible when two circuit judges divide and the district judge is the swing man. . . . Familiarity breeds contempt. I saw it happen. I didn't think that the quality of district judges equaled the quality of circuit judges. But no one questions him. After all, he is volunteering his services. It wouldn't be sporting to say it. . . . We have about a half dozen district judges who make a contribution. But most district judges defer to circuit judges. All we have is a body of sitting wrens. . . . Screening makes it possible to have only circuit judges sitting by reducing the number of sittings. That's a great by-product." After circuit expansion in 1978, the Justice Department proposed limiting designation of district or visiting circuit judges to absences of active members due to illness, disability, vacancies, or official business; and the Senate barred designated judges from composing a majority of the court except where regular members were disqualified.[26]

tive timetables of the Speedy Trial Act further delayed civil appeals, including civil rights.[34] If Congress enacts a new federal criminal code, prescient would be John Minor Wisdom's warning: "After 1978, the deluge."[35] Workloads already justified three circuits of nine judges each for this region. Expanded appellate capacity would soon be absorbed by new district judgeships, each of which generates about forty appeals annually. Split or not, the Deep South states, at recent levels of docket growth, might well require fifty judges by the late 1980s.[36]

The 5th circuit, along with the 9th, thus brings the traditional system of federal appeals to a crossroads. The court, having exhausted initial remedies of visiting judges and enlargement in the late 1960s, pressed modernization beyond the physical limits of judges and the tolerance of critical constituencies. Its experience highlights the limits of what Courts of Appeals can do alone as well as the bounds of internal reorganization as an answer to the appeals explosion. Cast into bold relief are fundamental questions about the maintenance of traditional judicial roles under chronic case inflation. Indeed, all three circuits, adapting independently to different circumstances, have more or less exhausted the alternatives that they exemplify and that they fashioned on their own. To each the question is not whether change is necessary but the form change will take. Because the remedies now available to them and other hard-pressed circuits will affect the whole system, we should ask which reforms are most promising and which should come first? Answers to these questions, like the conjunction of political values and judicial roles in the judges' votes, necessarily knit competing philosophies of the judicial function with the politics of court reform.

## Paths of Reform

There are four basic strategies to relieve overloaded circuit courts: more judges, geographic realignment, better management, and diversion of cases to other forums. No single approach is likely to accomplish much by itself, nor is each suitable for every circuit. Even all approaches in concert might not suffice for long. Each alternative is unpleasant and therefore unpalatable to important groups. Building potential coalitions in support of reform, consequently, may be the most difficult task of all.

### More Judges

The simplest, most straightforward response to rising workloads is to increase the number of judges. This step is also easiest politically.

The Judicial Conference surveys the manpower needs of federal courts every four years. Though slow to act, Congress increased the number of circuit judgeships to 97 in 1968 and, following a stall until Democrats recaptured the White House, to 132 a decade later. This expansion, coupled with 117 more district judges, was the largest single increase in national history. Every circuit was authorized at least one additional judgeship. The D.C. and 2d circuits were enlarged to 11 members and the 5th to 26.[37]

Additional judicial manpower offers a quick fix for small circuits. Enlargement of larger ones, however, raises a galaxy of qualitative issues concerning the optimum size, number, and internal operations of circuit courts. Traditional wisdom is that small decision groups are the best way to foster the informal exchanges, collegiality, administrative flexibility, and personal accountability on which handcrafted appellate justice depends. Though Congress took the opposite tack, a large majority of federal judges regard size as the primary criterion of appellate organization and nine as the maximum feasible number of judges.[h][38]

The difficulty is that what may be optimum for effectiveness *within* Courts of Appeals may destabilize coherence *among* them. Adherence to the nine-judge standard, without more, will proliferate Courts of Appeals and burden the Supreme Court. The most overloaded circuits already exceed the nine-judge limit. Hardly had the Hruska Commission endorsed the rule of nine than the principle, as so often in the history of judicial reform, was "antiquated by events."[44] Escalation of appeals forced the Judicial Conference to recommend expansion beyond the desired limit not only in six of eleven circuits but even in the newly proposed divisions of the 5th![45]

Chief Justice Burger, sticking to the principle that ten or more judges is inherently unmanageable, favored splitting the 5th and 9th into three circuits each.[46] Many professionals agree with Judge J. Edward Lumbard that "there is much less danger to the character of the federal system in the creation of more circuits than there is in

---

[h] The rule of 9 was embraced officially by a special committee of the Judicial Conference in 1964 and by the Hruska Commission in 1974.[39] Chief Justice Burger espoused it repeatedly.[40] The council of the 2d circuit unanimously opposed "even the qualified court expansion" recommended by the Judicial Conference in 1974, Judge Friendly declaring that enlargement beyond 9 was acceptable "only as a last resort and with the greatest misgivings."[41] Similarly, in 1971, judges of the 5th circuit unanimously opposed expansion beyond 15 judgeships, calling it an "unworkable" solution that "would diminish the quality of justice"; and a majority to the east rebelled against 15 as "definitely six too many."[42] A majority of federal judges surveyed in 1972 also supported realignment or more circuits to preserve this principle.[43]

having some of our most important circuits become so unwieldy that the en banc procedure becomes unworkable, and flexible and informal means of supervising the administration of justice within the circuit are lost."[47] Even so, creating more circuits to keep them small obviously has limits. Projections of national needs range from twenty-two nine-judge circuits in 1981 up to thirty-five, some composed of single states, "within the very near future."[48] Whatever the effect on the prestige of the office, proliferation of this magnitude would aggravate the provincialism and conflicts in federal law that intermediate courts were designed to check.[49]

Hence, more judges is a deceptively simple solution. Additional judgeships were clearly needed in 1978, and perhaps more circuits, too.[50] The problem is how to organize growth without creating too large or too many courts. Relying on senior judges and visitors, second-class citizens excluded from administration and en bancs, is a variable makeshift, best adapted to relieving acute rather than chronic manpower shortages.[51] Enlarging courts, as the 5th and 9th circuits demonstrate, encourages production-line processing and bureaucratic controls. To avoid that by increasing the number of circuits aggravates intercircuit conflicts and the burdens on the Supreme Court. Other things being equal, the rule of nine would virtually compel creation of a new National Court of Appeals. Eventually, the strategy of more judges also becomes entangled in the political thicket of realigning judicial circuits.

*Geographic Realignment*

The objective of realignment is to equalize judicial resources in accordance with need. On the merits, a case can be made that circuit boundaries need revamping on a national scale. Few adjustments have been made in over fifty years, despite massive population shifts from hinterlands to coasts and wide variety in appellate demand. Citizens face unequal access to federal judicial services.[52] Disparities in workloads press upon the quality of judicial work. A majority of federal judges surveyed in 1972 believed geographic restructuring necessary, regardless of other improvements, to even the load.[53]

It is debatable whether reshuffling circuit boundaries, by itself, is worth the effort. The gains, to begin, are limited. No circuit appears to be underutilized. Realignment, unfeasible for compact circuits in New York and Washington, will provide only temporary relief for the most seriously overloaded circuits. The business remains. Nor will realignment correct systemwide ills. From the standpoint of national conflict resolution, it merely transforms intracircuit conflicts into intercircuit conflicts, thereby aggravating strains on the Supreme Court and pressures for a fourth tier.[54] To be weighed against the value of equalizing workloads, moreover, is the need for stable circuit law. Considering normal inertia against change, pride of place, and political stakes, it is scarcely surprising that the Hruska Commission's explorations of national realignment with bench and bar struck one dominant chord: "Leave us alone."[55]

The strongest case for realignment is to provide emergency relief for the critically overloaded circuits, the 5th and the 9th, pending more basic reforms. Splitting these two tribunals into four, as proposed by the Hruska Commission and the Senate, would allow essential growth in judicial manpower without overextending the size or number of circuits. What complicated questions of institutional design were policy issues of considerable moment. The nub of the problem in the 9th circuit is the concentrated population in Southern California. The Hruska Commission concluded that dividing California between two federal circuits was a lesser evil than an all-California circuit. This is hardly attractive as long as two federal circuits can decide the same state question differently under diversity jurisdiction.[56] More to the point, Californians are highly sensitive about precedents partitioning the state because of the implications for the control of water.

Race relations and energy policy were the stumbling blocks in the 5th circuit. For the past fifteen years the judges and their allies have battled over two basic models of appellate organization in the crisis of volume—traditional nine-judge courts requiring geographic splintering and a large, staff-assisted tribunal emphasizing the federalizing functions of a national court. Champions of division sharply attacked "jumboism" for its administrative headaches, impaired deliberations, and reduced cohesion.[57] Advocates of modernization, challenging division as a "fleeting and illusory solution" and expressing a "deathly fear" of proliferation, countered that a broad base of recruitment was essential to prevent capture of the court by segregationists and producer interests in oil and gas.[58] While the judges waffled on the issue in the early 1970s, a large majority favored partition both in 1964 and 1977, only to be blocked first in the Judicial Conference and later in the House of Representatives.[59]

Where to put Mississippi focused the options. Though joining the state with Louisiana and Texas in a new circuit would best balance uneven caseloads, Senator Eastland and the Eastern judges convinced the Senate in 1977 to align Mississippi with Alabama, Georgia, and Florida. This plan augured Texas and Louisiana judges passing exclusively on energy issues in the west, a more conservative majority toward civil rights, and the accession of James P. Coleman, the state's former governor, as chief judge in the east.[60] These prospects emboldened a dwindling minority of Texans—Brown, Gee, and Goldberg (plus senior judges Rives, Tuttle, and Wisdom, who could speak but not vote on the issue) to fight for expansion without division. House liberals followed suit.[61] The stalemate finally broke when the Omnibus Judges Act of 1978, following the 9th circuit's approach, separated questions of size from splits. Congress passed the buck by authorizing circuits over fifteen members to divide themselves administratively and to set their own rules for the number of members in en bancs. Old hands at this game, the 5th circuit council proposed in 1980 that Congress create a 5th circuit composed of Louisiana, Texas, and Mississippi and a new 11th circuit of Alabama, Georgia, and Florida. Meantime, the court would function as two administrative units, the judges serving circuitwide. As opposition faded in light of affirmative action appointments, Congress finally divided the circuit, effective in 1981.[62]

Plainly, realignment is to circuit courts what reapportionment is to legislatures, a political thicket that involves competing conceptions of institutional roles and public policy. That is why it happens so infrequently. The Hruska Commission itself originated in a political judgment, probably correct, that Congress was incapable of timely adjustment of circuit boundaries on a national scale. Splitting the 5th, even as a temporary Band-Aid, has twice ended in deadlock. The Commission and the Senate Judiciary Committee, both overwhelmingly populated by lawyers, repudiated enlargement and modernization as interim solutions, favored by the House; but rising appeals overcame their principles of appellate organization no less. In the long run, both the rule of nine and the old circuit of six states were plainly lost causes. Just as jumboists conceded the necessity of dividing the circuit in the 1980s, so neither more judges nor realignment alone will provide lasting relief. A three-way split became necessary before Congress could settle on two. National realignment following a nine-judge model by the 1980s would produce a structure that is "top heavy, parochial, and impossible to police by a single Supreme Court."[63] Consequently, some observers outside the South, seeing regionalism as the root of the evil, call for unification of Courts of Appeals into a single, national tribunal with rotating panels, a step that would undoubtedly add pressure for another appellate tier.[64]

Of all the methods of relieving overloaded circuits, realignment alone "offers the least promise."[65] About the best to be said is that it may buy time before Congress, confronting both jumboism and pro-

274 · Chapter Nine

liferation, must face up to basic questions of what Courts of Appeals should and can be expected to do, including "the imaginative use of new methods and procedures."[66]

*Better Management*

Improving court management involves increasing efficiency by rationing judge-time per case. The philosophy that improving court management will improve the quality of justice has long been an article of faith among American court reformers. Chief Justice Burger, for example, urges giving priority to "methods and machinery, to procedures and techniques, to management and administration of judicial resources, even over the much-needed reexamination of substantive legal institutions that are out of date."[67] This approach, appealing on the surface in terms of cost and simplicity, promises a further payoff of reducing delay, a worthy goal especially in criminal justice that cannot be drowned under false dichotomies of efficiency versus justice.

Everyone favors better management until the bills come due in terms of money, personnel, and treatment of litigants. Making courts more efficient is also easier said than done. Basically, efforts to do so tend to follow four paths: (1) working harder, (2) delegating administration to professional managers so judges can concentrate on adjudication, (3) streamlining adjudicatory procedures to reduce judicial energies expended per case, and (4) rationing judge-time according to priorities of function or subject (as in the Speedy Trial Act), so that energies are conserved for critical tasks. Together, these approaches encompass the general trend in the United States toward more centralized, bureaucratized, and professionally managed courts, of which the 5th and 9th circuits are prime federal examples.

While the room for improvement varies with each court, the three circuits are well along in better management. Apart from a few sluggards, circuit judges cannot be expected to work much harder. Until 1975, to be sure, for want of a uniform standard of what constitutes a case, the Administrative Office was slow to design a weighted caseload for appellate judges, parallel to that for district courts, from which minimum national standards of productivity per judge could be developed and enforced by "peer pressure."[68] Circuit judges, fearing external control, tend to resist quantitative measures or revealing individual records of work.[69] In the absence of common standards, outsiders can only accept Judge Bazelon's word that "we are working . . . our tails off."[70] Many judges contend they never worked harder; workloads commonly exceed fifty hours a week. If the job has not yet pressed them "to the point of exhaustion," as the

Chief Justice contends, the consensus is that they labor close to or beyond capacity.[71] Asking for more energy from judges is pumping a dry well.

The three circuits are also far along in administrative delegation and streamlined adjudication. All three tribunals have appointed professional circuit executives, from lists approved by a central board, to assist judges in court management.[72] As we have seen, they also pioneered various modes of internal modernization. Several improvisations have enduring value. Underlying them all is a mood of self-study and experimentation, often in collaboration with trial courts and professional administrators at both regional and national levels, that belies stereotypes of federal judges as ostriches, resistant to change. Circuit courts more than doubled their terminations (up 129%) between 1968 and 1979 without any increase in actual judges on the job.[73] Even discounting for "junk" litigation their productivity speaks for itself.

The problem is whether these measures of rationing judicial manpower impair appellate justice. Has the quest for greater efficiency displaced traditional goals of judicial self-government and handcrafted adjudication?

So far, the administrative risks are more potential than pressing, but they bear watching as reformers pursue managerial solutions somewhat uncritically. Peter G. Fish, a leading student of federal judicial administration, maintains that "from its inception, the hallmarks of the federal judiciary's administrative system have been independence, decentralization, and individualism."[74] Increasingly, however, the hallmarks are centralization, bureaucratization, and professionalization of judicial administration at the expense of judicial informality and autonomy. These general trends, rooted in external demands for efficiency, fiscal accountability, and professional standards of personnel management, have been accelerated by the law explosion. Centralization is evident at both national and regional levels. The Judicial Conference, making up for ineffective circuit councils, tends to be the management center of the federal judiciary, contrary to original design. Budgetary operations are centralized in the Administrative Office. Chief Justices, particularly Warren E. Burger, have asserted vigorous administrative leadership over the federal judiciary, down to the details of courtroom architecture.

Some chief judges, notably Lumbard, Brown, and Kaufman, also have made impressive marks as administrators at regional levels. Managing modern circuits is far more demanding than a generation ago. Besides monitoring their own dockets, Courts of Appeals are responsible for supervising federal defender programs, jury service, and wiretapping approved by courts below. As responsibilities and personnel grow, communication and internal coordination inevitably become more complex, requiring greater formalization and stronger bureaucratic controls. These in turn are both time consuming and potential sources of friction. A major complaint against jumboism in the 5th circuit, for instance, was that formal rules were supplanting professional norms and informal exchanges as the basis of court integration.

Further tensions may arise between competing professional orientations among new managers and the old. Not just court clerks or district judges face potential role conflict or loss of power. The collective dominance of circuit judges over court administration is also subject to erosion. It may exaggerate to say that "judges as a class are poor administrators," as one southern jurist declared, but federal judges traditionally have been ambivalent about their administrative responsibilities. Like professionals in other organizations, say hospital doctors or university professors, they seek the benefits of bureaucratization without having to supervise bureaucrats; and they resist administrative supervision from anyone but their peers.[75] The weaknesses of circuit councils, "rusty hinges" of administration by committee, reflect this ambivalence.[76] Injecting administrative specialists into largely informal processes of management also introduces a new dimension of bureaucratic politics into federal courts. "A court executive, whether he likes it or not, is concerned with politics."[77] Budgetary and calendar controls complicate relations between judges and managers. Modernized courts, like hospitals run by professional administrators, are institutions of "federated professionals," whose standards, interests, and loyalties, do not mesh automatically.[78] Given the overlap between administration and policy making, observed in Chapter Eight, it is uncertain whether the judges can keep the new professionals in their ideal state—on tap but not on top.

Thus far, most Courts of Appeals remain too small and informal for these potential strains to erupt into serious difficulties. Fears of staff intrusion Chief Justice Burger dismisses as "old wives' tales."[79] The experience of other institutions nonetheless warns that administrative modernization is no panacea. Better management is usually a euphemism for centralization, professionalization, and bureaucratization of court operations. These processes enhance potential role conflicts, professional rivalries, and subtle shifts of power. Courts of Appeals are clearly evolving into more complex organizations with increased delegation and formalization of administrative authority.

These may be small prices to pay for conservation of resources and judicial self-government. Still, in an era of combination and consolidation, it is not self-evident that Congress and the president are the only threats to judicial independence, nor that modern managerial techniques are inherently superior to coordinating and integrating federal courts by traditional means of mutual influence. There is a saying in public administration that the higher up the exercise of control the less effective the organization.[80] In view of the demonstrated interplay between court administration and policy making, the question for court reformers is how much management can be centralized and formalized without subverting the very values of collegiality, informality, and judicial independence they purport to defend.[i]

More worrisome than administrative relations is streamlined adjudication. Changing judicial roles in modern American society are likewise transforming the process of decision. The syndrome of case processing, bane of trial courts in this country, is beginning to infect federal appellate courts, as we saw in Chapter Five, even in their concepts of mission. As lawmaking takes precedence over the goals of uniformity and justice between the parties, so assembly lines are becoming the mode for error correction in large classes of litigation. All circuits in one way or another mass-produce decisions and ration judicial time. Is justice rationed in the bargain?

Screening and short-order opinions are the two most important time-savers. In principle, few lawyers or judges resist Judge John J. Parker's rationale for summary treatment: "no case and no sense."[82] The less that litigants or Congress filter frivolous cases from the appellate stream, the more critical become judicial methods of separating meretricious from meritorious federal claims. The critical issues center on the adequacy of gatekeeping, which may vary according to unique circuit conditions.

Screening, though "frankly an experiment imposed by necessity," is a method of limiting or eliminating oral argument for the purpose of reducing sittings and, above all, travel.[83] Because travel in geographically sprawling circuits consumes more judge-time than sittings and judicial conferences combined, screening maximizes time for judges to think and write in chambers.[84] Screening also cuts unnecessary travel and expense for litigants, which perhaps explains why lawyers of the 5th circuit objected less to screening than to order-type opinions.[85] Though individual judges differ widely in the

[i] Perhaps for these reasons, the Rockwell proposal for a centralized national executive to administer federal courts met the same fate as suggestions to unify Courts of Appeals.[81]

percentage of cases they decline to hear orally, many agree that appeals not requiring argument "stick out like a sore thumb."[86] Litigants are protected from one-man decisions by the requirement of unanimity for both denial of oral argument and decision on the merits.[87] While traditionalists may scoff at "hearings without anyone being heard," screening reduces circuit riding for judges and counsel alike without cutting appellate capacity.[88] The 5th circuit, as a result, relies far less than the others on wash outs and visiting judges.

What began as a tourniquet under emergency conditions is now a standard technique of docket control in all except the 2d circuit. Even there staff attorneys screen *pro se* petitions, while the judges follow the English practice of deciding cases with oral opinions from the bench, a practice that imposes little hardship where most litigants are near the court.[j] [89]

In effect, screening enables circuit judges of the 1970s to do what Supreme Court Justices did a century earlier: combat docket congestion by less circuit riding. The high court has declined to repudiate the device as a denial of due process or sound judicial administration.[91] Only isolated complaints developed, moreover, as long as judges did the screening and kept the fraction of decisions on briefs within the original target of about one-third—a common judicial estimate of insubstantial appeals.[k][92] When mounting appeals forced 5th circuit judges to delegate screening to their clerks and then to central staff attorneys, however, vigorous opposition crystallized on three counts.

First, the muzzle on lawyers was too tight. Over half of the 5th circuit's cases in the mid-1970s were decided without any oral argument. Only 8 percent received full time.[94] Reversing custom, the 3rd circuit recognized a right to oral argument only when a judge desired it.[95] Court expediency appeared to override the needs of litigants and traditions of oral advocacy.

---

[j] Oral decisions in the 2d circuit are a flexible surrogate for both screening and order-type opinions. "This little buzz business on the bench," Chief Judge Brown once remarked, presupposes advance preparation and judgment; but Chief Judge Kaufman countered that prior consultations are rare.[90] A judge in New York commented: "We gauge this as we go along. On one occasion the court didn't decide summarily when we noticed a girlfriend of a young lawyer in the audience. We made a quick check with a clerk, who told us that they were newlyweds and this was his first case in this court. So we waited and cut his head off the next morning."

[k] In the 5th circuit, for example, two circuit judges who originally opposed the practice became converts to it. A Federal Judicial Center survey showed that lawyers familiar with screening were less hostile to it than those in circuits without such experience.[93]

Second, too much judicial responsibility was delegated to clerks and central staff. It was bad enough that staff attorneys handled pro se work under judicial supervision. Under emergency conditions in 1974, the 5th circuit delegated screening to central staff attorneys in roughly 60 percent of the cases, including criminal, diversity, and some tax appeals.[96] Staff screening is a refinement of the pooled-clerk concept, a much-praised innovation in state appellate courts; but for federal appeals this recipe for crisis management aroused deep misgivings.[97] Some members conceded lack of time to read briefs until proposed classifications and per curiam orders were already prepared by their aides, thus violating a strong rule of the game.[98] Judges increasingly spent their time supervising decision making by others, including central staff attorneys responsible to the chief judge and the circuit council as a whole, rather than deciding themselves.

Beyond that, the safeguard of unanimity was not very comforting when the whole panel relied on the bench memo of the same staff attorney and decided without face-to-face conferences.[m] In the 5th circuit, 95 percent of summary decisions were made "round-robin style," by mail or phone. One-fourth received no explanation at all. Little wonder lawyers complained that the tribunal was no longer "a real court. . . . It is a judicial bureaucratic institution."[102] Judge-time was not only being rationed, but others were doing the rationing. What began as judicial gatekeeping to rationalize caseloads was becoming a staff operation under the nominal supervision of judges already complaining about excessive administrative burdens. Judges, as Brandeis had warned, were becoming administrators running "human machines." Eroded in the process was a basic norm of personal accountability: judges should do their own work.

Finally, screening raised the specter of unequal justice to underprivileged litigants.[103] Table 9.5 shows that the 5th circuit during the mid-1970s heard orally most tax and federal questions whereas the overwhelming number of prisoner petitions without counsel were treated summarily. So were most social security and direct criminal appeals. Efficiency experts might commend this as a rational allocation of judicial manpower, segregating for summary

---

[l] Excluded from screening were certain special classes, e.g., school desegregation and Chapter X bankruptcy cases.

[m] In the 8th circuit, by comparison, judges do the screening, and in the 3rd they regard face-to-face conferences as an "indispensable minimum" for summary disposition.[99] The 4th circuit requires a written opinion when oral argument is denied.[100] The 10th circuit, early pioneer of screening, eliminated staff recommendations on the merits to guard against excessive delegation.[101]

TABLE 9.5
Summary Calendar Percentage by Subject Matter, 5th Circuit
FY 1974-1976

| Subject Matter | Percentage without Oral Argument (Summary II) | | |
|---|---|---|---|
| | 1974 | 1975 | 1976 |
| Direct criminal | 61.9 | 55.6 | 60.0 |
| Prisoner cases | | | |
|   With counsel | 52.9 | 46.7 | 55.6 |
|   Without counsel | 91.9 | 90.3 | 85.9 |
| 2255 | | | |
|   With counsel | 54.2 | 82.9 | 92.0 |
|   Without counsel | 94.7 | 92.9 | 93.1 |
| Civil | | | |
|   Private civil (diversity) | 45.5 | 38.0 | 41.2 |
|   Private civil (federal question) | 25.6 | 30.3 | 29.8 |
|   U.S. civil | 35.6 | 29.0 | 31.9 |
|   Tax | 24.2 | 26.0 | 31.9 |
|   Bankruptcy | 43.3 | 52.9 | 46.7 |
|   NLRB | 37.8 | 46.5 | 53.8 |
|   Social Security | 71.4 | 63.2 | 63.3 |
|   Other agency | 33.3 | 35.5 | 46.9 |
|   Civil rights | 42.9 | 39.2 | 38.6 |
|   Admiralty | 52.3 | — | — |
| Sums | 54.9 | 51.2 | 53.4 |

SOURCE: Hearings on S. 11, S. 460 before the Senate Committee on the Judiciary, 95th Cong., 1st Sess. (1977), 604.

treatment routine appeals that would not benefit from oral argument. But who is to say what is junk litigation? Why were petitioners with counsel much more likely to be heard than those without?

Reduced opinion writing, often in the same cases, aggravated concern. For all the primacy of well-crafted opinions in judicial priorities, as seen in Chapter Five, the circuits wrote proportionately fewer of them. In 1975, only four cases in ten terminated in all circuits received signed opinions; one-fourth were terminated by per curiam opinions and over one-third without any.[104] These figures obscure informal explanation by oral opinions from the bench in the 2d circuit and unpublished memoranda intended solely for the parties in Washington; but form opinions, as the D.C. circuit discovered, apparently troubled southern attorneys more than screening.[105] Two-thirds of the lawyers in the Gulf states surveyed by the

Federal Judicial Center in 1972 thought that written explanations should become a due process requirement."[106] Otherwise, the assurance that at least one judge considered the appeal, the discipline that reasoned explanation imposes on decision makers, and the accountability to litigants and members of the bar, whom judges themselves regarded as their primary constituents, would be weakened. To little avail were rebuttals that short opinions, like Cicero's letter, take longer to compose or that circuit judges simply lack time to write in every case if they are to meet basic obligations of sound and timely adjudication, reserving opinions for legal points of precedential value.[108] More than any other emergency measures, staff screening and short-order opinions tipped the balance against the 5th circuit's "new look" and kindred practices elsewhere. The Hruska Commission, lawyers responding to lawyers, called on Congress to create more judges, more courts, and minimum national standards of appellate justice, including the right of every litigant to a written explanation of decisions, even if only a brief citation of precedent."[109]

Overload reveals the working priorities of any judiciary. Just as the 2d and D.C. circuits abbreviated procedures in keeping with their emphasis on opinion writing, so crisis management enabled the 5th circuit to "get the work out," satisfying law professors when they could.[112] In moderate doses, screening, central staffs, and restricted opinions are here to stay. Yet, these modes of better management at bottom mean rationing judge-time per case. And judge-time is the service people want. Recognizing these constraints, the Hruska Commission basically repudiated modernization in favor of a return to traditional models of appellate adjudication, however ironic it would be to impose minimum standards of adjudication by

---

[n] Selective publication of opinions creates problems of legal authority in some circuits, but the 2d circuit strictly suppressed oral opinions as precedents in *U.S. v. Joly*, 493 F. 2d 672, 676 (2d Cir. 1974), despite listing all cases in the *Federal Reporter*. Judge Bell called this a "nonproblem" in the 5th circuit because Rule 21 opinions, though reported, clearly lack authority. The Supreme Court declined to review the question whether counsel may be prohibited from citing unpublished opinions in *Do-Right Auto Sales, et al. v. United States Court of Appeals for the Seventh Circuit*, 429 U.S. 917 (1976).[107]

[o] Judge Bell, who originated Rule 21 opinions but ceased writing them in 1974, called this a "reasonable recommendation."[110] Colleagues were less certain. "If the Supreme Court can deny hundreds of petitions for certiorari without comment," said one circuit judge in 1970, "why can't we? A man is entitled to a right to appeal, not to a letter from the judges." Chief Judge Brown asked the Hruska Commission: "What are we here for? Are we to please litigants? Are we to make them feel good? . . . Are we psychiatrists who are supposed to ease people's feelings? Or are we to administer justice in an expanding field that puts great demands?"[111]

legislation or however doubtful their ability to relieve the pressure of quantity on quality without reducing intake at its source.

*Diversion*

The essential idea of diversion is to transfer nonessential judicial business to other and better forums. Whereas managerial reforms are commonly within the power of courts, diversion often requires legislation to change their jurisdiction. The Hruska Commission, guided by a premise of political feasibility, was barred by charter from examining jurisdictional options. This restriction prevented members from taking an integrated view of the federal judicial system. It also precluded consideration of a major strategy of reform: eliminating unnecessary work.

A substantial body of judges and critics regards the resulting institutional approach of the Commission as a tragic inversion of priorities. For them, the first order of business should be "averting the flood by lessening the flow."[113] While no one has yet suggested a judicial counterpart for "sunset" legislation, in which each federal activity must be justified periodically before renewal, the spirit is similar. Reducing nonessential business should precede organizational growth.

Proposals to divert federal court business are legion. They range from arbitration of civil disputes to alternatives for prosecution in nonviolent crimes.[114] Most laundry lists of suggestions, generally speaking, follow one or more of the following criteria: (1) federal jurisdiction, as Judge Friendly argued in his influential Carpentier lectures, should be scaled to important federal interests and functions that federal courts are "specially qualified to perform"; (2) overlapping jurisdiction should be curtailed; (3) remedies where possible should relieve all three levels of the federal judiciary at once and should not be directed toward one part without considering the impact on the others; and (4) the primary objective should be improving the quality of justice, not reducing court congestion per se.[115] Of the most promising alternatives, four proposals satisfy all these criteria.

ELIMINATING MANDATORY APPEALS   Chief Justice Burger urges abolition of appeals by right to the Supreme Court to safeguard its discretionary docket control.[116] The judges interviewed in this study overwhelmingly supported this move, though elimination ostensibly would aid the Justices at their expense and sacrifice sure access by civil rights groups for decisions of national scope. Time and again they denounced three-judge district courts as "a miserable way to do business"—an "abomination," "a monstrosity in concept and practice"—which they believed district judges disliked as well. Evidence was slim that regional courts were less sensitive to civil rights than their superiors. A procedure designed to speed significant appeals actually slowed them down because of scheduling problems. Emergencies could be handled by expedited appeal. Additional work for circuit courts would be offset by eliminating the inefficiencies of three federal judges doing the work of one during lengthy trials, not to mention steering by chief judges who assign the membership (see Chapter Eight, notes p and u). Gains in collective judgment at trial did not justify forcing the hand of the Supreme Court without benefit of prior appellate review. Whatever the loss in national appellate capacity, the Justices, not litigants, should decide which controversies require nationally binding rules.

While the number of cases is small, eliminating three-judge district courts would benefit the federal judiciary at every level. Certainly these circuit judges thought this privileged class of litigation should go. "It is an annoyance; it is unnecessary; it is outmoded; it is archaic."[117] "It is absurd on its face."

CURTAILING DIVERSITY JURISDICTION  The power of federal courts to adjudicate state questions in diversity of citizenship cases, for many federal judges, has also "outlived its usefulness."[118] Fears of local prejudice against nonresidents, which gave rise to this overlapping jurisdiction, have receded substantially as a result of the integration of national life and improved state judiciaries. Allowing removal for cause from state to federal courts, analogous to changes of venue, would protect litigants outside their states, without the redundancies, forum shopping, and discrimination bred by the present system. Many lawyers, it is true, defend diversity jurisdiction on grounds of local bias, convenience for multistate litigants, and superior quality of federal justice.[119] Because diversity suits constitute only 11 percent of circuit filings, and far less in the Supreme Court, they tax federal courts less at appellate levels, where the crunch is greatest. When the level of feared prejudice is unknown and some federal district judges see value in retention, what is to be gained by transferring these cases to overburdened state courts?[120]

The answer is that abolishing diversity jurisdiction is the least painful method to trim the fat without cutting into the muscle of federal judicial power. Diversity suits comprise one-fourth of the district courts' civil business and one-sixth of civil appeals arising from them to circuit courts.[121] Unlike prisoner petitions, these appeals cannot be dismissed as junk litigation that bloats caseload statistics without consuming much judicial energy. As we saw in Chapter Two, they generated greater appellate demand and apparently consumed a greater proportion of judge-time than any class except federal questions. Diversity cases are especially troublesome in larger circuits, because judges are expected to keep current with the laws of several states.[122] Assuming these experiences are common, both consumer demand for review and judicial resources expended were high in the very font of jurisdiction in which federal interests were least.

For the last half-century judicial leaders from Brandeis to Burger have pleaded that diversity jurisdiction is a luxury we no longer can afford.[123] Structural changes are likely to have negative effects in terms of delay, cost to litigants, and pressures to mass-produce decisions. Surrendering diversity jurisdiction, except for cases of demonstrated prejudice against nonresidents, offers most savings to federal courts at least cost to state judiciaries.

Though the impact on states would vary, it is instructive that not one state bar association, normally quick to defend state power, supports the American Law Institute's proposals for partial diversion of diversity jurisdiction.[124] The American Bar Association reiterated its support for retention in 1978, even as the House of Representatives, in a surprise move, voted to abolish diversity jurisdiction entirely.[125] If this response from the organized bar seems odd in light of the evidence, it reflects a central condition of federal courts. The roots of burdensome caseloads lie less in the organization and procedures of federal appellate courts than in inelastic and uneven demand for their services among different elements of the litigating public. Discriminating remedies for the ills of Courts of Appeals are primarily a political problem of setting priorities.

SPECIALIZATION   A less certain cluster of proposals to curtail circuit business is to divert appeals in technical subjects to experts, sitting either as panels of Courts of Appeals or as separate national tribunals. Specialization, notwithstanding the failure of the old Commerce Court, is no stranger to the federal judiciary. Specialized tribunals exist in military justice, taxation, and tort claims against the government as well as in patents and customs appeals.[126] Emergency Courts of Appeals have been established during periods of price control.[127] Specialization, as we saw in Chapter Eight, also occurs in circuit courts informally.

Proposals for further specialization have gained new currency both to enlarge national appellate capacity and to relieve congestion in lower courts. After the proposed National Court of Appeals fizzled in Congress, the Carter administration proposed and both houses passed a scaled-down version that would consolidate the Court of Claims and the Court of Customs and Patent Appeals into a new U.S. Court of Appeals for the Federal Circuit, adding to their appellate jurisdiction contract suits against the government. The Senate sponsors of this legislation, Edward M. Kennedy and Dennis De Concini, added a proposal to consolidate all appeals regarding civil taxation in a new U.S. Court of Tax Appeals, consisting of twelve current circuit judges to be chosen on a rotating basis by the Chief Justice; but the Senate deferred this proposal.[128] Still others urge a science court, an environmental court, and a national court of administrative appeals on the French model, perhaps evolving out of the D.C. circuit's current magnetic field.[129] To help lower courts, a Justice Department committee in the Ford administration, headed by Solicitor General Robert H. Bork, recommended restricting access of prisoners to federal courts and creating a new tier of tribunals to hear social security, welfare, and other regulatory claims.[130] Carter administration officials championed expanded authority for federal magistrates and alternatives to adjudication, such as no-fault automobile insurance, decriminalization, and arbitration, all with an accent on directing traffic away from federal courts.[131]

The variety and inventiveness of the proposals bespeak a tendency to create new institutions as a quick physic for court congestion in pet fields. Though each proposal raises highly complex issues, the arguments for and against specialization of appeals are similar, familiar, and divisive. Specialized appellate tribunals with national jurisdiction, proponents say, would provide faster, better informed, and more coherent national law in technical subjects such as patents and taxation, where forum shopping is severe. Opponents contend that the limited savings do not justify the risks of tunnel vision among experts. The patent and tax bars themselves champion review by generalists on grounds that their vexing subjects are cross-fertilized by other legal fields. National courts also risk ideological polarization and politicization of the appointing process.[132] Courts no less than regulatory agencies can become captives of the interests being regulated.[133] Then, too, would the best talent willingly serve as judges?

One way around these problems is to staff specialized courts with rotating circuit judges. Like the Hruska Commission, however, the judges interviewed in this study were skeptical of specialization.[134] They denounced special panels within Courts of Appeals as "horrible," "a terrible idea" inviting stagnation. A suggestion in the 5th circuit council to experiment with a standing criminal panel, rotating members every three months, drew only two votes. If it came to that, one judge commented, "I'd quit."

The judges were more willing to experiment with specialized tribunals in patents and taxation, where deficiencies were clearest, but like the bar at large they tended to divide over particulars. Patents were considered the best candidate for specialization. Lamenting the complexity of patent litigation, some judges challenged the alleged benefits of cross-pollination. "If an idea is obvious enough for me to understand it," one of them quipped, "it's not patentable." Were generalists being duped by specialists? As for a national tax court, the general reaction was a draw.[135] In the 5th circuit especially, several judges regarded the present system of filtering law questions through the Tax Courts to be working well enough to serve as a model for labor appeals, whose concentration on factual issues was frequently condemned as a great waste of time (see note r, this chapter). Because specialization in administrative appeals already abounds in Washington, there were suggestions that the D.C. circuit could evolve into a national labor or administrative court. This idea drew horrified looks in New York. On the whole, these judges appeared to prefer sister courts in patents and taxation to a National Court of Appeals above them. Serious support for specialization stopped there.

LIMITED DOCKET CONTROL   More popular was a related option of expanding their discretionary docket control.[p] Assuming that federal litigants should have the right to one appeal, advocates of this approach would confine routine factual review to lower courts and agencies in order to conserve circuit resources for allegations of gross error, prejudice, and inappropriate legal standards.[q]

Restricting access to Courts of Appeals would again follow a trail blazed by the Supreme Court a half-century ago. Several judges preferred this alternative to creating new circuits or a mini-Supreme Court, but inherent problems gave others pause.[138] For one thing, limiting rights to appeal would accelerate the trend toward more circuit lawmaking at the expense of checking functions. Predictable also would be proportionately more conflicts as circuit judges con-

[p] In 1969-1970, for example, 4 of 7 judges in the 2d circuit and 10 of 17 judges in the 5th circuit expressed a willingness to experiment with expanded certiorari powers as an alternative to further screening or proliferation of courts. In 1973, Chief Justice Burger also suggested leave-to-appeal procedure, used in England and Virginia, as an alternative to screening.[136]

[q] Some circuit judges assumed that due process required at least one appeal to a court; but Congress, with certain exceptions, has exempted decisions of the Veterans Administration from judicial review—an exemption now being challenged.[137]

centrated on close legal issues.¹³⁹ There was little consensus on the fields in which discretionary jurisdiction should obtain. The chief contenders were diversity cases, administrative appeals involving fact finding by experts previously reviewed, and prisoner petitions, where duplication, lack of finality, and squandered judicial resources are rampant.ʳ If most circuit judges were ready to unload diversity cases, not many were willing to put administrators on a par with trial courts as fact finders to whom appellate courts should defer. Relieving grievances at their source was undoubtedly preferable to having circuit courts search for needles of reversible error or civil rights violations in haystacks of repetitious prisoner petitions.¹⁴⁰ But because a few needles have pricked deep sores, some reeking of racism, many circuit judges were loath to choke off these remedies pending basic reforms of criminal processes.ˢ

Also unclear is how much judge-time certiorari procedures would save. The plain truth is that prisoner petitions, welfare claims, and

ʳ For example, one judge in the 5th circuit observed: "I'd pick the most important one of all—labor—the most colossal waste of time. The aperture of review is so narrow. To call upon us to read thousands of pages is the most colossal waste of time I know. If Congress wants an independent review of facts, let it create one with powers of certified legal questions to us. I don't want to be a fact finder. For the present I wouldn't move into limited cert. in the criminal field. Criminal law is in too much flux at present. Ten years from now I might be in a position to say, yes, like labor we've had it lo these many years.... Notice I haven't said we shouldn't take tax cases. We have Tax Courts, and tax law is geared to this system. So is the Labor Board, but they haven't developed concepts of law as in the tax field. I also think diversity jurisdiction should be much more limited than now. The old antiquated idea that you can't get justice in a state court is an old wives' tale. That's the only justification for diversity. In any case, they [state courts] don't have to pay attention to us except in the individual case, and if we come out differently, that's terrible because we have erred on their law."

ˢ Among the more imaginative proposals are the Carrington, Meador, and Rosenberg plan for unified review of all alleged errors shortly after trial with leave to appeal for prejudice, new evidence, and constitutional questions.¹⁴¹ A promising approach for prisoners' complaints, adopted in federal jails with wide approbation, is the Freund Committee's recommendation of prison ombudsmen or other in-house procedures to handle disputes, which federal courts, for want of better alternatives, attempt to process from afar.¹⁴² Such suggestions have the virtue of focusing on the right questions—how best to relieve grievances at their source—rather than on court congestion, even though the relief would be felt throughout the federal judiciary. For example, a program providing legal aid to prison inmates in six states cut sharply into court backlogs and the influence of "jailhouse lawyers." According to the Law Enforcement Assistance Administration, over 90% of the inmates' legal questions in 1974-1975 were settled by negotiation without court appearances.¹⁴³ The remaining 10% corresponds to some judges' rough estimates of prisoner petitions that merit certificates of probable cause.¹⁴⁴ In *Stone v. Powell* (428 U.S. 465 [1976]), the Burger Court restricted access via habeas corpus to challenge convictions on grounds of failure to exclude illegally obtained evidence.

the like get second-class treatment already. The overwhelming proportion are screened by staff and decided summarily. As the same personnel would probably assist judges in sorting cases for review, what would be gained by shifting from screening of mandatory appeals to selective docket control?[145] The answers mirror contending conceptions of appellate justice in the law explosion. Champions of modernization prefer screening and order-type opinions because they provide final judgment, at least nominally by three judges, on the merits of every appeal, whereas limited certiorari restricts rights to judicial review.[146] Is it necessary or wise to curtail access for the many in order to preserve oral argument, face-to-face conferences, and collegial deliberation for the few?[t]

On the other hand, if open access requires restricting deliberations, what is the point of review? Both mass production and docket control appear to put the convenience of courts before the interests of consumers. Why should minor disputes receive second-class treatment?[u][147]

In principle, no inconsistency exists between certiorari power and appeal by right.[148] The crux of the matter is gatekeeping. Someone must separate wheat from chaff in federal appeals if counsel refuse. Is it better for clerks and staff to filter cases under judicial supervision than to expand courts, contract their business, or create lesser tribunals so that judges can do it themselves? At what point does deciding what to decide overcome hearing and deciding appeals?[149] The same questions haunt federal courts at every level. And they illuminate how differing conceptions of judicial roles affect strategies of reform.

Though separating appellate functions is not always easy in practice, policing for error is more amenable to mass production or diversion than is lawmaking. The logic of checking functions and settling disputes implies more appeals, lawmaking and opinion writing less.[150] Federalizing functions impel a diverse recruitment base, if not national unification, which implies large courts and

[t] As a proponent of modernization declared: "We must find new ways. We can't survive with a system which gives the right to appeal to one court. The system will break down of its own weight. A super Court of Appeals or a junior-grade Supreme Court? The beneficiaries will be the rich, and the poor will lose out. That's why it's so important to consider various schemes, even at the expense of deliberation. I never do my best work while I deliberate. That's Frankfurter junk! I have confidence in my own judgment. Frankfurter crocheted."

[u] As one Nixon appointee said of prisoner petitions: "They are time consuming. But on the other hand I have never taken to the argument that cases consume too much time. God dammit—pardon my language—if you're in the penitentiary or about to lose money on a judgment, it doesn't sit too well to hear the court hasn't time. I think the court ought to take time."

modernization. As judges emphasize different goals, so they champion different tonics to shrink swollen dockets.

Yet, clearly, there is no simple cure for court congestion, nor one free of political choice. Each major remedy—more resources, realignment, modernization, and diversion—is a partial solution with distasteful implications. To divert will choke access to federal courts for selected interests. Not to divert, as Chief Justice Burger warns, makes more and larger institutions inevitable.[151] To combat that tendency, Burger has urged Congress to assess the impact of new programs on the federal judiciary.[152] The Supreme Court has not accepted the same discipline for its own decisions.[153] The Chief Justice's plea for appellate review of federal sentencing points up the essential dilemma, as Felix Frankfurter noted long ago, that the historic growth in federal authority, and its reflex in litigation, "will not stop."[154]

Any choice thus cuts to fundamentals: what are the appropriate roles of federal judges in the American polity? Rising tides of appeals reflect growing reliance on legal processes to protect individual rights and rising expectations of law as an instrument of social control. Precisely because Courts of Appeals are in the center of expanding conceptions of law and the judicial function, former Attorney General Bell and others argue that "the *role* more than the *condition* of the courts" offers most promise of decisive relief.[155] Strategies of court reform, as a result, ripple into larger issues of government overload in what President Carter condemned as an "over-lawyered and under-represented" society.[156] Historically, policy makers usually find it easier to increase institutional resources than to face up to fundamental questions of appropriate judicial functions and clienteles in American life. Congress remained true to form in 1978, buying time by expanding judgeships. But this option, like all others, involves a political judgment that necessarily impinges on the purposes and processes of Courts of Appeals, which are at once deeply rooted in American federalism and rapidly changing. In strategies of reform, no less than in theories of decision, judicial politics and judicial roles are necessarily joined.

## Conclusions

Proliferating laws in a litigious society proliferate appeals. The basic responses are to multiply judicial institutions, streamline their procedures, or restrict their roles. Has the crisis of volume reached the point where expanding judicial services must contract? Who decides—courts, Congress, clients—which path to take?

What makes specification of a discriminating agenda of reform so difficult are the lack of information to guide choices among unpleasant alternatives and, more fundamentally, the lack of political consensus about appropriate roles of federal judges in the United States. With all respect to the devoted band of lawyers, teachers, and jurists who have endeavored to launch timely reform, thus far few have offered coherent programs for the federal judiciary as a whole.[157] Action-oriented research to illuminate alternatives is only beginning to flower with the work of the Hruska Commission, the Federal Judicial Center, and the Justice Department's new Office for Improvements in the Administration of Justice. Not just scholars complain about inadequate information on the causes of caseload inflation, the loads judges can reasonably carry, or the likely effects of proposed changes.[158] While not written for the purpose of prescribing a specific plan of reforms, this study of Courts of Appeals in the federal judicial system should help put these problems into perspective.

The central concern has been tension between the purposes and organization of federal courts. Their mission of enforcing the supremacy and uniformity of federal law is allocated among the most decentralized institutions of the federal government. What keeps the federal judiciary from disintegrating? Why is harmony more dominant than discord in Courts of Appeals? Complicating these questions are changing judicial functions in the law explosion, which accentuate both lawmaking and case processing in Courts of Appeals as well as strain between those roles. Compounding the puzzle further are the diversity and informality of judicial relations in the flow of litigation. Though focusing on these three circuits in the late 1960s probably intensified the differences, we found that federal courts were, indeed, decentralized. Substantial variety flourished in court business and intercourt relations. Formal supervision, at both appellate levels, was limited, sporadic, and diversified. Pluralism marked appellate policy functions as Courts of Appeals participated in both national and regional policy networks. In the great mass of federal litigation, the intermediates were regional supreme courts, independent of direct control from the top. Spiraling caseloads and more judges can only reduce effective appellate oversight.

Were formal controls the only cement available, these trends would justify fears that the national judiciary is outgrowing its central nervous system.[159] Nevertheless, a broad view of Courts of Appeals in the federal judicial system, coupling court diversity with informal values and relations, gives less cause for alarm. For one thing, despite the localism and fragmentation of lower federal courts, horrendous pictures of besieged appellate courts fade sharply when account is taken of circuit gatekeeping. Though the odds of judicial review have fallen sharply in the last decade, from the standpoint of doctrinal control figures for court intake are deceiving. Circuit courts still review about 11 percent of cases terminated in district courts; and roughly a third of their decisions appealed reach the conference room of the Supreme Court, which hears over 5 percent of the total decided by the circuits.[160] Whether this supervision suffices depends partly on how much such ratios are artificially depressed by junk cases and partly on the presumed purposes of appeal. If circuit judges are correct that only one in ten of their cases presents lawmaking choices, and if one assumes further that the main purpose of Supreme Court review is to control the policy premises of subordinates in such situations, then 5-percent review may well suffice.[161] For purposes of national uniformity, there is no quantitative reason to presume that Supreme Court review is "patently inadequate."[162] Nor is the qualitative evidence yet convincing that Balkanization has reached a crisis stage warranting radical institutional surgery.[163] Overseers in the 1960s actually injected more conflict into the system than workers below. More judges and courts will increase the pressure for a fourth tier, but in many ways this oft-changing proposal has been "a solution in search of a problem," distracting attention from serious evils in lower federal courts.[164]

At regional levels consensus far outweighs conflict, both between levels and within Courts of Appeals. The apparent harmony is in some measure deceptive, but proof is scant that district courts and agencies are out of control. Otherwise, reversal rates would be much higher than they are. Far more worrisome than the prospects of runaway lower courts is the rush to judgment, the pressure of quantity on the quality of federal appeals.

Even with mass production, however, the pluralism of the federal judiciary should warn against projecting the problems of the most overloaded tribunals onto all of them. General conditions ill fit particular courts. It is a fallacy to assume that what ails one circuit afflicts the rest or that all are amenable to the same treatment. Not every circuit is overloaded or faces similar pressures. One cannot even assume that there are too many appeals. Just as subsidies are converting some urban circuits into automatic courts of error in criminal cases, so there may be insufficient appeals for effective enforcement of federal rights in some rural districts that need them most. Decentralization of federal judicial power means that remedies require cognizance of uniqueness.

It is also well to remember the strength of informal fetters on judicial discretion. Though the law explosion has eroded norms of appellate behavior, particularly as to en bancs and the distribution of work, shared values and informal relations are strong cohesives. For all their individualism, these circuit judges held common perceptions of their missions in adjudication as agents of the national government. They felt obliged to follow rulings of the Supreme Court and other precedents. Within Courts of Appeals their relations were guided by internalized norms and professional conventions, some carried over from experience as advocates, to control and minimize conflict within each group. Some structure even appeared in ostensibly random allocation of work, enabling members to accommodate competing goals of timely decisions and well-crafted opinions as well as seniority and specialization in a process of mutual influence.

The roles of circuit judges, of course, are not straitjackets. Tensions were most pronounced over the "stinking question" of lawmaking, the primacy of opinions, and criteria of holding en bancs. Spillover between administrative authority and influence in adjudication also collided with official theory of court organization. Still, these strains were largely over priorities on the margins of judicial activity. And the oft-mentioned clash between the judges' political ideologies and adjudicatory roles were softer than posited in either traditional or realist theories of appellate decision. On the contrary, political and professional orientations, far from being antithetical, were overlapping and mutually supporting ties in these tribunals. The effects of judicial attitudes on voting behavior were spasmodic, overlapping, and issue specific, a condition that intensified conflict in a few issues of public policy but moderated it in most. Elevated in significance were case contexts. This is precisely what we would expect of the political lawyers chosen to staff courts in between. Circuit judges were more alike than different, pragmatic men in the middle both professionally and politically. Therein lies primary glue in the federal judiciary. Shared and overlapping values among members of the interpretative community narrowed the range of conflict in intermediate courts and the aperture of essential Supreme Court review. The politics of judicial consensus, to put the matter starkly, made a system of *stare decisis* possible in national courts.

This interweaving of legal and political "cultures" points up the need to take an integrated view of Courts of Appeals in the federal judicial system if these tribunals are to be comprehended and improved.[165] Federal judicial capacity may be inadequate—regionally as well as nationally—but diagnosis and treatment are risky without taking into account the gatekeeping, diversity, and informality that prevail in practice. It is unsafe to propose relief for one part of the judicial system without considering the impact on the rest.

A systemic perspective has the paradoxical effect of narrowing issues and redefining goals. To recognize the pluralism within the federal judiciary is to scale down expectations of uniformity. Granted, "an inflexible execution of the national laws" across the land is a lasting dream of union, one fed as well by the ethical commitment to equal treatment of litigants.[166] Yet, even as a goal, there are limits to sameness within a "Nation of teeming nations." In the eternal tension between legal principles and particular cases, we do not expect different judges or juries to exercise uniform judgments in zones of reasonable doubt. Why should federal courts be held to higher standards? Kenneth M. Dolbeare, in a study of litigation in New York County, found that the notion of courts applying law to facts with standard results "cannot survive empirical testing in the courts of a single county under a single appellate court."[167] Uniformity of decision in every federal court in the United States is a mirage.

The goal itself must be accommodated with competing values. The price of uniformity is inflexibility. Decentralization is generally recognized in judicial administration as a spur to flexibility and creativity, but the formalism of legal theory bars us from striking realistic balances between uniformity and flexibility in adjudication. If the proper function of law is to provide a mechanism for peaceful resolution of disputes amid changing social conditions, as Grant Gilmore maintains, then law must be sufficiently loose and pluralistic to avoid paralysis.[168] The same logic holds for judging in national courts. Just as the doctrine of *stare decisis* enables judges to reconcile the values of continuity and change in a dynamic legal order, so decentralized interpretation of federal law permits Courts of Appeals to reconcile the uniform and diverse interests of 220 million people within the broad policy premises set by Congress and the Supreme Court.

Play in the joints is not merely unavoidable but healthy. Harmony, like certainty, is a question of degree. Coordination within broad policy premises, not conformity, is enough to fulfill the federalizing functions of national courts. Recognizing that the diffusion of national values to localities is a two-way street may relieve pressures for new judicial institutions to satisfy unrealistic goals. At least the diversity of conditions among federal courts should breed caution about what is amenable to regulation by uniform rules.[169]

If uniformity should be played down as an organizational objective, the informality of the federal judicial process needs to be played up. Just as informal constraints narrow the problem of cohesion among federal courts, so are they challenged by the trend toward mass production. A classic American response to governmental problems is to throw more money and personnel at them rather than to eliminate outmoded programs or reexamine goals. Yet, the importance of informal relations and internalized norms for judicial cohesion and accountability at every level warns against an uncritical rush to modernization and new institutions. By other names these mean formalization, centralization, and bureaucratization of services traditionally respected precisely because they were handcrafted rather than mass-produced. A normal tenet of organizations is the need for hierarchy to enforce institutional policies. Federal courts, combining a hierarchy of doctrine with decentralized administration, have nevertheless managed to coordinate their activities without heavy reliance on formal or external controls.[170] What makes this possible are internalized norms and informal processes of decision among equals who are not only kindred in outlook but are organized in groups small enough to reconcile independence with consensual, flexible rules of decision and administration. While moderate changes in federal judicial machinery are inevitable, a movement to more and larger tribunals, requiring extra professionals and formal controls, risks shifting the job of judging from adjudication to administering "human machines." Certainly, these steps seem imprudent without first exhausting less drastic alternatives. A go-slow policy is also in order given the inadequate knowledge, the unanticipated consequences of reorganization, and the faulty premise that administration is separable from policy making. Both jumboism and proliferation, in other words, should come last, not first. Spawning institutions with insufficient attention to the fit between purpose and process should be dreaded, as Learned Hand said of lawsuits, "beyond almost anything short of sickness and death."[171] Organizationitis is a dubious cure for appealitis.

The prudent course is a limited program of reforms geared to proven needs. A discriminating package would eliminate three-judge district courts and diversity jurisdiction and create specialized national appellate courts in fields where forum shopping is worst—patents and copyrights, civil taxation, and *perhaps* contract claims against the government. This approach, favored by the Carter administration and leading senators, is more likely of passage and less likely to inflict unanticipated damage than grandiose schemes.[172] Beyond this, conditions invite searching scrutiny of incentives to litigate and appeal, including the government's relitigation policy, as well as more experimentation with diversion, such as arbitration, grievance machinery closer to the source of disputes, and limited certiorari for Courts of Appeals. Just as litigant demand will at last come under close study, so the experience of larger circuits with expansion and "home rule" should be monitored carefully.[173] Freezing the size of circuits to an ideal number of judges is too inflexible, but problems of integrating and managing large appellate tribunals are such that jumboism is a risky way to combat parochialism in intermediate federal courts. The appropriate way is political—lodging responsibility squarely on appointing authorities to staff Courts of Appeals with qualified members capable of embracing the obligations of national office.

The compatibility of law and politics in circuit courts reinforces the old saw that men are more important than machinery. Because the processes of socialization and recruitment are so critical to court cohesion and the quality of decision, reformers rightly focus on those who staff federal courts. To fill a record increase in judgeships the Carter administration initiated a new procedure to meet twin goals of better qualified and more representative judges. Improving judicial qualifications is always in order. Affirmative action will be worthwhile in opening up predominately white, male institutions.[174] More open to skepticism is whether the new merit nominating commissions are better than traditional ways of achieving these objectives. Though full returns are not in, there is little proof so far that either method is inherently superior. Neither process will eliminate politics from judicial recruitment, nor should political experience be a disqualification in view of judicial functions. Nominating commissions may weaken senatorial patronage, but also diffuse responsibility. The crux of either method is how appointing authority is used.[175]

Finally, taking an integrated view of Courts of Appeals in the federal judicial system is to recognize that cutting judicial coats to human cloth is indeed "delicate business."[176] Whether it is better to create more judges, realign circuits, modernize courts, divert business, or some combination, all turns on competing conceptions of professional and political duty, which are not only entwined but in flux. Any strategy or blend of strategies necessarily affects the roles of courts and access of clientele groups. Consequently, a discriminating package of reforms, combining institutional tinkering with diversion and limited growth, as proposed here, may be harder to achieve than simply expanding physical resources. Federal courts, for all their tendency to fill its vacuums, are peculiarly vulnerable to the immobilism of American pluralist politics. Lacking a politically attentive constituency, they find it difficult to mobilize legislative coalitions strong enough to press judicial business onto the national agenda and to withstand counterattack by veto groups.

Leadership usually must come from judges themselves, at some cost to the theory of separation of powers and resentment over judicial lobbying.[177] Few proposals make much headway until problems boil, a condition that inhibits planning and inflates claims. Filling vacancies is tough enough.

It is fair to ask whether a political system that permits "near crisis" conditions to develop in its courts is capable of applying discriminating remedies. But in the last analysis there is no escaping the political process, nor should there be. The roles and organization of intermediate federal courts are at bottom political judgments about services that for many people are the most effective means of resolving disputes, enforcing federal rights, and holding officials to account. The bedrock of understanding is that for Courts of Appeals as for the Supreme Court, the joinder of politics and law permeates their roles, their rules, and their relations in the American polity.[178] The interesting questions are the mix. That is why maintaining the uniformity and supremacy of federal law, and the institutions that serve these goals, has never been sport for the short-winded—nor for lawyers and judges alone.

# Appendix 1
## Methodological Notes

Several methodological problems and considerations have been reserved for discussion in this Appendix. These include: (1) the flow of litigation and (2) rates of appeal discussed in Chapters Two and Three, (3) methods of randomization of panel and opinion assignments discussed in Chapter Eight, and (4) the interview schedule and questionnaire of circuit judges used throughout.

*The Flow of Litigation*

The universe of appeals in this study consists of all nonconsolidated cases, including original proceedings and appeals from administrative agencies, reported as having been decided by the three circuit courts after hearing or submission on briefs during fiscal years 1965, 1966, and 1967. That means 4,135 cases published in the *Federal Reporter*, plus 806 unpublished cases obtained from the Administrative Office of the United States Courts—a total of 4,941 cases. At the Supreme Court level, because 2 cases were unconsolidated and 2 were reported with decisions from other courts, the total was 4,945 appeals. Caseflow data for other years are from *Annual Reports of the Director of the Administrative Office of the United States Courts*, hereafter cited as AO *Annual Reports*.

There are several reasons for independent tracking of federal appeals through the circuits and Supreme Court. First, to determine what litigation the three Courts of Appeals formally controlled, it is necessary to know: (a) the decisions appealed to and reversed by each circuit court, and (b) the decisions appealed to and reversed by the Supreme Court *in the same cases*. Current reporting systems do not answer these questions. No compilation exists of original agency decisions from which to infer rates of appeal to the circuits. Most district court decisions go unpublished. Rates of reversal are also difficult to establish. Over 16 percent of these circuit decisions, including 40 percent of the D.C. circuit's cases, were not published in the *Federal Reporter*. The AO *Annual Reports*, which emphasize the productivity of courts at each level, are not designed to illuminate vertical relations among different tiers of the federal judiciary. The agency neither reports reversal rates by the Supreme Court nor links circuit reversals to specific subjects or tribunals below. Consequently, it is impossible to discern from aggregate AO reports who supports whom in what fields.

Second, because each court has a separate docket, estimates of appellate supervision usually rest on the convention that cases decided at different levels of the judicial system in any fiscal year are the same litigation, which ignores delay and varied growth rates in caseloads of up to 20 percent annually. Though this convention turns out to have produced less distortion in the mid-1960s than originally feared, one aim of the research was to estimate litigation flow free from this simplifying assumption. Third, the AO emphasizes the intake and pace of litigation more than decisions after hearing or submission on briefs. Such decisions are superior as a measure of judicial work to the more extensively reported data for cases commenced in each court. Hence, another research aim was to compare the decisional product of the three circuits and the Supreme Court, including policy outcomes, by linking appellate decisions after hearing or submission to their sources and subjects. Finally, the AO publishes no information on decisions by individual judges. Independent analysis was required to explore the distribution of work within Courts of Appeals as well as to compare judicial perceptions with behavior.

To meet these research objectives it became necessary to code each case and to track its disposition at both appellate levels. Appeals disposed of "after hearing or submission on briefs" are the unit of analysis. These decisions parallel those reported in Table B1 of AO *Annual Reports* and should be distinguished from AO data on "cases commenced" and "terminated" in U.S. Courts of Appeals. Approximately 28 percent of the cases filed in this period were disposed of without hearing and another 9 percent by consolidation. Cases disposed of by consolidation with a reported appeal were excluded, in conformity with AO practice, because their characteristics were too unknown for safe projection. The categories for the sources of appeals resemble AO classifications for "cases commenced" (see Table B3) and, where possible, follow the AO's breakdown of the subjects of appeals filed from U.S. district courts (see Table B7). The analysis thus provides comparable data for decisions after hearing. Some discrepancies should be noted, however. The AO excludes "original proceedings" from reversal rates (see AO *Annual Report* [1966], 152n); they are included here on grounds that several involved review of decisions made elsewhere.

Codes, like coral reefs, evolve incrementally. Attempts to distinguish law, fact, and value dissonance in the decisions failed. The worst omission was not following the AO category of appeals by source of civil jurisdiction, such as diversity, which limited comparison of rates of appeals in Chapter Two. For another effort to analyze the caseloads, decisions, and opinions of individual circuit judges in 1972-1973, though without names, see Hearing on S. 2991 before the Subcommittee on Improvements in Judicial Machinery of the Senate Judiciary Committee, 93rd Cong., 2d Sess. (1974), 101-39.

To collect the cases two coders leafed page by page through volumes 333-382 of the *Federal Reporter*, 2d series, in search of decisions of the three Courts of Appeals between July 1, 1964, and June 30, 1967. For each case found they prepared a worksheet containing information according to a numerical code. The information was then transferred onto computer cards for each case, verified, and stored on two tapes, one for courts and another for judges. This method presented two problems at the circuit level. First was consistency of coding by and between the coders. Fortunately, initial tests of intra- and intercoder reliability indicated that only four of forty broad classifications exceeded normal standards of reliability (i.e., 10% variance). To meet these problems, I discarded the area of challenge category (except for the gross distribution), double checked the coding for resistance, transformation of issues, intracourt bargaining, cross-court influence, and local D.C. cases as well as cases signaled by coders as puzzling or significant. In all, I reread over half the cases with signed opinions (1,417 of 2,474).

The second problem of unreported cases was overcome with the assistance of the AO. Through the courtesy of James A. McCafferty, the AO provided copies of its subject-matter code and a printout of cases decided by the three circuits during FY 1965-1967, from which unreported cases were isolated by matching the docket numbers of reported cases. For the unreported cases remaining (N = 806), AO information was sufficient to identify the subject, source, judges, and decision in each appeal, though not the policy outcome.

Similar procedures were used to track the circuit decisions at the Supreme Court. Coders paged through volumes 379-392 of *U.S. Supreme Court Reports* to glean appeals from the three circuits during this period. One case was found in volume 395. Cases with citations to courts below were matched to circuit decisions by hand; then the cases were analyzed and the information transposed to computer cards, one per case. For reliability, I double checked the coding of every Supreme Court case and the computer analysis by hand.

In addition, there were 464 cases listed in the reports as rising from the three circuits but without citations in circuit reports. Separate cards were made for these and added to the deck, though only 4 were accepted for review by the Justices. Thus, the estimates of appeals to and accepted by the Supreme Court in Chapter Three are derived from cases with circuit citations. Excluded were 35 cases consolidated at the Supreme Court, plus 460 cert. denials or dismissals and 4 cert. grants reported from these circuits in the same volumes of U.S. Reports without citations below. If we add these cases (N = 1,503), and adjust for a 22-case increment in petitions filed that remained pending in AO reports, our universe is 11 cases below the AO figure for certiorari petitions filed from the three circuits during the base period (N = 1,536). As a result of these adjustments, the rates of certiorari granted for circuit decisions after hearing did not change materially; but the rate of appeal to the high court in the base period shifted from 20 percent to 30 percent and the ratio of cert. grants to circuit decisions appealed became 7.3 percent. The ratio of circuit decisions after hearing appealed from the three tribunals to the Supreme Court, based exclusively on AO data and using the convention of identical years, was 32 percent in FY 1965-1967 and 25 percent in FY 1979. The all-circuit ratio in FY 1979 was 27 percent. The ratio of appeals granted in FY 1979 was 6.3 percent for the three circuits and 5.7 percent for all circuits. See AO *Annual Reports* (1975 and preliminary 1979), Tables B1 and B2.

In view of increasing nonpublication of circuit decisions, a few observations are in order regarding methods of estimating rates of appellate review of lower courts. For general estimates, conventional methods based on AO data, despite assumptions that decisions occurred in the same fiscal years, are reasonably satisfactory, except in situations of severe delay or rapidly accelerating demand. By itself, the assumption of simultaneity is insufficient ground for error (here 0.5%) to justify the opportunity costs of tracking cases in published reports, which require similar assumptions for unreported cases as well. For more specific estimates of litigation flow, however, which link courts vertically by subject and sources, neither AO reports nor published cases are adequate. Most problems of vertical linkage would be eliminated by a unified national docket in which each federal case is identified by the same docket number from start to finish. Short of that, many questions about intercourt relations and judicial behavior could be answered by improving access of scholars to information already in government hands. Data regarding the subjects, judges, and decisions in each federal case are reported to the AO but not published. This is not meant as criticism of the agency, which was very cooperative under constraints of limited resources, but rather to call attention to opportunities left fallow.

*Rates of Appeal*

Estimates of appellate demand from U.S. district courts to the three circuits, reported in Chapter Two, are based on unpublished federal court data for "contested judgments" in civil cases and convictions of guilt after trial in FY 1967-1970. Unfortunately, these data were not available for the base period, so we used data from the following four years, the latest available. Nor were the cases tracked individually in the stream of litigation. These measures consequently are not free from difficulty, but are preferable to those in common use because they better reflect the statutory authority governing federal appeals.

The essential problem is determining the baseline of appealable judgments. Using published district court opinions as the basis for calculating appellate court demand is unsatisfactory because the great majority of district court decisions are unpublished. Publication of decisions also has no bearing on the ability of parties to appeal (*Moore's Federal Practice*, 6, ¶54.02 [1976]). Relying on AO *Annual Reports* is also unsatisfactory because their published measures of district court activity lead to either underestimates or overestimates of demand in the appellate courts. For example, the AO reported that 11,893 appeals from district courts were commenced in the three circuits during FY 1967-1970. If *cases commenced* in district courts are taken as the basis for these appeals, the appeal rate would be 7 percent. If *trials completed* in district courts are taken as the baseline, the appeal rate jumps to 53 percent. Litigation that ends by settlement or abandonment in the trial courts makes the former estimate too restrictive; summary judgments and other appealable decisions rendered before or during trial make the latter estimate too expansive. Thus, the reported data provide biased bases for calculating rates of appeal from federal district courts.

In addition, the use of *appellate cases filed* as a measure of demand on appellate judges is problematic. Filings gauge clerk-work better than judge-work. Not every filing ripens into a decision by an appellate court. A superior measure of demand on appellate judicial resources is *cases decided after oral argument or submission on briefs*.

The rate of appeal is defined with greater precision as the ratio of the number of appeals to the number of appealable decisions reached in the district courts each fiscal year. In general, civil appeals are taken only from final judgments within the meaning of 28 U.S.C. §1291 (1970). Through 1970, the AO collected, but did not tabulate or report, information on the disposition of district court cases that corresponds to the requirements of the final judgment rule. Thus, all district court civil cases are divisible into two mutually exclusive categories: (1) dispositions by contested judgment; and (2) dispositions without contest or by consent. Cases classed as *contested judgments* form the critical base of appealable decisions for this analysis. Of course, not every termination of civil litigation in the district courts is a final judgment within the meaning of the statute; nor is every such termination appealable. The final judgment rule provides that appeals ordinarily will lie from judgments terminating litigation contested by the parties, but cases decided without contest (e.g., transfers, settlements, remands to other courts) are not appealable (C. Wright, A. Miller, and E. Cooper, *Federal Practice and Procedure: Jurisdiction* §§ 3855, 3914 [1976]). Default judgments and dismissals for failure to prosecute are appealable in principle, but the scope of review is limited. If defaults and failures to prosecute are included in the class of nonappealable actions, the category of "contested judgments" represents a sound operationalization of the final judgment rule in civil cases.

Several caveats are still in order. Some appeals are permissible prior to the termination of a case, 28 U.S.C. § 1292 (1970); but it is impossible to determine from AO data the frequency of such appealable orders or the number of appeals taken from them. The rates of appeal reported here are thus inflated to the extent that such interlocutory orders are excluded from the pool of appealable decisions.

Devising a rate of appeal for criminal cases is less complicated. The measure uses the familiar theoretical rationale of comparing direct criminal appeals to appealable criminal cases. The denominator of this ratio, appealable criminal decisions, is equivalent to the number of criminal convictions obtained by court or jury trial. Pleas of guilty are excluded because admissions of guilt entail a waiver of appeal to challenge convictions except for jurisdictional defects. Even this measure is not entirely problem free, however. Under certain conditions, the government can appeal the dismissal of a criminal case as long as jeopardy has not attached; and defendants can challenge the government's failure to live up to the terms of a plea bargain. See *Moore's Federal Practice*, 8, ¶203.06, n. 36; Wright, *Federal Practice and Procedure: Criminal* § 175 (1969); *Santobello v. New York*, 404 U.S. 257, 262 (1971). But these are relatively rare occurrences, and their absence from the measure should not mar the basic soundness of the findings. It should be noted that petitions filed by prisoners challenging their convictions on constitutional grounds or challenging the conditions of their confinement, following AO practice, are treated as civil matters and therefore reflected in the civil appeal rates.

The rate of appeal, both civil and criminal, is subject to another source of error. Data collected by the AO are in aggregate form. Because individual district court cases were not tracked to determine whether a case had been terminated by an appealable decision and whether an appeal had been filed from that decision, it is necessary to assume that contested judgments and appeals taken from them will be entered and filed in the same fiscal year. Obviously, some final decisions in the district courts and appeals from them will not coincide in the same year. This overlap (or underlap) is minimized here by using data for consecutive years.

The data on contested judgments were made available through the courtesy of James A. McCafferty of the AO, Jerry Goldman, and the Federal Judicial Center. Goldman also was coauthor of an article from which this section of the study draws heavily. I am deeply grateful to all of these parties for their assistance. For comparison of rates of appeals from all circuits in FY 1951-1960 and 1970 using similar data and measures, see Goldman's "Federal District Courts and the Appellate Crisis," *Judicature*, 57 (1973), 211-13.

## Panel and Opinion Assignments

The workloads of individual judges in Chapter Eight were randomized as follows. For panel assignments as reported in Tables 8.4-8.6, the expected frequencies were randomized according to the number of months served per judge. Judges sitting full-time for thirty-six months would be expected to have participated in 402 cases in the 2d circuit, 475 cases in the 5th circuit, and 208 cases in the D.C. circuit.

Elimination of judges on senior status who served part-time altered the observed-expected ratios, though not the rank order, especially among judges of the D.C. circuit. The ratios for 8 full-time judges only in 1,868 total cases were: McGowan 114%, Bazelon 113%, Burger 108%, Fahy 106%, Wright 105%, Danaher 94%, Leventhal 81%, Tamm 68%. Range: 46%.

The range in panel assignment ratios among full-time judges in the 2d circuit (Moore 123% to Anderson 85%) was 38%. The corresponding range in the 5th circuit (Tuttle 120% to Godbold 64%) was 56%.

To gauge specialization in panel assignments, the randomly expected frequencies were determined by multiplying each judge's total panel assignments by the proportion of the court's total cases in each field. The reported fields are contracts, torts, commerce, labor, taxation, personal status, crimes, and other, plus local in the D.C. circuit. These are the same fields analyzed in Chapters Two and Three, except that four criminal categories are consolidated here.

Chi-square one-sample tests for the distribution of panel assignments in these subjects were not statistically significant for any judge or field in the 2d or D.C. circuits. In the 5th circuit, by contrast, the distribution of panel assignments among the eight fields, correcting for continuity, df 7, yielded significant values for six judges:

Gewin, $N = 516$, $\chi^2 = 18.6$, $p < .01$; Goldberg, $N = 142$, $\chi^2 = 17.2$, $p < .02$; Jones, $N = 460$, $\chi^2 = 30.3$, $p < .001$; Rives, $N = 479$, $\chi^2 = 15.9$, $p < .03$; Thornberry, $N = 323$, $\chi^2 = 59.2$, $p < .001$; and Tuttle, $N = 611$, $\chi^2 = 22.2$, $p < .003$.

Similarly, $\chi^2$ one-sample values for the distribution of panel assignments by subject among judges of the 5th circuit, df 13, were significant in two general subjects: personal status, $N = 1,170$, $\chi^2 = 39.8$, $p < .001$; and taxation, $N = 663$, $\chi^2 = 23.93$, $p < .05$. For other subjects the values were: torts: $N = 739$, $\chi^2 = 10.8$, $p > .50$; commerce: $N = 460$, $\chi^2 = 9.846$, $p > .50$; labor: $N = 548$, $\chi^2 = 6.8$, $p > .90$; and crimes: $N = 507$, $\chi^2 = 28.2$, $p > .30$. Lest personal status and taxation be dismissed as isles of significance in a random sea, the odds that chance determined the whole matrix of panel assignments among 14 judges and 8 subjects in this circuit were less than 1 in 1,000. $N = 4,998$, df 91, $\chi^2 = 228.5$, $t = 7.92$, $p < .001$. Comparable whole matrix values for the 2d circuit were $\chi^2 = 49.6$, df 63, $p > .10$; D.C. circuit, $\chi^2 = 59.2$, df 88, $p > .10$.

For opinion assignments, the expected frequencies were determined by multiplying the total majority participations per judge times a weighting factor that adjusted the probabilities of three-person and two-person majorities by the mean dissent rate of all judges in each circuit in cases with signed opinions. The mean dissent rate in the 2d circuit was 4.54% and the weighting factor was 3.4% (95.5% × 33.3 + 4.5% × 50.0 = .3406). The mean dissent rate in the 5th circuit was 2.54%, and the weighting factor was .3372. The mean dissent rate in the D.C. circuit was 14.9%, and the weighting factor was .3579.

To adjust for small numbers, opinion assignments also were consolidated into economic versus personal status and criminal cases. This dimension roughly approximates the so-called distinction between property rights and human rights. The distributions of observed and randomly expected opinions (in parentheses) were statistically significant for only three judges, two in Washington and one in Houston, as follows. Bazelon: economic, 19 (31.9); personal status and criminal, 32 (22.2); other and local, 8 (5.4); $\chi^2 = 10.25$, df 2, $p < .01$. McGowan: economic, 45 (36.2); personal status and criminal, 14 (25.3); other and local, 8 (5.0); $\chi^2 = 9.51$, df 2, $p < .01$. Brown: economic, 90 (78.2); personal status and criminal, 19 (30.9); $\chi^2 = 6.35$, df 1, $p < .02$.

*The interview schedule and questionnaire*

Personal interviews were conducted by the author with thirty-five active and senior judges of the three circuits between 1969 and 1971, on a not-for-attribution basis. Certain remarks that the judges preferred to keep off the record remain so. Passages from the interviews quoted in the text are from the author's notes, not tape recordings. One retired Supreme Court Justice and the clerks of the three Courts of Appeals also were interviewed. No active judge and only two senior circuit judges from the case universe declined to be interviewed. (For a list of the respondents, see p. xx.) Additionally, all but one judge filled out a structured questionnaire, sometimes at the end of the interview in the author's presence but usually later, a procedure that proved necessary to save time. Every judge but one further responded to a follow-up, mailed questionnaire concerning their political attitudes *before* appointment to the federal bench.

The interviews, which ranged from thirty minutes to six hours for an average of about one-hundred minutes, emphasized in-depth responses to fairly open-ended questions. Consequently, not all questions were answered in every interview. Nor should the judges' job descriptions be regarded as a complete picture in judicial minds, let alone a map of action. Though little misunderstanding developed over the meaning of terms between the interviewer and the judges, in interview situations omissions can be as important as statements, and much is inevitably subsumed in remarks whose meaning must be grasped from context. An illustration was the colorful judge, harried by interruptions and too much lunch, who managed to answer a major question concerning the proper limits of judicial legislation by a lone remark: "That's a helluva way to run a railroad!" Context and other discussion left little doubt that he took a generous view of his lawmaking functions.

Multiple queries helped to guard against distorted inferences from single questions. Several trained graduate students also classified the critical responses independently of the author to help combat subjective classifications of the perceptual material in Chapters Four-Six. As the author's judgment controlled on the basis of demeanor evidence, however, subjectivity has not been entirely eliminated. A related warning should be raised about the structured questionnaire. Because the judges' understandings of terms, such as "very important," "important," and "not important," may vary in scope and intensity, their ratings are not necessarily comparable. All one can infer is that more judges than not ranked a given item accordingly. For discussion of interview techniques and inferences, see, for example, Lewis Anthony Dexter, *Elite and Specialized Interviewing* (Evanston: Northwestern University Press, 1970); Theodore L. Becker, "A Survey Study of Hawaiian Judges: The Effect on Decisions of Judicial Role Variations," *American Political Science*

*Review*, 60 (1966), 677-80, and exchange with S. Sidney Ulmer, *American Political Science Review*, 60 (1967), 1098-1101; and Thomas D. Ungs and Larry R. Baas, "Judicial Role Perceptions: A Q-Technique Study of Ohio Judges," *Law and Society Review*, 6 (1972), 343-66.

## Interview Schedule

name, circuit, date of interview

### A. Biographical
(Ask only items not available from *Who's Who*, etc.)

1. Where were you born? When?
   City
   County
   State

2. Where were you brought up?
                                Name                      Size
   Urban
   Suburban
   Rural

3. Religion:
   a. What is your religious preference?
   b. Same as parents'?

4. What was your father's occupation? Mother's occupation, if any?

5. Within your community, was your family considered upper, middle, or lower class?

6. Political party affiliation of parents?

7. Formal education: (Fill in unknown details, then evaluation.)
   Grammar school
   High school
   College
   Law school
   Other
   a. Standing in law school class?     Law review?
   b. How influential was your law school training on your subsequent career and legal thinking?
   c. Did any particular professor influence you?
   d. Do you have much contact with law school people now?

8. Occupations prior to becoming a judge on the U.S. Court of Appeals: (Positions, dates)
    a. Private
    b. Political
    c. Judicial
9. Would you please describe your practice as a lawyer?
    a. How long in practice?
    b. Type of practice?
        1. Urban/rural
        2. Criminal/civil
        3. Government, corporate, noncorporate, academic
        4. Size of firm
        5. Plaintiff/defendant
    c. Specialty?
    d. Martindale & Hubbell ratings?
    e. ABA ratings at appointment?
    f. Do you miss your practice?
10. Memberships: are you an active member of any
    a. Social or civic organizations?
    b. Professional organizations?
11. Political party affiliation? _____
    a. How active were you in party affairs before appointment?
        Voter
        Campaign worker          Campaign manager
        Financial contributor    Political adviser
        Party official           Candidate
12. Can you tell me how you first became interested in politics?
    a. Family
    b. University
    c. As lawyer
    d. Other
    e. Which was most important?
13. Can you tell me how you first became interested in serving as a judge?
    a. Family
    b. University
    c. As lawyer
    d. Other
    e. Which was most important?
14. Looking back, can you say whether you were more inclined toward a political or a judicial career?
15. What do you think were the most important factors in your appointment to this post? (Probe: party or professional route)
16. Did becoming a judge mean substantial loss of income for you?
17. Legislators often express ambition for a judgeship as a terminating point in a lawyer's career. Do you regard it as terminal?

## B. The Court of Appeals

Now, some questions about your job on the Court of Appeals

18. First, how would you describe the job of being a judge on the U.S. Court of Appeals—what are the most important things you should do here?
    a. Does the job differ from that of a federal district judge? How?
    b. Does the job differ from that of a Supreme Court Justice? How?
    c. Does the job differ from what you expected? How?

19. How influential is your court on public policy? (Finality, filtering?)
    a. Does your court have any special roles—i.e., roles different from the other circuits?
    b. What subjects appear most often in your court?
    c. Which are most important? Least important?
    d. Which interests you the most?

20. Have the demands on your court changed since you were appointed? Has the court won or lost support?

21. Judge Wyzanski once rated the 2d circuit as the "ablest court in the country." Does any circuit stand out today as the ablest? What about individual judges?

22. Circuit courts were one of the first government bodies to be organized on a regional basis. Do you consciously think of your job as being an intermediary between national and local outlooks or more as an arm of the national government?

23. Some people think circuit judges should be legal innovators, thus illuminating issues for the Supreme Court; others argue that circuit judges should merely apply the law, leaving legal innovation to legislatures and the Supreme Court. (Hand, Magruder, Parker) What do you think? (Cf. Q-18b.) Probe: Charles Clark once estimated that only 10% of the cases before a circuit court offer any real chance of creativity. Do you agree with that estimate?

24. In recent years there has been a lot of talk about factions or blocs on the Supreme Court. Do they exist on the circuit court? Why?
    a. How important are they?
    b. Is there much internal conflict?

25. How does the court manage to reach agreement? (Cf. USSC.)
    a. Is there much give and take among members of the court?
    b. Is there sufficient collegial deliberation?
    c. Does the opinion writer have extra responsibility in achieving agreement? (Probe: brokerage)
    d. Does the process differ in en banc cases?

26. Why is the rate of dissent lower on this court than the Supreme Court?
    (Probe for primary audiences of dissent, dissent as cue to review, etc.)
    a. What are the purposes of dissent on an intermediate appellate court?

27. Uniqueness
    a. 2d circuit—Your court has a unique procedure in which each judge circulates memorandum opinions in each case prior to conference. Would you please appraise the effects of this procedure? (Probe: on workload, quality, dissent rate, etc.)
    b. 5th circuit—Your court has been expanded in size beyond the maximum of nine judges once recommended by the Judicial Conference as the maximum feasible size for any appellate court. Would you please appraise the effects of this expansion? (Probe: on workload, quality, internal procedure, cooperation and conflict, etc.)
    c. D.C. circuit—Your court has unique responsibilities in reviewing appeals from the District of Columbia. Would you please appraise the effects of this responsibility on your role in the federal judicial system? (Probe: on workload, internal procedure, cooperation and conflict, etc.)

28. We hear much these days about overloaded dockets. Do you feel overloaded and overworked? How has the court responded? (Probe: increased summary disposition, specialization, quality, etc.)

29. Rules of the game
    a. We hear that every collegial court has its *unofficial* rules of the game, certain things that members do and must not do if they want the respect and cooperation of fellow members. Is this true? What are some of these rules that a member must observe to hold the respect and cooperation of his colleagues?
    b. What kinds of sanctions will be imposed on members who do not conform? (Cf. Musmanno dissent quashed.)

30. Are there judges on your court who are particularly effective in influencing other judges? What reasons account for their influence? (Probe for task and social leadership, expertness, seniority, personality, craftsmanship, etc. Cf. Q-24.)

31. Does the office of chief judge give the incumbent advantages in influencing other members? (Probe: administration, assignments.) Disadvantages?

32. We have noticed that your court uses visiting judges—both district and circuit judges—to sit on panels and write opinions. Would you please appraise the effects of this practice? (Probe: on workload, quality, cohesiveness, en banc cue, etc.)

33. Supreme Court Justices often mention a certain "freshman" period before they became a fully effective member of the court. Is this true on the Court of Appeals? How long does the period last?

34. How are panel and opinion assignments determined in this circuit? (Probe: do geography and specialization figure in panel or opinion assignments? Cf. Hutcheson in cases involving Texas law.)
35. Do you resent being reversed by the Supreme Court? Is it proper for a circuit court judge to take issue publicly with the Supreme Court?
36. In supervising district courts, how far should circuit judges advise or admonish district judges outside their written opinions? How effective is the judicial council of this circuit in supervising district court judges?
37. We have been told that legislatures and bureaucracies could not function without informal contacts which cut across formal, hierarchical chains of command. Is this true of federal courts? How important are informal contacts (e.g., judicial councils, bar meetings, socializing) for the development of federal law? (Probe: Hand advice to Medina on relations with district judges.)

## C. Judicial proprieties

Finally, let's turn to a few questions about judicial proprieties.

38. First, do you feel that the Canons of Professional Ethics adequately express the norms of the profession as to the conduct of federal judges? The norms of the general public?
39. Do the canons give clear enough guidance as to conflicts of interest? Are stricter standards necessary?
40. What is the chief problem facing your court?
41. What is the hardest part of your job?
42. What is the best part of your job?
43. That is the end of our questions. We would be grateful to know what you think of them. Have we missed anything of importance that scholars should study to understand Courts of Appeals?

## Courts of Appeals Study, Judges Questionnaire

1. In terms of equipping a man for the court, how would you rank the following experiences?

```
      moderately
      important
very            
important     not important
```

|  |  |  |
|--|--|--|
|  |  |  |
|  |  |  |
|  |  |  |
|  |  |  |
|  |  |  |
|  |  |  |
|  |  |  |

Extensive legal practice
Experience as a trial lawyer
Political experience
Experience in civic affairs
Prior judicial experience
Training in a leading law school
Bar association leadership

2. How would you rank the following factors in terms of their influence on your perception of issues and your decision in a case?

```
      moderately
      important
very            
important     not important
```

|  |  |  |
|--|--|--|
|  |  |  |
|  |  |  |
|  |  |  |
|  |  |  |
|  |  |  |
|  |  |  |
|  |  |  |

Nature of parties to the litigation
Professional standing of counsel
Oral arguments
Briefs of opposing counsel
Amicus curiae briefs
Independent research
Judicial conferences

3. How would you rank the following personal characteristics as they affect a judge's effectiveness on a circuit bench?

```
      moderately
      important
very            
important     not important
```

|  |  |  |
|--|--|--|
|  |  |  |
|  |  |  |
|  |  |  |
|  |  |  |
|  |  |  |
|  |  |  |
|  |  |  |
|  |  |  |
|  |  |  |

Personality
Intelligence
Integrity
Length of service
Learning or expertness
Craftsmanship
Party affiliation
Intensity of conviction
Willingness to compromise

312 · Appendix One

4. Judge Lumbard has estimated that the presentations of only one in five lawyers are "passable"; only one in ten he rated as "good." In your opinion, is his estimate too high or too low?

5. In reaching your decisions, how influential do you consider the following factors?

|very important|moderately important|not important| |
|---|---|---|---|
| | | | Law review article relevant to issue |
| | | | Community values |
| | | | Opinions of other members of panel |
| | | | Opinions of other judges, not members of panel |
| | | | Opinions of law clerks |
| | | | Opinions of respected members of the bar |
| | | | Opinions of interested groups |
| | | | Public opinion |

6. In reaching decisions how influential are these factors?

|very important|moderately important|not important| |
|---|---|---|---|
| | | | Your personal views of justice in the case |
| | | | Precedent when clear and relevant |
| | | | Precedent when unclear and uncertain |
| | | | What the public needs and demands |
| | | | Common sense |
| | | | Respect for the judgment and ability of the judge or administrator below |
| | | | Anticipated Supreme Court response |

7. When precedents are absent or ambiguous, what do you do? Please rank the following factors according to which you are most likely to follow in this situation.

|very important|moderately important|not important| |
|---|---|---|---|
| | | | Closest precedent in this circuit |
| | | | Closest precedent in any circuit |
| | | | Decision of most prestigious court |
| | | | The dictates of justice |
| | | | The views of the court's most expert member |
| | | | Apparent needs of public policy |
| | | | Anticipated Supreme Court response |
| | | | Public opinion |

8. In writing opinions, which audience are you most eager to reach?

|  very important  | moderately important | not important |  |
|---|---|---|---|
|  |  |  | Party litigants |
|  |  |  | Judges reversed or affirmed below |
|  |  |  | Supreme Court Justices |
|  |  |  | Other government officials |
|  |  |  | Members of the bar |
|  |  |  | Law schools |
|  |  |  | Interest groups |
|  |  |  | General public |

9. The approval of which group above gives you greatest personal satisfaction?

10. How far may a circuit judge go in recruiting quality judges for the federal judiciary?

(Please check *permissible* items)

1. Recommend names to Department of Justice
2. Advise Department of Justice on request
3. Recommend names to senators and other politicians
4. Advise senators and other politicians on request
5. Politick behind the scenes for qualified candidates
6. Politick openly for qualified candidates

11. How far may a circuit judge go in political activity?

(Please check *permissible* items)

1. Vote
2. Make campaign contribution
3. Attend party meeting
4. Advise politicians behind the scenes
5. Make public speeches in support of policies only
6. Endorse a candidate publicly
7. Recommend a candidate to a friend
8. Postpone retirement so his party can appoint a successor

12. How far may a circuit judge go in professional or civic activity?

(Please check *permissible* items)

1. Member of bar or civic organization
2. Contribute financially to bar or civic organization
3. President or committee head of bar association
4. President or committee head of civic organization
5. Trustee of hospital, art museum, university, etc.
6. Head of public investigating committee
7. Teach in an accredited law school

## Follow-up Questionnaire (By Mail)

*Before* you became a federal judge, how did you classify yourself according to political beliefs or values?

          ——conservative
          ——moderate
          ——liberal
          ——other

# The Business of the Supreme Court

## Appendix 2

### The Business of the Three Courts of Appeals
Distribution of Circuit Decisions by Subject, after Hearing or Submission, FY 1965-1967

### Rates of Appeal, Circuits to Supreme Court FY 1965-1967

### Distribution of Supreme Court Decisions from Three Circuits by Subject, FY 1965-1967 (Before Dismissal) After Hearing

| Subjects | 2d (N=1,357) n | 2d % | 5th (N=2,248) n | 5th % | D.C. (N=1,336) n | D.C. % | Three Circuits (N=4,941) N | Three Circuits % | Circuit Decisions Appealed to Supreme Court (N=4,945)* Total Decisions N | Rate Appealed % | Certiorari Petitions Granted (N=1,004) Total Certiorari Petitions n | Rate Granted % | Supreme Court (N=103) n | Supreme Court (N=103) % | Supreme Court (N=92) n | Supreme Court (N=92) % |
|---|---|---|---|---|---|---|---|---|---|---|---|---|---|---|---|---|
| CONTRACTS | 126 | 9.3 | 291 | 12.9 | 137 | 10.3 | 554 | 11.2 | 554 | 13.4 | 74 | 4.1 | 4 | 3.9 | 3 | 3.3 |
| Insurance | 18 | 1.3 | 118 | 5.2 | 18 | 1.3 | 154 | 3.1 | 154 | 11.0 | 17 | 0.0 | 0 | 0.0 | 0 | 0.0 |
| Marine | 15 | 1.1 | 14 | 0.6 | 1 | 0.1 | 30 | 0.6 | 30 | 20.0 | 6 | 0.0 | 0 | 0.0 | 0 | 0.0 |
| Negotiable instruments | 3 | 0.2 | 7 | 0.3 | 5 | 0.4 | 15 | 0.3 | 15 | 6.7 | 1 | 100.0 | 1 | 1.0 | 1 | 1.1 |
| Real property | 12 | 0.9 | 50 | 2.2 | 37 | 2.8 | 99 | 2.0 | 99 | 14.1 | 14 | 0.0 | 0 | 0.0 | 0 | 0.0 |
| Recovery and enforcement | 11 | 0.8 | 18 | 0.8 | 11 | 0.8 | 40 | 0.8 | 40 | 15.0 | 6 | 0.0 | 0 | 0.0 | 0 | 0.0 |
| Other contracts | 67 | 4.9 | 84 | 3.7 | 65 | 4.9 | 216 | 4.4 | 216 | 13.9 | 30 | 6.7 | 3 | 2.9 | 2 | 2.2 |
| TORTS | 187 | 13.8 | 333 | 14.8 | 95 | 7.1 | 615 | 12.4 | 615 | 19.7 | 121 | 6.6 | 9 | 8.7 | 8 | 8.7 |
| Marine-personal injury | 46 | 3.4 | 71 | 3.2 | 3 | 0.2 | 120 | 2.4 | 120 | 25.0 | 30 | 10.0 | 4 | 3.9 | 3 | 3.3 |
| Motor vehicle-personal injury | 18 | 1.3 | 56 | 2.5 | 15 | 1.1 | 89 | 1.8 | 89 | 11.2 | 10 | 10.0 | 1 | 1.0 | 1 | 1.1 |
| Other personal injury | 41 | 3.0 | 67 | 3.0 | 32 | 2.4 | 140 | 2.8 | 140 | 17.1 | 24 | 8.3 | 2 | 1.9 | 2 | 2.2 |
| Employer liability | 11 | 0.8 | 42 | 1.9 | 8 | 0.6 | 61 | 1.2 | 61 | 23.0 | 14 | 0.0 | 0 | 0.0 | 0 | 0.0 |
| Other torts | 71 | 5.2 | 97 | 4.3 | 37 | 2.8 | 205 | 4.1 | 205 | 21.0 | 43 | 4.7 | 2 | 1.9 | 2 | 2.2 |
| COMMERCE | 221 | 16.3 | 205 | 9.1 | 185 | 13.8 | 611 | 12.4 | 613 | 24.0 | 147 | 17.0 | 28 | 27.2 | 25 | 27.2 |
| Antitrust | 14 | 1.0 | 19 | 0.8 | 5 | 0.4 | 38 | 0.8 | 38 | 42.1 | 16 | 12.5 | 2 | 1.9 | 2 | 2.2 |
| Agriculture | 4 | 0.3 | 9 | 0.4 | 3 | 0.2 | 16 | 0.3 | 16 | 37.5 | 6 | 0.0 | 0 | 0.0 | 0 | 0.0 |

# The Business of the Supreme Court (cont.)

## Appendix 2 (cont.)
### The Business of the Three Courts of Appeals
*Distribution of Circuit Decisions by Subject, after Hearing or Submission, FY 1965-1967*

### Rates of Appeal, Circuits to Supreme Court

### Distribution of Supreme Court Decisions from Three Circuits by Subject, FY 1965-1967 (Before Dismissal) After Hearing

| Subjects | 2d (N=1,357) n | % | 5th (N=2,248) n | % | D.C. (N=1,336) n | % | Three Circuits (N=4,941) N | % | Total Decisions N | Rate Appealed % | Total Certiorari Petitions n | Rate Granted % | Supreme Court (N=103) n | % | Supreme Court (N=92) n | % |
|---|---|---|---|---|---|---|---|---|---|---|---|---|---|---|---|---|
| Bankruptcy | 84 | 6.2 | 79 | 3.5 | 0 | 0.0 | 163 | 3.3 | 163 | 10.4 | 17 | 23.5 | 4 | 3.9 | 4 | 4.3 |
| Food and drug | 3 | 0.2 | 4 | 0.2 | 3 | 0.2 | 10 | 0.2 | 11 | 36.4 | 4 | 50.0 | 2 | 1.9 | 2 | 2.2 |
| Patents | 14 | 1.0 | 26 | 1.2 | 27 | 2.0 | 67 | 1.4 | 67 | 25.4 | 17 | 5.9 | 1 | 1.0 | 1 | 1.1 |
| Copyright | 25 | 1.8 | 14 | 0.6 | 5 | 0.4 | 44 | 0.9 | 44 | 27.3 | 12 | 8.3 | 3 | 2.9 | 1 | 1.1 |
| Other commerce | 77 | 5.7 | 54 | 2.4 | 142 | 10.6 | 273 | 5.5 | 274 | 27.4 | 75 | 20.0 | 16 | 15.5 | 15 | 16.3 |
| LABOR | 156 | 11.6 | 243 | 10.8 | 97 | 7.3 | 496 | 10.0 | 497 | 17.9 | 89 | 7.9 | 7 | 6.8 | 7 | 7.5 |
| Fair Labor Standards Act | 1 | 0.1 | 34 | 1.5 | 5 | 0.4 | 40 | 0.8 | 40 | 7.5 | 3 | 0.0 | 0 | 0.0 | 0 | 0.0 |
| Social Security | 12 | 0.9 | 38 | 1.7 | 1 | 0.1 | 51 | 1.0 | 51 | 5.9 | 3 | 0.0 | 0 | 0.0 | 0 | 0.0 |
| Labor Reporting Act | 11 | 0.8 | 4 | 0.2 | 4 | 0.3 | 19 | 0.4 | 19 | 5.3 | 1 | 0.0 | 0 | 0.0 | 0 | 0.0 |
| Railway Labor Act | 5 | 0.4 | 17 | 0.8 | 13 | 1.0 | 35 | 0.7 | 35 | 31.4 | 11 | 9.1 | 1 | 1.0 | 1 | 1.1 |
| Labor relations acts | 114 | 8.4 | 140 | 6.2 | 70 | 5.2 | 324 | 6.6 | 325 | 19.7 | 64 | 6.3 | 4 | 3.9 | 4 | 4.3 |
| Other labor | 13 | 1.0 | 10 | 0.4 | 4 | 0.3 | 27 | 0.5 | 27 | 25.9 | 7 | 28.6 | 2 | 1.9 | 2 | 2.2 |
| TAXATION | 146 | 10.8 | 279 | 12.4 | 33 | 2.5 | 458 | 9.3 | 459 | 27.5 | 126 | 10.3 | 15 | 14.6 | 13 | 14.1 |
| Income tax | 88 | 6.5 | 136 | 6.0 | 20 | 1.5 | 244 | 4.9 | 244 | 23.4 | 57 | 7.0 | 4 | 3.9 | 4 | 4.3 |
| Tax fraud | 14 | 1.0 | 18 | 0.8 | 2 | 0.1 | 34 | 0.7 | 34 | 50.0 | 17 | 11.8 | 2 | 1.9 | 2 | 2.2 |
| Forfeiture and penalty | 0 | 0.0 | 12 | 0.5 | 1 | 0.1 | 13 | 0.3 | 13 | 7.7 | 1 | 0.0 | 0 | 0.0 | 0 | 0.0 |
| Other tax | 44 | 3.2 | 113 | 5.0 | 10 | 0.7 | 167 | 3.4 | 168 | 30.4 | 51 | 13.7 | 9 | 8.7 | 7 | 7.6 |
| PERSONAL STATUS | 175 | 12.9 | 518 | 23.0 | 121 | 9.1 | 814 | 16.5 | 814 | 20.3 | 165 | 9.7 | 16 | 15.5 | 16 | 17.4 |
| Civil rights | 11 | 0.8 | 100 | 4.4 | 2 | 0.1 | 113 | 2.3 | 113 | 23.0 | 26 | 15.4 | 4 | 3.9 | 4 | 4.3 |

*Circuit Decisions Appealed to Supreme Court (N=4,945)*
*Certiorari Petitions Granted (N=1,004)*

| Category | | | | | | | | | | | | | | | |
|---|---|---|---|---|---|---|---|---|---|---|---|---|---|---|---|
| Immigration and deportation | 23 | 1.7 | 8 | 0.4 | 3 | 0.2 | 34 | 0.7 | 29.4 | 10 | 40.0 | 4 | 3.9 | 4 | 4.3 |
| Suffrage | 2 | 0.1 | 41 | 1.8 | 2 | 0.1 | 45 | 0.9 | 6.7 | 3 | 0.0 | 0 | 0.0 | 0 | 0.0 |
| Civil rights removals | 3 | 0.2 | 27 | 1.2 | 0 | 0.0 | 30 | 0.6 | 10.0 | 3 | 66.7 | 2 | 1.9 | 2 | 2.2 |
| Prisoner petitions | | | | | | | | | | | | | | | |
| Habeas corpus | 99 | 7.3 | 210 | 9.3 | 37 | 2.8 | 346 | 7.0 | 24.9 | 86 | 5.8 | 5 | 4.9 | 5 | 5.4 |
| Mandamus | 9 | 0.7 | 25 | 1.1 | 27 | 2.0 | 61 | 1.2 | 14.8 | 9 | 0.0 | 0 | 0.0 | 0 | 0.0 |
| Parole review | 3 | 0.2 | 2 | 0.1 | 16 | 1.2 | 21 | 0.4 | 14.3 | 3 | 0.0 | 0 | 0.0 | 0 | 0.0 |
| Vacate sentence | 25 | 1.8 | 105 | 4.7 | 34 | 2.5 | 164 | 3.3 | 15.2 | 25 | 4.0 | 1 | 1.0 | 1 | 1.0 |
| CRIMES AGAINST PERSONS | 4 | 0.3 | 4 | 0.2 | 117 | 8.8 | 125 | 2.5 | 10.4 | 13 | 0.0 | 0 | 0.0 | 0 | 0.0 |
| Homicide | 0 | 0.0 | 2 | 0.1 | 45 | 3.4 | 47 | 1.0 | 10.6 | 5 | 0.0 | 0 | 0.0 | 0 | 0.0 |
| Kidnapping | 0 | 0.0 | 0 | 0.0 | 0 | 0.0 | 0 | 0.0 | 0.0 | 0 | 0.0 | 0 | 0.0 | 0 | 0.0 |
| Rape | 0 | 0.0 | 0 | 0.0 | 19 | 1.4 | 19 | 0.4 | 0.0 | 0 | 0.0 | 0 | 0.0 | 0 | 0.0 |
| Assault | 4 | 0.3 | 2 | 0.1 | 53 | 4.0 | 59 | 1.2 | 13.6 | 8 | 0.0 | 0 | 0.0 | 0 | 0.0 |
| CRIMES AGAINST PROPERTY | 74 | 5.5 | 153 | 6.8 | 250 | 18.7 | 477 | 9.7 | 24.1 | 115 | 6.1 | 9 | 8.7 | 7 | 7.6 |
| Robbery | 35 | 2.6 | 38 | 1.7 | 212 | 15.9 | 285 | 5.8 | 18.6 | 53 | 7.5 | 4 | 3.9 | 4 | 4.3 |
| Auto theft | 4 | 0.3 | 48 | 2.1 | 19 | 1.4 | 71 | 1.4 | 15.5 | 11 | 0.0 | 1 | 1.0 | 0 | 0.0 |
| Extortion | 0 | 0.0 | 1 | 0.0 | 1 | 0.1 | 2 | 0.0 | 50.0 | 1 | 0.0 | 0 | 0.0 | 0 | 0.0 |
| Fraud | 16 | 1.2 | 36 | 1.6 | 10 | 0.7 | 62 | 1.3 | 48.4 | 30 | 6.7 | 3 | 2.9 | 2 | 2.2 |
| Embezzlement | 1 | 0.1 | 5 | 0.2 | 1 | 0.1 | 7 | 0.1 | 14.3 | 1 | 0.0 | 0 | 0.0 | 0 | 0.0 |
| Forgery | 14 | 1.0 | 18 | 0.8 | 6 | 0.4 | 38 | 0.8 | 39.5 | 15 | 6.7 | 1 | 1.0 | 1 | 1.0 |
| Other property crimes | 4 | 0.3 | 7 | 0.3 | 1 | 0.1 | 12 | 0.2 | 33.3 | 4 | 0.0 | 0 | 0.0 | 0 | 0.0 |
| MORALS OFFENSES | 128 | 9.4 | 41 | 1.8 | 92 | 6.9 | 261 | 5.3 | 28.4 | 74 | 4.1 | 3 | 2.9 | 3 | 3.3 |
| Narcotics | 124 | 9.1 | 29 | 1.3 | 82 | 6.1 | 235 | 4.8 | 29.8 | 70 | 4.3 | 3 | 2.9 | 3 | 3.3 |
| White slave | 1 | 0.1 | 8 | 0.4 | 0 | 0.0 | 9 | 0.2 | 11.1 | 1 | 0.0 | 0 | 0.0 | 0 | 0.0 |
| Other sex | 1 | 0.1 | 0 | 0.0 | 4 | 0.3 | 5 | 0.1 | 0.0 | 0 | 0.0 | 0 | 0.0 | 0 | 0.0 |
| Obscenity (mail) | 2 | 0.1 | 0 | 0.0 | 1 | 0.1 | 3 | 0.1 | 33.3 | 1 | 0.0 | 0 | 0.0 | 0 | 0.0 |
| Gambling | 0 | 0.0 | 4 | 0.2 | 5 | 0.4 | 9 | 0.2 | 22.2 | 2 | 0.0 | 0 | 0.0 | 0 | 0.0 |
| MISCELLANEOUS OFFENSES | 37 | 2.7 | 25 | 1.1 | 19 | 1.4 | 81 | 1.6 | 30.9 | 25 | 20.0 | 6 | 5.8 | 5 | 5.4 |
| Escape | 1 | 0.1 | 1 | 0.0 | 1 | 0.1 | 3 | 0.1 | 0.0 | 0 | 0.0 | 0 | 0.0 | 0 | 0.0 |

## Appendix 2 (cont.)

### The Business of the Three Courts of Appeals
Distribution of Circuit Decisions by Subject, after Hearing or Submission, FY 1965-1967

### The Business of the Supreme Court (cont.)
Distribution of Supreme Court Decisions from Three Circuits by Subject, FY 1965-1967

Rates of Appeal, Circuits to Supreme Court (Before Dismissal) After Hearing

| Subjects | 2d (N = 1,357) n | % | 5th (N = 2,248) n | % | D.C. (N = 1,336) n | % | Three Circuits (N = 4,941) N | % | Circuit Decisions Appealed to Supreme Court (N = 4,945)* Total Decisions N | Rate Appealed % | Certiorari Petitions Granted (N = 1,004) Total Certiorari Petitions n | Rate Granted % | Supreme Court (N = 103) n | % | Supreme Court (N = 92) n | % |
|---|---|---|---|---|---|---|---|---|---|---|---|---|---|---|---|---|
| Weapons | 0 | 0.0 | 9 | 0.4 | 11 | 0.8 | 20 | 0.4 | 20 | 10.0 | 2 | 100.0 | 2 | 1.9 | 2 | 2.2 |
| Migratory birds | 0 | 0.0 | 1 | 0.0 | 0 | 0.0 | 1 | 0.0 | 1 | 0.0 | 0 | 0.0 | 0 | 0.0 | 0 | 0.0 |
| Selective Service | 10 | 0.7 | 7 | 0.3 | 0 | 0.0 | 17 | 0.4 | 17 | 23.5 | 4 | 25.0 | 1 | 1.0 | 1 | 1.1 |
| Bribery | 12 | 0.9 | 2 | 0.1 | 4 | 0.3 | 18 | 0.4 | 18 | 50.0 | 9 | 0.0 | 1 | 1.0 | 0 | 0.0 |
| Perjury | 14 | 1.0 | 5 | 0.2 | 3 | 0.2 | 22 | 0.4 | 22 | 45.5 | 10 | 20.0 | 2 | 1.9 | 2 | 2.2 |
| LOCAL | 0 | 0.0 | 0 | 0.0 | 54 | 4.0 | 54 | 1.1 | 54 | 1.9 | 1 | 0.0 | 0 | 0.0 | 0 | 0.0 |
| Domestic relations | 0 | 0.0 | 0 | 0.0 | 5 | 0.4 | 5 | 0.1 | 5 | 20.0 | 1 | 0.0 | 0 | 0.0 | 0 | 0.0 |
| Traffic | 0 | 0.0 | 0 | 0.0 | 1 | 0.1 | 1 | 0.1 | 1 | 0.0 | 0 | 0.0 | 0 | 0.0 | 0 | 0.0 |
| Other D.C. cases | 0 | 0.0 | 0 | 0.0 | 48 | 3.6 | 48 | 1.0 | 48 | 0.0 | 0 | 0.0 | 0 | 0.0 | 0 | 0.0 |
| OTHER | 103 | 7.6 | 156 | 6.9 | 136 | 10.2 | 395 | 8.0 | 395 | 13.7 | 54 | 9.3 | 6 | 5.8 | 5 | 5.4 |
| Sums | 1,357 | 100.0 | 2,248 | 100.0 | 1,336 | 100.0 | 4,941 | 100.0 | 4,945 | 20.3 | 1,004 | 9.2 | 103 | 100.0 | 92 | 100.0 |

NOTE: Slight discrepancies in percentages are caused by rounding error.

* The total number of circuit decisions becomes 4,945 to account for 2 circuit cases that were unconsolidated by the justices and 2 that were consolidated but treated separately with appeals from other circuits.

## Appendix 3
### Rates of Appeal from Contested Judgments in U.S. District Courts by Source of Civil Jurisdiction, FY 1967-1970*

| CIRCUIT | U.S. (Plaintiff) | | | U.S. (Defendant) | | | Federal Question | | | Diversity of Citizenship | | |
|---|---|---|---|---|---|---|---|---|---|---|---|---|
| | Appeals Filed n | Contested Judgments N | Rate of Appeal % | Appeals Filed n | Contested Judgments N | Rate of Appeal % | Appeals Filed n | Contested Judgments N | Rate of Appeal % | Appeals Filed n | Contested Judgments N | Rate of Appeal % |
| **2d** | 123 | 534 | 23.0 | 423 | 1,161 | 36.4 | 1,394 | 4,173 | 33.4 | 524 | 1,043 | 50.2 |
| Connecticut | 14 | 145 | 9.7 | 40 | 266 | 15.0 | 68 | 250 | 27.2 | 31 | 106 | 29.2 |
| New York | | | | | | | | | | | | |
| Northern | 8 | 51 | 15.7 | 27 | 77 | 35.1 | 133 | 593 | 22.4 | 19 | 50 | 38.0 |
| Eastern | 24 | 158 | 15.2 | 101 | 178 | 56.7 | 193 | 821 | 23.5 | 61 | 108 | 56.5 |
| Southern | 68 | 117 | 58.1 | 227 | 521 | 43.6 | 911 | 1,768 | 51.5 | 364 | 594 | 61.3 |
| Western | 7 | 46 | 15.2 | 20 | 98 | 20.4 | 77 | 683 | 11.3 | 19 | 32 | 59.4 |
| Vermont | 2 | 17 | 11.8 | 8 | 21 | 38.1 | 12 | 58 | 20.7 | 30 | 153 | 19.6 |
| **5th** | 322 | 3,354 | 9.6 | 1,011 | 4,547 | 22.2 | 1,976 | 8,955 | 22.1 | 1,061 | 4,338 | 24.5 |
| Alabama | | | | | | | | | | | | |
| Northern | 4 | 51 | 7.9 | 43 | 263 | 16.3 | 106 | 298 | 35.6 | 69 | 808 | 8.5 |
| Middle | 8 | 30 | 26.7 | 8 | 105 | 7.6 | 41 | 512 | 8.0 | 12 | 92 | 13.0 |
| Southern | 12 | 37 | 32.4 | 24 | 98 | 24.5 | 57 | 272 | 21.0 | 20 | 96 | 20.8 |
| Florida | | | | | | | | | | | | |
| Northern | 2 | 43 | 4.7 | 19 | 175 | 10.9 | 45 | 375 | 12.0 | 33 | 88 | 37.5 |
| Middle | 38 | 815 | 47.8 | 88 | 293 | 30.0 | 208 | 1,295 | 16.1 | 102 | 290 | 35.2 |
| Southern | 40 | 435 | 9.1 | 87 | 243 | 35.8 | 230 | 1,038 | 22.2 | 151 | 467 | 32.3 |
| Georgia | | | | | | | | | | | | |
| Northern | 15 | 121 | 12.4 | 178 | 1,235 | 14.4 | 121 | 452 | 26.8 | 78 | 383 | 20.4 |
| Middle | 14 | 56 | 25.0 | 33 | 107 | 30.8 | 46 | 148 | 31.1 | 42 | 180 | 23.3 |
| Southern | 6 | 67 | 9.0 | 14 | 111 | 12.6 | 52 | 376 | 13.8 | 15 | 135 | 11.1 |

## Appendix 3 (cont.)
### Rates of Appeal from Contested Judgments in U.S. District Courts by Source of Civil Jurisdiction, FY 1967-1970*

| CIRCUIT | U.S. (Plaintiff) | | | U.S. (Defendant) | | | Federal Question | | | Diversity of Citizenship | | |
|---|---|---|---|---|---|---|---|---|---|---|---|---|
| | Appeals Filed n | Contested Judgments N | Rate of Appeal % | Appeals Filed n | Contested Judgments N | Rate of Appeal % | Appeals Filed n | Contested Judgments N | Rate of Appeal % | Appeals Filed n | Contested Judgments N | Rate of Appeal % |
| (5th cont.) | | | | | | | | | | | | |
| Louisiana | | | | | | | | | | | | |
| Eastern | 23 | 295 | 7.8 | 69 | 270 | 25.6 | 325 | 1,443 | 22.5 | 162 | 552 | 29.3 |
| Western | 14 | 70 | 20.0 | 21 | 212 | 9.9 | 128 | 326 | 39.3 | 37 | 140 | 26.4 |
| Mississippi | | | | | | | | | | | | |
| Northern | 13 | 50 | 26.6 | 24 | 69 | 34.8 | 58 | 144 | 40.3 | 26 | 87 | 30.0 |
| Southern | 42 | 99 | 42.4 | 46 | 138 | 33.3 | 78 | 149 | 52.3 | 68 | 215 | 31.6 |
| Texas | | | | | | | | | | | | |
| Northern | 21 | 273 | 7.7 | 100 | 305 | 32.8 | 116 | 686 | 16.9 | 105 | 297 | 35.4 |
| Eastern | 12 | 58 | 20.7 | 32 | 213 | 15.0 | 76 | 249 | 30.5 | 46 | 161 | 28.6 |
| Southern | 30 | 260 | 8.3 | 85 | 358 | 23.7 | 183 | 883 | 20.7 | 44 | 179 | 24.6 |
| Western | 27 | 590 | 4.6 | 136 | 342 | 40.0 | 103 | 298 | 34.6 | 51 | 168 | 30.4 |
| Canal Zone | 1 | 4 | 25.0 | 4 | 10 | 40.0 | 3 | 11 | 27.3 | 0 | 0 | — |
| D.C. | 44 | 177 | 24.9 | 718 | 2,304 | 31.2 | 89 | 149 | 59.7 | 3 | 0 | — |
| Sums, three circuits | 489 | 4,065 | 12.0 | 2,152 | 8,012 | 26.9 | 3,459 | 13,277 | 26.1 | 1,588 | 5,381 | 29.5 |
| Sums, all circuits | 1,246 | 9,769 | 12.8 | 5,949 | 21,897 | 27.2 | 11,066 | 42,235 | 26.2 | 4,742 | 16,321 | 29.1 |

SOURCE: Data courtesy of Jerry Goldman and the Federal Judicial Center; AO Annual Reports, Table B7.
* Local jurisdiction excluded. Slight discrepancies in percentages are caused by rounding error.

## Appendix 3 (cont.)
### Rates of Appeal from Contested Civil Judgments and Convictions of Guilt in U.S. District Courts, FY 1967-1970*

Note: Numbers in parentheses cover FY 1969-1970

| CIRCUIT | Appeals Filed n | All Civil Contested Judgments N | Rate of Appeal % | Appeals Filed n | All Criminal Convictions after Trial N | Rate of Appeal % |
|---|---|---|---|---|---|---|
| 2d | 2,464 | 6,911 | 35.7 | 1,014 | 1,400 | 72.4 |
| Connecticut | 153 | 767 | 19.9 | (52) | (60) | (86.7) |
| New York | | | | | | |
| Northern | 187 | 771 | 24.3 | (18) | (20) | (90.0) |
| Eastern | 379 | 1,265 | 30.0 | (173) | (182) | (95.1) |
| Southern | 1,570 | 3,000 | 52.3 | (352) | (412) | (85.4) |
| Western | 123 | 859 | 14.3 | (26) | (42) | (61.9) |
| Vermont | 52 | 249 | 20.9 | (4) | (13) | (30.8) |
| 5th | 4,370 | 21,194 | 20.6 | 1,357 | 2,704 | 50.2 |
| Alabama | | | | | | |
| Northern | 222 | 1,420 | 15.6 | (35) | (40) | (87.5) |
| Middle | 69 | 739 | 9.3 | (31) | (68) | (45.6) |
| Southern | 113 | 503 | 22.5 | (26) | (42) | (61.9) |
| Florida | | | | | | |
| Northern | 99 | 681 | 14.5 | (22) | (50) | (40.0) |
| Middle | 436 | 2,693 | 16.2 | (72) | (102) | (70.6) |
| Southern | 508 | 2,183 | 23.3 | (128) | (180) | (71.1) |
| Georgia | | | | | | |
| Northern | 392 | 2,191 | 17.9 | (60) | (124) | (48.4) |
| Middle | 135 | 491 | 27.5 | (53) | (136) | (39.0) |
| Southern | 87 | 689 | 12.6 | (12) | (60) | (20.0) |
| Louisiana | | | | | | |
| Eastern | 579 | 2,560 | 22.6 | (41) | (112) | (36.6) |
| Western | 200 | 748 | 26.7 | (8) | (23) | (34.8) |
| Mississippi | | | | | | |
| Northern | 121 | 350 | 34.6 | (23) | (55) | (41.8) |
| Southern | 234 | 601 | 38.9 | (28) | (33) | (84.8) |
| Texas | | | | | | |
| Northern | 342 | 1,561 | 21.9 | (59) | (86) | (68.6) |
| Eastern | 166 | 681 | 24.4 | (9) | (19) | (47.4) |
| Southern | 342 | 1,680 | 20.4 | (57) | (124) | (46.0) |
| Western | 317 | 1,398 | 22.7 | (91) | (132) | (68.9) |
| Canal Zone | 8 | 25 | 32.0 | — | — | — |
| D.C. | 854 | 2,630 | 32.5 | 1,583 | 1,699 | 93.2 |
| Sums, three circuits | 7,688 | 30,735 | 25.0 | 3,954 | 5,803 | 68.1 |
| Sums, all circuits | 23,089 | 90,222 | 25.5 | 8,931 | 16,263 | 54.9 |

SOURCE: Data courtesy of Jerry Goldman and the Federal Judicial Center; AO *Annual Reports*, Table B1, and *Federal Offenders in United States Courts*, Table D7, 7a.

* Local jurisdiction excluded. Slight discrepancies in percentages are caused by rounding error.

## Appendix 4

Subjects of Circuit Court Decisions
after Hearing or Submission, FY 1965-1967
2d Circuit
(N = 1,357)

| SUBJECTS | Affirm n | % | Mixed n | % | Reverse n | % | Avoid n | % | Other n | % | Total N | % |
|---|---|---|---|---|---|---|---|---|---|---|---|---|
| CONTRACTS | 85 | 67.5 | 9 | 7.1 | 24 | 19.0 | 3 | 2.4 | 5 | 4.0 | 126 | 100.0 |
| Insurance | 12 | 66.7 | 2 | 11.1 | 3 | 16.7 | 0 | 0.0 | 1 | 5.6 | 18 | 100.0 |
| Marine | 13 | 86.7 | 0 | 0.0 | 1 | 6.7 | 1 | 6.7 | 0 | 0.0 | 15 | 100.0 |
| Negotiable instruments | 3 | 100.0 | 0 | 0.0 | 0 | 0.0 | 0 | 0.0 | 0 | 0.0 | 3 | 100.0 |
| Real property | 8 | 66.7 | 1 | 8.3 | 3 | 25.0 | 0 | 0.0 | 0 | 0.0 | 12 | 100.0 |
| Recovery and enforcement | 9 | 81.8 | 1 | 9.1 | 1 | 9.1 | 0 | 0.0 | 0 | 0.0 | 11 | 100.0 |
| Other contracts | 40 | 59.7 | 5 | 7.5 | 16 | 23.9 | 2 | 3.0 | 4 | 6.0 | 67 | 100.0 |
| TORTS | 134 | 71.7 | 13 | 7.0 | 35 | 18.7 | 3 | 1.6 | 2 | 1.1 | 187 | 100.0 |
| Marine-personal injury | 35 | 76.1 | 2 | 4.3 | 7 | 15.2 | 1 | 2.2 | 1 | 2.2 | 46 | 100.0 |
| Motor vehicle-personal injury | 14 | 77.8 | 0 | 0.0 | 4 | 22.2 | 0 | 0.0 | 0 | 0.0 | 18 | 100.0 |
| Other personal injury | 27 | 65.9 | 1 | 2.4 | 11 | 26.8 | 1 | 2.4 | 1 | 2.4 | 41 | 100.0 |
| Employer liability | 9 | 81.8 | 0 | 0.0 | 2 | 18.2 | 0 | 0.0 | 0 | 0.0 | 11 | 100.0 |
| Other torts | 49 | 69.0 | 10 | 14.1 | 11 | 15.5 | 1 | 1.4 | 0 | 0.0 | 71 | 100.0 |
| COMMERCE | 140 | 63.3 | 19 | 8.6 | 52 | 23.5 | 5 | 2.3 | 5 | 2.3 | 221 | 100.0 |
| Antitrust | 7 | 50.0 | 2 | 14.3 | 5 | 35.7 | 0 | 0.0 | 0 | 0.0 | 14 | 100.0 |
| Agriculture | 4 | 100.0 | 0 | 0.0 | 0 | 0.0 | 0 | 0.0 | 0 | 0.0 | 4 | 100.0 |
| Bankruptcy | 54 | 64.3 | 6 | 7.1 | 19 | 22.6 | 3 | 3.6 | 2 | 2.4 | 84 | 100.0 |
| Food and drug | 0 | 0.0 | 1 | 33.3 | 2 | 66.7 | 0 | 0.0 | 0 | 0.0 | 3 | 100.0 |
| Patents | 10 | 71.4 | 1 | 7.1 | 3 | 21.4 | 0 | 0.0 | 0 | 0.0 | 14 | 100.0 |
| Copyright | 15 | 60.0 | 3 | 12.0 | 6 | 24.0 | 1 | 4.0 | 0 | 0.0 | 25 | 100.0 |
| Other commerce | 50 | 64.9 | 6 | 7.8 | 17 | 22.1 | 1 | 1.3 | 3 | 3.9 | 77 | 100.0 |
| LABOR | 107 | 68.6 | 18 | 11.5 | 26 | 16.7 | 4 | 2.6 | 1 | 0.6 | 156 | 100.0 |
| Fair Labor Standards Act | 1 | 100.0 | 0 | 0.0 | 0 | 0.0 | 0 | 0.0 | 0 | 0.0 | 1 | 100.0 |
| Social Security | 9 | 75.0 | 0 | 0.0 | 3 | 25.0 | 0 | 0.0 | 0 | 0.0 | 12 | 100.0 |
| Labor Reporting Act | 7 | 63.6 | 0 | 0.0 | 2 | 18.2 | 1 | 9.1 | 1 | 9.1 | 11 | 100.0 |
| Railway Labor Act | 4 | 80.0 | 0 | 0.0 | 0 | 0.0 | 1 | 20.0 | 0 | 0.0 | 5 | 100.0 |
| Labor relations acts | 77 | 67.5 | 18 | 15.8 | 17 | 14.9 | 2 | 1.8 | 0 | 0.0 | 114 | 100.0 |
| Other labor | 9 | 69.2 | 0 | 0.0 | 4 | 30.8 | 0 | 0.0 | 0 | 0.0 | 13 | 100.0 |

## 2d Circuit (cont.)

| SUBJECTS | Affirm n | % | Mixed n | % | Reverse n | % | Avoid n | % | Other n | % | Total N | % |
|---|---|---|---|---|---|---|---|---|---|---|---|---|
| TAXATION | 106 | 72.6 | 12 | 8.2 | 27 | 18.5 | 0 | 0.0 | 1 | 0.7 | 146 | 100.0 |
| Income tax | 63 | 71.6 | 9 | 10.2 | 15 | 17.0 | 0 | 0.0 | 1 | 1.1 | 88 | 100.0 |
| Tax fraud | 13 | 92.9 | 0 | 0.0 | 1 | 7.1 | 0 | 0.0 | 0 | 0.0 | 14 | 100.0 |
| Forfeiture and penalty | 0 | 0.0 | 0 | 0.0 | 0 | 0.0 | 0 | 0.0 | 0 | 0.0 | 0 | — |
| Other tax | 30 | 68.2 | 3 | 6.8 | 11 | 25.0 | 0 | 0.0 | 0 | 0.0 | 44 | 100.0 |
| PERSONAL STATUS | 132 | 75.4 | 3 | 1.7 | 29 | 16.6 | 4 | 2.3 | 7 | 4.0 | 175 | 100.0 |
| Civil rights | 4 | 36.4 | 0 | 0.0 | 6 | 54.5 | 1 | 9.1 | 0 | 0.0 | 11 | 100.0 |
| Immigration and deportation | 13 | 56.5 | 0 | 0.0 | 5 | 21.7 | 1 | 4.3 | 4 | 17.4 | 23 | 100.0 |
| Suffrage | 1 | 50.0 | 0 | 0.0 | 1 | 50.0 | 0 | 0.0 | 0 | 0.0 | 2 | 100.0 |
| Civil rights removals | 3 | 100.0 | 0 | 0.0 | 0 | 0.0 | 0 | 0.0 | 0 | 0.0 | 3 | 100.0 |
| Prisoner petitions | | | | | | | | | | | | |
| Habeas corpus | 79 | 79.8 | 2 | 2.0 | 14 | 14.1 | 2 | 2.0 | 2 | 2.0 | 99 | 100.0 |
| Mandamus | 7 | 77.8 | 0 | 0.0 | 2 | 22.2 | 0 | 0.0 | 0 | 0.0 | 9 | 100.0 |
| Parole review | 2 | 66.7 | 0 | 0.0 | 1 | 33.3 | 0 | 0.0 | 0 | 0.0 | 3 | 100.0 |
| Vacate sentence | 23 | 92.0 | 1 | 4.0 | 0 | 0.0 | 0 | 0.0 | 1 | 4.0 | 25 | 100.0 |
| CRIMES AGAINST PERSONS | 4 | 100.0 | 0 | 0.0 | 0 | 0.0 | 0 | 0.0 | 0 | 0.0 | 4 | 100.0 |
| Homicide | 0 | 0.0 | 0 | 0.0 | 0 | 0.0 | 0 | 0.0 | 0 | 0.0 | 0 | — |
| Kidnapping | 0 | 0.0 | 0 | 0.0 | 0 | 0.0 | 0 | 0.0 | 0 | 0.0 | 0 | — |
| Rape | 0 | 0.0 | 0 | 0.0 | 0 | 0.0 | 0 | 0.0 | 0 | 0.0 | 0 | — |
| Assault | 4 | 100.0 | 0 | 0.0 | 0 | 0.0 | 0 | 0.0 | 0 | 0.0 | 4 | 100.0 |
| CRIMES AGAINST PROPERTY | 66 | 89.2 | 2 | 2.7 | 6 | 8.1 | 0 | 0.0 | 0 | 0.0 | 74 | 100.0 |
| Robbery | 31 | 88.6 | 1 | 2.9 | 3 | 8.6 | 0 | 0.0 | 0 | 0.0 | 35 | 100.0 |
| Auto theft | 4 | 100.0 | 0 | 0.0 | 0 | 0.0 | 0 | 0.0 | 0 | 0.0 | 4 | 100.0 |
| Extortion | 0 | 0.0 | 0 | 0.0 | 0 | 0.0 | 0 | 0.0 | 0 | 0.0 | 0 | — |
| Fraud | 13 | 81.3 | 1 | 6.3 | 2 | 12.5 | 0 | 0.0 | 0 | 0.0 | 16 | 100.0 |
| Embezzlement | 1 | 100.0 | 0 | 0.0 | 0 | 0.0 | 0 | 0.0 | 0 | 0.0 | 1 | 100.0 |
| Forgery | 13 | 92.9 | 0 | 0.0 | 1 | 7.1 | 0 | 0.0 | 0 | 0.0 | 14 | 100.0 |
| Other property crimes | 4 | 100.0 | 0 | 0.0 | 0 | 0.0 | 0 | 0.0 | 0 | 0.0 | 4 | 100.0 |
| MORALS OFFENSES | 112 | 87.5 | 1 | 0.8 | 13 | 10.2 | 1 | 0.8 | 1 | 0.8 | 128 | 100.0 |
| Narcotics | 110 | 88.7 | 1 | 0.8 | 11 | 8.9 | 1 | 0.8 | 1 | 0.8 | 124 | 100.0 |
| White slave | 1 | 100.0 | 0 | 0.0 | 0 | 0.0 | 0 | 0.0 | 0 | 0.0 | 1 | 100.0 |
| Other sex | 0 | 0.0 | 0 | 0.0 | 1 | 100.0 | 0 | 0.0 | 0 | 0.0 | 1 | 100.0 |

## 2d Circuit (cont.)

| SUBJECTS | Affirm n | % | Mixed n | % | Reverse n | % | Avoid n | % | Other n | % | Total N | % |
|---|---|---|---|---|---|---|---|---|---|---|---|---|
| Obscenity (mail) | 1 | 50.0 | 0 | 0.0 | 1 | 50.0 | 0 | 0.0 | 0 | 0.0 | 2 | 100.0 |
| Gambling | 0 | 0.0 | 0 | 0.0 | 0 | 0.0 | 0 | 0.0 | 0 | 0.0 | 0 | — |
| MISCELLANEOUS OFFENSES | 30 | 81.1 | 0 | 0.0 | 6 | 16.2 | 1 | 2.7 | 0 | 0.0 | 37 | 100.0 |
| Escape | 1 | 100.0 | 0 | 0.0 | 0 | 0.0 | 0 | 0.0 | 0 | 0.0 | 1 | 100.0 |
| Weapons | 0 | 0.0 | 0 | 0.0 | 0 | 0.0 | 0 | 0.0 | 0 | 0.0 | 0 | — |
| Migratory birds | 0 | 0.0 | 0 | 0.0 | 0 | 0.0 | 0 | 0.0 | 0 | 0.0 | 0 | — |
| Selective Service | 7 | 70.0 | 0 | 0.0 | 2 | 20.0 | 1 | 10.0 | 0 | 0.0 | 10 | 100.0 |
| Bribery | 8 | 66.7 | 0 | 0.0 | 4 | 33.3 | 0 | 0.0 | 0 | 0.0 | 12 | 100.0 |
| Perjury | 14 | 100.0 | 0 | 0.0 | 0 | 0.0 | 0 | 0.0 | 0 | 0.0 | 14 | 100.0 |
| OTHER | 83 | 80.6 | 2 | 1.9 | 16 | 15.5 | 2 | 1.9 | 0 | 0.0 | 103 | 100.0 |
| Sums | 999 | 73.6 | 79 | 5.8 | 234 | 17.2 | 23 | 1.7 | 22 | 1.6 | 1,357 | 100.0 |

NOTE: Slight discrepancies in percentages are caused by rounding error.

Appendix Four • 325

## Appendix 4 (cont.)
### Subjects of Circuit Court Decisions after Hearing or Submission, FY 1965-1967
### 5th Circuit
### (N = 2,248)

| SUBJECTS | Affirm n | Affirm % | Mixed n | Mixed % | Reverse n | Reverse % | Avoid n | Avoid % | Other n | Other % | Total N | Total % |
|---|---|---|---|---|---|---|---|---|---|---|---|---|
| CONTRACTS | 195 | 67.0 | 19 | 6.5 | 64 | 22.0 | 6 | 2.1 | 7 | 2.4 | 291 | 100.0 |
| Insurance | 74 | 62.7 | 7 | 5.9 | 30 | 25.4 | 4 | 3.4 | 3 | 2.5 | 118 | 100.0 |
| Marine | 9 | 64.3 | 0 | 0.0 | 4 | 28.6 | 1 | 7.1 | 0 | 0.0 | 14 | 100.0 |
| Negotiable instruments | 6 | 85.7 | 1 | 14.3 | 0 | 0.0 | 0 | 0.0 | 0 | 0.0 | 7 | 100.0 |
| Real property | 39 | 78.0 | 3 | 6.0 | 8 | 16.0 | 0 | 0.0 | 0 | 0.0 | 50 | 100.0 |
| Recovery and enforcement | 12 | 66.7 | 0 | 0.0 | 6 | 33.3 | 0 | 0.0 | 0 | 0.0 | 18 | 100.0 |
| Other contracts | 55 | 65.5 | 8 | 9.5 | 16 | 19.0 | 1 | 1.2 | 4 | 4.8 | 84 | 100.0 |
| TORTS | 217 | 65.2 | 15 | 4.5 | 88 | 26.4 | 5 | 1.5 | 8 | 2.4 | 333 | 100.0 |
| Marine-personal injury | 48 | 67.6 | 6 | 8.5 | 15 | 21.1 | 0 | 0.0 | 2 | 2.8 | 71 | 100.0 |
| Motor vehicle-personal injury | 35 | 62.5 | 1 | 1.8 | 17 | 30.4 | 0 | 0.0 | 3 | 5.4 | 56 | 100.0 |
| Other personal injury | 39 | 58.2 | 1 | 1.5 | 25 | 37.3 | 1 | 1.5 | 1 | 1.5 | 67 | 100.0 |
| Employer liability | 30 | 71.4 | 0 | 0.0 | 10 | 23.8 | 1 | 2.4 | 1 | 2.4 | 42 | 100.0 |
| Other torts | 65 | 67.0 | 7 | 7.2 | 21 | 21.6 | 3 | 3.1 | 1 | 1.0 | 97 | 100.0 |
| COMMERCE | 121 | 59.0 | 11 | 5.4 | 57 | 27.8 | 4 | 2.0 | 12 | 5.9 | 205 | 100.0 |
| Antitrust | 11 | 57.9 | 0 | 0.0 | 8 | 42.1 | 0 | 0.0 | 0 | 0.0 | 19 | 100.0 |
| Agriculture | 5 | 55.6 | 0 | 0.0 | 2 | 22.2 | 0 | 0.0 | 2 | 22.2 | 9 | 100.0 |
| Bankruptcy | 49 | 62.0 | 7 | 8.9 | 18 | 22.8 | 2 | 2.5 | 3 | 3.8 | 79 | 100.0 |
| Food and drug | 3 | 75.0 | 0 | 0.0 | 0 | 0.0 | 0 | 0.0 | 1 | 25.0 | 4 | 100.0 |
| Patents | 21 | 80.8 | 0 | 0.0 | 5 | 19.2 | 0 | 0.0 | 0 | 0.0 | 26 | 100.0 |
| Copyright | 9 | 64.3 | 1 | 7.1 | 4 | 28.6 | 0 | 0.0 | 0 | 0.0 | 14 | 100.0 |
| Other commerce | 23 | 42.6 | 3 | 5.6 | 20 | 37.0 | 2 | 3.7 | 6 | 11.1 | 54 | 100.0 |
| LABOR | 124 | 51.0 | 44 | 18.1 | 63 | 25.9 | 3 | 1.2 | 9 | 3.7 | 243 | 100.0 |
| Fair Labor Standards Act | 13 | 38.2 | 3 | 8.8 | 16 | 47.1 | 0 | 0.0 | 2 | 5.9 | 34 | 100.0 |
| Social Security | 24 | 63.2 | 1 | 2.6 | 9 | 23.7 | 1 | 2.6 | 3 | 7.9 | 38 | 100.0 |
| Labor Reporting Act | 2 | 50.0 | 1 | 25.0 | 1 | 25.0 | 0 | 0.0 | 0 | 0.0 | 4 | 100.0 |
| Railway Labor Act | 8 | 47.1 | 3 | 17.6 | 5 | 29.4 | 0 | 0.0 | 1 | 5.9 | 17 | 100.0 |
| Labor relations acts | 73 | 52.1 | 35 | 25.0 | 27 | 19.3 | 2 | 1.4 | 3 | 2.1 | 140 | 100.0 |
| Other labor | 4 | 40.0 | 1 | 10.0 | 5 | 50.0 | 0 | 0.0 | 0 | 0.0 | 10 | 100.0 |

## 5th Circuit (cont.)

| SUBJECTS | Affirm n | % | Mixed n | % | Reverse n | % | Avoid n | % | Other n | % | Total N | % |
|---|---|---|---|---|---|---|---|---|---|---|---|---|
| TAXATION | 201 | 72.0 | 22 | 7.9 | 50 | 17.9 | 2 | 0.7 | 4 | 1.4 | 279 | 100.0 |
| Income tax | 92 | 67.6 | 14 | 10.3 | 26 | 19.1 | 1 | 0.7 | 3 | 2.2 | 136 | 100.0 |
| Tax fraud | 13 | 72.2 | 2 | 11.1 | 3 | 16.7 | 0 | 0.0 | 0 | 0.0 | 18 | 100.0 |
| Forfeiture and penalty | 7 | 58.3 | 1 | 8.3 | 4 | 33.3 | 0 | 0.0 | 0 | 0.0 | 12 | 100.0 |
| Other tax | 89 | 78.8 | 5 | 4.4 | 17 | 15.0 | 1 | 0.9 | 1 | 0.9 | 113 | 100.0 |
| PERSONAL STATUS | 294 | 56.8 | 11 | 2.1 | 160 | 30.9 | 10 | 1.9 | 43 | 8.3 | 518 | 100.0 |
| Civil rights | 33 | 33.0 | 6 | 6.0 | 39 | 39.0 | 3 | 3.0 | 19 | 19.0 | 100 | 100.0 |
| Immigration and deportation | 7 | 87.5 | 0 | 0.0 | 0 | 0.0 | 0 | 0.0 | 1 | 12.5 | 8 | 100.0 |
| Suffrage | 9 | 22.0 | 1 | 2.4 | 23 | 56.1 | 3 | 7.3 | 5 | 12.2 | 41 | 100.0 |
| Civil rights removals | 11 | 40.7 | 2 | 7.4 | 11 | 40.7 | 0 | 0.0 | 3 | 11.1 | 27 | 100.0 |
| Prisoner petitions | | | | | | | | | | | | |
| Habeas corpus | 142 | 67.6 | 1 | 0.5 | 58 | 27.6 | 2 | 1.0 | 7 | 3.3 | 210 | 100.0 |
| Mandamus | 14 | 56.0 | 0 | 0.0 | 5 | 20.0 | 1 | 4.0 | 5 | 20.0 | 25 | 100.0 |
| Parole review | 2 | 100.0 | 0 | 0.0 | 0 | 0.0 | 0 | 0.0 | 0 | 0.0 | 2 | 100.0 |
| Vacate sentence | 76 | 72.4 | 1 | 1.0 | 24 | 22.9 | 1 | 1.0 | 3 | 2.9 | 105 | 100.0 |
| CRIMES AGAINST PERSONS | 3 | 75.0 | 0 | 0.0 | 1 | 25.0 | 0 | 0.0 | 0 | 0.0 | 4 | 100.0 |
| Homicide | 1 | 50.0 | 0 | 0.0 | 1 | 50.0 | 0 | 0.0 | 0 | 0.0 | 2 | 100.0 |
| Kidnapping | 0 | 0.0 | 0 | 0.0 | 0 | 0.0 | 0 | 0.0 | 0 | 0.0 | 0 | — |
| Rape | 0 | 0.0 | 0 | 0.0 | 0 | 0.0 | 0 | 0.0 | 0 | 0.0 | 0 | — |
| Assault | 2 | 100.0 | 0 | 0.0 | 0 | 0.0 | 0 | 0.0 | 0 | 0.0 | 2 | 100.0 |
| CRIMES AGAINST PROPERTY | 116 | 75.8 | 9 | 5.9 | 25 | 16.3 | 0 | 0.0 | 3 | 2.0 | 153 | 100.0 |
| Robbery | 28 | 73.7 | 2 | 5.3 | 7 | 18.4 | 0 | 0.0 | 1 | 2.6 | 38 | 100.0 |
| Auto theft | 37 | 77.1 | 0 | 0.0 | 11 | 22.9 | 0 | 0.0 | 0 | 0.0 | 48 | 100.0 |
| Extortion | 1 | 100.0 | 0 | 0.0 | 0 | 0.0 | 0 | 0.0 | 0 | 0.0 | 1 | 100.0 |
| Fraud | 25 | 69.4 | 4 | 11.1 | 5 | 13.9 | 0 | 0.0 | 2 | 5.6 | 36 | 100.0 |
| Embezzlement | 5 | 100.0 | 0 | 0.0 | 0 | 0.0 | 0 | 0.0 | 0 | 0.0 | 5 | 100.0 |
| Forgery | 15 | 83.3 | 3 | 16.7 | 0 | 0.0 | 0 | 0.0 | 0 | 0.0 | 18 | 100.0 |
| Other property crimes | 5 | 71.4 | 0 | 0.0 | 2 | 28.6 | 0 | 0.0 | 0 | 0.0 | 7 | 100.0 |
| MORALS OFFENSES | 33 | 80.5 | 1 | 2.4 | 6 | 14.6 | 0 | 0.0 | 1 | 2.4 | 41 | 100.0 |
| Narcotics | 25 | 86.2 | 0 | 0.0 | 4 | 13.8 | 0 | 0.0 | 0 | 0.0 | 29 | 100.0 |
| White slave | 6 | 75.0 | 0 | 0.0 | 1 | 12.5 | 0 | 0.0 | 1 | 12.5 | 8 | 100.0 |
| Other sex | 0 | 0.0 | 0 | 0.0 | 0 | 0.0 | 0 | 0.0 | 0 | 0.0 | 0 | — |

## 5th Circuit (cont.)

| SUBJECTS | Affirm n | % | Mixed n | % | Reverse n | % | Avoid n | % | Other n | % | Total N | % |
|---|---|---|---|---|---|---|---|---|---|---|---|---|
| Obscenity (mail) | 0 | 0.0 | 0 | 0.0 | 0 | 0.0 | 0 | 0.0 | 0 | 0.0 | 0 | — |
| Gambling | 2 | 50.0 | 1 | 25.0 | 1 | 25.0 | 0 | 0.0 | 0 | 0.0 | 4 | 100.0 |
| MISCELLANEOUS OFFENSES | 17 | 68.0 | 0 | 0.0 | 7 | 28.0 | 0 | 0.0 | 1 | 4.0 | 25 | 100.0 |
| Escape | 1 | 100.0 | 0 | 0.0 | 0 | 0.0 | 0 | 0.0 | 0 | 0.0 | 1 | 100.0 |
| Weapons | 4 | 44.4 | 0 | 0.0 | 5 | 55.6 | 0 | 0.0 | 0 | 0.0 | 9 | 100.0 |
| Migratory birds | 1 | 100.0 | 0 | 0.0 | 0 | 0.0 | 0 | 0.0 | 0 | 0.0 | 1 | 100.0 |
| Selective Service | 7 | 100.0 | 0 | 0.0 | 0 | 0.0 | 0 | 0.0 | 0 | 0.0 | 7 | 100.0 |
| Bribery | 2 | 100.0 | 0 | 0.0 | 0 | 0.0 | 0 | 0.0 | 0 | 0.0 | 2 | 100.0 |
| Perjury | 2 | 40.0 | 0 | 0.0 | 2 | 40.0 | 0 | 0.0 | 1 | 20.0 | 5 | 100.0 |
| OTHER | 115 | 73.7 | 3 | 1.9 | 27 | 17.3 | 3 | 1.9 | 8 | 5.1 | 156 | 100.0 |
| Sums | 1,436 | 63.9 | 135 | 6.0 | 548 | 24.4 | 33 | 1.5 | 96 | 4.3 | 2,248 | 100.0 |

NOTE: Slight discrepancies in percentages are caused by rounding error.

## Appendix 4 (cont.)
## Subjects of Circuit Court Decisions after Hearing or Submission, FY 1965-1967
## D.C. Circuit
(N = 1,336)

| SUBJECTS | Affirm n | % | Mixed n | % | Reverse n | % | Avoid n | % | Other n | % | Total N | % |
|---|---|---|---|---|---|---|---|---|---|---|---|---|
| CONTRACTS | 95 | 69.3 | 7 | 5.1 | 25 | 18.2 | 6 | 4.4 | 4 | 2.9 | 137 | 100.0 |
| Insurance | 12 | 66.7 | 1 | 5.6 | 5 | 27.8 | 0 | 0.0 | 0 | 0.0 | 18 | 100.0 |
| Marine | 1 | 100.0 | 0 | 0.0 | 0 | 0.0 | 0 | 0.0 | 0 | 0.0 | 1 | 100.0 |
| Negotiable instruments | 2 | 40.0 | 1 | 20.0 | 1 | 20.0 | 0 | 0.0 | 1 | 20.0 | 5 | 100.0 |
| Real property | 28 | 75.7 | 0 | 0.0 | 5 | 13.5 | 4 | 10.8 | 0 | 0.0 | 37 | 100.0 |
| Recovery and enforcement | 8 | 72.7 | 1 | 9.1 | 1 | 9.1 | 1 | 9.1 | 0 | 0.0 | 11 | 100.0 |
| Other contracts | 44 | 67.7 | 4 | 6.2 | 13 | 20.0 | 1 | 1.5 | 3 | 4.6 | 65 | 100.0 |
| TORTS | 61 | 64.2 | 3 | 3.2 | 25 | 26.3 | 1 | 1.1 | 5 | 5.3 | 95 | 100.0 |
| Marine-personal injury | 3 | 100.0 | 0 | 0.0 | 0 | 0.0 | 0 | 0.0 | 0 | 0.0 | 3 | 100.0 |
| Motor vehicle-personal injury | 8 | 53.3 | 1 | 6.7 | 5 | 33.3 | 1 | 6.7 | 0 | 0.0 | 15 | 100.0 |
| Other personal injury | 21 | 65.6 | 1 | 3.1 | 8 | 25.0 | 0 | 0.0 | 2 | 6.3 | 32 | 100.0 |
| Employer liability | 3 | 37.5 | 0 | 0.0 | 5 | 62.5 | 0 | 0.0 | 0 | 0.0 | 8 | 100.0 |
| Other torts | 26 | 70.3 | 1 | 2.7 | 7 | 18.9 | 0 | 0.0 | 3 | 8.1 | 37 | 100.0 |
| COMMERCE | 131 | 70.8 | 6 | 3.2 | 31 | 16.8 | 5 | 2.7 | 12 | 6.5 | 185 | 100.0 |
| Antitrust | 2 | 40.0 | 0 | 0.0 | 3 | 60.0 | 0 | 0.0 | 0 | 0.0 | 5 | 100.0 |
| Agriculture | 1 | 33.3 | 1 | 33.3 | 0 | 0.0 | 0 | 0.0 | 1 | 33.3 | 3 | 100.0 |
| Bankruptcy | 0 | 0.0 | 0 | 0.0 | 0 | 0.0 | 0 | 0.0 | 0 | 0.0 | 0 | — |
| Food and drug | 3 | 100.0 | 0 | 0.0 | 0 | 0.0 | 0 | 0.0 | 0 | 0.0 | 3 | 100.0 |
| Patents | 19 | 70.4 | 0 | 0.0 | 7 | 25.9 | 0 | 0.0 | 1 | 3.7 | 27 | 100.0 |
| Copyright | 5 | 100.0 | 0 | 0.0 | 0 | 0.0 | 0 | 0.0 | 0 | 0.0 | 5 | 100.0 |
| Other commerce | 101 | 71.1 | 5 | 3.5 | 21 | 14.8 | 5 | 3.5 | 10 | 7.0 | 142 | 100.0 |
| LABOR | 58 | 59.8 | 12 | 12.4 | 15 | 15.5 | 9 | 9.3 | 3 | 3.1 | 97 | 100.0 |
| Fair Labor Standards Act | 2 | 40.0 | 0 | 0.0 | 1 | 20.0 | 2 | 40.0 | 0 | 0.0 | 5 | 100.0 |
| Social Security | 0 | 0.0 | 0 | 0.0 | 1 | 100.0 | 0 | 0.0 | 0 | 0.0 | 1 | 100.0 |
| Labor Reporting Act | 2 | 50.0 | 0 | 0.0 | 1 | 25.0 | 0 | 0.0 | 1 | 25.0 | 4 | 100.0 |
| Railway Labor Act | 7 | 53.8 | 2 | 15.4 | 1 | 7.7 | 2 | 15.4 | 1 | 7.7 | 13 | 100.0 |
| Labor relations acts | 44 | 62.9 | 10 | 14.3 | 11 | 15.7 | 4 | 5.7 | 1 | 1.4 | 70 | 100.0 |
| Other labor | 3 | 75.0 | 0 | 0.0 | 0 | 0.0 | 1 | 25.0 | 0 | 0.0 | 4 | 100.0 |
| TAXATION | 19 | 57.6 | 1 | 3.0 | 7 | 21.2 | 4 | 12.1 | 2 | 6.1 | 33 | 100.0 |
| Income tax | 9 | 45.0 | 1 | 5.0 | 5 | 25.0 | 3 | 15.0 | 2 | 10.0 | 20 | 100.0 |
| Tax fraud | 2 | 100.0 | 0 | 0.0 | 0 | 0.0 | 0 | 0.0 | 0 | 0.0 | 2 | 100.0 |

## D.C. Circuit (cont.)

| SUBJECTS | Affirm n | % | Mixed n | % | Reverse n | % | Avoid n | % | Other n | % | Total N | % |
|---|---|---|---|---|---|---|---|---|---|---|---|---|
| Forfeiture and penalty | 1 | 100.0 | 0 | 0.0 | 0 | 0.0 | 0 | 0.0 | 0 | 0.0 | 1 | 100.0 |
| Other tax | 7 | 70.0 | 0 | 0.0 | 2 | 20.0 | 1 | 10.0 | 0 | 0.0 | 10 | 100.0 |
| PERSONAL STATUS | 73 | 60.3 | 1 | 0.8 | 33 | 27.3 | 8 | 6.6 | 6 | 5.0 | 121 | 100.0 |
| Civil rights | 1 | 50.0 | 0 | 0.0 | 0 | 0.0 | 0 | 0.0 | 1 | 50.0 | 2 | 100.0 |
| Immigration and deportation | 2 | 66.7 | 0 | 0.0 | 1 | 33.3 | 0 | 0.0 | 0 | 0.0 | 3 | 100.0 |
| Suffrage | 1 | 50.0 | 0 | 0.0 | 0 | 0.0 | 1 | 50.0 | 0 | 0.0 | 2 | 100.0 |
| Civil rights removals | 0 | 0.0 | 0 | 0.0 | 0 | 0.0 | 0 | 0.0 | 0 | 0.0 | 0 | — |
| Prisoner petitions | | | | | | | | | | | | |
| Habeas corpus | 18 | 48.6 | 0 | 0.0 | 13 | 35.1 | 5 | 13.5 | 1 | 2.7 | 37 | 100.0 |
| Mandamus | 13 | 48.1 | 1 | 3.7 | 11 | 40.7 | 1 | 3.7 | 1 | 3.7 | 27 | 100.0 |
| Parole review | 10 | 62.5 | 0 | 0.0 | 4 | 25.0 | 1 | 6.3 | 1 | 6.3 | 16 | 100.0 |
| Vacate sentence | 28 | 82.4 | 0 | 0.0 | 4 | 11.8 | 0 | 0.0 | 2 | 5.9 | 34 | 100.0 |
| CRIMES AGAINST PERSONS | 81 | 69.2 | 2 | 1.7 | 25 | 21.4 | 3 | 2.6 | 6 | 5.1 | 117 | 100.0 |
| Homicide | 33 | 73.3 | 1 | 2.2 | 8 | 17.8 | 1 | 2.2 | 2 | 4.4 | 45 | 100.0 |
| Kidnapping | 0 | 0.0 | 0 | 0.0 | 0 | 0.0 | 0 | 0.0 | 0 | 0.0 | 0 | — |
| Rape | 13 | 68.4 | 0 | 0.0 | 5 | 26.3 | 0 | 0.0 | 1 | 5.3 | 19 | 100.0 |
| Assault | 35 | 66.0 | 1 | 1.9 | 12 | 22.6 | 2 | 3.8 | 3 | 5.7 | 53 | 100.0 |
| CRIMES AGAINST PROPERTY | 205 | 82.0 | 5 | 2.0 | 27 | 10.8 | 3 | 1.2 | 10 | 4.0 | 250 | 100.0 |
| Robbery | 176 | 83.0 | 3 | 1.4 | 21 | 9.9 | 2 | 0.9 | 10 | 4.7 | 212 | 100.0 |
| Auto theft | 16 | 84.2 | 0 | 0.0 | 3 | 15.8 | 0 | 0.0 | 0 | 0.0 | 19 | 100.0 |
| Extortion | 1 | 100.0 | 0 | 0.0 | 0 | 0.0 | 0 | 0.0 | 0 | 0.0 | 1 | 100.0 |
| Fraud | 7 | 70.0 | 1 | 10.0 | 1 | 10.0 | 1 | 10.0 | 0 | 0.0 | 10 | 100.0 |
| Embezzlement | 0 | 0.0 | 0 | 0.0 | 1 | 100.0 | 0 | 0.0 | 0 | 0.0 | 1 | 100.0 |
| Forgery | 4 | 66.7 | 1 | 16.7 | 1 | 16.7 | 0 | 0.0 | 0 | 0.0 | 6 | 100.0 |
| Other property crimes | 1 | 100.0 | 0 | 0.0 | 0 | 0.0 | 0 | 0.0 | 0 | 0.0 | 1 | 100.0 |
| MORALS OFFENSES | 75 | 81.5 | 0 | 0.0 | 14 | 15.2 | 0 | 0.0 | 3 | 3.3 | 92 | 100.0 |
| Narcotics | 65 | 79.3 | 0 | 0.0 | 14 | 17.1 | 0 | 0.0 | 3 | 3.7 | 82 | 100.0 |
| White slave | 0 | 0.0 | 0 | 0.0 | 0 | 0.0 | 0 | 0.0 | 0 | 0.0 | 0 | — |
| Other sex | 4 | 100.0 | 0 | 0.0 | 0 | 0.0 | 0 | 0.0 | 0 | 0.0 | 4 | 100.0 |
| Obscenity (mail) | 1 | 100.0 | 0 | 0.0 | 0 | 0.0 | 0 | 0.0 | 0 | 0.0 | 1 | 100.0 |
| Gambling | 5 | 100.0 | 0 | 0.0 | 0 | 0.0 | 0 | 0.0 | 0 | 0.0 | 5 | 100.0 |

## D.C. Circuit (cont.)

| SUBJECTS | Affirm n | % | Mixed n | % | Reverse n | % | Avoid n | % | Other n | % | Total N | % |
|---|---|---|---|---|---|---|---|---|---|---|---|---|
| MISCELLANEOUS OFFENSES | 15 | 78.9 | 0 | 0.0 | 4 | 21.1 | 0 | 0.0 | 0 | 0.0 | 19 | 100.0 |
| Escape | 1 | 100.0 | 0 | 0.0 | 0 | 0.0 | 0 | 0.0 | 0 | 0.0 | 1 | 100.0 |
| Weapons | 10 | 90.9 | 0 | 0.0 | 1 | 9.1 | 0 | 0.0 | 0 | 0.0 | 11 | 100.0 |
| Migratory birds | 0 | 0.0 | 0 | 0.0 | 0 | 0.0 | 0 | 0.0 | 0 | 0.0 | 0 | — |
| Selective Service | 0 | 0.0 | 0 | 0.0 | 0 | 0.0 | 0 | 0.0 | 0 | 0.0 | 0 | — |
| Bribery | 3 | 75.0 | 0 | 0.0 | 1 | 25.0 | 0 | 0.0 | 0 | 0.0 | 4 | 100.0 |
| Perjury | 1 | 33.3 | 0 | 0.0 | 2 | 66.7 | 0 | 0.0 | 0 | 0.0 | 3 | 100.0 |
| LOCAL | 34 | 63.0 | 0 | 0.0 | 9 | 16.7 | 5 | 9.3 | 6 | 11.1 | 54 | 100.0 |
| Domestic relations | 1 | 20.0 | 0 | 0.0 | 2 | 40.0 | 2 | 40.0 | 0 | 0.0 | 5 | 100.0 |
| Traffic | 0 | 0.0 | 0 | 0.0 | 1 | 100.0 | 0 | 0.0 | 0 | 0.0 | 1 | 100.0 |
| Other D.C. cases | 33 | 68.8 | 0 | 0.0 | 6 | 12.5 | 3 | 6.3 | 6 | 12.5 | 48 | 100.0 |
| OTHER | 74 | 54.4 | 2 | 1.5 | 47 | 34.6 | 4 | 2.9 | 9 | 6.6 | 136 | 100.0 |
| Sums | 921 | 68.9 | 39 | 2.9 | 262 | 19.6 | 48 | 3.6 | 66 | 4.9 | 1,336 | 100.0 |

NOTE: Slight discrepancies in percentages are caused by rounding error.

## Appendix 5
### Sources of Supreme Court Decisions, FY 1965-1967
### 2d Circuit
### (N = 1,359)

| SOURCES | No Appeal n | No Appeal % | Appeal Declined n | Appeal Declined % | Affirm Circuit n | Affirm Circuit % | Mixed Circuit n | Mixed Circuit % | Reverse Circuit n | Reverse Circuit % | Avoid Circuit n | Avoid Circuit % | Other (Dismiss) n | Other (Dismiss) % | Total N | Total % |
|---|---|---|---|---|---|---|---|---|---|---|---|---|---|---|---|---|
| U.S. District Courts | 757 | 68.1 | 314 | 28.2 | 9 | 0.8 | | | 23 | 2.1 | 1 | 0.1 | 8 | 0.7 | 1,112 | 100.0 |
| Connecticut | 58 | 68.2 | 21 | 24.7 | 1 | 1.2 | | | 4 | 4.7 | | | 1 | 1.2 | 85 | 100.0 |
| New York | | | | | | | | | | | | | | | | |
| Northern | 41 | 71.9 | 15 | 26.3 | | | | | 1 | 1.8 | | | | | 57 | 100.0 |
| Eastern | 100 | 70.9 | 37 | 26.2 | 1 | 0.7 | | | 1 | 0.7 | | | 2 | 1.4 | 141 | 100.0 |
| Southern | 505 | 66.7 | 223 | 29.5 | 6 | 0.8 | | | 17 | 2.2 | 1 | 0.1 | 5 | 0.7 | 757 | 100.0 |
| Western | 32 | 68.1 | 14 | 30.0 | 1 | 2.1 | | | | | | | | | 47 | 100.0 |
| Vermont | 21 | 84.0 | 4 | 16.0 | | | | | | | | | | | 25 | 100.0 |
| Boards and Commissions | 149 | 76.0 | 41 | 20.9 | 2 | 1.0 | | | 4 | 2.0 | | | | | 196 | 100.0 |
| U.S. Tax Court | 44 | 66.7 | 19 | 28.8 | 1 | 1.5 | | | 2 | 3.0 | | | | | 66 | 100.0 |
| NLRB | 77 | 87.5 | 11 | 12.5 | | | | | | | | | | | 88 | 100.0 |
| CAB | 0 | — | 1 | 100.0 | | | | | | | | | | | 1 | 100.0 |
| FCC | 1 | 100.0 | 0 | — | | | | | | | | | | | 1 | 100.0 |
| FPC | 1 | 50.0 | 1 | 50.0 | | | | | | | | | | | 2 | 100.0 |
| FTC | 0 | — | 1 | 100.0 | | | | | | | | | | | 1 | 100.0 |
| Secretary of Agriculture | 0 | — | 0 | — | | | | | | | | | | | 0 | — |
| SEC | 2 | 100.0 | 0 | — | | | | | | | | | | | 2 | 100.0 |
| INS | 4 | 50.0 | 1 | 12.5 | 1 | 12.5 | | | 2 | 25.0 | | | | | 8 | 100.0 |
| Other boards and commissions | 20 | 74.1 | 7 | 25.9 | | | | | | | | | | | 27 | 100.0 |
| Original Proceedings | 50 | 98.0 | 0 | — | | | | | 1 | 2.0 | | | | | 51 | 100.0 |
| Other | 0 | — | 0 | — | | | | | | | | | | | 0 | — |
| Sums | 956 | 70.3 | 355 | 26.1 | 11 | 0.8 | 0 | — | 28 | 2.1 | 1 | 0.1 | 8 | 0.6 | 1,359 | 100.0 |

NOTE: Slight discrepancies in percentages are caused by rounding errors.

**Appendix 5** (cont.)

Sources of Supreme Court Decisions, FY 1965-1967
5th Circuit
(N = 2,249)

| SOURCES | No Appeal n | % | Appeal Declined n | % | Affirm Circuit n | % | Mixed Circuit n | % | Reverse Circuit n | % | Avoid Circuit n | % | Other (Dismiss) n | % | Total N | % |
|---|---|---|---|---|---|---|---|---|---|---|---|---|---|---|---|---|
| U.S. District Courts | 1,586 | 80.1 | 364 | 18.4 | 9 | 0.5 | 4 | 0.2 | 14 | 0.7 | | | 2 | 0.1 | 1,979 | 100.0 |
| Alabama | | | | | | | | | | | | | | | | |
| Northern | 66 | 89.2 | 7 | 9.5 | | | | | 1 | 1.4 | | | | | 74 | 100.0 |
| Middle | 45 | 75.0 | 14 | 23.3 | | | | | 1 | 1.7 | | | | | 60 | 100.0 |
| Southern | 49 | 89.1 | 6 | 10.9 | | | | | | | | | | | 55 | 100.0 |
| Florida | | | | | | | | | | | | | | | | |
| Northern | 32 | 84.2 | 6 | 15.8 | | | | | | | | | | | 38 | 100.0 |
| Middle | 152 | 80.9 | 33 | 17.6 | 2 | 1.1 | | | 1 | 0.5 | | | | | 188 | 100.0 |
| Southern | 198 | 76.7 | 53 | 20.5 | 1 | 0.4 | 1 | 0.4 | 5 | 1.9 | | | | | 258 | 100.0 |
| Georgia | | | | | | | | | | | | | | | | |
| Northern | 115 | 83.3 | 20 | 14.5 | 2 | 1.4 | | | 1 | 0.7 | | | | | 138 | 100.0 |
| Middle | 60 | 75.9 | 19 | 24.1 | | | | | | | | | | | 79 | 100.0 |
| Southern | 66 | 91.7 | 6 | 8.3 | | | | | | | | | | | 72 | 100.0 |
| Louisiana | | | | | | | | | | | | | | | | |
| Eastern | 170 | 78.3 | 44 | 20.3 | 1 | 0.5 | | | 1 | 0.5 | | | 1 | 0.5 | 217 | 100.0 |
| Western | 75 | 82.4 | 16 | 17.6 | | | | | | | | | | | 91 | 100.0 |
| Mississippi | | | | | | | | | | | | | | | | |
| Northern | 42 | 82.4 | 8 | 15.7 | | | | | 1 | 2.0 | | | | | 51 | 100.0 |
| Southern | 98 | 87.5 | 13 | 11.6 | | | 1 | 0.9 | | | | | | | 112 | 100.0 |

| | | | | | | | | | | | | | | |
|---|---|---|---|---|---|---|---|---|---|---|---|---|---|---|
| Texas | | | | | | | | | | | | | | |
| Northern | 148 | 83.6 | 24 | 13.6 | 1 | 0.6 | 1 | 0.6 | 2 | 1.1 | 1 | 0.6 | 177 | 100.0 |
| Eastern | 49 | 74.2 | 16 | 24.2 | — | — | 1 | 1.5 | — | — | — | — | 66 | 100.0 |
| Southern | 137 | 67.5 | 65 | 32.0 | 1 | 0.5 | — | — | — | — | — | — | 203 | 100.0 |
| Western | 79 | 84.0 | 13 | 13.8 | 1 | 1.1 | — | — | 1 | 1.1 | — | — | 94 | 100.0 |
| Canal Zone | 5 | 83.3 | 1 | 16.7 | — | — | — | — | — | — | — | — | 6 | 100.0 |
| *Boards and Commissions* | 170 | 77.6 | 41 | 18.7 | 2 | 0.9 | — | — | 6 | 2.7 | — | — | 219 | 100.0 |
| U.S. Tax Court | 47 | 74.6 | 16 | 25.4 | — | — | — | — | — | — | — | — | 63 | 100.0 |
| NLRB | 95 | 81.9 | 18 | 15.5 | 1 | 0.9 | — | — | 2 | 1.7 | — | — | 116 | 100.0 |
| CAB | 0 | — | 0 | — | — | — | — | — | — | — | — | — | 0 | — |
| FCC | 0 | — | 0 | — | — | — | — | — | — | — | — | — | 0 | — |
| FPC | 1 | 20.0 | 0 | — | 1 | 20.0 | — | — | 3 | 60.0 | — | — | 5 | 100.0 |
| FTC | 1 | 50.0 | 0 | — | — | — | — | — | 1 | 50.0 | — | — | 2 | 100.0 |
| Secretary of Agriculture | 0 | — | 0 | — | — | — | — | — | — | — | — | — | 0 | — |
| SEC | 0 | — | 0 | — | — | — | — | — | — | — | — | — | 0 | — |
| INS | 1 | 100.0 | 0 | — | — | — | — | — | — | — | — | — | 1 | 100.0 |
| Other boards and commissions | 25 | 78.1 | 7 | 21.9 | — | — | — | — | — | — | — | — | 32 | 100.0 |
| *Original Proceedings* | 47 | 100.0 | 0 | — | — | — | — | — | — | — | — | — | 47 | 100.0 |
| *Other* | 2 | 50.0 | 2 | 50.0 | — | — | — | — | — | — | — | — | 4 | 100.0 |
| *Sums* | 1,805 | 80.3 | 407 | 18.1 | 11 | 0.5 | 4 | 0.2 | 20 | 0.9 | 2 | 0.1 | 2,249 | 100.0 |

NOTE: Slight discrepancies in percentages are caused by rounding error.

## Appendix 5 (cont.)
### Sources of Supreme Court Decisions, FY 1965-1967
### D.C. Circuit
### (N = 1,337)

| SOURCES | No Appeal n | No Appeal % | Appeal Declined n | Appeal Declined % | Affirm Circuit n | Affirm Circuit % | Mixed Circuit n | Mixed Circuit % | Reverse Circuit n | Reverse Circuit % | Avoid Circuit n | Avoid Circuit % | Other (Dismiss) n | Other (Dismiss) % | Total N | Total % |
|---|---|---|---|---|---|---|---|---|---|---|---|---|---|---|---|---|
| U.S. District Courts | 932 | 89.4 | 100 | 9.6 | 2 | 0.2 | 1 | 0.1 | 7 | 0.7 | | | 1 | 0.1 | 1,043 | 100.0 |
| U.S. jurisdiction | 677 | 91.5 | 54 | 7.3 | 1 | 0.1 | 1 | 0.1 | 6 | 0.8 | | | 1 | 0.1 | 740 | 100.0 |
| D.C. jurisdiction | 255 | 84.2 | 46 | 15.2 | 1 | 0.3 | | | 1 | 0.3 | | | | | 303 | 100.0 |
| Boards and Commissions | 179 | 82.5 | 31 | 14.3 | 1 | 0.5 | | | 6 | 2.8 | | | | | 217 | 100.0 |
| U.S. Tax Court | 4 | 80.0 | 1 | 20.0 | | | | | | | | | | | 5 | 100.0 |
| NLRB | 49 | 79.0 | 13 | 21.0 | | | | | | | | | | | 62 | 100.0 |
| CAB | 19 | 79.2 | 5 | 20.8 | | | | | | | | | | | 24 | 100.0 |
| FCC | 52 | 86.7 | 7 | 11.7 | 1 | 1.7 | | | | | | | | | 60 | 100.0 |
| FPC | 6 | 75.0 | 0 | — | | | | | 2 | 25.0 | | | | | 8 | 100.0 |
| FTC | 5 | 62.5 | 2 | 25.0 | | | | | 1 | 12.5 | | | | | 8 | 100.0 |
| Secretary of Agriculture | 0 | — | 1 | 100.0 | | | | | | | | | | | 1 | 100.0 |
| SEC | 3 | 100.0 | 0 | — | | | | | | | | | | | 3 | 100.0 |
| INS | 1 | 100.0 | 0 | — | | | | | | | | | | | 1 | 100.0 |
| Other boards and commissions | 40 | 88.9 | 2 | 4.4 | | | | | 3 | 6.7 | | | | | 45 | 100.0 |
| Other D.C. agencies | 29 | 90.6 | 3 | 9.4 | | | | | | | | | | | 32 | 100.0 |
| Original Proceedings | 31 | 88.6 | 4 | 11.4 | | | | | | | | | | | 35 | 100.0 |
| Other | 9 | 90.0 | 1 | 10.0 | | | | | | | | | | | 10 | 100.0 |
| Sums | 1,180 | 88.3 | 139 | 10.4 | 3 | 0.2 | 1 | 0.1 | 13 | 1.0 | 0 | — | 1 | 0.1 | 1,337 | 100.0 |

NOTE: Slight discrepancies in percentages are caused by rounding error.

## Appendix 6
### Subjects of Supreme Court Decisions, FY 1965-1967
### 2d Circuit
### (N = 1,359)

| SUBJECTS | No Appeal n | % | Appeal Declined n | % | Affirm Circuit n | % | Mixed Circuit n | % | Reverse Circuit n | % | Avoid Circuit n | % | Other (Dismiss) n | % | Total N | % |
|---|---|---|---|---|---|---|---|---|---|---|---|---|---|---|---|---|
| CONTRACTS | 102 | 81.0 | 21 | 16.7 | 1 | 0.8 | | | 1 | 0.8 | | | 1 | 0.8 | 126 | 100.0 |
| Insurance | 13 | 72.2 | 5 | 27.8 | | | | | | | | | | | 18 | 100.0 |
| Marine | 12 | 80.0 | 3 | 20.0 | | | | | | | | | | | 15 | 100.0 |
| Negotiable instruments | 3 | 100.0 | 0 | — | | | | | | | | | | | 3 | 100.0 |
| Real property | 11 | 91.7 | 1 | 8.3 | | | | | | | | | | | 12 | 100.0 |
| Recovery and enforcement | 9 | 81.8 | 2 | 18.2 | | | | | | | | | | | 11 | 100.0 |
| Other contracts | 54 | 80.6 | 10 | 14.9 | 1 | 1.5 | | | 1 | 1.5 | | | 1 | 1.5 | 67 | 100.0 |
| TORTS | 134 | 71.7 | 49 | 26.2 | 1 | 0.5 | | | 3 | 1.6 | | | | | 187 | 100.0 |
| Marine-personal injury | 34 | 73.9 | 10 | 21.7 | | | | | 2 | 4.3 | | | | | 46 | 100.0 |
| Motor vehicle-personal injury | 17 | 94.4 | 1 | 5.6 | | | | | | | | | | | 18 | 100.0 |
| Other personal injury | 27 | 65.9 | 12 | 29.3 | 1 | 2.4 | | | 1 | 2.4 | | | | | 41 | 100.0 |
| Employer liability | 7 | 63.6 | 4 | 36.4 | | | | | | | | | | | 11 | 100.0 |
| Other torts | 49 | 69.0 | 22 | 31.0 | | | | | | | | | | | 71 | 100.0 |
| COMMERCE | 165 | 74.3 | 49 | 22.1 | 4 | 1.8 | | | 2 | 0.9 | | | 2 | 0.9 | 222 | 100.0 |
| Antitrust | 8 | 57.1 | 4 | 28.6 | 1 | 7.1 | | | 1 | 7.1 | | | | | 14 | 100.0 |
| Agriculture | 1 | 25.0 | 3 | 75.0 | | | | | | | | | | | 4 | 100.0 |
| Bankruptcy | 78 | 92.9 | 5 | 6.0 | 1 | 1.2 | | | | | | | | | 84 | 100.0 |
| Food and drug | 1 | 25.0 | 1 | 25.0 | 2 | 50.0 | | | | | | | | | 4 | 100.0 |
| Patents | 10 | 71.4 | 4 | 28.6 | | | | | | | | | | | 14 | 100.0 |
| Copyright | 16 | 64.0 | 6 | 24.0 | | | | | 1 | 4.0 | | | 2 | 8.0 | 25 | 100.0 |
| Other commerce | 51 | 66.2 | 26 | 33.8 | | | | | | | | | | | 77 | 100.0 |

## 2d Circuit (cont.)

| SUBJECTS | No Appeal n | % | Appeal Declined n | % | Affirm Circuit n | % | Mixed Circuit n | % | Reverse Circuit n | % | Avoid Circuit n | % | Other (Dismiss) n | % | Total N | % |
|---|---|---|---|---|---|---|---|---|---|---|---|---|---|---|---|---|
| LABOR | 126 | 80.8 | 28 | 17.9 | | | | | 2 | 1.3 | | | | | 156 | 100.0 |
| Fair Labor Standards Act | 1 | 100.0 | 0 | — | | | | | | | | | | | 1 | 100.0 |
| Social Security | 10 | 83.3 | 2 | 16.7 | | | | | | | | | | | 12 | 100.0 |
| Labor Reporting Act | 10 | 90.9 | 1 | 9.1 | | | | | | | | | | | 11 | 100.0 |
| Railway Labor Act | 4 | 80.0 | 1 | 20.0 | | | | | | | | | | | 5 | 100.0 |
| Labor relations acts | 91 | 79.8 | 22 | 19.3 | | | | | 1 | 0.9 | | | | | 114 | 100.0 |
| Other labor | 10 | 76.9 | 2 | 15.4 | | | | | 1 | 7.7 | | | | | 13 | 100.0 |
| TAXATION | 99 | 67.3 | 37 | 25.2 | 2 | 1.4 | | | 7 | 4.8 | | | 2 | 1.4 | 147 | 100.0 |
| Income tax | 62 | 70.5 | 23 | 26.1 | 1 | 1.1 | | | 2 | 2.3 | | | | | 88 | 100.0 |
| Tax fraud | 7 | 50.0 | 6 | 36.7 | | | | | 1 | 7.1 | | | | | 14 | 100.0 |
| Forfeiture and penalty | 0 | — | 0 | — | | | | | | | | | | | 0 | — |
| Other tax | 30 | 66.7 | 8 | 17.8 | 1 | 2.2 | | | 4 | 8.9 | | | 2 | 4.4 | 45 | 100.0 |
| PERSONAL STATUS | 110 | 62.9 | 56 | 32.0 | 3 | 1.7 | | | 6 | 3.4 | | | | | 175 | 100.0 |
| Civil rights | 8 | 72.7 | 2 | 18.2 | | | | | 1 | 9.1 | | | | | 11 | 100.0 |
| Immigration and deportation | 14 | 60.9 | 5 | 21.7 | 1 | 4.3 | | | 3 | 13.0 | | | | | 23 | 100.0 |
| Suffrage | 1 | 50.0 | 1 | 50.0 | | | | | | | | | | | 2 | 100.0 |
| Civil rights removals | 2 | 66.7 | 1 | 33.3 | | | | | | | | | | | 3 | 100.0 |
| Prisoner petitions | | | | | | | | | | | | | | | | |
| Habeas corpus | 61 | 61.6 | 34 | 34.3 | 2 | 2.0 | | | 2 | 2.0 | | | | | 99 | 100.0 |
| Mandamus | 5 | 55.6 | 4 | 44.4 | | | | | | | | | | | 9 | 100.0 |
| Parole review | 3 | 100.0 | 0 | — | | | | | | | | | | | 3 | 100.0 |
| Vacate sentence | 16 | 64.0 | 9 | 36.0 | | | | | | | | | | | 25 | 100.0 |
| CRIMES AGAINST PERSONS | 1 | 25.0 | 3 | 75.0 | | | | | | | | | | | 4 | 100.0 |
| Homicide | 0 | — | 0 | — | | | | | | | | | | | 0 | — |
| Kidnapping | 0 | — | 0 | — | | | | | | | | | | | 0 | — |

|  | C1 | % | C2 | % | C3 | % | C4 | % | C5 | % | C6 | % | Total | % |
|---|---|---|---|---|---|---|---|---|---|---|---|---|---|---|
| Rape | 0 | — | 0 | — |  |  |  |  |  |  |  |  | 0 | — |
| Assault | 1 | 25.0 | 3 | 75.0 |  |  |  |  |  |  |  |  | 4 | 100.0 |
| **CRIMES AGAINST PROPERTY** | 44 | 59.5 | 28 | 37.8 | 1 | 1.4 | 1 | 1.4 |  |  |  |  | 74 | 100.0 |
| Robbery | 21 | 60.0 | 13 | 37.1 | 1 | 2.9 |  |  |  |  |  |  | 35 | 100.0 |
| Auto theft | 4 | 100.0 | 0 | — | 0 | — |  |  |  |  |  |  | 4 | 100.0 |
| Extortion | 0 | — | 0 | — | 0 | — |  |  |  |  |  |  | 0 | — |
| Fraud | 8 | 50.0 | 7 | 43.8 | 1 | 6.3 |  |  |  |  |  |  | 16 | 100.0 |
| Embezzlement | 0 | — | 1 | 100.0 |  |  |  |  |  |  |  |  | 1 | 100.0 |
| Forgery | 9 | 64.3 | 5 | 35.7 |  |  |  |  |  |  |  |  | 14 | 100.0 |
| Other property crimes | 2 | 50.0 | 2 | 50.0 |  |  |  |  |  |  |  |  | 4 | 100.0 |
| **MORALS OFFENSES** | 76 | 59.4 | 50 | 39.1 | 2 | 1.6 |  |  |  |  |  |  | 128 | 100.0 |
| Narcotics | 73 | 58.9 | 49 | 39.5 | 2 | 1.6 |  |  |  |  |  |  | 124 | 100.0 |
| White slave | 1 | 100.0 | 0 | — | 0 | — |  |  |  |  |  |  | 1 | 100.0 |
| Other sex | 1 | 100.0 | 0 | — | 0 | — |  |  |  |  |  |  | 1 | 100.0 |
| Obscenity (mail) | 1 | 50.0 | 1 | 50.0 | 0 | — |  |  |  |  |  |  | 2 | 100.0 |
| Gambling | 0 | — | 0 | — | 0 | — |  |  |  |  |  |  | 0 | — |
| **MISCELLANEOUS OFFENSES** | 19 | 51.4 | 15 | 40.5 | 2 | 5.4 | 1 | 2.7 |  |  |  |  | 37 | 100.0 |
| Escape | 1 | 100.0 | 0 | — | 0 | — |  |  |  |  |  |  | 1 | 100.0 |
| Weapons | 0 | — | 0 | — | 0 | — |  |  |  |  |  |  | 0 | — |
| Migratory birds | 0 | — | 0 | — | 0 | — |  |  |  |  |  |  | 0 | — |
| Selective Service | 7 | 70.0 | 3 | 30.0 |  |  |  |  |  |  |  |  | 10 | 100.0 |
| Bribery | 5 | 45.5 | 6 | 54.5 |  |  |  |  | 1 | 9.1 |  |  | 11 | 100.0 |
| Perjury | 6 | 42.9 | 6 | 42.9 | 2 | 14.3 |  |  |  |  |  |  | 14 | 100.0 |
| **OTHER** | 80 | 77.7 | 19 | 18.4 | 2 | 1.9 | 1 | 1.0 |  |  | 1 | 1.0 | 103 | 100.0 |
| **Sums** | 956 | 70.3 | 355 | 26.1 | 11 | 0.8 | 28 | 2.1 | 1 | 0.1 | 8 | 0.6 | 1,359 | 100.0 |

NOTE: Slight discrepancies in percentages are caused by rounding error.

**Appendix 6** (cont.)

Subjects of Supreme Court Decisions, FY 1965-1967

5th Circuit

(N = 2,249)

| SUBJECTS | No Appeal n | % | Appeal Declined n | % | Affirm Circuit n | % | Mixed Circuit n | % | Reverse Circuit n | % | Avoid Circuit n | % | Other (Dismiss) n | % | Total N | % |
|---|---|---|---|---|---|---|---|---|---|---|---|---|---|---|---|---|
| CONTRACTS | 252 | 86.6 | 38 | 13.1 | 1 | 0.3 | | | | | | | | | 291 | 100.0 |
| Insurance | 108 | 91.5 | 10 | 8.5 | | | | | | | | | | | 118 | 100.0 |
| Marine | 11 | 78.6 | 3 | 21.4 | | | | | | | | | | | 14 | 100.0 |
| Negotiable instruments | 6 | 85.7 | 0 | — | 1 | 14.3 | | | | | | | | | 7 | 100.0 |
| Real property | 39 | 78.0 | 11 | 22.0 | | | | | | | | | | | 50 | 100.0 |
| Recovery and enforcement | 14 | 77.8 | 4 | 22.2 | | | | | | | | | | | 18 | 100.0 |
| Other contracts | 74 | 88.1 | 10 | 11.9 | | | | | | | | | | | 84 | 100.0 |
| TORTS | 274 | 82.3 | 54 | 16.2 | 3 | 0.9 | | | 1 | 0.3 | | | 1 | 0.3 | 333 | 100.0 |
| Marine-personal injury | 53 | 74.6 | 16 | 22.5 | 1 | 1.4 | | | | | | | 1 | 1.4 | 71 | 100.0 |
| Motor vehicle- personal injury | 49 | 87.5 | 6 | 10.7 | | | | | 1 | 1.8 | | | | | 56 | 100.0 |
| Other personal injury | 58 | 86.6 | 9 | 13.4 | | | | | | | | | | | 67 | 100.0 |
| Employer liability | 32 | 76.2 | 10 | 23.8 | | | | | | | | | | | 42 | 100.0 |
| Other torts | 82 | 84.5 | 13 | 13.4 | 2 | 2.9 | | | | | | | | | 205 | 100.0 |
| COMMERCE | 151 | 73.7 | 45 | 22.0 | 2 | 1.0 | 1 | 0.5 | 6 | 2.9 | | | | | 205 | 100.0 |
| Antitrust | 10 | 52.6 | 9 | 47.4 | | | | | | | | | | | 19 | 100.0 |
| Agriculture | 7 | 77.8 | 2 | 22.2 | | | | | | | | | | | 9 | 100.0 |
| Bankruptcy | 68 | 86.1 | 8 | 10.1 | 1 | 1.3 | 1 | 1.3 | 1 | 1.3 | | | | | 79 | 100.0 |
| Food and drug | 3 | 75.0 | 1 | 25.0 | | | | | | | | | | | 4 | 100.0 |
| Patents | 16 | 61.5 | 10 | 38.5 | | | | | | | | | | | 26 | 100.0 |
| Copyright | 12 | 85.7 | 2 | 14.3 | | | | | | | | | | | 14 | 100.0 |
| Other commerce | 35 | 64.8 | 13 | 24.1 | 1 | 1.9 | | | 5 | 9.3 | | | | | 54 | 100.0 |

| | | | | | | | | | | | |
|---|---|---|---|---|---|---|---|---|---|---|---|
| LABOR | 207 | 84.8 | 32 | 13.1 | 3 | 1.2 | | | 2 | 0.8 | 244 | 100.0 |
| Fair Labor Standards Act | 32 | 94.1 | 2 | 5.9 | | | | | | | 34 | 100.0 |
| Social Security | 37 | 97.4 | 1 | 2.6 | | | | | | | 38 | 100.0 |
| Labor Reporting Act | 4 | 100.0 | 0 | — | | | | | | | 4 | 100.0 |
| Railway Labor Act | 12 | 66.7 | 5 | 27.8 | 1 | 5.6 | | | | | 18 | 100.0 |
| Labor relations acts | 115 | 81.6 | 23 | 16.3 | 1 | 0.7 | | | 2 | 1.4 | 141 | 100.0 |
| Other labor | 7 | 77.8 | 1 | 11.1 | 1 | 11.1 | | | | | 9 | 100.0 |
| TAXATION | 206 | 73.8 | 69 | 24.7 | | | | | 4 | 1.4 | 279 | 100.0 |
| Income tax | 108 | 79.4 | 27 | 19.9 | | | | | 1 | 0.7 | 136 | 100.0 |
| Tax fraud | 9 | 50.0 | 8 | 44.4 | | | | | 1 | 5.6 | 18 | 100.0 |
| Forfeiture and penalty | 11 | 91.7 | 1 | 8.3 | | | | | | | 12 | 100.0 |
| Other tax | 78 | 69.0 | 33 | 29.2 | | | | | 2 | 1.8 | 113 | 100.0 |
| PERSONAL STATUS | 424 | 81.9 | 88 | 17.0 | 2 | 0.4 | 2 | 0.4 | 2 | 0.4 | 518 | 100.0 |
| Civil rights | 78 | 78.0 | 20 | 20.0 | | | 2 | 2.0 | | | 100 | 100.0 |
| Immigration and deportation | 7 | 87.5 | 1 | 12.5 | | | | | | | 8 | 100.0 |
| Suffrage | 39 | 95.1 | 2 | 4.9 | | | | | | | 41 | 100.0 |
| Civil rights removals | 25 | 92.6 | 0 | — | 1 | 3.7 | | | 1 | 3.7 | 27 | 100.0 |
| Prisoner petitions | | | | | | | | | | | | |
| Habeas corpus | 162 | 77.1 | 47 | 22.4 | 1 | 0.5 | | | | | 210 | 100.0 |
| Mandamus | 23 | 92.0 | 2 | 8.0 | | | | | | | 25 | 100.0 |
| Parole review | 1 | 50.0 | 1 | 50.0 | | | | | | | 2 | 100.0 |
| Vacate sentence | 89 | 84.8 | 15 | 14.3 | | | | | 1 | 1.0 | 105 | 100.0 |
| CRIMES AGAINST PERSONS | 3 | 75.0 | 1 | 25.0 | | | | | | | 4 | 100.0 |
| Homicide | 2 | 100.0 | 0 | — | | | | | | | 2 | 100.0 |
| Kidnapping | 0 | — | 0 | — | | | | | | | 0 | — |
| Rape | 0 | — | 0 | — | | | | | | | 0 | — |
| Assault | 1 | 50.0 | 1 | 50.0 | | | | | | | 2 | 100.0 |

5th Circuit (cont.)

| SUBJECTS | No Appeal n | % | Appeal Declined n | % | Affirm Circuit n | % | Mixed Circuit n | % | Reverse Circuit n | % | Avoid Circuit n | % | Other (Dismiss) n | % | Total N | % |
|---|---|---|---|---|---|---|---|---|---|---|---|---|---|---|---|---|
| CRIMES AGAINST PROPERTY | 98 | 64.1 | 51 | 33.3 | | | 1 | 0.7 | 2 | 1.3 | | | 1 | 0.7 | 153 | 100.0 |
| Robbery | 23 | 60.5 | 14 | 36.8 | | | 1 | 2.6 | | | | | | | 38 | 100.0 |
| Auto theft | 39 | 81.3 | 8 | 16.7 | | | | | | | | | 1 | 2.1 | 48 | 100.0 |
| Extortion | 0 | — | 1 | 100.0 | | | | | | | | | | | 1 | 100.0 |
| Fraud | 17 | 47.2 | 17 | 47.2 | | | | | 2 | 5.6 | | | | | 36 | 100.0 |
| Embezzlement | 5 | 100.0 | 0 | — | | | | | | | | | | | 5 | 100.0 |
| Forgery | 9 | 50.0 | 9 | 50.0 | | | | | | | | | | | 18 | 100.0 |
| Other property crimes | 5 | 71.4 | 2 | 28.6 | | | | | | | | | | | 7 | 100.0 |
| MORALS OFFENSES | 30 | 73.2 | 11 | 26.8 | | | | | | | | | | | 41 | 100.0 |
| Narcotics | 21 | 72.4 | 8 | 27.6 | | | | | | | | | | | 29 | 100.0 |
| White slave | 7 | 87.5 | 1 | 12.5 | | | | | | | | | | | 8 | 100.0 |
| Other sex | 0 | — | 0 | — | | | | | | | | | | | 0 | — |
| Obscenity (mail) | 0 | — | 0 | — | | | | | | | | | | | 0 | — |
| Gambling | 2 | 50.0 | 2 | 50.0 | | | | | | | | | | | 4 | 100.0 |
| MISCELLANEOUS OFFENSES | 19 | 76.0 | 3 | 12.0 | | | | | 3 | 12.0 | | | | | 25 | 100.0 |
| Escape | 1 | 100.0 | 0 | — | | | | | | | | | | | 1 | 100.0 |
| Weapons | 7 | 77.8 | 0 | — | | | | | 2 | 22.2 | | | | | 9 | 100.0 |
| Migratory birds | 1 | 100.0 | 0 | — | | | | | | | | | | | 1 | 100.0 |
| Selective Service | 6 | 85.7 | 0 | — | | | | | 1 | 14.3 | | | | | 7 | 100.0 |
| Bribery | 1 | 50.0 | 1 | 50.0 | | | | | | | | | | | 2 | 100.0 |
| Perjury | 3 | 60.0 | 2 | 40.0 | | | | | | | | | | | 5 | 100.0 |
| OTHER | 141 | 90.4 | 15 | 9.6 | | | | | | | | | | | 156 | 100.0 |
| Sums | 1,805 | 80.3 | 407 | 18.1 | 11 | 0.5 | 4 | 0.2 | 20 | 0.9 | 0 | — | 2 | 0.1 | 2,249 | 100.0 |

NOTE: Slight discrepancies in percentages are caused by rounding error.

**Appendix 6** (cont.)

Subjects of Supreme Court Decisions, FY 1965-1967

D. C. Circuit

(N = 1,337)

| SUBJECTS | No Appeal n | % | Appeal Declined n | % | Affirm Circuit n | % | Mixed Circuit n | % | Reverse Circuit n | % | Avoid Circuit n | % | Other (Dismiss) n | % | Total N | % |
|---|---|---|---|---|---|---|---|---|---|---|---|---|---|---|---|---|
| CONTRACTS | 126 | 92.0 | 11 | 8.0 | | | | | | | | | | | 137 | 100.0 |
| Insurance | 16 | 88.9 | 2 | 11.1 | | | | | | | | | | | 18 | 100.0 |
| Marine | 1 | 100.0 | 0 | — | | | | | | | | | | | 1 | 100.0 |
| Negotiable instruments | 5 | 100.0 | 0 | — | | | | | | | | | | | 5 | 100.0 |
| Real property | 35 | 94.6 | 2 | 5.4 | | | | | | | | | | | 37 | 100.0 |
| Recovery and enforcement | 11 | 100.0 | 0 | — | | | | | | | | | | | 11 | 100.0 |
| Other contracts | 58 | 89.2 | 7 | 10.8 | | | | | | | | | | | 65 | 100.0 |
| TORTS | 86 | 90.5 | 9 | 9.5 | | | | | | | | | | | 95 | 100.0 |
| Marine-personal injury | 3 | 100.0 | 0 | — | | | | | | | | | | | 3 | 100.0 |
| Motor vehicle-personal injury | 13 | 86.7 | 2 | 13.3 | | | | | | | | | | | 15 | 100.0 |
| Other personal injury | 31 | 96.9 | 1 | 3.1 | | | | | | | | | | | 32 | 100.0 |
| Employer liability | 8 | 100.0 | 0 | — | | | | | | | | | | | 8 | 100.0 |
| Other torts | 31 | 83.8 | 6 | 16.2 | | | | | | | | | | | 37 | 100.0 |
| COMMERCE | 150 | 80.6 | 25 | 13.4 | 2 | 1.1 | | | 8 | 4.3 | | | 1 | 0.5 | 186 | 100.0 |
| Antitrust | 4 | 80.0 | 1 | 20.0 | | | | | | | | | | | 5 | 100.0 |
| Agriculture | 2 | 66.7 | 1 | 33.3 | | | | | | | | | | | 3 | 100.0 |
| Bankruptcy | 0 | — | 0 | — | | | | | | | | | | | 0 | — |
| Food and drug | 3 | 100.0 | 0 | — | | | | | | | | | | | 3 | 100.0 |
| Patents | 24 | 88.9 | 2 | 7.4 | 1 | 3.7 | | | | | | | | | 27 | 100.0 |
| Copyright | 4 | 80.0 | 1 | 20.0 | | | | | | | | | | | 5 | 100.0 |
| Other commerce | 113 | 79.0 | 20 | 14.0 | 1 | 0.7 | | | 8 | 5.6 | | | 1 | 0.7 | 143 | 100.0 |
| LABOR | 75 | 77.3 | 22 | 22.7 | | | | | | | | | | | 97 | 100.0 |
| Fair Labor Standards Act | 4 | 80.0 | 1 | 20.0 | | | | | | | | | | | 5 | 100.0 |

## D. C. Circuit (cont.)

| SUBJECTS | No Appeal n | No Appeal % | Appeal Declined n | Appeal Declined % | Affirm Circuit n | Affirm Circuit % | Mixed Circuit n | Mixed Circuit % | Reverse Circuit n | Reverse Circuit % | Avoid Circuit n | Avoid Circuit % | Other (Dismiss) n | Other (Dismiss) % | Total N | Total % |
|---|---|---|---|---|---|---|---|---|---|---|---|---|---|---|---|---|
| Social Security | 1 | 100.0 | 0 | — | | | | | | | | | | | 1 | 100.0 |
| Labor Reporting Act | 4 | 100.0 | 0 | — | | | | | | | | | | | 4 | 100.0 |
| Railway Labor Act | 8 | 61.5 | 5 | 38.5 | | | | | | | | | | | 13 | 100.0 |
| Labor relations acts | 55 | 78.6 | 15 | 21.4 | | | | | | | | | | | 70 | 100.0 |
| Other labor | 3 | 75.0 | 1 | 25.0 | | | | | | | | | | | 4 | 100.0 |
| TAXATION | 28 | 84.8 | 5 | 15.2 | | | | | | | | | | | 33 | 100.0 |
| Income tax | 17 | 85.0 | 3 | 15.0 | | | | | | | | | | | 20 | 100.0 |
| Tax fraud | 1 | 50.0 | 1 | 50.0 | | | | | | | | | | | 2 | 100.0 |
| Forfeiture and penalty | 1 | 100.0 | 0 | — | | | | | | | | | | | 1 | 100.0 |
| Other tax | 9 | 90.0 | 1 | 10.0 | | | | | | | | | | | 10 | 100.0 |
| PERSONAL STATUS | 115 | 95.0 | 5 | 4.1 | | | 1 | 0.8 | | | | | | | 121 | 100.0 |
| Civil rights | 1 | 50.0 | 0 | — | | | 1 | 50.0 | | | | | | | 2 | 100.0 |
| Immigration and deportation | 3 | 100.0 | 0 | — | | | | | | | | | | | 3 | 100.0 |
| Suffrage | 2 | 100.0 | 0 | — | | | | | | | | | | | 2 | 100.0 |
| Civil rights removals | 0 | — | 0 | — | | | | | | | | | | | 0 | — |
| Prisoner petitions | | | | | | | | | | | | | | | | |
| Habeas corpus | 37 | 100.0 | 0 | — | | | | | | | | | | | 37 | 100.0 |
| Mandamus | 24 | 88.9 | 3 | 11.1 | | | | | | | | | | | 27 | 100.0 |
| Parole review | 14 | 87.5 | 2 | 12.5 | | | | | | | | | | | 16 | 100.0 |
| Vacate sentence | 34 | 100.0 | 0 | — | | | | | | | | | | | 34 | 100.0 |
| CRIMES AGAINST PERSONS | 108 | 92.3 | 9 | 7.7 | | | | | | | | | | | 117 | 100.0 |
| Homicide | 40 | 88.9 | 5 | 11.1 | | | | | | | | | | | 45 | 100.0 |
| Kidnapping | 0 | — | 0 | — | | | | | | | | | | | 0 | — |
| Rape | 19 | 100.0 | 0 | — | | | | | | | | | | | 19 | 100.0 |
| Assault | 49 | 92.5 | 4 | 7.5 | | | | | | | | | | | 53 | 100.0 |

| | | | | | | | | | | | | | |
|---|---|---|---|---|---|---|---|---|---|---|---|---|---|
| **CRIMES AGAINST PROPERTY** | 220 | 88.0 | 27 | 10.8 | 1 | 0.4 | | | | | 2 | 0.8 | 250 | 100.0 |
| Robbery | 188 | 88.7 | 22 | 10.4 | 1 | 0.5 | | | | | 1 | 0.5 | 212 | 100.0 |
| Auto theft | 17 | 89.5 | 2 | 10.5 | | — | | | | | | | 19 | 100.0 |
| Extortion | 1 | 100.0 | 0 | — | | | | | | | | | 1 | 100.0 |
| Fraud | 7 | 70.0 | 3 | 30.0 | | | | | | | | | 10 | 100.0 |
| Embezzlement | 1 | 100.0 | 0 | — | | | | | | | | | 1 | 100.0 |
| Forgery | 5 | 83.3 | 0 | — | | | | | | | 1 | 16.7 | 6 | 100.0 |
| Other property crimes | 1 | 100.0 | 0 | — | | | | | | | | | 1 | 100.0 |
| **MORALS OFFENSES** | 81 | 88.0 | 10 | 10.9 | | | | | | | 1 | 1.1 | 92 | 100.0 |
| Narcotics | 71 | 86.6 | 10 | 12.2 | | | | | | | 1 | 1.2 | 82 | 100.0 |
| White slave | 0 | — | 0 | — | | | | | | | | | 0 | — |
| Other sex | 4 | 100.0 | 0 | — | | | | | | | | | 4 | 100.0 |
| Obscenity (mail) | 1 | 100.0 | 0 | — | | | | | | | | | 1 | 100.0 |
| Gambling | 5 | 100.0 | 0 | — | | | | | | | | | 5 | 100.0 |
| **MISCELLANEOUS OFFENSES** | 18 | 94.7 | 1 | 5.3 | | | | | | | | | 19 | 100.0 |
| Escape | 1 | 100.0 | 0 | — | | | | | | | | | 1 | 100.0 |
| Weapons | 11 | 100.0 | 0 | — | | | | | | | | | 11 | 100.0 |
| Migratory birds | 0 | — | 0 | — | | | | | | | | | 0 | — |
| Selective Service | 0 | — | 0 | — | | | | | | | | | 0 | — |
| Bribery | 3 | 75.0 | 1 | 25.0 | | | | | | | | | 4 | 100.0 |
| Perjury | 3 | 100.0 | 0 | — | | | | | | | | | 3 | 100.0 |
| **LOCAL** | 53 | 98.1 | 1 | 1.9 | | | | | | | | | 54 | 100.0 |
| Domestic relations | 4 | 80.0 | 1 | 20.0 | | | | | | | | | 5 | 100.0 |
| Traffic | 1 | 100.0 | 0 | — | | | | | | | | | 1 | 100.0 |
| Other D.C. cases | 48 | 100.0 | 0 | — | | | | | | | | | 48 | 100.0 |
| **OTHER** | 120 | 88.2 | 14 | 10.3 | | | | | | | 2 | 1.5 | 136 | 100.0 |
| **Sums** | 1,180 | 88.3 | 139 | 10.4 | 3 | 0.2 | 1 | 0.1 | 13 | 1.0 | 1 | 0.1 | 1,337 | 100.0 |

Note: Slight discrepancies in percentages are caused by rounding error.

# List of Abbreviations

AO   Administrative Office of the United States Courts
AO *Annual Report*   *Annual Report of the Director of the Administrative Office of the United States Courts*
*Hearings*   U.S. Commission on Revision of the Federal Court Appellate System, *Hearings*, First Phase (1973) and Second Phase (1974-1975)
Hruska Commission   U.S. Commission on Revision of the Federal Court Appellate System

# Bibliographic Notes

**Preface**

1. *New York Times Co. v. U.S.*, 403 U.S. 713 (1971); *U.S. v. Nixon*, 418 U.S. 683 (1974); and *Alyeska Pipeline Service Co. v. The Wilderness Society*, 421 U.S. 240 (1975).

2. Felix Frankfurter and James M. Landis, *The Business of the Supreme Court: A Study in the Federal Judicial System* (New York: Macmillan, 1927).

3. See, for example, Burton M. Atkins, "The Effect of Panel Decision-Making on the United States Courts of Appeals: Theoretical and Empirical Considerations" (Ph. D. dissertation, University of Kentucky, 1970); Atkins, "Some Theoretical Effects of the Decision-Making Rules on the United States Courts of Appeals," *Jurimetrics Journal*, 11(1970), 13-23; Atkins, "Decision-Making Rules and Judicial Strategy on the United States Courts of Appeals," *Western Political Quarterly*, 25(1972), 626-42; Atkins and William Zavoina, "Judicial Leadership on the Court of Appeals: A Probability Analysis of Panel Assignment in Race Relations Cases on the Fifth Circuit," *American Journal of Political Science*, 18(1974), 701-11; Atkins and Justin J. Green, "Consensus on the United States Courts of Appeals: Illusion or Reality?" *American Journal of Political Science*, 20(1976), 735-48; Paul D. Carrington, "Crowded Dockets and the Courts of Appeals: The Threat to the Function of Review and the National Law," *Harvard Law Review*, 82(1969), 542-617; Mary H. Curzan, "A Case Study in the Selection of Federal Judges: The Fifth Circuit, 1953-1963" (Ph.D. dissertation, Yale University, 1968); Alvin Dozeman, "A Study of Selected Aspects of Behavior of the Judges of the U.S. Court of Appeals for the Tenth Circuit" (M.A. thesis, Michigan State University, 1960); Sheldon Goldman, "Voting Behavior on the United States Courts of Appeals, 1961-1964," *American Political Science Review*, 60(1966), 374, 375, n.6; Goldman, "Voting Behavior on the United States Courts of Appeals Revisited," *American Political Science Review*, 69(1975), 491-506; Goldman, "Conflict and Consensus in the United States Courts of Appeals," *Wisconsin Law Review*(1968), 461-82; Goldman, "Conflict on the U.S. Courts of Appeals, 1965-1971: A Quantitative Analysis," *University of Cincinnati Law Review*, 42(1973), 635-58; Louis S. Loeb, "Judicial Blocs and Judicial Values in Civil Liberties Cases Decided by the Supreme Court of the United States and the Court of Appeals for the District of Columbia," *American University Law Review*, 14(1965), 146-77; J. W. Peltason, *Fifty-Eight Lonely Men: Southern Federal Judges and School Desegregation* (New York: Harcourt, Brace & World, 1961); Francis M. Rich, Jr., "Role Perception and Precedent Orientation as Variables Influencing Appellate Judicial Decision-Making: An Analysis of the Fifth Circuit Court of Appeals" (Ph.D. dissertation, University of Georgia, 1967); Richard J. Richardson, "A Study of

the Judicial Process in Three United States Courts of Appeals, 1956-1961" (Ph.D. dissertation, Tulane University, 1967); Richardson and Kenneth N. Vines, "Review, Dissent and the Appellate Process: A Political Interpretation," *Journal of Politics*, 29(1967), 597-616; Richardson and Vines, *The Politics of Federal Courts: Lower Courts in the United States* (Boston: Little, Brown and Co., 1970); Robert H. Salisbury, "The United States Court of Appeals for the Seventh Circuit, 1940-1950: A Study of Judicial Relationships" (Ph.D. dissertation, University of Illinois, 1955); Marvin Schick, *Learned Hand's Court* (Baltimore: Johns Hopkins Press, 1970); Glendon Schubert, *Judicial Policy-Making*, rev. ed. (Chicago: Scott, Foresman, 1974); Kenneth N. Vines, "The Role of the Circuit Courts of Appeals in the Federal Judicial Process: A Case Study," *Midwest Journal of Political Science*, 7(1963), 305-19.

4. Warren E. Burger, "Annual Report on the State of the Judiciary," 96 S. Ct. 3, 6 (March 1, 1976). Hruska Commission, *Structure and Internal Procedures: Recommendations for Change* (Washington, D.C.: June 1975).

5. Stephen L. Wasby, "Extra Judges in 'The Court Nobody Knows': Some Aspects of Decision Making in the United States Courts of Appeals," paper presented at the annual meeting of the American Political Science Association, Washington, D.C., 1979, 1.

6. For helpful introductions, see David Easton, *A Systems Analysis of Political Life* (New York: John Wiley and Sons, 1965); Sheldon Goldman and Thomas P. Jahnige, *The Federal Courts as a Political System*, 2d ed. (New York: Harper & Row, 1976).

7. Easton, *Systems Analysis*, 29.

8. G. Edward White, *The American Judicial Tradition: Profiles of Leading American Judges* (New York: Oxford University Press, 1976), 2.

9. Frankfurter and Landis, *Business of the Supreme Court*, 3.

10. Lon L. Fuller, *The Morality of Law* (New Haven: Yale University Press, 1964), 170-77; Donald L. Horowitz, *The Courts and Social Policy* (Washington, D.C.: The Brookings Institution, 1977).

11. John C. Wahlke, Heinz Eulau, William Buchanan, and LeRoy C. Ferguson, *The Legislative System: Explorations in Legislative Behavior* (New York: John Wiley and Sons, 1962). Also see Goldman and Jahnige, *Federal Courts*, 33-42, 199-210; and Walter F. Murphy and Joseph Tanenhaus, *The Study of Public Law* (New York: Random House, 1972), 116-49.

12. For ambiguity in the term "function," see Theodore L. Becker, "Judicial Structure and Its Political Functioning in Society," *Journal of Politics*, 29(1967), 302-33; and Richard Lempert, "More Tales of Two Courts: Exploring Changes in the 'Dispute Settlement Function' of Trial Courts," *Law and Society Review*, 13(1978), 92-93.

13. Cf. the concept of personal as distinct from social role in Robert Hogan, *Personality Theory: The Personological Tradition* (Englewood Cliffs, N.J.: Prentice-Hall, 1976); Hogan and Carol Mills, "Legal Socialization," *Human Development*, 19(1976), 261-76.

14. Heinz Eulau, *Micro-Macro Political Analysis: Accents on Inquiry* (Chicago: Aldine, 1969), vii, 2.

15. Joel B. Grossman and Joseph Tanenhaus, eds., *Frontiers of Judicial Research* (New York: John Wiley and Sons, 1969), 12.

16. Dorothy Emmet, *Rules, Roles and Relations* (New York: St. Martin's Press, 1966), 172; Richard Lempert, "Norm-Making in Social Exchange: A Contract Law Model," *Law and Society Review*, 7(1972), 1-32.

17. *Baltimore Sun*, December 14, 1969, 12:1.

## One · Courts of Appeals in the Governing Process

1. The following discussion draws heavily from Felix Frankfurter and James M. Landis, *The Business of the Supreme Court: A Study in the Federal Judicial System* (New York: Macmillan, 1927); Carl McGowan, *The Organization of Judicial Power in the United States* (Evanston: Northwestern University Press, 1969); Gerhard Casper and Richard A. Posner, *The Workload of the Supreme Court* (Chicago: American Bar Foundation, 1976), 11-24; and Richard J. Richardson and Kenneth N. Vines, *The Politics of Federal Courts: Lower Courts in the United States* (Boston: Little, Brown and Co., 1970), ch. 2.

2. Charles Warren, "New Light on the History of the Federal Judiciary Act of 1789," *Harvard Law Review*, 37(1923), 49, 124; Henry J. Friendly, "The Historic Basis of Diversity Jurisdiction," *Harvard Law Review*, 41(1928), 483-510.

3. *Erie R.R. Co. v. Tompkins*, 304 U.S. 64 (1938).

4. McGowan, *Organization of Judicial Power*, 14-18.

5. Frankfurter and Landis, *Business of the Supreme Court*, 61-65.

6. Ibid., 21-30. See Richard E. Ellis, *The Jeffersonian Crisis: Courts and Politics in the Young Republic* (New York: Oxford University Press, 1971); The Oliver Wendell Holmes Devise History of the Supreme Court of the United States, Julius Goebel, Jr., I, *Antecedents and Beginnings to 1801* (New York: Macmillan, 1971); and Carl B. Swisher, V, *The Taney Period, 1836-64* (New York: Macmillan, 1974), 248-92. Cf. Mary K. B. Tachau, *Federal Courts in the Early Republic: Kentucky 1789-1816* (Princeton: Princeton University Press, 1978).

7. Frankfurter and Landis, *Business of the Supreme Court*, 30-55; Casper and Posner, *Workload of the Supreme Court*, 16.

8. Frankfurter and Landis, *Business of the Supreme Court*, 14, 60-65, 86. *Swift v. Tyson*, 41 U.S. (16 Pet.) 1 (1842).

9. Quoted in Warren, "New Light," 76.

10. Senate Committee on the Judiciary, *Legislative History of the United States Circuit Courts of Appeals and the Judges Who Served during the Period 1801 through March 1958*, 85th Cong., 2d Sess. (1958); H.R. 7665, 96th Cong., 2d Sess. (1980).

11. Frankfurter and Landis, *Business of the Supreme Court*, chs. 5-7. See Alpheus T. Mason, *William Howard Taft: Chief Justice* (New York: Simon & Schuster, 1964), 88-137.

12. 90 Stat. 1119 (1976).

13. 28 U.S.C. § 1291 (1970). AO *Annual Report* (preliminary 1979), Table B7, A-10.

14. AO *Annual Report* (preliminary 1979), Table B1, A-2. *National Citizens Committee for Broadcasting v. F.C.C.*, 555 F. 2d 938 (D.C. Cir. 1977); aff'd. 436 U.S. 775 (1978).

15. *Sierra Club v. E.P.A.*, 540 F. 2d 1114 (D.C. Cir. 1976).

16. *A.F.L.-C.I.O. v. Kahn*, 48 L.W. 2005 (1979); cert. denied, 48 L.W. 1001-2 (1979).

17. Peter Graham Fish, *The Politics of Federal Judicial Administration* (Princeton: Princeton University Press, 1973).

18. Howard M. Vollmer and Donald Mills, eds., *Professionalization* (Englewood Cliffs, N.J.: Prentice-Hall, 1966), 264-94. Eliot Friedson, *Professional Dominance: The Social Structure of Medical Care* (New York: Atherton Press, 1970).

19. Paul D. Carrington, Daniel J. Meador, and Maurice Rosenberg, *Justice on Appeal* (St. Paul: West Publishing Co., 1976), 2-3. See Arthur D. Hellman, "The Business of the Supreme Court under the Judiciary Act of 1925: The Plenary Docket in the 1970's," *Harvard Law Review*, 91(1978), 1709-1802.

20. J. Edward Lumbard, "Current Problems of the Federal Courts of Appeals," *Cornell Law Review*, 54(1968), 29, 32.

21. Frankfurter and Landis, *Business of the Supreme Court*, 187.

22. Lumbard, "Current Problems," 29.

23. 28 U.S.C. § 46 (1970).

24. Burton M. Atkins, "Decision-Making Rules and Judicial Strategy on the United States Courts of Appeals," *Western Political Quarterly*, 25(1972), 630. Also, Atkins, "Some Theoretical Effects of the Decision-Making Rules on the United States Courts of Appeals," *Jurimetrics Journal*, 11(1970), 13-23.

25. See, e.g., *Green v. Santa Fe Industries*, 533 F. 2d 1309, 1310 (2d Cir. 1976). Also, Burton M. Atkins, "Judicial Behavior and Tendencies towards Conformity in a Three Member Small Group: A Case Study of Dissent Behavior on the U.S. Courts of Appeals," *Social Science Quarterly*, 54(1973), 41-53; Atkins and Justin J. Green, "Consensus on the United States Courts of Appeals: Illusion or Reality?" *American Journal of Political Science*, 20(1976), 735-48.

26. See, e.g., *Armstrong v. Bd. of Educ. of Birmingham*, 323 F. 2d 333, 352-61 (5th Cir. 1963); 48 F.R.D. 141, 182 (1969). Burton M. Atkins and William Zavoina, "Judicial Leadership on the Court of Appeals: A Probability Analysis of Panel Assignment in Race Relations Cases on the Fifth Circuit," *American Journal of Political Science*, 18(1974), 701-11.

27. Abram Chayes, "The New Judiciary," *Harvard Law School Bulletin*, 27(1976), 23. See Chayes, "The Role of the Judge in Public Law Litigation," *Harvard Law Review*, 89(1976), 1281-1316; and Maurice Rosenberg, "Let's Everybody Litigate?" *Texas Law Review*, 50(1972), 1349-68.

28. See, e.g., *Alexander v. Holmes County Bd. of Educ.*, 387 U.S. 253 (1967); *James v. Wallace*, 406 F. Supp. 318 (M.D. Ala. 1976); *Wyatt v. Stickney*, 344 F. Supp. 373 (M.D. Ala. 1972); *O'Connor v. Donaldson*, 422 U.S. 563 (1975); *Hawkins v. Town of Shaw, Miss.*, 437 F. 2d 1286 (5th Cir. 1971); *New York Times*, November 13, 1976, 1:1; April 24, 1977, 1:2; and

*City of Mobile v. Bolden,* 100 S.Ct. 1490 (1980). Donald L. Horowitz, *The Courts and Social Policy* (Washington, D.C.: The Brookings Institution, 1977), 6-7. Cf. Theodore Eisenberg and Stephen C. Yeazell, "The Ordinary and Extraordinary in Institutional Litigation," *Harvard Law Review,* 93(1980), 465-517.

29. *Baker v. Carr,* 369 U.S. 186, 266, 270 (1962). Chayes, "Role of the Judge," 1292-96.

30. Omnibus Judges Act, Public Law 95-486 (1978); 92 Stat. 1629 (1978); 28 U.S.C. § 44, § 133 (1978).

31. Carrington et al., *Justice on Appeal,* 4-6; Casper and Posner, *Workload of the Supreme Court,* 27-62; Harry W. Jones, ed., *The Courts, the Public, and the Law Explosion* (Englewood Cliffs, N.J.: Prentice-Hall, 1965); Henry J. Friendly, *Federal Jurisdiction: A General View* (New York: Columbia University Press, 1973), 15-54; Richard A. Posner, *Economic Analysis of Law* (Chicago: University of Chicago Press, 1973), 333-56.

32. See, e.g., *Gideon v. Wainwright,* 372 U.S. 335 (1963); *Mapp v. Ohio,* 367 U.S. 643 (1961); *Miranda v. Arizona,* 384 U.S. 436 (1966); *Coleman v. Alabama,* 399 U.S. 1 (1970); *Argersinger v. Hamlin,* 407 U.S. 25 (1972); and *Apodaca v. Oregon,* 406 U.S. 404 (1972). *Fay v. Noia,* 372 U.S. 391 (1963); *Townsend v. Sain,* 372 U.S. 293 (1963).

33. Casper and Posner, *Workload of the Supreme Court,* 35-46. *Anders v. California,* 386 U.S. 738 (1967), and *Ferri v. Ackerman,* 100 S.Ct. 402 (1979).

34. S. 1437, 95th Cong., 1st Sess. (1977). See *New York Times,* February 3, 1978, A11:4; also Burger, C.J., *New York Times,* January 2, 1977, 1:8.

35. 347 U.S. 483 (1954); 349 U.S. 294 (1955). *New York Times,* April 24, 1977, 50:6. *Washington Post,* July 18, 1976, A6:8. Nathan Glazer, "Towards an Imperial Judiciary?" *The Public Interest,* 41(1975), 104-23. See Frank M. Johnson, Jr., "The Constitution and the Federal District Judge," *Texas Law Review,* 54(1976), 903, 916.

36. For recently enacted laws tending to increase caseloads of federal courts, see Hearings on S. 11, S. 460 before the Senate Committee on the Judiciary, 95th Cong., 1st Sess. (1977), 617. Also, see Carl McGowan, "Federal Jurisdiction: Legislative and Judicial Changes," *Case Western Reserve Law Review,* 28(1978), 517, 519n; and Lawrence Baum, Sheldon Goldman, and Austin Sarat, "Transformations in Appellate Activity: A Look at the Business of Three United States Courts of Appeals, 1895-1975," paper delivered at the annual meeting of the American Political Science Association, New York, 1978.

37. Norman H. Nie, Sidney Verba, and John R. Petrocik, *The Changing American Voter* (Cambridge: Harvard University Press, 1976). Also, Verba and Nie, *Participation in America: Political Democracy and Social Equality* (New York: Harper & Row, 1972).

38. Jerry Goldman, "Federal District Courts and the Appellate Crisis," *Judicature,* 57(1973), 211-13.

39. Frankfurter and Landis, *Business of the Supreme Court,* 3.

40. See, e.g., David L. Shapiro, "Federal Diversity Jurisdiction: A Survey and a Proposal," *Harvard Law Review,* 91(1977), 317-55.

41. Archibald Cox, *The Role of the Supreme Court in American Government* (New York: Oxford University Press, 1976), 36. Also see J. Woodford Howard, Jr., "Adjudication Considered as a Process of Conflict Resolution: A Variation on Separation of Powers," *Journal of Public Law*, 18(1969), 339-70.

42. See, e.g., Cox, *Role of the Supreme Court*, 99-118; Herbert Wechsler, "Toward Neutral Principles of Constitutional Law," *Harvard Law Review*, 73(1959), 1-35; Alexander M. Bickel, *The Supreme Court and the Idea of Progress* (New York: Harper & Row, 1970); Raoul Berger, *Government by Judiciary* (Cambridge: Harvard University Press, 1977), and references in notes 27, 28, and 35 of this chapter. Cf. Charles L. Black, Jr., *The People and the Court: Judicial Review in a Democracy* (New York: Macmillan, 1960); Johnson, "The Constitution," 903-16; Arthur S. Miller and Ronald F. Howell, "The Myth of Neutrality in Constitutional Adjudication," *University of Chicago Law Review*, 27(1960), 661-95; J. Skelly Wright, "The Role of the Supreme Court in a Democratic Society—Judicial Activism or Restraint?" *Cornell Law Review*, 54(1968), 1-28; and Wright, "Professor Bickel, the Scholarly Tradition, and the Supreme Court," *Harvard Law Review*, 84(1971), 769-805.

43. See, e.g., Horowitz, *Courts and Social Policy*; and Arthur Selwyn Miller and Jerome A. Barron, "The Supreme Court, the Adversary System, and the Flow of Information to the Justices: A Preliminary Inquiry," *Virginia Law Review*, 61(1975), 1187-1245.

44. See, e.g., *Report of the Study Group on the Caseload of the Supreme Court* (Washington, D.C.: Federal Judicial Center, 1972); Paul D. Carrington, "Crowded Dockets and the Courts of Appeals: The Threat to the Function of Review and the National Law," *Harvard Law Review*, 82(1969), 542-617; Carrington et al., *Justice on Appeal*, 185-224; James F. Blumstein, "The Supreme Court's Jurisdiction—Reform Proposals, Discretionary Review, and Writ Dismissals," *Vanderbilt Law Review*, 26(1973), 895-938; Paul A. Freund, "Why We Need the National Court of Appeals," *American Bar Association Journal*, 59(1973), 247-52; and Freund, "A National Court of Appeals," *Hastings Law Journal*, 25(1974), 1301; Shirley M. Hufstedler, "Courtship and Other Legal Arts," *American Bar Association Journal*, 60(1974), 545-48; William H. Rehnquist, "Whither the Courts?" *American Bar Association Journal*, 60(1974), 787-90; Hruska Commission, *Structure and Internal Procedures: Recommendations for Change* (Washington, D.C.: June 1975), 5-39, 76-188. Also, Symposium, "Federal Appellate Justice in an Era of Growing Demand," *Cornell Law Review*, 59(1974), 571-657. Cf. Charles L. Black, Jr., "The National Court of Appeals: An Unwise Proposal," *Yale Law Journal*, 83(1974), 883-99; William J. Brennan, Jr., "The National Court of Appeals: Another Dissent," *University of Chicago Law Review*, 40(1973), 473-85; Casper and Posner, *Workload of the Supreme Court*, and their "The Caseload of the Supreme Court: 1975 and 1976 Terms," *Supreme Court Review* (1977), 87-98; Arthur J. Goldberg, "One Supreme Court: It Doesn't Need Its Cases 'Screened,'" *New Republic*, February 10, 1973, 14-16; with reply by Alexander M. Bickel, February 17, 1973, 17-18; Eugene

Gressman, "The Constitution v. the Freund Report," *George Washington Law Review*, 41(1973), 951-70; Friendly, *Federal Jurisdiction*, 49-54; Donald P. Lay, "Why Rush to Judgment? Some Second Thoughts on the Proposed National Court of Appeals," *Judicature*, 59(1975), 172-79; Douglas A. Poe, John R. Schmidt, and Wayne W. Whalen, "A National Court of Appeals: A Dissenting View," *Northwestern University Law Review*, 67(1973), 842-56; S. Sidney Ulmer, "Revising the Jurisdiction of the Supreme Court: Mere Administrative Reform or Substantive Policy Change?" *Minnesota Law Review*, 58(1973), 121-55; Earl Warren, "Let's Not Weaken the Supreme Court," *American Bar Association Journal*, 60(1974), 677-80; and Peter Westen, "The Proposed National Court of Appeals: A Threat to the Supreme Court," *New York Review of Books*, February 22, 1973.

45. Chayes, "Role of the Judge," 1292. See *New York Times*, May 11, 1980, 36:1.

46. See, e.g., *Harris v. New York*, 401 U.S. 222 (1971); *U.S. v. Calandra*, 414 U.S. 338 (1974); *Stone v. Powell*, 427 U.S. 465 (1976); *Eisen v. Carlisle & Jacquelin*, 417 U.S. 156 (1974). Nathan Lewin, "Avoiding the Supreme Court," *New York Times Magazine*, October 17, 1976, 31.

47. Hruska Commission, *Structure and Internal Procedures* (June 1975).

48. Archibald Cox, *The Warren Court: Constitutional Decision as an Instrument of Reform* (Cambridge: Harvard University Press, 1968), 4-5.

49. David Easton, *A Systems Analysis of Political Life* (New York: John Wiley and Sons, 1965), 21. Frankfurter and Landis, *Business of the Supreme Court*, 2.

50. Blackstone, *Commentaries* 6; *The Federalist*, no. 78; and *Osborn v. Bank of the U.S.*, 22 U.S. (9 Wheat.) 738, 866 (1824).

51. See, e.g., Benjamin N. Cardozo, *The Nature of the Judicial Process* (New Haven: Yale University Press, 1921); Felix S. Cohen, "Transcendental Nonsense and the Functional Approach," *Columbia Law Review*, 35(1935), 809-49; Karl N. Llewellyn, *The Common Law Tradition: Deciding Appeals* (Boston: Little, Brown and Co., 1960).

52. Julius Stone, *Legal System and Lawyers' Reasonings* (Stanford: Stanford University Press, 1964), 264; Vernon K. Dibble and Berton Pekowsky, "What Is and What Ought to Be: A Comparison of Certain Characteristics of the Ideological and Legal Styles of Thought," *American Journal of Sociology*, 79(1973), 511-49.

53. Quoted in Alpheus T. Mason, *Harlan Fiske Stone: Pillar of the Law* (New York: Viking Press, 1956), 470n.

54. Richardson and Vines, *Politics of Federal Courts*, 142-44; Walter F. Murphy, *Elements of Judicial Strategy* (Chicago: University of Chicago Press, 1964), 12-36, 91-122; S. Sidney Ulmer, *Courts as Small and Not So Small Groups* (New York: General Learning Process, 1971); Glendon Schubert, *Judicial Policy-Making*, rev. ed. (Chicago: Scott, Foresman, 1974), ch. 1; and G. Edward White, *The American Judicial Tradition: Profiles of Leading American Judges* (New York: Oxford University Press, 1976).

55. Frankfurter and Landis, *Business of the Supreme Court*, 3.

56. Conference Report no. 92-1457, Legislative History, P.L. 92-489,

*United States Code Congressional and Administrative News* (1974), 3612.

57. Donald Black, "The Mobilization of Law," *Journal of Legal Studies*, 2(1973), 125-49.

58. Joel B. Grossman and Austin Sarat, "Litigation in the Federal Courts: A Comparative Perspective," *Law and Society Review*, 9(1975), 321-46. See Baum et al., "Transformations in Appellate Activity."

59. Hruska Commission, *Structure and Internal Procedures* (June 1975), 168.

60. Joel B. Grossman, *Lawyers and Judges: The ABA and the Politics of Judicial Selection* (New York: John Wiley and Sons, 1965); Harold W. Chase, *Federal Judges: The Appointing Process* (Minneapolis: University of Minnesota Press, 1972).

61. Wright, "Role of the Supreme Court," 11.

62. See remark of Brown, J., in J. W. Peltason, *Fifty-Eight Lonely Men: Southern Federal Judges and School Desegregation* (New York: Harcourt, Brace & World, 1961), 9-10.

63. Quoted in Archibald MacLeish and E. F. Prichard, Jr., eds., *Law and Politics and Occasional Papers of Felix Frankfurter* (New York: Capricorn Books, 1962), 15.

64. 347 U.S. 483 (1954).

65. Alpheus T. Mason, *Security through Freedom: American Political Thought and Practice* (Ithaca: Cornell University Press, 1955), 149.

66. Martin Shapiro, "Stability and Change in Judicial Decision-Making: Incrementalism or Stare Decisis?" *Law in Transition Quarterly*, 2(1965), 146.

67. Walter F. Murphy, "Lower Court Checks on Supreme Court Power," *American Political Science Review*, 53(1959), 1017-31.

68. Richard J. Richardson, "A Study of the Judicial Process in Three United States Courts of Appeals, 1956-1961" (Ph.D. dissertation, Tulane University, 1967), 85.

## Two · The Flow of Litigation in Three Courts of Appeals

1. *The Federalist*, no. 81 (New York: Random House, n.d.), 528.

2. For general discussion, see Julius Stone, *Legal System and Lawyers' Reasonings* (Stanford: Stanford University Press, 1964); Grant Gilmore, *The Ages of American Law* (New Haven: Yale University Press, 1977); and Donald L. Horowitz, *The Courts and Social Policy* (Washington, D.C.: The Brookings Institution, 1977).

3. See Richard J. Richardson and Kenneth N. Vines, *The Politics of Federal Courts: Lower Courts in the United States* (Boston: Little, Brown and Co., 1970). For parallel observations in other courts, see Gerhard Casper and Richard A. Posner, *The Workload of the Supreme Court* (Chicago: American Bar Foundation, 1976), 8, 27-32; and their "The Caseload of the Supreme Court: 1975 and 1976 Terms," *Supreme Court Review* (1977), 87-98; Martin A. Levin, *Urban Politics and Criminal Courts* (Chicago: University of Chicago Press, 1977), 2; and Wolf V. Heydebrand, "The Context of Public Bureaucracies: An Organizational Analysis of Federal District Courts," *Law and Society Review*, 11(1977), 759-821.

4. For longer-term trends of more uniformity in circuit dockets, including more public and less private law, see Lawrence Baum, Sheldon Goldman, and Austin Sarat, "Transformations in Appellate Activity: A Look at the Business of Three United States Courts of Appeals, 1895-1975," paper delivered at the annual meeting of the American Political Science Association, New York, 1978.
5. *Abramson v. Boedeker*, 379 F. 2d 741, 743 (5th Cir. 1967).
6. Martin Shapiro, "Decentralized Decision-Making in the Law of Torts" in S. Sidney Ulmer, ed., *Political Decision-Making* (New York: Van Nostrand Reinhold, 1970), 44-75; and Shapiro, "Toward a Theory of Stare Decisis," *Journal of Legal Studies*, 1(1972), 125-34.
7. *Hearings*, 2d Phase, II (1975), 959.
8. As quoted in Felix Frankfurter to Erwin N. Griswold, October 4, 1957. Frankfurter Papers, Manuscripts Division, Library of Congress.
9. Note, "Appealability in the Federal Courts," *Harvard Law Review*, 75(1961), 351, 353.
10. Cf. Will Shafroth, "Survey of U.S. Courts of Appeals," 42 F.R.D. 243-315 (1967); and "Survey of the United States Courts of Appeals," in Hearings on H.R. 7378 before the House Committee on the Judiciary, 92d Cong., 1st Sess. (1971), 192-227.
11. AO *Annual Report* (1978), Table B3, 298. See *Hearings*, 1st Phase, 98; Hearings on S. 11, S. 460 before the Senate Committee on the Judiciary, 95th Cong., 1st Sess. (1977), 634.
12. AO *Annual Report* (1961 and preliminary 1979), Table B1.
13. *Hearings*, 1st Phase, 92. For elimination of habeas corpus petitions from the D.C. Superior Court to federal district and circuit courts, see *Swedin v. Pressley*, 97 S.Ct. 1224 (1977), and criticism by the *Washington Post*, March 25, 1977, A26:1. Cf. Frankfurter, J., in *Dennis v. U.S.*, 341 U.S. 494, 525 (1951).
14. Carl McGowan, *The Organization of Judicial Power in the United States* (Evanston: Northwestern University Press, 1969), 11-18. Cf. Walter F. Murphy, "Lower Court Checks on Supreme Court Power," *American Political Science Review*, 53(1959), 1017; and Lawrence Baum, "Lower-Court Response to Supreme Court Decisions: Reconsidering a Negative Picture," *Justice System Journal*, 3(1978), 208-19.
15. See Henry J. Friendly, *Federal Jurisdiction: A General View* (New York: Columbia University Press, 1973), 15-54, 139-152; and Baum et al., "Transformations in Appellate Activity."
16. Richardson and Vines, *Politics of Federal Courts*, 127-29.
17. See Donald Black, "The Mobilization of Law," *Journal of Legal Studies*, 2(1973), 125-49.
18. Daniel Fiorino, "The Federal Courts and the Regulatory Process: The Cases of Natural Gas and Broadcasting" (Ph.D. dissertation, Johns Hopkins University, 1977), 271-94.
19. Horowitz, *Courts and Social Policy*, 226.
20. *Atlantic Refining Co. v. Public Service Commission of New York*, 360 U.S. 378 (1959). *U.S. v. Bowe*, 360 F. 2d 1 (2d Cir. 1966). *U.S. v. One Carton Positive Motion Picture Film*, 367 F. 2d 889, 904 (2d Cir. 1966).

21. For excellent analysis of circuit conflicts over patent policy, see Martin Shapiro, *The Supreme Court and Administrative Agencies* (New York: Free Press, 1968), 167-85; Friendly, *Federal Jurisdiction*, 153-55; and testimony of James B. Gambrell and Donald Dunner, *Hearings*, 2d Phase, II, 833-44. For forum shoppers' guides in other fields, see references in Paul D. Carrington, "Crowded Dockets and the Courts of Appeals: The Threat to the Function of Review and the National Law," *Harvard Law Review*, 82(1969), 542, 596-604; and Hruska Commission, *Structure and Internal Procedures: Recommendations for Change* (Washington, D.C.: June 1975), 76-168; and Kenneth C. Haas, "The Reactions of the U.S. Courts of Appeals to Supreme Court Prisoner's Rights Decisions: An Analysis of Conflict among the Circuits," paper presented at the annual meeting of the American Political Science Association, Washington, D.C., 1979.

22. Shapiro, *Supreme Court*, 95, 262.

23. Note, "Government Litigation in the Supreme Court: The Roles of the Solicitor General," *Yale Law Journal*, 78(1969), 1444, n. 10; William E. Brigman, "The Office of the Solicitor General of the United States" (Ph.D. dissertation, University of North Carolina at Chapel Hill, 1966), 28-66; Paul D. Carrington, "United States Appeals in Civil Cases: A Field and Statistical Study," *Houston Law Review*, 11(1974), 1101-23; Donald L. Horowitz, *The Jurocracy* (Lexington, Mass.: D. C. Heath, 1977); and Suzanne Weaver, *Decision to Prosecute: Organization and Public Policy in the Antitrust Division* (Cambridge: MIT Press, 1977).

24. Jerry Goldman, "Federal District Courts and the Appellate Crisis," *Judicature*, 57(1973), 211-13.

25. Warren E. Burger, "The State of the Judiciary—1975," *American Bar Association Journal*, 61(1975), 439-40.

26. See also David L. Shapiro, "Federal Diversity Jurisdiction: A Survey and a Proposal," *Harvard Law Review*, 91(1977), 317-55, esp. 319-24.

27. Black, "Mobilization of Law," 128. Carnegie Foundation Report, "A Step toward Equal Justice," as reported in the *Louisville Courier-Journal*, April 19, 1974, A8:1.

28. Seitz, C. J., in *Hearings*, 1st Phase, 39; 386 U.S. 738 (1967); and *Ferri v. Ackerman*, 100 S.Ct. 402 (1979).

29. Burger, "State of the Judiciary," 439; Goldman, "Federal District Courts," 213; Maurice Rosenberg, "Let's Everybody Litigate?" *Texas Law Review*, 50 (1972), 1349-68; and Rosenberg, "Anything Legislatures Can Do, Courts Can Do Better?" *American Bar Association Journal*, 62(1976), 587-90.

30. Goldman, "Federal District Courts," 213. Cf. Richard Lempert, "More Tales of Two Courts: Exploring Changes in the 'Dispute Settlement Function' of Trial Courts," *Law and Society Review*, 13(1978), 91-138.

31. See interview with Maurice Rosenberg, *The Third Branch*, 12(January 1980), 7. Cf. Irving R. Kaufman, "The Pre-Argument Conference: An Appellate Procedural Reform," *Columbia Law Review*, 74(1975), 1094-1104; and William Mack, "Settlement Procedures in the U.S. Court of Appeals: A Proposal," *Justice System Journal*, 1(1975), 17-42 (issue 2), with Jerry Goldman,

*An Evaluation of the Civil Appeals Management Plan: An Experiment in Judicial Administration* (Washington, D.C.: The Federal Judicial Center, 1977), and Goldman, "The Civil Appeals Management Plan: An Experiment in Appellate Procedural Reform," *Columbia Law Review*, 78(1978), 1209-40.

32. See AO *Annual Report* (1975), Table B1; (1978), Table 6, 165-66 (preliminary 1979), Table B1, A2. *Court Management Statistics* (1976), 323-25.

33. Black, "Mobilization of Law"; Joel B. Grossman and Austin Sarat, "Litigation in the Federal Courts: A Comparative Perspective," *Law and Society Review*, 9(1975), 321-46.

34. Walter F. Murphy, *Elements of Judicial Strategy* (Chicago: University of Chicago Press, 1964), 21.

35. See Casper and Posner, *Workload of the Supreme Court*, 27-32; Gregory J. Rathjen, "Lawyers and the Appeals Process: A Profile," *Federal Bar Journal*, 34(1975), 30-41; Maurice Rosenberg, "Devising Procedures That Are Civil to Promote Justice That Is Civilized," *Michigan Law Review*, 69(1971), 797-820; Marc Galanter, "Why the 'Haves' Come Out Ahead," *Law and Society Review*, 9(1974), 95-106, and Galanter, "Afterword: Explaining Litigation," *Law and Society Review*, 9(1975), 347-68; Austin Sarat and Joel B. Grossman, "Courts and Conflict Resolution: Problems in the Mobilization of Adjudication," *American Political Science Review*, 69(1975), 1200-17, and *New York Times*, January 12, 1979, D3.

36. See, e.g., National Advisory Commission on Criminal Justice Standards and Goals, *A National Strategy to Reduce Crime* (Washington, D.C.: 1973), 146-50; 154-57; Warren E. Burger, "Annual Report on the State of the Judiciary," 97 S.Ct. 4-5 (May 1, 1977), and *New York Times*, January 2, 1977, 1:8; *Thermatron Products, Inc.* v. *Hermansdorfer*, 423 U.S. 336 (1976). Seitz, C.J., *The Third Branch*, 8 (September 1976), 4.

37. See the references in note 21, this chapter.

38. Cf. Sheldon Goldman, "Conflict and Consensus in the United States Courts of Appeals," *Wisconsin Law Review* (1968), 461-82; and "Conflict on the U.S. Courts of Appeals, 1965-1971: A Quantitative Analysis," *University of Cincinnati Law Review*, 42(1973), 636. Richardson and Vines, *Politics of Federal Courts*, 134-38.

39. Richardson and Vines, *Politics of Federal Courts*, 127-29.

40. See, e.g., *Perry* v. *U.S.*, 347 F. 2d 813 (D.C. Cir. 1964); *U.S.* v. *Mitchell*, 354 F. 2d 767 (2d Cir. 1966). Also, *New York Times*, December 10, 1972, 55. *N.A.A.C.P.* v. *Thompson*, 357 F. 2d 831 (5th Cir. 1966). *Davis* v. *Bd. of School Commissioners of Mobile Co.*, 364 F. 2d 896 (5th Cir. 1966); *U.S.* v. *Mississippi*, 339 F. 2d 679 (5th Cir. 1964); *Bell* v. *Southwell*, 376 F. 2d 659 (5th Cir. 1967).

41. *Escobedo* v. *Illinois*, 378 U.S. 478 (1964). Cf. Friendly, J., in *U.S.* v. *Hall*, 421 F. 2d 540 (2d Cir. 1969), and Burger, J., in *Jackson* v. *U.S.*, 337 U.S. F. 2d 137, 141 (D.C. Cir. 1964). See Henry J. Friendly, "The Bill of Rights as a Code of Criminal Procedure," *California Law Review*, 53(1965), 929; and Friendly, "Fifth Amendment Tomorrow: The Case for Constitutional Change," *University of Cincinnati Law Review*, 37(1968), 671. For resistance in the 5th circuit, see, e.g., *Hall* v. *West*, 335 F. 2d 481 (5th Cir. 1964);

Cox v. Hauberg, 342 F. 2d 167 (5th Cir. 1965), cert. denied 381 U.S. 935 (1965); In re Brown, 346 F. 2d 903 (5th Cir. 1965). Alexander M. Bickel, "Impeach Judge Cox," New Republic, September 4, 1965, 153; J. W. Peltason, Fifty-Eight Lonely Men: Southern Federal Judges and School Desegregation (New York: Harcourt, Brace & World, 1961); and Charles V. Hamilton, The Bench and the Ballot: Southern Federal Judges and Black Voters (New York: Oxford University Press, 1973).

42. Cox, J., quoted in Killingsworth v. Enterprise and Quitman Consol. Sch. Districts, 403 F. 2d 181 (5th Cir. 1968). Cf. U.S. v. Jefferson Co. Board of Education, 372 F. 2d 836 (5th Cir. 1966) and Andrews v. City of Monroe, La., 370 F. 2d 925 (5th Cir. 1966). Also see U.S. v. Mississippi, 359 F. 2d 103 (5th Cir. 1966). For a similar episode in which Carswell, J., joined in reversing Scarlett, J., see Hillyer v. Dutton, 379 F. 2d 809 (5th Cir. 1967).

43. Jerome Frank, Courts on Trial (Princeton: Princeton University Press, 1949), 222-24.

44. Kenneth M. Dolbeare, "The Federal District Courts and Urban Public Policy," in Joel B. Grossman and Joseph B. Tanenhaus, eds., Frontiers of Judicial Research (New York: John Wiley and Sons, 1969), 391.

45. Among the few are the sources of 2d circuit appeals in FY 1966-1973, in Hearings, 1st Phase, 1055-56, 1061-62.

46. Quoted in Baum, "Lower-Court Response," 219, n. 36.

47. See, e.g., Halshyn v. U.S., 345 F. 2d 728, 730, n. 1 (D.C. Cir. 1965); Bishop v. U.S., 349 F. 2d 220 (D.C. Cir. 1965); and Salley v. U.S., 357 F. 2d 274 (D.C. Cir. 1966).

48. Nomination of Irving Ben Cooper, Hearings before the Senate Committee on the Judiciary, 87th Cong., 2d Sess. (1962), 361-75. See Joel B. Grossman, Lawyers and Judges: The ABA and the Politics of Judicial Selection (New York: John Wiley and Sons, 1965), 40-41.

49. See references in note 41, this chapter; David Wright Clark, "The Civil Rights Record of District Judge William Harold Cox" (Millsaps College, 1970); and New York Times, March 28, 1965, 25. For analyses of Carswell's record, see Cong. Rec., March 16, 1970, S 3777-3806; and March 26, 1970, S 4631-40.

50. See, e.g., Carr v. Montgomery Co. Bd. of Educ., 289 F. Supp. 647 (M.D. Ala. 1968); 402 F. 2d 782 (5th Cir. 1968); 395 U.S. 225 (1969). James v. Wallace, 406 F. Supp. 318 (M.D. Ala. 1976); Wyatt v. Stickney, 344 F. Supp. 373 (M.D. Ala. 1972). Frank M. Johnson, Jr., "The Constitution and the Federal District Judge," Texas Law Review, 54 (1976), 903-16.

51. See Robert I. Mendelsohn, "Survey of the United States Court of Appeals for the District of Columbia Circuit," Committee on the Administration of Justice, Court Management Study (Washington, D.C.: December 31, 1969), 69-70. Also, Cong. Rec., March 23, 1971, S 3590.

52. Richardson and Vines, Politics of Federal Courts, 134 and references in note 21, this chapter.

53. Lok v. I.N.S., 548 F. 2d, 37, 38 (2d Cir. 1977).

54. Richardson and Vines, Politics of Federal Courts, 53-54. See John

Minor Wisdom, "The Frictionmaking, Exacerbating Political Role of Federal Courts," *Southwestern Law Journal*, 21(1967), 411.

55. Nathan Lewin, "Avoiding the Supreme Court," *New York Times Magazine*, October 17, 1976, 31, 90.

56. See Barbara A. Curran, *The Legal Needs of the Public* (Chicago: American Bar Foundation, 1977).

57. *New York Times*, July 23, 1978, E18:1. Hruska Commission, *The Geographical Boundaries of the Several Judicial Circuits: Recommendations for Change* (Washington, D.C.: December 1973), 7.

58. Horowitz, *Courts and Social Policy*, 283.

59. Casper and Posner, *Workload of the Supreme Court*, 8.

60. *The Third Circuit Time Study* (Washington, D.C.: Federal Judicial Center, 1973); *Hearings*, 1st Phase, 51.

61. *Baltimore Sun*, July 7, 1971, A8.

62. Carl J. Friedrich, "Public Policy and the Nature of Administrative Policy," *Public Policy*, 1(1940), 3-24; Herbert A. Simon, *Administrative Behavior: A Study of Decision-Making Processes in Administrative Organization*, 3rd ed. (New York: Free Press, 1976), xx, xxxvi-xxxvii, 220-28. Also, Herbert Kaufman, *The Forest Ranger: A Study in Administrative Behavior* (Baltimore: Johns Hopkins Press, 1960), and Kaufman, *Administrative Feedback: Monitoring Subordinates' Behavior* (Washington, D.C.: The Brookings Institution, 1973).

## Three · The Flow of Litigation in the Supreme Court

1. Graham Allison, *Essence of Decision* (Boston: Little, Brown and Co., 1971), 67.

2. For example, three other remands and ten consolidations from the 2d and 5th circuits in this sample resulted from one 2d circuit reversal—*Marchetti v. U.S.*, 390 U.S. 39 (1968).

3. *Curtis Publishing Co. v. Butts*, 388 U.S. 130 (1967); *U.S. v. Wade*, 388 U.S. 218 (1967); *Gojack v. U.S.*, 384 U.S. 702 (1966); *Afroyim v. Rusk*, 387 U.S. 253 (1967); and *Red Lion Broadcasting Co. v. F.C.C.*, 395 U.S. 367 (1969).

4. There were three important civil rights decisions in the statutory category: *Georgia v. Rachel*, 384 U.S. 780 (1966); *Greenwood v. Peacock*, 384 U.S. 808 (1966); and *Pierson v. Ray*, 386 U.S. 547 (1967).

5. *Harris v. U.S.*, 390 U.S. 234 (1968). For continuity of the mix, see Gerhard Casper and Richard A. Posner, *The Workload of the Supreme Court* (Chicago: American Bar Foundation, 1976), 84-85; and their "The Caseload of the Supreme Court: 1975 and 1976 Terms," *Supreme Court Review*, (1977), 87-98.

6. For discussion of increasing power by reducing the range of discretion, see Walter F. Murphy, *Elements of Judicial Strategy* (Chicago: University of Chicago Press, 1964), 23; and Thomas Schelling, *The Strategy of Conflict* (Cambridge: Harvard University Press, 1960), ch. 1.

7. Frank, J., in *Choate v. Commissioner of Internal Revenue*, 129 F. 2d 684, 686 (2d Cir. 1942).

8. *Textile Mills Securities Corp. v. Commissioner of Internal Revenue*, 314 U.S. 326, 335 (1941).

9. See Note, "Government Litigation in the Supreme Court: The Roles of the Solicitor General," *Yale Law Journal*, 78(1969), 1442-81; William E. Brigman, "The Office of the Solicitor General of the United States" (Ph.D. dissertation, University of North Carolina at Chapel Hill, 1966); Paul D. Carrington, "United States Appeals in Civil Cases: A Field and Statistical Study," *Houston Law Review*, 11(1974), 1101-23; Donald L. Horowitz, *The Jurocracy* (Lexington, Mass.: D. C. Heath, 1977); and Suzanne Weaver, *Decision to Prosecute: Organization and Public Policy in the Antitrust Division* (Cambridge: MIT Press, 1977).

10. See *Annual Reports of the Attorney General of the United States* (FY 1965-1967), 42, 54, and 39 respectively.

11. The three losses were *Commissioner of Internal Revenue v. Tellier*, 383 U.S. 687 (1966); *Houston Contractors Assn. v. N.L.R.B.*, 386 U.S. 664 (1967); and *Commissioner of Internal Revenue v. Bosch*, 387 U.S. 456 (1967).

12. 388 U.S. 218 (1967), and 384 U.S. 808 (1966).

13. For substantial variations in the subject matter of the government's requests for review, see Brigman, "Office of the Solicitor General," 77.

14. See, e.g., Felix Frankfurter, "Mr. Justice Brandeis and the Constitution," *Harvard Law Review*, 45(1931), 33, 79.

15. Joseph Tanenhaus et al., "The Supreme Court's Certiorari Jurisdiction: Cue Theory," in Glendon Schubert, ed., *Judicial Decision-Making* (New York: Free Press, 1963), 111-32. Also see Neil T. Zimmerman, "The Decision to Decide: A Statistical Analysis of the Preliminary Decision-Making Process of the United States Supreme Court" (Ph.D. dissertation, University of California at Riverside, 1970); and S. Sidney Ulmer, William Hintze, and Louise Kirklosky, "The Decision to Grant or Deny Certiorari: Further Consideration of Cue Theory," *Law and Society Review*, 6 (1972), 637.

16. Richard J. Richardson and Kenneth N. Vines, *The Politics of Federal Courts: Lower Courts in the United States* (Boston: Little, Brown and Co., 1970), 150-56.

17. See, e.g., Bernard G. Segal in *Hearings*, 1st Phase (1973), 1095.

18. Felix Frankfurter, as quoted in Alexander M. Bickel, *The Supreme Court and the Idea of Progress* (New York: Harper & Row, 1970), 20.

19. For a similar estimate, see Richardson and Vines, *Politics of Federal Courts*, 150.

20. See Robert G. McCloskey, *The Modern Supreme Court* (Cambridge: Harvard University Press, 1972), 57, 118-19. *Harris v. U.S.*, 390 U.S. 234 (1968).

21. Richardson and Vines, *Politics of Federal Courts*, 134, 159.

22. *Kent v. U.S.*, 383 U.S. 541 (1966).

23. *U.S. v. Jefferson Co. Bd. of Educ.*, 372 F. 2d 836 (5th Cir. 1966), *en banc*

380 F. 2d 385 (5th Cir. 1967), *cert. denied*, 389 U.S. 840 (1967). *U.S. v. Barnett*, 346 F. 2d 99 (5th Cir. 1965).

24. Julius Stone, John Hinckley Memorial Lecture, Johns Hopkins University, March 15, 1977. See Julius Stone, *Legal System and Lawyers' Reasonings* (Stanford: Stanford University Press, 1964).

25. William Denman to Henry F. Ashurst, February 19, 1937. George W. Norris Papers, Manuscripts Division, Library of Congress. Courtesy of Jerry Goldman.

26. Carl J. Friedrich, "Public Policy and the Nature of Administrative Responsibility," *Public Policy*, 1(1940), 3-24. See Sheldon Goldman and Thomas P. Jahnige, *The Federal Courts as a Political System* (New York: Harper & Row, 1971), 189-97; Edward N. Beiser, "The Rhode Island Supreme Court: A Well-Integrated Political System," *Law and Society Review*, 8(1973), 167-82.

27. Robert L. Stern and Eugene Gressman, *Supreme Court Practice*, 4th ed. (Washington, D.C.: Bureau of National Affairs, 1969), 154-58. Also, see Bernard G. Segal, *Hearings*, 1st Phase, 129.

28. See District of Columbia Court Reform and Criminal Procedure Act of 1970, Public Law 91-358, 84 Stat. 473; *Alexander v. Holmes County Bd. of Educ.*, 396 U.S. 19 (1969); *Carter v. West Feliciana Parish School Bd.*, 396 U.S. 290 (1970); and *New York Times*, February 14, 1971, 25:1.

29. Richardson and Vines, *Politics of Federal Courts*, 161. Arthur D. Hellman, "The Business of the Supreme Court under the Judiciary Act of 1925: The Plenary Docket in the 1970's," *Harvard Law Review*, 91(1978), 1709-1803.

30. See Martin Shapiro, *Law and Politics in the Supreme Court* (New York: Free Press, 1964).

31. Alpheus T. Mason, *Harlan Fiske Stone: Pillar of the Law* (New York: Viking Press, 1956), 384.

32. Shapiro, *Law and Politics*, 41-42.

33. Felix Frankfurter to Hugo L. Black, February 8, 1939, as quoted in Mason, *Stone*, 470n.

34. See, e.g., *Pearson v. Northeast Airlines*, 309 F. 2d 553 (2d Cir. 1962), *cert. denied*, 372 U.S. 912 (1963); *Durham v. U.S.*, 214 F. 2d 862 (D.C. Cir. 1954); *Easter v. District of Columbia*, 361 F. 2d 50 (D.C. Cir. 1966); *Scenic Hudson Conference v. F.P.C.*, 354 F. 2d 608 (2d Cir. 1965), *cert. denied*, 384 U.S. 941 (1966); *U.S. v. Jefferson County Bd. of Educ.*, 372 F. 2d 836 (5th Cir. 1966), 380 F. 2d 385 (5th Cir. 1967), *cert. denied*, 389 U.S. 840 (1967); *Office of Communication, United Church of Christ v. F.C.C.*, 359 F. 2d 994 (D.C. Cir. 1966); *Environmental Defense Fund, Inc. v. Ruckelshaus*, 439 F. 2d 584 (D.C. Cir. 1971), not appealed, *Baltimore Sun*, January 16, 1971, A1; *Hawkins v. Town of Shaw, Miss.*, 437 F. 2d 1286 (5th Cir. 1971).

35. *Sierra Club v. Morton*, 405 U.S. 727 (1972); *Vermont Yankee Nuclear Power Corp. v. Natural Resources Defense Council, Inc.*, 435 U.S. 19 (1978). For an interesting example of interaction in the development of judicial, administrative, and legislative legal standards, see Philip L. Greenfield,

"The Politics of Air Pollution: A Study of Courts and Administrative Agencies as Supplementary Lawmakers" (M.A. thesis, Johns Hopkins University, 1979).

36. Felix Frankfurter and James M. Landis, *The Business of the Supreme Court: A Study in the Federal Judicial System* (New York: Macmillan, 1927), 2-3.

37. Richardson and Vines, *Politics of Federal Courts*, 143-45, 161; Allison, *Essence of Decision*, 67-92.

38. Donald L. Horowitz, *The Courts and Social Policy* (Washington, D.C.: The Brookings Institution, 1977), 283.

39. Hruska Commission, *Structure and Internal Procedures: Recommendations for Change* (Washington, D.C.: June 1975), 30-39. For discussion, see references in Chapter One, note 44.

40. Shirley M. Hufstedler, "Courtship and Other Legal Arts," *American Bar Association Journal*, 60(1974), 547.

41. William J. Brennan, Jr., "The National Court of Appeals: Another Dissent," *University of Chicago Law Review*, 40(1973), 479.

42. Stone, *Legal System*, 234, 267-85.

43. *Hearings*, 1st Phase, 15, 11. Erwin N. Griswold, "Rationing Justice—The Supreme Court's Caseload and What the Court Does Not Do," *Cornell Law Review*, 60(1975), 335, 338-44; Roger C. Cramton, "Federal Appellate Justice in 1973," *Cornell Law Review*, 59(1974), 571-73.

44. See Martin Shapiro, *The Supreme Court and Administrative Agencies* (New York: Free Press, 1968), 177-85.

45. Casper and Posner, *Workload of the Supreme Court*, 85-92. Cf. Hruska Commission, *Structure and Internal Procedures* (June 1975), 76-188; and Kenneth C. Haas, "The Reactions of the U.S. Courts of Appeals to Supreme Court Prisoner's Rights Decisions: An Analysis of Conflict among the Circuits," paper presented at the annual meeting of the American Political Science Association, Washington, D.C., 1979.

46. Carrington, "United States Appeals," 1105. Also Lay, J., in *Hearings*, 2d Phase, II, 903.

47. Carrington, "United States Appeals," 1104. For a complaint by Justice Blackmun about this practice, see *New York Times*, November 3, 1976, 71:4.

48. Donald P. Lay, "Why Rush to Judgment? Some Second Thoughts on the Proposed National Court of Appeals," *Judicature*, 59(1975), 175-76. Cf. Henry J. Friendly, *Federal Jurisdiction: A General View* (New York: Columbia University Press, 1973), 153-71, 176-90; and Burger, Blackmun, and White, J.J., *New York Times*, December 5, 1978, A18:1.

49. I am grateful to A. Leo Levin for suggesting this analogy.

50. Steven Flanders, Proceedings of a Conference on Social Science Research in the Courts (Denver: National Center for State Courts, January 20-22, 1977), 484; and Lawrence Baum, "Lower-Court Response to Supreme Court Decisions: Reconsidering a Negative Picture," *Justice System Journal*, 3(1978), 208-19.

51. Marvin Schick, *Learned Hand's Court* (Baltimore: Johns Hopkins Press, 1970), 170n.

52. I am grateful to Francis E. Rourke for this analogy. See Herbert A. Simon, *Administrative Behavior: A Study of Decision-Making Processes in Administrative Organization*, 3rd ed. (New York: Free Press, 1976), xx, xxxvi-xxxvii, 220-28. Also, Herbert Kaufman, *The Forest Ranger: A Study in Administrative Behavior* (Baltimore: Johns Hopkins Press, 1960), and Kaufman, *Administrative Feedback: Monitoring Subordinates' Behavior* (Washington, D.C.: The Brookings Institution, 1973).
53. *Hearings*, 2d Phase, II, 680-81.
54. Carrington, "United States Appeals," 1121. Also Casper and Posner, *Workload of the Supreme Court*.
55. *Hearings*, 1st Phase, 10, 651-52.
56. Ibid., 984.
57. Lay, "Why Rush to Judgment," 177.
58. Wyzanski, J., in Walter F. Murphy and C. Herman Pritchett, *Courts, Judges and Politics* (New York: Random House, 1961), 325.

## Four · **The Making of Circuit Judges**

1. See, e.g., Julius Stone, *Legal System and Lawyers' Reasonings* (Stanford: Stanford University Press, 1964), 21-62, 209-12; Karl N. Llewellyn, *The Common Law Tradition: Deciding Appeals* (Boston: Little, Brown and Co., 1960); Richard L. Richardson and Kenneth N. Vines, *The Politics of Federal Courts: Lower Courts in the United States* (Boston: Little, Brown and Co., 1970), 2-14, 173-77; Martin Shapiro, "Decentralized Decision-Making in the Law of Torts," in S. Sidney Ulmer, ed., *Political Decision-Making* (New York: Van Nostrand Reinhold, 1970), 44-75.
2. Henry J. Abraham, *The Judicial Process*, 3rd ed. (New York: Oxford University Press, 1975), 87-94. See Heinz Eulau and John D. Sprague, *Lawyers in Politics: A Study in Professional Convergence* (Indianapolis: Bobbs-Merrill, 1970); Richard S. Wells, "The Legal Profession and Politics," *Midwest Journal of Political Science*, 8(1964), 166-90; and Joseph A. Schlesinger, "Lawyers and American Politics: A Clarified View," *Midwest Journal of Political Science*, 1(1957), 26-39.
3. For trail-blazing conclusions of a movement toward professionalization of federal judges, see Rodney L. Mott, Spencer D. Albright, and Helen R. Semmerling, "Judicial Personnel," *Annals of the American Academy of Political and Social Science*, 167(1933), 143-55. In general, see Ernest Greenwood, "Attributes of a Profession," *Social Work*, 2(1957), 44-55; Howard M. Vollmer and Donald L. Mills, eds., *Professionalization* (Englewood Cliffs, N.J.: Prentice-Hall, 1966); and Wilbert E. Moore, *The Professions: Roles and Rules* (New York: Russell Sage Foundation, 1970).
4. Maurice Rosenberg, "The Qualities of Justice—Are They Strainable?" *Texas Law Review*, 44(1966), 1063-80. The literature on judicial selection is enormous. For useful bibliography, see Glenn R. Winters, ed., *Selected Readings in Judicial Selection*, rev. ed. (Chicago: American Judicature Society, 1973); and Craig R. Ducat and Victor E. Flango, "In Search of Qualified Judges: An Inquiry into the Relevance of Judicial Selection Research," paper

delivered at the annual meeting of the American Political Science Association, San Francisco, 1975.

5. Joel Ish, "A Model of Judicial Recruitment," unpublished ms., 1.

6. Richard A. Watson and Rondal G. Dowling, *The Politics of the Bench and the Bar* (New York: John Wiley and Sons, 1969), 16. Cf. Winters, *Selected Readings*; Herbert Jacob, "The Effect of Institutional Differences in the Recruitment Process: The Case of State Judges," *Journal of Public Law*, 13(1964), 104-19; and Bradley Canon, "The Impact of Formal Selection Processes on the Characteristics of Judges—Reconsidered," *Law and Society Review*, 6(1972), 579-93.

7. For theoretical foundations this linkage rests heavily on Kenneth Prewitt, *The Recruitment of Political Leaders: A Study of Citizen-Politicians* (Indianapolis: Bobbs-Merrill, 1970); and John L. Holland, *Making Vocational Choices: A Theory of Careers* (Englewood Cliffs, N.J.: Prentice-Hall, 1973). Also see Barbara Nachmann, "Childhood Experience and Vocational Choice in Law, Dentistry, and Social Work," *Journal of Counselling Psychology*, 7(1960), 243-50; and Basil Sherlock and Alan Cohen, "The Strategy of Occupational Choice: Recruitment to Dentistry," *Social Forces*, 44(1966), 301-13.

8. Nina Totenberg, "Will Judges Be Chosen Rationally?" *Judicature*, 60 (1976), 93.

9. Harold W. Chase, *Federal Judges: The Appointing Process* (Minneapolis: University of Minnesota Press, 1972); John R. Schmidhauser, *Judges and Justices: The Federal Appellate Judiciary* (Boston: Little, Brown and Co., 1979).

10. Prewitt, *Recruitment*, 7.

11. Sheldon Goldman, "Judicial Appointments to the United States Courts of Appeals," *Wisconsin Law Review* (1967), 186-214; Goldman, "Johnson and Nixon Appointees to the Lower Federal Courts: Some Socio-Political Perspectives," *Journal of Politics*, 34(1972), 935, 939. For further evidence of partisanship in judicial recruitment, see Chase, *Federal Judges*; and Sheldon Goldman, "Judicial Backgrounds, Recruitment, and the Party Variable: The Case of the Johnson and Nixon Appointees to the United States District and Appeals Courts," *Arizona State Law Journal* (1974), 211-22; and Goldman, "A Profile of Carter's Judicial Nominees," *Judicature*, 62(1978), 246-54.

12. Mott et al., "Judicial Personnel," 153. Goldman, "Judicial Backgrounds," 220; and Samuel Krislov, "Constituency versus Constitutionalism: The Desegregation Issue and Tensions and Aspirations of Southern Attorneys General," *Midwest Journal of Political Science*, 3(1959), 75-92.

13. Totenberg, "Will Judges Be Chosen Rationally?" 93.

14. *New York Times*, January 6, 1980, 12:18. Cf. Roger H. Davidson, *The Role of the Congressman* (New York: Pegasus, 1969), 41; and Donald R. Matthews, *U.S. Senators and Their World* (Chapel Hill: University of North Carolina Press, 1960), 33.

15. See Joel B. Grossman, *Lawyers and Judges: The ABA and the Politics of Judicial Selection* (New York: John Wiley and Sons, 1965).

16. See Goldman, "Judicial Backgrounds," 212.

17. Jerome E. Carlin, *Lawyers on Their Own* (New Brunswick, N.J.: Rutgers University Press, 1962), 18-23.

18. See James Willard Hurst, *The Growth of American Law* (Boston: Little, Brown and Co., 1950), chs. 12 and 13; Joel F. Handler, *The Lawyer and His Community* (Madison: University of Wisconsin Press, 1967); Jerome E. Carlin, *Lawyers' Ethics: A Survey of the New York City Bar* (New York: Russell Sage Foundation, 1966); Jerold S. Auerbach, *Unequal Justice: Lawyers and Social Change in Modern America* (New York: Oxford University Press, 1976), 41-73; Jack Ladinsky, "Careers of Lawyers, Law Practice and Legal Institutions," *American Sociological Review*, 28(1963), 47-54; and John P. Heinz, Edward O. Laumann, Charles L. Cappell, Terrence C. Halliday, and Michael H. Schealman, "Diversity, Representation, and Leadership in an Urban Bar: A First Report of a Survey of the Chicago Bar," *American Bar Foundation Research Journal* (1976), 717-85.

19. Cf. Grossman, *Lawyers and Judges*, 204. I am grateful to Edward Heck for suggesting this term.

20. Holland, *Making Vocational Choices*, 6.

21. Alpheus T. Mason, *William Howard Taft* (New York: Simon & Schuster, 1964), 717. Quote in William H. Harbaugh, *Lawyer's Lawyer: The Life of John W. Davis* (New York: Oxford University Press, 1973), 192.

22. Francis Biddle, *In Brief Authority* (New York: Doubleday & Co., 1962), 79-80. For loss of interest in politics by federal chief justices before their appointment, see J. Woodford Howard, Jr., "Judicial Biography and the Behavioral Persuasion," *American Political Science Review*, 65(1971), 704-15.

23. Felix Frankfurter to Eugene V. Rostow, June 15, 1955. Frankfurter Papers, Manuscript Division, Library of Congress.

24. Harold R. Medina to Richard Hartshorne, November 20, 1947. Medina Papers, Firestone Library, Princeton University.

25. Harold D. Lasswell, "The Selective Effect of Personality on Political Participation," in Richard Christie and Marie Jahoda, eds., *Studies in the Scope and Method of "The Authoritarian Personality"* (Glencoe, Ill.: Free Press, 1954), 197-225. For an interesting application of incentive theory, see Austin Sarat, "Judging in Trial Courts: An Exploratory Study," *Journal of Politics*, 39(1977), 368-98, and sources cited.

26. Holland, *Making Vocational Choices*, 9, 6.

27. Carlin, *Lawyers on Their Own*, 168.

28. Schlesinger, "Lawyers and American Politics." For the continuity of these incentives, see Seymour Warkov and Joseph Zelan, *Lawyers in the Making* (Chicago: Aldine, 1965), 12.

29. *New York Times*, June 27, 1969, 17.

30. See Chase, *Federal Judges*, 3-47; Mott et al., "Judicial Personnel."

31. *New York Times*, July 29, 1973, 40:3.

32. John R. Brown to James O. Eastland, July 10, 1968. Senate Judiciary Committee files, courtesy of Hugh E. Jones. Richard Harris, *Decision* (New York: E. P. Dutton & Co., 1971), 44-45. See Walter F. Murphy, "In His Own Image: Mr. Chief Justice Taft and Supreme Court Appointments," *Supreme*

*Court Review* (1961), 159-93; and Bruce Allen Murphy, "A Supreme Court Justice as Politician: Felix Frankfurter and Federal Court Appointments," *American Journal of Legal History*, 21(1977), 316-34.

33. Alpheus T. Mason and William M. Beaney, *American Constitutional Law*, 6th ed. (Englewood Cliffs, N.J.: Prentice-Hall, 1978), xiii.

34. Executive Order 11972. *U.S. Code Congressional and Administrative News*, 95th Cong., 1st Sess. (March 1977), 285.

35. See Peter G. Fish, "Questioning Judicial Candidates: What Can Merit Selectors Ask?" *Judicature*, 62(1978), 8-17; Larry C. Berkson, "The U.S. Circuit Judge Nominating Commission: The Candidates' Perspective," *Judicature*, 62(1979), 466-82. For affirmative action, see Robert J. Lipshutz and Douglas B. Huron, "Achieving a More Representative Federal Judiciary," *Judicature*, 62(1979), 483-85; Sheldon Goldman, "Should There Be Affirmative Action for the Judiciary?" *Judicature*, 62(1979), 488-94; and Peter G. Fish, "Evaluating the Black Judicial Applicant," *Judicature*, 62(1979), 495-501; Elliot E. Slotnick, "The Changing Role of the Senate Judiciary Committee in Judicial Selection," *Judicature*, 62(1979), 502-10; Charles Halpern and Ann Macrory, "Choosing Judges," *New York Times*, July 1, 1979, E21.

36. Berkson, "U.S. Circuit Judge Nominating Commission," 478-80; Slotnick, "Changing Role," 508-10. *Wall Street Journal*, October 23, 1978, 24.

37. See Goldman, "Should There Be Affirmative Action?"; Goldman, "A Profile of Carter's Judicial Nominees," *Judicature*, 62(1978), 246-54; and Larry Berkson, Susan Carbon, and Alan Neff, "A Study of the U.S. Circuit Judge Nominating Commission: Findings, Conclusions and Recommendations," *Judicature*, 63(1979), 104-29.

38. Sheldon Goldman, "Voting Behavior on the United States Courts of Appeals Revisited," *American Political Science Review*, 69(1975), 491-506.

39. Kenneth Prewitt and Heinz Eulau, "Social Bias in Leadership Selection, Political Recruitment, and Electoral Context," *Journal of Politics*, 33(1971), 293-315. For similar effects among lawyers, see Carlin, *Lawyers on Their Own*; Ladinsky, "Careers of Lawyers"; and Jack Ladinsky, "The Impact of Social Backgrounds of Lawyers on Law Practice and Law," *Journal of Legal Education*, 16(1963), 127-44. For a profile of southern lawyers, see Charles Y. Chai, "Recruitment Characteristics and Leadership Status of Urban Lawyers in the South: A Case Study of New Orleans," *Tulane Law Review*, 48(1974), 239-71.

40. Matthews, *U.S. Senators*, 44-45.

41. Senate Committee on the Judiciary, *Legislative History of the United States Circuit Courts of Appeals and the Judges Who Served during the Period 1801 through March 1958*, 85th Cong., 2d Sess. (1958), 7-10.

42. Harris, *Decision*, 110.

43. Warkov and Zelan, *Lawyers in the Making*, 3, 47. Matthews, *U.S. Senators*, 20.

44. For similar conclusions, see Goldman, "Judicial Backgrounds," 222. Quote in Matthews, *U.S. Senators*, 44.

45. See Mott et al., "Judicial Personnel"; Glendon Schubert and David J. Danelski, eds., *Comparative Judicial Behavior* (New York: Oxford Univer-

sity Press, 1969); Brian Abel-Smith and Robert Stevens, *Lawyers and the Courts: A Sociological Study of the English Legal System, 1790-1965* (Cambridge: Harvard University Press, 1967); and C. Neal Tate, "Paths to the Bench in Britain: A Quasi-Experimental Study of the Recruitment of a Judicial Elite," paper delivered at the annual meeting of the Western Political Science Association, Denver, 1974.

46. Matthews, *U.S. Senators*, 14-17.

47. Mott et al., "Judicial Personnel," 151.

48. Davidson, *Role of the Congressman*, 58. Kenneth E. Dawson and Kenneth Prewitt, *Political Socialization* (Boston: Little, Brown and Co., 1969), 58-59. For other estimates of geographic mobility among federal judges, see Richardson and Vines, *Politics of Federal Courts*, 72; and John D. Sprague, *Voting Patterns of the United States Supreme Court: Cases in Federalism 1889-1959* (Indianapolis: Bobbs-Merrill, 1968).

49. Mary H. Curzan, "A Case Study in the Selection of Federal Judges: The Fifth Circuit, 1953-1963" (Ph.D. dissertation, Yale University, 1968), 44-46, 51.

50. "An Afterword: Science and the Judicial Process," *Harvard Law Review*, 79(1966), 1604-28. From a large literature, see, for example, David W. Adamany, "The Party Variable in Judges' Voting: Conceptual Notes and a Case Study," *American Political Science Review*, 63(1969), 57-73; Don R. Bowen, "The Explanation of Judicial Voting Behavior from Sociological Characteristics of Judges" (Ph.D. dissertation, Yale University, 1965); Bradley Canon and Dean Jaros, "Dissent on State Supreme Courts: The Differential Significance of Characteristics of Judges," *Midwest Journal of Political Science*, 15(1971), 322-46; Sheldon Goldman, "Voting Behavior Revisited," and "Backgrounds, Attitudes and Voting Behavior of Judges," *Journal of Politics*, 31(1969), 214-29; Joel B. Grossman, "Social Backgrounds and Judicial-Decision Making," *Harvard Law Review*, 79(1966), 1551-64, and sources cited; also Grossman, "Social Backgrounds and Judicial Decisions: Notes for a Theory," *Journal of Politics*, 29(1967), 334-51; Stuart S. Nagel, "Political Party Affiliations and Judges' Decisions," *American Political Science Review*, 55(1961), 843-50; John R. Schmidhauser, "Stare Decisis, Dissent, and the Background of the Justices of the Supreme Court of the United States," *University of Toronto Law Journal*, 14(1962), 194-212; S. Sidney Ulmer, "Dissent Behavior and the Social Backgrounds of Supreme Court Justices," *Journal of Politics*, 32(1970), 580-98.

51. John Wahlke, Heinz Eulau, William Buchanan, and LeRoy C. Ferguson, *The Legislative System: Explorations in Legislative Behavior* (New York: John Wiley and Sons, 1962), 70. The following section draws heavily from Dawson and Prewitt, *Political Socialization*; Kenneth P. Langton, *Political Socialization* (New York: Oxford University Press, 1969); and Roberta S. Sigel, *Learning about Politics: A Reader in Political Socialization* (New York: Random House, 1970).

52. Robert T. Hogan and Carol Mills, "Legal Socialization," *Human Development*, 19(1976), 261-76. Also, Robert Hogan, *Personality Theory: The Personological Tradition* (Englewood Cliffs, N.J.: Prentice-Hall, 1976).

53. Langton, *Political Socialization*, 14-16; Sigel, *Learning about Politics*, 427-33. See Talcott Parsons, *The Social System* (Glencoe, Ill.: Free Press, 1951), 208.

54. Orville G. Brim, Jr., and Stanton Wheeler, *Socialization after Childhood: Two Essays* (New York: John Wiley and Sons, 1966), 3-7.

55. Ibid., 83-85; Dawson and Prewitt, *Political Socialization*, 75; and Leonore Alpert, Burton M. Atkins, and Robert C. Ziller, "Becoming a Judge: The Transition from Advocate to Arbiter," *Judicature*, 62(1979), 325-35.

56. Cf. Felix Frankfurter, "The Supreme Court in the Mirror of the Justices," *University of Pennsylvania Law Review*, 105(1957), 791, 785. On training programs, see Beverly Blair Cook, "The Socialization of New Federal Judges: Impact on District Court Business," *Washington University Law Quarterly* (1971), 253-79.

57. Among the few studies of judicial socialization are Cook, "Socialization of New Federal Judges"; Eulau and Sprague, *Lawyers in Politics*, 56-64; Alpert et al., "Becoming a Judge"; and Robert Carp and Russell Wheeler, "Sink or Swim: The Socialization of a Federal District Judge," *Journal of Public Law*, 21(1972), 359-93.

58. Allan Kornberg and Norman Thomas, "The Political Socialization of National Legislative Elites in the United States and Canada," *Journal of Politics*, 27(1965), 761-75.

59. Alpheus T. Mason, *Brandeis: A Free Man's Life* (New York: Viking Press, 1946), 88-95.

60. See Robert E. Lane, "Fathers and Sons: Foundations of Political Belief," *American Sociological Review*, 24(1959), 502-11.

61. Kornberg and Thomas, "Political Socialization," 774; Hogan, *Personality Theory*.

62. Cf. Matthews, *U.S. Senators*, 49.

63. Martin Mayer, *Emory Buckner* (New York: Harper & Row, 1968).

64. Matthews, *U.S. Senators*, 50-52. Davidson, *Role of the Congressman*, 49-62.

65. Kornberg and Thomas, "Political Socialization," 770.

66. Langton, *Political Socialization*, 84-119. Dan Lortie, "Laymen to Lawmen: Law Schools, Careers, and Professional Socialization," *Harvard Education Review*, 29(1959), 352, 363-67.

67. Davidson, *Role of the Congressman*, 50.

68. Mott et al., "Judicial Personnel," 149-55.

69. John T. Wold, "Political Orientations, Social Backgrounds, and Role Perceptions of State Supreme Court Judges," *Western Political Quarterly*, 27(1974), 239-48.

70. See Mott et al., "Judicial Personnel," 149-55. Herbert Jacob and Kenneth N. Vines, *Politics in the American States: A Comparative Analysis*, 2d ed. (Boston: Little, Brown and Co., 1971), 272-310; and Thomas Dye, *The Politics of Equality* (Indianapolis: Bobbs-Merrill, 1971), 166-71.

71. Krislov, "Constituency versus Constitutionalism," 84-92.

72. 347 U.S. 483 (1954); 349 U.S. 294 (1955).

73. Kenneth N. Vines, "Federal District Judges and Race Relations Cases in the South," *Journal of Politics*, 26(1964), 337-57.
74. Davidson, *Role of the Congressman*, 59-60.
75. Bell resignation, *Baltimore Sun*, July 27, 1976, A4 and December 23, 1976, A8; *Washington Post*, August 15, 1976, A3:7. For suit in the U.S. Court of Claims by several federal district and circuit judges seeking pay increases, see *Atkins v. U.S.*, 556 F. 2d 1028 (1977).
76. Richard F. Fenno, Jr., *Congressmen in Committees* (Boston: Little, Brown and Co., 1973), 199-202.
77. Grossman, *Lawyers and Judges*, 204.
78. Archibald Cox, *The Warren Court: Constitutional Decision as an Instrument of Reform* (Cambridge: Harvard University Press, 1968), 21-22.
79. Ira Sharkansky and C. Richard Hofferbert, "Dimensions of State Policy," in Jacob and Vines, *Politics in the American States*, 315-50.
80. Davidson, *Role of the Congressman*, 70.
81. Brim and Wheeler, *Socialization after Childhood*, 27-28.
82. Roscoe Pound, quoted in Rosenberg, "Qualities of Justice," 1063.

### Five • The Purposes of Courts of Appeals

1. Learned Hand to D. Lawrence Groner, May 31, 1946. Groner Papers, University of Virginia. Courtesy of Jerry Goldman.
2. Abram Chayes, "The Role of the Judge in Public Law Litigation," *Harvard Law Review*, 89(1976), 1281-1316.
3. Karl N. Llewellyn, *The Common Law Tradition: Deciding Appeals* (Boston: Little, Brown and Co., 1960), 19-61.
4. Henry J. Friendly, Book Review, *University of Pennsylvania Law Review*, 109(1961), 1040, 1045.
5. John C. Wahlke, Heinz Eulau, William Buchanan, and LeRoy C. Ferguson, *The Legislative System: Explorations in Legislative Behavior* (New York: John Wiley and Sons, 1962), 246.
6. See Lewis Anthony Dexter, *Elite and Specialized Interviewing* (Evanston: Northwestern University Press, 1970), ch. 5.
7. See, e.g., Wahlke et al., *Legislative System*, 245-66; Henry Robert Glick, *Supreme Courts in State Politics* (New York: Basic Books, 1971); and Kenneth N. Vines, "The Judicial Role in the American States," in Joel B. Grossman and Joseph Tanenhaus, eds., *Frontiers of Judicial Research* (New York: John Wiley and Sons, 1969), 461-85. For parallel questions, see Donald D. Jackson, *Judges* (New York: Atheneum, 1974), 303-25; and John T. Wold, "Political Orientations, Social Backgrounds, and Role Perceptions of State Supreme Court Judges," *Western Political Quarterly*, 27(1974), 239-48. For useful discussion, see Charles H. Sheldon, *The American Judiciary: Models and Approaches* (New York: Dodd, Mead and Co., 1974). For critiques of various methods of discerning role perceptions, see Thomas D. Ungs and Larry R. Baas, "Judicial Role Perceptions: A Q-Technique Study of Ohio Judges," *Law and Society Review*, 6(1972), 343-66; and Victor E.

Flango, Lettie M. Wenner, and Manfred W. Wenner, "The Concept of Judicial Role: A Methodological Note," *American Journal of Political Science*, 19(1975), 277-89.

8. Llewellyn, *Common Law Tradition*. Julius Stone, *Legal System and Lawyers' Reasonings* (Stanford: Stanford University Press, 1964).

9. Cf. the works of Wahlke, Glick, Vines, and Wold, cited in notes 5 and 7, this chapter; also, Austin Sarat, "Judging in Trial Courts: An Exploratory Study," *Journal of Politics*, 39(1977), 368-98.

10. For a similar view, see John J. Gibbons, in *Hearings*, 1st Phase (1973), 43. Also, Arthur J. Goldberg, *Hearings*, 2d Phase, I, 169.

11. Collins J. Seitz, *Hearings*, 1st Phase, 33.

12. *The Third Circuit Time Study* (Washington, D.C.: Federal Judicial Center, 1973).

13. For kindred tensions, see Lawrence B. Mohr, "The Concept of Organizational Goal," *American Political Science Review*, 67(1973), 470-81; Herbert L. Packer, "Two Models of the Criminal Process," *University of Pennsylvania Law Review*, 113(1964), 1-68; and Malcolm M. Feeley, "Two Models of the Criminal Justice System: An Organizational Perspective," *Law and Society Review*, 7(1973), 407-25.

14. Cf. Brandeis, J., in *Olmstead v. United States*, 277 U.S. 438, 485 (1928) with Learned Hand, *The Bill of Rights* (Cambridge: Harvard University Press, 1958), 70-71.

15. See works by Glick, Vines, and Wold in note 7, this chapter.

16. Wahlke et al., *Legislative System*, 259, 272; Roger H. Davidson, *The Role of the Congressman* (New York: Pegasus, 1969), 80; James David Barber, *The Lawmakers* (New Haven: Yale University Press, 1968).

17. Herbert A. Simon, *Administrative Behavior: A Study of Decision-Making Processes in Administrative Organization*, 3rd ed. (New York: Free Press, 1976), xx, xxxvi-xxxvii, 220-28.

18. See Marvin Schick, *Learned Hand's Court* (Baltimore: Johns Hopkins Press, 1970), 338-47.

19. For exceptional public criticisms of Warren Court tensions over criminal procedure, see Henry J. Friendly, *Benchmarks* (Chicago: University of Chicago Press, 1967), 235-84. Also, *New York Times*, November 10, 1968, 73. J. Edward Lumbard, "Criminal Justice and the Rule-Making Power," *West Virginia Law Review*, 70(1968), 143-54.

20. Schick, *Learned Hand's Court*, 11.

21. Cf. Rodney L. Mott, Spencer D. Albright, and Helen R. Semmerling, "Judicial Personnel," *Annals of the American Academy of Political and Social Science*, 167(1933), 143-49. For further evidence of limits on intercircuit communication, see Robert A. Carp, "The Scope and Function of Intracircuit Judicial Communication: A Case Study of the Eighth Circuit," *Law and Society Review*, 6(1972), 405, 407, 422.

22. Cf. *U.S. ex. rel. Stenno v. Denno*, 355 U.S. F. 2d 731 (2d Cir. 1966); 388 U.S. 293 (1967) with *Wade v. U.S.*, 358 F. 2d 557 (5th Cir. 1966); 388 U.S. 218 (1967).

23. Carl J. Friedrich, "Public Policy and the Nature of Administrative Responsibility," *Public Policy*, 1(1940), 3-24.

24. Cf. Jackson, *Judges*, 303-4; William D. Kitchin, *Federal District Judges: An Analysis of Judicial Perceptions* (Baltimore: Collage Press, 1978). Kenneth M. Dolbeare, *Trial Courts in Urban Politics* (New York: John Wiley and Sons, 1968).

25. Carp, "Scope and Function," 407.

26. See John M. Wisdom, "The Friction-Making, Exacerbating Political Role of Federal Courts," *Southwestern Law Journal*, 21(1967), 411.

27. Richard J. Richardson and Kenneth N. Vines, *The Politics of Federal Courts: Lower Courts in the United States* (Boston: Little, Brown and Co., 1970), 173-77.

28. For similar problems with the term "public policy," see Ira Sharkansky, *Policy Analysis in Political Science* (Chicago: Markham Publishing Co., 1970), 1-18.

29. Martin Shapiro, "Decentralized Decision-Making in the Law of Torts," in S. Sidney Ulmer, ed., *Political Decision-Making* (New York: Van Nostrand Reinhold, 1970), 44-75.

30. *New York Times*, October 12, 1975, 30:1. For the role of federal courts in enabling southerners to accept desegregation "without losing face," see Jimmy Carter's comment in Jack Bass and Walter de Vries, *The Transformation of Southern Politics: Social Change and Political Consequence since 1945* (New York: Basic Books, 1976), 406.

31. Dorothy Emmet, *Rules, Roles and Relations* (New York: St. Martin's Press, 1966), 138-66.

32. Arthur L. Goodhart, "Legal Procedure and Democracy," *Journal of the American Judicature Society*, 47(1963), 61. For judging as interest activity, see Craig R. Ducat and Victor E. Flango, "Toward an Integration of Public Law and Judicial Behavior," *Journal of Politics*, 39(1977), 49-50.

33. Chayes, "Role of the Judge," 1316. Beverly Blair Cook, "Role Lag in Urban Trial Courts," *Western Political Quarterly*, 25(1972), 234.

34. See Peter G. Fish, "Should Federal Appellate Judges Help Select Their Colleagues?" *Judicature*, 63(1979), 6-7, 44-45.

35. *New York Times*, April 7, 1973, 1:2.

36. See Walter F. Murphy, *Elements of Judicial Strategy* (Chicago: University of Chicago Press, 1964), ch. 7. Irving B. Kaufman, "Lions or Jackals: The Function of a Code of Judicial Ethics," *Law and Contemporary Problems*, 37(1970), 3-8. Cf. Jerome E. Carlin, *Lawyers' Ethics: A Survey of the New York City Bar* (New York: Russell Sage Foundation, 1966).

37. For a disclosure of stock holding by 5th circuit judges Brown and Jones in a gas rate-reduction case, see *Baltimore Sun*, October 15, 1969, A6.

38. For similar views of Justice Blackmun, see *New York Times*, July 14, 1975, 13:6.

39. Benjamin N. Cardozo, *The Growth of the Law* (New Haven: Yale University Press, 1924), 61.

## Six · Judicial Values and Judicial Votes

1. Donald L. Horowitz, *The Courts and Social Policy* (Washington, D.C.: The Brookings Institution, 1977).

2. Julius Stone, *Legal System and Lawyers' Reasonings* (Stanford: Stanford University Press, 1964).

3. Cf. Theodore L. Becker, *Political Behavioralism and Modern Jurisprudence* (Chicago: Rand McNally & Co., 1964), 11-26, 66; and Kenneth M. Dolbeare, *Trial Courts in Urban Politics* (New York: John Wiley and Sons, 1967), 69, with Glendon Schubert, *The Judicial Mind* (Evanston: Northwestern University Press, 1965), 12-15, 286-87. See Charles H. Sheldon, *The American Judicial Process: Models and Approaches* (New York: Harper & Row, 1974), 73-98; James L. Gibson, "Judges' Role Orientations, Attitudes and Decisions: An Interactive Model," *American Political Science Review*, 72(1978), 911-24; and Gibson, "Discriminant Functions, Role Orientations, and Judicial Behavior: Theoretical and Methodological Linkages," *Journal of Politics*, 39(1977), 984-1007.

For all the reliance on professionalism in justifications of judicial power over the years, the effort to examine systematically the relationships among judicial role orientations and behavior began with C. Herman Pritchett's *Civil Liberties and the Vinson Court* (Chicago: University of Chicago Press, 1954). Other published attempts include: Theodore L. Becker, "A Survey of Hawaiian Judges: The Effect on Decisions of Judicial Role Variations," *American Political Science Review*, 60(1966), 677-80; Victor E. Flango and Craig R. Ducat, "Toward an Integration of Public Law and Judicial Behavior," *Journal of Politics*, 39(1977), 41-72; Henry Robert Glick, *Supreme Courts in State Politics: An Investigation of the Judicial Role* (New York: Basic Books, 1971), 42-51; Joel B. Grossman, "Role-Playing and the Analysis of Judicial Behavior: The Case of Mr. Justice Frankfurter," *Journal of Public Law*, 11(1962), 285-309; and Grossman, "Dissenting Blocs on the Warren Court: A Study in Judicial Role Behavior," *Journal of Politics*, 30(1968), 1068-90; Dorothy B. James, "Role Theory and the Supreme Court," *Journal of Politics*, 30(1968), 160-86; Dean Jaros and Robert I. Mendelsohn, "The Judicial Role and Sentencing Behavior," *Midwest Journal of Political Science*, 11(1967), 471-88; and Kenneth N. Vines, "The Judicial Role in the American States: An Exploration," in Joel B. Grossman and Joseph Tanenhaus, eds., *Frontiers of Judicial Research* (New York: John Wiley and Sons, 1969), 461-85.

4. John C. Wahlke, Heinz Eulau, William Buchanan, and LeRoy C. Ferguson, *The Legislative System: Explorations in Legislative Behavior* (New York: John Wiley and Sons, 1962); and Roger H. Davidson, *The Role of the Congressman* (New York: Pegasus, 1969). Cf. Warren E. Miller and Donald E. Stokes, "Constituency Influence in Congress," *American Political Science Review*, 57(1963), 45-56; Heinz Eulau and Katherine Hinckley, "Legislative Institutions and Processes," in James A. Robinson, ed., I, *Political Science Annual* (Indianapolis: Bobbs-Merrill, 1966), 85-189; Ronald D. Hedlund and H. Paul Friesema, "Representatives' Perceptions of Constituency Opinion,"

*Journal of Politics*, 34(1972), 730-52; and Jack R. Van Der Slik, "Role Theory and the Behavior of Representatives," *Public Affairs Bulletin*, 6(Public Affairs Research Bureau, Southern Illinois University, March-April 1973), 1-11. Also, cf. James N. Rosenau, "Private Preferences and Political Responsibilities: The Relative Potency of Individual and Role Variables in the Behavior of U.S. Senators," in J. David Singer, ed., *Quantitative International Politics* (New York: Free Press, 1968), 22-27; and Glen H. Stassen, "Individual Preference versus Role-Constraint in Policy-Making," *World Politics*, 25(1972), 96-119.

5. See references in note 3, this chapter. Also Charles H. Sheldon, "Perceptions of the Judicial Roles in Nevada," *Utah Law Review* (1968), 355-67; Thomas D. Ungs and Larry R. Baas, "Judicial Role Perceptions: A Q-Technique Study of Ohio Judges," *Law and Society Review*, 6(1972), 343-66; and John T. Wold, "Political Orientations, Social Backgrounds, and Role Perceptions of State Supreme Court Judges," *Western Political Quarterly*, 27(1974), 239-48.

6. Cf. Wold, "Political Orientations"; Glick, *Supreme Courts in State Politics*; and Vines, "Judicial Role."

7. 347 U.S. 483 (1954).

8. *Durham v. United States*, 214 F. 2d 862 (D.C. Cir. 1954); *United States v. Jefferson County Bd. of Educ.*, 372 F. 2d 836 (5th Cir. 1966), 380 F. 2d 385 (5th Cir. 1967), cert. denied, 389 U.S. 840 (1967).

9. See references in notes 3 and 5, this chapter. Also, William D. Kitchin, *Federal District Judges: An Analysis of Judicial Perceptions* (Baltimore: Collage Press, 1978).

10. Interview, *U.S. News and World Report*, August 21, 1972, 39.

11. Charles E. Clark and David M. Trubek, "The Creative Role of the Judge: Restraint and Freedom in the Common Law Tradition," *Yale Law Journal*, 71(1961), 262.

12. Ibid., 256n. Cf. Benjamin N. Cardozo, *The Nature of the Judicial Process* (New Haven: Yale University Press, 1921), 164; Cardozo, *The Growth of the Law* (New Haven: Yale University Press, 1924), 60-61; Henry J. Friendly, "Reactions of a Lawyer—Newly Become Judge," *Yale Law Journal*, 71(1961), 222; and Karl N. Llewellyn, *The Common Law Tradition: Deciding Appeals* (Boston: Little, Brown and Co., 1960), 25.

13. See references in notes 3, 5, and 9, this chapter.

14. Cf. Becker, *Political Behavioralism*, 99.

15. Burger, "Interview," 40.

16. Miller and Stokes, "Constituency Influence," 56.

17. William J. Goode, "A Theory of Role Strain," *American Sociological Review*, 25(1960), 483-96.

18. Richard Lempert, "Norm-Making in Social Exchange: A Contract Law Model," *Law and Society Review*, 7(1972), 1-32.

19. See, e.g., Reed C. Lawlor, "Personal Stare Decisis," *Southern California Law Review*, 41(1967), 73-118; Glendon Schubert, *The Judicial Mind Revisited* (New York: Oxford University Press, 1974), 20; and Vernon K. Dibble and Berton Pekowsky, "What Is and What Ought to Be: A Compari-

son of Certain Characteristics of the Ideological and Legal Styles of Thought," *American Journal of Sociology*, 79(1973), 511-49.

20. Archibald Cox, *The Warren Court: Constitutional Decision as an Instrument of Reform* (Cambridge: Harvard University Press, 1968), 20-23.

21. Cf. Wold, "Political Orientations," 243; and Vines, "Judicial Role," 478-79.

22. Wold, "Political Orientations," 241-42.

23. See references, note 3 this chapter. Whereas Becker (*Political Behavioralism*, 66) and Dolbeare (*Trial Courts*, 69) considered judicial role perceptions as a major independent variable in the judicial process, Schubert (*Judicial Mind*, 286-87) subsumed them under individual attitudes and ideologies. Pritchett (*Civil Liberties*, chs. 10, 11) conceptualized role perceptions as intervening variables between individual values and votes. Cf. Walter F. Murphy and Joseph Tanenhaus, *The Study of Public Law* (New York: Random House, 1972), 108-9.

24. See M. Brewster Smith, "A Map for the Analysis of Personality and Politics," *Journal of Social Issues*, 24(July 1968), 15, 25. Alan A. Stone, Book Review, *Harvard Law Review*, 86(1973), 1352-64.

25. Kenneth P. Langton, *Political Socialization* (New York: Oxford University Press, 1969), 15.

26. See Ungs and Baas, "Judicial Role Perceptions." Mirra Komarovsky, "Some Problems in Role Analysis," *American Sociological Review*, 38(1973), 649-62.

27. See J. Woodford Howard, Jr., "On the Fluidity of Judicial Choice," *American Political Science Review*, 62(1968), 43-56.

28. John D. Sprague, *Voting Patterns of the United States Supreme Court: Cases in Federalism, 1889-1959* (Indianapolis: Bobbs-Merrill, 1968), 31.

29. Paul D. Carrington, Daniel J. Meador, and Maurice Rosenberg, *Justice on Appeal* (St. Paul: West Publishing Co., 1976), 2-3.

30. Gibson, "Judges' Role Orientations," 917-23. Also, Gibson, "Discriminant Functions," 1001-3.

31. Cf., e.g., Samuel C. Patterson, "Legislative Leadership and Political Ideology," *Public Opinion Quarterly*, 27(1963), 399-410; Schubert, *Judicial Mind*, chs. 7-9; and Glick, *Supreme Courts*, 49.

32. Stuart Nagel, "Political Party Affiliation and Judges' Decisions," *American Political Science Review*, 55(1961), 843-50, and Nagel, "Ethnic Affiliations and Judicial Propensities," *Journal of Politics*, 24(1962), 92-110; Vines, "Judicial Role," 479-480; and Glick, *Supreme Courts*, 49.

33. See Hubert M. Blalock, *Social Statistics*, 2d ed. (New York: McGraw-Hill, 1972), 220-28.

34. See Sidney Siegel, *Nonparametric Statistics for the Behavioral Sciences* (New York: McGraw-Hill, 1956), 42-47, 179; and Blalock, *Social Statistics*, 424.

35. Cf. Gibson, "Judges' Role Orientations," 914-16.

36. For similar hypotheses, see Vines, "Judicial Role," 478.

37. Cf., e.g., ibid., 478-85; Glick, *Supreme Courts*, 49-51; and Gibson, "Judges' Role Orientations," 917-21; Gibson, "Discriminant Functions," 1000-7.

38. Cf. Sheldon Goldman, "Voting Behavior on the U.S. Courts of Appeals Revisited," *American Political Science Review*, 69(1975), 493.

39. Gibson, "Discriminant Functions," 1005.

40. Miller and Stokes, "Constituency Influence," 56.

41. I am grateful to J. Randall Smith for assistance with the multivariate analysis. See Leo A. Goodman, "Causal Analysis of Data from Panel Studies and Other Kinds of Surveys," *American Journal of Sociology*, 78(1973), 1135-91; James A. Davis, "Hierarchical Models in Multivariate Contingency Tables: An Exegesis of Goodman's Recent Papers," in Herbert L. Coster, ed., *Sociological Methodology 1973-1974* (San Francisco: Jossey-Bass Publishers, 1974); and Yvonne M. M. Bishop, Stephen E. Feinberg, and Paul W. Holland, *Discrete Multivariate Analysis: Theory and Practice* (Cambridge: MIT Press, 1975). Cf. Gibson, "Judges' Role Orientations," and "Discriminant Functions."

42. Robert G. McCloskey, *The Modern Supreme Court* (Cambridge: Harvard University Press, 1972), 50.

43. Cardozo, *Nature of Judicial Process*, 16-17.

44. Cf. references in note 32, this chapter. Also see Sheldon Goldman, "Voting Behavior on the United States Courts of Appeals, 1961-1964," *American Political Science Review*, 60(1966), 374-83; and Goldman, "Voting Behavior Revisited," 491-506.

45. Cf., e.g., Nagel, "Political Party Affiliation"; Vines, "Judicial Role," 478; and David W. Adamany, "The Party Variable in Judges' Voting: Conceptual Notes and a Case Study," *American Political Science Review*, 63(1969), 57-73.

46. For parallel conclusions using simulation techniques, see Werner F. Grunbaum, "Analytical and Simulation Models for Explaining Judicial Decision-Making," in Grossman and Tanenhaus, *Frontiers of Judicial Research*, 307, 329-30. Also, see Gibson, "Judges' Role Orientations" and "Discriminant Functions."

47. Cf. Langton, *Political Socialization*, 15; Smith, "Map For Analysis," 25; Murphy and Tanenhaus, *Study of Public Law*, 109; Joel B. Grossman, "A Model for Judicial Policy Analysis," in Grossman and Tanenhaus, *Frontiers of Judicial Research*, 410; and David J. Danelski, "Conflict and Its Resolution in the Supreme Court," *Journal of Conflict Resolution*, 11(1967), 71-86.

48. Mark De Wolfe Howe, ed., *Holmes-Pollock Letters*, 2d ed. (Cambridge: Harvard University Press, 1961), I, xxxii.

49. Judith N. Shklar, *Legalism* (Cambridge: Harvard University Press, 1964).

50. Horowitz, *Courts and Social Policy*, 64. For similar conclusions regarding the Supreme Court, see Doris Marie Provine, "Case Selection in the United States Supreme Court," paper presented at the annual meeting of the American Political Science Association, Washington, D.C., 1979.

51. Burton M. Atkins and Justin J. Green, "Consensus on the United States Courts of Appeals: Illusion or Reality?" *American Journal of Political Science*, 20(1976), 735-48.

52. For evidence of overlapping policy and role values in the Supreme Court, see Flango and Ducat, "Toward an Integration," 41-72.

53. Henry J. Friendly, "Of Voting Blocs, and Cabbages and Kings," *University of Cincinnati Law Review*, 42(1973), 673, 677.

54. Dolbeare, *Trial Courts*, 69. Cf. references in note 23, this chapter.

55. Kenneth Prewitt, Heinz Eulau, and Betty H. Zisk, "Political Socialization and Political Roles," *Public Opinion Quarterly*, 30(1966-1967), 569-82.

56. See Glick, *Supreme Courts*; Vines, "Judicial Role"; and Wold, "Political Orientations."

57. Rodney L. Mott, Spencer D. Albright, and Helen R. Semmerling, "Judicial Personnel," *Annals of the American Academy of Political and Social Science*, 167(1933), 143-55. *Baltimore Sun*, September 23, 1978, A11. See 79 F.R.D. 187(1978); and *The Third Branch*, 11(October 1979), 1-2.

58. Kitchin, *Federal District Judges*; Greg A. Caldiera and John T. Wold, "Routine Decision-Making in Five California Courts of Appeal," forthcoming in *Polity*. For suggestive discussion, see Richard J. Richardson and Kenneth N. Vines, *The Politics of Federal Courts: Lower Courts in the United States* (Boston: Little, Brown and Co., 1970); Kenneth N. Vines, "Federal District Judges and Race Relations Cases in the South," *Journal of Politics*, 26(1964), 337-57; and Samuel Krislov, "Constituency versus Constitutionalism: The Desegregation Issue and Tensions and Aspirations of Southern Attorneys General," *Midwest Journal of Political Science*, 3(1959), 75-92.

59. Stassen, "Individual Preference," 118-19.

60. Herbert A. Simon, *Administrative Behavior: A Study of Decision-Making Processes in Administrative Organization*, 3rd ed. (New York: Free Press, 1976), xx, xxxvi-xxxvii, 220-28.

61. Friendly, "Reactions," 228.

62. Ronald Dworkin, "The Model of Rules," *University of Chicago Law Review*, 35(1967), 14-46; Dworkin, "Hard Cases," *Harvard Law Review*, 88(1975), 1057-1109.

63. Cardozo, *Nature of Judicial Process*, 17, 21.

64. Martin Shapiro, "Toward a Theory of Stare Decisis," *Journal of Legal Studies*, 1(1972), 125-34.

### Seven · Consensus and Conflict in Circuit Courts

1. From a rich literature see, e.g., Carl A. Auerbach, Willard Hurst, Lloyd K. Garrison, and Samuel Mermin, *The Legal Process*, 2d ed. (San Francisco: Chandler Publishing Co., 1961), chs. 5, 6, and 8; Walter F. Murphy, *Elements of Judicial Strategy* (Chicago: University of Chicago Press, 1964), 37-90; and S. Sidney Ulmer, *Courts as Small and Not So Small Groups* (New York: General Learning Process, 1971). See Sidney Verba, *Small Groups and Political Behavior* (Princeton: Princeton University Press, 1961).

2. See Heinz Eulau, "The Informal Organization of Decisional Structures in Small Legislative Bodies," *Midwest Journal of Political Science*, 13(1969), 351-54.

3. Burton M. Atkins, "Decision-Making Rules and Judicial Strategy on the United States Courts of Appeals," *Western Political Quarterly*, 25(1972), 628-29.

4. Ibid., 630. Also, Burton M. Atkins, "Some Theoretical Effects of the Decision-Making Rules on the United States Courts of Appeals," *Jurimetrics Journal*, 11(1970), 13-23; and Atkins, "Judicial Behavior and Tendencies towards Conformity in a Three Member Small Group: A Case Study of Dissent Behavior on the U.S. Court of Appeals," *Social Science Quarterly*, 54(1973), 44.

5. A. Lamar Alexander, Jr., Note, "En Banc Hearings in the Federal Courts of Appeals: Accommodating Institutional Responsibilities," Part I, *New York University Law Review*, 40(1965), 596-97. Justin J. Green and Burton M. Atkins, "Designated Judges: How Well Do They Perform?" *Judicature*, 61(1978), 358-70.

6. See Sheldon Goldman's articles: "Conflict and Consensus in the United States Courts of Appeals," *Wisconsin Law Review* (1968), 461-82; "Conflict on the U.S. Courts of Appeals, 1965-1971: A Quantitative Analysis," *University of Cincinnati Law Review*, 42(1973), 635-58; "Voting Behavior on the United States Courts of Appeals, 1961-1964," *American Political Science Review*, 60(1966), 374-83; "Voting Behavior on the United States Courts of Appeals Revisited," *American Political Science Review*, 69(1975), 491-506. Also, Herbert Jacob and Kenneth N. Vines, *Politics in the American States: A Comparative Analysis*, 2d ed. (Boston: Little, Brown and Co., 1971), 300.

7. Richard F. Fenno, Jr., "The House Appropriations Committee as a Political System: The Problem of Integration," *American Political Science Review*, 56(1962), 310.

8. Martin Shapiro, "Toward a Theory of *Stare Decisis*," *Journal of Legal Studies*, 1(1972), 125-34; Rensis Likert, "A Motivational Approach to a Modified Theory of Organization and Management," in Mason Haire, ed., *Modern Organization Theory* (New York: John Wiley and Sons, 1959), 184-217.

9. John C. Wahlke, Heinz Eulau, William Buchanan, and LeRoy C. Ferguson, *The Legislative System: Explorations in Legislative Behavior* (New York: John Wiley and Sons, 1962), 11, 141-43.

10. Ibid.

11. Ibid., 141. Also, Donald R. Matthews, *U.S. Senators and Their World* (New York: Vintage Books, 1960), 92-117; Fenno, "House Appropriations Committee"; Allan Kornberg and Norman Thomas, "The Political Socialization of National Legislative Elites in the United States and Canada," *Journal of Politics*, 27(1965), 961; Charles M. Price and Charles G. Bell, "The Rules of the Game: Political Fact or Academic Fancy," *Journal of Politics*, 32(1970), 839-40; and Henry Robert Glick, *Supreme Courts in State Politics: An Investigation of the Judicial Role* (New York: Basic Books, 1971), 55-68.

12. George Homans, *The Human Group* (New York: Harcourt, Brace, 1950), 315.

13. Wahlke et al., *Legislative System*, 141-43.

14. See, e.g., James E. Langer and Steven Flanders, *Comparative Report on Internal Operating Procedures of U.S. Courts of Appeals* (Washington, D.C.: Federal Judicial Center, March 28, 1973).

15. Ulmer, *Courts as Small Groups*, 1. Also Thomas G. Walker, "Judges in Concert: The Influence of the Group on Judicial Decision Making" (Ph.D. dissertation, University of Kentucky, 1970).

16. Jacob and Vines, *Politics in the American States*, 300.

17. Ulmer, *Courts as Small Groups*, 13. Also, Atkins, "Judicial Behavior," 43. For a bibliography of dissent literature, see Sheldon Goldman, "Conflict on Courts of Appeals," 639, n. 10.

18. Murphy, *Elements of Judicial Strategy*, 43-49.

19. David W. Rohde, "A Theory of Formation of Opinion Coalitions in the U.S. Supreme Court," in Richard G. Niemi and Herbert F. Weisberg, *Probability Models of Collective Decision Making* (Columbus, Ohio: Charles E. Merrill, 1972), 165-78.

20. Goldman, "Conflict and Consensus," "Conflict on Courts of Appeal," "Voting Behavior," and "Voting Behavior Revisited." Cf. Doris Marie Provine, "Case Selection in the United States Supreme Court," paper presented at the annual meeting of the American Political Science Association, Washington, D.C., 1979.

21. Burton M. Atkins and Justin J. Green, "Consensus on the United States Courts of Appeals: Illusion or Reality?" *American Journal of Political Science*, 20(1976), 735-48.

22. Glick, *Supreme Courts*, 55-56; John T. Wold, "Internal Procedures, Role Perceptions and Judicial Behavior: A Study of Four State Courts of Last Resort" (Ph.D. dissertation, Johns Hopkins University, 1972), 214-24. Lewis F. Powell, Jr., "What the Justices Are Saying . . . ," *American Bar Association Journal*, 62(1976), 1454.

23. 28 U.S.C. § 46 (1970). Brown, C.J., in Hearings on H.R. 7378 before Subcommittee no. 5 of the House Committee on the Judiciary, 92d Cong., 1st Sess. (1971), 99-100.

24. Steven Flanders and Jerry Goldman, "Screening Practices and the Use of Para-Judicial Personnel in a United States Court of Appeals: A Study of the Fourth Circuit," *Justice System Journal*, 1(1975), 6-13.

25. *Hearings*, 1st Phase, 351, 415-16, 102-3. In general, see Thomas B. Marvell, *Appellate Courts and Lawyers: Information Gathering in the Adversary System* (Westport, Conn.: Greenwood Press, 1978).

26. See Harold R. Medina, "The Decisional Process in the U.S. Court of Appeals, Second Circuit," *New York Law Journal*, February 18-20, 1963.

27. Ellen J. Miller, "Puisne Judges," *Harvard Law School Bulletin* (Fall 1975), 22-25. Also, see Daniel M. Taubman, "The Clerkship Experience," *Harvard Law School Bulletin* (Fall 1975), 27-31. Powell, "What the Justices Are Saying," 1454.

28. See Flanders and Goldman, "Screening Practices"; and Medina, "Decisional Process."

29. Alpheus T. Mason, *The Supreme Court from Taft to Warren* (Baton Rouge: Louisiana State University Press, 1958), 201.

30. *New York Times*, February 6, 1975, 65:2-3.

31. Marvin Schick, *Learned Hand's Court* (Baltimore: Johns Hopkins Press, 1970), 96.

32. Ibid., 98.

33. Medina, "Decisional Process."

34. Schick, *Learned Hand's Court*, 98.

35. Note, "The Second Circuit: Federal Judicial Administration in Microcosm," *Columbia Law Review*, 63(1963), 889. J. Edward Lumbard, "Current Problems of the Federal Courts of Appeals," *Cornell Law Review*, 54(1968), 35-38; and Irving R. Kaufman, "The Pre-Argument Conference: An Appellate Procedural Reform," *Columbia Law Review*, 74(1974), 1094-1103.

36. Schick, *Learned Hand's Court*, 219-304. See, e.g., *Walters v. Moore-McCormack Lines, Inc.*, 312 F. 2d 893, 896 (2d Cir. 1963); *Armstrong v. Bd. of Educ. of Birmingham*, 323 F. 2d 333, 352 (5th Cir. 1963); *Gray v. U.S.*, 319 F. 2d 725 (D.C. Cir. 1963). Charles M. Lamb, "Warren Burger and the Insanity Defense—Judicial Philosophy and Voting Behavior on a U.S. Court of Appeals," *American University Law Review*, 24(1974), 91-128.

37. Albert Hirschman, *Exit, Voice and Loyalty: Responses to Decline in Firms, Organizations and States* (Cambridge: Harvard University Press, 1970). Joel B. Grossman, "Dissenting Blocs on the Warren Court: A Study in Judicial Role Behavior," *Journal of Politics*, 30(1968), 1068. Cf. Fenno, "House Appropriations Committee," 317.

38. Auerbach et al., *Legal Process*, 357, n. 1.

39. For contrary views of the workload hypothesis, cf. Sheldon Goldman, "Voting Behavior Revisited," 493n; and Atkins and Green, "Consensus on Courts of Appeals," 746.

40. For samples of bloc analysis from a huge literature, see references in notes 3, 4, 6, 31, and 37, this chapter. Also, Charles M. Lamb, "Exploring the Conservatism of Federal Appeals Court Judges," *Indiana Law Journal*, 51(1976), 257-79. Cf. Henry J. Friendly, "Of Voting Blocs, and Cabbages and Kings," *University of Cincinnati Law Review*, 42(1973), 673-77; Grossman, "Dissenting Blocs," 1068; Goldman-Grossman exchange, *Journal of Politics*, 31(1969), 214; Walter F. Murphy, "Courts as Small Groups," *Harvard Law Review*, 79(1966), 1565; Walter F. Murphy and Joseph Tanenhaus, *The Study of Public Law* (New York: Random House, 1972), 159-76; John D. Sprague, *Voting Patterns of the United States Supreme Court: Cases in Federalism, 1889-1959* (Indianapolis: Bobbs-Merrill, 1968); and Ulmer, *Courts as Small Groups*.

41. Grossman, "Dissenting Blocs," 1078-80. Cf. Eulau's nonpolar decision structure, "Informal Organization," 348.

42. *Singleton v. Jackson Municipal Sep. Sch. Dist.*, 419 F. 2d 1211 (5th Cir. 1970).

43. Cf. subsequent en bancs in which 15 judges splintered in several directions: *Cismeros v. Corpus Christi Ind. Sch. Dist.*, 467 F. 2d 142 (5th Cir. 1972); *U.S. v. Texas Educ. Agency*, 467 F. 2d 848 (5th Cir. 1972).

44. For empirical support of these conclusions, see Goldman, "Conflict on Courts of Appeals," 640-56; *Washington Post*, March 28, 1971, B2; Atkins, "Decision-Making Rules," 634; Lamb, "Exploring Conservatism," and Lamb, "Warren Burger and the Insanity Defense," 124.

45. See, e.g., *Borum v. U.S.*, 380 F. 2d 595, 598 (D.C. Cir. 1967), in which J. Skelly Wright charged that a dissent by Warren E. Burger "exceeded normal limits."

46. Murphy, *Elements of Judicial Strategy*, 37-38. Also, J. Woodford How-

ard, Jr., "On the Fluidity of Judicial Choice," *American Political Science Review*, 62(1968), 43-56.

47. *Singleton v. Jackson Municipal Sep. Sch. Dist.*, 419 F. 2d 1211 (5th Cir. 1970).

48. *Armstrong v. Bd. of Educ. of Birmingham*, 323 F. 2d 333, 352 (5th Cir. 1963).

49. *Ross v. Sirica*, 380 F. 2d 557 (D.C. Cir. 1967).

50. Learned Hand to Charles E. Clark, April 18, 1957. Clark Papers, Yale Law School. Courtesy of Jerry Goldman.

51. For the concept of collegial deliberation, see Henry M. Hart, Jr., "Foreword: The Time Chart of the Justices," *Harvard Law Review*, 73(1959), 84-100.

52. 28 U.S.C. § 46 (1970). Alexander, "En Banc Hearings." See Note, "En Banc Review in Federal Circuit Courts: A Reassessment," *Michigan Law Review*, 72(1974), 1637-55; Note, "En Banc Procedures in the Federal Courts," *University of Pennsylvania Law Review*, 111(1962), 220-31; and Hruska Commission, *Structure and Internal Procedures: Recommendations for Change* (Washington, D.C.: June 1975), 60-63. Albert B. Maris, "Hearing and Rehearing Cases in Banc," 14 F.R.D. 91 (1953).

53. Cf. Wisdom, J., in *U.S. v. Cox*, 342 F. 2d 167, 185 (5th Cir. 1965).

54. *Hearings*, 1st Phase, 103.

55. AO *Annual Reports* (1955), 89 and (1976), 276.

56. Langer and Flanders, *Comparative Report*, 57-60. See Richard J. Richardson and Kenneth N. Vines, *The Politics of Federal Courts: Lower Courts in the United States* (Boston: Little, Brown and Co., 1970), 40-43; and Charles Alan Wright, "The Overloaded Fifth Circuit: A Crisis in Judicial Administration," *Texas Law Review*, 42(1964), 953-56.

57. For a more extensive analysis of the judges' views, see J. Woodford Howard, Jr., "Decision-Making Procedures in U.S. Courts of Appeals for the 2d and 5th Circuits" (Washington, D.C.: Federal Judicial Center, 1972), 1-10.

58. Cf., e.g., statements of Brown, Wisdom, Godbold, Gewin, Clark, Coleman, Morgan, and Bell, J.J., in *Hearings*, 1st Phase, 142, 353, 375, 392-417, and 448. Also, see *Hearings*, 2d Phase, I (1974) and II (1975); and Hearings on S.11, S. 460 before the Senate Committee on the Judiciary, 95th Cong., 1st Sess. (1977), 612-13.

59. Hearing on S.J. Res. 122 before the Subcommittee on Improvements in Judicial Machinery of the Senate Committee on the Judiciary, 92d Cong., 2d Sess. (1972), 107-8; Hearings on S.J. 729 before the Subcommittee on Improvements in Judicial Machinery of the Senate Committee on the Judiciary, part 2, 94th Cong., 1st Sess. (1975), 209-12.

60. Cf. Hearing on S.J. Res. 122, 70, 102-3; and *Hearings*, 1st Phase, 392; Hruska Commission, *Structure and Internal Procedures* (April 1975), 93; Hruska Commission, *The Geographical Boundaries of the Several Circuits: Recommendations for Change* (Washington, D.C.: December 1973), 6-11.

61. Omnibus Judgeship Act, Public Law 95-486 (1978); 92 Stat. 1633 (1978); 28 U.S.C. § 46 (1978). See *The Third Branch*, 10(September 1978), 1, 3; *The Third Branch*, 12 (May 1980), 3; H.R. 7665, 96th Cong., 2d Sess. (1980).

62. For analysis of communications in other circuits, see Robert A. Carp, "The Scope and Function of Intra-Circuit Judicial Communication: A Case Study of the Eighth Circuit," *Law and Society Review*, 6(1972), 405-26; and Stephen L. Wasby, "Communications within the Ninth Circuit Court of Appeals: The View from the Bench," *Golden Gate University Law Review*, 8(1977), 1-25.

63. *Hearings*, 1st Phase, 403.

64. Langer and Flanders, *Comparative Report*, 57-58.

65. 419 F. 2d 1211 (5th Cir. 1970).

66. AO *Annual Report* (1978), Table 8, 167. *Hearings*, 1st Phase, 393.

67. *Hearings*, 1st Phase, 364. 28 U.S.C. § 48 (1970).

68. *Green v. Santa Fe Industries*, 533 F. 2d 1309, 1310 (2d Cir. 1976). *Hearings*, 1st Phase, 380.

69. *Hearings*, 1st Phase, 149, 167-68, 380, 382.

70. Ibid., 149, 652.

71. Godbold, J., ibid., 377. Bell, J., Hearings on S.J. 729, 32-33.

72. Friendly, "Of Voting Blocs," 676.

73. Richardson and Vines, *Politics of Federal Courts*, 125; Alexander, "En Banc Hearings," 583-84; Atkins, "Decision-Making Rules," 632-42.

74. *Western Pacific R.R. Corp. v. Western Pacific Railroad Co.*, 345 U.S. 247 (1953); *Walters v. Moore-McCormack Lines*, 312 F. 2d 893, 897 (2d Cir. 1963); *Borass v. Village of Belle Terre*, 476 F. 2d 806 (2d Cir. 1973); *Zahn v. International Paper Co.*, 469 F. 2d 1033 (2d Cir. 1972); *I.B.M. v. U.S.*, 480 F. 2d 293 (2d Cir. 1973).

75. *Frady v. U.S.*, 348 F. 2d 84 (D.C. Cir. 1965).

76. Brown C.J., in *Hearings*, 2d Phase, II, 878; letter from a 5th circuit judge, not for attribution, to John R. Brown, June 15, 1973, courtesy of Hruska Commission staff.

77. Cf. Friendly and Moore, J.J., in *Indussa Corp. v. S. S. Ranborg*, 377 F. 2d 200, 204, 206 (2d Cir. 1967).

78. See *Eisen v. Carlisle & Jàcquelin*, 479 F. 2d 1005, 1020 (2d Cir. 1973); and *Green v. Santa Fe Industries*, 533 F. 2d 1309, 1310 (2d Cir. 1976).

79. Jerome Frank, *Law and the Modern Mind* (New York: Brentano's, 1930), 111.

80. Shirley M. Hufstedler, "Courtship and Other Legal Arts," *American Bar Association Journal*, 60(1974), 545, 546.

81. Canon 19, Canons of Judicial Ethics (ABA, 1924), as quoted in Auerbach et al., *Legal Process*, 359.

82. Cf. Atkins and Green, "Consensus on Courts of Appeals," 746-47.

83. Robert H. Jackson, *The Supreme Court in the American System of Government* (Cambridge: Harvard University Press, 1957), 16. Powell, "What the Justices Are Saying," 1454.

## Eight · **Leadership in the Allocation of Work**

1. Craig R. Ducat and Victor E. Flango, "Affective and Effective Leadership on State Supreme Courts: The Role of the Chief Judge," paper delivered

at the annual meeting of the American Political Science Association, Chicago, 1974; David J. Danelski, "The Influence of the Chief Justice in the Decisional Process of the Supreme Court," in Thomas P. Jahnige and Sheldon Goldman, eds., *The Federal Judicial System* (New York: Holt, Rinehart and Winston, 1968), 147-60; Robert L. Kahn and Elise Boulding, eds., *Power and Conflict in Organizations* (New York: Basic Books, 1964); Robert Tannenbaum, Irving R. Weschler, and Fred Massarik, *Leadership and Organization: A Behavioral Science Approach* (New York: McGraw-Hill, 1961); and Sidney Verba, *Small Groups and Political Behavior* (Princeton: Princeton University Press, 1961).

2. Donald R. Matthews and James A. Stimson, *Yeas and Nays: Normal Decision-Making in the U.S. House of Representatives* (New York: John Wiley and Sons, 1975), 45; and Helmut Norpoth, "Explaining Party Cohesion in Congress: The Case of Shared Policy Attitudes," *American Political Science Review*, 70(1976), 1156-71.

3. Samuel J. Eldersveld, *Political Parties: A Behavioral Analysis* (Chicago: Rand McNally & Co., 1964); and Arnold S. Tannenbaum, ed., *Control in Organizations* (New York: McGraw-Hill, 1968), 9. See Lawrence B. Mohr, "The Concept of Organizational Goal," *American Political Science Review*, 67(1973), 470-81.

4. Charles M. Price and Charles G. Bell, "The Rules of the Game: Political Fact or Academic Fancy?" *Journal of Politics*, 32(1970), 839-55. See Herbert B. Ascher, "The Learning of Legislative Norms," *American Political Science Review*, 67(1973), 499-513; Richard F. Fenno, Jr., *Congressmen in Committees* (Boston: Little, Brown and Co., 1973); Allan Kornberg and Norman Thomas, "The Political Socialization of National Legislative Elites in the United States and Canada," *Journal of Politics*, 27(1965), 761-75; and James D. Barber, *The Lawmakers: Recruitment and Adaptation to Legislative Life* (New Haven: Yale University Press, 1965).

5. Robert Carp and Russell Wheeler, "Sink or Swim: The Socialization of a Federal District Judge," *Journal of Public Law*, 21(1972), 359-93. Also, see Leonore Alpert, Burton M. Atkins, and Robert C. Ziller, "Becoming a Judge: The Transition from Advocate to Arbiter," *Judicature*, 62(1979), 325-35; and Henry J. Friendly, "Reactions of a Lawyer—Newly Become Judge," *Yale Law Journal*, 71(1961), 218-38.

6. See J. Woodford Howard, Jr., "On the Fluidity of Judicial Choice," *American Political Science Review*, 62(1968), 43-56; Howard, "Adjudication as a Process of Conflict Resolution: A Variation on Separation of Powers," *Journal of Public Law*, 18(1969), 339-70; William J. Brennan, Jr., "The National Court of Appeals: Another Dissent," *University of Chicago Law Review*, 40(1973), 473, 484. James E. Clayton, *The Making of Justice* (New York: E. P. Dutton & Co., 1964), 158.

7. See Felix Frankfurter, "Some Observations on the Nature of the Judicial Process of Supreme Court Litigation," *Proceedings of the American Philosophical Society*, 98(1954), 233, 239.

8. Hruska Commission, *Structure and Internal Procedures: Recommendations for Change* (Washington, D.C.: June 1975), 68. See *New York Times*,

April 6, 1975, 16:3; and proposed Federal Courts Improvement Act of 1979, S. 1477, 96th Cong., 1st Sess. (1979), § 45 (a).

9. E. Barrett Prettyman, "The Duties of a Circuit Chief Judge," *American Bar Association Journal*, 46(1960), 633.

10. Ibid., 633-36; Burton M. Atkins and William Zavoina, "Judicial Leadership on the Court of Appeals: A Probability Analysis of Panel Assignment in Race Relations Cases on the Fifth Circuit," *American Journal of Political Science*, 18(1974), 701, 702; J. Edward Lumbard, "Current Problems of the Federal Courts of Appeals," *Cornell Law Review*, 54(1968), 29, 42-43; and John C. Wahlke, Heinz Eulau, William Buchanan, and LeRoy C. Ferguson, *The Legislative System: Explorations in Legislative Behavior* (New York: John Wiley and Sons, 1962), 191.

11. Prettyman, "Duties of a Chief Judge," 633.

12. Cf. Danelski, "Influence of the Chief Justice"; and Ducat and Flango, "Affective and Effective Leadership," 3, 8-10.

13. Fenno, *Congressmen in Committees*, 145-47, 172-73.

14. Lumbard, "Current Problems," 43. See Will Shafroth, "Survey of the United States Courts of Appeals," 42 F.R.D. 243 (1967).

15. Fenno, *Congressmen in Committees*, 46-47, 156, 288-91.

16. Henry J. Friendly, "Of Voting Blocs, and Cabbages and Kings," *University of Cincinnati Law Review*, 42(1973), 675.

17. *Hearings*, 2d Phase (1975), II, 878.

18. Maurice Rosenberg, "The Qualities of Justices—Are They Strainable?" *Texas Law Review*, 44(1966), 1063, 1067.

19. Cf. S. Sidney Ulmer, "Leadership in the Michigan Supreme Court," in Glendon Schubert, ed., *Judicial Decision-Making* (New York: Free Press, 1963), 15.

20. Heinz Eulau, "The Informal Organization of Decisional Structures in Small Legislative Bodies," *Midwest Journal of Political Science*, 13(1969), 341, 348-57. Wahlke et al., *Legislative System*, 193-215; and references in note 2, this chapter.

21. Eulau, "Informal Organization," 364.

22. Cf. Donald R. Matthews, *U.S. Senators and Their World* (Chapel Hill: University of North Carolina Press, 1960), 95-97.

23. Hruska Commission, *Structure and Internal Procedure* (June 1975), 60.

24. *Armstrong v. Bd. of Educ. of Birmingham*, 323 F. 2d 333, 352-61. (5th Cir. 1963); Robert I. Mendelsohn, "Survey of the United States Courts of Appeals for the District of Columbia circuit," Committee on the Administration of Justice, Court Management Study (Washington, D.C.: 1969), 76-81; 48 F.R.D. 181 (1969).

25. Burton M. Atkins, "Opinion Assignments on the United States Courts of Appeals: The Question of Issue Specialization," *Western Political Quarterly*, 27(1974), 409-10, 425-28.

26. Friendly, "Of Voting Blocs," 675.

27. 323 F. 2d 333, 352-61 (5th Cir. 1963). For Judge Wisdom's rebuttal that sittings were governed by "pure chance," see *New York Times*, July 31, 1963, 12:4.

28. *Hearings*, 1st Phase, 145, 639.

29. Cf. Mendelsohn, "Survey of Courts of Appeals," 79-80.

30. Hearings on S. 11, S. 460 before the Senate Committee on the Judiciary, 95th Cong., 1st Sess. (1977), 646. See, e.g., 48 F.R.D. 181 (1969); *U.S. News and World Report*, August 16, 1965, 66; and *Washington Post*, June 15, 1969, F1.

31. Cf. Paul D. Carrington, "Crowded Dockets and the Courts of Appeals: The Threat to the Function of Review and the National Law," *Harvard Law Review*, 82(1969), 542, 587-96.

32. Cf. Wahlke et al., *Legislative System*, 197.

33. Fenno, *Congressmen in Committees*, 81-83, 94-97. Matthews, *U.S. Senators*, 162.

34. Atkins and Zavoina, "Judicial Leadership," 702.

35. Thomas G. Walker, "Behavioral Tendencies in the Three Judge-District Court," *American Journal of Political Science*, 17(1973), 407-13.

36. Sheldon Goldman, "Conflict on the U.S. Courts of Appeals, 1965-1971: A Quantitative Analysis," *University of Cincinnati Law Review*, 42(1973), 647. See John P. McIver, "Scaling Judicial Decisions: The Panel Decision-making Process of the U.S. Courts of Appeals," *American Journal of Political Science*, 20(1976), 749-61.

37. Goldman "Conflict on Courts of Appeals," 649-51. See Charles Lamb, "Exploring the Conservatism of Federal Appeals Court Judges," *Indiana Law Journal*, 51(1976), 275-79.

38. Goldman, "Conflict on Courts of Appeals," 641, 648, 655.

39. 323 F. 2d 333, 352-61 (5th Cir. 1963).

40. Atkins and Zavoina, "Judicial Leadership," 702-11.

41. 323 F. 2d 333 (5th Cir. 1963). Michael W. Giles and Thomas G. Walker, "Judicial Policy-Making and Southern School Segregation," *Journal of Politics*, 37(1975), 916-36.

42. Atkins and Zavoina, "Judicial Leadership," 706-9. See Richard J. Richardson and Kenneth N. Vines, "Review, Dissent and the Appellate Process: A Political Interpretation," *Journal of Politics*, 29(1967), 597, 612.

43. *U.S. v. Jefferson Co. Bd. of Educ.*, 372 F. 2d 836 (5th Cir. 1966); J. W. Peltason, *Fifty-Eight Lonely Men: Southern Federal Judges and School Desegregation* (New York: Harcourt, Brace, & World, 1961); and Note, "Judicial Performance in the Fifth Circuit," *Yale Law Journal*, 73(1963), 90-133.

44. Charles Alan Wright, "The Overloaded Fifth Circuit: A Crisis in Judicial Administration," *Texas Law Review*, 42(1964), 949-82.

45. For three-judge court workloads between FY 1965 and 1972, see Hearing on S.J. Res. 122 before the Subcommittee on Improvements in Judicial Machinery of the Senate Committee on the Judiciary, 92d Cong., 2d Sess. (1972), 65.

46. Prettyman, "Duties of a Chief Judge," 636.

47. Walter F. Murphy, *Elements of Judicial Strategy* (Chicago: University of Chicago Press, 1964), 63-90.

48. See Arthur H. Dean, John Minor Wisdom, and Jerome I. Chapman, "A

Tribute to Chief Judge Elbert P. Tuttle," *Cornell Law Review*, 53(1967), 1-25. *Washington Post*, June 14, 1968, A18:1.

49. See J. Woodford Howard, Jr., *Mr. Justice Murphy: A Political Biography* (Princeton: Princeton University Press, 1968), 267. Cf. David W. Rohde, "Policy Goals, Strategic Choice and Majority Opinion Assignments in the U.S. Supreme Court," *Midwest Journal of Political Science*, 16(1972), 652-82; and Gregory J. Rathjen, "Policy Goals, Strategic Choice, and Majority Opinion Assignments in the U.S. Supreme Court: A Replication," *American Journal of Political Science*, 18(1974), 713-24.

50. 28 U.S.C. § 45 (b). See Seitz, J., in Hearing on S. 2991 before the Subcommittee on Improvements of Judicial Machinery of the Senate Committee on the Judiciary, 93rd Cong., 2d Sess. (1974), 280.

51. Hearing on S. 2991. For 5th circuit, see *Hearings*, 1st Phase, 638-39. See S. 1477, 96th Cong., 1st. Sess. (1979), § 45 (b).

52. Cf. John J. Parker, "Improving Appellate Methods," *New York University Law Review*, 25(1950), 1, 12.

53. Harold R. Medina, "The Decisional Process in the U.S. Court of Appeals, Second Circuit," *New York Law Journal*, part two, February 19, 1963.

54. *Hearings*, 1st Phase, 147, 164.

55. See Goldman, "Conflict on Courts of Appeals," 640-41.

56. See references in notes 50 and 51, this chapter. Cf. Justin J. Green and Burton M. Atkins, "Designated Judges: How Well Do They Perform?" *Judicature*, 61(1978), 358-70.

57. See Atkins, "Opinion Assignments," 416-18.

58. For collapsing procedure, see Sidney Siegel, *Nonparametric Statistics for the Behavioral Sciences* (New York: McGraw-Hill, 1956), 178-79.

59. Atkins, "Opinion Assignments," 417, 424-27. Also, see H. Stephen Whitaker, "The Florida Supreme Court: Internal Procedures," *Government Research Bulletin*, 4 (Tallahasee: Institute of Government Research, Florida State University, 1967), 5.

60. *New York Times*, December 21, 1976, 24:1.

61. Siegel, *Nonparametric Statistics*, 68-75, 250.

62. Atkins, "Opinion Assignments," 417.

63. Ibid., 413-14.

64. Goldman, "Conflict on Courts of Appeals," 640.

65. See Atkins, "Opinion Assignments," 424-27.

66. Ibid.

67. See references in notes 47 and 49, this chapter. Also, Burton M. Atkins, "Decision-Making Rules and Judicial Strategy on the U.S. Courts of Appeals," *Western Political Quarterly*, 25(1972), 626-42.

68. For a parallel concept of "stratarchy," see Harold D. Lasswell and Abraham Kaplan, *Power and Society* (New Haven: Yale University Press, 1950), 219-20; and discussion in Eldersveld, *Political Parties*, 8-11.

69. Cf. Hruska Commission, *Structure and Internal Procedures* (April 1975), 108-9; and (June 1975), 68, 177.

70. See the proposed Federal Courts Improvement Act of 1979, S. 1477, 96th Cong., 1st Sess. (1979).

71. Public Law 95-486 (1978); 92 Stat. 1633 (1978); 28 U.S.C. § 46 (c) (1978).

72. Hruska Commission, Structure and Internal Procedures (June 1975), 60-63.

73. Public Law 95-486 (1978); 92 Stat. 1633 (1978); 28 U.S.C. § 41 (1978). See The Third Branch, 10(September 1978), 1, 3.

## Nine · **Strategies of Reform**

1. Julius Stone, Legal System and Lawyers' Reasonings (Stanford: Stanford University Press, 1964), 209.

2. Donald L. Horowitz, The Courts and Social Policy (Washington, D.C.: The Brookings Institution, 1977), 254, 261, 268.

3. J. Skelly Wright, "Professor Bickel, the Scholarly Tradition, and the Supreme Court," Harvard Law Review, 84(1971), 769, 793. For evidence of variety, see David L. Shapiro, "Federal Diversity Jurisdiction: A Survey and a Proposal," Harvard Law Review, 91(1977), 317-55; Wolf V. Heydebrand, "The Context of Public Bureaucracies: An Organizational Analysis of Federal District Courts," Law and Society Review, 11(1977), 759-821; and New York Times, January 7, 1980, 1:1.

4. Felix Frankfurter and James M. Landis, The Business of the Supreme Court: A Study in the Federal Judicial System (New York: Macmillan, 1927), 2.

5. Louis D. Brandeis to Felix Frankfurter, February 6, 1925, as quoted in Jerry Goldman, "Jurisdictional Politics and the Federal Courts" (Ph.D. dissertation, Johns Hopkins University, 1974), 219.

6. Shirley M. Hufstedler, "Courtship and Other Legal Arts," American Bar Association Journal, 60(1974), 546.

7. Hearings, 1st Phase (1975), 976.

8. Public Law 95-486 (October 20, 1978); 92 Stat. 1629-34 (1978); 28 U.S.C. § 44 (1978).

9. AO Annual Reports (1978), Table B2, 296; and (preliminary 1979), Table B2, A-5. Cf. Hearings, 2d Phase, II, 681.

10. AO Annual Reports (1978), 156, and (preliminary 1979), Table B1, A-2 and 2.

11. See, e.g., Hearings, 2d Phase, I, 106-17. Rehnquist, J., in New York Times, August 10, 1976, 18:5. Bell resignation, Baltimore Sun, July 27, 1976, A4, and December 23, 1976, A8. See Washington Post, August 15, 1976, A3:7.

12. "Annual Report on the State of the Judiciary," 96 S. Ct., 3, 6 (March 1, 1976). Also see New York Times, May 11, 1980, 36:1.

13. Hearings, 1st Phase, 450. Hearings on S. 729 before the Subcommittee on Improvements in Judicial Machinery of the Senate Committee on the Judiciary, 94th Cong., 1st Sess., part 2 (1975), 33.

14. New York Times, June 27, 1978, 1:4; and September 2, 1979, 23:6. Hearings, 1st Phase, 1080.

15. *New York Times*, January 2, 1977, 32:1. Kaufman, C.J., *The Third Branch*, 8(September 1976), 4.

16. AO *Annual Reports* (1978), Table B1, 293-94, and (preliminary 1979), Table B1, A-2.

17. Cf. Irving R. Kaufman, "The Pre-Argument Conference: An Appellate Procedural Reform," *Columbia Law Review*, 74(1974), 1094-1103; and Jerry Goldman, *An Evaluation of the Civil Appeals Management Plan: An Experiment in Judicial Administration* (Washington, D.C.: Federal Judicial Center, 1977), and Goldman, "The Civil Appeals Management Plan: An Experiment in Appellate Procedural Reform," *Columbia Law Review*, 78(1978), 1209-40.

18. *Hearings*, 1st Phase, 1067. Hearing on S. 2991 before the Subcommittee on Improvements in Judicial Machinery of the Senate Committee on the Judiciary, 93rd Cong., 2d Sess. (1974), 6, 282, 286-88; and Hearings on S. 11, S. 460 before the Senate Committee on the Judiciary, 95th Cong., 1st Sess. (1977), 583.

19. Wright, J., *Hearings*, 1st Phase, 81, 98. Bazelon, C.J., *The Third Branch*, 8(June 1976), 7. Hearings on S. 11, 633-34.

20. Hearings on S. 11, 634.

21. *Hearings*, 1st Phase, 103-5.

22. Ibid., 2d Phase, I, 451. David L. Bazelon to Joseph D. Tydings, February 11, 1969 in Senate Committee on the District of Columbia, *Crime in the District of Columbia: Implementing the Suggestions of the President's Commission on Crime*, 91st Cong., 1st Sess. (1969), 55-56.

23. Hearings on S. 11, 647; *Hearings*, 1st Phase, 103.

24. AO *Semi-Annual Report of the Director* (1976), 2; Hearings on S. 11 (1977), 634.

25. *Hearings*, 1st Phase, 1039. AO *Annual Report* (1977), Table B4, 308, and (preliminary 1979), Table B4, A-8.

26. *Judicature*, 62(1978), 255. See the proposed Federal Courts Improvement Act of 1979, S. 1477, 96th Cong., 1st Sess. (1979), § 46 (b).

27. Hruska Commission, *The Geographical Boundaries of the Several Judicial Circuits: Recommendations for Change* (1973), 2. 62 F.R.D. 223 (1973). For a narrative of screening procedures, see *Hearings*, 1st Phase, 156-57. For an explanation of screening, see *Isbell Enterprises, Inc. v. Citizens Casualty Co. of N.Y.*, 431 F. 2d 409 (5th Cir. 1970).

28. Hruska Commission, *Geographical Boundaries*, 6.

29. Ibid.

30. Hearings on S. 729 (1975), 32.

31. *Baltimore Sun*, July 27, 1976, A4. Also see note 11, this chapter.

32. Senate Report no. 94-404, 94th Cong., 1st Sess. (1975), 6, 17. Also Godbold, J., *Hearings*, 1st Phase, 376.

33. Hearings on S. 11 (1977), 625.

34. Ibid., 594. *The Third Branch*, 8(June 1976), 7. See *The Third Branch*, 10(May 1978), 3; *Baltimore Sun*, November 19, 1977, B1.

35. *Hearings*, 1st Phase, 360.

36. Ibid., 159, 327, 637. Hearings on S. 11 (1977), 623. See Burger, C.J., "Annual Report on the State of the Judiciary," 97 S. Ct. 8 (May 1, 1977).

37. Public Law 95-486 (October 20, 1978); 92 Stat. 1629-34(1978); 28 U.S.C. § 44 (1978).

38. Federal Judicial Center, Report on Response of Federal Judges to Questionnaire on Appellate Litigation (January 21, 1972), 3. For general discussion of size and alternative principles of appellate court organization, see Paul D. Carrington, Daniel J. Meador, and Maurice Rosenberg, *Justice on Appeal* (St. Paul: West Publishing Co., 1976), 138-84; 185-224. Also, Alan Betten, "Institutional Reform in the Federal Appellate Courts," *Indiana Law Journal*, 52(1976), 63-95.

39. *Proceedings of the Judicial Conference of the United States* (March 16-17, 1964), 15. Hruska Commission, *Structure and Internal Procedures: Recommendations for Change* (Washington, D.C.: June 1975), 55-59.

40. Warren E. Burger to Roman L. Hruska, May 29, 1975, in Hruska Commission, *Structure and Internal Procedures* (June 1975), 177. Also ABC Broadcast, July 5, 1977.

41. Kaufman, C.J., in Hearing on S. 2991 (1974), 282; and Friendly, C.J., in Hearing on S.J. Res. 122 before the Subcommittee on Improvements in Judicial Machinery of the Senate Committee on the Judiciary, 92d Cong., 2d Sess. (1972), 151.

42. Hearings on S. 2990 before the Subcommittee on Improvements in Judicial Machinery of the Senate Committee on the Judiciary, 93rd Cong., 2d Sess., part 1 (1974), 73. *Hearings*, 1st Phase, 392. For debate over the nine-judge standard, cf. Hufstedler, J., in Hearings on S. 729 (1975), 88, 91; and remarks of Sen. Quentin N. Burdick, Sen. Roman L. Hruska, and A. Leo Levin in Hearing on S. 2991 (1974), 77-79.

43. See Federal Judicial Center, Report on Response of Federal Judges, 2-3.

44. Frankfurter and Landis, *Business of the Supreme Court*, 49.

45. Hearings on S. 729 (1975), 5-8.

46. "Annual Report on the State of the Judiciary," 97 S. Ct. 8 (May 1, 1977).

47. J. Edward Lumbard, "Current Problems of the Federal Courts of Appeals," *Cornell Law Review*, 54(1968), 29, 44.

48. For projections, cf. Brown, J., in *Hearings*, 1st Phase, 642; and Senate Report no. 94-513, 94th Cong., 1st Sess. (1975), 10-11; quote, William P. Westphall in Hearings on S.J. Res. 122 (1972), 101.

49. For Justice Frankfurter's fear that inflating judgeships would deflate the office, see *Lumbermen's Mutual Casualty Co. v. Elbert*, 348 U.S. 48, 59 (1954).

50. Cf. Geoffrey Hazard, "After the Trial Court—the Realities of Appellate Review," in Harry W. Jones, ed., *The Courts, the Public, and the Law Explosion* (Englewood Cliffs, N.J.: Prentice-Hall, 1965), 80-81; and Senate Report no. 94-513 (1975), 11. Also, see Quentin N. Burdick, "Federal Courts of Appeals: Radical Surgery or Conservative Care," *Kentucky Law Journal*, 60(1972), 807-16.

51. See Justin J. Green and Burton M. Atkins, "Designated Judges: How

Well Do They Perform?" *Judicature,* 61(1978), 358-70; "News," *Judicature,* 62(1978), 255; and Stephen L. Wasby, "Extra Judges in 'The Court Nobody Knows': Some Aspects of Decision Making in the United States Courts of Appeals," paper presented at the annual meeting of the American Political Science Association, Washington, D.C., 1979.

52. Richard J. Richardson and Kenneth N. Vines, *The Politics of Federal Courts: Lower Courts in the United States* (Boston: Little, Brown and Co., 1970), 43-45. See Alvin Rubin, "Views from the Lower Court," *U.C.L.A. Law Review,* 23(1976), 448, 452; and Stephen L. Wasby, "Inconsistency in the United States Courts of Appeals: Dimensions and Mechanisms for Resolution," *Vanderbilt Law Review,* 32(1979), 1343-73.

53. See Federal Judicial Center, Report on Response of Federal Judges, 4.

54. *Hearings,* 1st Phase, 356-57, 974-76, 979.

55. Ibid., 54, 646.

56. For excellent discussion, see Arthur D. Hellman, "Legal Problems of Dividing a State between Federal Judicial Circuits," *University of Pennsylvania Law Review,* 122(1974), 1188-1281.

57. *Hearings,* 1st Phase, 392-95. See, e.g., Bell, Clark, Goldberg, J.J., in *Hearings,* 1st Phase, 452-55, 403, 657, and 392-417 generally. Also Ainsworth, J., Hearing on S. 2991 (1974), 222, 232, and Hearings on S. 2990 (1974), 109-26.

58. See, e.g., Wisdom, J., in *Hearings,* 1st Phase, 353-61; and 2d Phase, II, 880.

59. Hearing on S.J. Res. 122 (1972), 107-8. Richard T. Rives to Robert F. Kennedy, May 19, 1964, reprinted in Rives to William J. Weller, May 6, 1975, Hearings on S. 729 (1975), 209-10. For 10-3 votes favoring enlargement and division, but a 7-6 majority against enlargement without division in 1977, see Hearings on S. 11 (1977), 612-13.

60. See Hruska Commission, *Geographical Boundaries,* 5-10; *New York Times,* March 27, 1978, A18:1; Hearings on S. 11 (1977); and Charles R. Haworth, "Circuit Splitting and the 'New' National Court of Appeals," *Southwestern Law Journal,* 30(1976), 839-86.

61. *New York Times,* May 18, 1978, B9:1, and June 19, 1978, A15:5.

62. Public Law 95-486 (1978); H.R. Report no. 96-1390, 96th Cong., 2d Sess. (1980), 4-5; H.R. 7665, 96th Cong., 2d Sess. (1980).

63. Hruska Commission, *Geographical Boundaries* (1973), 3. Quote, Brown, C.J., in *Hearings,* 1st Phase, 534. See note 48, this chapter.

64. See, e.g., *Hearings,* 1st Phase, 112; Frederick Weiner, "Federal Regional Courts: A Solution for the Certiorari Dilemma," *American Bar Association Journal,* 49(1963), 1169-74; remarks of Robert A. Leflar, Hearings on S.J. Res. 122 (1972), 159-61. Carrington et al., *Justice on Appeal,* 222-23; Hearings on S. 729 (1975), 92. Also see note 81, this chapter.

65. Friendly, J., as quoted in *Hearings,* 1st Phase, 656.

66. Brown, C.J., in Hearings on H.R. 7378 before Subcommittee no. 5 of the House Committee on the Judiciary, 92d Cong., 1st Sess. (1971), 100.

67. Warren E. Burger, "Deferred Maintenance of Judicial Machinery," *LEAA Newsletter,* 1(May 1971), 8. Also, Mark W. Canon, "The Federal Judi-

cial System: Highlights of Administrative Modernization," *Criminology*, 12(1974), 10-24. For skepticism about this approach, see, e.g., James A. Gazell, "Three Principal Facets of Judicial Management," *Criminology*, 9(1971), 131-53; Lucinda Long, "Some Second Thoughts about Court Administrators," paper presented at the annual meeting of the American Political Science Association Chicago, 1976; Carl Baar, "Will Urban Trial Courts Survive the War on Crime?" in Herbert Jacob, ed., *The Potential for Reform of Criminal Justice* (Beverly Hills: Sage Publications, 1974), 331-52; and David L. Bazelon, "New Gods for Old: 'Efficient' Courts in a Democratic Society," *New York University Law Review*, 46(1971), 653-74.

68. For standardization of *pro se* petitions, cf. AO *Annual Report* (1975), 173 and Brown, C.J., in *Hearings*, 1st Phase, 638. Quote, Bell, J., *Hearings*, 1st Phase, 483.

69. For an exception, see Hearings on S. 11 (1977), 602.

70. Ibid., 649.

71. *New York Times*, July 24, 1978, A7:6.

72. For complaints about this procedure, see Lay, J., in *Hearings*, 2d Phase, II, 912. Also see John T. McDermott and Steven Flanders, *The Impact of the Circuit Executive Act* (Washington, D.C.: Federal Judicial Center, 1979).

73. AO *Annual Reports* (1978), Table 1, 157 and (preliminary 1979), 2, Table B1, A2.

74. Peter G. Fish, Hearings before the Subcommittee on Separation of Powers of the Senate Committee on the Judiciary, *The Independence of Federal Judges*, 91st Cong., 2d Sess. (1971), 291. See Fish, *The Politics of Federal Judicial Administration* (Princeton: Princeton University Press, 1973).

75. Gazell, "Three Principal Facets," 145. See Howard M. Vollmer and Donald L. Mills, eds., *Professionalization* (Englewood Cliffs, N.J.: Prentice-Hall, 1966), 264-94 and sources cited; Eliot Friedson, *Professional Dominance: The Social Structure of Medical Care* (New York: Atherton Press, 1970); and Richard H. Hall, "Professionalization and Bureaucratization," *American Sociological Review*, 33(1968), 92-104.

76. Peter G. Fish, "The Circuit Councils: Rusty Hinges of Federal Judicial Administration," *University of Chicago Law Review*, 37(1970), 203-41. Cf. J. Edward Lumbard, "The Place of the Federal Judicial Councils in the Administration of the Courts," *American Bar Association Journal*, 47(1961), 169-72; and Steven Flanders and John T. McDermott, *Operation of the Federal Judicial Councils* (Washington, D.C.: Federal Judicial Center, 1978). Also see S. 1477, 96th Cong., 1st Sess. (1979).

77. Ernest C. Friesen, Edward C. Gallas, and Nesta M. Gallas, *Managing the Courts* (Indianapolis: Bobbs-Merrill, 1971), 113.

78. Long, "Some Second Thoughts," 7. See references, note 75, this chapter.

79. *The Third Branch*, 4(February 1972), 2.

80. Arnold S. Tannenbaum, "Control and Effectiveness in a Voluntary Organization," *American Journal of Sociology*, 67(1961), 33-46. See Rensis Likert, "A Motivational Approach to a Modified Theory of Organization and

Management," in Mason Haire, ed., *Modern Organization Theory* (New York: John Wiley and Sons, 1959), 184-217.

81. "A Management and Systems Survey of the United States Courts," a report prepared by North American Rockwell Information System Co. for the Federal Judicial Center (1970). Also see Carl Baar, "Reorganization of the Federal Judicial System," *Judicature*, 55(1972), 282-87.

82. John J. Parker to Elliott Northcutt and Morris Soper, May 29, 1936, as quoted in William C. Burris, "John J. Parker and Supreme Court Policy: A Case Study in Judicial Control" (Ph.D. dissertation, University of North Carolina at Chapel Hill, 1964), 223-24. See report, *Attorney Attitudes toward Limitation of Oral Argument and Written Opinion in Three U.S. Courts of Appeals* (Washington, D.C.: Federal Judicial Center, 1974); excerpts in *The Third Branch*, 7(February 1975), 2; Hruska Commission, *Structure and Internal Procedures* (June 1975), 42-43, 49-52; and Jerry Goldman, *Attitudes of United States Judges toward Limitation of Oral Argument and Opinion-Writing in the United States Courts of Appeals* (Washington, D.C.: Federal Judicial Center, 1975); excerpts in *The Third Branch*, 7(May 1975), 6.

83. Warren E. Burger, "Report on the Federal Judicial Branch" to the American Bar Association (August 6, 1973), 6. For general discussion, see references, note 27, this chapter and Charles R. Haworth, "Screening and Summary Procedures in the United States Courts of Appeals," *Washington University Law Quarterly* (1973), 257-326; Steven Flanders and Jerry Goldman, "Screening Practices and the Use of Para-Judicial Personnel in a U.S. Court of Appeals: A Study of the Fourth Circuit," *Justice System Journal*, 1(1975), 1-16; and Note, "Screening of Criminal Cases in the Federal Courts of Appeals: Practice and Proposals," *Columbia Law Review*, 73(1973), 77-105.

84. *Hearings*, 1st Phase, 47.

85. Ibid., 2d Phase, II, 683. See *Attorney Attitudes*, note 82, this chapter.

86. *Hearings*, 2d Phase, II, 873; 1st Phase, 350, 367.

87. Ibid., 1st Phase, 639, 486.

88. Ibid., 487, 399.

89. *Internal Operating Procedures of United States Courts of Appeals* (Washington, D.C.: Federal Judicial Center, 1973), 30. See Donald H. Zeigler and Michele G. Hermann, "The Invisible Litigant: An Inside View of Pro Se Actions in the Federal Courts," *New York University Law Review*, 47(1972), 157-257.

90. *Hearings*, 1st Phase, 641. Hearing on S. 2991 (1974), 309.

91. *U.S. v. Ambers*, 416 F. 2d 942 (5th Cir. 1969), *cert. denied*, 396 U.S. 1039 (1970).

92. See, e.g., Bell, J., *Hearings*, 1st Phase, 453; 2d Phase, II, 683.

93. *Hearings*, 1st Phase, 452; 2d Phase, II, 695, 683.

94. Ibid., 1st Phase, 155, 453; 2d Phase, II, 873, 890; Hearings on S. 11 (1977), 604.

95. *Hearings*, 1st Phase, 37.

96. Ibid., 510; 2d Phase, II, 870.

97. See, e.g., Daniel J. Meador, *Appellate Courts: Staff and Process in the Crisis of Volume* (St. Paul: West Publishing Co., 1974); N. O. Stockmeyer, Jr., "RX for the Certiorari Crisis: A More Professional Staff," *American Bar Association Journal*, 59(1973), 846-50.

98. Cf. remarks of Coleman, Morgan, Gewin, and Clark, J.J., in *Hearings*, 1st Phase, 416.

99. Ibid., 2d Phase, II, 993; quote, Seitz, C.J., *Hearings*, 1st Phase, 38.

100. Ibid., 2d Phase, II, 716, 721.

101. Ibid., 977.

102. Cicero Sessions, *Hearings*, 1st Phase, 335. Cf. Wisdom and Wright, J.J., *Hearings*, 1st Phase, 367 and 102-3. For a defense of screening and Rule 21 opinions, see Brown, C.J., *Hearings*, 1st Phase, 505, 509-40.

103. Ibid., 2d Phase, II, 953.

104. AO *Annual Report* (1975), Table 9, 184.

105. See *N.L.R.B.* v. *Amalgamated Clothing Workers of America*, 430 F. 2d 966 (5th Cir. 1970).

106. Hruska Commission, *Structure and Internal Procedures* (June 1975), 49. Cf. *Attorney Attitudes*, note 82, this chapter.

107. *Hearings*, 2d Phase, II, 678. Cf. *Taylor* v. *McKeithen*, 407 U.S. 191 (1972); and David Dunn, "Unreported Decisions in the U.S. Courts of Appeals," *Cornell Law Review*, 63(1977), 128-48; and William L. Reynolds and William M. Richman, "The Non-Precedential Precedent—Limited Publication and No-Citation Rules in the United States Courts of Appeals," *Columbia Law Review*, 78(1978), 1167-1208.

108. Aldisert, C.J., *Hearings*, 2d Phase, II, 933, 708.

109. Hruska Commission, *Structure and Internal Procedures* (June 1975), 50-52.

110. *Hearings*, 2d Phase, 683.

111. Ibid., 1st Phase, 640.

112. For primacy of decision-making over opinion-writing functions, see statements of Arthur J. Goldberg and Gibbons, J., in *Hearings*, 2d Phase, I, 169, and 1st Phase, 43. Also, see David Neubauer, "Judicial Role and Case Management," *Justice System Journal*, 4(1978), 223-32.

113. Henry J. Friendly, "Averting the Flood by Lessening the Flow," *Cornell Law Review*, 59(1974), 634-57.

114. See, e.g., proposals of the Carter administration to improve federal civil justice, *The Third Branch*, 11(March 1979), 2; and Hearing on S. 1819 before the Subcommittee on Improvements in Judicial Machinery of the Senate Committee on the Judiciary, 95th Cong., 1st Sess. (1977), 1-2.

115. Quote, Friendly, J., Hearings on H.R. 7378 (1971), 66. See Henry J. Friendly, *Federal Jurisdiction: A General View* (New York: Columbia University Press, 1973), 1-14. Also, see, e.g., Paul D. Carrington, "Crowded Dockets and the Courts of Appeals: The Threat to the Function of Review and the National Law," *Harvard Law Review*, 82(1969), 542-617; and remarks of Wright and Wisdom, J.J., *Hearings*, 1st Phase, 80-91, 353-61; and Gee, J., Hearings on S. 729 (1975), 53.

116. Burger to Roman L. Hruska, May 29, 1975, Hruska Commission,

*Structure and Internal Procedures* (June 1975), 176; *The Third Branch*, 7(March 1975), 1, and 11(March 1979), 2. See 90 Stat. 1119 (1976); and Bennett Boskey and Eugene Gressman, "Recent Reforms in the Federal Judicial Structure—Three-Judge District Courts and Appellate Review," 67 F.R.D. 135 (1975).

117. Kaufman, C.J., Hearing on S. 2991 (1974), 305. See David P. Currie, "The Three-Judge District Court in Constitutional Litigation," *University of Chicago Law Review*, 32(1964), 1-79.

118. Wisdom, J., *Hearings*, 1st Phase, 362.

119. See, e.g., John P. Frank, "For Maintaining Diversity Jurisdiction," *Yale Law Journal*, 73(1963), 7-13; and Jerry Goldman and Kenneth S. Marks, "Diversity Jurisdiction and Local Bias: A Preliminary Empirical Inquiry," *Journal of Legal Studies*, 9(1980), 93-104.

120. Shapiro, "Federal Diversity Jurisdiction."

121. AO *Annual Report* (1978), Table B7, 304-5 and Table C4, 326, 328.

122. Hearings on S. 729 (1975), 50.

123. Brandeis to Frankfurter, February 6, 1925, in Goldman, "Jurisdictional Politics." Burger, C.J., "Annual Report on the State of the Judiciary," 97 S. Ct. 6 (May 1, 1977). See Friendly, *Federal Jurisdiction*, 139-52 and sources cited; and Thomas D. Rowe, Jr., "Abolishing Diversity Jurisdiction: Positive Side Effects and Potential for Further Reforms," *Harvard Law Review*, 92(1979), 963-1012.

124. Victor E. Flango and Nora F. Blair, "The Relative Impacts of Diversity Cases on State Trial Courts," *State Court Journal*, 2(1978), 20-26. Hearings on S. 729 (1975), 54. For Carter administration proposals to abolish diversity jurisdiction except for alienage, see *The Third Branch*, 11(March 1979), 2; S. 679, 96th Cong., 1st Sess. (1979).

125. H.R. 9622, 95th Cong., 2d Sess. (February 28, 1978). *New York Times*, March 1, 1978, 42:1; and *The Third Branch*, 10(March 1978), 1. See S. 679, 96th Cong., 1st Sess. (1979).

126. For upgrading the status of bankruptcy judges as adjuncts of district courts, see Public Law 95-598 (1978), and discussion in *The Third Branch*, 10(November 1978), 1-2; and Carroll Seron, *Judicial Reorganization: The Politics of Reform of the Federal Bankruptcy Court* (Lexington, Mass.: D. C. Heath, 1978).

127. Robert A. Kagan, *Regulatory Justice: Implementing a Wage-Price Freeze* (New York: Russell Sage Foundation, 1978).

128. For various versions of the proposed Federal Courts Improvement Act of 1979, see S. 677, S. 678, and S. 1477, 96th Cong., 1st Sess. (1979); *The Third Branch*, 11(March 1979), 2; 11(April 1979), 2; 12(October 1980), 4-5; H.R. 3806, 96th Cong., 2d Sess. (1980); and Edward M. Kennedy, "The Federal Courts Improvement Act," *Judicature*, 62(1979), 8-13. For other alternatives, see *Wall Street Journal*, September 14, 1978, 3:4; Carrington, "Crowded Dockets," 574-80, 587-96, 604-12; Clement F. Haynsworth, "A New Court to Improve the Administration of Justice," *American Bar Association Journal*, 59(1973), 841-45; and Erwin N. Griswold, "The Need for a Court of Tax Appeals," *Harvard Law Review*, 57(1944), 1153-92.

394 • Notes, Chapter Nine

129. See, e.g., *The Third Branch*, 8(October 1976), 3, 7. Arthur Kantrowitz, "Proposal for an Institution for Scientific Judgment," *Science*, 156(1967), 763-64; Scott C. Whitney, "The Case for Creating a Special Environmental Court System," *William and Mary Law Review*, 14(1973), 473; 15(1973), 33; Carrington et al., *Justice on Appeal*, 217-22; Report of the President's Advisory Council on Executive Organization (Ash Committee), *A New Regulatory Framework* (1971), 53-55. Cf. David P. Currie and Frank I. Goodman, "Judicial Review of Federal Administrative Action: Quest for the Optimum Forum," *Columbia Law Review*, 75(1975), 1-88.

130. *New York Times*, February 1, 1977, 15:8.

131. *New York Times*, February 11, 1977, A12:3. *Baltimore Sun*, November 5, 1977, A9. For Pound conference, see *The Third Branch*, 8(April 1976), 1, 2; 8(October 1976), 1, 2. Also see the Dispute Resolution Bill, S. 957, which passed the Senate but failed in the House, during the 95th Congress; S. 237, 96th Cong., 1st Sess. (1979) regarding magistrates; and the proposed Federal Courts Improvement Act of 1979, S. 678, 96th Cong., 1st Sess. (1979), summarized in *The Third Branch*, 11(March 1979), 2, and 11(April 1979), 1-2, and Kennedy, "Federal Courts Improvement Act," 8-13.

132. Simon Rifkind, "A Special Court for Patent Litigation? The Danger of a Specialized Judiciary," *American Bar Association Journal*, 37(1951), 425-26; *Hearings*, 2d Phase, I, 148.

133. Lawrence Baum, "Judicial Specialization, Litigant Influence, and Substantive Policy: The Court of Customs and Patent Appeals," *Law and Society Review*, 11(1977), 823-50.

134. Hruska Commission, *Structure and Internal Procedures* (June 1975), 60, 28-30.

135. Cf. Friendly, *Federal Jurisdiction*, 161-71.

136. Burger, C.J., "Report on the Federal Judicial Branch" to the American Bar Association (August 6, 1973), 6.

137. 38 U.S.C. § 4005 (1970). *New York Times*, May 21, 1978, 18:1. See Robert P. Davis and Paul Nejelski, "Justice Impact Statements: Determining How New Laws Will Affect the Courts," *Judicature*, 62(1978), 18-27.

138. See, e.g., *Hearings*, 1st Phase, 354; 2d Phase, II, 928; Hearings on S.J. Res. 122 (1972), 42.

139. Stephen C. Halpern and Kenneth N. Vines, "Institutional Disunity, the Judges' Bill and the Role of the U.S. Supreme Court," *Western Political Quarterly*, 30(1977), 471-83.

140. See, e.g., Burger, C.J., "Report on the Federal Judicial Branch," 7-10; Griffin B. Bell, quoted in *Baltimore Sun*, December 13, 1976, A4; and Henry J. Friendly, "Is Innocence Irrelevant? Collateral Attack on Criminal Judgments," *University of Chicago Law Review*, 38(1970), 142-72. For criminal appeals generally, see Carrington et al., *Justice on Appeal*, 56-120.

141. Carrington et al., *Justice on Appeal*, 103-20.

142. See, e.g., *Report of the Study Group on the Caseload of the Supreme Court* (Washington, D.C.: Federal Judicial Center, 1972), 47-48; *Hearings*, 2d Phase, I, 327; and 1st Phase, 362.

143. *LEAA Newsletter*, 7(April 1978), 3, 11. *Baltimore Sun*, January 3, 1978, A3:1.

144. Brown, C.J., *Hearings*, 1st Phase, 645. For an estimate that only 1 percent of prisoner petitions were granted in 1970, see Report of the Committee on Prisoner Petitions, Federal Judicial Center (January 10, 1972), 4-6.

145. See, e.g., Hearing on S.J. Res. 122 (1972), 133; and Hearings on S. 729 (1975), 51.

146. Brown, C.J., in Hearings on H.R. 7378 (1971), 119; *Hearings*, I, 540.

147. Paul Nejelski, "Do Minor Disputes Deserve Second Class Justice?" *Judicature*, 61(1978), 102-3.

148. *Hearings*, 1st Phase, 354.

149. Shirley M. Hufstedler, "Comity and the Constitution: The Changing Role of the Federal Judiciary," *New York University Law Review*, 47(1972), 841, 850.

150. See remarks of Mary Schroeder, J., Transcript of Proceedings, Conference on Social Science Research in the Courts (National Center for State Courts, 1977), 129; William H. Rehnquist, "Whither the Courts," *American Bar Association Journal*, 60(1974), 787-90; and Neubauer, "Judicial Role."

151. Burger to Hruska, May 29, 1975, in Hruska Commission, *Structure and Internal Procedures* (June 1975), 177-78. Burger, "Reducing the Load on 'Nine Mortal Justices,' " *New York Times*, August 14, 1975, C31:6.

152. Warren E. Burger, "State of the Federal Judiciary, 1972," *American Bar Association Journal*, 58(1972), 1049-50; 97 S. Ct. 4 (May 1, 1977). See Davis and Nejelski, "Justice Impact Statements," 18-27.

153. Cf. the Judicial Conference's opposition to broader access to citizens charging government officials with acts of discrimination (*New York Times*, March 11, 1978, 16:1); and *Monell v. New York City Dept. of Social Services*, 98 S. Ct. 2018 (1978).

154. *New York Times*, January 2, 1977, 1:1. Quote, Hearings on S. 729 (1975), 47.

155. *Baltimore Sun*, November 5, 1977, A9.

156. *Washington Post*, May 5, 1978, A1:4.

157. For the notable exception of Judge Friendly, see Friendly, J., Hearings on H.R. 7378 (1971); Friendly, *Federal Jurisdiction*; and Friendly, "Averting the Flood."

158. See, e.g., Bell, J., in *Hearings*, 2d Phase, II, 688. Earl W. Kintner, Hearings on H.R. 7378 (1971), 58-59. Also, Geoff Gallas, "Court Reform: Has It Been Built on an Adequate Foundation?" *Judicature*, 63(1979), 28-38.

159. Carrington, "Crowded Dockets," 596.

160. AO *Annual Report* (preliminary 1979), Tables B7, C1, 45 and B2; and *Hearings*, 2d Phase, II, 681.

161. For a similar view, see Bell, J., in *Hearings*, 2d Phase, II, 681. Also Herbert A. Simon, *Administrative Behavior: A Study of Decision-Making Processes in Administrative Organization*, 3rd ed. (New York: Free Press, 1976), xx, xxxvi-xxxvii, 220-28; Herbert Kaufman, *The Forest Ranger: A Study in Administrative Behavior* (Baltimore: Johns Hopkins Press, 1960),

and Kaufman, *Administrative Feedback: Monitoring Subordinates' Behavior* (Washington, D.C.: The Brookings Institution, 1973).

162. Hufstedler, "Courtship and Other Legal Arts," 547.

163. Gerhard Casper and Richard A. Posner, *The Workload of the Supreme Court* (Chicago: American Bar Foundation, 1976), 85-92; and their "The Caseload of the Supreme Court: 1975 and 1976 Terms," *Supreme Court Review* (1977), 87-98; Paul D. Carrington, "United States Appeals in Civil Cases: A Field and Statistical Study," *Houston Law Review*, 11(1974), 1101. Cf. Hruska Commission, *Structure and Internal Procedures* (June 1975), 4-30, 76-168; Erwin N. Griswold, "Rationing Justice—The Supreme Court's Caseload and What the Court Does Not Do," *Cornell Law Review*, 60(1975), 335-54; and Burger, White, and Blackmun, J.J., *New York Times*, December 5, 1978, A18:1.

164. Coffin, C.J., as quoted in *The Third Branch*, 8(December 1976), 8. For extensive literature on the proposed National Court of Appeals, see Chapter One, note 44.

165. Richardson and Vines, *Politics of Federal Courts*, 173-77.

166. Alexander Hamilton, *The Federalist*, no. 81 (New York: Random House, n.d.), 528. See Donald P. Lay, "Why Rush to Judgment? Some Second Thoughts on the Proposed National Court of Appeals," *Judicature*, 59(1975), 177-79.

167. Kenneth M. Dolbeare, *Trial Courts in Urban Politics* (New York: John Wiley and Sons, 1967), 126-27. Gallas, "Court Reform," 30-31.

168. Grant Gilmore, *The Ages of American Law* (New Haven: Yale University Press, 1977), 108-11.

169. Horowitz, *Courts and Social Policy*, 283.

170. Martin Shapiro, "Decentralized Decision-Making in the Law of Torts," in S. Sidney Ulmer, ed., *Political Decision-Making* (New York: Van Nostrand Reinhold, 1970), 44-75.

171. As quoted by Jerome Frank, " 'Short of Sickness and Death': A Study of Moral Responsibility in Legal Criticism," *New York University Law Review*, 26(1951), 547.

172. S. 677 and 678, 96th Cong., 1st Sess. (1979). See references in notes 128 and 131, this chapter.

173. *New York Times*, January 12, 1979, D3; and interview with Maurice Rosenberg, *The Third Branch*, 12(January 1980), 7.

174. Ibid., May 5, 1978, A15, and January 29, 1979, A16.

175. Cf. *Baltimore Sun*, November 29, 1978, A20; and Steven Flanders, "Senator Sarbanes Is Quite Right," *Baltimore Sun*, December 27, 1978, A17; Symposium, "Federal Judicial Selection: The Problems and Achievements of Carter's Merit Plan," *Judicature*, 62(1979), 465-510; Anthony Lewis, "A Dubious Reform," *New York Times*, January 18, 1979, A21; and Larry Berkson, Susan Carbon, and Alan Neff, "A Study of the U.S. Circuit Judge Nominating Commission: Findings, Conclusions and Recommendations," *Judicature*, 63(1979), 104-29.

176. Warren E. Burger, as quoted in *Baltimore Sun*, July 6, 1971, 1:8.

177. For criticism by Senator Dennis De Concini of Chief Justice Burger's lobbying over the bankruptcy bill and Burger's reply, see *New York Times*, November 19, 1978, 39:1; and *Baltimore Sun*, October 26, 1978, A11.

178. C. Herman Pritchett, "The Development of Judicial Research," in Joel B. Grossman and Joseph Tanenhaus, eds., *Frontiers of Judicial Research* (New York: John Wiley and Sons, 1969), 42.

# Index

abstention, 147
access to courts, 14-15, 17, 20, 271, 285, 288-89, 295
accountability, 83, 279, 281, 294
Achilles, 145
Adams, Brooks, 19
adjudication, 8-10, 13-14, 83, 127, 157, 226, 257, 262, 274-75, 281, 293
administrative agencies, xxi, 26, 32, 43-47, 64, 133, 149, 297-98, 331-34. *See also individual agencies*
administrative appeals, xix, xxiv, 6, 12, 20, 24-27, 31-32, 34, 46, 55, 60, 70, 76, 265, 286-87, 297, 331-34
administrative law, 30, 72, 76, 250
Administrative Office of the United States Courts (AO), 7, 24, 26, 34, 58, 274-75, 297-303; *Annual Reports* of, 12, 26-27, 35-36, 58, 266-67, 297-98, 301, 321
admiralty, 32, 55, 76, 144, 149, 206, 230, 234, 253, 280
affirmative action, 101, 243-44, 252, 273, 295
*Afroyim v. Rusk*, 59
agriculture, 315, 322, 325, 328, 335, 338, 341
Ainsworth, Robert A., Jr., xx, 49-50, 140, 195, 237, 242-45, 249
Alabama, xix, 10, 45, 145, 214, 272-73; Middle District, 319, 321, 332; Northern District, 35, 37, 319, 321, 332; Southern District, 47, 51, 319, 321, 332
Alaska, 145
Ali, Muhammad, 56
Allgood, Clarence W., 49
Allison, Graham, 57
American Bar Association, 18, 129, 154, 284; Standing Committee on the Federal Judiciary, 50, 93, 95, 108
American Judicature Society, 94
American Law Institute, 94, 284
*Anders v. California*, 11, 37
Anderson, Robert P., xx, 139, 194, 236, 239, 303

antitrust, 62-63, 66, 76, 315, 322, 325, 328, 335, 338, 341
appellate capacity, 14; regional, 32-33, 41, 55, 79, 83-84, 219-20, 262-69, 278, 290-92; national, 21, 79-84, 188, 283-86, 290-92
arbitration, 282, 285, 294
Arkansas, 4
*Armstrong v. Bd. of Educ. of Birmingham*, 243
assault, 317, 323, 326, 329, 337, 339, 342
Atkins, Burton M., 194, 241, 250
Atlanta, Ga., 252
Attorney General (U.S.), 96, 252
attorneys general (state), 117
Austin, Tex., 92
Australia, 3
auto theft, 29, 317, 323, 326, 329, 337, 340, 343

Baas, Larry R., 306
Bail Reform Act of 1968, 8, 11
bankruptcy, 5, 12, 26-27, 31, 33, 61, 65-66, 72, 200, 279-80, 316, 322, 325, 328, 335, 338, 341
bar, members of and associations, 17, 93-94, 100, 119, 133, 142, 151-52, 154-55, 169, 196, 198, 281, 284
bargaining, 193-97, 208-9, 219
Barnett, Ross, 73, 244
Bartels, John R., 48
Bastian, Walter M., 141, 196, 238, 249, 254
Bazelon, David L., xx, 93, 102, 139, 141, 196, 204, 206, 209, 235, 238-41, 248, 253, 255, 274, 303-4
Becker, Theodore L., 305
Bell, Griffin B., xx, xxv, 82, 93, 118, 140, 195, 217, 237, 239, 241-45, 248, 250-52, 268, 281, 289
Biddle, Francis, 95
Bill of Rights, 11
Black, Hugo L., 16
Blumenfeld, M. Joseph, 48
Board of Patent Appeals, 52

## 400 · Index

Bonsal, Dudley B., 48
Bootle, William A., 49
Bork, Robert H., 285
Brandeis, Louis D., 92, 109, 133, 200, 262, 279, 284
Brennan, Stephen W., 48, 50
Brennan, William J., Jr., 80, 223
Brewster, Leo, 50
bribery, 63, 318, 324, 327, 330, 337, 340, 343
briefs, 197-200; amicus curiae, 60, 199
Brown, John R., xx, 24, 100, 139-40, 195, 227-29, 233-35, 237, 239, 241-46, 248, 251, 253, 268, 273, 275, 278, 281, 304
*Brown v. Bd. of Educ.*, 13, 19, 117, 138, 160
Bruchhausen, Walter, 48
Bryan, Frederick van Pelt, 48
Buchanan, William, xxii
Buckner, Emory, 110
bureaucratization, 7, 9, 14, 79, 271, 274-76, 279, 294
Burger, Warren E., 141, 163, 166, 196, 204, 206, 209, 223, 238-39, 241, 253-55, 257, 263, 270, 274-76, 282, 284, 286-87, 289, 303
Burger Court, 14, 53, 78, 176, 201
Burke, Harold P., 48

calendars, 136, 212, 233, 276
California, 272
Cameron, Benjamin F., 147, 204, 206, 209, 229, 233, 237, 241-42, 244-45
Canal Zone, xix, 45, 320-21, 333
Cannella, John M., 48
Cardozo, Benjamin N., 156, 165, 180, 188, 223
Carl, Jerome, 98
Carpentier lectures, 282
Carrington, Paul D., 81, 287
Carswell, G. Harrold, xx, xxv, 49-50, 55, 93, 100, 137, 197, 231
Carter, Jimmy, 101, 289
Carter administration, 14, 285, 294-95
Cashin, John M., 48
Casper, Gerhard, 11
Catholics, 102-3, 167
centralization, 276, 294
certiorari, writ of, 58, 63-68, 73-74, 77, 81, 193, 281, 286-88, 294
Chayes, Abram, 9

Chicago, Ill., 98
Chicago and Northwestern Railroad, 94
chief judges, U.S. Courts of Appeals, 6-8, 222, 243, 253, 273, 279, 283; formal powers, 226-29, 255-58; influence on adjudication, 225-34, 245-48, 252-58; workloads, 227-28, 239-40, 248. *See also* Courts of Appeals, allocation of work in
Chief Justices (U.S.), 6-7, 95, 226, 263, 275, 285
Choate, Emett C., 49
Christenberry, Herbert W., 49
Cicero, 281
Circuit Courts of Apeals (U.S.), 5
circuit executives, 7, 275-76
Circuit Judge Nominating Commissions, 18, 101, 295
circuit judges, 21, 87-88, 98, 101, 106, 111, 117, 136-37, 141, 165, 169, 184, 217, 269
  ages, 102, 106, 119, 239
  ambitions for judgeships, 17, 90, 95-99, 108, 111-13, 116-18, 121-22
  attitudes, xviii, 19, 117, 261; toward judicial lawmaking, 159-73, 175-88; toward being reversed by Supreme Court, 139-41
  birthplaces, 105-7
  collective responsibility, 135, 205, 209
  dissent rates, 190-91, 193-96
  educational backgrounds, 93-94, 105-6, 113
  ethnic backgrounds, 102-3
  experience in government, 91-93, 97, 113-15, 121
  freshmen, 193, 209, 229, 233, 239, 242-44, 248-52, 257. *See also* circuit judges, socialization, of freshmen
  independence, 115-18, 136-42, 165, 189-90, 220
  judicial discretion, xviii, 18, 21, 23, 25, 75, 87, 122, 150, 167, 186-89, 195, 219-20, 263; formal controls on, xviii, 23, 41, 54-56, 79-84, 87, 122, 150, 290-94; informal controls on, 41, 75, 81-84, 87, 120, 122, 125, 156-57, 187, 191-97, 219-20, 234, 255-57, 291-94

judicial opinions, 136-37, 199-203, 213, 215-16, 220, 223-27, 230, 247-50, 279; assignments of, 192, 201, 222, 226, 234-39, 247-58, 292, 297, 303-4; craftsmanship in, 230, 255; leadership in, 142-44, 225-32, 247-58; oral opinions, 199, 202, 265, 267, 278, 280-81; order-type opinions, 199, 202, 267-68, 277, 280-81, 288; per curiam opinions, 14, 60, 74, 236-38; priority of, 24-25, 127-31, 134, 157, 187, 203, 257, 280-81, 292; slip opinions, 213, 215-16, 267; solo opinions, 211-12, 215, 248; unpublished opinions, 267, 281

judicial role orientations, xviii, xx-xxiv, 20-22, 79, 83-84, 87-89, 108, 117, 120-27, 129, 263, 288; *community roles*, 125-26; as agents of national government (areal roles), xvii, 3-4, 20, 23, 41, 77-78, 82-84, 113, 117, 123, 125-26, 144-48, 156, 184, 191, 219-20, 222, 244, 246, 256, 262, 277, 288, 292-93, 296; as participants in community affairs, 150-57, 222; *consensual roles*, 84, 192-221, 294; and norm of equal work, 201, 232, 235, 239, 246-49, 255, 257; *decisional roles*, 126, 159-88; as innovators, 160-62, 165, 167-70, 175-80, 186; as interpreters, 161-63, 167-70, 175-77, 179, 186; as realists, 161-63, 168-71, 175-77; political, professional, and social backgrounds and, 167-70; voting behavior and, 170-88, 298; *purposive roles*, 14, 39, 125-45, 156-57, 187, 191, 196, 222, 290-91; as adjudicators, 127-32, 134, 151, 153, 223, 292; as administrators, 127, 131-32; as educators, 127, 133-34; as lawmakers, 127, 132-33, 140; as ritualists, 127, 129-31, 134, 153

occupational mobility, 105-7

perceptions, xxiii, 305-6; of collegial deliberation, 211-15; of cross-court influence, 142-44; of elements of decision, 164-65, 196; of en bancs, 190, 215-20; of freshman socialization, 223-25; of give and take, 195, 203, 207-10; of influence on public policy, 147-50; of lawmaking opportunities, 165-66, 187, 291; of leadership on Courts of Appeals, 192, 226-32; of legal factors in decisions, 198-200; of panel and opinion assignments, 226-27, 232-35; of permissible activity in recruiting federal judges, 154; of permissible civic activity, 153-56; of permissible political activity, 153; of permissible professional activity, 153-56; of precedent in decisions, 164-65; of preparation for judgeships, 119-20, 151; of related actors in decisions, 150-52; of reversal by Supreme Court, 139-42; of voting blocs, 205-7; of workloads, 264, 268, 274

personalities, xxiii, 18, 87, 95-97, 105, 120, 123, 137, 166-67, 179-80, 224, 226, 229-31

political orientations, xxiii, 18-19, 84, 87-88, 129, 159, 166-89, 230, 247, 269, 295, 314; as conservatives, liberals, and moderates, 18, 115-17, 121, 170, 172-74, 176, 179, 181; professional orientations and, xviii, 18-19, 21-22, 75, 84, 87, 108, 116-17, 121, 167-72, 178-88, 219, 258, 261, 292; social backgrounds and, 115-17, 120-23, 167-72, 181-84; voting behavior and, 170-88, 298

political participation, 90-93, 96, 108, 115, 121-22, 153-55, 169

political party affiliations, 90, 106, 122, 159, 169-70, 230; voting behavior and, 170, 181-83

precedent orientations, 81, 112, 138, 145, 156, 160-67, 186-88, 191, 292

professional backgrounds, 92-96, 111-13, 117-19; as attorneys in private practice, 94, 96, 98, 110, 113-14, 118-19, 124, 168-69; as political lawyers, 95, 101, 106, 113, 121, 123, 169, 188, 292; as judges, 92-93, 96, 113, 119, 134, 159, 168-69; attitudes toward judicial lawmaking and prior judicial experience, 168-69; voting behavior and, 181-83

circuit judges (cont.)
  professional orientations, xviii, 18-19, 22, 84, 87-89, 108, 112-13, 118-23, 134, 141, 150-57, 159, 167-72, 176, 276, 292, 295; voting behavior and, 176, 179-88
  recruitment, xxiii, 75, 78, 86-102, 112-24, 145-46, 154-57, 168-70, 184-86, 188, 272, 288-89, 295; elements of, 16-19, 89-102, 121; paths to circuit courts and, 88-89, 112-18, 122, 168, 185; politics in, 17-19, 88, 90-95, 99-101, 112, 116-18, 120, 161, 166-67, 295; professionalism in, 17-19, 88-90, 93-95, 101, 108, 116-17; reciprocity in, 87-89, 95-99, 101, 113-15, 121-24
  reference groups, 112, 123, 126, 152-57
  religious affiliations, 102-3, 105, 168
  salaries, 98
  senior judges, 115, 190, 201, 213, 239, 247-48, 256, 258, 265, 267, 271, 303-5
  social backgrounds, 88, 93, 102-7, 122-23, 181-83, 185, 224; class origins, 102-5, 159, 167-68; voting behavior and, 181-83
  socialization, xxii, 19, 84, 87-89, 102-24, 156-57, 166-67, 172, 184, 188, 295; agents of, 106, 108-9; anticipatory, 84, 88-89, 107-8, 112, 120-22, 146-47, 170, 192, 223; evaluation of, 119-20; of freshmen, 107, 123-24, 135, 192, 222-25, 229, 239, 255, 257; occupational (on-the-job training), 84, 107, 112, 222-25; political, 102-16, 120-24; professional, 84, 102-16, 120-24; stages of, 106-12, 121-24
  specialization, 165, 201, 222-25, 230-32, 234-35, 240-57
  turnover, 18, 75, 190
  values, xxi, xxiii, 18-19, 21-22, 33, 41, 89, 113, 115-18, 120-23, 141, 219, 292; voting behavior and, 116, 167-88, 261, 292; work assignments and, 240-46, 250-58
  vocational development, 87-90, 93-99, 101, 105-6, 111-24, 168
  voting behavior, 106, 116, 159, 169-88, 223, 261

  workloads, 25, 98, 193, 197, 200, 205, 210, 240, 253, 256, 264, 268-75, 303. See also Courts of Appeals, caseloads; Courts of Appeals, decisions
circuit judicial conferences, 213, 216
circuit judicial councils, 6, 7, 212-13, 226, 270, 273, 276, 279
circuit riding, 4, 200, 212, 215, 277-78
Civil Aeronautics Board, 32, 44-47, 65, 331, 333-34
civil appeals, 5, 26-29, 35-37, 39, 52, 65, 298, 315-30, 338-43
Civil Appeals Management Plan, 38, 265
civil liberties, 29, 60, 91
civil rights, 13, 30, 60, 163, 226, 269, 282-83, 287, 316, 323, 326, 329, 336, 339, 342; in 5th circuit, xix, 29, 32, 37, 41-42, 52-53, 62-64, 66-67, 72-73, 99-100, 106, 147-50, 166, 204, 206, 229, 240-46, 251-52, 267, 269, 273, 280, 316-17, 326, 339; in three-judge district courts, 240, 245, 256, 283; voting behavior and, 173-77, 179-80, 182-85, 187
Civil Rights Act of 1964, 5, 69
Civil Rights Commission, 148
civil rights removals, 70, 147, 244, 317, 323, 326, 329, 336, 339, 342
Civil War, 4-5
Clarie, T. Emmet, 48
Clark, Charles, xx
Clark, Charles E., 147, 165, 202-4, 207, 210, 228
Clark, Tom C., xx
Clayton, Claude F., 49-50
Clean Air Act of 1970, 32
Coleman, James P., xx, 92, 140, 195, 215, 237, 242-45, 250-52, 273
Columbia University Law School, 93-94
commerce, 30, 60-61, 163, 240, 252, 303-4, 315, 322, 325, 328, 335, 338, 341
Commerce Court (U.S.), 284
Commission on Revision of the Federal Court Appellate System (Hruska Commission), xvii, 17, 55, 80, 213-14, 232, 257, 263, 268, 270, 272-73, 281-82, 285, 290
compliance, 19-20, 25, 70, 246
conflict of interest, 197
Congress (U.S.), xvii, xxiv, 4-9, 11, 13-16, 20, 27-28, 32, 37, 77, 92, 106, 113, 162,

165, 191, 197, 213-14, 222, 240, 250-58, 262-63, 269-71, 273, 277, 281, 285, 287, 289
*Congressional Record*, 109
Connally, Ben C., 49
Connecticut, xix, 44, 104, 115, 213, 319, 321, 331
Constitution (U.S.), 4-5, 88, 138, 163; constitutional questions, 28, 60, 77, 147
consumer protection, 13
contested judgments, 34, 37, 82, 301-3, 319-21
contracts, 29-30, 60-61, 71-72, 240, 252-53, 285, 294, 303, 315, 322, 325, 328, 335, 338, 341
Cooper, Edward H., 302
Cooper, Irving Ben, 48, 50
copyrights, 62-63, 66, 173, 175, 177, 179-80, 182-83, 294, 316, 322, 325, 328, 335, 338, 341
Corcoran, Howard F., 51
Cornell University Law School, 93
Court of Appeals for the Federal Circuit (proposed), 285
Court of Claims (U.S.), 285
Court of Customs and Patent Appeals (U.S.), 284-85
Court of Emergency Appeals (U.S.), 284
Court of Tax Appeals (proposed), 285-86
court reform, 14, 18-19, 157, 259; politics of, xxiv-xxv, 269-73, 282, 284-86, 289-90, 295-98; strategies of, 261-96
Courts of Appeals (U.S.), xvii, xix-xxv, 3-44, 52-91, 96, 118-39, 142-50, 161, 163, 165-66, 169, 187-97, 220-26, 230-32, 235, 239-40, 247, 255, 257-58, 261-64, 269-70, 273-77, 284-87, 289-343
    administration, 6-8, 13, 16, 20, 123, 131-32, 142, 189, 222, 226-28, 255-58, 264, 268-71, 274-79, 281-82, 294; policy making and, 8, 225-32, 246-50, 255-58, 276-77, 292, 294
    allocation of work in, xviii, 21-22, 185, 221, 232, 292; experience and, 240, 249-50, 256-57; norm of equality and, 201, 232, 248-49, 256; opinion assignments and, 192, 201, 222, 226, 234-39, 247-58, 292, 297, 303-4; panel assignments and, 192, 222, 226, 228-29, 232-47, 254-58, 303-4; panel rotation and, 9, 171, 184, 187-90, 193-94, 197, 219-20, 225, 231-35, 247, 255-57, 285-86, 297; randomness in, 9, 209, 228-29, 232-35, 239, 241-47, 256
    autonomy, xvii, 7-8, 23, 33, 40, 52-58, 63, 71-75, 78-79, 125, 138-45, 156, 189, 196, 290
    business, xviii, 23-33, 54-56, 71, 78-79, 148-49, 282, 290, 298, 315-43; compared with Supreme Court's, 59-63, 69, 74, 315-18; variety of, 23, 31, 34-35, 40, 54-56, 79, 220, 261, 290-93
    caseloads, 9-14, 26-28, 30, 83, 214, 232, 290; decision making and, 79-80, 198-200, 205, 217, 264-69, 277-82; overload in, xix, 14-15, 21, 28, 83, 131, 150, 244-46, 249, 262-74, 281, 289, 291
    cohesion, xviii, xxii-xxiii, 3, 211; among circuits, 8-9, 18-19, 21-23, 59, 75, 79, 83, 87, 89, 122-25, 144, 170, 185-91, 207, 221, 261, 268, 270-72, 276, 292-95; within circuits, 8-9, 41, 83, 100, 115-17, 192, 218-19, 222, 257-58, 270-72
    collegial deliberation in, xxi, 9, 103, 195, 208, 211-21, 270, 276-77, 288
    conflict in, xviii, 3, 8-9, 21-22, 42, 52, 67-71, 77, 79, 107, 123, 157, 193-96, 204-7, 253, 261, 267, 286-87; among circuits, 8, 17, 21-22, 52, 67-71, 81-83, 185, 218, 271, 291-93; within circuits, 9, 21-22, 67-70, 83, 185, 189-222, 257, 291-92, 294; roles and, 129, 157, 159-88
    consensus in, xviii, 3, 21-22, 69, 83, 87, 107, 123, 134, 157, 184-93, 210, 261, 287, 290-91
    constituencies, xxi, 13-17, 19-21, 31-32, 53-54, 62, 79, 89-90, 101, 110, 121-23, 126, 133, 145-47, 150-57, 268-69, 281, 289, 295
    decision making in, 14, 19, 79, 213, 222, 262-69, 281; bench memoranda and, 198, 200, 279; formal procedures of, 191-92, 213, 216, 220, 247, 256, 261, 276-77, 294; informal methods of conflict resolution and, 123, 148, 191-97,

Courts of Appeals (U.S.) (cont.)
213, 216-21, 271, 276-77, 293-94;
informality of, 21-22, 54, 75, 81-84,
87, 125, 156, 191-97, 220, 232, 234,
255-57, 261-62, 277, 284, 290,
292-94; mass production and, 9, 14,
77, 79-80, 83, 187, 214, 263, 265,
267-68, 271, 277, 284, 288, 291,
294; models of, 79, 172, 178-79,
182, 186; peer pressure and, xxiii,
122, 191, 201, 274; persuasion and,
203, 208-9, 225; preparation for,
197-200, 279; pressure of quantity
on quality of, 14, 125, 212, 262-65,
271, 274, 282-83, 291, 295; rules of,
187, 189-91, 197, 201, 218, 258,
294; situational factors in, 165-66,
171, 181-84, 186-87, 231, 292; as
small groups, 16, 166-67, 189-223,
258, 261

decisions, 35, 41-56, 321-30; finality
and, 57-59, 68, 71, 73-75, 78, 82-83,
291, 315-18; impact of, 19, 133,
148-50; integrity of, 197; policy
outcomes of, 24, 52-55, 159, 178-83,
185, 188, 194, 219, 240; solo decisions, 202, 278; summary decisions, 14, 199, 202, 279-80

dissent rates in, 42

environments, xxi, 13, 15-22, 82-88,
106, 121-23, 145, 150, 155-57, 211,
245-46, 261; political settings and,
xviii, xxi, xxv, 3, 13, 15-21, 186,
289

external controls on, 21, 87, 122,
261, 274, 294

functions, xvii-xix, xxi-xxii, 2-8,
16-18, 20, 23, 25, 75-84, 115, 123-
34, 184, 187, 191, 219, 224, 262-63,
269, 274, 288-90, 295-96; in administration, 6-8, 13, 16, 127, 131-32;
changes in, 9-16, 28, 37-38, 56, 79,
83-84, 125, 131-32, 150, 153, 156-
57, 262-63, 277, 288-90; compared
with district courts and Supreme
Court, 76, 134-37, 145, 186-87, 199,
224; in conflict resolution, 5, 76-78,
83, 217, 277, 288; in enforcement of
national law, xvii-xxi, 3-4, 13, 20,
23, 31-41, 77-78, 82-84, 117, 123,
125-26, 144-50, 156, 184, 191,
219-20, 222, 244, 246, 256, 262,
277, 288, 290-93, 296; in error correction, 7, 20, 25, 28, 54, 56, 70,
76-78, 80, 82-83, 128-29, 131, 218,
262, 272, 277, 286, 288-89, 291,
293; in filtering and gatekeeping,
42, 54, 77-78, 144-45, 288, 291; in
finality, 24, 55-59, 68, 71, 73-75, 78,
82-83, 145, 290-91, 315-18; in lawmaking, 15-16, 25, 54, 78-80, 82-83,
131-33, 153, 159-88, 217, 262, 277,
286, 288, 292, 305; strategies of reform and, 79-84, 295-96

history, 3-8

jurisdiction, xxi, 3-8, 16-17, 35, 56,
186, 191, 261, 282-85, 288, 294,
319, 334

leadership among, 142-45, 148-50,
299

leadership in, xviii, 139, 189-90,
192, 221-22; adjudicative, 142-44,
148-49, 225-32, 239-40, 246-50;
administrative, 225-29, 275-76; relationship between, 8, 222, 225-32,
240, 246-50, 255-58, 276-77, 292,
294

organization, xxi, 3-10, 16-17, 23,
78, 145, 213-14, 219, 228, 232, 255,
263-64, 269-73, 284, 289-90, 292-
94, 296

policy making by, 6, 18-20, 31-33,
39, 51-56, 76, 78, 82, 131, 150, 161,
163-65, 186-88, 217, 219-20, 263,
272-73, 292, 298; networks of, 41,
57, 62, 78-79, 290; priority of, 83,
129, 131-33, 157, 212, 217, 220,
262, 267, 287-88, 292

problems and prospects, xvii, xxiv-
xxv, 9-15, 21-22, 39, 262-69

productivity, 239, 262-63, 265-69,
274-75

professionalism in, xxii, 22, 41, 87,
89, 101, 113, 118-23, 125, 134, 140,
150-57, 167, 169-72, 176, 189, 191,
220, 229-30, 232, 235, 276

rates of appeal to, 10-13, 25-41,
43-46, 53-55, 73-74, 77, 82-83,
262-63, 291, 297-303, 319-21

size, xix, 11-12, 26, 146, 191, 213-14,
258, 268-73, 289, 295

specialization among, 25, 29-32,

51-56, 62-63, 66-67, 71-73, 76, 78-79, 137, 148-49, 284-86, 290, 293-94
  strategies of reform, 261-96
  supervision of district courts and agencies, xvii-xviii, 3, 7, 21-56, 69, 74-84, 128-29, 261, 290-92, 296, 298
  uniqueness, xxi, 22-23, 72, 84, 181, 291
  *See also* numbered circuits
Cox, Archibald, 15, 64
Cox, William H., 42, 50-51, 56, 117, 229, 245
Crete, 53
crimes against persons, 30, 61, 317, 323, 326, 329, 336, 339, 342
crimes against property, 30, 51, 61, 317, 323, 326, 329, 337, 340, 343
criminal appeals, 5, 13, 26-34, 40, 43, 56, 149, 204, 240, 250, 274, 287; in Courts of Appeals, 26-37, 44, 46, 51-56, 61-62, 78, 82, 149-50, 163, 207, 218, 246, 249-54, 263, 265-69, 279-80, 315-21, 323-24, 326-33, 336-40, 342-43; growth of, 11-13, 40, 262; panel and opinion assignments in, 240, 246, 249-54, 303-4; rates of, 33-40, 302-3, 321; in Supreme Court, 60-65, 71, 76-78, 316-18, 336-37, 339-40, 342-43; voting behavior in, 173-77, 179-80, 182, 185. *See also* District of Columbia Circuit, business; Fifth Circuit, business; Second Circuit, business
Criminal Justice Act of 1964, 11, 37
criminal law, 76, 230, 249
criminal procedure, 11, 31, 62, 72, 209
criminal responsibility, 149, 166
Croake, Thomas F., 48
cue theory, 67, 222
Curran, Edward M., 51
*Curtis Publishing Co. v. Butts*, 59
Curzan, Mary H., 106

Danaher, John A., 115, 141, 196, 209, 238, 253-54, 303
Davidson, T. Whitfield, 50-51
Davis, John W., 95
Dawkins, Benjamin C., Jr., 49
Dawson, Archie Owen, 48
de Gaulle, Charles, 155

decentralization, 8, 17-18, 21-23, 54, 83, 188-89, 275, 290-91, 293
DeConcini, Dennis, 285
delay, 264, 267, 274, 283-84
demand for appellate services, xxi, 5, 9-15, 17, 21, 23, 33-41, 54-57, 63-68, 80, 82, 97, 123, 217, 220, 263-64, 271, 281, 284, 288, 291, 294-95, 300-301, 319-21; inelasticity of, 64, 68, 71, 284
Democratic National Convention, 110
Democrats, 90, 96, 99, 169, 181, 270
Denman, William, 73
Department of Health, Education, and Welfare, 132
Department of Justice, 6, 14, 34, 96, 99, 130, 154, 268, 285; Civil Liberties Unit, 47; Office for Improvements in the Administration of Justice, 14, 290
Department of State, 93
Department of the Treasury, 93
desegregation, xix, xxiv, 9-10, 63, 71, 75, 78, 99-100, 123, 132, 146, 149-50, 206, 214, 216, 244, 279
Dexter, Lewis A., 305
dissensus, 185, 194-96, 207, 219, 221, 232, 257, 291
dissent, 42, 60, 67, 144, 166, 176, 185, 190-91, 193-96, 202, 205, 208, 210, 219, 223, 225, 231; functions of, 205-6. *See also* circuit judges, dissent rates; Courts of Appeals, dissent rates in
district attorneys (state), 92, 114
district courts (U.S.), xvii, xxii, 4-6, 10, 12-13, 16, 20, 24, 34-35, 44-47, 52, 64, 106, 113, 122, 131, 135, 137, 155-57, 186, 291, 298, 300-301, 331-34; finality of, 39-40, 82, 291. *See also* three-judge district courts; *and individual district courts listed by state*
district judges (U.S.), 4, 19-20, 99, 106, 125, 134-37, 168-69, 224, 231, 248, 268-70, 283; reversal of, 47-52
District of Columbia, 29, 34-35, 52, 233, 254, 265
District of Columbia Board of Tax Appeals, 26, 46
District of Columbia Circuit, U.S. Court of Appeals for, xix-xx, xxiv, 5, 18, 26-43, 46-47, 50-53, 55-56, 58-59, 61, 63-65, 67, 70, 72, 75-76, 78, 91-93, 100, 102-7, 113, 115-17, 122-23, 141-44, 148-49,

District of Columbia Circuit (cont.)
  160-61, 166, 190, 206-9, 211-12, 217, 222, 224, 227, 233, 238-41, 248-49, 253-54, 263-67, 270, 280-81, 285-86, 297, 303-4, 309, 315-18, 320-21, 328-30, 334, 341-43
  business, 26-33, 46, 61-62, 263, 265-67, 315-18, 320-21, 328-30; administrative appeals, 26, 32, 46, 55, 265, 285, 334; criminal appeals, 26-27, 29-30, 34, 43, 52-53, 71-72, 78, 166, 204, 209, 249, 253-54, 316-18, 321, 328-30
  conflict in, 100, 123, 161, 193, 204, 206-7, 209, 249, 267
  decisions, 27, 38-43, 46-47, 50-51, 263, 265-67, 321, 328-30; policy outcomes of, 42, 46-47, 52-53, 55, 71-72, 148-50; process of, 265-67; "wash outs" in, 38, 265, 267
  delay in, 266-67
  dissent in, 42, 193, 196, 304
  en bancs in, 218
  jurisdiction, xix, 32, 72; local, 27, 35-36, 46, 72, 75, 240, 265, 267, 303-4, 318, 320-21, 330, 334, 343
  opinion assignments in, 238, 248-49, 253-54, 303-4
  panel assignments in, 233-34, 238-41, 245, 303-4
  productivity, 263, 265-67
  rates of appeal to, 34-38, 41, 320-21
  recruitment to, 100
  size, xix, 263, 270
  supervision of district courts and agencies, 29-33, 35-43, 46-47, 50, 52, 55, 319-21, 334
  supervision of, by Supreme Court, 58-59, 61-65, 70-72, 76, 141, 315-18, 334, 341-43
District of Columbia Court of Appeals, 12, 27
District of Columbia Court Reorganization Act, 265
diversion, 282-89, 294-95
diversity jurisdiction, 3-6, 28, 35-37, 55-56, 82, 234, 272, 279, 283-84, 287, 294, 298, 319-20
docket congestion, xvii, 20, 264-65, 278, 282, 284-85, 287-89
docket control, 5, 41-42, 57, 77, 83, 165, 193, 278, 286-89, 291, 294-95

Dolbeare, Kenneth M., 293
domestic relations, 318, 330, 343
Dooley, Joseph B., 49
Dooling, John F., Jr., 48
due process, 15, 286
*Durham v. U.S.*, 161
Dyer, David W., xx, 49-50, 140, 193, 195, 231, 237, 239, 242-45, 248

Eastland, James O., 99, 272
economic regulation, 6, 9-10, 62, 64, 246, 249, 253, 304
Edgerton, Henry W., 141, 196, 238, 241, 249, 254
Eighth Circuit, U.S. Court of Appeals for, 5, 143, 279
Eisenhower, Dwight D., 99-100, 110
Eleventh Circuit, U.S. Court of Appeals for, xix, 5, 214, 273
Elliott, J. Robert, 50
Ellis, Frank B., 50
Ellsworth, Oliver, 5
embezzlement, 31, 62, 317, 323, 326, 329, 337, 340, 343
*Empire Rayon Yarn Co. v. American Viscose Corp.*, 208
employee injuries, 173-80, 315, 322, 325, 328, 335, 338, 341
employer liability, 315, 322, 325, 328, 335, 338, 341
en bancs, 9, 42, 67, 70, 77, 83, 190-93, 205-11, 213, 215-20, 226, 230, 258, 271, 273, 292; purposes of, 195, 211, 217-20; transformation of, 211, 213, 216-20, 292
energy regulation, 13, 214, 272
England, 10, 286
environmental protection, 6, 9, 13, 30-32, 56, 78
Environmental Protection Agency, 6
equity, 10, 14
error correction, 7, 20, 25, 54, 56, 70, 76-78, 80, 82-83, 129, 131, 262, 277, 286, 288, 291
escape, 317, 324, 327, 330, 337, 340, 343
*Escobedo v. Illinois*, 42
Estes, Joe Ewing, 49
Eulau, Heinz, xxii
expertise, 165, 201, 222-25, 230-32, 234-35, 240-57. *See also* circuit judges, specialization; Courts of Appeals, specialization among

extortion, 31, 62, 317, 323, 326, 329, 337, 340, 343

factionalism, 205-7
Fahy, Charles, xx, 93, 115, 141, 144, 196, 209, 238-40, 248, 254, 303
Fair Labor Standards Act, 30, 52-53, 63, 316, 322, 325, 328, 336, 339, 341
Federal Bureau of Investigation, 47
Federal Communications Commission, 6, 29, 32, 44-47, 65, 144, 331, 333-34
Federal Energy Regulatory Commission, 6
Federal Judicial Center, 7, 35, 278, 281, 290, 303
federal judicial system, xxi, 1, 8, 79, 84, 282, 290, 292
Federal Maritime Commission, 70, 72
*Federal Offenders in United States Courts*, 35
Federal Power Commission, 30, 32, 44-47, 65, 70, 72, 331, 333-34
federal questions, 35, 67, 75, 279, 319-20
*Federal Reporter*, 24, 142, 281, 297, 299
federal rules of procedure, 7-8, 28, 55, 163, 191-92, 265
Federal Trade Commission, 32, 44-46, 65, 331, 333-34
federalism, xvii, 4, 146-47, 289
Federalists, 4
Feinberg, Wilfred, xx, 139, 194, 233, 236, 239, 248
Ferguson, LeRoy C., xxii
Fifth Amendment, 31, 61, 72
Fifth Circuit, U.S. Court of Appeals for, xix-xx, 18, 26-42, 45-47, 49-52, 55, 58-59, 61-64, 67, 70, 72, 75, 78, 83, 91-93, 98-100, 102-7, 113, 115-16, 122, 128, 130-32, 137-38, 140-44, 146-50, 160-62, 166, 179, 187, 193, 197-98, 206-7, 211, 213-18, 224, 227-29, 231, 233, 235, 237, 239, 241-56, 264-74, 277-81, 285-87, 303-4, 309, 315-21, 325-27, 332-33, 338-40
   business, 26-37, 45, 61-62, 150, 263, 265-69, 315-21, 325-27, 332-33, 338-40; administrative appeals, 26, 30, 32, 45-47, 52, 70, 332-33; civil rights, xix, 29, 32, 37, 41-42, 52-53, 62-64, 66-67, 72-73, 99-100, 106, 147-50, 166, 204, 206, 229, 241-46, 251-52, 267, 269, 273, 280, 316-18, 326, 339; criminal appeals, 26-27, 29-30, 34-35, 37, 39, 52-53, 64, 72, 268-69, 280, 316-18, 321, 326-27, 339-40
   conflict in, 193, 204-6, 209, 215-18, 244, 256
   decisions, 38-41, 43, 46-47, 49-51, 263, 321, 325-27; policy outcomes of, 45-47, 52-53, 55, 70-72, 148-50; process of, 197-99, 201-2, 219, 266-69, 277-82; "wash outs" in, 265
   delay in, 266-67
   dissent in, 42, 193, 195, 304
   division of, xix, 5, 213-15, 269-73
   en bancs in, 213, 215-18, 220, 231
   leadership in, 142-44, 148, 227-28, 239, 243-56, 275
   opinion assignments in, 234-35, 237, 247-54, 303-4
   panel assignments in, 197, 209, 233, 235, 237, 239, 241-47, 252-54, 303-4
   productivity, 26, 213, 266-69, 277-81
   rates of appeal to, 34-39, 41, 319-21
   recruitment to, 99-100, 271
   screening in, 197-98, 213, 215, 220, 233, 247, 267-68, 277-81, 288
   size, xix, 26, 213-14, 267-71, 273
   supervision of district courts and agencies, 29-33, 35-43, 45-47, 49-53, 55, 319-21, 332-33
   supervision of, by Supreme Court, 58-59, 61-64, 66-67, 70-72, 140, 315-18, 332-33, 338-40
filtering, xvii, 56, 77-78, 131, 160, 218, 277, 283. *See also* gatekeeping
finality, xvii, 7-8, 23-25, 39-40, 43, 55-59, 73-75, 77-78, 82, 128, 130-31, 136, 138, 145-46, 149, 287-88
firearms, *see* weapons
First Circuit, U.S. Court of Appeals for, 143, 215
Fish, Peter G., 275
Fisher, Joe J., 50
Florida, xix, 45, 214, 272-73, 319, 321, 332; Middle District, 37, 319, 321, 332; Northern District, 319, 321, 332; Southern District, 37, 66, 319, 321, 332
Foley, James T., 48
Foley Square (New York City), xxv, 130, 142, 212

food and drug cases, 31, 62-63, 316, 322, 325, 328, 335, 338, 341
forfeitures and penalties, 316, 323, 326, 329, 336, 339, 342
forgery, 62, 317, 323, 326, 329, 337, 340, 343
Fort Sumter, S.C., 206
Fort Worth, Tex., 216
forum shopping, xxii, 17, 33, 55, 283, 285, 294
Founding Fathers, 4
Fourth Circuit, U.S. Court of Appeals for, 143-44, 148, 228, 279
France, 88, 122
Frank, Jerome, 147, 204
Frankfurter, Felix, xvii, xxii, 1, 8, 10, 16, 79, 82, 95, 262, 288-89
Franklin, Benjamin, 110
fraud, 66, 317, 323, 326, 329, 337, 340, 343
Freund (Paul A.) Committee, 287.
Friendly, Henry J., xx, 72, 92, 94, 139, 144, 194, 208, 217, 229, 231, 236, 240, 248, 250, 255, 270, 282
Fuller, Lon L., 106
Fulton, Charles B., 49
Fusaro, A. Daniel, xx

Gallup poll, 149
gambling, 317, 324, 327, 329, 337, 340, 343
Garza, Reynaldo G., 49
Gasch, Oliver, 51
gatekeeping, 16, 42, 54, 131, 160, 277, 279, 288, 291-92. See also filtering
Gee, Thomas G., 273
*General Electric Co. v. Gilbert*, 69
generalists, 95, 201, 232, 235, 257, 285
George Washington University Law School, 93
Georgetown University Law School, 93
Georgia, xix, 45, 93, 214, 272-73, 319-21, 332; Middle District, 49-50, 320-21, 332; Northern District, 49, 319, 321, 332; Southern District, 37, 47, 50-51
Gewin, Walter P., xx, 94, 140, 195, 237, 241-46, 250-52, 304
Gibson, Ernest W., 48
Gilmore, Grant, 293
Glick, Henry R., 173
Godbold, John C., xx, 140, 195, 217, 237, 239, 241-45, 248, 303

*Gojack v. U.S.*, 59
Goldberg, Irving L., xx, 140, 193, 195, 223, 235, 237, 241-46, 248, 273, 304
Goldman, Jerry, 34-35, 303
Goldman, Sheldon, 240-41
Great Britain, 122
Great Depression, 17, 93, 110
Green, Justin J., 194
*Greenwood v. Peacock*, 64
Griswold, Erwin N., 81
Grooms, Harlan H., 49
Gulf of Mexico, 147, 280-81

habeas corpus, 26, 31, 53, 61, 65-66, 317, 323, 326, 329, 336, 339, 342
Hamilton, Alexander, 15, 23
Hand, Augustus, 47, 142
Hand, Learned, 77, 82, 125, 130, 133, 142, 147, 200, 210, 294
Hannay, Allen B., 49
Hart, George L., Jr., 51
Harvard University Law School, 93, 95, 103, 112, 117
Hatch Act, 91, 153
Hawaii, 145
Haynsworth, Clement F., Jr., 155, 197
Hays, Paul R., xx, 91, 94, 139, 193-94, 236, 240, 250, 253, 255
Henderson, John O., 48
Herlands, William B., 48
Holmes, Oliver Wendell, Jr., 25, 166, 184
Holtzoff, Alexander, 47, 50-51
Homans, George, 192
homicide, 317, 323, 326, 329, 336, 339, 342
Hooper, Frank A., 49
House of Representatives (U.S.), 16-17, 272-73, 284
Houston, Tex., 37, 47, 105, 206, 248, 304
Howard University Law School, 94
Hruska, Roman L., 103
Hruska Commission, see Commission on Revision of the Federal Court Appellate System
Hufstedler, Shirley M., 80, 83
Hughes, Charles Evans, 6
Hughes, Everett C., 85
Hughes, Sarah T., 49
Hunter, Edwin F., Jr., 49
Hutcheson, Joseph C., Jr., 98, 140, 148, 195, 228, 231, 234-35, 237, 242-45, 248-49, 251-52

Index · 409

immigration, 5, 30, 32, 53, 55, 62-63, 66, 70, 72, 76, 241, 317, 323, 326, 329, 336, 339, 342
Immigration and Naturalization Service, 32, 44-46, 53, 70, 331, 333-34
*in forma pauperis*, 42, 60, 64
Ingraham, Joe McD., 49-50
innovation, 20, 28, 138, 157, 159-67, 176, 188, 216-17, 268
insanity defense, 31, 161
insurance, 33, 62-63, 285, 315, 322, 325, 328, 335, 338, 341
intercourt relations, xviii, xxi, 23-25, 33, 41-84, 134, 138-50, 261, 290-94, 299-300
interest groups, 20, 150-52
Internal Revenue Service, 17
Interstate Commerce Commission, 241, 245
interviews, xix-xx, 297, 304-10
Ish, Joel S., 89

Jackson, Robert H., 220
Jacksonville, Fla., 216
Japan, 122
Javits, Jacob K., 100
Jeffersonians, 4
Jews, 102, 167
Johnson, Frank M., Jr., 49-51, 137
Johnson, Lyndon B., 100, 244
Jones, Warren L., xx, 140, 195, 237, 239, 241-46, 251, 304
Jones, William B., 51
judicial activism, 5, 9-11, 13, 125, 129, 159-61, 163, 169, 175-77, 179, 184
judicial administration, *see* Courts of Appeals, administration; Courts of Appeals, leadership
judicial behavior, xxiv, 15, 19, 25, 116, 126, 163, 169, 171, 176, 184, 186, 300. *See also* circuit judges, voting behavior
Judicial Conference (U.S.), 6-7, 154, 163, 213, 226, 270, 272-73, 275
judicial conferences, 38, 163, 192, 198-99, 201-2, 204, 209, 211-12, 279, 288
judicial decision, theories of, xxii, xxiv, 3, 22, 89, 150-51, 159, 167, 171, 176, 181, 184-87, 261, 289, 292-93. *See also* Courts of Appeals, decision making in; Courts of Appeals, decisions
judicial functions, 9, 15, 20, 23, 28, 41, 82-84, 118, 137, 263, 282, 289. *See also* Courts of Appeals, functions
judicial independence, 3, 6, 15, 88-89, 122, 138-45, 150, 189-90, 209, 226, 275, 277
judicial lawmaking, xxiii, 15-16, 20, 25, 71, 78, 80, 83, 126, 132-34, 138, 150, 153, 156, 159-63, 165-67, 169, 171-72, 176-77, 184-87, 262, 277, 286, 288, 290-92, 305. *See also* circuit judges, attitudes, toward judicial lawmaking; circuit judges, voting behavior; Courts of Appeals, functions
judicial manpower, 213, 265, 269-70, 272, 275, 279-80, 295
judicial policy making, xxi, 8, 13-16, 18-19, 87, 150, 153. *See also* Courts of Appeals, policy making by; judicial lawmaking; Supreme Court, policy making by
judicial role perceptions, xix, xxii-xxiv, 84, 112-13, 121-23, 184-86, 200, 295, 305-6; strategies of reform and, 288-89; voting behavior and, 170-88, 292. *See also* circuit judges, judicial role orientations; circuit judges, perceptions
judicial roles, xxi, 9-10, 15-16, 18, 21-22, 56, 87-89, 108, 117, 120-24, 129, 145, 159-60, 166, 170-71, 187-88, 223, 261, 269, 288-89; defined, xxii-xxv, 125-26. *See also* circuit judges, judicial role orientations; judicial role perceptions
judicial selection, *see* circuit judges, recruitment
judicial self-restraint, 125, 166, 169, 219
judicial temperament, 95-96, 137
judiciaries (state), 3, 5, 11, 117, 122, 130, 147, 166, 279, 283-84, 287; supreme courts, 7, 92, 134, 160, 162, 186, 193
Judiciary Acts: (1891), 5, 190; (1925), 77-78, 262
juries, 98, 276, 302

Kaufman, Irving R., xx, 53, 139, 194, 218, 236, 239-40, 248, 275, 278
Keech, Richmond B., 47, 51
Kennedy, Edward M., 285
Kennedy, John F., 93, 100, 244
Kennedy, Robert F., 96, 113
kidnapping, 62, 317, 323, 326, 329, 336, 339, 342

King Minos, 53
Kornberg, Allan, 112

labor relations, 17, 29-32, 51-56, 61-64, 66, 70-72, 76, 78, 174-75, 177, 180, 182, 240, 250, 252-53, 287, 303-4, 316, 322, 325, 328, 336, 339, 341-42
Labor Reporting Act, 316, 322, 325, 328, 336, 339, 342
Landis, James M., xvii, xxii, 1, 8, 79
Lasswell, Harold D., 96
law clerks, 92, 114, 151, 198, 200, 202, 209, 233, 248-49, 279, 288
Law Enforcement Assistance Administration, 287
law explosion, 9-11, 26, 55, 75, 80-81, 142, 188, 199, 220, 244, 258, 262, 264, 269, 275, 288, 291-92
law of the circuits, 33, 52, 55, 79, 144, 187, 190, 219, 272
law schools, 111-12, 119, 148, 151-52, 155, 167-68
lawyers, see bar
leadership, xviii, 82, 87-88, 97, 105, 120-21, 156. See also Courts of Appeals, leadership
League of Nations, 110
legal culture, xxii, 87, 144, 148, 150, 186, 188, 292
legal profession, 93-95, 107-8, 118, 120, 157, 240
legal realism, xxi, 15, 21-22, 87, 166-69, 187
legislatures (state), 113
legitimacy, 14-15, 190
Lempert, Richard, 166
Leventhal, Harold, xx, 92, 141, 196, 207, 238, 241, 249, 254, 303
Levet, Richard H., 48
Liberal Party, 91
Lieb, Joseph P., 49
litigants, 150-52. See also demand for appellate services
litigation flow, xvii-xix, xxv, 1, 15, 17, 21, 127, 143, 261, 290-91, 297-300, 315-21; in Courts of Appeals, 23-56; in Supreme Court, 57-84
Llewellyn, Karl N., 163
localism, 3-4, 14, 79, 146, 148, 156, 271, 290, 293, 295
Lortie, Dan, 112
Louisiana, xix, 45, 272-73, 320-21, 332;
Eastern District, 47, 66, 320-21, 332; Western District, 320-21, 332; Supreme Court of, 186
Lumbard, J. Edward, xx, 72, 92, 139, 194, 222, 225, 227, 229, 231, 233, 236, 239-40, 248, 250, 252, 270, 275
Lynne, Seybourn H., 49

McCafferty, James A., 299
McCloskey, Robert G., 179
McGarraghy, Joseph C., 51
McGohey, John F. X., 48
McGowan, Carl, xx, 94, 116, 141, 196, 207, 238-39, 248-49, 253-55, 303-4
McLean, Edward C., 48
MacMahon, Lloyd F., 48
McRae, William A., Jr., 49
Madison, James, 162
magistrates, 285
Maine, 4
management, see Courts of Appeals, administration
mandamus, 26, 317, 323, 326, 329, 336, 339, 342
Manton, Martin T., 210
Marbury v. Madison, 138
Marshall, Burke, 96
Marshall, John, 15, 144
Marshall, Thurgood, 64, 103, 139, 193-94, 236, 240
Martindale-Hubbell Law Dictionary, 94, 307
Matthews, Burnita S., 51
Matthews, Donald R., 102, 111
Meador, Daniel J., 287
Medina, Harold R., xx, 96, 139, 194, 236, 247-49, 310
Mehrtens, William O., 49
Meredith, James H., 244
Metzner, Charles M., 48
Miami, Fla., 37, 105
migratory birds, 31, 62, 318, 324, 327, 330, 337, 340, 343
Miller, Arthur, 302
Miller, Warren E., 178
Miller, Wilbur K., 141, 196, 238, 249, 254
Miranda v. Arizona, 163
miscellaneous offenses, 317, 324, 327, 330, 337, 340, 343
Mishler, Jacob, 48
Mississippi, xix, 10, 37, 45, 73, 92, 99, 147, 206, 272-73, 320-33; Northern Dis-

trict, 45, 320-21, 332; Southern District, 37, 45, 47, 51, 320-21, 332
Mississippi River, 214
Mitchell, John, xxv
Mize, Sidney C., 50-51
modernization, 267-69, 272-77, 281, 288-89, 294-95
Moore, Leonard P., xx, 92, 139, 194, 208, 236, 239-40, 248, 250, 252, 303
*Moore's Federal Practice*, 301-2
morals offenses, 29, 317, 323, 329, 337, 340, 343
Morgan, Lewis R., xx, 49-50
Mott, Rodney L., 115, 186
Mt. Olympus, 76
Murphy, Frank, 223
Murphy, Thomas F., 48
Musmanno, Michael A., 205

Nagel, Stuart S., 173
narcotics, 29, 61-62, 66, 317, 323, 326, 329, 337, 340, 343
National Court of Appeals (proposed), 80-81, 271, 284-88, 291
National Labor Relations Board, 6, 17, 32, 44-46, 65-66, 70, 173, 175, 280, 287, 331, 333-34
national law: Balkanization of, 8, 33, 55, 79, 81-82, 190, 210, 257, 263, 291; nationalization of, 23, 53-54, 118, 145-50, 156, 261; uniformity of, 3-5, 14, 17, 20-23, 41, 71, 73-74, 79-84, 125, 145-47, 159, 185, 190, 219-20, 261-62, 290-93, 296
nationalism, 145-47
natural gas, 32, 52, 72, 76
negotiable instruments, 62-63, 315, 322, 325, 328, 335, 338, 341
New Deal, 6
New England, 105
New Jersey, Supreme Court of, 186
New Orleans, La., 37, 47, 100, 213, 216
New York, xix, 37, 42, 44, 52, 56, 82, 91, 100, 105, 130-31, 142-43, 149, 186, 190, 204-7, 212-13, 217-18, 228, 248, 252, 271, 278, 286, 319, 321, 331; Eastern District, 100, 319, 321, 331; Northern District, 319, 321, 331; Southern District, 35, 50, 66, 100, 319, 321, 331; Western District, 319, 321, 331
New York City, 10, 100
New York County, 293

New York Court of Appeals, 116, 169, 186
Ninth Circuit, U.S. Court of Appeals for, 83, 143, 258, 264, 268-74
Nixon, Richard M., xxiv-xxv, 75, 99-100, 147, 162, 264, 288
Noel, James L., Jr., 49
*North Carolina Utilities Commission* v. *F.C.C.*, 144
Northwestern University Law School, 93-94

obscenity, 32, 62, 317, 324, 327, 329, 337, 340, 343
Olivier, Laurence, xxiv
ombudsmen, 10, 287
Omnibus Judges Act of 1978, 258, 262, 265, 270, 273
opinions, *see* circuit judges, judicial opinions
oral argument, 14, 192, 197-99, 213, 216-18, 233, 247, 265-68, 277-80, 288
original proceedings, 12, 27, 44-46, 331-34

Palmieri, Edmund L., 48
Pan American Airways, 94
Parker, John J., 148, 277
Parkinson's law, 218
parole, 5, 26, 63, 317, 323, 326, 329, 336, 339, 342
patents, 33, 52, 55, 62-63, 71, 81, 173-75, 177, 179-80, 182-83, 234, 284-86, 294, 316, 322, 325, 328, 335, 338, 341
patronage, 101, 122, 295
Paulson, Nathan J., xx
Pennsylvania, Supreme Court of, 205
perjury, 318, 324, 327, 330, 337, 340, 343
personal injuries, 31, 137, 173-75, 177, 180, 183, 241, 315, 322, 325, 328, 335, 338, 341; marine, 31, 61, 72; motor vehicle, 63
personal status cases, 29-30, 61, 240, 242, 250, 252, 303-4, 316-17, 323, 326, 329, 336, 339, 342
Philadelphia, Pa., 144
Pine, David A., 51
Plato, 107
plea bargaining, 32, 40, 302
pluralism, 3, 21, 54, 57, 79, 185, 220, 290-91, 293

political culture, xxii, 87, 148, 156, 188, 292
Port, Edmund, 48
Posner, Richard A., 11
Pound, Roscoe, xxiii
Powell, Lewis F., Jr., 220
precedent, xxiii, 41, 57, 129, 163-65, 184, 187, 281, 292. See also circuit judges, precedent orientations; stare decisis
premises of decision, 56, 82, 138, 147, 156, 185, 187, 228, 291, 293
presidents (U.S.), xvii, xxiv, 13, 15, 17, 90, 99, 101, 277
Prettyman, E. Barrett, 141, 196, 225-26, 238
Prewitt, Kenneth, 90
prisoner petitions, 11-12, 14, 26-27, 29-30, 52, 173-77, 179-80, 182, 184, 241-42, 244, 246-47, 279-80, 283, 287-88, 317, 323, 326, 329, 336, 339, 342
private civil cases, 12, 27, 29
Privy Council, 210
pro se petitions, 198, 278-79
professionalization, 19, 89, 118-23. See also circuit judges, professional orientations; Courts of Appeals, professionalism in
prosecutors, 92
Protestants, 103, 105
public defenders: state, 92, 114; U.S., 276
public opinion, 19, 149-52, 165
Putnam, Richard J., 49

questionnaire, 297, 304-5, 311-14

race relations, 78, 133, 214, 244, 272
Railway Labor Act, 316, 322, 325, 328, 336, 339, 342
rape, 317, 323, 326, 329, 337, 339, 342
Rayfiel, Leo F., 48
real property, 29, 62, 315, 322, 325, 328, 335, 338, 341
realignment, 146, 215, 269, 271-74, 289, 395
reapportionment, 5, 9, 63, 71, 226, 273
Reconstruction, 4
recovery and enforcement, 315, 322, 325, 328, 335, 338, 341
recruitment, see circuit judges, recruitment
*Red Lion Broadcasting Co. v. F.C.C.*, 59
Reed, Stanley, 92

reference groups, 90, 110, 112, 123, 126, 148, 150-52, 156-57, 217
regionalism, 8-9, 20, 23, 33, 41, 52, 55, 57, 63, 71-75, 77-81, 122, 126, 142, 145-47, 150, 156, 181, 190, 220, 246, 271-73, 290-92
remands, 43, 73
Republicans, 96, 99, 169, 181
research design, xviii-xix, 297-314
resistance by lower courts, 28, 42, 72, 83, 299
reversal rates, 25, 38-62, 68-75, 297-98; of administrative agencies, 43-47, 70-72, 331-43; of U.S. circuit judges, 139-41; of U.S. Courts of Appeals, 57-62, 68-75, 83, 331-43; of U.S. district courts, 43-47, 82-83, 322-30; of U.S. district judges, 47-52
Richardson, Richard J., 42, 67, 71
right of appeal, 5, 286-88
Rives, Richard T., xx, 140, 144, 195, 237, 239, 241-46, 250-51, 273, 304
Robb, Roger, xx, 104
robbery, 62, 317, 323, 326, 329, 337, 340, 343
Robinson, Spottswood W., III, xx, 51, 94, 102, 141, 196, 207, 238
Rockwell report, 277
Rogers, Henry W., 210
role conflict, 127, 160, 166, 187, 232, 246, 276
role lag, 153
role perceptions, see judicial role perceptions
role strain, 123, 166, 187, 290
Roosevelt, Franklin D., 169
Roosevelt, Theodore, 19
Rosenberg, Maurice, 287
Rosling, George, 48
Rostow, Eugene V., 95
routine, 15, 76, 78, 80, 136-37, 187, 193, 220, 222, 280, 286
rule of anticipated reactions, 56, 75, 82, 138, 145, 156, 164-65
rule of law, 15, 144
rule of nine, 213, 215, 270-71, 273
rules of the game, 192, 195-205, 207, 220, 222-23, 226, 232, 246, 255-56, 279
Ryan, Sylvester J., 48, 50

Santa Fe, N.M., 115
*Santobello v. New York*, 302

Scarlett, Frank M., 50
Schick, Marvin, 203
Schweinhaut, Henry A., 47, 51
screening, 14, 34, 42, 77-78, 80, 191-92, 265; in 5th circuit, 197-98, 213, 215, 220, 233, 247, 267-68, 277-81, 288; in Supreme Court, 60-76, 138
searches and seizures, 30, 70
Second Circuit, U.S. Court of Appeals for, xix-xx, xxv, 18, 26-40, 42-50, 52-53, 55, 58-66, 70, 72, 75, 91-93, 103-7, 113, 115-16, 122, 130, 132-33, 136, 139, 141-44, 147-49, 161-63, 166, 187, 190, 193-94, 198, 202-3, 206, 208, 211-13, 216, 219, 222, 224-25, 227, 232, 234, 236, 239-41, 248-50, 253-54, 264-67, 270, 278, 280-81, 286, 303-4, 309
  business, 26-34, 44, 61-62, 149, 163, 263, 265-67, 315-24, 331, 335-37; administrative appeals, 26, 32, 44, 70, 72, 331; criminal appeals, 26-27, 29-30, 34, 39, 43, 52, 62, 72, 265, 316-18, 321, 323-24, 336-37
  conflict in, 42, 122, 162, 166, 193-94, 203, 205, 208, 210, 217-19
  decisions, 38-40, 42-44, 47-48, 263, 321-24; policy outcomes of, 46, 52-53, 70, 72, 149; process of, 198, 265-67; voting memoranda in, 136, 202-3, 212-13, 219, 265; "wash outs" in, 38, 265
  dissent in, 42, 193-94, 304
  en bancs in, 166, 217-19
  leadership in, 142-44, 148, 222, 225, 227, 231, 254, 275
  opinion assignments in, 236, 248-50, 253-54, 303-4
  panel assignments in, 232-33, 235-36, 239-41, 245, 303-4
  productivity, 263, 265-66
  rates of appeal to, 34-36, 39, 319-21
  recruitment to, xxv, 100, 113
  size, 263, 265, 270
  supervision of district courts and agencies, 29-33, 35-40, 42-44, 46-48, 50, 52, 55, 319-21, 331
  supervision of, by Supreme Court, 58-59, 61-66, 70-72, 76, 139, 315-18, 331, 335-37
Secretary of Agriculture, 32, 44-46, 331, 333-34

Securities and Exchange Commission, 6, 32, 44-46, 331, 333-34
selective service, 33, 318, 324, 327, 330, 337, 340, 343
Selma, Ala., 244
Senate (U.S.), xvii, 16, 104, 227-28, 247, 258, 268, 272, 285
Senate Judiciary Committee, 99-100, 273, 280
senatorial courtesy, 99-100
senators (U.S.), xxiv-xxv, 16-17, 104, 111, 115, 154, 187, 294
seniority, 201, 222-23, 225, 229-30, 232-40, 255-58, 292; in opinion assignments, 247-49, 252-56; in panel assignments, 239-40, 244, 248-49, 256
sentencing, 11, 26, 40, 289, 317, 323, 326, 329, 336, 339, 342
separation of powers, xxiii, 10, 17, 97, 159, 296
Seventh Circuit, U.S. Court of Appeals for, 143
Shapiro, Martin, 33-34, 78
Sheehy, Joseph W., 49
Sibley, Samuel H., 148
Simon, Herbert, 82
Simpson, Bryan, xx, 49-50, 104, 140, 193, 195, 237, 242-43
*Singleton v. Jackson Municipal Sep. Sch. Dist.*, 206, 209, 216
Sirica, John J., 47, 51
Sixth Circuit, U.S. Court of Appeals for, 143, 234, 247
Sloan, William Boyd, 49
Smith, J. Joseph, xx, 92, 104, 115, 139, 193-94, 236
Smith, Sidney O., Jr., 49
Sobeloff, Simon E., 228
social role, xxii-xxiii, 107, 150, 171
social security, 14, 30, 32-33, 63, 71, 279-80, 285, 316, 322, 325, 328, 336, 339, 342
socialization, *see* circuit judges, socialization
Solicitor General (U.S.), 34, 64-65, 81, 93, 95
South, 30, 37, 99, 105, 113, 117, 128, 147, 149, 156, 161, 204, 239, 248, 269
Spears, Adrian A., 49
specialization, *see* circuit judges, specialization; Courts of Appeals, specialization among; expertise

Speedy Trial Act, 11, 40, 269, 274
staffs, 200, 233, 268, 272, 279, 281, 288; staff attorneys, 7, 198, 278-79, 281
standing, 10, 16, 30-31
*stare decisis*, 23, 73, 80-82, 121, 128, 138, 156, 160, 162-64, 166-67, 188, 292-93. See also circuit judges, precedent orientations
Stassen, Glen H., 187
Statue of Liberty, 32
Stokes, Donald E., 178
Stone, Harlan Fiske, 92, 223
Stone, Julius, 73, 261
*Stone v. Powell*, 287
suffrage and elections, 30, 52-53, 60, 63, 66, 241, 317, 323, 326, 329, 336, 339, 342
Sugarman, Sidney, 48
Sunbelt, 37
Supreme Court (U.S.), xvii, 3-15, 17-21, 23-24, 28, 37, 50, 91, 95, 99-100, 102-3, 119, 128, 132-33, 137-39, 141, 146, 149, 151, 155, 159-60, 163-64, 166, 184-85, 190-91, 196, 200-201, 204-6, 208, 217-20, 223, 225-26, 246-47, 257, 262-63, 270-73, 281-83, 286, 289, 296-97
  business, 5, 12, 18, 21, 57, 63-77, 331-43; compared with Courts of Appeals, 23, 57, 59-63, 69, 74, 315-18
  decisions, 58-59, 189, 219; policy outcomes of, 64, 68-73, 76; rules of, 67, 70
  dissent rate, 60
  functions, 3-8, 10-11, 63, 67-71, 75-76, 80-84, 138, 272, 288-89, 292-93
  policy making by, 63, 67, 70, 75-76, 79-80, 293; priority of, 68-71, 75-76, 80-84, 138, 217, 220, 262, 291
  rates of appeal to, 10-13, 57-69, 72-74, 77, 80-84, 291, 297-303, 315-19, 331-43
  screening in, 60-77, 138
  supervision of lower courts, xviii, 18, 20-21, 57-84, 87, 120, 144, 148, 188-89, 219, 273, 290-300, 315-18, 331-43
Supreme Court Justices, 4-5, 7, 20, 60, 62, 64, 66-67, 78, 134, 138, 142, 146, 152, 163, 166, 188, 193, 278, 283; socialization of, 223-24
Suttle, Dorwin W., 49
Swan, Thomas W., 95, 139, 142, 147, 194, 236

Taft, William Howard, 5, 95, 223
Tamm, Edward A., xx, 47, 51, 94, 141, 196, 238-39, 241, 248, 254, 303
Tanenhaus, Joseph, 67
Tax Courts (U.S.), 26, 32, 44-46, 70, 287, 331, 333-34
taxation, 17, 29-32, 55, 60-62, 64, 71-72, 78, 81, 175, 182, 234, 240-41, 247, 250, 252-53, 279-80, 284-86, 294, 303-4, 316, 323, 326, 328, 336, 339, 342; income tax, 31, 52, 65-66, 76, 173-77, 180, 182-83, 316, 323, 326, 328, 336, 339, 342; tax fraud, 30, 62, 65-66, 316, 323, 326, 328, 336, 339, 342
Tenney, Charles H., 48
Tenth Circuit, U.S. Court of Appeals for, 5, 143, 279
tenure, 168
Texas, xix, 45, 235, 272-73; Eastern District, 320-21, 333; Northern District, 51, 320-21, 333; Southern District, 47, 66, 320-21, 333; Western District, 320-21, 333
Third Circuit, U.S. Court of Appeals for, 131, 143-44, 278-79
Thomas, D. Holcombe, 50-51
Thomas, Norman, 112
Thornberry, Homer, xx, xxv, 49-50, 92, 100, 140, 195, 237, 241-46, 250-51, 304
three-judge district courts (U.S.), 63, 226, 229, 256, 282-83, 294; assignments to, 240-41, 245-46, 256
Timbers, William H., 48, 50
torts, 29-30, 60-61, 71-72, 240, 252-53, 284, 303-4, 315, 322, 325, 328, 335, 338, 341
traffic cases, 318, 330, 343
transformation of issues, 30-31, 42, 62, 299
transitivity, 171, 181
trial courts, 92, 114, 134-36, 162, 166, 275, 277, 287
Truman, Harry S, 110, 169
Tuttle, Elbert P., xx, 93, 139-40, 144, 148,

193, 195, 228-29, 231, 233, 237, 241-46, 248, 250-52, 255, 273, 293, 303-4
Tyler, Harold R., Jr., 48

Ulmer, Sidney S., 306
Ungs, Thomas D., 306
United Nations, 92-93, 114
U.S. attorneys, 92, 113, 168; assistants, 113
U.S. litigation, 64, 294, 319; civil, 12, 27-28, 280
U.S. Supreme Court Reports, 299
U.S. v. Jefferson Co. Bd. of Educ., 161, 244
U.S. v. Wade, 59, 64, 144
University of Michigan Law School, 93

Vanderbilt, Arthur T., 259
Vermont, xix, 35, 37, 44, 47, 213, 319, 321, 331
Veterans Administration, 286
Vietnam War, xxiv
Vinci, Leonardo da, 161
Vines, Kenneth N., 42, 67, 71, 173
Vinson Court, 71
Virginia, 286; Supreme Court of, 116, 169, 186
visiting judges, 42, 142, 190, 215, 226, 265, 267-69, 271, 278
voting blocs, 190, 195, 205-7, 240-41
Voting Rights Act, 5

Wadsworth, Edward W., xx
Wahlke, John C., xxii
Wagner Act, 52
Walsh, Leonard P., 51
Warren, Earl, xxv, 99, 137, 155, 223
Warren Court, 11-12, 53-54, 60, 71-72, 75, 81, 140, 175
Washington, George T., 141, 196, 238, 249, 254

Washington, D.C., xx, 4, 7, 28-29, 32, 37, 42, 47, 52-53, 55-56, 71, 82, 100, 103, 105-6, 116, 129, 143, 145, 149, 161, 190, 193, 197, 199, 204, 206-7, 212, 230, 233, 239, 248, 253, 271, 280, 304
Waterman, Sterry R., xx, 94, 139, 144, 194, 208, 225, 236, 240, 252-53
weapons, 61-63, 318, 324, 327, 330, 337, 340, 343
Weinfeld, Edward, 48, 50
welfare, 32, 285, 287-88
Welles, Orson, xxiv
West, E. Gordon, 49
white slavery, 317, 323, 326, 329, 337, 340, 343
Whitehurst, George W., 49
Widener, H. Emory, Jr., 144
Wilson, Woodrow, 109-10
wiretapping, 276
Wisdom, John Minor, xx, xxv, 140, 144, 193, 195, 215, 237, 239, 241-45, 250-53, 255, 269, 273
Wold, John T., 116, 169
Wolf v. Barkes, 208
workman's compensation, 33, 53, 63
World War I, 5
World War II, 17
Wright, Charles Alan, 302
Wright, J. Skelly, xx, 93-94, 100, 113, 141, 196, 209, 238, 248, 254-55, 303
Wyatt, Inzer B., 48
Wyzanski, Charles E., Jr., 308

Yale University Law School, 93, 112
Young, George C., 49
Youngdahl, Luther W., 47, 51

Zampano, Robert C., 48
Zavoina, William, 241

**Library of Congress Cataloging in Publication Data**

Howard, J  Woodford.
  Courts of appeals in the Federal judicial system.

  Bibliography: p.
  Includes index.
  1. Appellate courts—United States.   2. United States. Court of Appeals for the Second Circuit.
  3. United States. Court of Appeals for the Fifth Circuit.   4. United States. Court of Appeals for the District of Columbia Circuit.   5. Judicial process—United States.   I. Title.

KF8750.H68      347.73'24      80-7529
ISBN 0-691-07623-5
ISBN 0-691-10100-0 (pbk.)

**LIBRARY OF DAVIDSON COLLEGE**